A Passion for Justice

A Passion for Justice

An Introductory Guide to the Code of Canon Law

G. J. Woodall

GRACEWING

First published in 2011

Gracewing
2 Southern Avenue, Leominster
Herefordshire HR6 0QF

UK ISBN   978 085244 478 8

NIHIL OBSTAT 23 October 2009 Fr Peter Vellacott LL.B, STB, JCL *Censor deputatus*

IMPRIMATUR   28 October 2009, (Appendix 1 & 2) 6 January 2010,
(Appendix 3) 29 July 2010
Rt Rev. Malcolm McMahon OP
Bishop of the Diocese of Nottingham, England

This book was submitted for review by Gracewing Ltd, intended as an introductory commentary and overview of the 1983 Code of Canon Law that aims not only to state what the law is, but to show its role or purpose, its origin and its meaning for the Church today.

Application has been made for copyright permission for use of the English translation provided in *The Code of Canon Law* (Collins, London, 1983), prepared by The Canon Law Society of Great Britain and Ireland in association with The Canon Law Society of Australia and New Zealand and The Canadian Canon Law Society, in the text of this work; it is also used in the Tables, but the layout of the tables, as well as addition and emphases, are those of the author.

Typeset by
Action Publishing Technology Ltd, Gloucester, GL1 5SR

Contents

Foreword   xix
List of Tables   xvii
Introduction   1
**Chapter 1   The Function of Canon Law and the Revision of the
        Code**   7
1. Introduction   7
2. Law, Justice and the Church   7
3. Law and the Community of the Baptized   11
4. Canon Law and Theology   15
5. The Historical Sources of Canon Law   18
    a. Scriptural Foundations of Canon Law   18
    b. Canons and Decretals   20
    c. The *Corpus iuris canonici* or Body of Canon Law   24
    d. Some Initial Conclusions   29
6. The Codification of Canon Law and the Revision of the Code   29
    a. Codification and the Code of 1917   29
    b. The Revision of the Code: The Principles Involved   31
    c. The Revision of the Code and the Second Vatican Council   36
    d. The Structure of the Revised Code for the Latin Church   40
    e. The Fundamental Law of the Church ('*Lex fundamentalis*')   40
    f. The Promulgation of the Code of 1983   43
7. Conclusion   45

Chapter 2   General Norms (Book I of the Code)   46
1. Introduction   46
2. Persons in the Church and their Juridical Status   46
    a. Juridical Status in the Church   46
    b. Physical Persons in the Church   53
    c. Moral Persons and Juridical Persons in the Church   58
3. Laws in the Church: Their Promulgation and Main Features   61
    a. The Promulgation of Laws   61
    b. The Proper Subjects of the Code of 1983   63

c. The Manner of Promulgation   63
d. The Entry into Force of the Law and the 'vacatio legis'   64
e. A Formal Amendment to the Code   64
f. Canonical Norms outside the Code   65
g. The Extent of Ecclesiastical Laws   66
4. Acts in Canon Law: Legislative, Administrative and Judicial   67
   a. The Distinction of Powers   67
   b. Legislative Acts   68
   c. Judicial Acts   68
   d. Executive or Administrative Acts   69
5. Offices in the Church   76
   a. The Concept of 'Office' in the Church   76
   b. The Provision of Offices: Appointments   77
   c. Different Ways of Making Appointments   78
   d. Loss of Office   78
6. Conclusion   80

Chapter 3   The People of God (Book II of the Code),
Part I: Christ's Faithful   81
1. Introduction   81
2. The Rights and Duties of the Christian Faithful as a Whole   81
3. The Rights and Duties of the Lay Faithful   87
   a. The Foundation of their Rights and Duties   87
   b. Some Comments on these Rights and Duties   87
4. The Clerical State   92
   a. The Reform of Orders and Ministries   92
   b. The Incardination of Clergy   93
   c. The Formation of Clergy   96
   d. The Specific Rights and Duties of Clergy   103
5. Loss of the Clerical State   104
   a. Ways of Losing the Clerical State   104
   b. Loss of the Clerical State and the Question of Celibacy   107
   c. Consequences of the Loss of the Clerical State   108
6. Personal Prelatures   108
7. Associations of Christ's Faithful   109
8. Conclusion   110

Chapter 4   The People of God (Book II of the Code), Part II: The Church's Hierarchical Structure, I: The Supreme Authority   111

1. Introduction   111
2. The Meaning of the Supreme Authority of the Church   111
3. The Role of the Papacy   114
   a. The Petrine Office or Function   114
   b. Election to the Petrine Office   118
4. Collegiality: Bishops as Part of the Supreme Authority   121
   a. The Source of the 'Power' of Bishops   121
   b. The College of Bishops   122
   c. Ecumenical Councils and Synods of Bishops   123
5. The Cardinals (cc. 349–359)   128
6. The Roman Curia   130
7. Papal Legates (cc. 362–367)   135
8. Conclusion   135

Chapter 5   The People of God (Book II of the Code), Part II: The Church's Hierarchical Structure, II, Particular Churches   136

1. Introduction   136
2. Particular Churches   136
   a. Particular Churches Equivalent to Dioceses   136
   b. The Diocese as a Particular Church   137
3. The Bishop in the Particular Church   140
   a. The Divine Institution of the Episcopacy and Pastoral Care   140
   b. The Selection of Bishops   142
   c. The Responsibilities of Diocesan Bishops   145
   d. The Resignation of the Diocesan Bishop   148
   e. The Functions of Other Bishops   148
   f. Special Arrangements for a Vacant and for an Impeded Diocese   149
4. Groupings of Dioceses   150
   a. Ecclesiastical Provinces   150
   b. Episcopal Conferences   151
5. Diocesan Structures   152
   a. Diocesan Synods   153
   b. The Diocesan Curia   153
6. Parishes and their Priests   162
   a. The Canonical Nature of the Parish   162
   b. The Parish Priest   166
   c. Parochial Vicars or Assistant Priests   174

7. Other Figures of Importance in the Diocese   174
    a. Vicars Forane (Deans)   174
    b. Rectors   176
    c. Chaplains   177
8. Conclusion   177

**Chapter 6   The People of God (Book II of the Code),
Part III: Institutes of Consecrated Life and Societies of
Apostolic Life**   178
1. Introduction   178
2. Institutes of Consecrated Life in General   178
    a. The Nature of the Consecrated Life   178
    b. Recent Canonical Developments   179
    c. An Analysis of Key Canons (cc. 207, 573)   182
    d. Other Norms on Institutes of Consecrated Life in General   184
3. Institutes of Consecrated Life and Societies of Apostolic Life:
Particular Norms   192
    a. Definitions and Distinctions in Institutes and Societies   192
    b. Houses of Religious Institutes and of Societies of
Apostolic Life   193
    c. Governance   197
    d. Admission and Initial Formation   200
    e. Profession of the Evangelical Counsels (cc. 654–658)   203
    f. Continuing Formation (cc. 659–661)   204
    g. Incardination   205
    h. Rights and Duties of Persons in Institutes or in Societies   205
    i. Separation from Institutes and Societies   208
4. Conclusion   209

**Chapter 7   The Teaching Function of the Church
(Book III of the Code)**   210
1. Introduction   210
2. The Preliminary Canons   210
    a. An Analysis of the Key Canon (c. 747)   210
    b. The Other Preliminary Canons and the Church's
Magisterium   213
3. The Ministry of the Word   219
    a. Preaching   220
    b. Catechesis   222
4. The Missionary Work of the Church and the Ministry of the
Word   224

5. Catholic Education   225
   a. Parental Responsibilities and Rights   225
   b. Catholic Schools   226
   c. Catholic Universities   226
6. Social Communications   227
7. The Profession of Faith and Oath of Fidelity   227
8. Conclusion   229

**Chapter 8   The Sanctifying Function of the Church (Book IV
of the Code), Part I, Liturgy and the Sacraments in General**   231
1. Introduction   231
2. Sacraments and Faith: Response to God's Word   232
   a. Some Implications of Conciliar Teaching   232
   b. The Church and the Liturgy   233
3. Preliminary Canons on the Church's Sanctifying Function   235
   The Meaning of the Sanctifying Function   235
   The Sanctifying Function: Sacred Ministers and Lay Faithful 235
4. The Sacraments in General   240
   a. An Analysis of Canon 840   240
   b. Equality of Status and Diversity of Function   242
   c. The Bishops' Role in the Sacraments and the Holy See   243
   d. Other Norms for the Sacraments in General   244
5. The Valid Celebration of the Sacraments   246
   a. The Distinction between Validity and Liceity   246
   b. The Conditions for Sacramental Validity in General   246
   c. The Valid Celebration of the Sacraments in Particular   248
   d. The Duty of Reverence and of Due Care over the
      Sacraments   249
   e. The Conditional Administration of the Sacraments   249
6. Conclusion   254

**Chapter 9   The Sanctifying Function of the Church (Book IV
of the Code), Part I: The Sacraments, II, The Sacraments
of Initiation**   255
1. Introduction   255
2. The Preliminary Canons on Baptism   255
   a. The Lawful Celebration of Baptism   255
   b. Revised Norms for Adult Baptism: Preparation for Baptism 256
   c. Canonical Requirements for Infant Baptism   260
   d. Other Preliminary Norms for Baptism (Adult and Infant)   261
   e. Sponsors at Baptism   264
   f. The Theological Significance of Baptism   264

g. Registration and the Baptismal Register   265
h. The Postponement or Deferral of Baptism   266
3. The Sacrament of Confirmation   267
a. The Conciliar Background   267
b. An Analysis of Canon 879   267
c. The Matter and Form of Confirmation   268
d. The Minister of Confirmation   268
e. The Proper Candidate for Confirmation   271
f. Reception into Full Communion with the Catholic Church   271
g. Sponsors at Confirmation   272
h. Registration of Confirmation   272
i. Juridical Effects of Confirmation   273
j. The Timing of Confirmation and Sacramental Initiation   273
4. The Sacrament of the Eucharist   274
a. The Nature of the Eucharist: The Preliminary Canons   274
b. The Celebration of the Eucharist: General Aspects   279
c. The Valid Celebration of the Eucharist   281
d. The Licit Celebration of the Eucharist   281
e. The Minister of Holy Communion   284
f. The Administration of Viaticum   284
g. Participation in the Eucharist   285
h. The Reservation of the Blessed Sacrament   287
i. *Communicatio in sacris*   287
j. Offerings for Masses   290
k. The Extra-ordinary Form of the Mass   291
5. Conclusion   294

**Chapter 10   The Sanctifying Function of the Church (Book
IV of the Code), Part I: The Sacraments, III, The Sacraments
of Healing**   295
1. Introduction   295
2. The Sacrament of Reconciliation   295
a. Doctrinal Foundations of Canonical Norms on
Reconciliation   295
b. An Analysis of Key Canons (cc. 959-961)   298
c. Abuses in the Sacrament of Reconciliation   302
d. The Minister of Reconciliation and Confessional Faculties   306
e. Responsibilities of Confessors   308
f. Offences against the Sacrament of Reconciliation   310
g. The Duties of the Penitent   311
h. Indulgences   312

3. The Sacrament of the Anointing of the Sick   314
   a. The Significance of the Sacrament of Anointing the Sick   314
   b. The Introductory Canon (c. 998)   316
   c. The Administration of the Sacrament of the Sick   317
4. Conclusion   319

**Chapter 11 The Sanctifying Function of the Church (Book IV
of the Code), Part I: The Sacraments, IV, The Sacrament of
Holy Orders**   320
1. Introduction   320
2. An Analysis of the Key Canons (cc. 1008–1009, 1012)   320
3. The Celebration of Holy Orders: Conditions of Validity   325
4. The Liceity of Ordinations   328
   a. Laws Applying to Ordinations in all Degrees of Sacred
      Order   328
   b. Further Laws Applying to Ordination to the Episcopate   329
   c. Further Laws on both Diaconal and Presbyteral
      Ordinations   330
   d. The Ordaining Bishop   330
   e. Dimissorial Letters   331
   f. Proper Candidates for Sacred Orders   333
   g. Canonical Irregularities and Simple Impediments   338
   h. Ordination and Homosexual Persons   341
   i. Documentation and Investigations Required for
      Ordination   342
   j. Registration and Proof of Ordination   343
5. Conclusion   343

**Chapter 12 The Sanctifying Function of the Church (Book IV
of the Code), Part I: The Sacraments, V, The Canon Law of
Marriage – The Nature of Marriage**   344
1. Introduction   344
2. A Historical Perspective on Marriage   344
   a. Roman Law and Marriage   344
   b. Augustine and the Good of Marriage   345
   c. Disputes over Consent and Consummation   346
   d. St Thomas Aquinas   346
   e. The Council of Trent and the Roman Catechism   347
   f. Magisterial Interventions prior to the Second Vatican
      Council   347
3. The Second Vatican Council and its Aftermath   349
   a. The Second Vatican Council   349

b. The Magisterium of Paul VI and of John Paul II   351
4. Biblical Indications and the Canonical Doctrine of Marriage   352
   a. The Old Testament   352
   b. The New Testament   353
5. The Preliminary Canons on Marriage   358
   a. The Need for Pastoral Care for those Marrying and for the Married   358
   b. The Canonical Nature of Marriage   358
   c. Matrimonial Consent   364
   d. Further Comments on the Preliminary Canons   366
6. Conclusion   369

Chapter 13   The Sanctifying Function of the Church (Book IV of the Code), Part I: The Sacraments, VI, The Canon Law of Marriage – Impediments to Marriage and Matrimonial Consent   370
1. Introduction   370
2. Impediments to Marriage in General   370
   a. The Meaning of a (Diriment) Impediment   370
   b. The Declaration and Establishment of Impediments   371
   c. Dispensation from Impediments to Matrimony   372
3. Particular Impediments to Marriage   375
   a. Age (c. 1083)   375
   b. Impotence (c. 1084)   375
   c. *Ligamen* – Bond of a Previous Marriage (c. 1085)   378
   d. Disparity of Cult/Worship (c. 1086)   380
   e. Sacred Orders (c. 1087)   381
   f. Perpetual Public Vow of Chastity in a Religious Institute (c. 1088)   383
   g. Crimes (cc. 1089–1090)   383
   h. Relationships (cc. 1091–1094)   383
4. The Nature of Matrimonial Consent   386
5. Defects in Matrimonial Consent   388
   a. Incapacity to Exchange Consent (c. 1095)   388
   b. Ignorance (c. 1096)   393
   c. Error of Person and of Quality of Person (c. 1097)   394
   d. Deceit (c. 1098)   395
   e. Radical Error Determining the Will (c. 1099)   397
   f. Simulation of Consent (c. 1101)   398
   g. Conditional Consent (c. 1102)   401
   h. Force and Grave Fear (c. 1103)   402
   i. Knowledge/Opinion about Nullity of a Union (c. 1100)   402

j. Consent in Difficult Circumstances   403
6. Consent and Preparation for Marriage   404
7. Conclusion   405

**Chapter 14   The Sanctifying Function of the Church (Book IV
of the Code), Part I: The Sacraments, VII, The Canon Law
of Marriage – Canonical Form and Other Questions**   406
1. The Canonical Form of Marriage   406
    a. The Origin of Canonical Form   406
    b. The Key Canon on the Form of Marriage (c. 1108)   408
    c. Official 'Assistance' at Weddings   408
    d. Further Requirements of Liceity and the Official Church
        Witnesses   412
    e. Those Bound by the Canonical Form of Marriage (c. 1117) 412
    f. Mixed Marriages (cc. 1124–1125)   414
    g. The Secret Celebration of Marriage (cc. 1130-1133) 416
    h. Registration and Proof of Marriage (c. 1121)   416
2. Other Features of Marriage Law   417
    a. The Effects of Marriage   417
    b. The Rectification of Invalid Unions   420
    c. The Separation of the Spouses   422

**Chapter 15   The Sanctifying Function of the Church (Book IV
of the Code), Parts II and III: Places,Times, VII, Other Acts of
Divine Worship**   429
1. Non-sacramental Acts of Worship (Book IV, Part II)   429
    a. Sacramentals   429
    b. The Liturgy of the Hours   430
    c. Funerals   431
    d. The Cult of the Saints: Images and Relics   432
    e. Vows and Oaths   432
2. Sacred Places and Sacred Times (Book IV, Part III)   433
    a. Sacred Places   433
    b. Sacred Times   436
3. Conclusion   438

**Chapter 16   The Temporal Goods of the Church (Book V of the
Code)**   439
1. Introduction   439
2. Scripture and Church Involvement with Temporal Goods   439
    a. The Missionary Work of the Church (2 Cor. 8:1–5; 9:1–9) 439
    b. Support for the Clergy (2 Thess. 3:7–9; 2 Cor. 11:7–11) 440

c. Facilitating Works of Charity (Acts 2:42–7; 4:35–7)   440
d. Temporal Goods and Worship   440
e. The Need for Accountability and the Prevention of Abuses   440
3. Historical Perspectives on Temporal Goods   441
4. The Second Vatican Council and Temporal Goods   443
5. The Preliminary Canons on Temporal Goods   444
6. The Acquisition (and Retention) of Temporal Goods   447
   a. Natural and Positive Law   447
   b. Donations from the Faithful   447
   c. Sacred Objects and Goods   450
   d. Wills and Foundations   451
7. The Administration of Temporal Goods   452
   a. Responsible Administrators   452
   b. Administration and Finance Committees   453
   c. Administration of Goods in General   454
   d. Fund for the Support of the Clergy   455
8. Alienation of Temporal Goods   456
   a. The Role of Contracts   456
   b. The Key Principle for the Alienation of Goods   457
   c. Further Norms   458
   d. Advice and Specific Regulations   458
   e. A Problematic Development   459
9. Temporal Goods and Pious Foundations   460
10. Conclusion   461

**Chapter 17   Penal Law: Sanctions in the Church (Book VI of
the Code)**   463
1. The Reason for Penal Law in the Church   463
2. The Nature of Canonical Crimes and of Canonical Penalties   464
3. The Subjects of Canonical Penalties   465
   a. An Analysis of Canon 1321   465
   b. The Question of Personal Imputability   466
4. Types of Penal Sanction   470
   a Censures   470
   b. Expiatory Penalties   474
   c. Penal Remedies   476
   d. Penances   477
5. The Application of Penalties   477
6. The Cessation of Penalties   482
7. Particular Crimes and Particular Penalties   484
   a. Offences against Religion and against the Unity of the
      Church   484

b. Offences against Authorities and the Freedom of the
   Church   485
c. Offences of Usurpation of Office or Abuse of Office   485
d. Offences of Falsehood   486
e. Offences against Special Obligations   486
f. Offences against Human Life and Liberty   487
g. General Norm (c. 1399)   488
8. More Serious Crimes ('*graviora delicta*')   488
  a. Crimes against the Eucharist   489
  b. Crimes against the Sacrament of Penance   490
  c. Crime with a Minor   490
9. Special Faculties and the Congregation for the Clergy, 2009   491
10. Conclusion   494

Chapter 18   Procedural Law (Book VII of the Code)   495
1. The Importance of Procedural Law   495
2. Trials in General (Part I)   496
  a. Some General Remarks   496
  b. The Competent Forum   496
  c. Grades or Instances of Tribunals   497
  d. The Judicial Process – Procedures for Contentious Trials   498
  e. The Discipline of the Tribunal   500
3. The Contentious Trial (Part II)   502
  a. The Introduction of a Case   502
  b. The Instruction of the Case   503
  c. The Conclusion of the Case   506
  d. The Oral Contentious Process   509
4. Special Judicial Processes or Types of Contentious Trials
   (Part III)   509
  a. Matrimonial Processes: Investigation of the Nullity of a
     Marriage   509
  b. The Legal Separation of Spouses   517
  c. Processes for Dissolution of a Non-consummated Marriage   518
  d. Dissolution of a Non-sacramental Marriage   518
  e. Declaration of the Presumed Death of a Spouse   520
5. Procedures for the Declaration of Nullity of Sacred Orders   520
6. Ways of Avoiding Trials   521
7. Procedures in Penal Law (Part IV)   521
  a. Judicial and Administrative Processes   521
     The Preliminary Investigation   524
     The Course of the Penal Process   525
     Appeal or Recourse   526

b. Action for Restitution (Reparation of Damages) 527
c. Some Observations relating to Clerical Sexual Abuse of
    Minors 527
8. Recourse against Administrative Acts (Part V) 543
    a. Preliminary Recourse or Petition 543
    b. Special Acts of Recourse 544
9. Conclusion: The Pastoral Care of Souls (c. 1752) 545

Conclusion 547
Appendix 1: Reception of Former Anglican Communities 549
Appendix 2: Two Changes to the Code 554
**Appendix 3: Procedures: Clerical Sexual Abuse of Minors and
    Other Grave Crimes** 557
Index of Modern Authors 563
General Index 566

List of Tables

1. The Codes of 1917 and 1983   41
2. Persons in the Church (cc. 96, 204 and 849)   48
3. Rights and Duties of all the Faithful (cc. 208–223)   84
4. The Rights and Duties of the Lay Faithful   88
5. The Specific Rights and Duties of Clergy   105
6. A. The Supreme Authority in General (c. 330)   112
   B. The Papacy (c. 331)   116
   C. The Synod of Bishops (c. 342)   125
7. A. The Diocese as a Particular Church (cc. 368–369)   138
   B. The Bishops (c. 375)   141
8 A. The Parish (c. 515 § 1–3)   163
   B. The Parish Priest (c. 519)   167
9 A. The Consecrated Life   183
   B. The Consecrated Life as a State of Life (c. 588)   187
   C. Religious and Secular Institutes / Societies of Apostolic Life   194
   D. Schema of the Canons 573–746   195
10. The Teaching Function of the Church   211
11. A. The Sanctifying Function of the Church – Sacred Liturgy   236
    B. The Sacraments of the Church   241
    C. The Validity of the Sacraments in Particular I   250
    D. The Validity of the Sacraments in Particular II   251
12. The Sacrament of the Eucharist   276
13. The Sacrament of Penance (Reconciliation)   300
14. The Sacrament of Holy Orders   321
15. The Canon Law of Marriage   360
16. The Temporal Goods of the Church   445
17. A. The Nature of Penal Law   468
    B. The Subjects of Penal Sanctions   471
    C. The Application of Penalties   478
18. A. Procedures in Cases of Nullity of Marriage   510
    B. Procedures in Penal Law   522

Foreword

Three years ago saw the twenty-fifth anniversary of the promulgation of *The Code of Canon Law* (*Codex iuris canonici*), the code of laws which governs those of us of the Latin rite of the Catholic Church. This took place on 25 January 1983, and the new code came into force on the First Sunday of Advent later that year, on 27 November. Proclaimed as law by Pope John Paul II on the very anniversary of John XXIII's announcement that there was to be a second Vatican Council and that the 1917 Code of laws was to be revised, it is a very significant anniversary.

The intention had been to produce this introductory guide to the 1983 Code in time for that anniversary. However, the work involved made that impossible. Perhaps the delay can be seen as somewhat fortuitous in some ways. The Church is, of course, the living body of the community of the baptized in Christ and in the Holy Spirit on the journey to eternal communion in them with the Father. We who belong to the Church on earth continue to seek to respond to this exalted vocation amid the changes, hopes and difficulties of life. The law does not stand still and even the 1983 Code is not a static reality, but an instrument of justice of this pilgrim people. Since 2008 the lifting of the excommunications on the four bishops ordained illicitly by Mgr Lefebvre caused some considerable discussion. Last year some changes were introduced by Pope Benedict XVI to deal more effectively with some clergy who are living at serious odds with the responsibilities of the clerical state. This last year has been marked by repeated scandals of clerical sexual abuse of minors and relevant canonical procedures are again under review. The lived reality of the Church requires us to seek to improve what are human ways of trying to be just towards one another and towards others. The slightly later appearance of this work has meant that some attention has been accorded to these questions.

I wish to express my sincere gratitude to my family, living and dead, for the example and encouragement I have received in my faith, in the priesthood and in my work for the Church. I thank too the many parishioners whom I have tried to serve over the years, as well as former and present students. It was, in part, former students who urged the writing of this work.

A very special word of thanks must go to Fr Peter Vellacott, JCL, a fellow priest of the Diocese of Nottingham, who undertook the laborious, painstaking task of proofreading the text. He pointed out many errors and made a number of very helpful suggestions and I am truly indebted to him for all he did. Needless, to say, any mistakes which remain are entirely my own responsibility.

G. J. Woodall
22 February 2011
Feast of the Chair of St Peter

Introduction

In 2008 we celebrated the twenty-fifth anniversary of *The Code of Canon Law* for the Latin Church, promulgated or officially established as law by Pope John Paul II on 25 January 1983. This feast day of the Conversion of St Paul was the anniversary of the date on which Pope John XXIII had proclaimed that there would be a second Vatican Council. The new Code was due to come into effect on the first Sunday of Advent later that year on 27 November 1983. None of this was coincidence; this 'new Code' was the completion of the revision of the first Code of Canon Law, that of 1917, for which the Council had called and it represents the transfer into law of many of the perspectives and provisions of that Council. In the words of Pope John Paul II, when he promulgated or established this Code as law:

> It is very much to be hoped that the new canonical legislation will be an effective instrument by means of which the Church may be able to perfect itself according to the spirit of the Second Vatican Council and show itself ever more equal to the task of carrying out its salvific role in the world.[1]

While a 'celebration' of a code of laws might strike many people as odd, hopefully this book may help to show that there is much in this Code to value, that it constitutes a digest of the Church's understanding of itself, as elaborated in the Council between 1962 and 1965, and that it offers real assistance to all of us in the Church as we seek to serve the Church and our world in the ways of justice in fulfilling the mission entrusted to us at our baptism by Jesus Christ.

At first sight law seems opposed to the Gospel, even conjuring up images of Jesus confronting the Pharisees. It appears to restrict our liberty and our initiative, suggesting numerous rules imposed from

---

[1.] John Paul II, Apostolic letter *motu proprio, Sacrae disciplinae legis*, 25 January 1983, in *Codex iuris canonici*, Libreria editrice Vaticana, 1983, xiii.

above, with little obvious connection with evangelization or with promoting justice and peace in our world. Older priests may recall, fondly or regretfully, detailed attention to some aspects of law in their preparation for the priesthood years ago in a way not emulated more recently. The Code of Canon Law of 1983, or that of 1990 for the Eastern Catholic Churches, cannot replace the Bible, revelation or the theology and doctrine of the Council, but it can perhaps complement them as an authentic instrument at the service of the Church and of the world in our time.

It is not entirely obvious why the Church needs to have a set of laws. Why not do without them and rely on the Holy Spirit? Although the community of believers founded by Our Lord as the People of God of the New Testament is a community of those seeking holiness and eternal life with God, we live as a community also here on earth. Individuals and groups within the Church may have a different understanding of what the Holy Spirit is prompting at any given time. Some interpretations of what we ought to be doing and of how we ought to live on a regular basis may well be incompatible with one another and perhaps even with the Gospel. This is not a phenomenon unique to our time. The early Church had to settle the question of whether new converts would have to undergo the Jewish legal ritual of circumcision or not. The Council of Jerusalem decided that this was not necessary and must not be required of them (Acts 15:5–29). Incidentally, this decision was fully sustained by Peter, whatever his initial thoughts may have been; it was a conciliar decision of the College of the Apostles, based on the Gospel, and resulted in a church law to be followed in admitting new members to the Christian community.

The word 'canon' means 'norm' or 'rule'. In origin it meant a 'stick', which was used to measure things. It is used in various contexts within the Church: the 'canon' of Scripture, the 'canon' of the faith or *regula fidei*, the 'canons' who follow a rule of life, such as the Augustinian canons, and 'canon law'.[2] 'Canon law' is the expression used for the Church's norms or rules which are part of its legal or juridical structure and which regulate its practice. They are connected to the concept of 'justice', justice within the Church between its various members, justice between the Church and other persons as individuals, justice between the Church and the various States in existence, and so on.

Questions arise about how to proclaim the Gospel or about how to

---

[2.] J. A. Coriden, *An Introduction to Canon Law*, revised edn, Paulist, New York, Mahwah, NJ, 2004, 3.

give witness to it in parish communities. What is the role of a parish pastoral council in relation to this clearly Christian duty? Is it compulsory, what is its legitimate role, how ought it to relate to the parish priest? Practical issues concerning who may baptize a child can lead to unnecessary conflict, if the purpose of a law is not understood. A priest who has had a great influence on a particular family might be asked to conduct the baptism, but the parish priest is responsible for baptisms in the parish. It would be regrettable were this to become a matter of power or control, since the parish priest is properly charged with this responsibility in order to ensure the proper pastoral preparation for the sacrament (which has nothing to do with power and control). If it concerns a family of practising Catholics, with every reason to judge that the child is likely to be brought up to practise the faith, and provided the other priest is not under some canonical sanction, there is no canonical reason for the parish priest to refuse permission for the other priest to proceed.

More complicated is the situation of a woman whose husband has been assaulting her sporadically or more systematically and who is a real threat to her and to her children and who asks a priest about nullity of marriage procedures. To be told that they had been married in a Catholic church with a nuptial Mass and that, therefore, there is nothing to be done betrays ignorance on the part of the priest both about nullity and about other procedures. An enquiry about the nullity of the marriage could be undertaken, although its outcome cannot be guaranteed. The possibility of a canonical legal separation might be considered. The particular priest may well not be in a position to know detailed procedures and should avoid predicting their outcome, but he should at least refer the matter to an expert in canon law and follow the advice given; otherwise, there is no proper pastoral care of the woman and family concerned.

We are all too well aware of major problems of sexual abuse by clergy, especially of minors. There are canonical norms and procedures which were simply not followed by many bishops over recent decades (they have been revised recently, but were often not implemented). What constitutes a crime in canon law and how is it to be dealt with canonically (apart from any proceedings under civil law, if relevant)? It might be thought we should not have crimes and sanctions in canon law, but recent scandals demonstrate that we need some such laws to protect people and to act on their behalf when they are victims of such crimes. On the other hand, laws have to be properly established (or promulgated) or they are not truly laws at all; some procedures developed in Britain in the Catholic Church after the Nolan Report on child sexual abuse were not in conformity with canon law. Where specific laws are needed or desired, it is important that they be proper laws. Proper laws and legal procedures are necessary to try to avoid crimes being committed, to make possible effective action on behalf of victims, and to ensure proper legal protection in ensuing procedures for anyone alleged to be responsible for perpetrating such crimes. Here the need for bishops to seek and to follow expert canonical advice in formulating and implementing effective laws in harmony with the law of the Church as a whole is essential.

These few instances may indicate that canon law has to do with what is real and important in the Church and in our world. The advice of those who understand it and who are expert in it can be useful or necessary at times to all of us, laity and clergy, as we strive to fulfil our vocation as followers of Christ. This commentary, hopefully, will show the value of the Code of Canon Law as an instrument of justice and as an instrument of the Gospel. However, it is not designed to be a detailed commentary of a highly technical nature, of the sort which experts themselves would consult. Such commentaries already exist and may be consulted with profit.[3] The aim here is more limited, namely to furnish an introductory commentary, such as may be useful to those in the Church who are not lawyers themselves, but who might like to understand something of this matter or who might need some guidance on a particular issue at a level which is serious and reliable, but which is also accessible to people in general, to laity and clergy. It is hoped that it may be of value to seminarians who are studying the Church's law as they prepare for the priesthood, to those preparing for permanent diaconate, to those entering the consecrated life. Those living and working in parishes, involved in various aspects of diocesan life, in religious or secular institutes, societies of apostolic life or in personal prelatures, may find this introduction helpful too. Perhaps, those who studied the Code of 1917 but never really came to grips with the current Code or those who never saw the point of canon law at all in their seminary days may discover the approach here more positive, more theological, than what they remember. The

---

[3.] Cf., The Canon Law Society of Great Britain and Ireland, in association with the Canadian Canon Law Society, G. Sheehy, R. Brown, D. Kelly and A. McGrath (eds) and F. Morissey (consultant ed.), *The Canon Law: Letter and Spirit: A Practical Guide to the Code of Canon Law*, Chapman, London, 1995; J. P. Beal, J. A. Coriden and T. J. Green (eds), *New Commentary on the Code of Canon Law: an entirely new and comprehensive commentary by Canonists from North America and Europe, with a new translation of the Code*, study edn, Paulist, New York, Mahwah, NJ, 2000.

aim here is not just to state what the law is, but to show its role or purpose, its origin and its meaning, presupposing no former or detailed knowledge.

It will be noticed that not all parts of the Code receive equal treatment. The Code is divided into seven books, of very unequal lengths. The first book deals with general norms of canon law, treating fundamental elements, which are then reflected in, and which are to be applied to, all the laws of the Church. These general norms will be examined because of their fundamental role, but in a generic way, to demonstrate why they are there and how they function. The last book (Book VII) is on procedural norms, also necessary in that the right way of going about implementing laws is an aspect of justice; these will be presented in their essentials, to show why they are needed and to give some examples of how they work. Nevertheless, their detailed application is a matter for specialists and treatment here will be selective.

On the other hand, the two longest books in the Code are those on the People of God (Book II) and on the sacraments (Book IV) and these will receive more careful attention. They have to do more directly with the life we lead in the Church generally and are likely to be of broader and deeper interest to the readers for whom this introductory commentary is written. The shorter books, on the teaching function of the Church (Book III), on the temporal goods of the Church, possessions, finances, etc., (Book V) and on penal law, canonical crimes and sanctions (Book VI), will also be assessed quite fully.

Since this Code of laws was called for when the Second Vatican Council was announced and since it is explicitly intended to put into legal form what that Council taught, it will not be surprising that there are many ways in which theology (the discipline which studies God, the Church and its life and work) influenced the Code. Part of the purpose of this book is to show those connections. Yet, a person might be forgiven for opening the Code of 1983 and for being bemused at the 1752 laws with which they were confronted. One means of trying to make sense of this multitude of laws which is employed here is to focus on the 'key canons' to each section, usually their opening canons. A schematic presentation of these is offered in tables, to highlight key theological and legal concepts and to give an orientation of the corresponding section. To be able to grasp these initial, but crucial points already provides an understanding of much else. What might seem daunting at first sight should begin to make sense. Once that happens, this instrument of the Gospel and of justice can be appreciated for what it is and can then serve its purpose in the life and work of the Church of Jesus Christ in our time.

Chapter 1

The Function of Canon Law and the Revision of the Code

1. Introduction

Canon law and law in general may seem to some to be a series of laws which have fallen down from heaven, to be followed with blind obedience, a restriction upon our liberty, imposed by someone more powerful than we are, an intrusion which we may be inclined to resent. That was certainly not how the Jewish people understood the law of God in the Old Testament. There it was seen as a gift and as a privilege, to make them wise and prudent, a sign of God's closeness to his people (Dt. 4:7–8; Ps. 147:20). On the other hand, merely following a set of laws cannot bring salvation; that comes from God in Jesus Christ through the Holy Spirit, to be received and lived out in a faith in Christ which is put into action, remaining always God's free gift which we do not earn (Rom. 4: 20–8).

2. Law, Justice and the Church

The Church is the community of the baptized in Jesus Christ, united to him by the Holy Spirit and in him united to the Father. One justification which has been put forward for the existence of canon law is that every society or community needs to regulate its activities and behaviour in an ordered way if it is to live in peace; wherever there is society, there is also law, according to an ancient saying (*'ubi societas, ibi lex'*). Like any other society, then, the Church needs its organization and system of law for its own specific community. It is similar to other forms of society in that it has a law, but differs from them in that it has its own law. This concept of canon law is not unreasonable. It underpins what is known as public ecclesiastical law (*'ius publicum ecclesiasticum'*) or the way the Church relates to other organized social groups or states. An expression which the Catholic Church has used about itself in the past and which recurs in the Second Vatican Council, but one which is often misunderstood, is that the Church constitutes a 'perfect society' ('*societas perfecta*'). Too often this is taken to mean that the Church is perfect in all respects and is contrasted with the defects of individuals or procedures which all too often are to be found. The Second Vatican Council taught both that the Church is perfectly holy and that it remains always in need of sanctification. Insofar as it is united to Jesus Christ in the Holy Spirit, and it never ceases to be so united, then it is and cannot but be perfectly holy. However, although some individuals live truly holy lives and manifest the holiness of the Church in their exemplary living, individuals and groups, human procedures and practices within the Church can and do fail to live up to the call we all have to be holy, so such persons within the Church do not reflect its holiness and give a counter-witness to it; thus, the Church, in most of its members, needs to grow in holiness. The expression 'perfect society' does not refer to this distinction; rather, it means simply that the Church constitutes a society distinct from other groupings of society, especially states, 'perfect' in the sense that it has, and that it is entitled to have, an organization of its own, independent from them, with its own system of laws. We shall see this reflected a number of times in the Code, where the 'innate right' of the Church to its own hierarchical structure, to its own system of penal laws, and such like, is affirmed. In the past, it is true that it was often considered necessary for the Church to operate as an independent state of a significant kind (the Papal States). Yet, it is not the Church's normal purpose directly to govern states; the Vatican City State is a very small entity, assuring the Church of a real measure of independence and the basis for much of the central work which the Church truly needs to do to fulfil its mission of spreading the Gospel.

Proclaiming and living the Gospel of Christ requires, amongst other things, some organized ways of looking after people (we have dioceses and parishes very largely). Questions of how to prepare for baptism and the other sacraments, their proper reception, how to foster and coordinate the preaching of the Gospel, how we ought to cooperate with one another in the Church, how finances needed for the Church's mission are to be arranged and properly used, are among some of the matters which need this kind of structure and order. Were everything to be left to haphazard initiatives, many people would go uncared for in the Church; duplication and conflict would be more likely. This means that there would be real injustices done to people. The common good of the community of the Church demands some organization. A system of laws, independent of the laws and governments of states, which have their own proper role and apparatus, is designed to serve the common good of the Church in its mission of transmitting the Gospel of the Lord.

It could hardly suffice, as a justification for the existence of canon law, to invoke the saying that every society needs law; this is true, but it is insufficient. It matters very much what sort of law is envisaged and what sort of society it is to serve. As the society of the People of God, of those baptized in Christ to be bearers and servants of the Gospel, it is indispensable that its society strive for justice and that its laws be at the service of justice. Justice involves giving everyone their due ('*suum cuique*' – 'to each his own'). It is much broader than law, which does not extend to all moral obligations rooted in justice, as with many of the details of parents' moral responsibility to care for a sick child. Law has to be concerned with the common good of people and not every aspect of what is good for individuals.

On the other hand, there are different conceptions of what is good for people, different ways of looking at the common good, at justice and at what it means to give everyone their due. Many societies in the past considered that slavery was right or normal and thought justice was served by maintaining people in that condition, with a minority of 'citizens' enjoying a different and better form of 'justice'. More recently, some have taken justice to mean above all the maintenance of an economic system based on the possession of goods and property, to the point where those without were systematically deprived of access to many of the goods of the earth. The ideological imposition of 'justice' through class hatred and class war in communism or through extreme nationalist and racialist policies has led to the most appalling abuses of the human person. All of these have had their systems of 'law' to promote and to impose their version of 'justice', according to the underlying rationale they adopted.

A democratic system of government may well seem to be the best way of trying to protect against such abusive systems and, for this reason at least, is to be preferred to autocratic, dictatorial or authoritarian regimes. However, democracy does not guarantee what is objectively morally right, nor can it guarantee authentic justice.[1]

A tendency in recent decades, within many democratic societies, has been that of advancing particular causes by means of well-organized groups of lobbyists, media campaigns and other propaganda to assert so-called 'rights' in the name of 'justice', even to the point

---

[1] John Paul II, Encyclical letter, *Centesimus annus*, 1 May 1991, nn. 46–7.

9

where a 'right' to marriage of homosexual couples has been claimed under conventions on human rights or where a 'right' for a woman to have 'access' to a 'legal and safe abortion' has been proposed in a resolution before the European Parliament.[2] Laws actually in existence or proposed do not automatically enshrine what is just and the mere fact that a society, even a democratic society through a majority decision, enacts laws does not make them right or obligatory in conscience.

Canon law must be grounded in justice, but that justice is to be rooted in what can be discerned not as the will of certain groups, even of dominant ones, in a society, but as what is truly good and just as such. Law which is declared or established by human beings is not a reflection of justice if it expresses only the good of a group (partial or even party good), but only where it accords with the common good of all. That common good in turn cannot be identified simply with what most people want or decide; that may result in a majority law oppressing an ethnic or cultural minority, pretending to impose or permit what is of its nature morally wrong. It can only be grounded on what is fundamentally good in each and all of its basic aspects, good for each and for all, what is due to each and to all human beings simply because they are human beings, their true and integral good. This good can be discerned when our reason operates correctly ('right reason' or '*recta ratio*') and not in a prejudiced, selfish or partial manner.[3] Authentic human laws thus always reflect and protect basic human goods (life, health, justice, marriage, truth, religious liberty, and so on); they never contradict the basic elements of our true and integral good as human beings nor the moral responsibilities which arise in their regard, which are part of natural moral law and which are recognized by right reason.[4] To serve justice, then, all human laws must serve the common good, understood in the way just described. If they violate this condition, they are not true laws and they lack the full force of law.

[2.] Resolution of the Parliamentary Assembly of the Council of Europe, Strasbourg, on 'Access to safe and legal abortion' (doc. 11537), 16 April 2008, accessed 12 July 2009, 'webmaster, assembly@coe.int'.

[3.] St Thomas Aquinas, *Summa theologiae*, I–II, q. 90, a. 1: 'A law is a certain rule or measure of acts, according to which someone is led to act or is restrained from acting. Yet, something is called a law from its having binding force, because it obliges (us) in regard to our acts. The rule and measure of acts is reason, which is the first principle of human acts ...' (The translations are mine, unless otherwise stated.)

[4.] G. Grisez, *The Way of the Lord Jesus*, I, *Christian Moral Principles*, Franciscan Herald Press, Chicago, 1983, 121–34.

There does not seem to be a law which is not just; hence to the extent that it stems from justice, it has something of the character of law. In human affairs, though, something is said to be just from its being right in accordance with the rule of reason, for the first rule of reason is natural law ... Therefore, every human law has the character of law insofar as it is derived from the law of nature; if, in fact, it disagrees with natural law in anything, it will not now be law, but a corruption of law.[5]

Canon law is one example of human law, of law established by human beings in many of its provisions, and so it must protect and promote this common good in the interests of justice.[6] This it is to do first of all, in regard to the particular society for which it is particularly designed, those who are baptized in Christ, more specifically Catholics and, in the 1983 Code, Catholics of the Latin rite of the Church. Yet, it is to serve the common good, and the elements of the authentic human good to which it relates, of all Christians and of all people. It contradicts neither this fundamental human good nor its essential elements and so it does not contradict what are true and authentic human rights.

While canon law is directed to the specific communities mentioned, it does not remove what truly are basic human rights from anyone, although, of course, it will concern itself with the conduct of people who have given up the exercise of certain rights for the purpose of serving the Gospel in a specific way (as with those who renounce the natural right to marry, to give a particular witness to the over-riding importance of the Gospel and of the eternal life it proclaims by living a celibate life or living under a vow of consecrated chastity).

3. Law and the Community of the Baptized

If canon law must enshrine the demands of justice and must stand at the service of the common good, these realities cannot be understood simply on the basis of what pertains in society at large. The particular community which it is to serve, as an instrument of justice, is the Church as the community of the baptized and especially that of the

---

[5.] St Thomas Aquinas, *Summa theologiae*, I–II, q. 95, a. 2.
[6.] Ibid., I–II, q. 90, a. 2: 'However, since each part is ordered to the whole, as the imperfect is to the perfect, ... it is essential that law properly relate to our common ordering to happiness ... Thus, since law may be said primarily to be that which is in accordance with the order which is directed towards the common good, it follows necessarily that any particular command of law whatsoever, concerning some specific behaviour, does not have the character of law unless it is itself in accordance with the order which is directed towards the common good; therefore, every law is ordered to the common good.'

Latin Catholic Church. It will become clear very quickly that there are considerations which necessarily pertain to canon law, which would hardly make sense in society more broadly, except in what is a significant aspect, namely, that of giving witness to the degree of coherence with which Christians live out the demands of the Gospel. Inevitably, the Church's law must concern itself with the things of God, with spiritual realities, with eternal life and happiness or beatitude (blessedness), although the object of its laws will always be the way human beings are or ought to be related to those spiritual realities, in terms of being part of the common good of the People of God. In fact, all law reflects the understanding of life which is shared by those who devise it. All law ought, in reality, to be guided by and be based upon that happiness or state of blessedness, which is the destiny of all of us, according to the plan of God.[7] This is especially true of canon law and constitutes one of its most distinctive features. Some of its provisions are said to be of divine law, so that these are 'declared' or 'expressed' in the Church's law, rather than being 'established' as laws, while other provisions are truly human laws, being made by human law-givers, the Pope and at times others insofar as they are competent. Both elements are to reflect the divine origin and mission of the Church.

Here we see a specifically theological purpose and function of canon law, which in no way detracts from what has been said about justice and the common good, but which stems from the specific character of the people who form the community for which this law exists, most directly the community of the Church, of those baptized in Christ. Already in the Old Testament there had been a preoccupation with justice as an indispensable dimension of the Covenant between God and his chosen people, Israel. God, as the Creator, had brought people into existence, as the pinnacle of his work of creation, creating them in his image and likeness (Gen. 1:26–8), with the vocation to be united with one another in a society which was built upon marriage (Gen. 1:27, 2:23–5), subduing the fact of the earth to place its resources at the disposal of all, and to be united with him in the seventh-day rest (Gen. 1:26–31). The sexual differentiation between male and female was the basis of a complementarity between them. The fundamental equality of all human beings, which God's act of creation implies, provides a deep theological foundation for the justice which must rest at the basis of all law. It is reflected in the 'charter' of the Covenant, which God had

---

7. Ibid., I–II, q. 90, a. 2.

offered to the Hebrews after liberating them (Ex. 19:3–6), in his mercy and compassion (Ex. 3:7–10; 6:5–6), from the oppression of slavery and saving them through water and in the desert, through the ten words, the Decalogue or Ten Commandments (Ex. 20:1–17; Dt. 5:1–22). Apart from the specific ways in which people are called to worship God, these ten words, the foundation of all morality and justice, are capable of being recognized as true and as binding in conscience by all whose reason is functioning correctly, on the basis of 'right reason' and, indeed, form the cornerstone of many systems of law for that very reason. Here we see that the demands of justice are an indispensable part of belonging to the community of believers of the People of God. This crucial link is reinforced by particular, casuistic laws or laws dealing with particular situations, in which justice towards those in the community who are least able to defend themselves, the poor, widows, orphans and strangers, is demanded as a sign of fidelity to the Covenant (Ex. 22:20–4; Dt. 24:6, 10–15, 17–21). God reveals himself repeatedly as the God of justice and those responsible for the administration of justice, of laws, are to ensure that the poor and the weak are not exploited, but that justice is done.

Those who were representatives of God in his dealings with Israel were to assure his people of justice. Thus, King David was rebuked for his injustice in committing adultery with Uriah's wife and then in having Uriah murdered (2 Sam. 12:1–10). The prophets proclaimed God's justice against those who were swindlers (Amos 5:24; 8:4–8). In the Psalms God is often called the 'God of justice', who would assure his people of justice, insisting on just judgments in courts without bribery and corruption (Ps. 1:6; 14:2, 5; 57:1–2; 74:1–2, 7; 81:1–8; 93:20–1; 98:4; 118).

In the New Testament the New Covenant, established in and through Jesus, reveals the unlimited compassion of God towards us and saves us from the slavery of sin and of death through his resurrection. Embracing that gift in faith, through baptism (Mk. 1:14–15; Acts 2:38; Rom. 6:1–11), we become part of the New People of God, the Church. In this society or community, too, justice is a requirement of how we are to live in communion with Christ, since to live otherwise is a serious contradiction of our relationship with him and of the Covenant. Indeed, our justice has to be profound, going beyond that of the Scribes or the Pharisees or else we will never enter the kingdom of heaven (Mt. 5:17–20). It has to be reflected in the way we treat one another, since to despise others or hold them in contempt is to be gravely unjust and to open up the road which leads to hatred and murder (Mt. 5:21–6). Justice will be done by God who judges justly,

13

as the parable of the rich man and Lazarus shows (Lk. 16:19–31). The fundamental equality of all the baptized, of the People of God of the New Covenant, rests on the saving action of Christ, on his granting us a share in that victory of his. It is this basic equality which calls for relationships of justice between us, such that to be unjust towards the poor or towards other groups entails violating the Covenant, putting ourselves outside the bond of union with Christ (Jas. 2:1–13). As St Paul puts it:

> You are all of you, sons of God through faith in Christ Jesus. All baptized in Christ, you have all clothed yourselves in Christ and there are no more distinctions between Jew and Greek, slave and free, male and female, but all of you are one in Christ Jesus. (Gal. 3:26–8)

The mystery of our salvation through the death and resurrection of Christ and our relationship to him in the Holy Spirit and through them with our heavenly Father are realities crucial to what the Church itself is. Properly speaking, it is not even the community of those who have been baptized, but it is that community, across history, in their union with Christ in the Spirit. Without Jesus Christ, there is no Church and without the Holy Spirit, there is no Church. Canon law has to be rooted in these sacred mysteries, as it seeks to order our relationships in justice for the common good of the People of God.

The Church is a mysterious reality, a spiritual reality, but one also visible in time and through history. The Church is to allow Christ, the light of the nations, to shine on all people through the Gospel and it is 'like a sacrament, or a sign and instrument of intimate union with God and of the unity of the whole human race'.[8] Already, the nature of the Church as both an invisible and spiritual reality and as a visible community on earth emerges. 'This is the one Church of Christ, one, holy, Catholic and Apostolic ... constituted and structured in this world as a society, subsists in the Catholic Church.'[9] The higher justice, beyond that of the Scribes and the Pharisees, is new because it is in Christ. Canon law is to reflect the specific nature of the Church, at the service of this superior justice and its fulfilment in the loving communion of heaven in Christ. It is to help to structure and order this

---

[8.] Second Vatican Council, Dogmatic Constitution on the Church, *Lumen gentium*, 21 November 1964, n. 1: *Sacrosancta oecumenica Concilium Vaticanum II: constitutiones, decreta, declarations*, Secretariae Concilii oecumenici Vaticani II, Typis polyglottis vaticanis, 1974. All references to the Latin text of the Council, its authentic text, are taken from this edition; translations are mine, unless otherwise indicated.

[9.] Ibid., n. 8.

community of the baptized, as it responds to its Christ-given mission of proclaiming the Gospel to all people, so that all may share in the glory of his resurrection. The Church is at the service of this deepening communion with God in Christ and, in him, with all the baptized. In its mission of preaching the Gospel to all people, it is to promote this communion with all people, since all are called to salvation.[10]

4. Canon Law and Theology

Since the first Code of Canon Law in 1917, its theological character has been brought out much more, to emphasize its role in relation to the Church and its mission of salvation. The German canonist, Klaus Mörsdorf, had examined the first Code of the Church from this perspective, in relation to the Word of God which is to be preached and the sacraments which are celebrated and which are means of uniting the faithful more fully with Our Lord.

On the other hand, there are different schools of canon law, with varying outlooks. The lay school of Italian canonists, of whom C. Jemolo and E. Dieni were typical, recognize the peculiar position of the Church as having a spiritual dimension, but insist that canon law is a juridical reality. Anything which cannot be fitted into such categories is classified as 'meta-juridical' or beyond the scope of law, for example, the Spirit, grace.[11] Often highly critical of what they see as the role of the Roman Curia, this school treats canon law as a specific system of law on a par with civil law; it is part of legal science, often seen to be at the service of people in the Church (perhaps more sociologically in terms of what they may want or consider they 'need'). It would not necessarily involve taking truths of revelation or doctrinal truths more generally as normative for the law.

The juridical nature of canon law is the focus of the *Opus Dei* school of Navarre, whose experts include J. Hervada, J. I. Arieta and P. Lombardía.[12] However, their approach is very notably different from

---

[10.] Ibid., nn. 13, 40–1.

[11.] For example, E. Dieni, *Tradizione 'juscorporalistica' e codificazione del matrimonio canonico*, Giuffré, Milan, 1999; Jemolo was a prominent writer of this school after the 1917 Code.

[12.] For example, Hervada and Lombardía have edited a bi-lingual text and commentary as an 'exegetical' commentary on the Code of 1983 (Latin-Spanish), *Commentario exegético del código de derecho canónico*, EUNSA, Pamplona, 1996: cf. the 2nd, revised English edition E. Caparros, M. Thériault and J. Thorn (ed.), *Code of Canon Law Annotated*, Wilson and Lafleur, Montréal, Midwest Theological Forum, Woodbridge, 2004.

that of the Italian lay canonists. The Navarre school neither denies nor considers unimportant the theological and doctrinal roots of canon law; quite the opposite. They do think of it, however, as essentially juridical in that the legal consequences or implications of the truths of the faith are the proper object of canon law, as distinct from the various branches of theology, from which canon law is technically independent.

Another way of understanding canon law is to examine it from a historical perspective. This can involve going to its sources in the past to trace the reasons for particular laws, how they have developed in the meantime and what they may imply at present. Conversely, existing laws can be traced backwards to their sources and to the circumstances which may have given rise to them. The historical approach to canon law is associated with J. Gaudemet and with J. Werckmeister, among others.[13]

The Munich school of Mörsdorf and of his followers has no doubt that canon law has to occupy itself with such juridical realities, but it emphasizes the theological bases of laws more directly. Mörsdorf had structured his analysis of canon law around an understanding of the theology of the Church, ecclesiology, especially emphasizing the importance of word and sacrament in the mission and in the building up of the Church itself, seeing canon law as a 'theological discipline with a juridical method'. This self-consciously theological approach to canon law has been embraced by many more recently, notably by E. Corecco, who considered canon law primarily from the perspective of 'communion' ('communio'), stemming from the sacraments of baptism and of order, that communion being present in the particular Church and in the universal Church, with canon law both expressing and serving to build up that communion.[14]

There is no doubt that the 1983 Code has more explicit theological references than did its predecessor of 1917. One approach to this has been to see the role of canon law as grounded in an understanding of the Church, but as basically related to the administration of the sacraments, in its origins. Its expansion beyond such a function has been seen by some as excessive, with the consequent suggestion

---

13. For example, J. Gaudemet, *Église et cité: Histoire du droit canonique*, Cerf, Paris, 1994.

14. M. Wijlens, *Theology and Canon Law: The Theories of Klaus Mörsdorf and Eugenio Corecco*, Univ. Press of America, Lanham, New York, London, 1992; A. Cattaneo, 'The Contribution of Eugenio Corecco to Canon Law: A Key to Understanding' in G. Borgonovo and A. Cattaneo (eds), E. Corecco, *Canon Law and Communio: Writings in the Constitutional Law of the Church*, Libreria editrice Vaticana, 2004, 36–44 at 36–41.

that it should play a more restricted role.[15] For L. Örsy, canon law is related to theology by dealing with the implications of faith and in directing actions stemming from faith, whereas theology is concerned more with seeking to understand faith.[16]

G. Ghirlanda reflects upon the mystery of the Church not only in regard to its divine origin, its origin in revelation, and its essentially theological foundations, without which canon law cannot be understood, but also as necessarily a historical reality, the People of God, making its way through history and seeking to live out that mystery. While never reducing the mystery to the concrete, historical form in which it is to be lived, this latter dimension, with specifically human forms of institution and law, cannot be ignored without turning the Church into something unreal. Both divine law and human (ecclesiastical) law which make up canon law reflect these two inseparable dimensions of the Church.[17]

As can be seen, there is a richness of approaches here to what canon law is and to how it can be approached. They are not necessarily all mutually incompatible. The structuring of the common good in the interest of justice, both within the community of the Church and more generally, and at the service of the Church's communion and mission, rooted in Jesus Christ and in his Gospel, are essential aspects of the Church's law. The Second Vatican Council asked for canon law to 'take into account the mystery of the Church', as set out in the Dogmatic Constitution on the Church.[18] That text highlights the spiritual and the visible dimensions of the Church, as inseparable from one another, as the following extracts indicate:

- Christ 'ever sustains here on earth his Holy Church, the community of faith hope and charity, as a visible organization through which He communicates truth and grace to all'.

- The society structured with hierarchical organs and the mystical Body of Christ, the visible society and the spiritual community, the earthly Church and the Church endowed with heavenly goods ... form one complex reality, which coalesces from the divine and human element.

[15.] P. Huizing, 'Reflections on the System of Canon Law', *The Jurist*, 42 (1982), 239–76.
[16.] L. Örsy, 'Integrated Interpretation or the Role of Theology in the Interpretation of Canon Law', *Studia canonica*, 22 (1988), 245–64.
[17.] G. Ghirlanda, *Il diritto nella Chiesa: mistero di comunione*, 4th revised edn, Paoline, Cinisello Balsamo; Pontificia Università Gregoriana, Rome, 2006, 34–5, n. 19.
[18.] Second Vatican Council, Decree on Priestly Training, *Optatam totius*, n. 16.

– This is the only Church of Christ, which in the Creed we profess to be one, holy, Catholic and apostolic ... This Church, constituted and organized as a society in this world, subsists in the Catholic Church, governed by the Successor of Peter and by the Bishops in communion with him, granted that many elements of sanctification and of truth are found outside its common structures, which as properly gifts of Christ to the Church, lead towards Catholic unity.[19]

5. The Historical Sources of Canon Law

After this synopsis of what canon law is, it will be useful to look next at its sources and at its history, at least in a summary form, to be able to appreciate better how it has emerged and how it may serve the purposes we have just outlined.

a. Scriptural Foundations of Canon Law

The sources of canon law go back to the Scriptures of the New Testament, even though the term 'canon law' does not appear there. The fact that canon law is based upon the revelation given by God in Christ and transmitted by the Church does not mean that every item of canon law can always or easily be referred to a specific biblical text, but it does mean that the Church's law rests ultimately upon these sacred foundations. The Scriptures do not provide canon law as we know it, but, among the moral norms which are given, there are some which can be discerned to have the function which canon law later came to have, of regulating the Church insofar as it is a visible society, for its good order and the common good of its members, including the facilitation of its missionary activity of spreading the Gospel. Perhaps some of these functions may be detected in the following texts:

Mt. 19:1–10 (Mk. 10:1–10; Lk. 16:18)

Jesus's teaching, challenging to his Jewish listeners and to the Apostles themselves on the indissolubility of marriage and prohibition of divorce is the basis of the Catholic Church's refusal to accept that those who are in a valid, sacramental and consummated marriage may truly divorce and so re-marry.

[19.] *Lumen gentium*, n. 8.

Acts 15:19–20

The Council of Jerusalem dealt with a critical issue of how far former Jewish practices, especially circumcision, were to be required of new converts, particularly in the Greek world. Its conclusions became normative for the early Church, were designed not only to foster its good order and avoid possibly serious dissension and division, but also and primarily to facilitate effective evangelization by jettisoning as compulsory what was not essential (circumcision) in favour of what was essential (reliance upon the grace of Christ and avoidance of idolatry and fornication).

1 Cor. 7:12–16

Paul decided on the basis of his Apostolic authority (in an act of moral Magisterium) that, for marriages involving the non-baptized, indissolubility was to be observed, unless the non-believer prevented the believer from living (the faith) in peace, in which case there could be a separation. No permission to re-marry was involved. This is not just moral teaching, but it is also a matter of Church order and relates to the sacrament (of baptism). Thus, it can also be regarded canonically and became the basis in later canon law of the so-called 'Pauline privilege'.

1 Cor. 11: 4–6, 33–4

A man is forbidden to wear a veil when praying, but a woman is required to do so or to have her head shaved, both as a matter of respect. Christians are to respect one another, especially the poor, and to avoid greed and drunkenness in connection with the celebration of the Eucharist. The regulations about dress and hairstyle seem to have been time-conditioned laws.

1 Tim. 2:8–12; 3:2–12

Women were not to wear braided hair or jewellery or expensive clothes; nor were they to teach men. The conditions needed to be a 'presiding elder' (or 'priest') were laid down: such a person was neither to have been married more than once nor to be a neophyte nor a heavy drinker, and was to be courteous, peaceable, a good teacher, who looked after his own family well and was of good reputation. This is perhaps significant for the fact that canon law would later include laws on the position of people in the Church, on the basis of the sacrament of Holy Orders.

b. Canons and Decretals

Apart from scriptural sources of what became canon law, it is very difficult to be sure what gave rise to canon law, especially in a period of sporadic, but intense persecution and before the law was systematized. Nevertheless, the authority of the *Didache,* of the *Apostolic Tradition* of Hippolytus, and of the Fathers of the Church in general, is evident from many citations found in collections of canons handed down.[20] Given early Church concerns about order and about the celebration of baptism and of the Eucharist, it is not surprising that these were a focus for its laws at the time.

After the toleration of Christianity by Constantine in 313 and its establishment as the official religion of the Empire by Theodosius in 380, the collapse of the Roman Empire in the West, as well as Constantine's transfer of the capital to Byzantium earlier in 330, meant that Eastern influence was strong, particularly through the Emperors. The *Code* of Theodosius and the *Digest* of Justinian showed that the Emperors sought to decide matters of law for the Church, as well as for civil society, although there was a distinction, since *nomos* signalled a civil law and *kanon* law for the Church. Civil law had some influence on canon law, too, because the Roman lawyers (Modestinus, Ulpian, as well as Justinian) had such a developed system of law. Yet, much of this was lost to the West in the Dark Ages. As the Church expanded after persecution had ended, the move from towns to countryside meant bishops ordained priests to assist them in looking after much larger numbers of people. Regulations concerning admission to and the administration of sacraments, such as baptism, Eucharist and Penance developed too.

Law was often part of texts which were doctrinal in nature and was often not distinguished adequately from doctrine. As barbarian invasion and conquest severely disrupted the West, the fragmentation affected not only church discipline, but the awareness of and access to laws. Nevertheless, laws were produced from ecumenical (general) or provincial synods of bishops, and from the popes, whose primacy was acknowledged in various respects and to varying degrees. Constantine had called the first great ecumenical Council at Nicaea in 325. Not only did this clarify teaching on the divinity of Christ, but it appended its decisions as rules to be implemented and observed, as canons. Laws

---

20. J. Gaudemet, 'Les sources du Décret de Gratien', *Revue de droit canonique,* 48 (1998), 247–59 at 249–53.

introduced by the decision of councils were called 'canons'.[21] Many of the councils were provincial or regional: in Spain (Elvira 300 and a series at Toledo until 703), Gaul (Arles, 314) and Africa (Carthage, 348). Laws established by the popes were called 'decretals'.[22] The number of such decretals increased in the fifth century, for example, those of (or perhaps slightly earlier than) Pope Gelasius I (492–96), dealing with the primacy of the Roman Pontiff, the duty to accept the four ecumenical Councils held to date and the duty to accept the writings of specified Fathers, while rejecting the doctrines of heretical authors.[23]

The decretals rested on the authority of the Pope as the successor of Peter, who was consulted on that account about matters of concern. The decretals both demonstrated and fostered the exercise of papal authority. The problems with such a system of laws, apart from the weakness of the Church in being able to coordinate and enforce them, was that they grew up in different situations and were not ordered, which made it hard to make efficient and effective use of them. One of the important developments was, therefore, the growth of 'collections' of canon laws. The earliest collections were simply arranged or compiled on the basis of their chronological origin, providing the most up-to-date version in the latest texts, but they were still very difficult to use effectively.[24] Then, there were attempts to produce systematic collections. Such collections were disseminated on a somewhat erratic basis to other areas, as the political conditions of the times permitted. Some of the more important of the collections were the following:

The Antiochene Collection, the 'Tripartita' and the 'nomocanons'. In the East the codification of Justinian in his *Digest* in the sixth century was a great source of canon as well as civil law. Since Theodosius had declared Christianity the official religion of the Empire in 380, the Christian Emperors legislated for the Church as well as for the State. An early collection of canon laws in Antioch in the fourth century had

---

[21.] For example, Nicaea (325): Denzinger-Schönmetzer, *Enchiridion symbolorum, declarationum et definitionum de rebus fidei et morum*, 36th edn, Herder, Barcelona, Freiburg-im-Breisgau, Rome, 1976, nn. 127–9; J. Neuner and J. Dupuis, *The Christian Faith in the Doctrinal Statements of the Catholic Church*, 2nd edn, Mercier, Dublin & Cork, 1976, nn. 7–8.

[22.] For example, The 'Tome of Damasus': DS, nn. 152–77; ND, *The Christian Faith*, n. 306.

[23.] 'Decretum Gelasianum', DS, nn. 350–4.

[24.] P. Erdo, *Storia delle fonti del diritto canonico*, Marcianum, Venice, 2008, 30–9: German original, *Die Quellen des Kirchenrechts: Eine geschichtliche Einführung*, Frankfurt-am-Main, 2002.

pre-dated Justinian, but later on a systematic collection of laws was produced; the *Tripartita* of the sixth century dealt with ecclesiastical laws in Justinian and in later texts, organizing the canons into three parts on clergy, bishops and religious, on offices and church matters, and on actions against heretics, Jews and pagans.[25] By the eleventh century the East had *Collectiones nomocanonum* or collections of civil laws and of canon laws, organised systematically. However, the contact between East and West in these centuries was limited.

In the West the key collections included:
The *Dionysiana*: Dennis the Little (Dionysius exiguus) at Rome in the time of Gelasius I and afterwards, was asked by the Pope to compile an ordered set of laws, probably in the years after Gelasius, in the early sixth century. He produced a list of canons from the Greek Councils, translated into Latin, and added a number of decretals. Not only did he distinguish between canons and decretals, with two separate books on each, but he produced some systematic material and also purified the texts of doctrinal comment to produce a juridical work, although the work is seen by some as chronological, rather than systematic, in nature.[26] When Charlemagne asked Pope Hadrian for legal guidelines, an updated version was sent in 774 (the *Dionysiana-hadriana*).[27]

Hispana (Isidoriana): The early seventh century saw a collection of canons from the synods of Toledo by Isidore of Seville. Canonical collections in Spain ceased after the Islamic conquests of 711. The collection was mainly chronological and was used in other countries.

The Dacheriana: This was a collection discovered by D'Achéry in the 1680s. It stems from the ninth-century Carolingian period near Lyons and is based on a combination of the Dyonisiana-Hadriana and the Isidoriana (Hispana). It is a systematic, rather than a chronological, collection of laws and deals especially with penance, procedural law and the clergy.[28]

The Vetus gallica: This ninth-century collection of provincial councils,

---

[25] C. Van de Wiel, *History of Canon Law*, Peeters, Eerdmans, Louvain, 1991, 42–3.

[26] Ibid., 47–9; P. Vadrini et al., *Droit canonique*, 2nd edn, Dalloz, Paris, 1999, 5.

[27] J. A. Coriden, *An Introduction to Canon Law*, revised edn, Paulist, New York, Mahwah, NJ, 2004, 15.

[28] Erdo, *Storia delle fonti ...*, 77.

for example, of Arles, was a systematic collection from about 600; it dealt with church reform.

The Decretum of Burchard of Worms, 1022: This is one of the most important texts of the time, not least because it collected together the Dionysiana-Hadriana, the Pseudo-Isidoriana and two ninth-century texts, the *Anselmo dedicata* and the *Libri duo de synodalibus causis*. The first, dedicated to an archbishop of Milan, concerned the relationship between bishops and monasteries, papal primacy, and other matters. The second was the result of a diocesan investigation in Trier, under Reginald of Prüm, of the clergy (one book) and of the laity (the second book), with formulae for excommunication which the bishop could use on his visitations.[29] Burchard was especially concerned to stress the role of the bishop and was to insist on limiting the role of lay powers. In an age of Viking and Saracen attacks, forms of feudalism had begun to develop and nobles protecting a certain territory had often sought priests or monks for spiritual assistance or powerful abbots had exercised such a role themselves, often giving house and land (a benefice) in return for the spiritual services to be rendered to them and to the people under them (office). Since the control of powerful lay leaders over the Church had arisen in this way, the provision of benefices in relation to offices threatened the proper autonomy of the Church and the spiritual work of the clergy.[30] His Decree gathers material from penitential books from Ireland, as well as matrimonial laws; it deals with clerical celibacy and generally with the reform of the Church which the eleventh century was to witness.

Tripartita, Decretum and Panormia of Ives of Chartres, 1095: Ives of Chartres produced a list of papal decretals from Clement I to Urban II and extracts from the canons of councils. The *Decretum* used a good deal of Burchard of Worms, but was chronological and difficult to use. The *Panormia* was more systematically organized. Ives argued for papal primacy, for the primacy of the spiritual over the temporal, but incorporated the laws of secular rulers where they did not conflict with those of the Church and urged cooperation between Church and State. He also provided much in the latter work which was of value in juridical practice.[31]

[29.] Ibid., 87.

[30.] Van de Wiel, *History of Canon Law*, 69–71.

[31.] J. Gaudemet, *Les sources du droit canonique VIIIe–XXe siècle*, Cerf, Paris, 1993, 95–7; Erdo, *Storia delle fonti*, 98–100.

False decretals: These were issued especially in the ninth century and associated with the names of important bishops or Church Fathers, for example. the Pseudo-Isidorian decretals. The pressure for church authorities to liberate themselves from secular power after the dependencies of the fractured political situation following Charlemagne and Otto the Great and in the throes of attacks from Norsemen, Saracens and Hungarians, led to efforts to reinforce claims not just to papal primacy, but to papal control of central Italy and superiority over the Emperor (as manifested by the *Dictatus Papae* of Gregory VII of 1075), which stated, amongst other things, that 'the Roman Pontiff alone has universal rule' and that 'the Roman Pontiff may impose and depose'.[32] The practice of feudal lords granting part of their land for the building of a chapel, engaging a priest to fulfil a particular duty there (*officium*) and allowing him the benefit of that land or dues (*beneficium*), however understandable in a context of the need for protection from invasion and attack, undermined the proper autonomy of the Church. The problem of *simony*, of buying spiritual benefits, was a further difficulty. Efforts to reform clergy morals, including the imposition of celibacy as a rule in the Western Church, the election of the Pope predominantly by the cardinals, the refusal of lay investiture under Gregory VII, made it a tense time in which legal and doctrinal justification was at a premium. From the ninth century false decretals, such as the Donation of Constantine of the Papal States, had been elaborated, some of which were used in collections, although unwittingly, by this time.

c. The **Corpus iuris canonici** *or Body of Canon Law*

The great Roman lawyer, the Emperor Justinian, had produced a massive compendium of civil laws, known as the 'Body of Civil Law' or *Corpus iuris civile*. The Body of Canon Law consisted of two main parts, Gratian's Decree and the decretals of Gregory IX and certain subsequent materials.

Gratian's *Decretum*
In the twelfth century, the first university in Europe, Bologna, was established and it focused, amongst other things, upon law, both civil and canon law. Its greatest figure for canon law was Gratian, whose

---

[32.] Gregory VII, 'Dictatus Papae' in G. Barraclough, *The Medieval Papacy*, Thames and Hudson, 1967, 87, nn. 2 and 12 of the papal text.

mastery of the sources of canon law was such that he was held to be the Master of canon law and was known often just as the 'Master'. A 'master's degree' meant exactly that, that someone was a true master of the sources of their subject, to the point of being able to analyse them systematically and accurately, with the authority of a profound expert. Master Gratian of Bologna was the first scientific canon lawyer. His massive and detailed work, the *Concordia discordantium canonum*, known more usually as Gratian's *Decretum* or the *Decretum Gratiani* of 1140 was not just another collection of canon laws. In this '*Agreement of discordant canons*' he provided a critical analysis of the texts he found. What is known as the 'Twelfth Century Renaissance' not only saw the development of universities, especially at Bologna and at Paris, but in Bologna the focus on law was fostered by the discovery, earlier in the century, of Justinian's *Digest* of civil law, which Gratian used in compiling his Decree.

Gratian collated earlier materials in a structured fashion, quoting his authorities and giving their texts, but what was so new was his commentary on the texts and his analysis of them in a systematic and scientific study of the laws he arranged. He assessed sources, considered conflicting statements in various collections and argued the case for one interpretation rather than another. Master Gratian was a teacher of canon law, master of his sources and the most important, authoritative interpreter of canon law the Church had yet seen or, perhaps, has ever seen. Together with what followed in the next century, his Decree was to be the basis of the Church's canon law until 1917. Even though Gratian was the 'father of canon law', his work was the work of a professor of law; it was not law itself, was never formally authorized, never officially promulgated. Yet, it was the basis of subsequent papal decretals and of the study of canon law itself. In practice, it provided assistance to the lawyer popes such as Alexander III (1159–81), Innocent III (1198–1216), Gregory IX (1227–41) and Innocent IV (1243–54), as they extended papal influence, not least through encouraging reference to Rome of disputes and questions about the Church or about church rights with respect to the State.

The very title of the work shows Gratian's intention of bringing the inherited, disparate and often contradictory laws (*discordantium canonum*) into some sort of order, so that they could be understood, used and applied. His method was dialectical, a method used by Arab philosophers who transmitted Aristotle to Europe about this time, which helped to foster this approach in Scholastic theology as a whole. He compared previous legal statements and sources, whom he listed, giving extensive or complete presentations and, where there were discrepancies in the sources or where there were disputed current issues to which they needed to be applied, he gave his own evaluations or sayings (the 'dicta Gratiani'). Gratian sought to analyse the law on the basis of the place and time of their origin or promulgation, their meaning and the extent of their validity, so that he conducted a truly juridical science, with both a scientific presentation and analysis of law and its practical application too.

Although Gratian established canon law as a discipline distinct from theology, he was a theologian too. He engaged in debate with the great theologian of the university of Paris, Peter Lombard, whose *IV Libri Sententiarum*, 'Four Books of the Sentences' or judgments, were his considered judgments on the theological matters of the day. In particular, the two great masters disagreed about what made a marriage indissoluble; for Peter Lombard it was the consent of the parties; for Gratian this was necessary, but not sufficient, since this had to be followed by carnal union for the marriage to be indissoluble (the 'consensus-copula' debate). Gratian's Decree is divided into three sections. The first part consists of *Distinctions* (101), divided into canons, the second of *Causae* (36), divided into questions, and the third, on consecration, a later addition perhaps by a disciple and successor, Paucapalea. The matters treated in part I are the sources of the law, the Church's hierarchy, qualities of those to be ordained, ordination, choice of bishops, and the duties of the clergy. Part II covers procedure, the prohibition of simony, the power of the bishop, matters of property, religious orders, marriage and confession.[33] Part III deals with other sacraments and liturgical matters. The first part deals with statements of what the law is, whereas the second begins from concrete cases to be examined and analysed, perhaps in lectures.[34]

It has recently been shown that the Decree was probably written in two stages, that there was an earlier, shorter version, perhaps more closely structured and with fewer repetitions and a later version, which incorporated points from the Second Lateran Council of 1139.[35] Although some parts of the *Decretum* are very well ordered, others are not. Insertions occur, e.g. on penance in the treatment of marriage. There are also comments called *paleae*, thought by some to have been the work of Paucapalea. Gratian also gives titles (rubrics) and other comments (*dicta*), where he expresses canonical doctrine. Gratian's

---

[33.] Van de Wiel, *History of Canon Law*, 99–102.

[34.] Gaudemet, *Les sources du droit canonqiue*, 110–14.

[35.] A. Winroth, 'Les deux Gratien et le droit romain', *Revue de droit canonique*, 48 (1998), 285–99.

Decretum was a private collection in the sense that it was never officially promulgated as the law of the Church as such. It relied for its validity on the origin of each of the laws it contained. Nevertheless, it covered a wide range of issues, which had been the concern of church law from the start. It was studied and commented upon by scholars called 'decretists' and was used by popes and bishops in juridical aspects of their work; it was of major significance.

The Decretals

The second half of the *Corpus iuris canonici* or of the Body of Canon Law consists of the Decretals, first of all of Gregory IX and then of some later popes. In the period after Gratian not only was there the commentary of his disciple Paucapalea, but there were further laws issued by the popes and these needed to be integrated into the system. Over the years five sets of compilations of papal decretals were made, which were 'integrated' into Gratian's *Decretum*, but which were in some instances only private compilations, while in other they were properly promulgated, as with the third compilation by Innocent III. Innocent III was also responsible for the Fourth Lateran Council of 1215, which promulgated many canons against heresies of the time, on the Schism with the Greeks, on penance (the duty to go to confession and the obligation of the seal of confession), on clandestine marriages and on simony.[36]

Pope Gregory IX commissioned the canonist, Raymond of Penyafort, to collect and organize in a systematic way papal decretals since the Decree of Gratian. He produced what are known as the *Decretals of Gregory IX* in five books. These were organized in a way parallel to the laws of Justinian (sources, persons, things, actions or procedures and penal law). In 1234 Gregory promulgated these five books, formally establishing them as laws, publishing them at the University of Bologna and perhaps at Paris. In addition to assembling and ordering papal decretals, he had integrated into these texts the canons of the Third and Fourth Lateran Councils, as well as some secular laws.[37] The purpose was to gather together all that had not been included in Gratian's *Decretum* and all that had been issued since, in a structured and harmonious way. The *Decretales* all had the force of papal law through Gregory's promulgation.[38] The commentators on these texts were the 'decretalists'.

---

[36] Fourth Lateran Council, DS, nn. 800–20.
[37] Gaudemet, *Les sources du droit canonique*, 127–31.
[38] Erdo, *Storia delle fonti*, 120–3.

A later compilation of laws, updated and systematized, came under Boniface VIII (1294–1303 – the *Liber sextus* or sixth book, following on from the five books of Gregory's *Decretals*, promulgated in 1298. A compilation under Clement V (1304-14), sometimes called the seventh book or *Liber septimus* or the *Clementinae* was issued in 1314, but was not fully promulagted and so lacked the full force of law. Boniface VIII had not only promulgated the *Liber sextus*, but had declared that other laws in conflict with them, before and after the *Decretum*, were abrogated (abolished) in line with the principle: '*Lex posterior derogat priori nisi expresse aliud dicatur*' (a later law removes a prior law unless the opposite is expressly stated), but not abrogating the *Decretum* itself, so that it retained its juridical value, even though as such it was not law.[39]

The combination of the *Decretum Gratiani* and of the *Decretales* of Gregory IX, whose book outside the decree (*Liber extra*) consisted of five books, together with the *Liber sextus*, with the Clementinae, constitute the *Corpus iuris canonici*, analogous to Justinian's *Corpus iuris civilis*, and remained the key reference point in canon law until the Code of 1917. Other laws were said to be '*outside*' this main reference point, the *Extravagantes* of John XXII (1316–34) and the later *Extravagantes communes* compiled privately in 1500–03 were added to the Corpus by Chappuis who compiled the latter. The decrees of the Council of Trent were the canons enforcing doctrinal teaching and church reform, but the Council expressly forbade commentaries upon them. This meant that the science of canon law was impeded after Trent, although there was a treatment of the place of canon law in Suarez.[40]

By the time of Pius X in the early twentieth century, there was a need to revise and update the Church's laws. Pius X asked Cardinal Gasparri, a great canonist of the time, to oversee this work. This resulted in the Pio-Benedictine Code (after Pius X and Benedict XV) or the *Codex iuris canonici* of 1917, the first Code of law for the Catholic Church. It lacked the detailed sources of the *Corpus*, which it abrogated (C.I.C. (1917), c. 6), but Gasparri produced several volumes of sources, the *Codicis iuris canonici fontes*, in which the sources of that Code can be found.[41]

[39.] Van de Wiel, *History of Canon Law*, 109–10.
[40.] F. Suarez, *De legibus ac Deo legislatore*, Coimbra, 1613, Book IV.
[41.] *Codex iuris canonici*, 1917, Typis polyglottis Vaticanis, c. 6.

d. Some Initial Conclusions

Even prior to 1917 the history of canon law in the Church indicates some important points to be kept in mind in the study of canon law. The Church's law is based on the Scriptures, the Fathers, Councils and papal teaching; it is rooted in theology and in the mission of the Church as given to it by Christ. Its laws may be universal or particular, but the Codes are mainly to provide universal law, law for the whole Church. Bishops or superiors of societies of consecrated life may issue laws for their own proper subjects, but only within what is permitted by the universal law. The lawgiver for the Church as a whole, at the human level, is the Pope. A law needs to be properly promulgated or officially issued and published as law by the proper lawgiver for it to be binding, since people cannot be bound by laws they cannot know. The overwhelming majority of the canons of the Code deal with the Church's mission, with the nature and structure of the Church (the responsibilities of different people and groups within it) and with the sacramental life of the Church (preparation for, celebration and meaning of the sacraments). This has always been the focus of the Church's canon law and remains so today in the Code of 1983.

6. The Codification of Canon Law and the Revision of the Code

a. Codification and the Code of 1917

The codification of the Church's law, in the first *Codex iuris canonici* or Code of Canon Law in 1917, in the Code we are studying, the *Codex iuris canonici* of 1983 for the Latin Church and the *Codex canonum ecclesiarum orientalium* (Code of Canons for the Eastern Churches) for the Eastern Catholic Churches of 1990, was not an obvious development. We have already noticed that one of the main difficulties with a system of written laws is that they can be difficult to compile and to order. Collections of laws, chronologically or systematically structured, may be hard to use. Laws on any particular issue may not easily be found or may be lost; some may have been devised for a specific historical purpose no longer relevant and may be effectively obsolete, while still being officially in operation. Since the *Corpus iuris canonici* of Gratian's *Decretum* and the later compilations of the *Decretales* of Gregory IX and of later laws all dated back to before the Reformation and since the canons of the Council of Trent and the laws of later popes had been added since, there was a real problem in making good or effective use of the Church's laws by the time of Pius IX in the mid-nineteenth century. There was a feeling that the Church was in danger of 'being overwhelmed' by too many laws.[42] This feeling, expressed to Pius IX before the First Vatican Council of 1869–70, had been reinforced during the Council itself. Pius's attempt to systematize penal law had proven to be an enormous task and then the political situation after the First Vatican Council had prevented any real progress. Pius X took the matter up later and in 1904 ordered the production of a *Code* of the Church's laws.[43]

Recognizing the need for a rationalization of the Church's laws did not mean automatically that there should be a code of laws. Some modern European states had adopted a codified system in imitation of the *Code Napoléon*, but some felt that the Church should retain its own distinctive system, to emphasize its spiritual mandate and purpose. Some thought that the approach used to date had the advantage of indicating the historical perspective in a way that a code could not. However, the clarity of a code was attractive and a number of states seemed to be able to work well with such a system. It was decided that there should be a code, but one which would not contain historical texts, either in whole or in part, as in previous documents, to ensure that the new text was manageable, precise and clear. The further decision that it would be structured around 'persons', 'acts' and 'procedures' immediately gave rise to suspicions that it was modelled on secular texts, since that structure was the structure of Justinian's *Corpus iuris civile*.[44] Some thought the codification to be unhistorical and untrue to the Church's tradition. Others considered it an attempt to reinforce papal influence and to emphasize the doctrines of the Church as a perfect society and of public ecclesiastical law to contrast it with secular states.[45] The Church would assert its right to conduct its proper mission, make its own laws, organize its own finances, independently of any state.[46] The Code was promulgated by Benedict XV

[42.] The French bishops, responding to requests for submissions connected to the forthcoming Vatican Council, had stated in 1865 that there was an urgent need for a revision and a reform of the Church's law. cf. P. Gasparri 'Praefatio' (Codicis iuris canonici), in P. Gasparri (ed.), Codex iuris canonici: praefatio, fontium adnotatione et indice analytico-alphabetico, Typis polyglottis Vaticanis, 1918, xxix.

[43.] Pius X, 'Arduum sane munus' motu proprio, 19 March 1904.

[44.] L. Kondratuk, 'Le Code de 1917: entre nécessité technique et catholicisme intransigeant', Revue de droit canonique, 51 (2001), 305–21 at 309.

[45.] Ibid., 310–13.

[46.] L. Gerosa, Le droit de l'Église, St Paul, Luxemburg, 1998, 86–9: original German Das Recht der Kirche, Padeborn, 1995.

at Pentecost, 1917, and was to come into force a year later.

The Code of 1917 was divided into five books: general norms, on persons, on things, on procedures and on crimes and penalties.[47] Various subdivisions, sometimes into parts, sections, titles and chapters are to be found. The structure of the Code, in its three central books, reflects the structure of Justinian's *Corpus iuris civile*, as his collected laws had come to be called, into persons, things, and acts. Objections which eventually arose against this Pio-Benedictine Code were that the sacraments were treated in the book on things, that attention to the laity was limited and that the treatment of penal law was excessively complicated.[48] Yet, the 1917 Code was a success, even though in need of revision by the time of John XXIII. The criticisms levelled at it were not really founded, not least since it did give the Church a workable, clear law, much needed, with ample historical reference points in Gasparri's '*Fontes*'.[49]

b. The Revision of the Code: The Principles Involved

The inevitable impact of yet more laws since 1917 and the need to rationalize the system was one consideration leading to the call for the Code to be revised. Some of the criticisms noted above were factors too.[50] Finally, on the very day and in the very speech in which he proclaimed that there was to be a Second Vatican Council, John XXIII called for the Code to be revised; the work of updating (*aggiornamento*) which the Council was to undertake was bound to have its effect on any revised Code. He set up a Pontifical Commission of Cardinals in 1963 to work on the revision, this being amplified by canonical experts by Paul VI in 1965, although it was not to proceed with the revision until after the Council had completed its work.

The Commission for the revision (re-thinking – *recognitio*) was to prepare the reform of the Code 'in the light of the decrees of the Second Vatican Council'. It was to be a 'consultative' body and was 'to offer technical opinions of a provisional character on any juridical

---

[47.] *Codex iuris canonici* (1917), contents: *Normae generales, de personis, de rebus, de processibus, de delictis et poenis.*

[48.] Gerosa, *Le droit de l'Église*, 74–5.

[49.] G. Sheehy, 'Reflections on the Current State of Law in the Church, with particular reference to the proposed Books I–III of the new Code', *Studia canonica*, 12 (1978), 199–210 at 202–4.

[50.] The laws since 1917 had been collected by X. Ochoa, *Leges Ecclesiae post CIC editae (1917–1985)*, Rome, 1966–87, often referred to simply as *Leges Ecclesiae.*

questions submitted to it'.[51] In other words, it was to draft the new Code, responding to merely technical issues put to it, exercising a restricted, technical and advisory role.

In the period immediately after the Council this Commission proposed ten principles upon which this work was to be based, principles approved by the Synod of Bishops of 1967.[52] These were simply listed to start with:

1. Preamble and juridical nature of the Code.
2. On the position of the external and internal forum in canon law.
3. On certain means of fostering pastoral care in the Code.
4. On incorporating special faculties into the Code itself.
5. On applying the principle of subsidiarity in the Church.
6. On protecting the rights of persons.
7. On devising procedures to protect subjective rights.
8. On the territorial ordering in the Church.
9. On reforming (*recognoscendo*) penal law.
10. On the new systematic structure of the Code.[53]

These ten principles for the revision of the Code were discussed and approved by the Synod of Bishops in 1967. There were also written observations made about the proposed principles and the proposed Code, stemming from the Commission's consultation with the bishops. It may be helpful to note the key issues raised by the bishops in their written submissions and the reaction to them, as reflected in the statement or report (*relatio*), of the chairman of the Commission.

The Juridical Character of the Code (n. 1)

Discussions and consultations in connection with the 1967 Synod of Bishops had shown some wanted the Code not just to be revised, but to be profoundly re-structured 'on the basis of the new mind and disposition in the Church' after Vatican II.[54] Some favoured a more theological document, others a properly legal document, which would

---

51. Synodus episcoporum, 3–8 April 1967, Pontificia commissio codicis iuris canonici recognoscendo *Communicationes*, 1 (1969), 5: Circular letter of Secretary of State, 25 March 1968, Ibid.

52. Ibid., 55–6.

53. Ibid., 55.

54. 'Relatio' of Cardinal Felici at the meetings of 30 September–4 October 1967, on the revision of the Code ('*Relatio circa "Principia quae Codicis iuris canonici recognitionem dirigant"*'), *Communicationes*, 2 (1969), 86–91 at 88: 'Declarationes propositae, quae traducere quaerunt principia respondentia novae menti et habitui in Ecclesia a Concilio Oecumenico instauratis …'

reflect the charity and pastoral care of the Church, but still a clear, precise text, not obscured by many exhortations.[55] The Commission sought a text, juridical in character, going beyond general principles of faith and morals, to enable the Christian faithful (*Christifideles*) to find in it a proper basis for their activity in the mission of the Church, including the protection of their rights and duties as individuals and as participants in the society of the Church more generally. Their text said that the juridical nature of the Code was postulated on 'the social nature of the Church, which was founded on the power of jurisdiction attributed to the hierarchy by Christ'.[56]

The Relationship between External and Internal Fora (n. 2)

This refers to the distinction between the internal forum, treating what is confidential as a matter of conscience, such as what a specific penitent confesses in the sacrament of reconciliation, and the external forum, treating what is a public matter, at least in principle. There was a concern not to confound moral and juridical norms; the Code's 'juridical character ... should distinguish clearly between how things should operate in the external forum and how they should work in the internal forum, so that, as far as possible, conflicts (between the two) may be eliminated'. The question should be studied further.[57] The Commission emphasized the juridical nature of 'those things which pertain to the external forum', but stressed the 'necessity of the internal forum', since it has flourished in the best law in the Church through the centuries. The two should be coordinated so that conflicts were reduced, especially as to sacramental and penal law.[58] The issue was to ensure that, as far as possible, canonical penalties would be a matter of the external forum, the normal forum of public and legal operation.[59]

[55.] '*Responsiones ad animadversiones circa "Principia quae Codicis iuris canonici recognitionem dirigant"*', *Communicationes*, 2 (1969), 92–8 at 94–5.

[56.] Acta commissionis: '*Principia quae Codicis iuris canonici recognitionem dirigant*', *Communicationes*, 2 (1969), 77–85, n. 1 at 78: '*Indolem*, dicimus, *iuridicam*, quam postulat ipsa natura socialis Ecclesiae, quae in potestate iurisdictionis ab ipso Christo hierarchiae tributae, fundatur' (emphases in original).

[57.] Ibid., 2 (1969), 95.

[58.] Acta commissionis, *Communicationes*, 2 (1969), 79, n. 2.

[59.] Coriden, *An Introduction to Canon Law*, 4.

The Place of Pastoral Care in the Code (no. 3)

While some bishops recognized the need for a clear, juridical text, many felt that pastoral care of the Church should be evident in the Code, since the 'care of souls is the supreme law of the Church and this should be the first and supreme principle of our laws'.[60] A plea was made for the law to be more concerned with equity, exhortation and pastoral care than with condemnation, unless the latter was truly necessary for the public good and for church discipline. Church laws concerned its supernatural end and should be consistent with it, but not all of them were directly related to that end; they should reflect temperance, moderation, charity and so be distinguished from secular laws.

Special Faculties and the Role of the Bishop (n. 4)

The Code should treat positively of the role of the bishop who was in charge of a diocese; he should be able to dispense from general laws, other than those reserved specifically to higher authorities. Greater subsidiarity for bishops and regions, compatible with the primacy of the Pope, was sought, but the limits were to be specified. Despite some uncertainty about how this would apply in the administration of justice, greater autonomy within a general procedural law was thought perhaps worth pursuing.[61]

The Principle of Subsidiarity (n. 5)

To foster the Church's pastoral mission there should be greater collaboration between 'all types of the faithful', clergy, religious and laity; the function ('*munus*') of the laity should be defined and fostered. Initial consultations had led to the call for the principle of subsidiarity to be applied more fully in the Church, but the request from some for the Council's doctrine to be extended in the Code, especially in regard to the laity, could not be accepted, since the Commission could not extend the Council's doctrine, although it was to keep it carefully in mind.[62]

---

[60] Cardinal Felici's '*Relatio*', *Communicationes*, 2 (1969), 89.

[61] '*Responsiones*', *Communicationes*, 2 (1969), 96.

[62] Ibid., 2 (1969), 96: 'Prae oculis habenda est doctrina Concilii. Non possumus illam extendere pro arbitrio. Immo oportet caute agere, ut spiritus Concilii revera servetur'.

The Rights of Persons (n. 6)

It was agreed that the Code should reflect the Council's teaching on the threefold mission (*munera*) of the Church's pastors of teaching, ruling and sanctifying the People of God. There was also agreement about the need to protect the rights of individuals, although the role of superiors had to be stated too.[63] The Commission located the rights of persons 'on the basis of the radical equality between all members of the faithful, which ought to thrive whether on account of human dignity or on account of the baptism they have received', something which 'commonly grounds the juridical status of all before the rights and duties, pertaining to different ecclesiastical functions, may be assessed'.[64]

Procedures to Protect Subjective Rights (n. 7)

The issue of devising a fundamental law, stating the rights of people in the Church, was raised. If such a fundamental law was to express basic principles, work on that and on the other areas of the Code would need to proceed together, the one informing the other.[65] The protection of subjective rights for all persons, superiors and subjects equally, was thought desirable, with a judicial procedure for the latter to defend their rights, if violated by the former. Hence, there should be a clear distinction between the legislative, executive and judicial functions.[66] There was a request for judicial processes, especially in matrimonial cases, to be shorter and more equitable and, although a matter specifically for the Pope, for delegation in cases of privilege of faith.[67]

The Territorial Ordering of the Church (n. 8)

The question was raised of arranging sections of the People of God, other than territorially, for the more effective pastoral care of certain groups, such as those belonging to particular national groups or to special rites. This seemed possible, although territorial division was considered normally the most effective.

[63.] Ibid., 97.

[64.] Acta commissionis: '*Principia*', *Communicationes*, 2 (1969), 82–3, n. 6: ' proponitur ut in futuro Codice ob radicalem aequalitatem quae inter omnes christifideles vigere debet, tum ob humanum dignitatem tum ob receptum baptisma, *statutm iuridicum* omnibus comune condatur, antequam iura et officia recenseantur quae ad diversas ecclesiasticas functiones pertinent' (emphasis in original).

[65.] '*Responsiones*', *Communicationes*, 2 (1969), 98.

[66.] Acta commissionis: '*Principia*', *Communicationes*, 2 (1969), 83, n. 7.

[67.] '*Responsiones*', *Communicationes*, 2 (1969), 97.

Reform of Penal Law (n. 9)

Pastoral care was a concern leading to the request that the Church's penal law be revised to make the corrective role of the law more prominent than severity, for sanctions to be imposed only when truly necessary for the good of the People of God and on account of the gravity of the crime committed.[68] The Commission noted that all accepted the need for reform of the penal law, but stated that no canonist could accept the abolition of all ecclesiastical penalties imposed by law, proper to a 'perfect society'. It may be noted here that recent scandals in the Church have underlined the unduly optimistic perspective of some people at the time. It may be regrettable that penal law is needed in the Church, but centuries of experience had shown it to be necessary; something which recent scandals have confirmed.

The Restructuring of the Code (n. 10)

The need for a restructuring of the Code was accepted on the basis of the 'mind and spirit of the Sacred Council and of the scientific requirements of canonical legislation'.[69] An issue much broader than that of the restructuring of the Code was whether or not there should be one or two Codes (for the Latin and Eastern Churches). Opinions were divided and the question was a long-standing one, but in preparing the principles, it was to be borne in mind that they should be capable of being applied equally to the Eastern Churches.[70]

c. The Revision of the Code and the Second Vatican Council

Since the revision of the Code was to take clear account of the work of the Second Vatican Council, work on revising the Code was deliberately delayed until the Council had concluded its work for this precise reason. Many aspects of the Council's teaching, of relevance to the Code, were theological and will receive attention as the need arises.

[68.] Cardinal Felici's 'Relatio', Communicationes, 2 (1969), 89–90: 'In poenis igitur statuendis legislator intendere curabit, ut quae reputet pro populi disciplina salutaria ac necessaria, ea sine asperitate decernat, et solum ob delicti gravitatem poena applicetur'.

[69.] Acta commissionis: 'Principia.', Communicationes, 2 (1969), 84–5, nn. 8–10: '... sive ad mentem et spiritum Decretorum Sacri Concilii, sive ad scientificas legislationis canonicae exigentias' (n. 10). The reference in n. 9 to the 'perfect society' will be noted.

[70.] 'Responsiones', Communicationes, 2 (1969), 98.

However, some features of the Council's teaching had a specifically juridical character, which was bound to have a bearing upon how the Code was to be revised.

We have already seen that the Church was presented as the 'one Church of Christ, subsisting in the Catholic Church, ... constituted and ordered as a society, ... ruled by the successor of Peter and by the bishops in union with him'.[71] This dogmatic constitution on the Church recalled the hierarchical structure of the Church, noting that Christ 'established a variety of ministries which are ordered to the good of the whole Body'; ministers having 'sacred power' are 'at the service of their brothers', so that all of them as the People of God, 'collaborating together in a free and ordered way for the same end, ... may attain salvation'.[72] The Lord wished his Church to be built up across the centuries and he established the Petrine office as the 'perpetual and visible principle and foundation of the unity of faith and communion', reflected in the doctrines of the primacy and of the infallibility of the Pope.[73] Christ's same purpose of establishing the Church as an instrument of salvation across the centuries explains why he chose twelve Apostles and instituted them as a college or stable body. 'sharing in his power', they were to make all peoples his disciples (prophetic function), make them holy (sanctifying function) and rule them (ruling function). Both the Petrine and the Apostolic mission were to endure through time.[74] Their ministry was perpetuated through the laying on of hands and the Apostolic succession, by which the bishops enjoy the 'fulness of the order of priesthood'. The sacred power and office of bishop comes from Christ through episcopal ordination (ordination as bishops); the episcopal office is not delegated by the Pope, rather, 'through their episcopal consecration are conferred (on the bishops) the ministry (function – *munus*) of sanctifying and also those (*munera*) of teaching and ruling'. On the other hand, this sacred power is linked to the hierarchical nature of the Church around the Petrine ministry, since, even if the sacred power comes from Christ via episcopal ordination, its exercise depends also on the bishops' communion with the Pope and the rest of the College. Thus, the power bishops receive through their episcopal ordination and the threefold office, ministry or function which goes with it, 'of its nature (*'natura sua'*)

[71.] *Lumen gentium*, n. 8.
[72.] Ibid., n. 18.
[73.] Ibid.
[74.] Ibid., nn. 19–20.

cannot be exercised except in hierarchical communion with the head of the College and with its members'.[75]

The Council issued a Decree on Bishops, 'on the pastoral function of bishops in the Church', *Christus Dominus*, which already translated this doctrine into juridical terms to a considerable extent, a text which was to be reflected in the 1983 Code.[76] We may note how the Holy Spirit and Christ are said to grant bishops sacred power and their functions, underlining the divine basis of both through episcopal ordination and under-scoring that they do not derive these from papal decision. To be noted, too, is the clear way that the jurisdiction of bishops and the actual exercise of what they are given in their ordination as bishops is dependent upon their full communion with the Pope, as the successor of Peter and supreme pastor of the universal Church, and on the communion with one another and with him.

Thus, 'in the Church of Christ, the Roman Pontiff, as the successor of Peter, to whom Christ entrusted the task of caring for his sheep and his lambs, enjoys by divine institution supreme, full, immediate and universal power', being the 'pastor of all the faithful for the common good of the universal Church and for the good of particular Churches ...', yet

> The bishops themselves, having been made such by the Holy Spirit, succeed to the place of the Apostles as pastors of souls and, one with the Supreme Pontiff and under his authority, have been sent to fulfil the perennial work of Christ, the Eternal Shepherd ... Through the Holy Spirit who has been given to them they are true teachers of the faith, Pontiffs and shepherds'.[77]

Within this communion with the Pope and with one another, bishops are to fulfil the function they have received 'through their episcopal consecration', in respect of the particular Church entrusted to them, usually a diocese. Their role as pastors in the universal Church is also recognized:

> By the power of their sacramental consecration and by their hierarchical communion with the head of the College (the Pope) and of its other members, they are constituted members of the Episcopal Body ... With the Roman Pontiff its Head and never apart from this Head, this

---

[75.] Ibid., n. 21.

[76.] Second Vatican Council, Decree on the pastoral function of Bishops in the Church, *Christus Dominus*, n. 3.

[77.] Ibid., n. 2.

(College of Bishops) is the subject of (enjoys) supreme and full authority in the universal Church.[78]

Bishops have 'all ordinary, special and immediate power necessary for the exercise of their pastoral office', without prejudice to the power of the Roman Pontiff and to any matters he may reserve to himself or to others.[79]

The juridical status of priests was considered at the Council too. They are those who 'assist the bishops'.[80] The ministerial or ordained priesthood 'differs in essence and not only in degree' ('essentia et non gradu tantum') from the 'common priesthood of all the faithful'. A priest 'by the sacred power he enjoys' (which can only come through Holy Orders, as did the sacred power of the 'fulness of priesthood' of bishops) 'builds up and rules the priestly people' and, 'acting in the person of Christ', he sanctifies them.[81] Although the text does not use the term 'sanctify', it is clear that this is meant.

Notice that the juridical status of the priest, in a way similar to that of the fullness of priesthood of the bishops, stems from the sacrament of Holy Orders. Here it relates to Orders as 'ad sacerdotium' or 'for the priesthood' (not of deacons – ad ministerium – 'for ministry'). The ministerial priesthood differs in kind or essence and not just in degree with regard to the 'royal priesthood of the faithful', but both are a 'sharing in the priesthood of Christ' and they are ordered or structured to one another. The Council deliberately avoided any use of the Lutheran terminology of 'priesthood of all believers', which implied a denial of the ministerial priesthood. The specific ministry or function of bishops and that of priests, at the service of the whole People of God, was articulated in terms of the threefold function of Christ's own ministry, of teaching, sanctifying and ruling.[82] It is very significant, given the call of the Commission for the Revision of the Code for it to be restructured (10th principle) that these three functions or *tria munera* were to figure in the Code of 1983, even in the way it was structured.

It is not the purpose of this work to examine the law of the Eastern Catholic Churches as such. A Code for these Churches had not emerged after 1917, although Cardinal Gasparri had done extensive work on it and sections of law on marriage, on procedures, on religious

---

[78.] Ibid., n. 4.

[79.] Ibid., 8.

[80.] *Lumen gentium,* n. 20.

[81.] Ibid., n. 10.

[82.] Ibid., n. 21. These are more fully elaborated in the Council's Decree on the Ministry of Priests, *Presbyterorum ordinis,* nn. 4–6.

Orders, on patrimonial law or property, on rites and on persons, had been promulgated.[83] The Second Vatican Council recognized the need for the laws of the Eastern Churches to be codified, but judged that this would have to take into account the doctrines of the Council itself. Nevertheless, the Council recognized the 'right and duty' of the Eastern Churches to govern themselves, according to their age-old traditions, taking account of the customs of the faithful and the good of their souls.[84] The project on Eastern law was resumed in the 1970s and the *Codex canonum ecclesiarum orientalium* was issued in 1990, a Code for the Eastern Churches (not Church, as had been planned in the 1920s). It was not divided into books, but reflected Eastern Church legal sources, using titles, chapters and canons.

d. The Structure of the Revised Code for the Latin Church

The consultation with bishops and with *periti* or experts from the universities and elsewhere from 1971 to 1978 was important, but there was not always time to allow people to examine the great detail before having to have responses in to the drafting Commission. The fact that the drafts were in Latin restricted the capacity of some to assess them effectively. Thirdly, there was not a very good response, perhaps because of other priorities and because canon law has had a very poor image in recent years.[85]

The 1983 Code was restructured, based on Vatican II, with seven books instead of the five of the 1917 Code, using the offices of teaching and sanctifying in place of Justinian's categories, reducing canons on penal law and reducing the total number of canons from 2414 in 1917 to 1752 (cf. Table 1).

e. The Fundamental Law of the Church (Lex fundamentalis)

There had been much talk of a fundamental law for the Church. If, though, there were to be two Codes, one for the Latin Church and one for the Eastern Churches, there would be much to be said for having a

---

[83.] *Crebrae allatae*, 22 February 1949, *Acta apostolicae sedis (AAS)*, 41 (1949), 89–117; *Sollicitudinem nostram*, 6 January 1950, *AAS*, 42 (1950), 5–20; *Postquam Apostolicis*, 9 February, 1952, *AAS*, 44 (1952), 65–152; *Cleri sanctitate*, 2 June 1957, *AAS*, 49 (1957), 433–603.

[84.] Second Vatican Council, Decree on the Eastern Churches, *Ecclesiarum Orientalium*, n. 3.

[85.] F. G. Morrisey, 'The Revision of the Code of Canon Law', *Studia canonica* 12 (1978), 177–98 at 180–3.

Table 1

The Codes of 1917 and 1983

	The Code of 1917		The Code of 1983
Book I	General Norms	Book I	General Norms
Book II	On Persons	Book II	On Persons
Part I	On Clerics	Part I	On the Faithful
Part II	On Religious	Part II	On the Hierarchical Constitution of the Church
		Section I	On the Supreme Authority of the Church
		Section II	On Particular Churches
Part III	On the Laity in the Church	Section III	On Institutes of Consecrated Life and Societies of Apostolic Life
		Book III	On the Teaching Function of the Church
Book III	On Things	Book IV	On the Sanctifying Function of the Church
Part I	On the Sacraments	Part I	On the Sacraments
Part II	On Sacred Times and Places	Part II	On other Acts of Divine Worship
Part III	On Divine Worship	Part III	On Sacred Times and Places
Part IV	On Ecclesiastical Magisterium	Book V	On the Temporal Goods of the Church
Part V	On Benefices and other Ecclesiastical Institutions		
Book IV	On Procedures	Book VI	On Sanctions in the Church
Part I	On Judgments	Part I	On Crimes and Sanctions in General
Part II	On Causes of Beatification and Canonisation	Part II	On Sanctions for Specific Crimes
Part III	On Various Procedures and on Applying Sanctions		
Book V	On Crimes and Punishments	Book VII	On Procedures
Part I	On Crimes	Part I	On Judgments in General
Part II	On Sanctions	Part II	On the Contentious Judgment
Part III	On Sanctions for Specific Crimes	Part III	On Certain Special Procedures
		Part IV	On the Penal Process
		Part V	On the Way to Make Recourse and on Removing and Moving Parish Priests

fundamental law applying to both and underlying both Codes. Such a law would need to be related closely to the Code(s) and so work on the Code and on the fundamental law proceeded at the same time in the 1970s. However, the Latin Code proceeded well ahead of the Eastern Code.

The question of a fundamental law was not an easy one. There was a fear that it would be like a constitution of a secular state, which might undermine both the distinctive nature of the Church's law for its distinctive mission and the position of the Pope as the supreme legislator. In fact, it was intended to state in the *Lex fundamentalis* that the decision as to whether a particular law contravened the fundamental law would be a matter for the Pope.[86] How such a fundamental law would relate to the new Code(s) in detail was unclear: whether it should ground other laws and be the basis for procedures for their revision, whether it should be a theological statement for later juridical texts or whether it should itself be a juridical text was not always agreed. These issues were not really resolved by the time the final draft of the Latin Code had been seen by the Pope and revised in the light of his observations. There was certainly a wish not to delay further the publication of the new Code to discuss these questions. The idea of a fundamental law was dropped very late in the day, although no clear, official explanation for this was given.[87]

In fact, the fundamental law was intended, amongst other things to safeguard the rights of the faithful. Some of its intended provisions are to be found in cc. 208–223 of the 1983 Code, where their rights are listed. The last of its drafts (1980), under the title of 'The Fundamental Canonical Law of the Universal Catholic Church', had the following structure:[88]

---

[86] A. Gauthier, 'The progress of the *"Lex Ecclesiae fundamentalis"'*, *Studia canonica* 12 (1978), 377–88 at 387.

[87] Ibid., 377–81.

[88] The 1980 Draft has been translated by Coriden; here just the outline is given. For the text itself, see Coriden, *An Intoduction to Canon Law*, 47–55.

Title 1		The Church
Chapter 1		On all the Faithful
	Article 1	Call and incorporation of persons into the Church
	Article 2	Rights and duties of the faithful
	Article 3	Different states of the faithful
Chapter 2		Hierarchical Structures of the Church
	Article 1	The Pope and the College of Bishops
	Article 2	Patriarchs and major Archbishops (Eastern Churches)
	Article 3	Individual bishops
	Article 4	Presbyters and deacons
Chapter 3		The Mission of the Church
Title 2		The Functions of the Church
Chapter 1		The Teaching Function of the Church
Chapter 2		The Sanctifying Function of the Church
Chapter 3		The Ruling Function of the Church
Final Norms		

Since it was never promulgated, it never became part of Church law.

f. The Promulgation of the Code of 1983

The Code for the Latin Church was promulgated through the Apostolic Constitution, *Sacrae disciplinae legis*, of John Paul II in 1983.[89] There are a number of points of immediate interest in the Pope's remarks. The Code was announced with the calling of the Second Vatican Council and explicitly was based upon its teaching, both Council and Code having the same basic concern for a 'renewal of Christian life'. The work leading to the revision had been conducted 'in an entirely collegial spirit', with Episcopal Conferences being consulted at various stages, involved in the process of revision and in terms of the content of the revised laws. The Code was promulgated by papal authority, as was necessary: 'In promulgating this Code today, we are conscious that this act stems from our Pontifical authority itself and so

---

[89.] The text is to be found at the beginning of the Code itself in the official translation prepared by the Canon Law Society of England and Wales, in collaboration with the Canon Law Society of Australia and New Zealand and the Canadian Canon Law Society, *The Code of Canon Law* (Collins, London, 1983). All references to this work are to the 2001 edition. The *motu proprio 'Sacrae disciplinae leges'* is to be found on pp. xi–xv. Both the Code and the *motu proprio* which promulgated it were issued on 25 January 1983, on the 24th anniversary of John XXIII's call for the revision of the 1917 Code.

assumes a primatial nature.' Referring to Divine grace, the authority of the Apostles Peter and Paul, and the requests of the bishops (an allusion to collegiality), the Pope states:

> By the supreme authority which is ours and by means of this Constitution which is ours, we promulgate this present Code as it has been compiled and reviewed. We order that it is to have the force of law for the whole Latin Church.

The Pope roots the Church's law in the Scriptures as the 'first source of the whole juridical and legislative tradition of the Church'. The Code seeks not to replace charity or grace, but simply to facilitate 'order in ecclesial society and in the lives of the individuals who belong to it'. It 'fully accords with the nature of the Church and with the ecclesiological doctrine of Vatican II, which it seeks to translate into canonical terms' and, indeed, is to be interpreted on the basis of the Second Vatican Council and especially its ecclesiology, although he considers that it is entirely in harmony with the Church's legislative tradition. John Paul II emphasizes key elements of that ecclesiology: the Church's image as 'People of God' and as 'communion', the inter-relationships of collegiality and primacy, between universal and particular Churches, the threefold mission of all including the laity, the rights and duties of the faithful and specifically of the laity and the pursuit of ecumenism. He judges a Code to be 'absolutely necessary' for the Church as a 'social and visible unit', for the 'properly ordered exercise' of the 'functions divinely entrusted to the Church', especially for the 'properly ordered exercise of 'sacred power' and 'administration of the sacraments', so that the relations of 'Christ's faithful are mutually reconciled in justice based on charity', and the 'rights of each safeguarded and defended' to strengthen common initiatives for the work of the Church. Canon law needs to be implemented; hence the need for an 'accurate' expression of norms, to rest upon 'sound juridical, canonical and theological foundations'.[90]

The Code was to come into force on the first Sunday of Advent, 1983. This long period between the promulgation and date of entry into force of the Code, a long 'holiday of the law' or *vacatio legis*, was needed for people to come to know what the laws were which they were to implement.

[90.] Ibid.

It should be noted that the Code does not contain all laws, even for the Latin Church. Particular laws in dioceses or in religious Orders or congregations of consecrated persons, always to be within the universal law, are obviously not included. Separate norms for beatification and canonization are operative (*Divinus perfectionis Magister*), as are most liturgical norms (*The Rites of the Catholic Church* and *Institutio generali: Missale romanum ... recognitum*), as well as the operations of the Roman Curia (*Pastor bonus*).[91]

7. Conclusion

From the first thoughts of rationalizing inherited laws in the late nineteenth century until today, some issues have remained constant in canon law, even if their form has altered. The need for law in the Church, its theological roots and its juridical character remain. The rights and duties of all the faithful and the inter-relationship between those rights and duties, rooted in baptism, and rights and duties of people in the Church based on their functions, rooted in Holy Orders, have become very important since the Second Vatican Council. How far the 1983 Code reflects this and other principles for the revision of its predecessor will be seen in what follows, as we examine how that Code may assist the Church in its mission to spread the Gospel of Christ.

[91.] John Paul II, Apostolic Constitution, *Divinus perfectionis magister*, 25 January 1983, *AAS* 75 (1983), 349–55; (American) National Conference of Catholic Bishops, *The Rites of the Catholic Church*, I and II (Pueblo, NY, 1976), approved by the Apostolic See; Congregation for Divine Worship and the Discipline of the Sacraments, *Institutio generalis: Missale romanum ... recognitum* (Libreria Editrice Vaticana, 2000); John Paul II, Apostolic Constitution, *Pastor bonus*, 28 June 1988, *AAS* 80 (1989), 841–923.

Chapter 2

General Norms
(Book I of the Code)

1. Introduction

Canon law is an instrument of justice for the People of God, to help them to live in harmony with one another and to live by the Gospel of Christ, discharging their responsibilities as members of the Church and bringing that good news also to those who do not yet know him. This appears in the history of canon law, in its codification and in the revision of the Code.

The Code of 1983, like that of 1917, begins with General Norms. This somewhat abstract feature, in common with any system of law, is a necessary prelude because what is contained here applies to all the laws of the Code and of the Church and determines their proper application to the concerns of the Church. For any particular law, we might ask what needs to be done for it to be put into operation, whether a specific way of dealing with it is correct, misguided or so defective as to render the whole action meaningless. To help to appreciate the importance of this section of the Code, the emphasis will be on understanding the main characteristics of some general features of canon law, with examples to illustrate the relevance of what, otherwise, may seem obscure.

2. Persons in the Church and their Juridical Status

a. Juridical Status in the Church

The Juridical Status of all the Baptized

We shall begin by thinking about persons in the Church, since laws are made for persons. In an age accustomed to talk of human rights, a very effective political device has been to assert as human rights what particular groups of people wish to see brought about, which

46

has led to legislation, statements and judicial sentences purporting to recognize and to require recognition of 'rights', to abortion, euthanasia, sexual unions outside marriage, and so on. None of these constitutes any true right at all, nor can any civil law truly establish such 'rights' in violation of natural moral law. True fundamental or basic human rights are such precisely because they are not established by being attributed by governments, judges or other bodies, but because they stem from the very fact that someone is a human being; they are ontologically grounded. Every human person, thus, has basic human rights to life, to bodily integrity, to reputation, to free speech, and so on, although certain restrictions upon the exercise of those rights can be justified in some circumstances, as when someone is incarcerated for a crime after a conviction through due process of law. The Church recognizes these rights; her evangelizing mission must avoid coercion which would violate the fundamental right of human persons to religious liberty. Its mission is directed to all persons, seeking to open their hearts and consciences to understand, accept and live by the full truth of the Gospel of Jesus Christ, to embrace the unlimited, 'great hope' that he is and that he alone offers.[1] Nor do Christians lose their basic human rights by being members of the Church, although some may choose to sacrifice a human right for the sake of living out the Gospel in a specific way, as when a celibate does not marry for the sake of the Kingdom or as when those in the consecrated life give up personal possessions to share a community life in the service of the Gospel.

In canon law, however, there is a further concept of 'person'. Canonically, as well as in civil law, it is usual to distinguish between 'physical persons' and 'juridical persons', the former being individual human beings and the latter specific groups or bodies of people, but, for canon law, all are members of the Church. Someone becomes a physical person, canonically speaking, by being baptized or, to put it another way, becoming a physical person in the Church is a juridical consequence of baptism. Examining two key canons (cc. 96 and 204 – see Table 2), will help us to grasp much about person, rights and responsibilities in the Church.

Our vocation to live in Christ by the power of the Holy Spirit and thus to come to the Father to share their perfect communion (Mt. 28:19–20; Acts 2:38; Jn. 3:3–7) is fundamental to our lives as disciples of Christ. This is initiated or brought about through baptism. This is

---

[1.] Second Vatican Council, Declaration on Religious Liberty, *Dignitatis humanae*, nn. 1, 2, 10; Benedict XVI, Encyclical letter, *Spe salvi*, 30 November 2007, nn. 30–1.

Table 2

Persons in the Church (cc 96, 204, 849)

Canon 96

By *baptism* one is (*homo est*)
- incorporated into the *Church of Christ*
and - constituted a person in it
- with *rights* and duties ... *proper to Christians*
- in accordance with one's status (*eorum condicionem*)
- *insofar* as
- they are in *ecclesiastical communion*
- *and unless*
- a *lawfully issued sanction* intervenes.

Canon 204 § 1

Christ's faithful (*Christifideles*) are those who
- since they are *incorporated into Christ <u>through baptism</u>*
- are *constituted* the *People of God*

For this reason - they *participate in their own way* (*suo modo*) ...
in the *priestly*
prophetic and
kingly
office <u>of Chris</u>t (*munera Christi*)

(and)   - they are called ... to *exercise the mission Christ*
entrusted to the Church to fulfil in the world,
each according to *his or her particular condition*
(*secundum propium cuiusque condicionem*).

Canon 849

By (*baptism*) people are
- *made like to Christ* by a indelible character
and   - are *incorporated into the Church.*

not just to go through a ritual, but truly to be united to Christ, the conqueror of sin and death, being immersed into him and into the mystery of his saving death and resurrection (Rom. 6:1–11; 1 Cor. 15:42–57). Baptism radically alters us, since through it Christ himself creates a communion between himself and each one of us in a deeply personal way, a relationship with him which we cannot simply undo; hence the indelible character which baptism brings about (cc. 845 § 1; 849). At the same time, this communion with the Lord brings with it inescapably a union with all who are baptized in him, a communion with all of us in the Church. This new reality is expressed by a new juridical status or standing in law in the Church.

Looking at c. 204 § 1, we see that the 'faithful in Christ' are identified as 'all those who have been baptized' and who enjoy certain rights and duties (cc. 208–223) as a result. Beyond the natural rights and duties we have as human beings, there arises this new category of rights and duties from the communion with Christ which he effects through baptism. This new juridical status of all the baptized is a fundamental category for canon law, for the concept of 'person', a subject of rights and duties in the Church. This canonical concept of 'person', already present in the Code of 1917 (c. 87), was preserved in the 1983 Code precisely to emphasize that canonical rights and duties stem from baptism.[2]

Canon 204 § 1 expresses the theological truth that baptism inserts us into Christ, makes us members of his Body or 'in-corp-orates' us into him and thus into his threefold mission as Priest, Prophet and Shepherd-King, inserting us into him who is of his nature perfectly holy or perfect priest, who proclaims the Gospel of God prophetically and who is that Gospel in person, and who is the true Shepherd-King who leads us to the Father. The baptized person, then, participates in Christ's holiness and in his threefold function or mission, belonging as a result of baptism to the common priesthood of the faithful (c. 836), with a vocation to holiness or to perfection, in and through prayer with Christ and in Christ. Participation in the prophetic mission stems from baptism and in confirmation he receives the specific gift of the Spirit in order to give witness prophetically to Christ before the world. The third *munus* of sharing the ruling or kingly function or mission is to be understood as one of being at service, the baptized exercising this function by the example of a good and holy life, perhaps in

---

[2.] E. Besson, *La dimension juridique des sacrements*, Pontificia Universita Gregoriana (hereafter referred to in text as P.U.G.), Rome, 2004, 126–8.

a less obvious way than the ruling function of sacred ministers, but something implied when charity is said 'to possess an intrinsic power of evangelization'.[3]

The key canons presenting the meaning of 'person' in the Church are 96 and 204. Their analysis, along with c. 849, brings out the juridical importance of baptism, by which someone is incorporated into Christ, becomes a member of his Body, of the People of God. Someone, already a human being with personal rights by virtue of their existence, becomes or, technically, is 'constituted' a person in the Church through baptism (c. 96), while someone without baptism lacks that personhood in the Church. In canon law the term 'constituted' is often used to mean that a particular law brings into being or 'constitutes' some new reality (so-called constitutive law), but here it is not the law which brings something into being, but the action of Christ through baptism which brings this about, a reality which the law does no more than recognize or declare. Our other key canon (c. 204 § 1) also recognizes or declares legally the consequence of baptism, but at the communitarian level of the Church as a whole, namely that through baptism people are 'constituted' the People of God or the Church. We see here, then, how baptism affects us personally and as new members of the community of the Church, how it inserts us into Christ and into the Church. Neither of these aspects is detachable from the other; they are inseparably connected, inseparably established or constituted by the fact of baptism itself.

The term 'Christian faithful', or *'christifideles'*, here applies to all those who are truly or validly baptized, not only to those who belong to the Catholic Church, so that, juridically, these canons have an ecumenical significance, which we shall examine later. It means that, in some way, all the baptized share or 'participate in' the three-fold mission or functions of Christ and of the Church, their active participation in the mission Christ entrusted to the Church in the world deriving from their baptism (c. 204 § 1). In fact, the rights and duties 'proper to Christians' stem from their being persons in the Church or from their baptism (c. 96); these apply to all baptized persons and only to baptized persons, to whom they are 'proper'.

The canonical effects of baptism, therefore, are profound. A fundamental unity and a fundamental equality between all baptized

---

[3.] John Paul II, Apostolic exhortation, *Ecclesia in Europa*, 28 June 2003, n. 84; cf. Benedict XVI, Encyclical letter, *Deus caritas est*, 25 December 2005, n. 24.

Christians stems from their baptism; hence we read 'Flowing from their rebirth in Christ, there is a genuine equality of dignity and action among all Christ's faithful' (c. 208).[4]

However, there are three key qualifications to be noted, which do not alter the fundamental equality of the baptized, but which concern real differences of function, according to the canonical condition of each person, the degree of their communion with the Catholic Church and whether or not they are under a canonical sanction (c. 96); these we shall consider shortly. Their juridical status can be varied also on the basis of Holy Order and/or of the profession of the evangelical counsels (whether they are consecrated persons) and/or whether they hold an office in the Church.

Juridical Status and the Sacrament of Order

The basic equality of all the baptized persons in the Church, is affected by whether, after baptism, they have received the sacrament of Holy Order in the presbyteral or episcopal degrees, whether they are priests or bishops. Someone validly ordained as a priest and in full communion with the Catholic Church has a different juridical status because he is not just different in the degree, but in the kind of priesthood he shares with Christ. Priestly ordination inserts him into Christ in a specifically different, though related, way from that of baptism, such that he now acts in the person of Christ ('*in persona Christi*'); when he says the words of consecration, absolution, confirmation, anointing of the sick under the right conditions, Christ acts through him to bring about the transformation of the bread and wine into the Body and Blood of Christ, to forgive sins, to seal with the Holy Spirit or to heal the person spiritually and perhaps physically. With episcopal ordination, this is true also of the bishop's acts of ordaining others.

In both cases, ordination brings about a transformed and enduring new relationship with Christ, a 'new and special consecration', not contrary to, but deepening and furthering that of baptism, this further incorporation into Christ and into his Church being the foundation of a new juridical status of the ministerial priest or bishop. The Code states that: 'By divine institution, among Christ's faithful, there are in the Church sacred ministers who in law are also called clerics' (c. 207 § 1). This reference to those in Holy Orders (including deacons)

---

4. The English text of the Code of 1983 will be that prepared by the Canon Law Society of Great Britain and Ireland in association with the Canon Law Society of Australia and New Zealand and the Canadian Canon Law Society, *The Code of Canon Law*, Collins, London, 1983, unless otherwise indicated.

emphasizes that they are not placed above the faithful, but are drawn from and remain members of the faithful, to act as ministers for them. To say that 'by law' they are clerics is a reference to ecclesiastical law, a distinction between juridical power which comes from the Church's ecclesiastical law and the sacred power which comes from their being transformed by Christ through ordination to the priesthood, as ministerial priests or as bishops.[5] Hence, those priests who are released from the duties of the clerical state ('laicized') do not lose the sacred power of priesthood, which they possess by divine gift, but they may not exercise it, except in danger of death.

Juridical Status through the Profession of the Evangelical Counsels
Although this is not the same as ordination and does not carry with it any transformation of sacred power, the profession of the evangelical counsels of poverty, chastity and obedience to live in a communal and stable state of life is another act which brings with it a new juridical status within the Church. This establishes a new configuration to Christ through 'a new and special consecration' (c. 573) beyond that established by baptism and different from that established by Holy Orders in the presbyteral and episcopal degrees. Such counsels 'belong to the holiness and mission of the Church'.[6] In a development of the theological doctrine contained in the Code of 1983, John Paul teaches: 'this means that the consecrated life, present in the Church from the beginning, can never fail to be one of her essential and characteristic elements, for it expresses her very nature'.[7] This underlines the Code's recognition of the fact that those who profess the evangelical counsels have a distinctive juridical status in the Church (c. 574), although one which is not sacramentally based.[8]

Underlying the legal distinctions are people (lay, clerical, consecrated) responding to their vocations in Christ in the one vocation of all in the Church; the law expresses this basic equality and the distinctions which arise by virtue of that call and response in the visible structures of the Church as juridical status.[9]

---

[5] J. A. Coriden, T. J. Green and D. E. Heinschel (eds), *The Code of Canon Law: A Text and Commentary*, Chapman, London, 1985, 132; cf., L. Villemin, *Pouvoir d'ordre et pouvoir de juridiction: histoire théologique de leur distinction*, Cerf, Paris, 2003, 194–7, 234–6.

[6] *Lumen gentium*, n. 44; John Paul II, Apostolic exhortation, *Vita consecrata*, 25 March 1996, n. 29.

[7] John Paul II, *Vita consecrata*, n. 29.

[8] G. Ghirlanda, *Il diritto nella Chiesa*, 55–62, nn. 34–7.

[9] Ibid., 55–6, n. 34.

b. Physical Persons in the Church

People become persons in the Church only through valid baptism, which gives them a fundamental dignity and equality grounding their rights and duties as proper to Christians. Alongside this common equality are distinctions of juridical status just noted, but the condition of each person, the degree of their communion with the Catholic Church and whether or not they are subject to a legal sanction in the Church affect the exercise of their rights and duties (c. 96).

Physical persons in canon law are those individuals who are persons in the Church, according to cc. 96 and 204. Those individuals who are baptized are, thus, physical persons in canon law, as distinct from juridical persons. Those who are not baptized are not persons in the Church. Of course, they are human persons and they interest canon law insofar as they have dealings with those who are persons in the Church, as for example, when marrying a non-baptized person (c. 1086), or insofar as they may be evangelized by those in the Church (c. 211) or can seek baptism (cc. 748, 864). Catechumens, those preparing for baptism, are not persons in the Church and do not have the rights and duties of Christians, but they do have some unspecified rights, 'are linked to the Church in a special way' (c. 206 § 1), while the Church is to have a special care for them (c. 206 § 2).

For those who are physical persons in the Church, the distinctions within the basic equality of all the baptized and the limitations upon the exercise of rights and duties are rooted in the following considerations.

Condition in Canon Law

Firstly, such rights and functions of all the baptized are to be discharged according to the 'condition' of each of them. The word 'status' in c. 204 is better translated as 'condition', since the Latin in that canon and in c. 96 uses 'condicionem' and since the term seems not to refer to whether someone is in the state of life of being a deacon, priest, consecrated or lay person, as in c. 207 § 2, where the Latin term is 'status'. The technical term 'condition' covers five categories: age, use of reason, domicile (where people live), relationships and rite. We shall say a little about each in turn.

Age

As in any society, age affects what people can do legally, since their capacity to make deliberate decisions or to perform morally imputable acts depends, amongst other things, on their age. In the Church it determines when certain rights may be exercised, when duties in principle become binding on a person, when certain acts which can be undertaken by or in regard to physical persons in principle can actually be undertaken.

Infants are those under the age of seven, the presumption being that at that age most children attain the use of reason at a basic level (c. 97 § 2). Prior to that age the law treats all children as infants; between seven and eighteen for most purposes they are minors and after eighteen for most purposes they are adults. The age of legal majority (adulthood) is set at eighteen (c. 97 § 1) for most acts, so that a person under that age, for example, cannot bequeath goods, while at eighteen a person has full exercise of his rights (c. 98 § 1), which previously are to be exercised on his behalf by a guardian according to the norms of local civil law, except where divine or ecclesiastical law determines otherwise (c. 98 § 2).

There are a number of exceptions set by canon law. A minor is treated as an adult, when seeking baptism from the age of fourteen (c. 863), technically not needing the consent of parents to be baptized. A female is considered a woman, able to marry at fourteen, a male considered a man and able to marry from the age of sixteen (c. 1083 § 1). In penal law a person is considered no longer a minor at the age of sixteen (c. 1323 § 1), with the exception of victims of sexual crimes where the age has recently been raised to eighteen, to allow those who commit sexual abuse against youngsters to be prosecuted under canon law for this canonical crime if the victim was under eighteen (and not only if under sixteen) at the time of the crime. Moreover, the ten-year period within which the crime can be prosecuted begins from the eighteenth birthday of the victim, perhaps recognizing that he or she was not able to pursue the matter before becoming an adult.[10]

Various minimum ages are listed, mainly relating to some specific vocations in the Church: entry into a novitiate at seventeen (c. 643), perpetual vows at twenty-one (c. 658), diaconal ordination in view of the priesthood at twenty-three (c. 1031 § 1), ordination of celibate permanent deacons and of priests twenty-five (c. 1031 §1 and 2) and ordination of married, permanent deacons at thirty-five (c. 1031 § 2).

Age limits defined by law for ecclesiastical offices (c. 184) cause the loss of the office (unless an exception is granted by the competent

---

[10.] John Paul II, Apostolic letter *motu proprio, Sacramentorum sanctitatis tutela*, 30 April 2001; cf., B. E. Ferme, '*Graviora delicta*: the apostolic letter MP sacramentorum sanctitatis tutela' in Z. Suchecki (ed), *Il processo penale canonico*, Lateran University Press, Rome, 2003, 365–82 at 370, 380–1.

authority), but only once the competent authority has communicated this in writing does this take effect (c. 186). Apart from the Pope, holders of most ecclesiastical offices reach this age limit at seventy-five. Cardinals are excepted, but those over eighty are not allowed to vote in elections for a new pope in Conclave.

Use of reason

As we have seen, the presumption of law is that a person attains the age of reason when he or she is seven years old, before which such a person is an infant in law (cc. 97–98). Someone who, in fact, is completely lacking in reason (amentia) is treated canonically as an infant (c. 99), the presumption of capacity (c. 97 § 2) being overturned by proof to the contrary. Marriage law has instances of this criterion being applied, since someone completely lacking in reason (c. 1095 § 1), one gravely lacking in judgment about the essential duties of marriage (c. 1095 § 2) or someone for psychological reasons incapable of taking on and living out the essential duties of marriage (c. 1095 § 3) cannot give valid consent. Likewise, if someone intending to marry by proxy has properly designated someone to exchange consent on his or her behalf, but becomes insane before the person designated exchanges that consent, such consent is invalid (c. 1105 § 4).

Domicile

Put simply, the parish or the diocese where someone lives affects the exercise of their rights and duties or where they are able to exercise them. A person acquires a domicile (place of dwelling) by intending to live there permanently or by actually living there for five years (c.102 § 1), quasi-domicile by intending to live there or actually living there for three months (c. 102 § 2). Thus, it is possible for someone to have both a domicile and a quasi-domicile at the same time, for example a student or a worker who works away from home several days a week. A person with neither (a *vagus*) acquires domicile for marriage purposes in the place where he actually lives (c. 1115).

The effect of domicile or quasi-domicile is to give a person in the Church his or her proper parish priest or pastor (c. 107). These days, people are more mobile and some prefer a priest from another parish to look after them pastorally. However, in terms of their rights and duties, the one who has the actual duty to care for them is their proper parish priest, of the parish in which they reside. Domicile has effects also in regard to the competence of Church tribunals: the domicile of an accused in the case of a trial (cc. 1408–1409), of the respondent for a marriage enquiry (c. 1673 § 2). It affects where baptism should normally take place: adults in their own parish, children in the parish of their parents (c. 857 § 2) or where a marriage may take place, permission of the proper parish priest being required for a wedding to take place outside the parish of both parties (c. 1115).

Relationships

This question is of importance in the light of the scandals of nepotism centuries ago, where popes, cardinals and bishops often gave positions to their own relatives, often when they were unsuitable. It is also relevant to marriage law, insofar as it was realized that close inter-marriage created problems in families, now recognized to be genetically based.

Relationships of consanguinity or blood relationships (c. 108) are said to be in the direct line when relating parents to children (first degree) and grandchildren (second degree) or in the collateral line when counting back via a common ancestor to brother and sister (second degree, two degrees counting via the parents), nephew and aunt (third degree), first cousins (fourth degree), and so on. Canonically, for marriage purposes, there is an impediment to marriage in all degrees of the direct line, an impediment of divine and natural law which cannot be dispensed and up to the fourth degree in the collateral line (of divine and natural law to the second degree, which cannot be dispensed, of natural and ecclesiastical law in the other degrees (c. 1091), which can be dispensed under certain conditions).

The background of nepotism explains why there is a prohibition on a bishop appointing a vicar general, episcopal vicar or member of the diocesan finance committee any relative of his up to the fourth degree in the collateral line (cc. 478 § 2; 492 § 3). There is also a prohibition on a bishop alienating church property to a relative up to the same degree (c. 1298). For obvious reasons of impartiality a judge may not accept a case involving a relative up to the fourth degree in the collateral line (c. 1448).

Affinity is the relationship which obtains between in-laws (c. 109) and there is an impediment to marriage in the direct line (c. 1092). Relatives of the bishop may not be appointed to the diocesan finance committee up to four degrees in the collateral line (c. 492 § 3). Spiritual relationship, between godparents and godchildren, no longer has any canonical effect. Adoption usually follows the local civil law, an example of the so-called 'canonization of civil law', but adopted persons are under an impediment to marriage if related in the direct line or up to the second degree in the collateral line (c. 1094).

Rite

Apart from liturgical rites, such as the Mozarabic rite of Toledo, the Ambrosian rite of Milan, the so-called Tridentine rite, there are rites of the Uniate Churches *sui iuris* (Greek, Russian, Ukrainian, Armenian, Maronite, Syrian) Catholic Churches, which operate under the 1990 Code of Canon Law for the Eastern Churches. Quite simply, the rite of baptized infants of the Latin rite is that of their parents; where one parent is of the Latin rite and the other not, it is the rite upon which they agree or the rite of the father and, if they cannot agree, then upon reaching fourteen the child can choose his or her rite (c. 111). Persons may change from one ritual Church to another by papal permission issued through a legal document called a rescript or by choosing to join the autonomous ritual Church of their spouse (c. 112).

Degree of Communion with the Catholic Church

Although persons in the Church are equal and possess rights through baptism, their right and ability to exercise of those rights depends, beyond the issue of their condition, upon the degree to which they are in communion with the Catholic Church, in union with the bishops and with the successor of Peter. The limitations implied here obviously concern the visible communion of the Church, since the law cannot regulate what is invisible. This visible communion and the extent to which it affects the exercise of the rights of physical and of juridical persons involves three main factors: the profession of faith, the sacraments, and ecclesiastical governance (cc. 96, 205).

In regard to the bonds of the profession of faith, of the creeds and of the dogmas of faith, Protestants, Reformers, Anglicans who deny a number of truths of the Catholic faith, are not in full communion with us on that basis.

As for the sacraments, either a number of the seven specific sacraments of the Church are not recognized as sacraments in other Christian ecclesial communities and/or some of the sacraments celebrated are not valid according to Catholic doctrine. Thus Protestants and Reformers do not recognize sacraments, other than baptism and Holy Communion, while the Anglican Communion as a whole or in part does not recognize all seven sacraments or does not do so in the sense that we do, although some of their ministers and people may do. However, the Catholic Church does not recognize the validity of sacraments in the Protestant, Reformed and Anglican communities apart from baptism and matrimony, since all the other sacraments, quite apart from what is believed in their regard, depend absolutely on a validly ordained priest and those communities either do not recognize the ordained priesthood as we do and/or their own orders are not valid; hence their 'ordained' ministers cannot confer validly any sacraments requiring priestly orders.

Thirdly, the exercise of the rights we all share in common as members of the Christian faithful depends also on there being full visible communion with the Catholic Church. Although there are no major doctrinal differences with the Orthodox Churches or with the followers of Mgr Lefebvre, there is no visible communion with the Pope. The other issue is whether persons, physical or juridical, are under a legitimately imposed sanction of the Church (c. 96); someone excommunicated or otherwise sanctioned cannot exercise full rights.

c. Moral Persons and Juridical Persons in the Church

Two other categories of person exist in church law, moral and juridical. For the Church to be able to conduct its mission, we cannot just rely upon the isolated efforts of individuals, of physical persons in the church, not even in cooperation based on goodwill. Some aspects of Church structures stem from the clear will of Christ, while others are needed or are useful. How the life of the Church is organized in dioceses, parishes, congregations of consecrated persons, how churches and property are to be obtained and maintained for the purposes of the Church's mission require some level of organization in church law. Individual physical persons could not assume the weight of responsibility for decisions or for finances. Groups of people under-taking such responsibilities need to be recognized as being able to act according to church law.

Moral Persons

The Catholic Church as such and the Apostolic See could be taken to be examples of juridical persons, but the Code calls them moral persons and states that they are such by reason of divine law (c. 113 § 1). The Catholic Church is in true continuity with the Church founded by Christ, the Church of Christ exists in the Catholic Church in all its fullness and indefectibly, although elements of the truth are also found outside the visible confines of the Catholic Church.[11] The insti-

---

[11.] Congregation for the Doctrine of the Faith, Declaration, *Dominus Iesus*, 6 August 2000, n. 16; ID., Responses to Questions on Certain Aspects of the Doctrine on the Church, *Responsa ad quaestiones*, 29 June 2007, responses 2 and 3.

tution of the Petrine office by Christ likewise means that the See of Peter, the Holy or Apostolic See, is of divine origin. This is partly to prevent them being considered wrongly as entities merely established by others in the Church, with the implication that they might be suppressed in the same way. During the revision of the Code, this point was made strongly, that they are moral persons and are not of the merely juridical order, that they are not brought into being by the Code, but are presupposed by it and recognized in it.[12]

Juridical Persons in General

The concept of 'juridical person' was introduced in 1983, largely on the basis of civil law systems. It is a reflection of public ecclesiastical law, that the Church, like a state, is also a perfect society, with its own autonomy and system of laws.[13]

Juridical persons are aggregates or groups of persons or things (c. 115 § 1), recognized as having rights and duties (c. 113 § 2), having juridical personality. The concept relates to people who act together in accordance with the mission of the Church (c. 114 § 1), in a way which goes beyond the purposes of the individuals who make up such groups. They need to act or it is useful for the Church that they do act as a group, as an entity, but they also have to have the means to support themselves and to function or they should not be established as juridical persons (c. 114 § 3). Examples of juridical persons would be parishes, dioceses, seminaries, congregations of consecrated persons.

There has to be a physical person who has the authority to act officially in the name of the group or juridical person. Such authority can arise from a person's office in the Church, so that the diocesan bishop acts for the diocese (or the person validly appointed acts on his behalf in certain respects, such as the financial secretary for finances), the rector for the diocesan seminary, the parish priest for the parish, the abbot for the monastery, and so on. Otherwise, a decree can be issued by the competent authority establishing who is the appropriate authority or agent for the specific juridical person (c. 118).

A key aspect of a juridical person is that it has to have a purpose which goes beyond that of individuals or physical persons and it must consist of at least three persons (c. 115 § 1). This is not to be overlooked, for example when bishops seek to establish a diocesan institute of

---

[12.] Scheme for the revised Code, 'De personis iuridicis' in *Communicationes*, IX (1977), 240–1: 'Ecclesiae Catholicae personalitas non est ordinis iuridici ... sed est moralis, et ideo in Codice iuris affirmari non debet, sed supponitur.'
[13.] Cf. P. Valdrini, *Droit canonique*, 105–6, nn. 174–5.

consecrated life, since one or two persons, perhaps intending to become more numerous, cannot be constituted as a juridical person, although, if the number subsequently falls below three, this does not suppress the entity (c. 120 § 2).[14] Decisions can be collegial (as with the canons of a cathedral chapter), non-collegial (in a diocese, parish or seminary, where the superior acts for the juridical person) or mixed when, at times, all the physical persons involved participate in a decision and at other times the superior decides (as in institutes of consecrated life), according to their constitutions (c. 115 § 2).[15]

A juridical person in the Church can be an aggregate of things (c. 115 § 3), as in the case of a Catholic bookshop, piety shop, a piece of property. It would have to serve the Church's mission in some real way, either in the form of piety or devotion, or of the apostolate or spreading the Gospel, or of charity (c. 114 § 2), and would have to be directed by a physical person who in law would act legally in its name (c. 118).

Public Juridical Persons

There are three conditions for an entity to be a public juridical person: it must be created by church authority, for a specific purpose of the common good (a Catholic school, the curia or central offices of the diocese, a retreat centre) and act officially in the name of the Church (c. 116 § 1), not under some other auspices.

Private Juridical Persons

If a group lacks even one of the three elements necessary to be a public juridical person, it could still be a private juridical person, but it would have to be fully in accordance with the mission of the Church and would need to have its statutes approved, and it would have to be explicitly erected by a decree of the competent ecclesiastical authority (cc. 116 § 2; 117). Once again, this should only be done when the purposes of the association are checked, their resources to carry out their task are verified, and their willingness to operate only in accordance with Catholic doctrine and discipline is verified, the latter being required before they may use the name 'Catholic' of their entity (c. 116). Private juridical persons might be bodies such as the Legion of Mary, the St Vincent de Paul Society, the Union of Catholic Mothers.

---

14. The Canon Law Society of Great Britain and Ireland, *The Canon Law: Letter and Spirit*, n. 232.
15. Ghirlanda, *Il diritto nella Chiesa.*, 113, n. 91.

Juridical persons cease to exist if they are lawfully suppressed or are inactive for over a hundred years (c. 120 § 1).

3. Laws in the Church: Their Promulgation and Main Features

In a democratic society human laws are made through a procedure such as a majority vote for the laws proposed in both Houses of Parliament, together with their ratification by the Head of State. Some way has to be established in all societies for people to know what actually is law because, otherwise, they can hardly be expected to abide by it. There are various lawmakers within the Catholic Church: a bishop of a diocese can legislate for the people under his pastoral care, a superior in a religious or secular institute or of a society of apostolic life can do so for their members, always provided that they are in accordance with the general or universal law of the Church. For this universal law, the supreme lawgiver is the Pope. Not everything he says is a matter of law; it may be a homily, it may teach and explain the faith, but only if it is clearly established as law does it have the force of law and does it bind as law. This is what is involved in the promulgation of laws. In what follows we shall deal mainly with the law of the Catholic Church as a whole, its universal law.

a. The Promulgation of Laws

We may imagine that informing people about a law is enough, letting them know about it through the media, but this is not so. Such information may be wrong or misleading; even if it is accurate in content, it is still not enough. For something to become law, it has to be issued by a legitimate superior, in this case the Pope, for his proper subjects, who are all members of the faithful or, in regard to the 1983 Code, more specifically Catholic faithful of the Latin rite, but it still has to be issued by him as law. Promulgation differs from merely publicizing information; with promulgation, something is officially proclaimed by the legitimate superior to be or to have the force of law.[16] 'For a law to have binding force' or for people to be under an obligation to obey it, according to Thomas Aquinas, it must be 'a command of reason designed to protect or to promote the common good and it must be applied to those who are to be ruled by it ... through this,

---

[16.] Cf. Ferme, 'Graviora delicta', 371–2.

that it is brought to their attention by its promulgation'.[17] Gratian had been clear that laws are instituted, or brought into being, by being promulgated, by being proclaimed as law publicly, being signed and approved according to the customs of the people.[18] F. Suarez had likewise insisted on promulgation for human laws to be established.[19] Their formula is adopted in the Code, although in the singular: 'The law is established by being promulgated' (c. 7). A law has to be a common command, applying to various people, whose content is just, and it needs to be stable, not merely a temporary arrangement of sheer convenience.[20]

Laws of the Church which would fall strictly into that category are those which are brought into being by the Pope, bishops of dioceses or other legitimate superiors; these are called merely ecclesiastical laws, for example how parishes are to be erected (c. 515 § 2) or who may be sponsors for those being baptized (c. 874 § 1). These ecclesiastical laws are merely human laws, analogous to laws established by governments, aiming to serve the common good and the promotion of the Gospel. They are to be distinguished from laws which are truly divine laws. The latter are laws given by God, either found in revelation such as those presented in Scripture, or of natural law, not part of revelation, but capable of being known by human reason when it functions correctly. The Church does not presume to say that it establishes laws which are in reality established by God; rather it declares them to be laws, for example that baptism is the means of becoming a member of the faithful (c. 849) or that the Church has the innate right to preach the Gospel (c. 747 § 1). This discernment of such divine laws in history on the part of the Church may give a particular form to the divine law, but its being law and its binding power stem from God, being declared, but not constituted as such by the Church.[21]

[17.] St Thomas Aquinas, *Summa theologiae*, I–II, q. 90, a. 4.

[18.] Gratian, *Concordia discordantium canonum* (*Decretum Gratiani*), Pars I, Dist. I, cap. 13, ad 2; Dist. IV, cap. 3 dictum post: 'Leges instituuntur cum promulgantur, firmantur, cum moribus utentium approbantur'.

[19.] F. Suarez, *De legibus ac Deo legislatore*, Coimbra, 1613, Lib. I, cap. XI, n. 6.

[20.] L. Vela, 'Legge ecclesiastica (*Lex ecclesiastica*)', in C. C. Salvador, V. De Paolis and G. Ghirlanda (eds), *Nuovo dizionario di diritto canonico*, Paoline, Cinisello Balsamo, 1993, 625–30 at 626.

[21.] J-P. Schouppe, *Le droit canonique: introduction générale et droit matrimoniale*, Story-scientia, Bruxelles, 1991, 82–8.

b. The Proper Subjects of the Code of 1983

The Code of 1983 deals with the universal laws of the Church which apply to those of the Latin rite (c. 1), with the separate Code of 1990 for Catholics of the Eastern Churches; hence the proper subjects of 'merely ecclesiastical laws' (those which are not divine laws) are not the faithful as a whole, but Catholics of the Latin rite: 'those baptized into the Catholic Church or received into it', with the exception which reminds us of the conditions noted above of age and of the use of reason, namely 'unless they lack the use of reason or (unless the law expressly states otherwise) they have not reached their seventh year' (c. 11). Ecclesiastical laws do affect others in certain dealings with Catholics, as when marrying a Catholic or in investigations of a marriage. Here it is true that many of the laws concerning marriage are truly divine laws, but some are ecclesiastical laws. Other examples would be where other people enter into some contracts with Catholic juridical persons, as when people work in a church where many of the norms of Book V of the Code might well be involved.

c. The Manner of Promulgation

Mere publication of information is not enough to make a law; promulgation means the legitimate superior making it known precisely as law to his proper subjects. For the universal laws of the Church, such as those in the Code, the normal way of promulgating them is through the *Acta apostolicae sedis* (the Acts of the Apostolic See), a volume which came into being in 1908. In the Middle Ages promulgation was often effected by pinning the laws to the doors of the major basilicas in Rome. The normal way for a diocesan bishop to promulgate laws is through his periodic communications to the clergy of the diocese, the *Ad clerum*, but he would have to make it clear in the text itself that he was enacting or promulgating law.

On the other hand, promulgation can take another form, even for universal laws, 'unless in particular cases another manner of promulgation has been prescribed' (c. 8). An instance of this was the norms on grave crimes, which were promulgated by an Apostolic letter *motu proprio* of 30 April 2001, not published in the *Acta apostolicae sedis*, being sent to the bishops of the world, expressly stating that they were being promulgated.[22]

[22.] Cf. Ferme, '*Graviora delicta*', 372: 'Quae omnia ab ipso Summo Pontifice adprobata, confirmata et promulgata sunt ... ' ('All the things approved, confirmed and promulgated by the Supreme Pontiff himself ...')

d. The Entry into Force of Law and the 'vacatio legis'

There is usually a lapse between promulgation and the entry into legal force of a law. This is designed to give people an opportunity to familiarize themselves with the new law, to become acquainted with what their responsibilities will be. The term given to this interval is the 'vacatio legis' (the 'holiday of the law', the law 'being on holiday' or not in force in the meantime).

Normally the universal law of the Church comes into force three months after its publication in the Acta apostolicae sedis (c. 8 § 1), other laws, such as a diocesan law promulgated through the Ad clerum coming into operation one month later (c. 8 § 2). This is what occurs usually and in the absence of any other indication. However, the Code of 1983 was promulgated on 25 January 1983, the anniversary of the calling of the Second Vatican Council and of the call for the revision of the Code by John XXIII in 1959, and the text of its promulgation stated that it would come into force on the first Sunday of Advent, 27 November 1983.[23] The Code of 1990 came into effect almost a year after its promulgation. The reason was to give people a chance to absorb the new laws before they came into effect. There can be occasions where the law comes into effect at the time it is promulgated, this being stated in the text of promulgation itself. An example was the norms on grave crimes, including the sexual abuse of minors, the urgency of the matter being such as to require immediate implementation.[24] Another example was the legal document dealing with abuses in the sacrament of reconciliation, which was also to come into effect on the day of its promulgation.[25]

e. A Formal Amendment to the Code

The texts just mentioned on grave crimes and on the sacrament of reconciliation are instances of new laws since the Code of 1983. However, there was a formal change to the Code introduced in 1998 by

---

[23.] John Paul II, Apostolic constitution, Sacrae disciplinae legis, 25 January 1983; to be found at the beginning of official publications of the Code of 1983; Id, Apostolic constitution, Sacri canones, 18 October 1990, stating that the Code for the Eastern Churches was to come into effect on 1 October 1991.

[24.] Cf. Ferme, 'Graviora delicta', 372 'Normae vim legis exerunt eadem die qua promulgatae sunt' ('The norms have the force of law from the same day on which they were promulgated').

[25.] John Paul II, Apostolic letter, motu proprio, Misericordia Dei, 7 April 2002, Acta apostolicae sedis, 94 (2002), 452–9.

another *motu proprio*, on doctrines of the faith. In 1989 there had been issued a Profession of Faith and a new Oath of Fidelity, to be recited and taken by those preparing to be ordained and by those taking up certain offices in the Church. One element involved in this seemed to the Pope in need of specific clarification from a canonical point of view, namely doctrines on faith or morals which were not solemnly defined, but which were taught definitively by the Church's teaching authority or Magisterium, were to be firmly accepted and held, to the point where one who rejects them goes against the teaching of the Catholic Church. Furthermore, there was also a specific allusion to this in an amendment to the penal law in the Code. Both amendments were ordered to be introduced into the Codes of 1983 and 1990. For the Code of 1983:

> Canon 750 ... will now consist of two paragraphs. The first will present the text of the existing canon, the second will contain a new text. Thus, the text in its completed form will read:
> Canon 750 § 1 ...
> § 2 'Furthermore, each and everything set forth definitively by the Magisterium of the Church regarding teaching on faith and morals must be firmly accepted and held, namely those things required for the holy keeping and faithful exposition of the deposit of faith; therefore, anyone who rejects propositions which are to be held definitively sets himself against the teaching of the Catholic Church.'
> Canon 1371 n. 1 of the Code of Canon Law will consequently receive an appropriate reference to canon 750 § 2, so that it will now read:
> 'Canon 1371 The following are to be punished with a just penalty:
> 1. A person who ... teaches a doctrine condemned by the Roman Pontiff or by an ecumenical Council or obstinately rejects the teaching mentioned in canon 750 § 2 or in canon 752 ...'[26]

f. Canonical Norms outside the Code

Although the Code establishes norms for the universal Church, it does not cover matters relating to liturgy, except very generally (c. 2), the operation of the Curia of the Holy See, procedures for beatification and canonization (c. 1403 § 1), and agreements such as Concordats with civil states (c. 3). We have also seen other instances of laws introduced since the Code.

[26.] John Paul II, Apostolic letter, *motu proprio*, *Ad tuendam fidem*, 28 May 1998, *Acta apostolicae sedis*, 90 (1998), 457–61, n. 4.

g. The Extent of Ecclesiastical Laws

It will be clear by now that, even when they have been properly promulgated, the extent to which some laws bind people is limited. Divine and natural laws bind everyone. Merely ecclesiastical laws bind those baptized and received into the Catholic Church, if they have the use of reason and are over the age of seven (c. 11). Pre-existing ecclesiastical laws are abrogated (completely removed) by the Code (c. 6 § 1), except where the contrary has been specified, as in c. 3. Normally, a new law neither abrogates nor derogates (removing some provisions, but not all) from an earlier one unless it states so expressly, as in c. 6, or unless the new law replaces the old one or is directly contrary to it (cc. 20–21). Laws concern the future and are not retro-active (c. 9), with a few exceptions, where someone's rights have been infringed or where there is a radical sanation of an act which was invalid, as in c. 1161. Particular laws, such as those promulgated by the diocesan bishop, oblige his proper subjects living or domiciled in the territory of the diocese (cc. 12–13), but not normally when the person is outside that territory. Thus, a person abroad is not bound to go to Mass on a day which is a holiday of obligation in his home diocese, but not in the place to which he has gone. Laws are neither invalidating nor incapacitating unless they specifically state this (c. 10). Failing to observe a law would always be illicit or illegal, but not always is it invalid. A priest saying Mass without the proper vestments could still truly celebrate Mass and confect the Eucharist, but one who did not use true bread or wine and / or who did not say the words of consecration would not have celebrated the Eucharist (it would be invalid). In terms of an incapacitating law, we may think of marriage, where the right of people to marry applies to those who are 'legally capable' of marriage (c. 1057 § 1), whereas a person who is incapable of assuming and of fulfilling the essential obligations of marriage, such as a person suffering from severe paranoia at the time of the wedding, cannot and does not marry (c. 1095 § 3). A woman is incapable of ordination to the priesthood (c. 1024).

Laws are to be interpreted according to canonical jurisprudence (how the laws are interpreted and applied in the highest tribunals of the Church), according to legitimate custom, according to the authentic interpretations of the lawgiver (or through those of the Pontifical Council for the Interpretation of Legislative Texts). Generally, laws are to be interpreted broadly, but where the rights of other people are directly involved and in penal cases, they are to be interpreted strictly (c. 18). We can see here the influence of the principles for the revision of the Code.

4. Acts in Canon Law: Legislative, Administrative and Judicial

This section may appear at first sight to be arid and abstract, but, if laws are not to remain a dead letter, if they are to serve the community, if the rights and duties of people who are persons in the Church (cc. 204–228) are to amount to very much, there has to be a mechanism to ensure that they are implemented. We could say that the principle for the revision of the Code that the rights of persons be specified and protected underlies much of this part of the Code.

a. The Distinction of Powers

Another principle for the revision of the Code, that of the separation, but of legislative, executive (or administrative) and judicial powers, appears not as a separation, but as a distinction, since all three powers lie in the Pope and the bishop of the diocese (c. 135 § 1). We have already seen the distinction between sacred power and juridical power. Sacred power derives from Christ by ordination to the priesthood or to the episcopate, whereas its actual exercise depends also on someone having the juridical power to conduct certain acts, which arises either in virtue of the office to which he is validly appointed or its being conferred by decree of the competent authority. Some juridical power does not require sacred power and thus does not require priestly ordination.

Of the three different types of juridical power, legislative power cannot be delegated from one person to another, unless the law specifically provides otherwise (c. 135 § 2) and judicial power can never be validly delegated (c. 135 § 3). Executive or administrative power, however, can be delegated in some circumstances; this is because it is a matter neither of creating new laws (legislative power) nor of judging others (judicial power), but of putting existing laws into effect (executive power). An example might be the possibility of delegating aspects of the pastoral care of a parish to a lay person in circumstances of serious and long-term deprivation; 'aspects' because the full pastoral care of a parish implies priestly orders, since no one but a priest can celebrate the Eucharist, absolve from sin or anoint the sick, and since lay people can at times 'cooperate' in the exercise of executive power (c. 129 § 2).[27]

[27.] F. J Urrutia, 'Delegation of the Executive Power of Governance', *Studia canonica*, 19 (1985), 339–55 at 343–44.

b. Legislative Acts

The power of legislation belongs to the supreme power, that is to the College of Bishops (the bishops of the Catholic Church in full communion with the Pope, together with the Pope and never apart from him), to the Pope himself as the supreme pastor of the universal Church. He enacts legislation for the whole Church by promulgating laws. Bishops in charge of dioceses can enact particular laws for their diocese (abbots and others equivalent in law to bishops in charge of dioceses for their proper subjects) by promulgating them, as we have seen, but not in contradiction to universal law; otherwise, the laws are invalid, which means that they have no force or are non-existent (c. 135 § 2). Laws made by the bishop of the diocese apply to those who are domiciled or who reside in the diocese, whereas laws made by major superiors of institutes of consecrated life or of societies of apostolic life of pontifical right apply personally to their subjects.[28] Vicars general and episcopal vicars do not have legislative power, without a special mandate (c. 134 § 3).[29]

Those who enjoy legislative power and only those, with the exception of a specific mandate (c. 30), can issue general decrees which provide for the common good of all those in a community which can receive law (c. 29). In other words, the Pope could issue a general decree or could mandate one of the Congregations of the Roman Curia to do so (c. 30), to legislate more precisely about some matter, specifying something already in the Code. The general decree of the Congregation for the Doctrine of the Faith in 2007, condemning as a crime of attempting to ordain a woman and specifying the punishment of both the woman and the 'ordaining' prelate under such a mandate, is an example.[30]

c. Judicial Acts

In terms of enforcing the laws of the Church through judicial means, the bishop of the diocese is the chief judge of the diocese, but he

---

[28.] J. A. Coriden, *An Introduction to Canon Law*, revised edn, Paulist, New York, Mahwah, 2006, 168.

[29.] Valdrini, *Droit canonique*, 163–5, nn. 257–8.

[30.] Congregation for the Doctrine of the Faith, General Decree regarding the Delict of Attempted Sacred Ordination of a Woman, 19 December 2007. It specified not only the mandate received from the Pope by virtue of c. 30, but the fact that the decree would come into force immediately upon its publication in *L'Osservatore romano*.

usually exercises this function through one properly qualified and validly appointed as his vicar judicial, who has such judicial power by virtue of his appointment, as do the various officials involved for their respective roles by virtue of their valid appointments. This power cannot be delegated (c. 135 § 3).

d. Executive or Administrative Acts

Our main concern in this section is with how the laws of the Church are to be implemented, how the rights and duties of persons in the Church are to be protected and exercised. This cannot be left to reactions of an emotional nature on given occasions; such individualism would lead to injustice with people in similar situations being treated differently. Justice and equity require something more systematic. In canon law administrative acts are acts which are intended to have juridical effects, to bring about something specific of canonical value.

General Administrative Acts

General decrees, if they are not legislative, but executive or administrative, are one means by which those having executive power can lay down further regulations as to how something is to be done in a particular field for those in regard to whom they exercise such power (cc. 31–32). Thus, the financial secretary of the diocesan finance committee, with that committee's approval, can issue norms as to when and how financial returns are to be made to the diocese by parishes and other entities. A directory issued by one of the Congregations of the Roman Curia might specify how catechetics are to be conducted, on the ministry and life of priests, on the permanent diaconate or on how the pastoral role of bishops is to be fulfilled.[31] Finally, general instructions can be issued, to indicate how the law ought to be observed more fully or more precisely (c. 34 § 1). A recent example would be the norms issued by the Congregation for Divine Worship and the Sacraments on correcting abuses in the celebration of the liturgy, for which John Paul II had called in a prior encyclical and which he approved and

---

[31.] Congregation for the Clergy, *Directory on the Ministry and Life of Priests*, 31 January 1994; ID., *Directory for Catechesis*, 15 August 1997; Congregation for Bishops, *Directory for Bishops*, 22 February 2004.

issued subsequently.[32] Neither the decrees nor the instructions take away from or derogate from the laws, but only have force insofar as they seek to foster the application of existing laws (cc. 31 § 1; 33 § 1; 34 § 2).

Individual or Singular Administrative Acts

There is a whole variety of such acts, but all of them concern the application of canon laws to particular cases or persons (individuals or groups, but not the whole community); hence, they are singular or individual and may not be extended more generally (c. 36 § 2). Where they apply to the external forum, or to what is open in principle to being known elsewhere, they are to be given in writing (c. 37). However, this does not relate to the nature of the act itself, but to the possibility of proving that something has been done; therefore, it is a question of liceity or legality, but not of validity.[33] Unless they are acts of the Pope or of an ecumenical council, they are subject to recourse; in other words, those who consider themselves to be unjustly treated by them or who consider them to be illegal have the right to exercise recourse (the equivalent for administrative acts to an appeal against a judicial decision considered to be unjust) to the superior responsible for the act and, if not satisfied by the response, to the Apostolic See.[34] This could relate to the appointment or transfer of parish priests and of others, the erection, suppression or major alteration of a parish, acts concerning the use of church money or property and so on.

Those capable of discharging singular administrative acts are those with executive power (c. 35), which, apart from the Pope and bishops in charge of dioceses and those in law equivalent to them (those with full and proper ordinary power), includes those who share vicariously in the executive power of the bishop, vicars general and episcopal vicars. They can issue singular administrative acts, but only 'within the limits of their competence' (c. 35): a vicar general for the diocese as a whole, a vicar episcopal for the area of his responsibility only, which may be an area of the diocese or a sphere of responsibility, according to the wishes of the diocesan bishop to whom they

---

32. Congregation for Divine Worship and for the discipline of the Sacraments, Instruction on certain Matters to be Observed or to be avoided regarding the Most Holy Eucharist, *Redemptionis sacramentum*, 25 March 2004, nn. 2, 186, the latter stating that these norms were to be observed 'immediately'; cf. John Paul II, Encyclical letter, *Ecclesia de Eucharistia*, 17 April 2003, n. 52.

33. A. Alvarez, 'Atto amministrativo singolare', I–II, in Salvador, De Paolis and Ghirlanda (eds), *Nuovo dizionario di diritto canonico*, 64–5.

34. Valdrini, *Droit canonique*, 212, n. 328.

are accountable. Where such acts might harm the rights of individuals or where there may be a question of legal proceedings against someone, these acts are to be interpreted strictly (c. 36 § 1). Such acts would usually take the form of a decree, precept, or rescript (c. 35), but could include a privilege (c. 76 § 1). We shall look now at some of these forms of administrative acts.

Singular or Individual Decrees

The 'competent executive authority' can issue a decree which is not a general decree covering everybody in the community (the diocese, the universal Church), but individuals or a particular group, 'for a particular case', and 'according to the norms of law' (c. 48). Such decrees are not responses to particular requests. For such acts there needs to be an assessment by the persons with the executive power of the facts or circumstances, an evaluation of whether the decision contemplated is appropriate and, if it can be done, a consultation with those whose rights may be affected by the act (c. 50).[35] It is to be made known 'in writing' and, if it contains a decision, it is to express, at least in summary form, the reasons for it (c. 51). It can be made known through an executor, deputed for the purpose (c. 54), who must discharge this duty according to the wishes of the one who mandates him or, if it would be illegal or inopportune to implement it, must make this known to the one who gave him the responsibility (c. 41).

A practical example may help us. Given the shortages of priests, it has become necessary to restructure some parishes. An *Ad clerum* from the bishop may sate that 'St. John's parish will be "looked after" by Fr. X', but 'looked after' has no canonical effect, since the priest concerned is not thereby appointed either as parish priest or as parish administrator of that parish and lacks the faculties which go with such an appointment. This would not be an 'amalgamation' of parishes in any event, but would still be canonically most inadequate even as a temporary expedient. Where there was a decision to amalgamate two parishes, for the validity of such an action, the bishop would have to consult the diocesan Council of priests; he is 'not' to make such a change 'unless he has consulted the Council of priests' (c. 515 § 2), the word 'unless' indicating that this pertains to the validity of the act (c. 39), showing that the consultation is obligatory; failure to consult when consultation is obligatory being a further basis for the invalidity of the act (c. 127 § 1). However, for a decree to

---

[35.] A. Alvarez, 'Decreto singolare' in Savador, De Paolis and Ghirlanda (eds), *Dizionario di diritto canonico*, 332.

be issued legally, and to avoid a successful challenge to it through a recourse, the provisions of c. 51 are to be followed. This means that the decree must be issued in writing and that the reasons for it be stated at least in summary form in the decree. Thus, the decree would need to state clearly that, in accordance with c. 515 § 2, the diocesan council of priests was consulted (their consent is not necessary) on such and such a date about the proposed amalgamation of St John and St Mary's parishes, the reasons being for this proposal being that ..., and having consulted those parishes in such and such a form in conformity with c. 50, it is hereby decreed that these two parishes are to be amalgamated as from such and such a date. The reasons might indicate the absence of priests able to be appointed as parish priests in the two parishes, the difficulties of providing pastoral care for some time in those parishes and the absence of any realistic prospect of the situation changing in the foreseeable future. Something generic for the whole diocese might be relevant, but a decree is a singular administrative act, even if connected to other similar decrees in other areas of the diocese, and specific reasons pertaining to the situation in the two parishes (why these and not others?) concerned should be given in the decree. Failure to do this exposes the diocese to recourse, first of all to the bishop, but if not satisfied, to the Congregation for Clergy by any physical or juridical person affected by the decision. A copy of the decree, properly signed and dated by the bishop and by the chancellor, should be communicated to the parish priests (and through them to the people) in both parishes (c. 54).

Precepts

A precept is a particular type of decree and has to be issued according to the criteria just outlined. The difference between a singular decree and a precept is that a precept is a command or a prohibition, given in lawful form by a legitimate superior to a single person or to a number of individuals, who are his proper subjects, to persuade him or them to behave in accordance with the law (c. 49). A bishop can compel a priest of his diocese to live in a particular place, such as a monastery, or not to live in a particular place, his existing parish, for serious reasons, but, if he judges that he ought to do this, it has to be done through the issuing of a precept, against which recourse may be had. Someone arriving unannounced at the door and requiring someone's departure within half an hour to a place in another part of the country used to be associated with the Soviet Union and the practice of internal exile. Regrettably, the entirely legitimate concern to protect children from sexual abuse by clergy has led some bishops to act in an entirely illegal manner, with no precept being issued. A proper precept must be issued, with a summary of the reasons contained in it, and a proper canonical procedure must be followed.

Rescripts, Privileges and Dispensations

Whereas decrees are not normally issued as answers to requests, rescripts (writing-back or replies) are responses to requests. A request for a favour would be made to the bishop or to the Holy See or other competent authority and the response would come in the form of a rescript. A rescript, then, is 'an administrative act issued in writing by a competent authority by which of its very nature a privilege, dispensation or other favour is granted at someone's request' (c. 59 § 1). It can be requested on someone else's behalf (c. 61).

In the past some privileges were obtained abusively through nepotism and some other privileges were passed on or 'communicated' to others (often within religious orders); fortunately, neither of these is possible at present. Privileges are grants of favour by the legislator (Pope or bishop of the diocese) to physical or juridical persons (c. 76 § 1). They can relate to persons, giving an individual a favour which goes beyond the law ('*praeter legem*'), such as an honorary position as a canon or as a monsignor. They can refer to places, such as particular indulgences granted in association with particular shrines or other privileges attaching to certain basilicas; for example, the basilica of St Paul outside the Walls in Rome had the privilege until recently of being an 'abbacy nullius', a territory not part of the Diocese of Rome, but directly under the Pope (not under the vicariate of the Diocese of Rome). Such privileges which go beyond the law, but which do not contradict it, are granted now by rescript.

Rescripts granting favours against the law ('*contra legem*') are involved when a dispensation is granted, relaxing a merely ecclesiastical law in a particular case, for good reasons (c. 85). Those with executive power (the Pope, diocesan bishop and those equivalent to him in law, including major superiors, as well as those who share that power, such as vicars general and episcopal vicars within the limits of their power – that is, only in the area of the diocese or only for the areas of diocesan life for which they have responsibility as episcopal vicars – or one to whom the power of granting dispensations has been formally delegated), can grant dispensations.

Dispensations cannot be granted for elements constitutive of institutes or of juridical acts (c. 86); laws which are constitutive bring something into existence and what is essential to the very existence of an institute (such as a religious or secular institute) and what is essential for the validity of an administrative act as such cannot be the object of dispensation. The diocesan bishop cannot dispense from procedural or penal laws, since these have to do with the rights of various people affected, or from dispensations reserved to the Holy See (c. 87 § 1).

The diocesan bishop can dispense from merely disciplinary laws, such as fasting and abstinence, and from universal laws relating to his own proper subjects (c. 87 § 1), from those reserved to the Holy See if recourse to the Holy See cannot be had and grave danger is occasioned by the delay, if it is a case where the Holy See normally dispenses (c. 87 § 2). He can dispense from diocesan laws and from laws of a provincial synod or of the conference of bishops, if it is for the spiritual welfare of the subject concerned (c. 88). Parish priests and others cannot grant dispensations unless this power is specifically granted to them (c. 89). Parish priests in England and Wales can grant the permission for mixed religion in relation to marriage (c. 1125), but that is not a dispensation under the 1983 Code and it certainly does not stretch to the dispensation from disparity of cult (c. 1086), which is a matter of validity and is reserved to the bishop.

Dispensations are not automatic and are not to be treated as such by those with the power to dispense. For any dispensation, there has to be 'a just and reasonable cause', consideration of the 'circumstances of the case' and of 'the importance of the law from which a dispensation is given' (c. 90 § 1). Otherwise, unless it is the legislator who grants the dispensation (the diocesan bishop or the Holy See for diocesan laws and not any vicars; the Pope for universal laws and not even the diocesan bishop), then the dispensation is 'unlawful and invalid' (c. 90 § 1) and thus the action undertaken on the basis of the dispensation is equally unlawful and invalid.

The Validity of Juridical Acts

Acts which do not meet the requirements of law are always illicit, illegal or unlawful, but some such acts are also invalid; in other words, they have no effects and are null. Only where the law makes it clear that something involves validity is validity in question (c. 10), something signalled for administrative acts where the law contain the terms 'if', 'provided that' or 'unless' entail matters of validity (c. 39). Those acts which are intended to produce juridical effects are called juridical acts. For the validity of juridical acts it is necessary that those performing them be legally capable, that the essential elements of the acts are present, that the proper form of the act is observed and that other formalities of law necessary for validity be observed (c. 124).

Factors which may render an act invalid are: irresistible force used against the person concerned (c. 125 § 1). Grave, unjust fear and/or deceit normally mean that the act is valid unless the law provides otherwise (c. 125 § 2); it would be invalid, if there were no other means of escape from the fear other than to proceed with an act such as marrying (c. 1103) or if the deceit were used to inveigle a person into marriage and pertained to something so central as seriously to threaten to disrupt marital life (c. 1098). Ignorance or error about the very substance of an act or concerning a condition *sine qua non* for undertaking the act make the act invalid (c. 126).

Where the law itself requires consent for the validity of an act, failure to obtain, in a proper way (convening a meeting of them all, unless the law provides otherwise) the consent of a majority of all those entitled or required to give their judgment renders the act invalid. The same is true if the law requires the advice of a particular body; if they are not consulted, the act is invalid (c. 127 § 1). Where the law requires the consent of certain persons as individuals, the superior's act is invalid if he or she does not ask their consent or acts against the consent of any or all of them (c. 127 § 2, 1°). Where it requires their advice, the act is invalid if they are not consulted; the superior is not obliged to follow the advice given, but should have a very good reason for going against the unanimous or majority opinion (c. 127 § 2, 2°). If consent or advice is sought, those to be asked are obliged to give their opinion sincerely (c. 127 § 3). This means that there can be no question of obedience interfering with an individual's judgment, that any attempt by any superior or other person to pressurize a person into giving a particular judgment is not only morally wrong, but illegal. The good of the Church as a whole and of the particular community of an institute, a diocese, a dicastery of the Holy See, demands this honesty of judgment in any consultation which pertains to a juridical act being undertaken.

Statutes and Regulations or Ordinances

When some entity is created, brought into being or 'constituted' in canon law, through what is called 'constitutive law', similar to a 'performative utterance', something which brings into being what it proclaims, the legal structure and what determines its purpose are to be found in constitutions and the legislation which erects them is a constitution. Thus, each institute of the consecrated life or society of the apostolic life has its own constitutions and so does the Roman Curia or the various offices of the Holy See.[36] However, the functioning of these entities is determined by particular statutes and the

---

[36] John Paul II, Apostolic Constitution on the Roman Curia, *Pastor bonus*, 28 June 1988.

more precise practicalities by ordinances or regulations (c. 94), as, for instance, on how meetings are to be organized and run (c. 95).

5. Offices in the Church

The last section of this chapter on General Norms deals with offices in the Church. It is important, first of all, to understand the concept of ecclesiastical office. It is not the case that anybody who does anything in a parish or in a community holds an office as such. Well-meaning but ill-considered acts formalizing people's roles in a parish, with some kind of formal document from the bishop, are unwise from the point of view of canon law and perhaps of civil law.

a. The Concept of 'Office' in the Church

An ecclesiastical office ('*officium ecclesiasticum*') is any charge, responsibility ('*munus*') of divine or ecclesiastical disposition which 'is established in a stable manner for a spiritual purpose' (c. 145 § 1), with the rights and the duties of the office being established by law or, if the office is created at the time it is conferred, by decree (c. 145 § 2). Thus, the office of bishop is a responsibility of divine disposition, willed by Christ, for the good of the Church, in a stable manner, and its rights and duties are specified in the Code. The importance of the office being established 'in a stable manner' is that authorities in the Church are not to 'create offices' just as they see fit or for their friends, but to serve a purpose in the Church's mission which of its nature is to continue, existing before someone is appointed to it and afterwards, unless, in the case of an office of merely ecclesiastical origin, it is eventually suppressed by church authority. It carries rights and duties, a point which is by no means insignificant, given the history of 'livings' or 'benefices' being attached to offices in centuries gone by, where the '*beneficium*' at times took precedence over the '*officium*' or duty (*officium* means 'duty'). An office is a matter of service to the Gospel and so to the community of the Church through exercising such a function or charge.[37]

In its concern to disassociate entitlements from offices, the Second Vatican Council had urged the abolition of benefices, with 'offices' to be 'conferred in a permanent fashion ... for a spiritual purpose'.[38] The Code replaces 'permanent' with 'stable'. Nor is the concept of office in the Code linked directly with sacred power, since lay persons

---

[37.] Ghirlanda, *Il diritto nella Chiesa*, 294–5, n. 294.
[38.] Second Vatican Council, *Presbyterorum ordinis*, n. 20.

can hold some offices, such as financial administrator or judge in an ecclesiastical tribunal, if properly qualified; those who are suitable are 'capable of being admitted to ecclesiastical offices which, according to law, they can discharge' (c. 228 § 1), those with outstanding qualities being 'capable of being experts or advisers in councils, to assist the pastors of the Church' (c. 228 § 2). The statements that such persons are 'capable' of being appointed is important, since it means they may validly be appointed (c. 10). Again the insistence upon the spiritual purpose of the office is to underline the fact that financial recompense, however just, is not to be the main focus of attention.

b. The Provision of Offices/Appointments

Only the proper ecclesiastical superior may make an appointment to an office in the Church (c. 147). There are different ways in which appointments may be made, but first of all we need to consider the conditions of validity for any and all appointments. These are that there must be canonical provision of the office (c. 146), which should be in writing (c. 156). Provision associated with simony is invalid (c. 149 § 3). An office requiring 'full care of souls', involving the exercise of priestly orders, for instance, parish priest, cannot be validly conferred on a man who is not yet a priest (c. 150). The person appointed must be in communion with the Church (c. 149 § 1). The office must be vacant at the time of appointment, unless it is an office with a time limit on it, in which case an appointment can be made within the six months prior to the vacancy arising and with effect from the date of the vacancy. Otherwise, the appointment is invalid because the office is not vacant and it does not become valid through a subsequent vacancy (c. 154).

There can be other conditions of validity attaching to particular offices in the Church, but there are further conditions pertaining to liceity. These should not be ignored, since they are for the good of the Church, for the proper and effective care of the People of God. The question of suitability for the office is especially significant and at times woefully neglected. Suitability relates to competence, experience and moral qualities in the person concerned, whether in regard to vicars general and episcopal vicars (c. 478 § 1), expertise in canon law for the vicar judicial (c. 1420 § 4) or the specific academic and moral requirements for appointments of those teaching, and by implication those directing, philosophical, theological and juridical sciences in seminaries (c. 253 § 1).

Nor should anyone be appointed simultaneously to two posts whose functions are incompatible with one another (c. 152), such as canon penitentiary (who has to operate in the internal forum) and vicar general (who operates in the external forum and who could be involved in procedures relating to someone with whom he has had to deal in the internal forum).

c. Different Ways of Making Appointments

There are four ways of making appointments (c. 147). Firstly, unless otherwise stated the diocesan bishop makes appointments by free conferral in his own diocese (c. 157); it is up to him to select and to appoint the right person, although he must observe procedures and norms just noted. Secondly, presentation: Where there is a right of presentation, usually based historically, the persons to be presented must be consulted and may refuse. The authority competent to make the appointment must judge the suitability of the one(s) to be presented and can refuse to allow their further presentation. When a number of people are presented, the latter judges the most suitable and selects that person (cc. 158–163). The office of bishop is usually one which involves the right of presentation of a number (three) candidates to the Holy See for selection of one of them. In days gone by governments used to exercise this right for various Church offices through arrangements in Concordats. This is not common today, but it applies to Switzerland in regard to bishops. A third possibility is election. When an office is filled through election, as in many insti-tutes of consecrated life or as in the case of the vacancy of the Holy See, those entitled to vote must do so in the requisite time, in a way which is free, secret, absolute and determinate (c. 172 § 1 and 2). Normally, the person elected has to accept the office in the case of institutes of consecrated life. (cc. 164–179). If someone is elected to become pope but he does not accept election, then he never was pope. Finally, there is postulation: if a person desired by electors is under an impediment which is normally dispensed and those electing judge this person more suitable than anyone else, they may 'postulate' this person to the competent authority which is to decide the matter (cc. 180–183).

d. Loss of Office

Loss of office can occur in one of various ways. Office can be lost when a time limit is reached, such as with a superior in office for a specified number of years, through the death of the incumbent or through reaching an upper age limit for the office, although there is no loss of office if the requirement is merely that a resignation be submitted, if that resignation is not accepted (cc. 184–186). Resignation at any time for a just cause or at a time required by law causes loss of office, if the resignation is accepted, where that is necessary (cc. 187–189). One case where resignation cannot be accepted is that of the Holy Father, since he has no earthly superior; his resignation would have to be in a form which made it clear that he had resigned. The normal way for priests to lose office is by being transferred; in the case of diocesan clergy who are parish priests this has to be in accordance with cc. 1748–1752 (cc. 190–191).

A further possibility is loss of office by removal. This is not the same as transfer, but it may be because the time has elapsed and the person has not moved or the office was at the discretion of the authority. It can be that someone is not able to discharge the office any more and refuses to resign, where there is a need to provide for the good of the people in the parish or elsewhere (as when someone is terminally ill and has been in hospital for several months and realistically cannot resume his duties, but who refuses to resign, cc. 1740–1747, c. 1741, 2°). Those who have left the clerical state, publicly defected from the Catholic faith or from communion with the Catholic Church or who have attempted even a civil marriage, are removed by the law itself (c. 194). Finally, office can be lost by deprivation. This can only be for having committed a canonical crime and has to be conducted according to law (c. 196).

A brief word needs to be said about the transfer of parish priests. The office of parish priest is specifically supposed to be a stable one and normally of indefinite length, to enable to him to come to know and to serve the people entrusted to his care (c. 522). Therefore, parish priests who are diocesan priests cannot simply be transferred at the whim of the bishop, who must follow the procedures of the Code, if he judges that it would be pastorally beneficial for a parish priest to serve in another parish. If the priest is unsuitable and this is a ruse to remove him, the bishop's actions are completely illegal, since he ought to have used the procedures for the removal of a person no longer suitable to be a parish priest and, in principle, it would be difficult to say he was suitable for appointment as a parish priest elsewhere, although circumstances may suggest otherwise. Analogously, this would apply to transfer from any office (c. 190 § 2).

The good of the People of God is the determining criterion for the bishop, but, where he judges a particular parish priest should be transferred from a parish 'which he governs satisfactorily' (c. 1748), he must propose the transfer to him 'in writing' and try to persuade him to accept (c. 1748), the priest concerned giving his reasons to the bishop 'in writing' if he does not accept (c. 1749). If the bishop still judges the he should transfer the priest (this presupposes that he give serious consideration to the reasons put forward by the priest), he should consider the pros and cons with the two priests appointed for such a purpose (c. 1742) and then, if he still believes he should proceed, try to convince the priest again (c. 1750). If this fails and the bishop still believes he should persevere, he is to issue a decree, declaring that, after a specified time, the parish shall be vacant (c. 1751 § 1), declaring the parish vacant when that time has elapsed without result (c. 1751 § 2). This, as we recall, is because an appointment of anyone else to an office which is not vacant is invalid (c. 153 § 1). He can then proceed to make an appointment in that parish.

These provisions do not apply to parish priests who belong to institutes of consecrated life because their profession of obedience involves their making 'a total offering of the will' to their superiors as a sign of their total dedication to Christ in the Church.[39] For diocesan priests, the promise of obedience to the bishop does certainly imply a readiness to cooperate with what he judges right for the good of the Church and certainly precludes any deliberate awkwardness by the priest, but the law itself lays down these procedures for the good of the People of God and also to prevent any abuse by a bishop. The episode in Galloway diocese twenty years ago of three priests not accepting a transfer and of the bishop attempting to appoint them to parishes which were not vacant led to the Holy See supporting the priests and not the bishop. They were not being disobedient; the bishop had failed to follow the law.[40] A number of bishops have been reluctant perhaps to transfer parish priests for fear of something similar happening, but there is no need for anxiety. If the law is followed, even in a difficult case, there will be no problem.

6. Conclusion

Having clarified some concepts and procedures which affect all canon law, we shall now turn to the People of God, first of all to the faithful as a whole, to evaluate the position of the new Code in their regard.

---

[39] Second Vatican Council, Decree on the Renewal of the Religious Life, *Perfectae caritatis*, n. 23.

[40] Statement by Bishop Maurice Taylor of Galloway regarding the transfer of three priests to other parishes, following a decision by the Apostolic Signatura in which it accepted fully the bishop's discernment in the matter, but, 'as far as procedure was concerned, (it) found in favour of the three priests', the procedure followed not being sufficient where a priest was unwilling to transfer, 10 November 1995, *Canon Law Newsletter*, 104 (1995), 22–3, document V, nn. 2.3 and 8.

Chapter 3

The People of God

(Book II of the Code)

Part I: Christ's Faithful

1. Introduction

In this chapter we examine the longest book of the Code, that dealing with the People of God, the Church, as a whole and also in their various different sections, with reference to their various rights, responsibilities and functions in the life of the Church. Canon law seeks to facilitate the implementation of the Church's mission in its various dimensions, so that it is fulfilled effectively and with proper respect for the place and role of all in the Church.

2. The Rights and Duties of the Christian Faithful as a Whole

The principles upon which the Code was to be revised had included one of expressing the rights and duties of all the persons in the Church and another of ensuring that the rights of persons should be effectively protected. The idea of a fundamental law articulating those rights had been abandoned, perhaps to avoid a conflict between individuals and groups with such rights interpreting them as an instrument to use against divinely established features of the Church, including the Magisterium.[1]

Whatever the reasons for its abandonment, some elements of what might have been included in such a fundamental law were in fact incorporated into the list of rights and duties of the Christian faithful, especially in cc. 208–223 of the 1983 Code. Being created in the image and likeness of God (Gen. 1:26–8), every human being has

---

[1] Cf. P. Valdrini, *Droit canonique* 2nd edn, Dalloz, Paris, 1999, 37–8, nn. 63–4.

a fundamental dignity and equality, which are neither conceded nor conferred by any government, grounding natural rights which are to be recognized, protected and fostered by all governments. The Church defends such rights.

Beyond the basic or natural rights of all human beings, there are rights and duties 'proper to Christians', which belong to physical persons in the Church, arising from their being baptized, being 'by baptism ... incorporated into the Church of Christ and constituted a person in it' (c. 96), as part of the people of God (c. 204). This common equality of all the baptized, the faithful (c. 204), pertains to their juridical status as baptized, as persons in the Church. The actual exercise of their rights and duties depends upon the condition of each individual ('*condicionem*' – cc. 96, 204 § 1), the degree of their communion with the Catholic Church on the basis of their profession of faith, the sacraments and ecclesiastical governance, and whether or not they are under a legitimately imposed sanction (cc. 96, 205).

These rights and duties which pertain in principle to all members of the faithful stem from the consecration we receive through baptism, by which we are 'made like to Christ' (c. 849). Sharing Christ's total consecration to the Father in the Spirit through grace and through our response of faith, we are all called to share his perfect holiness.[2] We have seen that juridical status in the Church is further specified, according to whether someone has received ordination to the priesthood or to the episcopate or whether someone has professed the evangelical counsels. Nevertheless, these distinctions which affect the functions and offices we perform in the Church do not alter our common dignity as members of the faithful. Thus, there are some rights and duties which are common to all members of the faithful, rooted in our common baptism and in our common status as physical persons in the Church, whereas other rights and duties refer to particular groups of lay faithful, clerics and those in the consecrated life. We shall consider each of these groups in turn.

These inter-related aspects, based in key canons examined earlier (cc. 96, 204, 205, 207), are reflected in the first canon on the rights and duties of the faithful as a whole (c. 208). 'Flowing from their rebirth in Christ (i.e., baptism) there is a genuine equality of dignity and action among all Christ's faithful (by which) they all contribute to the building up of the Body of Christ, each according to his or her condition ('*condicionem*') and function ('*munus*')' (c. 208). The common

---

[2.] G. Ghirlanda, *Il diritto nella Chiesa, mistero di comunione: Compendio di diritto ecclesiale*, 4th edn, Paoline, Milano, P.U.G., Rome, 2006, 91–4, nn. 66–7.

dignity of all baptized Christians is to be respected not just because they are human beings, but specifically as persons in the Church. This common dignity among the baptized, among 'all Christ's faithful', extends to 'action'; in other words, it extends to a positive duty to recognize, permit and foster their active participation in the mission of the Church ('by which they all contribute to the building up of the Body of Christ'). This very important right of persons in the Church must not be impeded, but facilitated.

The limitations mentioned are that this right is to be exercised according to the 'condition' of people and their 'function' or role in the Church. We noted above that 'status' should be translated as 'condition' (c. 96), but 'office' (c. 208) is misleading because it is not the technical concept of an ecclesiastical office ('officium') which is in mind, but the particular function or responsibility ('munus') which people have in the Church, which is related to their juridical status. As always, it is the Latin text of the Code which is normative and not any vernacular translation. Depending on people's function or responsibility ('munus'), which can vary through a new and special consecration to Christ of a sacramental kind through priestly orders and/or of a non-sacramental kind through the profession of the evangelical counsels, their rights and duties may differ. Depending on their 'condition' (age, use of reason, domicile, relationships and rite), their actual exercise of the rights and duties they have in common as members of the faithful will vary. Other relevant factors of the profession of faith, the degree of communion with the Catholic Church and penal sanctions (cc. 205, 207) also affect the discharge of their rights and duties.

With these qualifications, the truth of fundamental dignity as persons in the Church and in acting to promote the mission of the Church remains prominent. It will be useful to summarize the rights and duties common to all members of the faithful, on the basis of canons 208–223 (Table 3). In this table the rights and duties as stated in the Code have been indicated, together with duties clearly implied by the assertions of particular rights, as in cc. 217, 219–220, as well as the rights clearly implied by the duties expressed in cc. 209–210. The whole of this section is to be interpreted in the light of c. 208, and of cc. 204–207. Furthermore, the generic observations in c. 223 underpin not the existence, but the exercise, of all rights and duties in the Church.

From the rights and duties listed, the key role of the Church's mission, in which all have the right to active participation, is evident (cc. 209 § 2, 210, 211, 215, 216), in the communion of the Church in its teaching, sacramental life and discipline (cc 209, 212–214, 216–218,

Table 3

Rights and Duties of all the Faithful (cc. 208°V223)

Rights of all the faithful	*Duties of all the Faithful*
to live in communion with the Church § c. 209 § 1	to preserve communion with the Church c. 209 § 1
to fulfil their responsibilities to the universal Church particular Church to which a person belongs (particular eastern Church/ diocese of Latin Church) c. 209 § 2	to carry their responsibilities to the universal Church particular Church to which a person belongs (particular Eastern Church/ diocese of Latin Church) c. 209 § 2
to strive, according to condition, to lead a holy life oneself promote the growth of the Church promote the holiness of the Church c. 210	to strive, according to condition, to lead a holy life oneself promote the growth of the Church promote the holiness of the Church c. 210
to spread the Gospel to all people c. 211	to strive to ensure Gospel reaches all people c. 211
to make known to pastors spiritual needs c. 212 § 2	to give Christian obedience to teaching and rules from pastors c. 212 § 1
to make views known to pastors for good of the Church, according to own knowledge, competence and position c. 212 § 3	to make views known to pastors for good of the Church c. 212 § 3
to make such views known to other faithful, but ... c. 212 § 3	(to make such views known to faithful) with respect for: integrity of faith and morals reverence for pastors the common good the dignity of individuals c. 212 § 3
to receive spiritual assistance from their pastors, especially through the word of God and the sacraments c. 213	
to worship God according to their own rite c. 214	
to establish freely and direct associations and hold meetings to serve charity pious purposes Christian vocations in the world c. 215	

Rights of all the faithful – contd.	Duties of all the Faithful – contd.
to promote and support apostolic action on their own initiative but according to their status and condition, although no-one may use the title 'Catholic' without the consent of the proper ecclesiastical authority c. 216	to obtain consent from ecclesiastical authorities before using the title 'Catholic' for any associations established c. 216
to receive a Christian education promoting personal maturity knowing and living the mystery of salvation (faith and morals) c. 217	to seek to promote their own personal maturity knowledge of the faith and morals a life coherent with the mystery of salvation c. 217
(those engaged in sacred sciences) to research freely in areas where they are expert to express opinions freely in such areas prudently and with due allegiance to the Magisterium c. 218	(those engaged in sacred sciences) to express opinions freely in such areas prudently and with due allegiance to the Magisterium c. 218
not to be coerced into choosing a state of life (vocation) c. 219	not to coerce others into choosing a state of life (vocation) c. 219
to retain a good reputation free from unlawful harm c. 220	not to harm another's reputation unlawfully c. 220
to protect their privacy c. 220	not to violate another's right to privacy c. 220
to vindicate and defend their rights before a Church tribunal c. 221 § 1	
to be judged according to law and equity if called before a Church tribunal c. 221 § 2 not to suffer canonical penalties except according to law c. 221 § 3	
	to provide for the needs of the Church for what is needed for divine worship for apostolic work for charitable work for the worthy support of its ministers c. 222 § 1 to promote social justice c. 222 § 2 to provide from own resources for needs of the poor c. 222 § 2

In exercising their rights the faithful are to have regard for:
- the common good of the Church
- the rights of others
- their own duties towards others (c. 223 § 1)
Ecclesiastical authority may regulate the exercise of rights for the common good (c. 223 § 2).

223). The autonomy of the Eastern Churches is defended (cc. 209 § 2; 214). There are serious implications for those responsible for education in the Church from the fact that the faithful have the right to receive a Christian education, including knowing the faith and its moral demands, as well as living by them (c. 217), since this requires that catechesis be presented in an integral manner, faithful to the deposit of faith, guarded in particular by the Magisterium. The principles for the revision of the Code had also spoken of the need for rights to be protected effectively; the insistence upon the fact that all have the right to bring matters of importance to the attention of Church pastors is significant (c. 212), but so too is the right to defend their interests, to be judged and punished only in accordance with law, before the Church's tribunals (c. 221). Not only duties relating to social justice (cc. 222 § 2, 223), but responsibilities to sustain financially the work of the Church, with a summary of the only purposes for which the Church may hold temporal goods (c. 222 § 1; Book V of the Code) are incorporated in this broad panorama.

The question has been raised whether or not some of the duties asserted here for all Christians are strictly juridical duties at all.[3] Certainly, the duties to seek our own sanctification, the growth of the Church and the holiness of the Church as a whole (c. 210), as well as that to promote social justice (c. 222), are moral duties incumbent upon all Christians, but juridical duties as such have to relate to external acts and not just to internal dispositions, although the latter can have important juridical consequences, to dealings between human beings rather than between man and God. Nevertheless, such rights and duties are important as background to other norms in the Code. However, it might be possible to consider these duties and rights from a properly juridical perspective, in regard to external behaviour and to inter-personal relations, in the sense that such duties being affirmed implies that others in the Church, whether as individuals, as groups or as those in positions of authority in the Church have no right to prevent or impede individual members of the faithful who seek to promote their own and the Church's holiness and the Church's growth, provided that they seek to realize these objectives in accordance with the other norms in the Code.

[3.] L. Müller, *Fede e diritto: Questioni fondamentali di diritto canonico*, Europress, Lugano, 2006, 211–22.

3. The Rights and Duties of the Lay Faithful

a. The Foundations of their Rights and Duties

The next section of the Code deals with the rights and duties of the 'lay faithful', as distinct from the clerical faithful and before treating those in the consecrated life. This terminology reminds us that we are concerned with those who are baptized, not just with anyone who happens to be in the Church or area with an interest or an opinion. The rights and duties of the lay faithful are additional (c. 224) to those which they enjoy in common with all members of the faithful (cc. 208–223). Their rights are reinforced by the Code, which states forcefully that lay people 'are deputed by God to the apostolate through baptism and confirmation' (c. 225 § 1); regrettably, the translation omits 'by God', which underlines a divine vocation and commission, based in baptism, for which the person is specifically strengthened and sealed by the Holy Spirit through confirmation, to spread and live by the Gospel. This incorporation into Christ and into the Church through baptism is the basis for various lay vocations.[4] The Code's recognition of this implies that ministers of the Church cannot forbid or impede it, but must facilitate it, although in accordance with the law.

The rights and duties noted in this section reflect also the divinely instituted distinction of the faithful into the lay faithful and the clerical faithful, arising from the sacrament of Holy Orders (c. 207 § 1). Grounded sacramentally and theologically in Christ's will, this distinction is neither a mere sociological convenience nor merely a human arrangement for the Church's *'bene esse'* or well being, but is part of its *'esse'*, of its very being and nature. The rights and duties specific to the lay faithful (c. 224) are listed in Table 4.

b. Some Comments on these Rights and Duties

The apostolate which is specific to the lay faithful is particularly directed to those spheres where these members of the faithful find themselves in the secular world (cc. 225, 227). Their special role in spreading the Gospel is there, in their homes and workplaces, in centres of social exchange and recreation; while all in the Church are to evangelize the world in which we live, this 'secular character' of

---

[4.] John Paul II, Apostolic exhortation, *Christifideles laici*, 30 December 1988, n. 10.

Table 4

The Rights and Duties of the Lay Faithful

Rights of the Lay Faithful	Duties of the Lay Faithful
to make known the message of salvation, especially where lay persons are the only ones in a position to spread the Gospel, and to bring others to know Christ – c. 225 § 1	to make known the message of salvation, especially where lay persons are the only ones in a position to spread the Gospel, and to bring others to know Christ – c. 225 § 1
	(as a special obligation) to 'permeate and perfect the temporal order of things with the spirit of the Gospel', according to their *condition*, thereby giving witness of Christ, especially – in secular business and – in exercising secular functions c. 225 § 2
for the married, in keeping with their (specifically married) vocation: – to build up the People of God through marriage and the family c. 226 § 1 – and to educate their children, a serious obligation, primarily theirs, relating especially, but not exclusively, to their religious education, according to the Church's teachings c. 226 § 2	for the married, in keeping with their (specifically married) vocation: – to build up the People of God through marriage and the family c. 226 § 1 – and to educate their children, a serious obligation, primarily theirs, relating especially, but not exclusively, to their religious education, according Church's teachings c. 226 § 2
to have the freedom in secular affairs common to all citizens, but exercising this right within limits: – their actions being permeated by the spirit of the Gospel, not by merely secular priorities – respecting Magisterial teaching – avoiding presenting their own opinions as the teaching of the Church. c. 227	
if 'suitable' (*idonei*), lay people are 'capable' (*habiles*) of being admitted to 'ecclesiastical offices' (*officia*) and 'functions' (*munera*) which, according to law, they may discharge c. 228 § 1	

if outstanding in the relevant knowledge, prudence and integrity, members of the lay faithful are capable of being experts and/or advisors even in councils (eg., diocesan or of the Holy See), according to law, to assist the sacred pastors

c. 228 § 2

to acquire knowledge of Christian teaching appropriate to their capacity and *condition* in order to be able:
- to live by that teaching
- to proclaim it
- to defend it
- to play their part in the apostolate

c. 229 § 1

to obtain teaching on the faith sufficient to be able to discharge their various roles, including living the Gospel, promoting and defending the faith and sharing in the apostolate

c. 229 § 1

to study sacred sciences at ecclesiastical institutions and to obtain degrees from them   c. 229 § 2
if suitable, to teach sacred sciences in such institutions   c. 229 § 3

for suitable lay men, according to provisions of Episcopal Conferences, to receive the stable lay ministries (*ministeria*) of lector and/or acolyte. (This does not give a right to sustenance or remuneration from the Church).

c. 230 § 1

to exercise the temporary functions (*munera*) of lector, commentator or cantor

c. 230 § 2

where Church needs require and ministers are not available, lay people can exercise certain functions (*munera*) in the ministry of the word, presiding over liturgical prayers, baptising and/or distributing Holy Communion

c. 230 § 3

Those pledged to special service in the Church to receive proper formation, remuneration, insurance, healthcare and social security   c. 231 § 1 and 2

the lay vocation is particularly theirs.[5] The Code, no more than the Second Vatican Council, envisages the lay apostolate as bringing everyone into the sanctuary; by what they say and do in their ordinary lives people are to sanctify themselves and the world. The vocation of Christian marriage is a good example; the couple are called to spread the Gospel especially through marriage and the family, their task of education and rearing children reflecting the Church's theological tradition that procreation implies a special responsibility also for religious education. For two baptized spouses, this vocation is further rooted in the sacrament of matrimony.[6] The principle of subsidiarity, one of the principles for the revision of the Code, operates here in the reassertion of the primary right and duty of parents to educate children, with others assisting, not replacing, them (c. 226 § 2).

The right of lay people to obtain sufficient teaching in the faith to be able to promote it, defend it and fulfil their apostolate once more challenges the quality of catechetics. Lay persons are also to be admitted to study Scripture, theology and canon law, where they are properly qualified and to teach such subjects where they meet the requirements of suitability (c. 229). The possibility of some members of the lay faithful being experts (theological, financial, psychological) is recognized (c. 228). Those who meet the requirements of suitability are legally capable (c. 10) of being appointed to a church office (c. 146), provided that it does not presuppose the exercise of priestly orders. Thus, members of the lay faithful, as physical persons in the Church (cc. 96, 204), can be appointed as financial secretary to the diocesan finance committee or another member of it, as judges, advocates, defenders of the bond in an ecclesiastical tribunal or as auditors assisting it, and so on, provided they are in full communion with the Church and their lives are not at odds with Church doctrine. Beyond the many lay people capable of such functions, there are many more discharging responsibilities and exercising rights as Christian faithful in family life and in their apostolate in the world in which they live and work.

These canons use categories we have seen in treating the general norms of the Code. Some lay persons may become lecturers in pontifical institutes, some lay men may become stable ministers in the Church as lectors or acolytes, other lay persons may exercise temporary functions, reading or administering the Eucharist, or others may fulfil

---

5. Ibid., n. 15; cf. G. Ghirlanda, 'Laico' in C. C. Salvador, V. De Paolis and G. Ghirlanda, *Nuovo dizionario di diritto canonico*, San Paolo, Cinisello, 1993, 612–19 at 613–14.
6. John Paul II, *Christifideles laici*, n. 23.

some limited and specified functions in the liturgy when there is a real need and ministers are not available (c. 230). However, there are criteria of suitability for all of these instances, which are not to be ignored and treated lightly, for the good of the Church. Notice the distinction between lay men possibly being admitted to stable ministries of lector or acolyte, including responsibilities for catechesis and animating the liturgy in the case of the former and of assisting at the altar and of exposing the Blessed Sacrament in certain instances in the case of the latter.[7] This is reserved to men by present church discipline, since these ministries were and are conferred upon those training to be priests; this possibility can operate only after a canonically valid decision of the Bishops' Conference (c. 230 § 1). The temporary functions or responsibilities of reading and distributing Holy Communion can be conferred on those who meet the requirements of suitability, but it is to be noted that these functions are of their nature temporary; cases where people may have been told they were appointed for life or situations where such people are effectively there for life are contrary to church law.[8] The Synod on the Word of God in the Life of the Church which has just ended has urged that the stable lay ministry of lector be open to women members of the faithful (implying that the ministry of acolyte be open to them too); this presents no doctrinal problem, since these ministries, even if still rightly conferred upon those training to be priests, are specifically lay ministries.[9] The last canon of this section (c. 231) brings the Church's social doctrine into canon law. Those who have an office in the Church and those employed by the Church have the right to a proper formation, but also to a just wage or salary, meaning a family wage or salary, and social insurance arrangements.

[7.] Ghirlanda, 'Laici', 617.

[8.] Congregation for Divine Worship and the Discipline of the Sacraments, Instruction, *Redemptionis sacramentum*, 25 March 2004, n. 155.

[9.] XII Ordinary General Assembly of the Synod of Bishops on 'The Word of God in the Life and Mission of the Church', October 2008, *Propositiones*: 'It is hoped that the ministry of lectorate may be opened also to women, so that their role of being announcers of the Word may be recognized in the Christian community' (my translation from the Italian). Such a proposal was not found either in the *Lineamenta* or outline preparatory document when it dealt, with the word in liturgy and prayer, chapter 2, n. 22, or with the Word in the life of the believer, n. 25, or in the subsequent working preparatory document, the *Instrumentum laboris*, prior to the Synod, in its treatment of various ministries and specifically of the office of lay persons, chapter 8, nn. 5–6.

4. The Clerical State

Based upon the fundamental equality of all members of the faithful
(c. 208), the clerical state is treated in the Code in the context of the
People of God. This does not make diaconate and priesthood matters
of democratic designation, since both involve a divine vocation from
Christ through the Church, but it does emphasize the basic reference
to baptism, to the vocation of all to sanctity and to the common priesthood of all the faithful. This reinforces the concept of service of the
People of God by those in sacred orders.

a. The Reform of Orders and Ministries

The juridical status of those members of the faithful who receive the
sacrament of Holy Orders is different from that of those who remain
as lay faithful; they become 'sacred ministers'. This represents a
change in canon law; previously, men became clerics when receiving
their first tonsure and there had been seven orders, analogous to
the seven sacraments, with minor orders (porter, exorcist, lector and
acolyte) and major orders (sub-diaconate, diaconate, priesthood),
major orders alone having been called also sacred orders.[10] The
Second Vatican Council had wished to simplify aspects of the liturgy,
particularly where developments had occurred over the centuries
whose significance was not always clear to people.[11] One instance of
such a simplification related to the structure of orders, the distinction between minor and major orders being abolished, with only
major or sacred orders remaining, although the sub-diaconate was
to be abolished. The reform retained the positions of lector and
acolyte, but as lay ministries, not orders.[12] They are at present
reserved to lay men (c. 230 § 1), although the Synod of Bishops just
ended has recommended that women members of the faithful be
admitted as lectors.[13] The bishop can appoint someone to the office
of exorcist or can depute a priest to act (on specific occasions) in

---

[10.] Benedict XV, *Codex iuris canonici* (1917), c. 949.

[11.] Second Vatican Council, Constitution on the Sacred Liturgy, *Sacrosanctum Concilium*,
n. 62.

[12.] Paul VI, Apostolic letter, *motu proprio, Ministeria quaedam* ('Reform of the discipline
of first tonsure, minor orders and subdiaconate'), 15 August, 1972, *Acta apostolicae
sedis*, 64 (1972), 529–34, nn. 1–6; cf. A Flannery (ed.), *Vatican Council II: The Conciliar
and Post-Conciliar Documents*, I, Fowler Wright, Leominster, 1980, 427–32.

[13.] XII Ordinary General Assembly of the Synod of Bishops on 'The Word of God in the
Life and Mission of the Church', *Propositiones*, n. 7.

that function, but it is neither an order nor a specific, stable ministry as such.

The Council wished not only to simplify the structures, but to recognize certain ministries as suitable for lay men, even if they were not proceeding towards ordination. It further wished that those who were proceeding to ordination (including to the permanent diaconate, restored at the behest of the Council) exercise the ministries of lector and acolyte in the Church so that they might gain experience in these ministries of reading and teaching and of assisting at the altar, as part of the preparation for permanent diaconate or for (transitional) diaconate and priesthood. These were judged highly appropriate also in the light of the association of word and sacrament which the Council sought to foster through the liturgical reforms it instigated. It was judged that those preparing for the priesthood should be free to assess whether or not they had a vocation.[14] They should not become clerics too soon in their formation, which should be more clearly a time of discernment by them, their bishop or other superiors and those responsible for their training.[15]

b. The Incardination of Clergy

After these reforms it is clear that a man becomes a cleric at ordination to the diaconate and not before. The practice of describing religious, even women religious, as 'reverend' has been discontinued too. Clerics, though, are not to be ordained just to do as they please; they are to serve the Church. Hence, the Church has sought to avoid clergy being 'acephalous' ('headless'), responsible to no one, and 'girovagi' ('wandering clerics') are not allowed (c. 265).[16] This is why no one may be ordained as a deacon or priest without being ordained for specific service: in a diocese, in an institute of consecrated life (religious or secular), although for a secular institute there has to be a special concession from the Apostolic See, since he would normally be incardinated into the particular Church or diocese (c. 266 § 3), in a society of apostolic life which has the faculty for this, or in a personal prelature (c. 265).

These canons emphasize the fact that ordination is always a matter of service ('diakonia') to the Church, of the People of God and of a specific portion of them as the proper superior decides; it is never

---

[14.] Cf. John Paul II, Apostolic exhortation, *Pastores dabo vobis*, 25 March 1992, nn. 36, 69.
[15.] Paul VI, *Ministeria quaedam*, n. 11.
[16.] J. A. Coriden, *An Introduction to Canon Law*, revised edn, Paulist, New York, Mahwah, 2006, 66.

a matter of personal privilege or operating on one's own terms. Secondly, to become a member of the clergy or to be ordained as a priest means to become part of an 'order', a sacred order, a specific group of persons with such functions, serving the communion of the Church. This has become the canonical reality, directly linked to ordination to the diaconate, of 'incardination' into a specific diocese, or other entity just noted (c. 265). By the juridical act of incardination this service of the Church is 'organized' or 'delimited' in that a particular person's service is orientated towards, rooted in, and committed to a particular part of Christ's people. Both to avoid wandering clergy and to ensure the proper and effective service of the People of God, it is strictly forbidden for a bishop to ordain a man without a need or purpose, without a possible canonical mission for him to fulfil in the Church, in the entity into which he will be incardinated (c. 269) or to exercise elsewhere for a time, by request or agreement of his ordinary. A canonical mission is not the same as incardination, but is linked to it; it specifies the particular office or task to be fulfilled for a given period of time. The reason it can be elsewhere for a time is that the needs of the universal Church are also to be considered by all, including diocesan bishops; hence a priest of a diocese could be asked by his bishop and others responsible, and could agree, to work as a lecturer in a seminary elsewhere, in a missionary capacity in another diocese, in one of the dicasteries or departments of the Roman Curia or Holy See, for a definite or for an unspecified period of time. This would not alter his incardination.

A good presentation of the role of incardination is found in recent norms relating to preparation for the permanent diaconate: 'Incardination is the juridical bond which has ecclesiological and spiritual force, insofar as it expresses the ministerial dedication of the deacon to the Church.'[17] Incardination cannot occur apart from diaconal ordination (c. 266 § 1–3), except where someone is already a cleric and so is incardinated elsewhere, to where he lawfully transfers. It is distinct from perpetual profession by which someone becomes a permanent member of an institute of consecrated life, since only clerics can be incardinated anywhere and diaconal ordination is the only way to become a cleric. Perpetual profession has to precede diaconal ordination in such institutes, unless it is a case of an existing

---

[17.] Congregation for the Clergy, 'Directory for the Ministry and Life of Permanent Deacons', *Acta apostolicae sedis*, 90 (1998), 879–926 at 880: 'Incardinatio est vinculum iuridicum quod vim ecclesiologicum et spiritualem habet quatenus exprimit dedicationem ministerialem diaconi Ecclesiae.'

cleric making perpetual profession in accordance with c. 266. In that case he is incardinated into that institute at perpetual admission and at that moment is excardinated from a diocese or other entity in which he was incardinated (c. 268 § 2).

The valid transfer from one diocese or other legal entity to another, occurs when both bishops agree and give letters of incardination/excardination (c. 267 § 1); excardination only occurs at the moment of incardination into the new diocese, to avoid acephalous, wandering clerics (c. 267 § 2). Where a cleric has moved to another diocese and worked there lawfully for five years (with the permission of both bishops), he is incardinated into the new diocese by the law itself after five years, if he has written to both bishops to say he intends to do this and if neither has written back in four months to reject his request (c. 268 § 1). This is a matter of validity.

Historically, the problems associated with wandering clerics goes back into the Middle Ages. The problems of pluralism and absenteeism, dealt with in the reforms of the Council of Trent, showed that even the appointment of priests and bishops did not resolve all difficulties, since there were too many for the proper service of people and since often those appointed did not attend to their duties as they should have done. This was not unconnected with the system of benefices, where the attachment of offices to land, titles and/or income meant that often there was more concern with what individual priests could gain from appointments than with how they could serve the Church.[18] This indicates that canon law is not a panacea for difficulties in the Church. It is necessary to regulate the life of the Church and especially to assure the effective and proper pastoral care of the People of God, but the personal commitment, integrity and diligence of those ordained and appointed are indispensable.

The 1917 Code's regulations on incardination were strict because of the concern to avoid unattached clergy ('*cardo*': 'hinge'; incardination: attached to a diocese). However, the pastoral needs of the Church as a whole in the years which followed showed a need for a level of adaptation, especially as regards the service of the universal Church. Hence, the current norms allow some flexibility, without excardination. The danger of being too rigid with the regulations and thereby of compromising the proper care of people in the Church is a real one.[19] The Second Vatican Council sought to attend to this, resulting

---

[18.] J. Gaudemet, *Le droit canonique*, Cerf, Fides, Paris, 1989, 39.
[19.] P. Valdrini, 'Le droit des personnes dans l'Église' in Valdrini *et al.* (ed.), *Droit canonique*, 59–62, nn. 106–113.

in the norms in the Code.[20] Bishops can permit priests to work in another diocese for a specified or even indefinite period of time, while remaining incardinated in the original diocese, but only with the written agreement of the bishop of the diocese where he would work (c. 271 § 1–2). This is one way of serving the needs of the Church in areas where there is a shortage of clergy: a bishop is not to refuse a request from a suitable priest for such an assignment, except where his own diocese is in grave need (c. 271 § 1). During this time the cleric is answerable to both and can be recalled, with the agreement not being renewed, at the behest of either (c. 271 § 3).

c. The Formation of the Clergy

The Code deals mainly with the formation of priests (only c. 236 is specifically on permanent deacons and there is nothing explicit on the formation of bishops). Placing these canons not in the treatment of Magisterium, as in the 1917 Code, but in the section on sacred ministers, places the focus on the threefold functions (*tria munera*) of the priest, linked to those of Christ and of the Church.[21] Treating formation at the start of the canons on the clerical state and the many canons dedicated to it shows its 'primordial importance'.[22]

Apart from the reform of the ministries and orders and the time and manner of becoming a cleric, for priestly formation the Code recommends minor seminaries (c. 234), permits formation outside of the seminary in some instances (c. 235 § 2), but especially seeks to locate such preparation for priesthood in a major seminary (c. 235 § 1). The poor education and morals of many clergy prior to and at the time of the Reformation was a source of great scandal, poor preaching and inadequate pastoral care. Seminaries established after that Council were designed to combat and to prevent such abuses.

The Main Features of a Seminary

The seminary, therefore, is to foster intellectual training in faith and doctrine (cc. 248; 252, 256),[23] philosophy and theology (cc. 250–252),

---

20. Second Vatican Council, Decree on the Pastoral Office of Bishops, *Christus Dominus*, n. 6; Decree on the Life and Ministry of Priests, *Presbyterorum ordinis*, n. 10; Paul VI, Apostolic letter, *motu proprio*, *Ecclesiae sanctae*, 6 August 1966, nn. 1-5; see A. Flannery (ed.), *Vatican Council II: The Conciliar and Post-Conciliar Documents*, 591ff.

21. Valdrini, *Droit canonique.*, 58–9, n. 104.

22. Gaudemet, *Le droit canonique*, 38–9.

23. John Paul II, *Pastores dabo vobis*, nn. 51–6.

liturgy (c. 256), human formation,[24] pastoral formation (cc. 255, 258)[25] and is also to provide spiritual preparation (cc. 244–245).[26] The latter requires the provision of a spiritual director chosen by the seminarian, to guide him to discern whether or not he has a vocation to the priesthood, as well as confessors (not necessarily the same person as an individual's spiritual director). The important distinction between the internal forum and the external forum, the confessor and the spiritual director operating in the former (cc. 239 § 2–3; 240 § 1) and the rector and other formation staff operating in the latter is to be maintained; thus the rector may not ask the opinion of a confessor or of a spiritual director about the suitability of a particular seminarian for ministries, candidacy or ordination (c. 242 § 2) He may not hear the confession of a seminarian unless specifically asked to do so by the student (c. 985). The spiritual formation is to be centred around the daily Eucharist, nurturing frequent use of the sacrament of reconciliation, devotion to Our Lady, retreats, and the like (c. 246).

The Promise of Celibacy for the Kingdom

There is to be specific attention to the preparation of students for the responsibilities of lifelong celibacy for the Kingdom (cc. 247 § 1, 277 § 1).[27] This is to concern the reasons for priestly celibacy, its appropriateness for the priestly life and especially the ideals it enshrines for the specific configuration of the priest to the Person of Christ. It is to involve also an esteem for the married state and for the gift of sexuality itself. A consideration of the personal qualities needed to live the celibate life as a specific way of nurturing wholehearted devotion to Christ and so an availability for the service of his Church is to be fostered too. This is part of the discernment of the vocation to celibacy which needs to be assessed alongside the question of a vocation to priesthood, since they are not identical, even if they are closely linked. There needs to be a realistic reflection also on the responsibilities which this vocation involves, not least the responsible way of conducting life as a priest, not behaving in a way which might endanger fidelity to celibacy nor giving scandal. The fundamental reason for celibacy being associated with priesthood is Christological (Christ's own celibate life, with his ability to relate to people of both sexes and of all kinds in conducting his mission without any improper behaviour). The ecclesiological

---

24. Ibid., nn. 43–4.
25. Ibid., nn. 57–9.
26. Ibid., nn. 45–50.
27. Ibid., n. 44.

purpose of celibacy, that the priest put himself at the disposal of the Church and of its mission in a way which may be more difficult if he had to worry about a wife and family (cf. 1 Cor 7:25–40) and its eschatological function of pointing to something so important as to warrant and explain to us the sacrifice entailed (implying a life which in fact does put Christ and the Kingdom first) need to be appreciated for the promise of celibacy to be meaningful in relation to the priesthood.[28] This requires a positive appreciation both of sexuality and of marriage, with neither fear nor scorn. Without these ideals the value of celibacy will not be understood and it cannot be lived out effectively if it is seen as a mere law or disciplinary rule. It is highly appropriate for the priesthood, but is not essentially linked to it, since there have been many priests in the past who were married, since Eastern Churches continue to observe the discipline prior to celibacy becoming normative in the Latin Church of permitting married men to be ordained priests (but not bishops), but not allowing priests to marry, and since dispensations can be granted for married men to be ordained in the Latin Church as has happened with some former Anglican and Lutheran ministers. The practical evaluation by the individual seminarian, assisted by prayer and by his spiritual director, remains essential to a proper discernment, whether he judges realistically that he has the capacity to live in basic peace in the celibate state, since grace builds on nature, but does not alter it fundamentally. A person who is psychologically and affectively immature is unsuitable for such a life.[29] Neither the person himself nor those responsible for his formation should delude themselves in that regard; 'nor should anyone pretend that grace supplies for the defects of nature in such a man'.[30] If a seminarian considers that he cannot live without the intimacy, also sexual, of a woman, then this would be a sign that he has a vocation not to celibacy, but to marriage, which means he ought neither to make the promise of celibacy nor let himself be ordained a priest.

[28.] Paul VI, Encyclical letter, *Sacerdotalis caelibatus*, 24 June 1967, *Acta apostolicae sedis*, 59 (1967), 657–97, nn. 19–26, 33–4.

[29.] Congregation for Catholic Education, *Orientamenti per l'utilizzo delle competenze psicologiche nell'ammissione e nella formazione dei candidati al sacerdozio*, 29 June 2008, n. 2.

[30.] Paul VI, *Sacerdotalis caelibatus*, n. 64.

The Selection of Students for the Seminary

The selection of students for seminary is to have regard to their status; they must have been baptized and confirmed (c. 241 § 2) and have the necessary intellectual, human, moral and spiritual qualities (c. 241 § 1). Special care is to be taken before a bishop or other superior accepts someone who has been dismissed from another place of formation (c. 241 § 3).[31]

These points may seem obvious, but both the bishop or other superior who wishes to send someone to a seminary and the rector of the seminary have an obligation to verify, by obtaining valid certificates, that a man has been validly baptized and confirmed. The assessment of the qualities of the one seeking admission need careful assessment too, more so in an age when there is a shortage of priests in many areas and where bishops may be tempted to take people too easily: 'I think he should have a chance' is not a good enough evaluation of someone's suitability to go to seminary, especially when subsequent judgments can be taken too lightly at times.

There is a very legitimate concern these days to avoid admitting to seminary anyone who may turn out to be (or already to have acted as) a paedophile. The danger of abuse of children and/or of young people justifies and requires stringent criteria already at the selection stage. Often these days, dioceses, institutes and societies engage psychologists to conduct much more thorough investigations than were done in the past. These are very costly (well over £1,000.00 per candidate assessed in view of the priesthood or of the permanent diaconate, I believe) and, where they succeed in identifying a major problem, this would be justified. However, other dimensions of discernment also apply and need to be taken equally seriously. The criteria which might well be used in assessing someone for a post would include not only at least minimal academic ability, but evidence of commitment and perseverance in what has been undertaken before.

A further criterion has been specified recently by the Congregation for Catholic Education, namely, that a person who practices homosexual acts, who has deeply rooted homosexual tendencies or who supports the 'gay culture' ought not to be admitted either to a seminary or to sacred orders, although someone could be admitted who had not engaged in any homosexual act for at least three years (presumably referring to someone with a transient or superficial tendency

---

[31.] Cf. Congregation for Catholic Education, *Orientamenti per l'utilizzo...*, n. 16.

only).[32] This regulation has attracted criticism, as might have been expected. The text does refer to recent problems which have arisen among priests and seems to refer to scandals of paedophilia. It has to be recognized that most homosexual persons are not paedophiles and that the bulk of paedophile abuse is heterosexual and often incestuous. However, the majority of those Catholic priests who have been convicted of crimes of paedophilia have been homosexual.[33] Thus, it would be seriously irresponsible of the Catholic Church not to address this specific problem in its selection and evaluation of candidates for the priesthood; that is what the recent norms attempt to do. More broadly, homosexual persons may be relatively settled during their time in seminary, but there have been cases of priests being under pressure from their living circumstances or from their pastoral work giving way to their passions or resuming former types of behaviour entirely at odds with Catholic doctrine on homosexual acts and with the implications of the complete continence required by clerical celibacy, causing, amongst other things, scandal by their behaviour.

Formation in the Seminary

The rector is appointed by the bishop for a diocesan seminary, by the bishops responsible for an inter-diocesan seminary (cc. 243, 253 § 1) or by those responsible to the Holy See for a pontifical seminary. He is the person responsible for acting in the name of the juridical person of the seminary (c. 238 § 2). He is responsible for advising bishops on the appointment of seminary staff, who must be morally upright and who must have at least a canonical licence in any theological, philosophical or juridical science they are to teach (c. 253 § 1). Under the guidance of the bishop(s) responsible (c. 259) or of the Holy See, he is responsible for the day-to-day running of the seminary (c. 260) and, with the

---

32. Congregation for Catholic Education, *Instruction concerning the Criteria for the Discernment of Vocations with regard to Persons with Homosexual Tendencies in view of their Admission to Seminary and to Holy Orders*, 4 November 2005, n. 2. Cf. B. Kiely, Homosexuality: Science, Morality and Discipline', *Seminarium*, new series XVVII (2007), 685–700 at 698–9.

33. Cf. M. P. Kafka, 'Sexual Molesters of Adolescents: Ephebophilia and Catholic Clergy: A Review and A Synthesis' in R. K. Hanson, F. Pfäflin and M. Lütz (eds), *Sexual Abuse in the Catholic Church: Scientific and Legal Perspectives: Proceedings of the Conference 'Abuse of Children and Young People by Catholic Priests and Religious' (Vatican City April 2–5, 2003)*, Libreria editrice Vaticana, 2004, 51–9 at 54. The distinction between 'ephebophilia' for those sexually drawn to adolescents and 'paedophilia' for those drawn to very young children, is not always made; I refer generically to paedophilia.

assistance of the seminary staff, to ensure that the norms he devises in accordance with the charter of formation of the Bishops' Conference, are observed (c. 261). Apart from matters to do with marriage, effectively the rector operates in place of the parish priest in regard to those for whom he is responsible in the seminary (c. 262). He is responsible for the upkeep of the premises (c. 263).

The norms of canon law will only be effective if they are implemented. The scandals over paedophilia seem in part to lie behind the recent systematic visitations being conducted under the auspices of the Congregation for Catholic Education in the various seminaries of the United States. The norms listed above delineate the responsibilities of bishops and of rectors in relation to the appointment of staff and the running of seminaries. When bishops are personal friends of the rector, the possibility of an objective evaluation of the rector and of the seminary is not rendered impossible, but there is a real risk that it may be compromised. At issue here are not just these current scandals, but much more also. The criteria of c. 253 are essentially twofold, academic and moral. While it may be understandable that a person about to complete a licence or a doctorate in Scripture, theology or canon law may be dispensed and appointed where there is urgent need, it would be altogether wrong for someone with no licence in anything to be appointed to a seminary to teach those subjects and scandalous were such a person to be made dean of studies in the seminary, responsible not only for organizing the programme of studies, but for monitoring the academic progress of students and for granting them exemptions from courses on the basis of judgments he could hardly be competent to make.

The other criterion specified in c. 253 § 1, that 'only those ... of outstanding virtue' be appointed, is an example of a canon which might have been better reformulated, since not many people may be able to match such an ideal. Yet, it should not be considered a mere moral exhortation rather than a juridical norm, since it is directly concerned with the juridical act of making an appointment to an office in the Church. It implies at least a negative criterion, namely, that no one who has conducted themselves in a way which is clearly incompatible with the obligations of celibacy or with the obligations of justice should be appointed to any position on the staff of a seminary or be allowed to teach in a seminary. A self-denying statement, confirming that he has never conducted himself in such a way as to be in clear violation of the obligations of celibacy or of justice, or in such a way as to bring disrepute upon the Church, should be required of everyone teaching in a seminary. A similar statement from the rector in regard to each member of staff appointed, or engaged, to teach courses at the seminary, and from the bishop in regard to the rector, should be required. Such statements should be signed and made conditions of appointment and of retaining an appointment in a seminary.

We have noticed the attention to psychologists in the selection process for seminaries. The increasing tendency for psychologists to be involved in seminary training is perhaps largely as a response to the crisis over sexual abuse. Some involvement can be very helpful, but certain dangers need to be avoided. Not all psychologists are clinical psychologists, able to diagnose and treat conditions which have been diagnosed. All psychologists, however competent they may be and however good they may be as persons, need to be very careful neither to violate nor to blur the line between internal and external fora. The insistence on this distinction in regard to the spiritual director has been noted. While it is true that the absolute confidentiality of the seal of confession only applies in the sacramental internal forum, or where such confession is involved, the confidentiality of the non-sacramental internal forum is such that the rector is forbidden to ask the spiritual director his opinion about a particular seminarian's suitability to proceed to candidacy for orders (which replaced tonsure), ministry (lector and acolyte) or ordination (diaconate and presbyterate/ priesthood). Indeed, the spiritual director should refrain from comment on students at meetings of the formation team, other than matters of mere information (for example, whether someone has come out of hospital).

Analogously, if a psychologist is engaged in the seminary and is part of the formation team, this means he is operating in the external forum. He should not give guarantees or intimations of confidentiality to seminarians, since he is required to make judgments and so to contribute to decisions about their suitability in the preparation for priesthood. Much less should there be any suggestion that group discussions with such a psychologist are subject to confidentiality. They should not be equated and made analogous to group therapy sessions. While it is one thing to encourage honest discussion about preparation for the priesthood, pastoral prospects and issues, it is quite another matter if seminarians feel constrained to 'open up' in public in such a group about their feelings, reactions, and the like in the presence of a psychologist, perceived to be analysing them. No such psychologist should be a member of the formation staff of a seminary in the external forum; a member of the latter should not operate as a psychologist with students individually or in groups.

There are occasions when the formation staff of a seminary may consider that a psychological referral would be necessary or at least useful. In such a case, it would be prudent and right to contact the person's bishop or other superior. If it were judged necessary for the individual's continuing formation, he could be required to submit to an assessment or counselling session as a condition of remaining in formation, but he would have the right of recourse to the rector or to the bishop and, if not satisfied, against the rector's decision to his bishop and against the bishop's decision to the Congregation for Education. However, every seminarian is morally responsible for undertaking fully his own part in his own formation and for collaborating fully with those responsible for him. Should such an evaluation or counselling be judged necessary or advisable, the seminarian should not be constrained nor 'urged' to go to a psychologist on the formation staff in the seminary; indeed, he should not be allowed to go to that person, however good he (or she) might be. Rather, he should be able to go to a psychologist of his choosing (from a list approved or proposed by the rector), but on condition that the report eventually prepared be sent only to the rector or to that seminarian's spiritual director; the student should see the report.[34]

d. The Specific Rights and Duties of Clergy

Much of what pertains to the rights and duties of clergy is scattered through the Code, but here some of the key rights and duties are put forward. Given the experience of past centuries with benefices, nepotism, pluralism and absenteeism, the Code places duties first and only then rights. The rights mentioned are very few, to just remuneration, to be appointed to offices requiring the exercise of orders, to associate with other clergy for purposes in keeping with their state of life, and to take an annual holiday. The right to appointment needs to be understood as a right in principle (a priest is not barred from such offices as is one without priestly orders), but actual appointment depends upon each individual's suitability for the office concerned.

Much of what is said in the Code about the specific rights and duties

---

[34.] The document of the Congregation for Catholic Education, promulgated on 29 June 2008, seems to confirm these judgments: *Orientamenti per l'utilizzo...*, (requiring the informed consent of the candidate (n. 5)), excluding such a psychologist from the formation team (n. 6), choice by the seminarian among approved psychologists if there is a need for evaluation (n. 12), clear respect for the different roles of the internal/external forum (nn. 13–15), while encouraging careful assessment, also psychological, of candidates in harmony with spiritual and moral formation (nn. 3, 6, 9–10).

of the clergy, since their rights and duties as members of all the faithful remain (c. 224), pertains to the secular clergy and especially to priests. However, there are clear references to the duties of deacons, as well as indications of what may not apply to permanent deacons. The specific rights and duties of the clergy are listed in Table 5.

There are analogies between secular clergy and those in institutes of consecrated life in regard to responsibilities of obedience, celibacy implying perfect continence and a simple life to emulate poverty, as well as in the duty to promote fraternal charity, akin to a specific responsibility to fraternal life among consecrated persons (c. 602). Other responsibilities concern the life of prayer, the duty to foster one's own holiness, to pray the full Divine Office every day (except permanent deacons), which is a specific obligation to pray for the whole Church in this way assumed at the diaconate. Priests are urged to celebrate the Eucharist each day (it is not a strict obligation), the recent tendency to abandon this long-standing tradition in the Latin Church being implicitly criticized in the renewed appeal for priests to celebrate the Eucharist each day, if possible.[35]

Methods of fostering pastoral work, remote and more direct, are listed (cc. 279–284) and the incompatibility of various roles, activities and organizations with the life of the priest, at least in principle, are recalled (cc 285–289).

5. Loss of the Clerical State

a. Ways of Losing the Clerical State

It is often said: 'once a priest, always a priest' and the same might be said for a deacon and for a bishop. This is because being a deacon, priest or bishop depends upon ordination and a change which ordination brings about in the person ordained by Christ, uniting that person to Christ in a new and deeper consecration. Especially in the priestly and episcopal degrees, this can be neither undone nor repeated, which is what is meant by saying that the sacrament of Holy Orders imparts a character (c. 845 § 1). However, the concept of the clerical state is a juridical category and so there can be alterations there. In the past, it used to be said that people were 'promoted' to orders in their seven

---

[35.] John Paul II, Encyclical letter, *Ecclesia de Eucharistia*, 17 April 2003, n. 11; Congregation for Divine Worship and for the Discipline of the Sacraments, Instruction, *Redemptionis sacramentum*, 25 March 2004, n. 110.

Table 5
The Specific Rights and Duties of Clergy

Rights of Clergy	Duties of Clergy
to just remuneration　c. 281	obedience: to obey the Pope and also his proper ordinary (promise at diaconate and priestly ordination)　c. 273 including accepting appointment to an office within the ordinary's jurisdiction, unless there are grave reasons against this　c. 274 § 1 though only a priest may accept an office requiring exercise of sacred orders　c. 274 § 2
to be appointed (in principle) to offices requiring the exercise of sacred power (priestly order)s　c. 274 § 1	celibacy: to observe 'perfect and perpetual continence for the sake of the Kingdom' (promise at diaconate ordination) to remain close to Christ with an undivided heart to dedicate themselves more freely to the service of God and neighbour　c. 277 § 1 to behave prudently in regard to those who might be a threat to continence or who might cause scandal　c. 277 § 2
(for secular clergy) to join associate with others for purposes compatible with their state in life　c. 278	simplicity of life (poverty): to follow a simple life　c. 282 § 1 hopefully, using goods beyond their needs for the good of the Church or for charity　c. 282 § 2
to take an annual holiday c. 283 § 2	fraternal cooperation: with other clerics, since all share in the presbyterate (of the diocese), to build up that brotherhood and to be united in prayer　c. 275 § 1, perhaps sharing a form of community life　c. 280
	to promote the mission of the laity in the Church and in the world　c. 275 § 2 to foster their own holiness: as 'consecrated to God by a new title' through ordination and as 'stewards of the mysteries of Christ', this is a special duty　c. 276 § 1 by: faithfully fulfilling pastoral duties　c. 276 § 2, n. 1

Table 5 (continued)

Rights of Clergy	Duties of Clergy
	nourishing themselves spiritually from the Lord's Word and the Eucharist; priests should celebrate and deacons attend Mass daily · · · c. 276 § 2 n. 2
	reciting the Divine Office daily for the good of the Church, in its entirety (for priests and transitional deacons), in part as laid down by the Bishops' Conference for permanent deacons · · · c 276 § 2, n. 3
	making a retreat regularly, as particular law lays down · · · c. 276 § 2, n. 4
	praying mentally, receiving the sacrament of penance, honouring Our Lady, etc. · · · c. 276, § 2, n. 5
	avoiding associations incompatible with clerical state · · · c. 278 § 3
	to foster pastoral work by continuing to study sacred sciences · · · c. 279 § 1
	attending pastoral courses · · · c. 279 § 2
	keeping up with other sciences as needed · · · c. 279 § 3
	not being absent from diocese for a long time without permission · · · c. 283 § 1
	wearing 'suitable ecclesiastical dress', as determined by Episcopal Conference except permanent deacons · · · c. 284 *
	not to assume public office without permission · · · c. 285 § 3*
	not to engage in commerce or business without permission · · · c. 286*
	not to be active part in political parties or trade unions, except where needed, in the judgment of Church authority, to defend the Church's rights or protect the common good · · · c. 287 § 2*
	not to engage in the administration of goods of lay people or in secular offices, etc · · · c. 285 § 4*
	not to undertake military service · · · c. 289 § 1
	not to undertake civic offices, unless their ordinaries have decreed otherwise · · · c. 289 § 2
	*not binding on permanent deacons unless particular law states otherwise · · · c. 288

levels.[36] Someone was said to be 'reduced to the lay state' or 'laicized'.[37] Out of respect for the lay faithful, this kind of terminology is not used these days. Not only that, but, theologically, there is a difference of function within the one body of all the faithful. Nowadays, we speak more of the 'loss of the clerical state'. Let us examine the key canon on this matter (c. 290):

> Sacred ordination, once validly received, never becomes invalid. A cleric, however, loses the clerical state:
> – by a judgment of a court or an administrative decree, declaring the ordination invalid (c. 290, n. 1)
> – by the penalty of dismissal, lawfully imposed (c. 290, n. 2)
> – by a rescript of the Apostolic See … (c. 290, n. 3)

In the first case, the person was never ordained. The second can only occur after the commission of a canonical crime, which the individual admits or which he is proven to have committed, for which that is a proper penalty. A rescript, we recall, is an administrative act by which an answer is given to a request or a petition. It is noted in c. 290 § 3 that a rescript granting a request to be relieved of the obligations of the clerical state is not granted to deacons except 'for grave reasons' and to priests except 'for very grave reasons'.

b. Loss of the Clerical State and the Question of Celibacy

The loss of the clerical state does not imply a dispensation from celibacy. This is so except for the instance mentioned in c. 290 § 1, the nullity of the ordination (c. 291). The reason for this, theologically, is that celibacy is related to priesthood not intrinsically, but extrinsically; it is appropriate for priests to be celibate, presuming that they have the vocation both to priesthood and, distinctly, to celibacy. Therefore, it is not automatically dispensed, if someone loses the clerical state. However much the discipline of the Church requires celibacy of those called to be priests in the Latin rite ('Clerics are obliged …', c. 277 § 1), it is a matter of a specific vocation as such ('Celibacy is a special gift of God …', c. 277 § 1). The fact that this is an appropriate way of life for the priest, rather than inevitably and necessarily linked to sacred ordination, means that the loss of the clerical state (c. 290) does not of itself remove the duties of celibacy (c. 291), which makes it illicit for

---

[36.] *Codex iuris canonici* (1917), cc. 992, 993, 994 § 1, § 2 and § 3, 995 § 1, 996 § 1, § 2 and § 3, 998 § 1 and § 3, 1001 § 1.
[37.] Ibid., cc. 211–214, especially c. 212 § 1.

a cleric to marry. A specific dispensation from the duties of celibacy would need to be sought and obtained before he could marry (c. 291).

c. Consequences of the Loss of the Clerical State

Although celibacy is not directly affected by loss of the clerical state (c. 292) – hence 'without prejudice to can. 291', there are some canonical consequences which do follow upon loss of that state, where this occurs 'in accordance with the law' (c. 292). The former cleric no longer enjoys the rights of the clerical state, nor is he bound by the duties of that state (c. 292). He is 'prohibited from exercising the power of order' (c. 292). This is entirely consistent with the point that he does not lose his power of order as such; a valid ordination 'never becomes invalid' (c. 290). The sacred power, sacred reality, remains permanently (order entails a 'character'), but the juridical reality is changed in that loss of the clerical state. The only exception to the exercise of order is noted in this canon itself, namely that a cleric in priestly orders may and ought to exercise the power of order in absolving a repentant sinner in danger of death (hence 'without prejudice to can. 976' – c. 292). He is automatically deprived of all offices and of all delegated power, for instance, to assist at weddings (c. 292). Returning to the clerical state for one who has lost that state is possible only by rescript, in answer to a petition, from the Apostolic See (c. 293).

6. Personal Prelatures

This is a new section in canon law, dealing with a reality not previously known. It seems to have been devised to cater for the organization, *Opus Dei*. A personal prelature is similar to a diocese, but it is not territorial; rather it is 'personal'. It has the purpose of providing for the pastoral care of members of a society or particular groups in different regions (such as *Opus Dei*) by assuring them priests and deacons (c. 294). Since this will entail working in dioceses, there is a need to consult the Episcopal Conferences concerned, but the personal prelature is erected by the Apostolic See and does not come under the diocesan bishop as such, being ruled by its own bishop, personal prelate (c. 294). The personal prelate is the ordinary of those clergy belonging to the personal prelature. He can establish seminaries and ordain clergy for work in the prelature, incardinating them into the prelature to work within it (c. 295 § 1); they are not acephalous (cf., c. 265). The prelate is responsible for their spiritual formation and for their upkeep (c. 295 § 2).

The particular statutes of the personal prelature are to define the way in which lay people may be associated with and cooperate with the work of the prelature, specifying their rights and duties (c. 296), as well as establishing how members of the prelature are to work and cooperate with local bishops in particular churches (dioceses) where the prelature works or wishes to work; these require the consent of the local ordinary of the place (c. 297).

7. Associations of Christ's Faithful

We have noted that the faithful have a right to associate together for a number of purposes of prayer, charitable work, apostolic work such as evangelization, catechesis or caring for the sick. If the association operates just as such, wanting no formal recognition from the Church, that is possible; it remains a private voluntary body, with no formal canonical status (c. 299). If it wants recognition by the Church, it has to have statutes, stating its purpose, how its members are chosen, how it operates and how it is directed (which would include how it finances its activities), which need to be approved by the competent church authority (c. 304 § 1). No association may call itself Catholic without the consent of that competent authority (c. 300). If associations are established by the Church as such, they are called 'public' (c. 301 § 3), if under the direction of a priest, presupposing the exercise of priestly orders and approved by competent authority, they are called 'clerical associations' (c. 302), while associations connected with, and seeking to follow aspects of, the spirituality of the order to which they are attached (men being the first order, women religious the second order) are often called third order (c. 303). Formally private associations and public associations are to operate in conformity with church doctrine on faith and morals and are subject to canonical visitation (c. 305 § 1); all are subjected to the Holy See and diocesan associations and associations working in a diocese are subject to the diocese (c. 305 § 2). A private association which has not been constituted a juridical person cannot be the subject of rights and duties as an association, although the faithful associated together can acquire property, make contracts and act through a proxy (c. 310).

The competent authorities which can establish public associations are the Holy See, the Bishops' Conference or the bishop of the diocese (c. 312) by means of a decree, which thus constitutes it a juridical person (c. 313). No one who has publicly defected from the Catholic faith, or is not in communion with the Church or who is excommunicated can validly be a member of a public association (c. 316 § 1);

any such person already in such an association, after being warned, is dismissed (c. 316 § 2). Private associations operate according to their statutes, but can acquire juridical personality (c. 312); the competent authority has the right to ensure that they function according to the common good, that their resources are used for the ends of the association, to confirm any spiritual director they select and to suppress the association in case of grave harm (cc. 323–326). Lay members of the faithful should value associations with spiritual purposes, especially those which operate in the secular sphere; associations should cooperate with one another and moderators should ensure that members are properly formed (cc. 327–329).

8. Conclusion

In this chapter on Part I of Book II of the Code, we have assessed the rights and duties of the faithful as a whole, of the lay faithful and of the clergy. We have noted the general position of personal prelatures. In the next chapter we shall consider the hierarchical structure of the Church. It will enable us to see how the Church operates to fulfil its mission from Christ at various levels.

Chapter 4

The People of God

(Book II of the Code)

Part II: The Church's Hierarchical Structure
I: The Supreme Authority

1. Introduction

After considering Part I of Book II on the rights and duties of the faithful as a whole, of the lay faithful and of the clergy, we turn now to the structures of the Church in Part II. In this chapter we shall treat the supreme authority in the Church and in the next the bishop and diocese, and the parish.

2. The Meaning of Supreme Authority of the Church

An analysis of the key canon (c. 330) on the supreme authority (Table 6A), which encapsulates the theology of the laws which follow and which provides a basis for understanding them, reveals a parallel between the position of Peter and the Roman Pontiff, his successor, on the one hand and between the College of the Apostles and the College of Bishops on the other. Equally, there is a parallel between the relationship between Peter and the College of Apostles and that between the Pope and the College of Bishops. Furthermore, this structure or constitution of the Church is not a matter of human arrangement or convenience for the mere good running of the Church (its 'bene esse'), but rather it is of divine origin and establishment, as a matter of what belongs to the Church of its nature or of its being (its 'esse'). This is an example of divine law, established by God and declared as law in the Code, as a fundamental aspect of the law of the Church, an element in its very constitution as willed and brought into being by Christ. It reflects the doctrine of

Table 6

The Supreme Authority in the Church

Table 6A

The Supreme Authority in General (c. 330)

'Just as, *by the Lord's institution ('statuente Domino'),*
        the Blessed Peter
            and the other Apostles
                constitute *one College,*

on the same basis (*'pari ratione'*),
        the Roman Pontiff, the successor of Peter,
            and the bishops, successors of the Apostles,
                are *joined together* between themselves.'

the Second Vatican Council, whose exact wording is found in the canon.[1]

The parallels drawn in c. 330 reflect both a connection and a distinction. The specific character of the Apostles, as those selected by Christ from among the disciples and 'sent' by him, is that they were chosen to be witnesses to him, to what he had said and done, and above all to the fact that he had risen from the dead, although they were not witnesses to the resurrection itself, a mysterious reality beyond direct human grasp. Encounter with the Risen Lord and thus an ability to testify to the truth of the resurrection were central to Paul's unique experience on the Damascus road (Acts 9:5–18; 1 Cor. 15:8; Gal. 1:2, 15–24) and to the criteria for selecting Barsabbas and Matthias as suitable candidates to replace Judas (Acts 1:15–26). The bishops are designated the 'successors of the Apostles', not of any particular apostle, but of all of them, through Apostolic succession to hand on this Apostolic faith.[2] In a similar way, Peter was chosen by Jesus, with a specific mission and role in the Church.

In the Code, the Petrine office of the Roman Pontiff ('bridge-builder', priest), involves him uniquely acting as a vicar of Christ (taking the place as earthly representative), of the one true Mediator between God and man. Even so, the bishops, by divine will and as successors of the Apostles, are truly 'pontiffs' or 'vicars of Christ', since, with the help of priests and deacons, they exercise the three functions of Christ of teaching, sanctifying and ruling, 'presiding over the flock in the place of God'.[3] We have seen how the concept of 'communion' in Christ by the Holy Spirit as our way to the Father, fundamental to the ecclesiology of the Second Vatican Council, operates in the way people become members of the faithful through baptism, are constituted persons in the Church, with rights and duties, to collaborate with those with specific functions in the Church by reason of their sacred orders and or of the office they hold in the service of this salvific mystery. Here we see another dimension of 'communion', one which involves both the unique position of the Petrine office and the office of the bishops, which is inseparable from it.[4] The new Conciliar

---

[1.] Second Vatican Council, Dogmatic Constitution on the Church, *Lumen gentium*, n. 22.
[2.] G. Ghirlanda, *Il diritto nella Chiesa: mistero di comunione: compendio di diritto ecclesiale*, 4th revised edn, Paoline, Milan, P.U.G., Rome, 2006, 531, n. 695.
[3.] *Lumen gentium*, n. 20: '… loco Dei presidentes gregi'.
[4.] E. Corecco, 'Aspects of the Reception of Vatican II in the Code of Canon Law' (1985) in a collection of his articles in G. Borgonovo and A. Cattaneo (eds), *Canon Law and Communio: Writings on the Constitutional Law of the Church*, Libreria editrice Vaticana, 1999, 222–83 at 255–7; cf. G. N. Smith, *The Canonical Visitation of Parishes: History, Law and Contemporary Concerns*, P.U.G., Rome, 2008, 129–32.

perspective on orders and ministries affected bishops, previously said to be 'consecrated', but in the Council and in the Code said to be 'ordained' or 'consecrated' and to possess 'the fulness of Holy Orders'.[5] This roots their position clearly in the action of Christ through the sacrament of Holy Orders in the episcopal degree, so that they are not mere delegates of the Pope, although they cannot exercise jurisdiction apart from him. Thus, c. 330 is crucial to a proper understanding both of the specific role of the Pope and of the collegial role of all the bishops in union with him, both of the collegial nature of the relationship between them and of his primatial function too. As Pope John Paul II put it,

> Therefore, on the basis of this communion, as binding together the universal Church, the hierarchical constitution of the same Church is also both explained and effected (brought into being); that Church, which was endowed by the Lord Himself with a nature *at one and the same time collegial and primatial.*[6]

Both the Petrine ministry and the Apostolic ministry of the Church in every age are both rooted in the Lord's will and action in instituting them, they are complementary and both are necessary to the Church. Both aspects of c. 330 are to be borne in mind in what follows.

3. The Role of the Papacy

a. The Petrine Office or Function

The Petrine office in the Church is presented in the Code after it deals with the faithful in general (cc. 96, 204, cc. 208–231) and after it deals with those in sacred orders (cc. 232–293); the Pope is located within the Church and within the episcopate, within the College of Bishops, a fundamental point of reference of c. 330. On the other hand, he derives neither his position nor his authority as the successor of Peter from these relationships. The 'divine institution' of the Petrine office and the place of the Roman Pontiff are reflected in a number of ways in

---

5. Second Vatican Council, *Lumen gentium*, n. 21; Decree on Bishops, *Christus Dominus*, n. 4.
6. John Paul II, Apostolic Constitution on the Roman Curia, '*Pastor bonus*', 28 June 1988, *Acta apostolicae sedis* 80 (1988), 841–912, at 842–4, art. 2: 'Habita igitur ratione huius communionis universam Ecdclesiam veluti conglutinantis, etiam hierarchica eiusdem Ecclesiae constitutio explicatur atque ad effectum deducitur; quae *collegiali simul ac primatiali* natura ab ipso Domino praedita est ...' (emphases in the original).

these canons and especially in canon 331 (Table 6B). Several points of note call for attention here:

The divinely established nature of the office

The Petrine office in the Church or the papacy is of 'divine institution' (c. 330) and is 'committed by the Lord' to Peter (c. 331); in other words, it comes from no human authority. 'Uniquely' assigned to Peter and not to any other Apostle, certainly as an Apostle, a witness to Christ, he was chosen by Christ as head of the Apostolic College. Since that office was to be transmitted to his successors, it is part of what God has revealed in Christ, part of what the Church hands on of all that she is and believes.[7] The abiding presence of this office reinforces the fact that this was a gift of Christ to his Church, for the whole of its existence and mission on earth.

The Primacy of the Pope

Since the Pope is a member of the College of Bishops, but is also its head, the collegial and simultaneously primatial roles of the Petrine office emerge anew (c. 331). The specification here that his power is 'full, immediate, universal, ordinary power' means that it stems from his office or function ('*munus*') as Bishop of Rome, the successor of Peter. The word '*munus*' evokes the three functions ('*tria munera*') of Jesus, of the Church and of every baptized person, of teaching, sanctifying and governing as a shepherd. Significantly, this canon and those which follow do not use '*officium*', which could betoken a merely ecclesiastical office to which someone was appointed by another or by others in the Church. The papal office or function is not that at all, but is rooted in Christ and entails a unique sharing in his mission, a unique function ('*munus*') within the Church in service of the common good, of its communion and of its mission. The titles noted in these canons reflect this special God-given office or function: constituted by the Lord (c. 330), the Pope is uniquely or alone the successor of Peter, continuing this function in a different period of history. He is 'bishop of the Church of Rome' (c. 331), in whose office this function 'permanently abides', thus assuring continuity of this essential mark of the Church in it Apostolicity in every age. He is the 'head of the College of Bishops', a function reflecting both primacy and collegiality. He is the 'Vicar of Christ' and 'universal Pastor of the Church here on earth', indicating unequivocally his subordination to the real Head of the Church, Jesus Christ, but at the same time his role of acting in his

---

7. Second Vatican Council, Constitution on Divine revelation, *Dei Verbum*, nn. 6–7.

115

Table 6B

The Papacy (c. 331)

'The *office/function* (*'munus'*) *uniquely* committed *by the Lord*
    to *Peter*, first of the Apostles
        to be *transmitted* to his successors
            abides in the *Bishop* of the Church of *Rome*.

    He is the *head* of the *College of Bishops*
        the *Vicar of Christ* and
           Pastor of the *universal Church* on earth

    Consequently, by virtue of his *office* (*'munus'*)
        he has   – *supreme,*
                – *full,*
                – *immediate,*
                – *universal* and
                – *ordinary*
      power in the Church and

    he can always exercise this power.'

Name and with his authority as the shepherd or pastor of the Church throughout the world, once more ensuring its unity in all its essential dimensions of belief, moral teaching and life, liturgy and sacraments. As 'ordinary', the Pope's power is not delegated from anyone else, but comes from Christ as such. As 'full', it is not a share in ordinary power as might occur with someone responsible for a particular sector of activity only. As 'immediate', it means that he does not have to operate through anyone else, not even another bishop. As 'universal', this is true in all dioceses and other parts of the world. The text adds that the Pope is 'always free to exercise' this power. In other words, it is certainly a very strong statement of a primacy, which is far more than a mere primacy of honour. This 'ordinary power', 'pre-eminent', not just for the universal Church in general, but for all particular Churches (non Latin Catholic Churches and all dioceses and parts of the Latin Church), derives also from his 'office' (c. 333 § 1). It is up to him to decide whether to exercise it collegially or personally (c. 333 § 2).

The Papacy and Collegiality

We can see that the role of papal primacy is closely connected to collegiality, since it 'reinforces and defends the proper, ordinary and immediate power of the bishops' (c. 333 § 1).[8] This can be understood in some ways as a defence of their role against unjust interference by civil authorities, as well as a statement that he derives his power and authority from Christ, not from the bishops.

Nevertheless, it would be a mistake to imagine that the Pope's power is absolute.[9] He is at the service of the Church ('servus servorum Dei': 'servant of the servants of God'), obliged by the faith of the Church, by Tradition which he is to guard and by the previous judgments of the Magisterium where these have been infallibly proposed.[10] He is also bound morally by the responsibilities of collegiality to work in communion with the Bishops, although he is not canonically bound to a particular way of operating in this regard (c. 333 § 2) and is not subject to any bishop. In 'fulfilling his office' the Pope 'is always joined in full communion by the

---

[8.] Ghirlanda, *Il diritto nella Chiesa* ..., 532, n. 696.

[9.] J. A. Coriden, *An Introduction to Canon Law*, revised edn, Paulist, New York, Mahwah, 2004, 72.

[10.] J. Alfaro, 'Theology and Magisterium' in R. Latourelle and G. O'Collins (eds), *Problems and Perspectives in Fundamental Theology*, Paulist, New York, Ramsey, 1982, 341–56 at 347–8.

other bishops and indeed by the whole Church' (c. 333 § 2), since Peter was to strengthen his brothers in unity (Jn. 21:15–17), making him the point of reference for that unity. Conversely, this collegial communion does not prevent him from deciding whether to exercise the Petrine office personally or collegially (c. 333 § 2). Of course, this power does enable him to intervene in certain grave cases for the common good of the whole Church, even against a particular bishop of a diocese. This would only be done in any direct way very rarely, where there was a real and serious need. Very often, the Pope exercises his specific functions as Pope to sustain and support bishops and communities of the Church in more indirect ways and in areas where they are not easily able to defend themselves. We can think of John Paul II's efforts on behalf of the Church in communist countries, Benedict XVI's efforts towards the Church in China, the efforts of both on behalf of the religious freedom of Catholics in Islamic countries. More generally, the Pope's legislative, administrative and judicial powers are used both in terms of primacy and of collegiality to reinforce the communion of the Church as a whole, the universal Church which is present in and through the various particular Churches.[11]

There is neither appeal nor recourse against a judgment or decree of the Roman Pontiff (c. 333 § 3). This stems from the supreme authority and universal ordinary power he possesses 'by virtue of his office' ('*munus*') (cc. 331, 332 § 2, 333 § 1, 2, 334). In other words, he derives neither his authority nor his power from the Church as a whole, nor from the bishops nor from the College of Bishops, but from the Lord himself. This divine origin of this office or function does not preclude, but implies, a cooperation with the other bishops in College, in synods, and so on (c. 334). The rejection of Conciliarism, the claim that a general council of the Church was superior to the Pope at the Council of Constance (1413–17), can also be seen to be reflected in this text. Hence, in a vacancy of the See of Peter, there are to be no innovations in the governance of the Church, but the special norms for such an occasion are to be applied (c. 335).

b. Election to the Petrine Office

The Pope obtains his position as Pope in one of two ways (c. 332 § 1): if he is a bishop already, his valid election and acceptance of the result constitutes him in office. If he is not yet a bishop, his valid election and

---

11. *Lumen gentium*, n. 23.

acceptance of the result is to be followed immediately by his episcopal ordination and at that point he assumes his office. Thus, the office of the Pope is that obtained through election (cf. cc. 145, 169–172) and acceptance by the one elected (c. 178) by one already in, or now ordained to, episcopal orders (c. 332 § 1).[12] There can be no question of the election being confirmed, since there is no earthly superior to the Pope. Similarly, he can never give his resignation to any human superior (since there is none), nor is it subject to acceptance. However, a novelty in this Code is that there is provision for the Pope to resign; he needs to resign in writing in a way which clearly manifests the fact that he has resigned (c. 332 § 2).

Although we have used the term 'office' here, the Code does not do so. It says that the Roman Pontiff 'obtains full and supreme power in the Church' (c. 332 § 1) in the way described. Yet, the general norms we have seen on obtaining ecclesiastical office are reflected in this canon, in the ways just noted.

When a pope dies or resigns, there is a vacancy of the Holy See. During this period, nothing is to be done which would interfere with the prerogatives of the Pope, no new initiatives are permitted and the work of the Roman Curia can only operate on the basis of standard procedures for handling matters which come before them. Any ecumenical council, such as the Second Vatican Council, has to cease to function once the death of the Pope becomes known and all acts taken from that moment on are invalid (c. 340). Any synod of bishops which might be in session likewise has to cease to function immediately upon receiving news of the death of the Pope, any subsequent acts being invalid (c. 347 § 2). In either case, the new Pope has to decide whether or not the ecumenical council or the synod of bishops is to continue (not when or how unless he decides affirmatively). Pope Paul VI decided to continue the Second Vatican Council, interrupted by the death of John XXIII. These norms clearly reflect the dogma on general councils not being above the Pope.

Those cardinals who are over eighty years old cannot vote in a papal election, but of the 115–120 who are to be in a conclave there needs to be a two-thirds majority to elect a new pope.[13] The renewed norms of John Paul II envisaged a decision on the basis of a simple majority in

---

[12.] John Paul II, Apostolic Constitution on the vacancy of the Apostolic See and on the election of a new pope, *Universi Dominici gregis*, 25 February 1996, nn. 88–90.
[13.] Ibid., nn. 70, 75.

the second week in a conclave (after the 11th day and the 34th vote)[14] if a decision had not yet been reached, even between the two who had received highest number of votes if the cardinals so agreed.[15] However, although the 2005 conclave operated under those norms, it did not reach the point where a simple majority became an issue; Benedict XVI was elected very quickly and with a majority of over two-thirds. In fact, this particular provision had led to some disquiet about the possibility of a simple majority and, after examining the matter, the new norms of John Paul II were modified by Benedict XVI, to require a two-thirds majority at whatever point in the conclave a pope is elected, for that election to be valid.[16] For canonical validity there must be no simony or attempting to 'buy' an office,[17] no other improper influences from groupings, promises, or the like among the cardinals,[18] nor from outside groups, including civil authorities,[19] and the procedural norms have to be followed in secret ballots.[20] John Paul II abolished the selection of the new pope by 'acclamation', 'inspiration' or 'compromise', making a valid election the only method of selection and as a matter of validity.[21] This was one of the most significant changes he introduced.[22]

It should be noted that the election of a pope requires the consent of the person; thus, if someone were elected, but did not accept, he would never have been pope. The requirement of episcopal ordination, if the individual is not already a bishop, clears up a theological debate of the past. Once a person validly elected has accepted election, if he is already a bishop or once he is ordained a bishop, he enjoys

---

14. P. G. Marcuzzi, 'Il Conclave e l'elezione del Romano Pontefice: Legislazione vigente' in Office of Liturgical Celebrations of the Supreme Pontiff, *Sede Apostolica vacante: storia – legislazione – riti, luoghi e cose*, Libreria editrice Vaticana, 2005, 131–43 at 137–8.

15. John Paul II, *Universi Dominici gregis*, nn. 62–86. A two-thirds' majority of the Cardinal electors present is needed for a pope validly to be elected, although (at a point in the second week) this can go to an absolute majority, even, if the Cardinal electors so decide, with the choice limited to the two persons with the highest number of votes in the preceding scrutiny: n. 75.

16. Benedict XVI, Apostolic letter, *motu proprio, De aliquibus mutationibus* on the election of the Roman Pontiff, 11 June 2007, suppressing n. 75 of *Universi Dominici gregis*. The alteration came into effect immediately by order of the same *motu proprio*.

17. John Paul II, *Universi Dominici gregis*, n. 78.

18. Ibid., n. 82.

19. Ibid., nn. 79–83.

20. Ibid., nn. 62, 77.

21. Ibid., n. 62.

22. Marcuzzi, 'Il Conclave ... Legislazione vigente', 135.

all the prerogatives of the Roman Pontiff from that moment.[23] This is before the Mass of inauguration, which is a liturgical celebration of the beginning of his Pontificate which has, in fact, already begun.

4. Collegiality: Bishops as Part of the Supreme Authority

b. The Source of the 'Power' of Bishops

Despite the strong presentation of papal primacy in these canons, the proper role of the bishops is also to be seen, reinforcing this major focus of the Second Vatican Council's ecclesiology. Thus, bishops are truly successors of the Apostles and their union with the Pope is analogous to the union of the Apostles and Peter in the Apostolic College (c. 330). They do not derive their sacred power from the Pope; they do not obtain their 'proper, ordinary and immediate power' (c. 333 § 1) from the Pope, but, through their episcopal ordination or consecration, from the Lord himself. This is also the key Christological source of their belonging to the College of Bishops, even though this also depends upon their being in full communion with the Pope.

On the other hand, the particular Churches, presided over by diocesan bishops, are intrinsically united to the one, holy, Catholic and Apostolic Church not by their choosing to be so, but by the action of Christ. All these elements are to be found in each and every particular Church and the universal Church is present in all of them; the universal Church flows from the particular Churches, but they also flow from the universal Church.[24] The unity of the episcopate under the Pope is also an aspect of this essential mark of the Church.[25]

[23.] John Paul II, *Universi Dominici gregis*, n. 88: 'After his acceptance (of his election), one who has already received episcopal ordination is immediately Bishop of the Roman Church, true Pope and Head of the College of Bishops; he acquires by that fact full and supreme power over the universal Church and he can exercise that power. If, on the other hand, the one elected lacks the Episcopal character, he is immediately to be ordained bishop' (my translation): 'Dopo l'accettazione, l'eletto che abbia già ricevuto l'ordinazione episcopale, è immediatamente Vescovo della Chiesa Romana, vero Papa e Capo del Collegio Episcopale; lo stesso acquista di fatto la piena e suprema potestà sulla Chiesa universale, e può esercitarla. Se, invece, l'eletto è privo del carattere episcopale, sia subito ordinato Vescovo.'

[24.] Congregation for the Doctrine of the Faith, Letter to the Bishops of the Catholic Church on some aspects of the Church understood as Communion, *Communionis notio*, 15 May 1992, n. 9.

[25.] Ibid., nn 12–15.

b. The College of Bishops

The 'supreme authority' of the Church is not the Pope alone, but also includes the 'College of Bishops', which, however, is not the College of Bishops without the Pope or in opposition to him, but only with him and in communion with him, 'in union with its head and never without this head' (c. 336). This body of the bishops of the Catholic Church in union with the Pope is the successor to the College of Apostles (c. 330), by virtue of 'their episcopal ordination or consecration and of their hierarchical communion with one another' and it has 'full and supreme power in the Church' (c. 336). This canon underlines the fact that this is of divine institution also by the fact that the College of Apostles 'perseveres continuously' or in an uninterrupted fashion (with and never without the successor of Peter) in the College of Bishops and so 'exists also as a subject of supreme and full power in the universal Church' (c. 336). Thus, the bishops derive their sacred power from Christ through their episcopal ordination, but their communion with one another, including with the Pope, is essential to their legal or juridical capacity (cf. c. 10) to hold the episcopal office and to exercise it.

The College of Bishops operates for the good of the universal Church, as its supreme authority, in a number of ways:

– in an Ecumenical Council (c. 337 § 1)

This can only be called by the Pope, who presides over it directly or through others whom he designates, who alone can suspend, transfer or dissolve it (c. 338 § 1), except were he to die while it was in progress, in which case it would be suspended by virtue of the law itself until his proper successor decided either to continue with it (as did Paul VI with the Second Vatican Council) or to dissolve it (c. 340). The Pope decides on the matters to be discussed and the order of business. Other bishops may propose additional items, but these have to be approved by the Pope before they can be included (c. 338 § 2). The Pope has to approve (confirm) and promulgate the decrees of such a council or other similar body or they have no binding force (cc. 338 § 1, 341). At an ecumenical council all bishops have the right and duty to participate and have a deliberative vote (may vote on decisions – c. 339 § 1), which have to be approved and promulgated by the Pope before they can be binding (c. 341), although other people who are not bishops may take part in the council, to exercise whatever role the Pope determines (c. 339 § 2).

– in Collegial action, dispersed throughout the world

This means when there is a truly collegial act, promoted or accepted as such by the Roman Pontiff (c. 337 § 2). This would involve communication with the bishops on some issue(s), a consultation with them, such that their opinion would be obtained. Some indication of collegial action of this kind can be seen in John Paul II's condemnation of the direct killing of the innocent, of direct abortion and of direct euthanasia, in each case adding '... in communion with the bishops of the Catholic Church',[26] referring to his 'consultation' with them (n. 62) on the moral issues touching human life, when he had written asking their cooperation 'in the spirit of episcopal collegiality'.[27]

– in other ways

The Pope would determine other ways in which the College of Bishops could operate collegially to serve the needs of the universal Church (c. 337 § 3).

– through the Synod of Bishops (c. 342ff.)

The work of the College of Bishops for the universal Church can also be effected through this new instrument of collegiality, which has emerged since the Second Vatican Council. When there is a synod of bishops, representing bishops from all over the world, which deals with the affairs of the universal Church, this event has some collegial significance. This will not be the same if there is a regional synod of bishops, from one continent, treating the affairs of that area. Nor is a synod of bishops, even for the universal Church, an event as profoundly and clearly collegial as an ecumenical or general council.

c. Ecumenical Councils and Synods of Bishops

Both of these entities are instruments of collegiality. Ecumenical or general councils of all the bishops in union with the Pope have been a feature of the Church since the early centuries. They are to assist the Pope in the exercise of his primatial role and so are collegial in the discharge of the responsibilities of the supreme authority of the Church, in which these bishops also share.

The synod of bishops, introduced after the Second Vatican Council, is an instrument of collegiality, but it is not always operated on the

---

[26.] John Paul II, Encyclical letter, *Evangelium vitae*, 25 March 1995, nn. 57, 62, 65.
[27.] Ibid., nn. 5, 62.

universal scale (c. 345), in that there have been special synods for Africa, Asia, America, Europe and Oceania; such synods are 'special sessions' of the synod (c. 346 § 3). However, most of the synods of bishops have been for the universal Church, either in ordinary general sessions (c. 346 § 1) or, when there is a particular or urgent need, in extraordinary general session (c. 346 § 2). The synod of bishops is not a meeting of all bishops, but, according to canon 342 (Table 6C), it is a group or even a committee ('*coetus*') of bishops. Its clear purpose is to foster the cooperation between the successor of Peter and the bishops; in other words, it has a specifically collegial function, which at the same time confirms the importance of the bishops in their function of serving the universal Church and not only their own particular churches (or dioceses for the Latin Church). Once again, however, this body, much less than a general or ecumenical council, is not above the Pope and it is there to 'assist' him by means of its 'counsel' or 'advice' and in 'considering' questions. Synods of bishops do not take decisions, much less decisions binding upon the Pope or upon the universal Church. It is a consultative and not a deliberative body, unless the Pope specifically requests this in particular instances and then he has to ratify any decisions (c. 343).

We have seen that the bishops derive their role as members of the College of Bishops sacramentally from being ordained as bishops, from Christ himself, but their communion with one another as bishops derives not only from this, but also from their relationship with the successor of Peter. This is a requirement of their being able to function in the Church as bishops; without this they are not members of the College of Bishops (c. 331) and so their relationship with the successor of Peter, the Pope, is 'constitutive' of their being members of that College and, as Corecco puts it, 'The relationship of communion of the bishops between themselves is derived from the constitutive relationship of communion which each individual bishop holds with the Pope as the head of the college.' This means that, although operating through synods of any description forms part of the function of a bishop, this can only be exercised practically to the extent that it includes directly or indirectly the head of the College of Bishops, the Pope.[28]

The topics treated, 'faith and morals' and also 'ecclesiastical discipline' (c. 342), are the proper subject matter of the Church's Magisterium, echoing the explicit teaching of the Councils of Trent, Vatican I and Vatican II. The 'mission of the Church in the world'

[28.] Corecco, 'Ontology of Synodality' (1990) in *Canon Law and Communio*, 341–68 at 359.

Table 6C

The Synod of Bishops (c. 342)

'The Synod of Bishops is a *group* of bishops
    selected from different parts of the world

        to *promote* the close *relationship* between
        the *Roman Pontiff* and the *Bishops* (who)
           by their counsel
           assist him
                – in the defence and development of faith and morals and
                – in the preservation and strengthening of ecclesiastical
                  discipline.

      They also *consider questions* concerning
          – the mission of the Church in the world.'

recalls the further focus of the Second Vatican Council. In other words, the functions of the synods are not only advisory, but are specifically linked to the magisterial functions inherent in the episcopacy and to questions of church discipline also inherent in that function, which the synods are designed to strengthen and reinforce in a collegial manner.

Here, too, a concern to avoid any insinuation of Conciliarism can be detected. The collegial function of the College of Bishops is united simultaneously to the primatial function of the Pope (c. 333 § 1),[29] which the former is not to compromise. The canons on the synods (cc. 342–347) reflect those on ecumenical councils (cc. 338–341), with the key distinctions that an ecumenical council is one where all and only Catholic bishops in full communion with the Pope have a right to sit and vote (c. 339 § 1), whereas the synod is only of a selection of them (c. 342), whose selection is to be ratified by the Pope who can add others also (c. 344, n. 2), and that the ecumenical council has a deliberative function, whereas that of a synod is limited to a consultative role (cc. 339 § 1; 343). Otherwise, in both cases, it belongs to the Pope to decide whether and when to call a council or a synod (cc. 338 § 1; 344 n. 1), to settle the matters to be discussed there and the order in which they are addressed (cc. 338 § 2; 344 nn. 3–4), to preside over it personally or through others (cc. 338 § 1, 344, n. 5), to conclude, transfer, suspend or dissolve it (cc. 338 § 2, 344, 6°). If the Holy See becomes vacant during either an ecumenical council or a synod of bishops, it is suspended by the law itself until the next Pope decides whether to continue with it or to dissolve it (cc. 340; 347 § 2) and any decisions after news reaches it are invalid.[30] When a synod of bishops is concluded, 'the function entrusted in it to bishops and other members ceases' (c. 347 § 1).

The synods of bishops, meeting in ordinary general session since 1967, have examined current problems relating to faith and the question of atheism, priestly ministry, justice in the world, evangelization, catechetics, the family, reconciliation, the laity, priests, the consecrated life, bishops, the Eucharist, and in October 2008, the Word of God in the life of the Church. There is now a permanent secretariat (c. 348) which operates between synods, doing preparatory work and work consequent upon each synod.

The normal process for synods is that, once a theme is decided by the Pope, arrangements are made for episcopal conferences to elect representatives, representatives of religious institutes of consecrated

---

29. John Paul II, *Pastor bonus*, art. 2.
30. John Paul II, *Universi Dominici gregis*, n. 34.

life are also elected, and other bishops may be appointed by the Pope, with 'experts' ('*periti*') often being brought in too (c. 345). An outline or discussion document ('*Lineamenta*') is circulated to bishops for their observations, in the light of which a 'working document' ('*Instrumentum laboris*') is produced and circulated and a set of propositions for discussion at the synod is produced. The discussions at the synod are in full session or in groups. Afterwards, the synod's secretariat issued three texts, approved by the Pope, but from 1975 onwards the recommendations ('*Propositiones*') of the synod have been sent to the Pope, who eventually issues an Apostolic exhortation on the matter discussed in his own name.[31]

Although some may feel that the roles of the curial bishops (who are bishops with a specific responsibility for the common good of the universal Church) and others and/or of the general secretariat may be too great, the synod of bishops is a good instance of collegiality in cooperation with the Pope, of the successors of the Apostles in communion with that one of their number who is the successor of Peter. There is a danger of considering it as a mere political instrument, as if democratic voting were the issue in the face of an 'autocracy' of the Pope. This is a total misunderstanding of the nature of the Church, of the profound ecclesiology of the Second Vatican Council and of the structures of councils and synods. Indeed, an awareness of such a possible misunderstanding seems to lie behind the decision to avoid using the term 'representatives' of the bishops who would attend such synods in the Code, although that term had been used by Paul VI when he had established the institution of synods; the theological sense in which a bishop might represent the local Church being too susceptible to a political interpretation if the term were used in a directly juridical sense.[32]

A deliberative vote is possible and proper in an ecumenical council because it is a gathering of all the bishops with the Pope, but especially because it is a testimony of faith from each particular Church

---

[31.] Initial post-synodal documents produced by the secretariat of the Synod and approved by the Pope were: *Ratione habita*, 28 October 1967; *Ultimis temporibus*, 30 November 1967 and *Convenientes ex universo*, 30 November 1971. Apostolic exhortations following ordinary general Synods of Bishops are: *Evangelii nuntiandi*, 8 December 1975; *Catechesi tradendae*, 16 October 1979; *Familiaris consortio*, 22 November 1981; *Reconciliatio et paenitentia*, 2 December 1984; *Christifideles laici*, 30 December 1988; *Pastores dabo vobis*, 25 March 1992; *Vita consecrata*, 25 March 1996; *Pastores gregis*, 16 October 2003; *Sacramentum caritatis*, 22 February 2007.

[32.] P. Valdrini, 'La constitution hiérarchique de l'Église' in P. Valdrini *et al.* (eds), *Droit canonique*, 2nd edn, Dalloz, Paris, 199, 121–89 at 130–1, n. 213.

in the person of the bishop (representatives of bishops have no deliberative vote), an act of discernment about the faith and its implications; even then, it is not a matter of a majority opinion, but of the 'convergence of the bishops with the Pope'.[33] With a consultative vote, too, it is not just that not all the bishops are there so that the College of Bishops is not represented in its totality, but the People of God more generally are reflected in it, in part through the preparatory processes, in part perhaps through the bishop's knowledge of his people, of their charisms and of their sense of the faith, although it is not the opinion of the particular Church until he has given his own judgment.[34] Institutions such as the synod of bishops are set up by the supreme authority to foster the communion of the Church as a whole, while respecting the legitimate diversity with the fundamental communion.[35]

5. The Cardinals (cc. 349–359)

The cardinals, some of whom are prefects or heads of the congregations of the Roman Curia, assist the Pope in the running of the universal Church. Chosen from across the world, they have an advisory role either as a group or college in consistory or individually. They elect the Pope, according to special norms, though they have no vote if they are over eighty years of age.[36] They have no sacramental basis and belong to a structure of purely ecclesiastical law.[37]

For centuries they have been chosen to help the Pope in caring for the universal Church, since one man cannot do everything required for the common good.[38] From the sixth century, some of the priests in some of the key churches ('cardo-cardinis': hinge, key) of the Diocese of Rome and then deacons from some key groupings of parishes of the diocese were chosen to help the Pope with his tasks: hence, cardinal priests and cardinal deacons, titles still used even though cardinals are now always actually bishops or are to be ordained bishops (c. 351 § 1). Dispensation from episcopal ordination is possible where someone is made a cardinal as an honour for work done and where there is

---

33. Corecco, 'Ontology of Synodality', 363–4.
34. Ibid., 364–7.
35. Congregation for the Doctrine of the Faith, *Communionis notio*, nn. 15–16.
36. John Paul II, *Universi Dominici gregis*, n. 33.
37. L. Gerosa, *Le droit canonique*, St Paul, Luxembourg, 1998, 308–9.
38. John Paul II, *Pastor bonus*, nn. 3–5.

no real responsibility.[39] From the eighth century some bishops from the dioceses outside of the Diocese of Rome ('sub-ubicarian' dioceses) were made cardinals for the same reason, in their case attached to dioceses directly linked to the Diocese of Rome. Attachment to the Diocese of Rome was judged necessary to be able to help the Pope in his work and so the Roman Curia also grew up in this way. After the Council of Trent sought to have cardinals appointed from elsewhere, to facilitate the government of the universal Church, attachment to the Diocese of Rome remains in the titles associated with churches in the diocese (ubicarian) or with dioceses outside Rome, in the obligation of cardinals working in the Roman Curia to reside in those areas, and in that of other cardinals to come to Rome whenever called by the Pope (c. 356) The total number of 'cardinal electors', under eighty years old and so those able to vote in a papal conclave (c. 349), was fixed at seventy in the past, but by order of Paul VI in 1975 and confirmed by John Paul II, it is now 'no more than 120'.[40]

The juridical source of the powers of the cardinals is that of the Diocese of Rome, to which they are attached through their titular churches.[41] Their main functions are electing a new pope, according to special norms (c. 349) and of assisting the Pope in his running of the universal Church (c. 356). This may be done as a college of cardinals, since they form a 'special College' or a 'College of their own' (c. 349), as when the Pope calls them together in a 'Consistory', through their service of the Holy See, working full time or otherwise in the dicasteries or departments of the Roman Curia, or as individuals as the Pope may need them. They should offer their resignation at seventy-five (c. 354), but remain cardinal electors until they are eighty. Finally, it is obvious that the College of Cardinals continues to exist and to operate during a vacancy of the Holy See, although only in strict accordance with the special norms laid down (c. 359), whereas the College of Bishops as such does not exist during such a vacancy, since it cannot exist without or apart from its head, the Pope (c. 336).

[39.] Recent examples would include the following Jesuit cardinals: Avery Dulles, Albert Vanhoye, Ugo Navarette.

[40.] John Paul II, *Universi Dominici gregis*, n. 33; cf., Paul VI, Apostolic Constitution, *Romano pontifice eligendo*, 1 October 1975 .

[41.] Valdrini, 'La constitution hiérarchique ...', 132, n. 215.

6. The Roman Curia

The word '*curia*' refers to the institutions in the diocese or elsewhere in the Church where those appointed assist the bishop or the institute of consecrated life or society of apostolic life or, in this case, the Pope, to discharge their duties ('*curare*': 'to take care of', 'to be responsible for'). The term 'Roman Curia' has been used for centuries to mean those appointed to assist the Pope in the discharge of his responsibilities as the supreme pastor of the universal Church. Although it might be more logical these days to use the term 'Roman Curia' for the 'Vicariate of Rome', the equivalent 'curia' to help the Pope as Bishop of Rome to discharge his responsibilities in the Diocese of Rome, with 'Apostolic Curia' being used for the curia of the universal Church, we shall continue to use 'Roman Curia' as has been customary in relation to the universal Church.

The Roman Curia covers the Secretariat of State (which functions as an organ of the Church, as well as being the foreign service of the Vatican state), congregations, tribunals (all called dicasteries) and two other institutes (for the papal household and for liturgical celebrations). Of medieval origin, the Roman Curia was reorganized by Pius X in 1908 to tackle a confusion of roles and to distinguish operations of the internal forum from those of the external forum and contentious cases from non-contentious cases. Paul VI reformed the Roman Curia in the light of the Second Vatican Council, to involve diocesan bishops more so as to better understand the needs of the particular Churches (dioceses), internationalizing the personnel, and so on.[42] The more detailed norms for the operation of the Roman Curia are 'defined in special law' (c. 360) of John Paul II's reform, in the Apostolic Constitution, *Pastor bonus*, of 1988. However, the key to understanding the Roman Curia is the statement in the Code that:

> the Supreme Pontiff
>   usually conducts the business of the *universal* Church
>   through the Roman Curia
>   which acts – *in his name* and
>   – *by his authority*
>   for the *good* and *service* of the *Churches*
>   (c. 360)

In this section of the Code the 'Apostolic See' or 'Holy See' means

---

42. Cf. Paul VI, Apostolic Constitution, *Regimini Ecclesiae universae*, 15 August 1967; Valdrini, 'La constitution hiérarchique ...', 136–7, nn. 219–20.

not just the Pope, but the Roman Curia (c. 361). The Pope 'usually' operates through the Roman Curia, but does not have to do so. The Curia acts 'in his name and by his authority', for the 'common good' of the Church. This 'service' to the 'Churches', to dioceses and other particular Churches, is a service both of collegiality and of papal primacy, both instruments of the Church's communion. This emerges from the first of the general norms of *Pastor bonus*:

> The Roman Curia is the assembly of dicasteries and institutions which help the Roman Pontiff in the exercise of his supreme pastoral office for the good and service of the universal Church and of the particular Churches, an exercise by which the unity of faith and the communion of the People of God are strengthened and the proper mission of the Church in the world is fostered.[43]

This key article demonstrates that the Roman Curia is a juridical structure, but that its function is rooted in the nature and mission of the Church. This ecclesiological service concerns not only the universal Church, but also assisting the bishops in their particular churches, to foster the unity and the communion of the Church itself. It has a threefold function: as ecclesial, it draws its power from the Pope and serves the universal Church and the bishops; as ministerial, it is an instrument of the Pope, and, as vicarious, it derives its power (normally administrative, but also judicial) from the Pope and exercises it only on his behalf, not in its own right.[44] The Curia's exercise of this vicarious ordinary power emphasizes its character of service both to the Pope and to the bishops.[45]

The Roman Curia as a whole seeks to work with the particular Churches, obtaining reports of any local synods and seeking the views of bishops in preparing documents which may be relevant to them.[46] The five-yearly reports by diocesan bishops of their dioceses to the Holy See are connected to their visits '*Ad limina Apostolorum*' ('to the thresholds of the Apostles', to the basilicas and tombs of Ss Peter and Paul). These are intended to reinforce hierarchical communion, collegial cooperation and proper pastoral concern for the needs of the Churches and of the universal Church.[47] Advice and help are offered, which can be very useful to bishops with particular concerns in their

---

43. John Paul II, *Pastor bonus*, art. 1.
44. Ghirlanda, *Il diritto nella Chiesa ...*, 555, n. 732.
45. John Paul II, *Pastor bonus*, art. 8.
46. Ibid., art. 26.
47. Ibid., art. 28–30.

dioceses, although there may be a need at times to correct malpractice.

The functions of the dicasteries or departments include the following. The Secretariat of State (first section) deals with particular Churches and (the second section) handles relations between the Vatican City State and other States.[48] The Congregation for the Doctrine of the Faith is to promote and defend doctrine on faith and morals throughout the world; whatever touches this material comes within its competence,[49] including correcting teachings which are erroneous.[50] It is to act also where 'more serious crimes concerning morals or the celebration of the sacraments' are involved, declaring or imposing canonical penalties where the law requires.[51] It deals with privilege of faith marriage cases.[52] The Congregation for Divine Worship and for the Discipline of the Sacraments has responsibility for areas of the liturgy, especially of the sacraments (other than those under the C.D.F.) for liturgical books, translations, music and art, as well as for dealing with liturgical abuses.[53] It deals with non-consummated marriages[54] (art. 67) and invalidity of sacred ordinations.[55] The Congregation for the Causes of Saints follows special norms on beatification and canonization and whose procedures at the diocesan level have been recently updated.[56] The Congregation for Bishops deals with the nomination and appointments of bishops, 'Ad limina' visits, relations with episcopal conferences, and such like.[57] The Congregation for the Clergy deals with the formation, ordination and exercise of ministry, the distribution of priests, councils of priests, parishes, the administration of the temporal goods of the

---

48. Ibid., art. 40–7.
49. Ibid., art. 48
50. Ibid., art. 49–51.
51. Recent norms promulgated by John Paul II in a 'motu proprio' of 30 April 2001, *Sacramentorum sanctitatis tutela*' dealt with these more serious crimes and specified procedures to be followed; cf. B. A. Ferme, '*Graviora delicta*: The Apostolic Letter, *Sacramentorum sanctitatis tutela*' in Z. Suchecki (ed.), *Il processo penale canonico*, Lateran University Press, Rome, 2001, 365–82 at 370–3.
52. John Paul II, *Pastor bonus*, art. 53.
53. Ibid., art. 62–6; Congregation for Divine Worship and for the Discipline of the Sacraments, Instruction on Certain Matters to be avoided in the Celebration of the Eucharist, *Redemptionis Sacramentum*, 25 March 2004.
54. John Paul II, *Pastor bonus*, art. 67.
55. Ibid., art. 63, 68.
56. Ibid., art. 71–4; Congregation for the Causes of Saints, Instruction on the procedures for undertaking investigations in dioceses or in eparchies relating to the causes of saints, *Sanctorum Mater*, 17 May 2007.
57. John Paul II, *Pastor bonus*, art. 75–82.

Church, and catechesis and with dispensations from the obligations of the clerical state (since 2006).[58] The Congregation for Institutes of the Consecrated Life and Societies of the Apostolic Life, deals with their erection, suppression, federations, formation of members, constitutions and statutes of each institute or society.[59] The Congregation for Seminaries and Institutes of Studies (often called Catholic Education) deals with seminaries, Catholic universities and Catholic schools.[60] The Congregation for the Evangelization for Peoples (formerly Propaganda Fide) handles all matters concerning missionary territories. The Congregation for Eastern Churches treats matters relating to Eastern Catholic Churches. There are various Pontifical Councils, for example for the Laity, for the Family, for Christian Unity, for the Authentic Interpretation of Legislative Texts, for Latin America, for Pastoral Care in Health. Although not technically part of the Curia, there are also Academies (of Science and, since 1994, for Life), whose purpose is largely to study and to advise bishops and other bodies in the Roman Curia and elsewhere on developments and issues of relevance.

Although the work of the Roman Curia is largely administrative, it also has a judicial function. There are three tribunals or courts, specifically constituted as such. The Apostolic Penitentiary deals with cases of conscience in the internal forum, sacramental (confession) and non-sacramental and can issue dispensations and sanations (rectifying or 'healing at the root' certain situations).[61] This is a very definite instance of the Church's law being at the service of the 'salvation of souls' as its 'supreme law' (c. 1752). The urgency of some matters, such as in the danger of death of a person, is such that the Apostolic Penitentiary continues to function even during the vacancy of the Apostolic See for that precise reason; Pius XI had said that the salvation of souls was not to be interrupted.[62] The Penitentiary ensures that there are enough confessors in the major Roman basilicas, with special faculties. It is also responsible for indulgences.[63] The Roman Rota is normally the appeals tribunal at second or third instance; it has responsibility also for the Church's jurisprudence, the way the laws are applied and the

---

[58.] Ibid., art. 93–8.

[59.] Ibid., art. 105–11.

[60.] Ibid., art. 112–16.

[61.] Ibid., art. 117–18.

[62.] P. G. Marcuzzi and S. Ardito, 'La sede vacante: Legislazione vigente' in *Sede Apostolica vacante …*, 91–101 at 98–101 and footnote 63: Pius XI, Apostolic Constitution, *Quae divinitus* 1935, *Acta apostolicae sedis*, 27 (1935), 112, n. 12.

[63.] John Paul II, *Pastor bonus*, art. 119–20.

consistency of judgments and in this way especially to assist the work of lower tribunals in the Church. It also judges individual bishops, major religious superiors and others who have no superior other than the Holy Father.[64] The other main tribunal is the Apostolic Signatura, which is the supreme court of appeal in the Church, with one exception. It judges cases where it is alleged that procedures have not been followed or laws have not been applied correctly in the Roman Rota or in the dicasteries of the Holy See; it decides the competence of different tribunals in the Church, as where political situations or lack of expert personnel in a given area mean that a local tribunal does not exist or cannot function easily in a given case.[65] The one exception concerns cases of the gravest crimes, usually against the sacraments and including the sexual abuse of minors, reserved exclusively to the Congregation of the Doctrine of the Faith in its capacity as a tribunal.[66]

Bishops from various parts of the world are appointed as members of the various bodies of the Roman Curia. Expert 'consultors' advise particular dicasteries on matters of importance and of relevance. This assists the Pope in his work as primate and it fosters both collegiality between bishops and the Pope and collaboration of the faithful in the work and mission of the Church. The Congregation for the Doctrine of the Faith has competence over any matter of doctrine or to the extent that doctrine is involved, giving it a certain precedence over other dicasteries. However, it is the Secretariat of State which deals with the day-to-day matters directly concerning the Holy Father, coordinates the working of the Roman Curia, as well as treating relations between the Holy See and particular Churches and other states.[67] Congregations of the Holy See make decisions and tribunals make judgments in the name of the Pope and with his authority, within the limits of their power; such decisions are made in the 'ordinary' or 'normal' way ('in forma ordinaria'). Some decisions are taken by the Pope himself and often cannot be taken by anyone else; these are issued properly by him in a 'specific way' ('in forma specifica').

These various structures are for the good of the universal Church and serve both the primatial and the collegial dimensions of the supreme authority of the Church. There has been progress since Paul VI sought to involve bishops more in this work and to make the Roman Curia

---

[64.] Ibid., art. 126–30.
[65.] Ibid., art. 121–5.
[66.] John Paul II, *Sacramentorum sanctiatis tutela*, 2001: B. Ferme, '*Graviora delicta* ...', 381–2.
[67.] John Paul II, *Pastor bonus*, art. 39–47.

more international. The fact that its working language is no longer Latin, but Italian, may have assisted this process in one respect, but may have limited it also. Accusations arise at times of ambition, power, excessive centralization and bureaucracy. The Church is always holy in that the Holy Spirit never deserts it and in that there are always members of the Church living good and holy lives, but it is always to be made holy in that we can and do sin and err.[68] This would be as true of those who work in the Roman Curia and of those who work elsewhere in the Church.

7. Papal Legates (cc. 362–367)

These are nuncios and other official representatives of the Catholic Church who liaise with the bishops of an area or region, with episcopal conferences and with governments. They serve the Church's unity, especially between the particular Church and the Apostolic See (cc. 363 § 1, 364). They assist in the transmitting of names for the selection of bishops, they collaborate with bishops and with bishops' conferences in the mission of the Church, in ecumenism and in inter-religious dialogue (c. 364). They also represent the Vatican City State as ambassadors or nuncios to civil governments (cc. 363 § 1, 365).

8. Conclusion

Having examined the nature of the supreme authority of the Church and the main forms in which it is exercised, it remains now to consider the more familiar aspects of the Church's hierarchical structure through the particular Churches, in the Latin Church dioceses.

[68.] Second Vatican Council, *Lumen gentium*, n. 8.

Chapter 5

The People of God

(Book II of the Code)

Part II: The Church's Hierarchical Structure
II: Particular Churches

1. Introduction

The second section of Part II of Book II of the Code of Canon Law deals with particular Churches, which in the Latin Church, to which this Code applies, means mainly dioceses (c. 368), particular Eastern Churches being treated in their own Code of 1990. This chapter will focus upon the diocese and its structures, as well as upon parishes, to see how the common good of the Church and the rights and duties of all the faithful in the service of the Gospel are addressed and promoted at these levels of the community of the baptized.

2. Particular Churches

a. Particular Churches Equivalent to Dioceses

In the Latin Church 'particular Church' normally refers to a diocese, but it applies also to the following entities, which, canonically, are largely 'equivalent to' dioceses (c. 368). A 'territorial prelature', formerly called a 'prelature of nothing', is a territory which is not part of a diocese, often established because it lacked the resources to be a diocese as such or to make special arrangements for something like a pilgrimage shrine outside a diocese. It relates to 'a certain portion of the People of God' (c. 370). A 'territorial abbey', previously known as an abbacy of nowhere, goes back to when abbots were put in a position similar to that of bishops over people, 'a certain portion of the people of God' (c. 370), living in the immediate area of the abbey. Such was the Basilica of St Paul's outside the Walls in Rome until 2005, when it became part of the Diocese of Rome.[1] In both cases, the grouping of people is territorial and the one responsible is a prelate or an abbot who 'governs it as a bishop, as its proper pastor' (c. 370), the prelate or abbot having 'proper' rather than 'vicarious' ordinary power in their regard. A 'vicariate apostolic' is a territory 'not yet a diocese' (c. 371 § 1), but which it is hoped may become one, under a vicar apostolic, appointed by the Pope and exercising power 'vicariously'. This structure exists often in missionary territories and at times in places where the political situation would militate against the erection of a diocese, as in parts of the Islamic world. An 'apostolic prefecture' is a stage prior to a territory becoming a vicariate apostolic, when the Congregation for the Evangelization of Peoples appoints a 'prefect' for a territory or for a group of people with 'vicarious' powers, who 'governs it in the name of the Supreme Pontiff' (c. 371 § 1). Finally, an 'apostolic administration permanently established' would be where the Holy See does not proceed yet to establish a diocese, often for political reasons, or where it does not wish to appoint a bishop to a vacant see for some reason. This differs from the apostolic administration of a vacant or impeded diocese, which is of its nature temporary and where there is the intention to appoint a bishop as soon as possible. In a permanently established apostolic administration, the one appointed also exercises power vicariously on behalf of the Pope (c. 371 § 2).

b. The Diocese as a Particular Church

The diocese is the usual particular Church in the Latin Church, on which the structures noted above are aligned. A careful analysis of the key canons (cc. 368–369) presented in Table 7A reveals the central features of a 'particular Church' as articulated at the Second Vatican Council, from which c. 369 is taken almost verbatim.[2] Particular Churches are under a diocesan bishop, to whom they are entrusted by the Pope (cc. 375 § 2, 376). They are constituted or established as particular Churches on the basis of the Gospel, by the Word of God and by the sacraments in and through which the Holy Spirit of Christ is operative, gathered together by and adhering to the diocesan bishop who has the fulness of Christ's priesthood through his episcopal ordination and who is in full communion with the Pope and College

---

[1.] Cf. John Paul II, Decree, *Vetustissimam abbatiam*, 11 July 1981; Benedict XVI, Apostolic letter *motu proprio, L'antica e venerabile Basilica*, 31 May 2005, nn. 4–5.
[2.] Second Vatican Council, Decree on Bishops, *Christus Dominus*, n. 11.

Table 7A

The Diocese as a Particular Church (cc. 368–369)

A *diocese* is
    – 'a *"particular Church"*,

        one *in* which and *from which*
        the *one* and *only Catholic Church* exists' (c. 368).

    'a *portion* of the *People of God*

        entrusted to a *bishop*
        with the cooperation of the *presbyterium*

        to be *shepherded* by *him* in such a way that,

        adhering to him and
        gathered by him
            – through the *Gospel* and
            – through the *Eucharist*
            – in the *Holy Spirit*

            it *constitutes* a *particular Church*

            in which there *exists* (*"inest"*) and operates
                the *One*
                Holy
                Catholic and
                Apostolic
                    Church of Christ' (c. 369).

of Bishops (c. 375 § 2).[3] The diocese, then, is a part or 'portion of the People of God', around the bishop as locus of communion, built up by the Gospel and the sacraments, whose pastoral care requires the collaboration of the priests of the diocese, the presbyterate.[4]

The one Church of Christ, which 'truly subsists in the Catholic Church',[5] is truly found in each and every particular Church, having all the 'marks of the Church' of Christ as One, Holy, Catholic and Apostolic (c. 369). It is maintained indefectibly by the Holy Spirit, through whom Christ is with the Church until the end of time.[6] Not only is the One Catholic Church truly present 'in' each particular Church, but it also exists 'from' each particular Church (c. 368); it does not exist apart from them or above them, but the universal Church and the particular Churches mutually abide in one another.[7] This means that each Christian recognizes himself or herself as a 'new person' in Christ through baptism and seeks to live as part of the 'communion' of the Church, not independently, but according to the criterion of faith. Even more than that, the communion of the particular Churches with the universal Church implies neither the former being submerged by the latter, nor a democracy which produces just what people want, but a faith-based communion of life in Christ, which implies in turn a readiness to put personal desire at the service of the Gospel, not just by free personal decision, but rather putting the faith into action as a communion of the Church rooted in that Gospel, in Christ. 'Communion does not stand in service of activity, but it is activity that is in service of life in communion.'[8] The mutual or reciprocal relationship of the universal Church and each particular Church implies that, just as the universal Church exists 'in' and 'from' the particular Churches, so particular Churches 'exist in and from the universal Church'.[9] The latter is neither the sum of

---

3. John Paul II, Apostolic exhortation on bishops in the Church, *Pastores gregis*, 16 October 2003, n. 8.
4. L. Gerosa, *Le droit de l'Église*, St Paul, Luxembourg, 1998, 310.
5. Second Vatican Council, Dogmatic Constitution on the Church, *Lumen gentium*, n. 8; Decree on Ecumenism, *Unitatis redintegratio*, n. 4.
6. *Lumen gentium*, n. 23.
7. Gerosa, *Le droit de l'Église*, 62–4, 309–11.
8. E. Corecco, 'Synodal or Democratic Structure of the Particular Church?' in G. Borgonovo and A. Cattaneo (eds), *Canon Law and Communio: Writings on the Constitutional Law of the Church*, Libreria editrice Vaticana, 1999, 70–102 at 73–6, 91–4, especially 93.
9. Congregation for the Doctrine of the Faith, Letter to the Bishops of the Catholic Church on some Aspects of the Church understood as Communion', *Communionis notio*, 28 May 1992, n. 9.

the various particular Churches, nor a federation of such Churches, nor the result of the communion between such Churches, since in its essential mystery the Church precedes them.[10] Not to recognize this is to have a reductive, unilateral understanding of 'communion', which entails the inseparable, reciprocal union of particular and universal.[11]

3. The Bishop in the Particular Church

a. The Divine Institution of the Episcopacy and Pastoral Care

In a way which is analogous to the relationship between the particular and the universal Church, the College of Bishops in its fundamental unity is not the result of individual bishops being combined together, nor an outcome of their communion, but is in itself an essential mark of the Church in its unity, 'one which precedes the office of being the head of a particular Church'.[12] By virtue of his episcopal ordination, the bishop acquires a new juridical status in the Church, reflecting his new sacred power of the fullness of the priesthood, so that he brings the fullness of the apostolic office into the particular Church, simultaneously assuring it of its catholicity and so assuring the Church of this mutual immanence in his person.[13] The diocesan bishop, the local ordinary of the diocese with 'full' and 'proper' responsibility for its care (c. 375), embodies these realities (Table 7B). The two paragraphs of c. 375 demonstrate clearly that the bishop is not essentially a delegate of the Pope, but derives his office, his capacities and his functions directly from God through his episcopal ordination or consecration, by the Holy Spirit. The essential condition ('by ... nature') of being in communion with the Pope and with the other members of the College of Bishops, of the particular Church and the universal Church being immanently united, is there too.[14] The 'canonical mission' the bishop receives from the Pope is not then a delegation of power as such, since he receives 'full, ordinary and immediate power' (c. 381) through his episcopal ordination; it is an instrument necessary for

---

[10.] John Paul II, Apostolic letter on Episcopal Conferences, *motu proprio, Apostolos suos,* 21 May 1998, n. 8; ID., *Pastores gregis,* n. 8.

[11.] *Communionis notio,* n. 8.

[12.] *Apsotolos suos,* n. 12; *Pastores gregis,* n. 8.

[13.] Gerosa, *Le droit de l'Église,* 311.

[14.] Second Vatican Council, *Lumen gentium,* n. 21; Decree on Bishops, *Christus Dominus,* n. 11.

Table 7B

The Bishop (c. 375)

'By *divine* institution

    bishops succeed the *Apostles through* the *Holy Spirit* given them
and are constituted
        – *pastors,*
        – *teachers* of doctrine
        – *priests* of sacred worship and
        – *ministers* of governance (c. 375 § 1).

By their episcopal *consecration*

    they receive the *offices* of
        – *sanctifying*
        – *teaching* and
        – *ruling*

    which by their *nature* can only be exercised
in *hierarchical communion* with

        – the *head* of the *College* and
        – its *members* (c. 375 § 2).

the exercise of that power and for the unity of the Church in which alone it can properly be exercised.[15] The prominence given to the threefold function of the bishops recalls the Apostles of whom they are the successors. The character of the Church as such is reflected in this canon.

b. The Selection of Bishops

It is for the Pope to appoint bishops freely or to confirm those elected (c. 377 § 1) in line with the general norms we have seen for appointments to ecclesiastical offices (c. 147). In the early centuries of the Church not much is known about how bishops, successors of the Apostles, were chosen, except that it seems the participation of the faithful as a whole may have been involved. The Council of Nicaea in 325 specified that the bishops of a province were to be responsible for the election of suitable candidates; abuses of nepotism led to the Pope playing a more decisive role after the Council of Trent.[16]

There is no doubt that the criteria of suitability for the office of bishop need to be taken seriously. Indeed, the criteria of suitability for any ecclesiastical office need to receive much more attention than they sometimes do, for the good of the Church. The criteria for being a bishop stem from the New Testament (1 Tim. 3:1–7). Celibacy for priests in the Latin Church and especially for bishops makes the criterion of not being married more than once and of caring well for his family (3:2, 4) no longer relevant. The criterion of not being a neophyte (3:5) or new convert implies being a member of the faithful (baptized). Being someone of an impeccable character requires him to be temperate, discrete, courteous, hospitable, kind and peaceable, not a heavy drinker, hot-tempered nor a lover of money (3:2–3). These features would be reflected in him having a good reputation (3:7). The criterion of managing his family well may imply an element of responsibility in regard to material goods, to money. That he must be a good teacher (3:2) implies knowledge of the faith and an ability to proclaim it effectively, necessary for the teaching function he would perform precisely as a bishop. The operation of simony (Acts 8:18–24), attempting to buy an office, renders any appointment acquired in this way totally invalid (c. 149 § 3); as distinct from a desire to serve the Church as a bishop (1 Tim. 3:1), this implies that someone prepared to try to 'influence' and 'bring

---

[15.] G. Ghirlanda, *Il diritto nella Chiesa: mistero di comunione: Compendio di diritto ecclesaiale* 4th edn, revised, Paoline, Milan, P.U.G., Rome, 2004, 291–2, n. 291.

[16.] Ibid., 569–70, n. 749.

about' his own appointment as a bishop is unsuitable to be a bishop.

According to the present Code, the criteria of suitability are that a man be at least thirty-five years old and have been a priest for at least five years (c. 378 § 1, 3°–4°), be 'outstanding' in faith, good morals, zeal for souls, wisdom, prudence and other human virtues, and possess other, unspecified gifts suitable for the office (1°), have a good reputation (2°) and hold a doctorate or licentiate in theology, Scripture or canon law or be 'well versed' in these disciplines if he does not have those academic qualifications (5°). Here we can see reflected the Scriptural criteria of faith, moral uprightness, a good reputation and implied a capacity to proclaim the Gospel. Norms issued prior to the revision of the Code and so prior to this canon spoke also of good judgment, stability of character, a sense of sacrifice and a social sense also of cooperation, solid attachment to the orthodoxy of the faith, devotion to the Holy See and fidelity to the Magisterium.[17] Although, technically, these precise criteria of suitability are abrogated by the Code, the unspecified 'other gifts' appropriate for the office of bishop (c. 378 § 1, 1°) would surely include such eminently just criteria.

The mechanism for selecting bishops varies. In Germany, Austria and Switzerland, cathedral chapters elect bishops, whose election needs to be confirmed by the Pope (c. 377 § 1) before there can be a valid appointment.[18] Some Concordats regulate aspects of the process in some countries, so that in Italy, apart from the sub-ubicarian sees (for Cardinal bishops), no non-Italian is to be appointed bishop; the State is to be informed of the persons nominated.[19]

It is for the nuncios or papal legates to conduct enquiries about the suitability of candidates, from bishops and perhaps from priests and other members of the faithful, as they judge appropriate. This is done under the pontifical secret. This should enable the Holy See to make a balanced and informed judgment. Names of possible candidates are to be proposed every three years by groups of bishops in ecclesiastical provinces (under a metropolitan or archbishop), although at times this may be from the conference of bishops, by discussion with one another and in secret (c. 377 § 2). Any diocesan bishop (bishop in charge of a diocese) can propose candidates independently of this and should put forward at least three names, if he seeks an auxiliary bishop – one who

---

[17.] J-B. D'Onorio, *La nomination des évêques: procédures canoniques et conventions diplomatiques*, Tardy, Paris, 1986, 33, referring to Paul VI, Constitution, *Episcopi facultas*, 25 March 1972, *Acta apostolicae sedis*, 64 (1972), 387–91.

[18.] Ghirlanda, *Il diritto nella Chiesa ...*, 570–1, n. 750.

[19.] Ibid., 571, n. 751.

helps but without right of succession (c. 377 § 2, 4). For a diocesan bishop or a coadjutor bishop (who helps the diocesan bishop and who has right of succession), the papal legate or nuncio must seek the opinions of the metropolitan and bishops of the province, members of the college of consultors and of the cathedral chapter and others as he judges fit (c. 377 § 3) to send a list of names ('*terna*') to the Holy See (the Congregation for Bishops).

It is to be noted that rights of presentation, election, and designation of candidates which do not already exist for historical reasons cannot be acquired in the future (c. 377 § 5). Furthermore, the Apostolic See has the exclusive right to accept or reject those nominated, presented or elected, having also the definitive judgment over who is to be appointed, even if it be someone not on the *terna* prepared (c. 378 § 2). This has been done in some notable instances, where groups of bishops have perhaps tried to engineer someone's appointment or someone's exclusion.[20]

These norms reflect historical vicissitudes and remind us that the laws of the Church need to respond to different situations. The criteria of suitability remain fundamental. While norms seek to preclude any form of nepotism, simony or political influence, dangers are inherent in the sinful condition of the human race and in the concupiscence consequent upon original sin; ambition and power-seeking are not unknown. Even less dramatic considerations urge that suitability be carefully judged. The nuncio has a delicate, but very important task; we know how damaging it is when bad mistakes are made. Nuncios are to collaborate with bishops in a country or region and these bishops have a key part to play in proposing names to the Holy See. Nuncios need to be sufficiently independent of the bishops to make objective judgments and recommendations for the good of the particular and of the universal Church. There is a danger inherent in the present system of like proposing like, but cloning bishops, less now through nepotism than through promoting friends, is not to be encouraged. On the one hand, the administrative experience of someone closely involved in working with the bishops, such as the secretary to the Bishops' conference in a given territory, can be useful, but it would be very regrettable if that position came in effect to be a 'career path' to the episcopacy.

Someone not yet ordained a bishop is to receive episcopal orders

---

20. D'Onorio, *La nomimation des évêques* ..., 34.

within three months of receiving apostolic letters of appointment and before taking possession of the cathedral (c 379). Before taking office the bishop must recite the profession of faith and swear the oath of fidelity to the Apostolic See (c. 380).

b. The Responsibilities of Diocesan Bishops

The responsibilities of bishops in general can be summarized as follows. They are to care for the Catholic faithful, those of other rites, ecumenical affairs and the unbaptized; thus they have a universal pastoral care (c. 383). A diocesan bishop has a particular responsibility to care for his priests, with whom he is joined in the *presbyterium* of the diocese as his 'helpers' and 'counsellors', defending their rights, seeing that they fulfil their duties, ensuring that they have the means to attend to their spiritual and intellectual lives, as well as assuring their livelihood and welfare (c. 384). This is especially so when he entrusts to them a new canonical mission or office, but also when they retire and continue in a new way to function in the presbyterate; his care for them then, in sickness or in other times of need, being part of the responsibility he accepts for them at their priestly ordination.[21] He is to foster vocations (c. 385), teach, preach and defend the faith (c. 386), promote and protect the sacramental life of the Church, fostering holiness (c. 387), saying Mass for the people of the diocese on Sundays and holydays, presiding at the Eucharist at the cathedral especially on major feasts (cc. 388–389, 395 § 3) and protecting against abuses in the liturgy (c. 392 § 2). He is to govern the Church according to law (cc. 391–393), nurturing the apostolate (c. 394) and making pastoral visitations in the diocese (cc. 396–398). He is to preserve the unity of the universal Church and is to make the 'ad limina' visits and reports to the Apostolic See (cc. 395, 399–400). He is urged to offer his resignation at seventy-five years of age or if too ill to function (c. 401).

These duties correspond to the bishop's functions of teaching, sanctifying and ruling as a shepherd. In regard to the teaching function, this involves him preaching regularly as the main teacher of the diocese, implying that he be properly formed and that he continue his formation, that he prepare homilies well. It involves him presiding at the liturgy in the diocese and especially in the cathedral, seat of his teaching authority. It entails a duty of vigilance over preaching and teaching in the diocese, firmly defending the integrity of the faith

---

[21.] *Pastores gregis*, n. 47.

(c. 386 § 1–2).[22] It involves him taking care that catechetics is well conducted, with catechists thoroughly prepared on the basis of the Church's faith and teachings, that schools and other institutes in the diocese operate in accordance with the fullness of Catholic doctrine and discipline and acting to warn and even remove those who do not abide by these norms.[23] It involves responsibility for books used for liturgy, for prayer and (textbooks) for religious education.

The sanctifying function of the diocesan bishop presupposes that he be a man of prayer, rooted in the Word of God,[24] who takes care of his spiritual life through the Liturgy of the Hours, of the Eucharist and of the other sacraments, as well as by regular reception of the sacrament of reconciliation, through personal retreats, and through a pattern of life coherent with these commitments, with a style of life which reflects poverty by avoiding ostentation, the perfect continence of celibacy and interior and exterior adherence to the faith and teaching of the Church and to the Holy Father. His sanctifying function is fulfilled through his prayers, through the Mass he is obliged to say personally for the people of the diocese every Sunday and on holydays of obligation (cc. 388–389), and especially at major liturgical functions in the cathedral, seat and symbol of his position, manifesting in his person the fullness of priesthood in glorifying God and in promoting the sanctification of the people.[25] It develops too through his active support for the particular vocations of the faithful and of their spiritual lives in general (c. 387). In these ways he can enable the faithful as a whole to fulfil their duties and exercise their rights in developing a spiritual life in the service of the Church's mission (cc. 210, 213–214).

The responsibilities of the diocesan bishop for governing the diocese as a shepherd are extensive. He has duties to all the faithful in the diocese, especially to those in special needs (the sick, the young, those in exile), Catholics of other rites, non-Catholic Christians, non-Christians and those of no faith (c. 383). There is a particular responsibility attaching to his own priests, to know them personally, defend their rights (c. 384), ensure that they fulfil their duties, provide for their support, sustain their spiritual lives and their continuing formation. The bishop is responsible also for enabling the faithful to fulfil their duties and exercise their rights (cc. 209–211, 213–216) to spiritual life,

---

[22.] P. Valdrini, 'La constitution hiérarchique de l'Église' in P. Valdrini *et al.* (eds), *Droit canonique*, 2nd edn, Dalloz, Paris, 1999, 121–89 at 151, n. 239.

[23.] *Pastores gregis*, nn. 29, 31.

[24.] Ibid., n. 28.

[25.] Ibid., nn. 32–4, 36–7.

to play their part in the apostolate in a way which is coordinated (c. 394). He is to guard against abuses in faith and discipline, in the liturgy and in the administration of the goods of the Church (c. 392 § 1–2). The obligation of residence in the diocese (c. 395 § 1) is both to avoid the abuse of absenteeism and to ensure the proper and effective care of those entrusted to him as diocesan bishop (c. 1752), with a specific duty to celebrate the Eucharist in the cathedral on Christmas Day, in Holy Week or on Easter Sunday, Pentecost and Corpus Christi (c. 395 § 3), since here he manifests especially the unity of the particular Church around his person as its particular pastor. He is to give an account of his ministry in quinquennial reports to the Holy See, by whom he is also sustained and from whom he can seek advice, on the occasion of fulfilling his duty to visit the Pope and the tombs of Peter and Paul, the visit 'ad limina Apostolorum' every five years (cc. 400 § 1, 395 § 2).

The diocesan bishop is to undertake official visitation of the diocese at least every five years either personally or with the help of coadjutor or auxiliary bishops or even vicars general or episcopal (c. 396 § 1).[26] This applies especially and principally to parishes, but also to other churches, to institutes of consecrated life of diocesan right and parishes or other institutions operated by institutes of pontifical right but only to the extent that these are specifically part of the pastoral apostolate of the diocese (c. 397 § 2). He is to visit Catholic institutions such as schools, youth centres, and so on (c. 397 § 1). These visitations are to enable him to see what is happening, to foster the more effective realization of the Church's mission in these various areas by encouragement and by direction, but they are essentially the time when the bishop is personally present among his people, fulfilling his various functions.[27] They are to be conducted with 'due diligence' and cannot simply be cursory, as an adjunct to a visit for confirmation (c. 398).[28]

The visitation of the whole diocese has to be undertaken within a five-year period (c. 396 § 1), but the word 'annually' means that it cannot be confined to one year out of the five, with visitation ignored in the other years. Although the diocesan bishop can be assisted by others mentioned and even by priests, this should not be delegated on

---

[26.] G. Ghirlanda, 'Vescovo diocesano' in C. C. Slavador, V. De Paolis and G. Ghirlanda (eds), *Nuovo dizionario di diritto canonico*, San Paolo, Cinisello, 1993, 1114–20 at 1116–19.

[27.] *Pastores gregis*, n. 46.

[28.] G. N. Smith, *The Canonical Visitation of Parishes: History, Law and Contemporary Concerns*, P.U.G., Rome, 2008), 164–5.

a regular basis, since the bishop is the principle of unity of the particular Church of the diocese and this cannot be manifested if he does not undertake the visitation personally. Only coadjutor and auxiliary bishops should be delegated for this assistance in any regular way (c. 408 § 1–2).[29] Serious reasons such as ill health, political circumstances, the burden of other legitimate responsibilities which he has (but if he cannot function effectively as bishop of the diocese, he should seek some more permanent solution), or the enormous size of the diocese may justify using the assistance indicated, but, even then, he should make some of the visitations himself.[30] Perhaps, in that event he should visit at least parishes in rotation.

d. The Resignation of the Diocesan Bishop

When aged seventy-five the diocesan bishop is urged to offer his resignation to the Holy See, although the Pope does not have to accept it (c. 401 § 1). If he is too ill or for some other reason is not able to discharge his functions properly, he is 'earnestly recommended' to offer his resignation (c. 402 § 2). Once such a resignation is accepted, the see becomes vacant and so a successor can be validly appointed, although in the meantime arrangements are made for the care of the diocese during the vacancy of the see.

e. The Functions of Other Bishops

A coadjutor bishop is appointed to help a bishop who is ill or who has some other difficulty in running the diocese and he has the right to succeed the diocesan bishop, doing so when the latter's resignation is accepted, when he dies or is removed; he should be appointed vicar general (cc. 403 § 3, 406, 409 § 1). In preference to other bishops, he is to be given responsibilities which the diocesan bishop cannot discharge (c. 408 § 2). A coadjutor or an auxiliary who is appointed in pressing circumstances, even with special faculties, is to work closely with the diocesan bishop, who is to consult them on matters of importance for the good of the diocese (cc. 407 § 1; 403 § 2). A duty to consult exists here, given the reference to c. 403 § 2 and the use of 'let them consult one another' 'sese ... consulant' (c. 407 § 1), means that it is under pain of invalidity (cc. 39, 127 § 2, 2°).

With other 'auxiliary bishops' consultation is urged, but not required:

[29.] Ibid., 149, 152.
[30.] Ibid., 150–1.

he 'may wish to consult them' – 'consulere velit' (c. 407 § 3). These help a diocesan bishop, but do not have a right to succeed him. Auxiliary bishops should be appointed vicar general, episcopal vicar (cc. 403 § 3, 406). If the diocesan bishop dies or otherwise loses office, the auxiliary retains only the functions he had and is to work under the diocesan administrator (c. 409 § 2). An emeritus is a retired bishop (cc. 185, 402 § 1), who is to be provided for in a worthy manner, the responsibility falling primarily on the diocese he has served, but the episcopal conference seeing to it that he is cared for properly (c. 402 § 2). He loses his office at retirement, along with its rights and duties; indeed, it is usually to relieve him of the burdens of office that he becomes 'emeritus'. However, he remains a full member of the College of Bishops by reason of episcopal ordination and communion with the Apostolic See, can be chosen as a full member of a synod of bishops, and he must be consulted on matters of importance, so that he is to receive papers from the Holy See, especially from the Pope, to be properly informed of such matters.[31] A titular bishop is not a diocesan bishop; he may work in the Roman Curia or be an auxiliary, but has a title of an ancient diocese (c. 376).

f. Special Arrangements for a Vacant and for an Impeded Diocese

If a bishop is too ill to run a diocese or cannot do so because he is in prison or otherwise incapable, but has not resigned, the diocese is said to be 'impeded' (c. 412). The coadjutor, an auxiliary bishop, vicar general or episcopal vicar (according to a list established by the diocesan bishop soon after taking over the diocese, renewed every three months and kept secretly by the chancellor, and communicated to the metropolitan) assumes responsibility (c. 413 § 1) or, if there is no list, the college of consultors chooses a priest to do this (c. 413 § 2). That person has the powers of diocesan administrator until the see ceases to be impeded, either when the bishop resumes direction or, if he resigns, when a new bishop takes over (c. 414). Such a person is to inform the Holy See as soon as possible of his appointment.[32]

[31.] F. D'Ostilio, I vescovi emeriti e l'istituzione giuridico dell' 'emeritato', Libreria editrice Vaticana, 2000, 34–8, including footnote 74, referring to the resolution of a 'dubium' by the Pontifical Council for the Interpretation of Legislative Texts of 2 July 1991; cf. L. G. Wrenn, 'The possibility of Bishops Emeriti being elected by their Conference as Members of the Synod of Bishops', Authentic Interpretations on the 1983 Code, Canon Law Society of America, Washington, DC, 1993, 62–3, n. 24.

[32.] E. Olivares, 'Sede episcopale impedito' in Nuovo dizionario di diritto canonico, 976–7.

The diocese is 'vacant' if the diocesan bishop loses his office by death, acceptance of his resignation, transfer or removal (c. 416); he functions as diocesan administrator until he takes over another diocese, if he is transferred (c. 418). Once the see is vacant, the auxiliary bishop senior by appointment is to summon the college of consultors or, if there is no auxiliary, they are to meet to appoint a diocesan administrator (c. 419), informing the Holy See immediately in the case of the death of the diocesan bishop. In the meantime the senior auxiliary bishop or the college of consultors has the powers of vicar general (c. 462).[33] The diocesan administrator cannot be someone who has already been presented for that see (as a possible bishop) nor can he be contemporaneously the financial secretary to the diocesan council for economic affairs (often called in English the trustees), so that, if that latter is chosen (which requires that he be a priest), and he accepts, he is to be replaced as financial secretary (c. 423 § 2). The diocesan administrator has the rights and duties of a diocesan bishop, except where the law says otherwise, but can make no innovations (c. 428), since his function is temporary as a 'caretaker' (c. 428). He ceases to function when a new bishop takes possession of the diocese (c. 430 § 1).[34]

4. Groupings of Dioceses

This section has been placed deliberately in the part of the Code dealing with particular Churches and no longer as an intermediary between the supreme authority (in which it had been considered to share to some extent) and dioceses as particular Churches. It thus reflects the ecclesiology of communion and of the elements of the Church existing in each particular Church. The purpose of the structures below is not merely administrative, but specifically to foster 'common pastoral action' between particular Churches in the same area and to foster cooperation between the bishops of those dioceses (c. 431 § 1).[35]

a. Ecclesiastical Provinces

These are groups of dioceses with juridical personality, established, combined or suppressed only by the Supreme Authority of the Church, as also with 'regions' combining more than one province.

[33.] Ibid., 977.
[34.] Ibid., 15–16.
[35.] Valdrini, 'La constitution hiérarchique ...', 180–1, nn. 281–2.

The aim is to foster common pastoral action (cc. 431–433) and also deeper communion not only between the bishops of the area, but between the particular Churches involved.[36] A province is under a 'metropolitan' (archbishop), responsible for seeing that faith and discipline are observed, conducting visitation if a suffragan bishop (all other dioceses of the province are 'suffragan' dioceses) neglects this, seeing to the appointment of a diocesan administrator in situations noted above. He wears the *pallium*, a strip of white wool with six black crosses, received from the Pope, as symbol of this office, indicating especially union with the Apostolic See and fraternal or brotherly concern for the suffragan bishops and their dioceses (cc. 435–437).[37]

b. Episcopal Conferences

This is a 'permanent institution', with juridical personality, in a certain country or other territory, for the common good of the Church there, established, altered or suppressed only by the Supreme Authority of the Church (cc. 447–449). It involves all diocesan, coadjutor and auxiliary bishops of the area as proper members (c. 450). Only diocesan bishops or those equivalent to them in law (such as apostolic administrators, vicars apostolic) have deliberative votes; auxiliary and coadjutor bishops have consultative or deliberative votes, according the conference's own statutes, but not if it concerns altering the statutes (c. 454).

Episcopal conferences can issue general decrees, if there are two-thirds voting in favour, but these need to be reviewed by the Apostolic See and to be lawfully promulgated before they oblige (c. 455 § 1–3). Except where provided by universal law, the authority of the diocesan bishop remains intact (c. 455 § 4); in other words, the conference normally cannot oblige a diocese if the diocesan bishop does not approve of the decree. More recent norms governing episcopal conferences, intended to tighten regulations and to prevent aberrations, require that:

1) doctrinal declarations be unanimously approved,
2) no other body (commission) can exercise Magisterium,
3) for other types of intervention the doctrinal commission of the conference must be explicitly authorized by its permanent council, and
4) the conference's norms are to be amended to include these present norms.[38]

---

[36] *Pastores gregis*, n. 62.
[37] Valdrini, 'La constitution hiérarchique …', 181–2, n. 283.
[38] *Apostolos suos*, section IV, which contains the specific canonical norms, art. 1–4.

A number of functions pertain to these conferences: to coordinate collections for charitable purposes, to prepare draft translations of liturgical texts, etc. One of the aims of John Paul II's norms, in *Apostolos suos*, was to restrain conferences where individual diocesan bishops were not in agreement with policy decisions, to insist that only bishops of a diocese have a deliberative vote, unless statutes determine otherwise and to prevent the importance of the role of the diocesan bishop from being obfuscated by non-episcopal officials, such as secretaries.

Furthermore, such conferences do not take the place of a provincial synod or council, although the conference can call a particular council of the whole territory of the conference (c. 439 § 2). The latter can be called by the majority of the bishops of the province so deciding, except when the metropolitan see is vacant, and it is presided over by the metropolitan (cc. 439 § 1, 440 § 1–2, 442 § 2). It must involve the Church of the dioceses at various levels: all diocesan, coadjutor and auxiliary bishops have the right to be present (c. 443 § 1), with priests, institutes of consecrated life, societies of apostolic life, lay faithful being involved. It can establish legislation for the province on faith, morals, ecclesiastical discipline, provided it is in conformity with the universal law of the Church. However, only the bishops have a deliberative vote, while others properly involved have only a consultative vote (c. 443 § 1, 3–4). Even then, the norms cannot be promulgated unless and until these have been subject to revision by the Holy See, to assess whether or not they conform to universal law or liturgical norms, and so have received the *'recognitio'* (confirmation after revision) of the Holy See (cc. 445–446).[39]

5. Diocesan Structures

In a way that is analogous to the structure and operation of the Roman Curia, this section of the Code can appear at first sight to be a matter of mere administration and bureaucracy. However, it is essential to the life of the People of God if we are to fulfil our specific vocations within the Church in a way which is coordinated and which truly contributes to the common good of the Church as a whole in its service of Christ. Leaving things to those who may be well-meaning is not enough. It is important to understand how the particular Church of the diocese should function in the service of the Gospel.

[39.] Pontifical Council for the Interpretation of Legislative Texts, *La natura giuridica e l'estensione della 'recognitio' della Santa Sede*, 28 April 2006, *Communicationes*, 38 (2006), 10–17, n. 4.

a. Diocesan Synods

These are councils of priests and lay faithful called for the good of the particular Church and to assist the bishop. They are occasional events and not permanent structures. It is for the diocesan bishop to decide if and when to call such a synod, after consulting the council of priests (cc. 460–461) and only he (not any vicar nor even a diocesan adminis-trator) can convene a diocesan synod (c. 462 § 1). Such a synod must include any coadjutor and auxiliary bishops, as well as vicars general and episcopal vicars, canons of the cathedral, members of the council of priests, lay members of the faithful and representatives from insti-tutes of consecrated life and societies of apostolic life present in the diocese to be elected as the diocesan bishop specifies, vicars forane (often called 'deans' in England and Wales) and two priests from every vicariate forane, one to attend and another to substitute for him should the need arise (c. 463). The diocesan bishop is to preside at the synod (c. 462 § 2) and, although all groups are to be represented (c. 463), only the diocesan bishop can legislate, everyone else having only a consultative vote (c. 466). All questions proposed are to be a matter of free discussion by members of the synod (c. 466). However, since the synod exists only to serve the good of the diocese and to assist the bishop in regard to that good (c. 460) and since the particular Church cannot exist nor function except in reciprocal in-dwelling with the universal Church in the communion of all particular Churches, it follows that what is incompatible with Catholic faith, with the Church's Tradition as such should not be an object of discussion at such a synod. Otherwise, there is real danger of misunderstanding not only by participants, but by other members of the particular Church and beyond, perhaps nurturing unrealistic and indeed improper expectations, none of which can benefit the Church. The diocesan bishop, therefore, should be vigilant about which questions are to be discussed if he calls such a synod.

b. The Diocesan Curia

The Diocesan Curia ('*curare*': to care for) is those institutions and persons who assist the bishop in the administration of the diocese and in the judicial work of the diocese (c. 469); for judicial aspects there are procedures in Book VII of the Code to be followed; for administration, the norms in this section of Book II apply (c. 472). Appointments to the Curia are to be made by the diocesan bishop (c. 470). The pastoral care of the portion of the People of God entrusted to the diocesan bishop requires coordination. He can appoint a moderator of the diocesan curia, if he judges it wise to ensure coordination; if so, he must be a priest (c. 473 § 2) and he should be a vicar general unless circumstances suggest otherwise (c. 473 § 3). If the moderator is not a vicar general, his capacities are limited to such administrative coordination. Another means available to help the bishop coordinate the pastoral care of the diocese is an episcopal council, made up of his vicars general and episcopal (c. 473 § 4), he himself being responsible for coordinating activity between himself and them (c. 473 § 1). The Chancellor of the Curia is responsible for counter-signing juridical acts, which the bishop must sign and for notifying the moderator of these (c. 474). We shall examine some key features of the Curia:

The Vicar General

A coadjutor bishop and auxiliary bishops should be vicars general or at least episcopal vicars. Such a 'vicar' acts on behalf of the diocesan bishop who has 'proper ordinary power' by virtue of his office. The vicar general has 'vicarious ordinary power', acting with the bishop's authority as his substitute, but only in administrative acts (neither for judicial nor for legislative acts, nor in the teaching or sanctifying roles of the bishop).[40] He has such power 'generally', for the whole diocese, not just for an area of responsibility (c. 479 § 1). A vicar general, normally only one, must be appointed (c. 475 § 1), being a priest over thirty years old with a doctorate or licentiate in theology, Scripture or canon law or being well versed in these, being of sound doctrine, prudent and experienced (c. 478 § 1). He must not also be appointed canon penitentiary, since the two offices are incompatible, involving a conflict of internal and external fora, nor must he be related to the bishop up to the fourth degree of consanguinity in the collateral line (c. 478 § 2). If he is not a bishop, he is to be appointed for a specified, limited time (c. 477 § 1). When absent, the bishop may appoint another in his place (c. 477 § 2), but this is a matter of formal appointment, not just a statement that a particular priest is to 'look after the diocese' for a particular period; the latter would result in his acts, for example dispensations, being invalid, since he lacks the office on which they depend. The vicar general is to cooperate with the bishop in coordinating the work of the diocese (c. 473 § 2), keep him informed of what he does, and never act against him (c. 480). His power ceases on expiry of the term of office or when the see becomes vacant (c. 481 § 1).

---

40. J. A. Coriden, *An Introduction to Canon Law*, revised edn, Paulist, New York, Mahwah, 2004, 92–3.

Episcopal Vicars

These exercise 'vicarious ordinary power', but only over the area of the diocese or the area of responsibility (cc. 476, 479 § 2), specified in a valid decree of appointment. Within those limits, the conditions of appointment, criteria of suitability and the relationship to the diocesan bishop are those which apply to the vicar general. If the episcopal vicar responsible for a specific area cannot be contacted and it is a question of a dispensation which he would be able to grant, a vicar episcopal for another area cannot validly issue the dispensation; either the bishop or the vicar general or another person specifically delegated the power to grant such a dispensation must be contacted.

Moderator of the Curia

This optional appointment has been considered above.

The Chancellor

The main function of the Chancellor ('*cancellarius*': gate-keeper) is to arrange and keep secure the documents, records of the Curia. He is automatically a notary (cc. 482–483), who is to sign and authenticate official documents, keeping them in an ordered archive (c. 487 § 1). There is also to be a secret archive, to which only the bishop (diocesan administrator) has the key (cc. 485–490). In fact, the Chancellor should be a qualified canonist, since he should prepare and/or verify documents such as decrees of the diocesan bishop, which he (or another notary) must sign for them to be legally operative, as well as providing the bishop with canonical advice, if there is no canonist among his vicars general or episcopal. His office does not cease with the vacancy of the see; indeed he must witness and authenticate the letters of appointment from the Holy See of a new bishop, as well as witness the latter's profession of faith and swearing of the oath in the liturgical ceremony which precedes his instalment.

The Archivist and other Notaries

Other archivists and notaries may be appointed (c. 484), to keep documents in an ordered manner and in conditions of secrecy, including historical, parish and diocesan documents, providing those who have a right of access with that access under the conditions laid down by general law and by the bishop (cc. 484, 487–488, 491). The bishop is to have a secret and secure archive of his own (cc. 489–490).

155

The Diocesan Finance Committee and Financial Administrator

A financial committee (sometimes called 'trustees' in England) with three 'members of the faithful' expert in finance and civil law, is to be appointed by the bishop for five years; no one related to the bishop up to the fourth degree of consanguinity being appointed (c. 492). A financial administrator or secretary is to be appointed by the bishop, after hearing the opinion of both the college of consultors and the finance committee, for five years (renewable), to be someone of expertise in finance and of outstanding integrity (c. 494 § 1). This procedure is to be followed each time his appointment is renewed.[41] The English text says 'after consulting' these two bodies, which would imply a question of the validity of the appointment if there were no formal consultation (c. 127 § 2). The Latin text does not use *'consulere'* nor any of the terms specifically indicating matters of validity (c. 37); it says 'after hearing' (*'auditis'*) them. This might mean consultation is a question only of liceity, which would make the appointment illegal if there were no consultation, leaving open a challenge through recourse. Yet, the duty to consult is often expressed in the Code through the word *'audire'*.[42] A real duty to consult is seen here and so a matter of validity.[43] This financial administrator is not to be removed from this office during his period of service except for a grave reason and after consultation with both of these bodies (c. 494 § 2). The responsibilities of the committee and of the administrator are to prepare a budget and accounts annually, to check the accounts for the preceding year provided by the financial administrator (cc. 493, 494 § 4), to administer the goods of the diocese, and to observe and ensure the observance of the norms on temporal goods throughout the diocese (Book V of the Code). The fact that the financial administrator is to give an annual report to the finance committee means that he is not a member of it, much less someone delegated by the bishop to preside over it (c. 492 § 1); this is because he is accountable to it (c. 494 § 3).

Nevertheless, the committee has a real degree of independence from the bishop; it must give consent to acts of extraordinary expenditure

---

[41.] Olivares, 'Economo diocesano' in *Nuovo dizionario di diritto canonico*, 437.

[42.] M. Wijlens, 'Juridic Acts (cc. 124–128)', in J. P. Beal, J. A. Coriden and T. J. Green (eds), *New Commentary on the Code of Canon Law: An Entirely New and Comprehensive Commentary by Canonists from North America and Europe, with a revised English translation of the Code*, Canon Law Society of America Study Edition, Paulist, New York, Mahwah. NJ, 2000, 177–83 at 181–2.

[43.] B. A. Cusack, 'The Internal Ordering of the Particular Church (cc. 464–572)', in Beal et al. (eds), *New Commentary on the Code of Canon Law ...*, 610–740 at 651.

and for the alienation of temporal goods of a certain value (cc. 1277, 1292) and he must consult it before appointing or removing a financial administrator (c.494 § 2), before levying taxes on public juridical persons (c. 1263) or undertaking major administrative acts (c. 1277).[44]

The Vicar Judicial ('*Officialis*') and other Tribunal Personnel

The bishop is the judge in the diocese or group of dioceses (c. 1426) in cases in which he himself is not personally involved; he can exercise this judicial power personally or through a vicar judicial or '*Officialis*' (c. 1419). The bishop must appoint a vicar judicial (c. 1420 § 1) and may appoint assistant vicars judicial, all priests, at least thirty years old, of good repute, with a doctorate or licentiate in canon law (c. 1420 § 3–4). There should be other judges appointed, for specific (renewable) periods of time; although the time is to be specified in the appointment (c. 1422), a specific time is not laid down by law because the office, of its nature, requires stability.[45] They do not cease to function if the see is vacant and cannot be removed by the diocesan administrator (c. 1420 § 5), not even with the approval of the college of consultors,[46] although they need to be confirmed in position by the new bishop (c. 1420 § 5).

The vicar judicial and other judges appointed carry out the judicial aspects of the bishop's responsibilities, the vicar judicial and assistant vicars judicial having vicarious ordinary power in this sphere only (and are not truly local ordinaries). The bishop can judge cases himself, but is recommended not to do so, apart from in exceptional cases.[47] The fact that the vicar judicial 'constitutes one single tribunal with the bishop' (c. 1420 § 2) means that there can be no appeal to the bishop over a matter judged by the tribunal. It is to be noted that, although many cases handled by diocesan tribunals concern marriage, there is no such thing as a 'marriage tribunal' known to canon law; the diocesan tribunal (or inter-diocesan or regional tribunal) has a broader reference and is competent to deal with a range of matters. Although the vicar judicial and the diocesan tribunal are treated in Book VII of the Code, it is useful to note this aspect of the bishop's

---

[44.] Valdrini, 'La constitution hiérarchique ...', 167–8, nn. 263–263/1.

[45.] Pontifical Council for Legislative Texts, Instruction on Tribunals handling causes of Nullity of Marriage, *Dignitas connubii*, 25 January 2005, art 44; K. Lüdicke and R. E. Jenkins, *Dignitas connubii: Norms and Commentary*, Canon Law Society of America, 2006, 88, n. 3: original German by K. Lüdicke, *Die Eheprozeßordnung der katholischen Kirche: Text (Latein und Deutsch) und Kommentar*, Ludgerus, Essen, 2005.

[46.] *Dignitas connubii: Norms ...*, 88, n. 4.

[47.] *Dignitas connubii*, art. 22; *Dignitas connubii: Norms*, 84–5, n. 6.

responsibilities and the place of the vicar judicial and of the tribunal in the diocesan Curia. This very delicate area of serving the People of God in the pursuit of truth and justice, demands that only those highly qualified and competent be appointed.

Juridically established Councils and the Pastoral Care of the Diocese

Since the Second Vatican Council, a number of bodies have grown up in the Church, many at diocesan level; some of these are specifically required by law, such as the diocesan council of priests and the college of consultors, others are optional, such as the episcopal council and the diocesan pastoral council, while yet other bodies are not envisaged by the law as such at all, but offices or commissions for liturgy, youth work, social justice and the like have developed. The latter type of structure can be very useful, but juridically it rests entirely on the bishop's decision and is directly accountable to him. There has been much confusion about the respective roles of those bodies which are juridically envisaged by the law. The episcopal council was left optional (c. 473 § 4), apparently to avoid making the government of the diocese fundamentally collegial and thus undermining the position of the bishop. Such a council has often helped greatly the coordination between diocesan bishop and vicars general and episcopal, but the lack of a council of priests in France led to that council being expanded in personnel beyond what the law envisages.[48] In fact, the law requires every diocesan bishop to establish two entities new to canon law in recent decades: the council of priests and the college of consultors (cc. 495 § 1, 502 § 1, cf. 501 § 2–3).

The Council of Priests

This is to represent the *presbyterium* (cc. 495 § 1, 498–499), being a council of priests and not of clergy (excluding deacons), especially the secular priests of the diocese and often those others working in the diocese (c. 498). It is there to 'assist' the bishop in the running of the diocese and is spoken of as the 'bishop's senate' (c. 495 § 1). This was a term used earlier of the cathedral chapter, from which the council of priests emerged when the Second Vatican Council sought a more representative body to reflect the needs of the diocese than the chapter which was nominated by the bishop.[49] The council is rooted in the

---

[48.] Valdrini, 'La constitution hiérarchique ...', 166, n. 261.

[49.] G. Ghirlanda, 'Consiglio presbiterale' in *Nuovo dizionario di diritto canonico*, 305–9 at 305–6.

priests' sharing the ministerial priesthood with the bishop. It is to meet only when the bishop calls it, to discuss what he asks of it. Its role is only consultative (c. 500 § 1–2), but it has to be consulted over the erection, suppression or major alteration of parishes (c. 515 § 2). It ceases to exist if the see is vacant, the college of consultors assuming its duties (c. 501 § 2).

The council of priests can be dissolved if it neglects or abuses its role, but it has to be reconstituted within a year (c. 501 § 3), which shows the importance the Code attaches to it. To be an effective instrument of assistance to the bishop, it must represent the diocese, not just numerically, but geographically (to identify the needs of distinct areas) and so that the different ministries in the diocese may be considered (c. 499). It is to help the bishop to know the diocese as a lived reality, so that he may provide for it more effectively.

The council of priests is to have its own statutes, to be approved by the diocesan bishop (c. 496). This would settle how the council is to be made up. All secular priests incardinated in the diocese have a right to vote (c. 498 § 1 n.1), which includes those working outside the diocese, as well as secular priests working in the diocese but incardinated elsewhere, priests of institutes of consecrated life or societies of apostolic life or, although the Code does not mention it, of a personal prelature working in the diocese (c. 498 § 1 n. 2), while for other priests domiciled there, it would depend on the statutes (c. 498 § 2). Often there is an election, according to statutes, to choose a good number of the members of the council (about half), but then there are those who are members in virtue of their office, (for example, the vicar general, some of the vicars episcopal, the financial administrator), and others appointed by the bishop (c. 497). The council is to be renewed over a five-year period (c. 501 § 1), perhaps with some members being replaced at one time and others at another, to ensure a level of continuity and stability. The diocesan bishop decides when to call the council and decides or approves what it is to discuss; it can never act without him and ceases when the see is vacant (cc. 500, 501 § 2).

Unlike the episcopal council which assures cohesion, but which is optional, the council of priests has an obligatory and more precise role, through which it shares in the ruling function of the bishop. This can be quite a large area of responsibility, since the diocesan bishop 'is to consult' the council on 'more serious matters' (c. 500 § 2); he 'is to hear their opinion' ('*audiat*') on these issues, depending upon the statutes. The council has only a consultative vote, but, if on some matters the bishop had to obtain their consent (c. 500 § 2), which means he must formally seek that consent and, if he did not do this or does not obtain the consent of the majority, his action on the matter in hand would be invalid (c. 127 § 1). The matters where the diocesan bishop must consult the council of priests are: before deciding to hold a diocesan synod (c. 461 § 1), erect, suppress or radically alter a parish (c. 515 § 2), what is to happen to offerings made by the faithful on the occasion of fulfilling a parochial function (c. 531), whether or not to establish a pastoral council in each parish (c. 536 § 1), deciding to build a new church (c. 1215 § 2), serious reasons for judging that a particular church not be used any longer for divine worship and be used for secular purposes (c. 1222 § 2) and levying a tax on public juridical persons subject to his authority (c. 1263).[50] At present the universal law does not specify any case where the consent of the council of priests is required.[51]

The College of Consultors

This is chosen by the bishop from among the members of the council of priests and it is to consist of six to twelve priests, appointment being for five years (c. 502 § 1). There is no election to the college. When the see is impeded or vacant, they elect a diocesan administrator who acts in place of the bishop when the see is vacant (c. 421 § 1) or, if there is no coadjutor bishop and if the diocesan bishop has not established a list of substitutes for such an eventuality,[52] they elect another priest when the see is impeded (c. 413); until the appointment of the diocesan administrator or of that other priest, the senior priest (by ordination) of the college presides over the college (c. 502 § 2). The episcopal conference can decide that the chapter of canons fulfil the functions of the college of consultors (c. 502 § 3). This tends to happen more in countries where the chapter has a more explicit role also in regard to civil powers. The Bishops' Conference of England and Wales has just made this determination, but the college of consultors normally, and not the chapter of canons, has this responsibility.

Presided over by the bishop (or diocesan administrator under c. 502 § 2), the opinion of the college should be heard ('*auditis*') before appointing or removing a financial administrator (c. 494 § 1–2). For actions contemplated of great significance for the financial state of the diocese it 'must hear' its 'advice' or 'counsel' ('*consilium ... audire debet*' – c. 1277), for acts of extra-ordinary administration its consent must be obtained ('*consensu eget*', c. 1277) and for alienating temporal goods of the Church of a value beyond the minimum established by

---

50. Valdrini, 'La constitution hiérarchique ...', 156–8, nn. 248–9 and footnote 3, p. 157.
51. Ghirlanda, 'Consiglio presbiterale', 307.
52. Olivares, 'Collegio dei consultori' in *Nuovo dizionario di diritto canonico*, 201–2.

the Bishops' Conference, its consent must be obtained ('*consensu eget*', c. 1292 §, 1, 4). These decisions are concerned with finance and with the temporal goods of the Church. In fact, the Code calls the diocesan council for economic affairs also to be heard or consulted or to give its consent in these cases, but it does not specify the order in which the two bodies are to work. Perhaps it makes more sense for the council for economic affairs to be approached first, since it has the technical expertise relevant to the cases in hand, which might inform the judgments of the college of consultors.[53]

The college of consultors has to be kept to a minimum of six and a maximum of twelve members (c. 502 § 1), which makes it more manageable than the council of priests and more easily called. Although both are concerned with assisting the bishop in the pastoral care of the diocese, perhaps the council of priests has a function more of giving general orientations, whereas the college of consultors has a more precise role in advising the bishop on particular decisions.[54]

The Chapter of Canons

These are to celebrate the more solemn liturgical functions in the cathedral (c. 503). They have an advisory role, according to statutes laid down by the bishop. They may undertake the role of the college of consultors, if the episcopal conference (not the diocesan bishop on his own) so decides (c. 502 § 3). Their role is more significant in countries such as Germany, Austria and Switzerland, where they have a role in relation to the selection of bishops of presenting names to the Holy See.

The Canon Penitentiary

A canon penitentiary is to be selected from among the chapter of canons (or another priest appointed if there is no chapter – c. 508 § 2), to act in the 'sacramental internal forum' (confession), and has faculties to absolve from '*latae sententiae*' censures, which have not been declared and which are not reserved to the Apostolic See (c. 508 § 1). He has ordinary faculties (including the faculty to absolve from the censures just noted) and can absolve diocesans and non-diocesans in the diocese and diocesans outside the diocese; he cannot delegate his faculties (c. 508 § 1). Since he operates in the internal forum, this office may not be combined with that of vicar general or of episcopal vicar (c. 478 § 2), who function in the external forum.

---

53. Valdrini, 'La constitution hiérarchique ...', 158–9, n. 250 and footnote 3, p. 158.
54. Ibid.

Diocesan Pastoral Council

The Code provides the option of there being a diocesan pastoral council, a body of the faithful of the diocese to offer advice on the pastoral affairs of the diocese (c. 511–512), lapsing when the see is vacant (c. 513) and having only a consultative vote (c. 514). This differs from the other bodies noted above; it is an optional body, it is for strictly pastoral advice, but presumably it would have a large contingent of lay people in it.

6. Parishes and their Priests

The particular Church no less than the universal Church, mutually inherent in one another, is to serve the mission of the Gospel, to unite people ever more fully in Jesus Christ. The various diocesan structures we have examined are to serve that purpose and are not merely elements of a bureaucracy. In the life of the particular Church or diocese it is 'the parish' which is 'the community, pre-eminent among all the other communities present in his diocese, for which the bishop has primary responsibility; it is with the parish above all that he must be concerned'.[55] This does not mean that he is to act as the parish priest, but that the parish must be the centre or heart of the bishop's attention, since it is in this context that most of the faithful live out their responsibilities in the Church.

a. The Canonical Nature of the Parish

While the universal Church and the particular Church (diocese) are mutually immanent, the parish is essentially part of the diocese. The relevant key canon (c. 515) merits close attention (Table 8A). Once more we see pastoral care as the supreme norm of canon law (c. 1752). A parish concerns the faithful, the baptized, especially those who are Catholics. It is 'part' of the diocese, under the diocesan bishop; it has no independent existence, but it is not something which depends upon the whim of the bishop, since it has 'stable' existence (c. 515 § 1), unless and until it is changed in accordance with law (c. 515 § 2). The parish priest is united to the bishop in the presbyterate of the diocese and, as such, he accepts the responsibility given to him by the bishop to care for that part of the faithful who belong to that parish. Since the parish has juridical personality (c. 515 § 3), he is the agent who

---

55. *Pastores gregis*, n. 45.

Table 8A

The Parish (c. 515 § 1–3)

'A *parish* is a certain community of *Christ's faithful*
    stably established
        within a *particular Church*

    whose *pastoral care*
        under the *diocesan bishop* is entrusted
            to a *parish priest*
                as its *proper pastor*' (c. 515 § 1).

'The diocesan *bishop alone* can
    – *establish*,
    – *suppress* or
    – *notably alter* parishes,
        although only after *consulting* the Council of Priests' (c. 515 § 2).

The parish has '*juridical personality*' (c. 515 § 3).

properly acts in its name, as long as he has taken possession of the parish and as long as he remains in office (c. 532). To be their 'proper pastor' means that he, not the bishop, is directly responsible for their care, the latter intervening on the basis of subsidiarity if they are not adequately cared for. It does not mean that no one else may ever care for them, but that the parish priest has specific responsibility for them. Once again we see how canon law is important for specifying how people's rights (to hear the Gospel, receive the sacraments, and so on) are to be respected and observed; without some such arrangements there would be no way of making those rights concrete, of ensuring that responsibilities were discharged. This is equally true of the mission of the Church as such which the parish, under the guidance of the priest, is to serve. The concepts of authority as 'service' and of subsidiarity are relevant to norms on the parish. The connection with the bishop ('under the authority of the bishop') is underlined in the 1983 Code in a way that it was not earlier.[56] This helps to stress the cooperation of the presbyterate with the bishop and the fact that the parish priest is neither independent nor isolated.

In the light of this key text, we see why the 'diocesan bishop alone' can establish, suppress or notably alter parishes. Bringing a parish into existence can be a sign of the Church's growth, but nowadays there are many cases of parishes either being suppressed or altered in a notable way, combining or otherwise significantly re-structuring them. The term 'clustering' is another regrettable neologism of our time, distinguished by a vagueness which renders it unsuitable for the canonical precision required in handling these important matters which affect people's sensitivities and lives quite profoundly. Bishops need to avoid loose formulae such as 'will look after' a particular area, a parish or part of a parish. As we saw earlier, consultation needs to have taken place with those whose rights are to be affected, the parishioners of the parishes involved in any planned significant alteration and, as a matter of the validity of the act changing the status of parishes, consultation with the diocesan council of priests must have occurred in a formal way, the validity of the act in this case being signalled by the word 'although' only after consulting the council of priests (c. 515 § 2), whose consent, however, is not necessary. Properly issued decrees, including reference to the formal acts preceding the decision, together with the dates on which they occurred and an indication of the specific reasons for the decision to make the alteration should be

---

[56.] J-C. Périsset, *Le nouveau Code de droit écclésial: Commentaire du Code de droit canonique: Le peuple de Dieu: La paroisse*, Tardy, Paris, 1989, 23–4, 33.

included in the relevant decrees, signed by the bishop and authenticated by the chancellor or other notary. Anything less would render the act invalid (if the council of priests were not consulted) or illegal if other matters were omitted, which would leave the bishop exposed to possible recourse by anyone adversely affected by his action. As long as there are still parishioners, a parish cannot be suppressed as such, but it could be amalgamated with another, a major alteration of both, but then the procedures noted and the documentation of the various consultations and decisions need to be observed.[57]

The Code has to allow for various eventualities. Other arrangements have to be made for some communities where there are not enough priests (c. 516). Placing some parishes together under a number of priests jointly (often called a 'team ministry') is one, but then there must be a moderator appointed by the diocesan bishop (not simply chosen by the priests involved), who has responsibility for coordinating pastoral care (c. 517 § 1); again this is a canonical device to ensure that people's needs and rights are met.

Since the faithful have the right to 'full pastoral care' (c. 213), there needs to be a priest with the faculties to care for them, even if circumstances make it necessary to entrust 'a share in the exercise of their pastoral care' to a deacon or to someone else (c. 517 § 2). Only a priest can celebrate the Eucharist, forgive sins, anoint the sick and, in certain cases, confirm; anything less is not to provide 'full' pastoral care for people. It is entirely misguided to imagine that arrangements involving deacons or even lay persons in a 'share' in pastoral care are a true or a desirable substitute for a priest or that this pertains to the 'rights' of lay faithful. Certainly, there is a right to fulfil their mission in the Church and to participate in caring for others also in parish life, but their true right is to receive 'full pastoral care', which can only be had from a priest.

Although a parish is normally territorial, relating to the persons living in a particular geographical part of a diocese, it can be personal – a parish priest for an ethnic or a national group, a military parish and so on (c. 518). The aim is to ensure proper, full pastoral care for people in particular circumstances which make the normal provision unsuitable or impracticable.

A parish may be entrusted to a clerical religious institute or society of apostolic life, for a time or indefinitely, but a specific parish priest (or moderator if there is a group for a number of parishes) is to be

---

[57.] Cf. P. Kitchen, 'The Alteration of Parishes', *Canon Law Newsletter*, 151, September 2007, 68–76.

appointed (cc. 520 § 1–2). In such cases, all priests concerned and especially the moderator must 'take possession', as indicated below (c. 542). The duties pertaining to priests fall on all of them, their coordinated fulfilment of them being assured by the moderator (c. 543). If one of them becomes ill or is otherwise incapable of functioning, the parish does not become vacant; if it is the moderator, the bishop is to appoint a new moderator (c. 544).

b. The Parish Priest

The Canonical Significance of the Parish Priest

It will be useful to consider the key canon (c. 519) in Table 8B. The pastoral care, which it is the key purpose of canon law to foster, is assured for the community of the parish through the responsibility which the parish priest has (and any assistant priests, deacons and lay faithful who are to assist him) to provide it. He does this on a Christological and an ecclesiological basis, in exercising the 'ministry of Christ' in which he shares under and with the bishop. His ministry of full pastoral care is rooted sacramentally in Holy Orders in the presbyteral degree, in his ministerial priesthood, and in the threefold functions of sanctifying, teaching and ruling (or leading) which he is to exercise precisely as a priest. This is done, in collaboration with the others mentioned, 'in accordance with the law', as a reflection of what the Church is and what we are called to be, as the way in which the proper pastoral needs of all can be met in the community of Christ. Since Jesus was priest, prophet and king, exercising a sanctifying, teaching and ruling (pastoral) function, the Church likewise has the same threefold 'munera' or functions, found in the offices of the Pope and of the bishop. As a co-worker with the bishop in the presbyterate of the diocese, the priest, by his ordination as a priest, also exercises these three functions.

Appointment and 'Taking Possession' of the Parish

A priest has to be in sacred orders before he can be validly appointed a parish priest (c. 521 § 1), sound in doctrine and morally good, suitable for the parish to which he is to be appointed after the bishop considers the circumstances, discussing them with the vicar forane (dean), and perhaps with others (cc. 521 § 2–3. 524); the appointment has to be made by the diocesan bishop (c. 523), implying that other procedures have been followed properly if it is a parish priest being transferred from another parish (cc. 1748–1751) and in any case that a valid decree

Table 8B

The Parish Priest (c. 519)

'The parish priest,
      as proper *pastor*
         of the *community entrusted* to him

  exercises *pastoral care* (over them)
      under the *authority* of the diocesan *bishop*
         whose <u>*ministry of Christ*</u> he is called to *share*

so that, *for this community* he may
      carry out the *offices* of
         – *teaching*
         – *sanctifying* and
         – *ruling*

      with the *cooperation* of other *priests* and *deacons* and
      the *assistance* of *lay members of Christ's faithful*
         in *accordance* with the *law*' (c. 519).

of appointment is issued. The discussion with the vicar forane (dean) is required, but a strict canonical duty to 'consult', implying that the appointment would be invalid if this were not done, seems not to be at issue; the Latin texts says *'audiat'* (c. 524) or should 'hear' the views of the latter.[58] However, this is part of the bishop verifying (c. 521 § 3) the suitability of the priest concerned to become parish priest or at least to become such in a particular parish (c. 521 § 2). These criteria of suitability (c. 521 § 1–2) are not to be taken lightly, for the good of the people concerned.

The new parish priest assumes responsibility for the parish after taking possession (induction) or having been dispensed by the bishop from it (c. 527). This is not a mere formality; it avoids absenteeism, up to that point the priest has no responsibility for the parish. Through this act he acquires an office of pastoral care which is stable and from which he can only be removed or transferred according to law, all because the needs of the people are such that they have a right to someone as parish priest who can come to know them and their needs, which requires a reasonably long period of time, in order to be able to meet them effectively, with the assistance of others. This is why the appointment of parish priest is to be for an indefinite period of time or, if the episcopal conference has decreed it for a specified number of years; in the latter case, however, a decree of that conference to be valid has to have the *'recognitio'* of the Holy See, which will not be given if the time specified is less than several years.

During the vacancy of the see or when it is impeded, a diocesan administrator can put a priest already nominated as parish priest 'in possession' (c. 525) and, only if the see has been vacant or impeded for more than a year, appoint a parish priest (c. 525). A parish priest is normally to be parish priest of one parish only, but he may be appointed to this position in regard to more than one parish, due to the shortage of priests (c. 526).

The Parochial Administrator

When the parish priest cannot fulfil his duties because of exile, imprisonment, illness, and so on, a parochial administrator is to be appointed by the diocesan bishop as soon as possible (cc. 539–541). He has all the rights and duties of the parish priest, unless the bishop determines otherwise, but he must make no major changes and must

---

58. J. A. Renken, 'Parishes and Pastors (cc. 515–44)' in Beal *et al.* (eds), *New Commentary on the Code of Canon Law ...*, 673–724 at 695; B. F. Griffin, 'Parochial Vicars (cc. 545–552)', Ibid., 725–40 at 733.

give an account to the parish priest when he returns. In the period before such a parochial administrator is appointed, the temporary care of the parish falls upon the most senior assistant priest or upon a priest designated by the bishop.

The parochial administrator, for some reason called by some a 'priest-in-charge', is different from the parish priest juridically in the sense that he operates for a temporary period, *ad interim*. The indications given above may justify the appointment of such an administrator. Other considerations which may warrant such a temporary appointment are where a priest may be only recently ordained and lack experience to be appointed parish priest or where someone with problems was being given an opportunity to see how he would manage. However, the use of a parochial administrator as a way to avoid appointing a parish priest or in a systematic way in the diocese is a gross abuse of the law and especially of the right of the people of the parish to full pastoral care, for which the law provides explicitly that there be a parish priest with stability of appointment over several years. Should a priest find himself in this position (certainly, if it endures beyond two years) or even parishioners find themselves in such a predicament, he or they would be advised to write to the bishop explicitly asking him to appoint a parish priest; if he refuses or does not do so without good reason, they may exercise recourse against the decision by writing to him and asking him to change his decision and, if this is refused unjustifiably or is ignored, they may exercise their right of hierarchical recourse by writing to the Holy See, to the Congregation for Clergy.

One instance where a parochial administrator should be appointed as such is where the parish priest is on holiday and there is no assistant priest. The priest concerned needs to be assessed for suitability, including following the norms for the protection of children where it concerns a priest from outside the diocese. The decree of appointment should state the dates between which he is to administer the parish and specify any conditions, as to remuneration, health insurance, residence and particular responsibilities to be discharged. By means of such an appointment, the priest concerned has all the faculties he needs to operate, which is not the case without such an appointment.

These various conditions are designed to serve the 'community of the faithful' for whom the parish priest is the 'proper pastor' (c. 519). The threefold functions he has to discharge for those people entrusted by the bishop to his specific care: a hierarchical aspect of his duties. It is those faithful who live within, have a domicile or are wanderers staying in his geographical parish or who are part of his personal parish (c. 107) who are the community for whom he is the proper pastor: a communitarian aspect of his duties (cc. 515 § 1, 519).[59]

The Main Responsibilities of the Parish Priest

The responsibilities of the parish priest listed in cc.528–530 and in some other canons are extensive. In a way which is analogous to that of the diocesan bishop, this does not mean that he has to fulfil them all on his own and in his own person, although he has to do much in that respect, especially for the duties which especially fall upon him as parish priest (c. 530), but he is to 'ensure' that these various duties are effectively fulfilled. This implies collaboration with others, especially in the parish, under the authority of the bishop and in accordance with the law. In this way, he attends to his teaching, sanctifying and ruling (serving) functions.

Rather than seeing here a list of mere duties, a theological and juridical perspective on the role of the parish priest provides a much better understanding of what is involved. The concept of the parish as a specific 'part of the particular Church' entrusted to the care of the parish priest (c. 515 § 1) recalls the Second Vatican Council's emphasis upon the parish as a community of the faithful, who belong to the faithful of the particular Church or diocese as a whole, itself rooted in the communion of the universal Church and of all the particular Churches, a community entrusted to a parish priest as one of the principal collaborators of the bishop; it is a special example of community apostolate in the life of the Church.[60] The parish is a particular portion of the faithful under the care of a parish priest, in union with the bishop in the particular Church; these are the 'constitutive elements' of a parish from this ecclesiological Conciliar perspective, reflected here in the Code. The parish priest is considered not just juridically, as in 1917, but precisely as collaborating with the bishop in the three functions of Christ and of the Church of teaching, sanctifying and ruling. Thus, the responsibilities of the parish priest in cc. 528–530 are very clearly expressions of this service of a community of the faithful, grounded in word and sacrament, to build up that communion of life and of apostolate in the mission of the Church.[61]

The parish priest is to 'ensure' the following in respect of his

---

59. Périsset, *La paroisse*, 50–2.
60. Gerosa, *Le droit de l'Église*, 318–19; cf. Second Vatican Council, Constitution on the Sacred Liturgy, *Sacrosanctum Concilium*, n. 42; *Christus Dominus*, n. 30; Decree on the Lay Apostolate, *Apostolicam actuositatem*, n. 10.
61. Gerosa, *Le droit de l'Église*, 318–21.

teaching function: that the Word of God is proclaimed in its entirety to all parishioners, that the lay faithful are instructed in the truths of the faith, especially through the homily, to help in catechesis, the promotion of the apostolate, also in regard to social justice, care for the Catholic education of children and the young, and that efforts are made to bring the Gospel to those who do not practise or who do not profess the true faith (c. 528 § 1). In respect of his sanctifying function, he is to: 'ensure' that the Eucharist is the heart of the parish assembly of the faithful, foster devout celebration of the sacraments, especially of the Eucharist and penance, lead people in prayer, including in their families, and promote their active participation in the sacred liturgy, direct the parish liturgy under the authority of the diocesan bishop and guard against abuses (c. 528 § 2). In regard to his pastoral activity of service and his governing function, he is to 'ensure': that he gets to know people entrusted to his care, through family visiting, sharing their worries and sorrows, that he corrects those in error prudently, that the sick and especially the dying are cared for through the sacraments, that he seek out the poor, suffering, lonely, exiles and those in special difficulties and that marriage and family life are fostered (c. 529 § 1). He is to promote the specific role of the laity in the Church's mission, fostering their associations for religious purposes, collaborate with the bishop and the presbyterate, nurture a concern for the parish among the faithful, that they see themselves as members of the particular and of the universal Church, promoting its unity (c. 529 § 2).

Especially (not exclusively) entrusted to the parish priest are the following functions: to administer baptism, confirmation (in danger of death), viaticum and anointing of the sick, including the Apostolic blessing, to assist at marriages and give the nuptial blessing, to conduct funerals, to bless the baptismal font at Eastertime, and conduct processions and blessings outside the church, to lead the more solemn celebrations of the Eucharist on Sundays and on holydays of obligation (c. 530). Other responsibilities include: to give offerings to the parish, unless intended for himself personally (c. 531), to act on behalf of the juridical person of the parish (c. 532), to reside in the parish and not be absent for over a week, other than for annual holidays and retreat without contacting the bishop (c. 533 § 1–2), preventing absenteeism and facilitating a more effective care of his people, among whom he lives and whom he serves more easily, to offer Mass each Sunday and holydays for the people of the parish or, if on occasion unable to do this, to cause it to be said (c. 534), to keep registers and make prompt and careful entries for baptisms, confirmations, marriages, funerals, entering into the baptismal registers confirmation and issues of status (marriage, ordination, perpetual profession) and to prepare valid certificates, sealed with a parish seal (c. 535).

The responsibility of the parish priest presented in these lists, which are not exhaustive, is designed to facilitate the effective pastoral care of the people specifically entrusted to him as their specific pastor. The nucleus of those duties is the list given in c. 530, but, even here, the term 'reserved' to the parish priest is avoided, in order not to risk the invalidity of acts important for the well-being of the people if another priest were to undertake them. On the other hand, the fact that another priest would be acting illegally in undertaking at least some of those acts without the requisite authorization of the parish priest is intended to safeguard and reinforce his role as the proper pastor of the people who form that part of the particular Church entrusted to his specific and proper pastoral care.[62] Normally, the parish priest is the one who is to ensure, for example, proper preparation for the sacraments; in principle and in fact he should be disposed to allow another priest in good standing to celebrate a baptism of a relative or of a friend, but the abuse of a former parish priest constantly returning to his previous parish to the point where he celebrates many funerals or more weddings than the new parish priest is certainly to be avoided. A diocesan bishop should intervene to clarify matters in favour of the priest he has appointed, if that were to occur.

Official Bodies in the Parish

The Code presents two bodies to assist the parish priest in his ministry, one of them, the parish committee for economic affairs, is compulsory, whereas the other, the parish pastoral council, is optional, unless it is made compulsory through a decree of the diocesan bishop, after having heard the opinion of the diocesan council of priests (c. 536 § 1).

The Parish Pastoral Council

The parish pastoral council is perhaps more widely known and is very common in fact. A bishop may certainly encourage or even require parishes to establish such councils and indeed they have many valuable uses. They are to have statutes, promulgated by the bishop, but these have to be in accordance with universal law. The council is expressly a pastoral council; it is there for the lay faithful, whose specific vocation and role (c. 210) the parish priest is to foster (c. 529 § 2), to be represented on this council and to participate 'one with him'

---

62. J. Diaz, 'Parroco' in *Nuovo dizionario di diritto canonico*,758–64 at 762–3.

in fostering the pastoral care of the people of the parish (c. 536 § 1). It has absolutely no right to enter into specifically financial questions, which are the specific province of the parish finance committee, which is compulsory. Specific ways of promoting the pastoral care of the parish, in liturgy, spiritual life, parish groups, apostolate, are certainly matters which can and should be discussed, with objectives and plans for how to bring these about also being considered.

When it is wrongly understood, as if it were a way to limit the legitimate and proper actions of the parish priest or to function as if he and perhaps others were specifically accountable to it or as if it were a form of democratic decision-making body, then it does not foster the communion of the Church in the parish nor with the particular Church of the diocese nor with the universal Church. Some regrettable developments in this direction led to a document being issued by various dicasteries of the Holy See on the matter. Before turning to them, the Code itself states explicitly that the parish pastoral council is 'presided over by the parish priest' (c. 536 § 1) and 'has only a consultative vote' (c. 536 § 2). The latter means that its vote is neither deliberative nor binding, but it has an enormous value when the council operates as it should in authentic harmony and collaboration. The tendency to distinguish between a parish priest who is 'president' of the council and a lay 'chair person' has no foundation in law; quite the opposite, since the clear intention of the Code is that the parish priest be more than a figurehead president (the expression *'cui parochus preest'* means 'over which the parish priest presides'), but he is the only one who does so. The equivalent noun *'praeses'* can be translated as 'president' or as 'chair person', but it is a distortion to portray it as permitting both, especially where the parish priest is then reduced to a figurehead.

In the light of abuses which emerged over the years the Vatican instruction stated clearly that the deliberations and decisions of the parish pastoral council are 'invalid' if the parish priest does not preside or approve.[63] It is very important to collaborate fully with parishioners, to ensure that their needs are met, that their positive contribution to the work and mission of the Church, to various aspects of the lay apostolate are fostered and that their rights in these regards and in regard to their active participation in the mission of the Church are respected.

[63.] Various Congregations of the Roman Curia, 'Instruction on certain questions regarding the Collaboration of the Non-Ordained Faithful in the Sacred Ministry of Priests', 15 August 1997, Vatican, 1997, art. 5 § 2–3.

The Parish Finance Committee or Committee for Economic Affairs

This is a body which the parish priest must establish (c. 537). It is to produce accounts annually with a report to the parish, to discuss items of major expenditure with them and with the diocese (c. 537). Clearly, it has to be composed of persons in the Church, members of the faithful in full communion with the Catholic Church (cc. 204–205, 207). It is to be established according to the norms of universal and diocesan law. The latter would settle how many members there are to be. The function of the committee is to 'help the parish priest in the administration of the goods of the parish' (c. 537), even though he remains the agent who acts on behalf of the juridical person of the parish (cc. 515 § 3, 532). This function, however, implies that the criteria of suitability for appointment include competence in finances and/ or in buildings. Such a body would be involved in verifying that accounts have been presented to an official auditor each year, suggesting budgets and plans for the future, as well as being consulted about decisions of importance concerning the acquisition, administration and alienation of Church goods, which will be examined in more detail in Book V of the Code.

c. Parochial Vicars or Assistant Priests

These can only be validly appointed if they are in the 'sacred order of priesthood' (c. 546); the bishop is to consult the parish priest and the vicar forane first (c. 547). They are to collaborate with the parish priest and under his authority, caring for all aspects of the parish, though they do not have the obligation of the Mass for the people of the parish. An assistant priest cares for the parish if there is no parish priest or other person appointed as parochial administrator (cc. 545–549). As appointed by the bishop to assist in the pastoral care of the parish, he is not a servant of the parish priest, who must enable him to work for the pastoral care of the people, with guidance and encouragement, since he is the principal collaborator of the parish priest in that work; conversely, the parochial vicar must collaborate positively with the latter.

7. Other Figures of Importance in the Diocese

a. Vicars Forane (Deans)

The vicar forane, dean or archpriest (c. 553 § 1) goes back to the idea of someone under the diocesan bishop having a particular responsibility

174

for parishes and churches outside the main cities, in the countryside or in 'outlying' areas ('*foras*': 'in an outlying area'). In the past and certainly in the Code of 1917 they had a role of 'intermediary' between the bishop and priests generally in the diocese, even appearing in the Code in that position between the one and the other. This function can now be said to have been superseded, one fulfilled more by vicars episcopal nowadays.[64] Now, the vicar forane is treated after the section on parish priests and assistant priests, indicating perhaps a key part of his role as coordinating pastoral activity at a level which goes beyond the single parish and the function of having a proper care for the priests of the vicariate or deanery. He is a pastoral vicar and is not a local ordinary.

The bishop does not have to have vicars forane or deans, but, if he judges that he should have them, then he should make an appointment, after hearing the opinions of the priests involved in the pastoral ministry in that deanery (c. 553 § 2), a change from previous practice when the bishop simply made an appointment. The law does not lay down how this is to be done; but it could involve an election, which the bishop perhaps might confirm, or it could involve their proposing three names from among whom he might choose; diocesan law should make these specifications and the bishop should really consider the matter with the council of priests. The presupposition is that the person chosen would be a priest actually involved in pastoral care in that area of the diocese, since he would share the problems of the area and know the area well enough to be able to fulfil his tasks; he has to be judged 'suitable' in the light of time and place (c. 554 § 1). He is appointed for a fixed period of time to be settled by diocesan statutes (c. 554 § 2), but can be removed by the bishop for a serious reason (c. 554 § 3).

The duties of the vicar forane are as follows: to promote and coordinate common pastoral action in the vicariate (deanery), to see that clerics (including deacons) lead a life in keeping with their state and fulfil their duties carefully, to ensure that the liturgy is celebrated according to liturgical norms, that churches and furnishings are appropriate for the Eucharist and other liturgical celebrations, that the Blessed Sacrament is properly kept, that parish registers are properly maintained and securely kept, that ecclesiastical goods are properly administered, that the presbytery (priest's house) is looked after carefully (c. 555 § 1), that he encourage clergy to attend lectures,

---

[64] J. Diaz, 'Vicari foranei' in *Nuovo dizionario di diritto canonico*,1121–8 at 1124–5.

theological meetings, conferences, that the spiritual needs of clergy in the area, especially those in difficult circumstances, are met (c. 555 § 2), that sick clergy receive spiritual and material help, that clergy who die receive a decent funeral and that parish and personal belongings are securely and properly attended to (c. 555 § 3). He is to visit the parishes in the vicariate (deanery), as arranged by the bishop (c. 555 § 4).

Many of these aspects of care are not automatically addressed in other ways. Without becoming in any way a policeman, the vicar forane can be of enormous help to priests in the deanery. Attending to parish registers may seem banal, but they are legal documents in canon law. People's well-being is affected, their proper pastoral care compromised by carelessness and at times downright neglect, leaving those seeking marriage without proper proof of baptism, certificates in preparation for confirmation not being available because the registers were not maintained, causing distress for the family concerned. The neglect of the premises is a failure in the administration of the goods of the Church, often leading to far greater costs and more serious problems in the future; tactful advice can also help protect the individual's health at times.

The elements of surveillance, as over the liturgy, presuppose that the vicar forane knows and follows the norms himself, which is not always the case and which is a factor to be evaluated in making a judgment about suitability for appointment. Similarly, joint pastoral action will be facilitated on various matters, such as preparation for sacraments, if what the Church expects is followed; cooperation will be understandably more limited if what is proposed or undertaken is inadequate or wrong.

The care of sick clergy is a matter of real concern. It should be taken for granted that a sick priest will receive the Eucharist daily, even be helped to celebrate the Eucharist if or when possible, that he be offered the sacraments of reconciliation and anointing, quite apart from practical questions of where and how he may live while ill. The value of the vicar forane's involvement in the procedures after death, relating to the dead priest's funeral, family and possessions, as well as relating to what belongs to the parish, is obvious.

b. Rectors

Rectors are entrusted with the care of churches which are not parish churches (c. 556), appointed by the bishop, even if presented by superiors of a religious institute (c. 557). They are not to perform

176

those liturgical functions which are proper to the parish priest (c. 530) without his permission and, according to requirements such as in the case of a marriage, delegation (c. 558), although the bishop can require that certain liturgical functions be held in the church, as need arises (c. 560).

c. Chaplains

A chaplain 'is a priest to whom is entrusted in a stable manner the pastoral care, at least in part, of some community or special group' (c. 564), normally appointed by the local ordinary (c. 565), ensuring he has faculties. if not by law then by special delegation, to hear confessions, anoint, confirm in danger of death those entrusted to his care (c. 566 § 1), those who are chaplains to hospitals, prisons or at sea having faculties also to absolve in those situations from *latae sentientiae* penalties neither reserved nor declared (c. 566 § 2). A chaplain to a religious congregation is to be appointed only after the bishop has consulted the superior and the chaplain is not to involve himself in their internal affairs (c. 567 § 1–2). The bishop is to try to ensure that groups not easily able to be cared for by the parish priest (migrants, seafarers) have a chaplain (c. 568), those in the armed services having special laws (c. 569). If there is a non-parochial church attached to the community, normally the chaplain is to be appointed rector (c. 570).

The recent tendency to appoint lay persons as 'chaplains' is improper; no one can be a chaplain who is not a priest (c. 564) because that person is incapable of providing full pastoral care. Institutions which do this which are under some responsibility to the state should be appointed as 'assistants' to a chaplain, with appropriate arrangements being made for a priest to be available at certain times, to whom that person acts as an assistant in canonical terms.

8. Conclusion

Having examined the structure of the hierarchy and seen how the faithful operate within those structures, it is time to look at institutes of consecrated life and societies of apostolic life, the third and last section of Book II.

Chapter 6

The People of God

(Book II of the Code)

Part III: Institutes of Consecrated Life
and Societies of Apostolic Life

1. Introduction

The last section of Book II on the People of God deals with institutes of consecrated life and societies of apostolic life. Most of the canons in this section relate to religious institutes of consecrated life (cc. 607–709), with fewer for secular institutes (cc. 710–730) and fewer still for societies of apostolic life (cc. 731–746), although in many respects the latter are assimilated to religious institutes of consecrated life. The first part of the section, though, treats institutes of consecrated life (religious and secular) in common.

2. Institutes of Consecrated Life in General

a. The Nature of the Consecrated Life

The Code of 1917 gave a generic treatment of those committed to the Christian life through vows under the title of the 'religious'. Even before the Second Vatican Council, the inadequacy of this arrangement was signalled when Pius XII gave recognition to 'secular institutes'. For all its efforts to look at things anew, the Council was somewhat ambiguous in dealing with the consecrated life; placing all under the title of 'religious'. To understand the Code in this area, we need consider what the consecrated life as such is.

Consecration in the Life of Jesus

Jesus consecrated himself to the Father's will, to the salvation of the world throughout his life on earth and to the point of dying on the

Cross and of bestowing the life of heaven through his resurrection. His perfect, unconditional and unlimited love of the Father and of all in the world meant that his obedience to the Father's will was absolute, though entirely free. This self-emptying (Phil. 2:5–11) is indicated not only by his obedience, but by his poverty or his detachment from possessions to love more fully and unrestrainedly, and by his celibate chaste, agapaic love from an undivided heart. This consecration of Jesus (Jn. 10:18; 17:19; Heb. 5:1–10) is fundamental to the consecrated life in the Church.

Consecration in the Life of the Disciples of Christ

All Christ's disciples are called to respond to the love he has shown to all, to love one another as he has loved us (Jn. 13:34; 15:12), by consecrating themselves to him and by sharing in his high priestly consecration of himself to the Father's will (Jn. 17:11–19). That consecration is a call to total dedication in love of God and of neighbour; which implies a total conversion of life or *metanoia*, a handing over of oneself to Christ in faith (Mk. 1:14–15). With the ascension and the coming of the Holy Spirit, this encounter of faith occurs through baptism by which we are immersed into or consecrated to Christ in his Paschal mystery, incorporated into him and into his Church (cc. 96, 204, 849). This baptismal consecration is strengthened through confirmation, both imparting a 'character' (c. 845 § 1) or establishing a relationship with Christ which cannot be 'undone', although we are capable of rejecting its implications. This consecration is strengthened and deepened in a specific way through the sacrament of Holy Order which also imparts a 'character'; especially through the new and sacred consecration, 'by a new title' (c. 276 § 1), of priestly orders.

The consecrated life involves a person's 'new and further consecration', after baptismal consecration, but it is not a sacred one; it stems from the personal response to a vocation to a deeper, distinct consecration, to a particular state of life in the Church. Received in the name of the Church, it is created by profession of the evangelical counsels, a juridical rather than a sacred consecration.

b. Recent Canonical Developments

The Code of 1917 and 'Religious'

The Code of 1917 treated all forms of the consecrated life under the rubric of the 'religious': 'The religious state or the stable way of living in common by which the faithful, besides (observing) the precepts common to all (members of the faithful), undertake to keep also the evangelical counsels through vows of obedience, chastity and poverty, is to be held in honour by all.'[1] Here a distinct state of life among baptized is recognized, since those living it have to come from among the faithful; it is to be honoured by all in the Church because the evangelical counsels were lived by Jesus and are commended in the Gospel.

The religious life delineated by the 1917 Code would not cover the consecrated life as it is lived by some in the Church now, such as secular persons wishing to live in the midst of the world a consecrated life rooted in the evangelical counsels. The common life would make this impossible for those in families or for others not capable of it or not called to community life. Vows would seem to preclude those with a particular apostolate which might conflict with some of the technical responsibilities of vows as such. Pius XII had recognized 'secular institutes' with a distinctive status of their own. Apart from associations whose members pursue holiness by life in common, secular institutes have an internal constitution and hierarchical structure of government which,

> by a complete dedication limited by no other bonds which they require of their members properly so called by the profession of the evangelical counsels for the sake of exercising ministries and the apostolate, approach more closely in terms of their substance the canonical states of perfection, ... especially societies without public vows, insofar as, though they do not have life in common as religious, they have other external forms of that life.[2]

He expanded on this a year later:

> Nothing will be lacking from the full profession of Christian perfection, solidly grounded in the evangelical counsels and truly religious as to its substance, but this perfection is to be exercised and witnessed in the world and, therefore, it must be accommodated to the secular life in all things which are licit and which are compatible with the duties and works of this same perfection.[3]

[1.] Benedict XV, *Codex iuris canonici* (1917), c. 487.

[2.] G. Ghirlanda, 'Vita consacrata' in C. C. Salvador, V. De Paolis and G. Ghirlanda (eds), *Nuovo dizionario de diritto canonico*, San Paolo, Milan, P.U.G., Rome, 1993, 1139–46 at 1139.

[3.] Pius XII, Apostolic *motu proprio*, 'Primo feliciter', 12 March 1948, *Acta apostolicae sedis*, 40 (1948), 283–6 at 284–5, II: 'Nihil ex plena christianae perfectionis professione, evangelicis consiliis solide fundata et quoad substantiam vere religiosa, detrahendum erit, sed perfectio est *in saeculo* exercenda et profitenda; ac proinde, cum vita saeculari in omnibus quae licita sunt et quae cum eiusdem perfectionis officiis et operibus componi valent, accommodetur oportet.'

The Contribution of the Second Vatican Council

In both of these texts secular institutes are distinguished from religious as to the common life and public vows, but they are recognized as 'substantially' like religious in some forms of their life. Not surprisingly, then, the Second Vatican Council treated the consecrated life in the section on the religious, after its fundamentally important teaching on the universal call to holiness.[4] Judging sanctity as not just for priests and religious implied a more nuanced approach. Christian marriage was a vocation, for which two baptized Christians were 'sanctified by a special sacrament'.[5] On the consecrated life, the Church, under the Holy Spirit, had set up 'stable forms of living' by the three evangelical counsels and 'various forms of life, solitary and common' to foster Christian perfection in brotherly communion for the good of the Church. People living this type of life come from both clergy and laity, but 'not as a middle way between the clerical and lay state'.[6] This life, 'rooted in the life of baptism', which the consecrated person 'seeks to live … out more deeply by the evangelical counsels', liberates those who follow it from habitual concerns to witness to heavenly realities and to the life of the resurrection as superior to earthly realities and more closely imitates the form of life lived by Christ himself, perpetually representing this in the life of the Church.[7]

The Christological, ecclesiological and prophetic-eschatological significance of the consecrated life, grounded in baptism, emerges from Conciliar teaching. However, the ambiguity of the Council's terminology remains: the consecrated life was said to be like the 'religious' life in the chapter '*De religiosis*' ('On the religious'). It spoke of 'the religious state', 'religious profession', 'religious' becoming strangers to their fellow human beings and exhorting the 'religious' about their vocation.[8] On the other hand, it uses the term 'religious' in a broader sense than did the 1917 Code, since in the Council it includes members of societies who do not take vows.[9] Some clarification was introduced when it was stated explicitly that secular institutes 'are not religious institutes', but imply 'a true and complete profession of the evangelical counsels', a 'consecration' to live in the world, preserving

---

[4.] Second Vatican Council, Dogmatic Constitution on the Chuch, *Lumen gentium*, n. 39.
[5.] Ibid., n. 35.
[6.] Ibid., n. 43.
[7.] Ibid., n. 44.
[8.] Ibid., nn. 43, 45–6.
[9.] S. Recchi, 'De natura consecrationis per consilia evangelica in codice adumbratio', *Periodica de re canonica*, 83 (1994), 33–43 at 34.

their 'proper and particular character as secular'.[10] The Council gave
general norms not just for religious, but for 'those who live a life in
common without vows' and for 'secular institutes'.[11] This foreshad-
ows the treatment of religious and secular institutes of consecrated
life and societies of the apostolic life in the 1983 Code.

c. An Analysis of Key Canons (cc. 207, 573)

Membership of the Church through baptism (cc. 96, 204) is the basis of
equality for all Christ's faithful, within which the distinction between
'sacred ministers' constituted such through sacramental ordination
and lay faithful is a matter of 'divine institution' (c. 207 § 1). From this
canon and c. 573 (Table 9A), we see that consecrated persons come
from both lay and clerical members of the faithful, confirming the
Council's teaching that they are not in an 'intermediate state'.[12] They
can only come from the faithful, a further consecration to Christ only
being possible for those already baptized and confirmed. They are not
confined to religious, since they include those who profess the evangelical counsels of poverty, chastity and obedience through sacred
bonds 'other than vows' (c. 573 § 2). Their consecration to God through
vows or other forms of profession is a non-sacramental consecration,
but their state of life is part of the Church and is part of the Church's
mission, which it promotes.

The first part of c. 573, in contrast to 1917, shows the impact of the
Council: other forms of profession, and not only vows, constitute
people in the consecrated life, but it has to be in a stable form of life, not
something sporadic or conditional. The canon presents Christological,
ecclesiological, pneumatological (role of the Spirit) and eschatological
features of this life in the mission of the Church. Love of God is both a
motivation in the vocation of the consecrated life and a key aspect of
its implementation as a deepening of baptismal consecration effected
by God through the Holy Spirit to render the person able to witness to
Christ in the mission of the Church in this further consecration.[13] The
evangelical counsels, reflecting the scriptural foundations of the consecrated life in its various forms, are notably associated not only with
love of God, but with the perfection of charity as love of neighbour.

[10.] Second Vatican Council Decree on the Religious Life, *Perfectae caritatis*, n. 11.

[11.] Ibid., n. 1.

[12.] Ibid., n. 43.

[13.] G. Ghirlanda, *Il diritto nel mistero della comunione: Compendio di diritto ecclesiale*, 4th
revised edn, Paoline, Milano, P.U.G., Rome, 2004, 182–3, n. 161.

Table 9A

The Consecrated Life

Canon 207 § 2

'Drawn from both groups (i.e., sacred ministers and lay faithful c. 207 § 1)
are those of *Christ's faithful* who
  professing the *evangelical counsels*
  – through *vows*
  – or *other sacred bonds* recognized and approved by the Church
    are *consecrated to God* in their own *special way*
    and *promote* the *salvific mission* of the Church.
Their <u>state,</u>
        although it does not belong to the hierarchical structure of the Church,
            does *belong* to its *holiness.'*

Canon 573 § 1

'Life *consecrated* though the *profession* of the *evangelical counsels* is a *stable form of
  living* in which
    – the *faithful* follow *Christ* more closely under the action of the *Holy Spirit*
    – and are totally dedicated to God, supremely loved.

By a *new and special title* they are *dedicated* (i.e, consecrated)
    to seek the *perfection* of charity
        in the *service of God's kingdom* for
            – the honour of God
            – the building up the Church
            – and the salvation of the world.

They are a splendid *sign* of the Church
    as they *foretell heavenly glory.'*

Canon 573 § 2

'*Christ's faithful freely* assume *this form of life*
    in *institutes of the consecrated life*
        canonically established by the *competent authority.*

By *vows* or *other sacred bonds*
    they *profess the evangelical counsels*
        of *chastity, poverty* and *obedience*
            according to the laws of their own institutes.
Because of the *charity* to which these counsels lead,
    they are linked in a special way to the *Church* and its mystery.'

The free, personal response to any divine vocation, brought out in pursuit of a 'stable form of life' (c. 573 § 1), makes this more than a private, individual matter. It indicates a life in an institute, canonically set up by the proper authority of the Church, governed in turn by the laws of these institutes, the particular constitutions of the institute as a whole and the statutes of each house. These characteristics apply both to religious and to secular institutes of consecrated life, a fact which is underlined by the fact that the profession of the evangelical counsels does not have to be by vows, nor by a public profession; members of secular institutes do not make public profession of such counsels.[14] The free personal response to a vocation is a matter of irrevocable choice once profession is permanent; even temporary profession involves sacred 'bonds', implying special 'links' to the Church. The counsels are not an end in themselves; uniting the consecrated person more deeply to Christ, they 'lead to charity', love of God and of neighbour, especially in the institute concerned.[15]

d. Other Norms on Institutes of Consecrated Life in General

We note now how the 1983 Code expounds these key characteristics of the consecrated life in other canons and how the apostolic exhortation after the Synod of Bishops on the consecrated life develops doctrine still further.

The Consecrated Life as a State of Life (c. 574 § 1–2, 588)

Persons professing the evangelical counsels in institutes of consecrated life enjoy a 'state ... which belongs to the life and holiness of the Church' which is to be fostered by all (c. 574 § 1). Thus, the consecrated life is not a marginal aspect of the Church's life, but is preserved always by God's grace (c. 575). 'Some of Christ's faithful are specially called by God to this state, so that they benefit from a special gift in the life of the Church and contribute to its mission, according to the spirit and purpose of each institute' (c. 574 § 2). Those baptized ('faithful') called to this way of life are called by God in a vocation to which they need to be able freely to respond (c. 573 § 1), but for which they receive a divine gift or charism, adapted to the role they are to fulfil in the mission of the Church. Their special vocation is more radical than that received through baptism and confirmation, implying a

---

[14.] G. Sheehy *et al.* (ed.), *The Canon Law: Letter and Spirit*, Chapman, London, 1995, n. 1124.

[15.] E. Gambari, *I religiosi nel codice: Commento ai singoli canoni*, Ancora, Milan, 1986, 96–7.

deepening of the baptismal consecration in a more complete confor-
mation to Christ, in a vocation which is not a necessary or automatic
consequence of the baptismal vocation. The latter requires neither
celibacy nor a specific detachment from goods nor obeying a superior
in following the evangelical counsels.[16] Unlike the marriage of two
baptized persons or Holy Orders, it is not a further sacramental consecration; it is a non-sacramental, institutional, juridical consecration
through the counsels. The life of consecrated persons is a specific state
of life, which 'of its very nature is neither clerical nor lay' (c. 588 § 1);
the lay, clerical and consecrated states of life are complementary in
the life of the Church.[17] Already the Council had said the religious
life belongs 'essentially to the life and holiness of the Church', while
the *Instrumentum laboris* of the 1994 Synod of Bishops had portrayed
the consecrated life as an 'essential element of the Church, rooted in
revelation itself and not simply part of the historical experience of the
Church, ... part of the essence of the Church, that is to say of its very
being ('*esse*') and not just of its well-being ('*bene esse*').'[18] The Apostolic
exhortation after the Synod, *Vita consecrata*, states very strongly that
the consecrated life 'belongs indisputably to the life and holiness of
the Church', which '... means that the consecrated life, present in the
Church *from the beginning, can never fail* to be one of her *essential* and
characteristic elements, for it expresses her very *nature'.* Underlining its
distinctive place, John Paul II adds that: 'The idea of a Church made
up only of sacred ministers and lay people does not therefore conform
to the intentions of her divine Founder, as revealed in the Gospel and
in the other writings of the New Testament'.[19] Here we find a key
development of theological and canonical doctrine, since the consecrated life is stated to be part of one of the essential or indefectible
'marks of the Church' (one, *holy,* Catholic and Apostolic'), not by mere
historical circumstance, but by the intention of Christ himself, as part
of revelation reflected in Scripture, in the Church from the start, and
indefectibly an essential part of her holiness and life, to reveal the
Church's holiness and foster its mission in a special way.[20]

[16.] John Paul II, Apostolic exhortation, *Vita consecrata*, nn. 14–15, 18–19, 30.
[17.] Ibid., n. 31.
[18.] G. Ghirlanda, 'Dimensione ecclesiologica della vita consacrata nel sinodo dei vescovi del 1994', *Periodica de re canonica,* 84 (1995), 655–86 at 656–7: 'elemento essenziale
della Chiesa radicata nella rivelazione stessa e non semplicemente come esperienza
storica ecclesiale ... In questo modo tale stato fa parte dell'essenza della Chiesa, cioè
del suo essere e non solo del suo ben'essere'.
[19.] John Paul II, *Vita consecrata*, n. 29; emphases in the original.
[20.] Ibid., nn. 32, 46–7.

On the other hand, individual members of institutes of consecrated life cannot but be either lay or clerical, those in sacred orders being clerical and those not in such orders being lay, but having a distinctive state of life which is an essential part of the Church. As for the institutes as such, a religious institute of consecrated life is directed by clerics and presupposes the exercise of orders, while a lay or secular institute of consecrated life (Table 9B) does not presuppose the exercise of orders (c. 588 § 2–3).

The Role of the Evangelical Counsels (cc. 575, 598)

The evangelical counsels are not mere human constructs, but are an instance of what is revealed, 'based on the teaching and example of Christ' and 'a divine gift which the Church received from the Lord', of what he handed on to the Church for our good and for our salvation.[21] They are a gift 'which, by His grace, it preserves always' (c. 575). Each institute, 'taking into account its own special character', is 'to define in its constitutions the manner in which these evangelical counsels ... are to be observed in its way of life' (c. 598 § 1), each member being bound to observe them faithfully, according to those constitutions (c. 598 § 2). These counsels in the consecrated life cannot be lived by people as isolated individuals, but this is done in a way common to all in each institute, through bonds recognized by the Church as ways of following Christ and of being more closely conformed to him.[22] We turn now to each of these counsels in turn.

Chastity (c. 599)

Chastity implies 'perfect continence observed in celibacy'; there may be no genital sexual intercourse and members are to remain unmarried. Embraced 'for the sake of the Kingdom of heaven' as 'a sign of the world to come', it is to be 'a source of greater fruitfulness from an undivided heart'. Such Christological and eschatological motives have an ecclesiological dimension, since they are to be lived out in contemplative prayer or in apostolic activity. The 'undivided heart' demands that prayer be at the centre of the consecrated life for all (in different ways), since the love which unites the consecrated person more deeply to Christ depends on a life of prayer, nor will it bear fruit for the Church's mission if it is not nurtured and rooted in that prayer. Such chaste love in the consecrated life is referred to the purest, perfect love of the Trinity, a love 'above every other love'

[21.] *Dei verbum*, nn. 2, 4, 7.
[22.] John Paul II, *Vita consecrata.*, n. 10–11, 13, 18.

Table 9B

The Consecrated Life as a State of Life (c. 588)

'In itself the consecrated life is neither lay nor clerical' (c. 588 § 1)

A *clerical institute* is one which,

    by reason of
(1) the end or purpose intended by
    (a) the founder
    or by reason of
    (b) lawful tradition

(2) - is governed by clerics
(3) - *presumes* the *exercise of Orders*

    and

(4) - is recognized as such by
    ecclesiastical authority,
    (c. 588 § 2).

A *lay institute* is one which is

(4) recognized as such by
    ecclesiastical authority,

because, by its
(1) nature, character and purpose,
    defined by

    (a) its founder or
    (b) lawful tradition,

(3) its *proper role* does *not presume*
    the *exercise of Orders* (c. 588 § 3).

from an undivided heart. This virtue of chastity implies a mastery of self, not as repression of sexual instincts or passion, but precisely in not allowing such passions to dominate and enslave, channelling them into morally upright and fulfilling service of others in ways which avoid genital expression, legitimate only in marriage. This does require a certain mastery of self and a maturity in the affective life, to be verified in those seeking the consecrated life.[23] Chastity is a counter-witness to a hedonistic culture, which risks reducing the person in his or her sexuality to an object.[24] The love of consecrated chastity is analogous and complementary to conjugal love; its unitive meaning lies in the person's deeper union with Christ and its real but non-genital fruitfulness is to be found in the life and mission of the Church.

Poverty (c. 600)

The evangelical counsel of poverty, lived in imitation of Christ, means to be poor in reality (not living better than others or giving a counter-witness) and poor in spirit (without arrogance), to be sober (literally and by living without undue comforts), industrious (hardworking, not idle) and dependent on others in the use of goods, according to the proper law of the institute. This is an area where 'just autonomy' and 'subsidiarity' are significant. Not all institutes can live poverty in the same way. A monk who is part of a religious community owns nothing for himself, but shares all with the community. In congregations with a more active apostolate members may need to own money or property for the sake of the institute's work and/or for his or her daily living, especially true of those in secular institutes. On the other hand, someone earning a wage or a salary may well be required or expected by the institute to contribute a certain percentage to the institute for its work. Poverty is designed to ensure simplicity of life, at risk in ways of behaving among some in institutes today, and to foster charity towards others in the institute and beyond, at times in direct service of the poor, always as a witness against the idolatry of money and possessions.[25]

[23.] Congregation for Institutes of Consecrated Life and for Societies of Apostolic Life, *Directives on Formation in Religious Institutes*, 2 February 1990, nn. 39–41.

[24.] John Paul II, *Vita consecrata*, n. 88; cf. J. Redford, *Born of a Virgin: Proving the Miracle from the Gospels*, St Paul's, London, 2007, 189.

[25.] John Paul II, *Vita consecrata*, nn. 89–90.

Obedience (c. 601)

The evangelical counsel of obedience requires a spirit of faith and love (not slavish abjection) in following Christ (which the commands of superiors should foster). It obliges the submission of the will to one's lawful superiors who act in the place of God 'when they issue commands, following their proper constitutions'; it involves a real obedience, but one conditional on these factors. Superiors may not command at will, much less become dictatorial over other members. All authority is to be conducted in a spirit of service. Obedience then is not a contradiction of freedom, but assists the attainment of true freedom, related to objective truth and moral values.[26] Difficulties at present can lead some institutes to submerge authority and obedience in a consensus, which at times may reflect the most vociferous or the most dominant. Yet, a proper exercise of authority is needed for the common good of each institute and for that of the Church which it serves. This implies a true obedience to the legitimate commands of a person's proper superior(s), the will of God being mediated through such commands.[27] Such human authority is to facilitate service of Christ; it is above all a spiritual authority, called to respect the dignity of others and help them to overcome difficulties, a question of fidelity to the particular charism of the institute, so that all may 'think with the Church' ('sentire cum Ecclesia'). This requires obedience by the superior to Christ, to the Holy Father, to the Church's law and to the particular law of the institute, so that the superior be seen to be docile to the will of God (c. 618).[28] The fostering of dialogue, of common discernment is to help all participate in the service the institute seeks to render to the Church and to its mission, but the superior has to have the courage to take decisions necessary for the common good and should then be obeyed.[29] Obedience is not blind; quite the opposite, but it should not automatically be assumed that an individual's perspective is correct and that the superior is wrong, especially without regard to the real needs and concerns of others. A true freedom is to be found in following the will of God through such a human mediation of that will; even where a subject sees things better than the superior, perhaps after dialogue obedience shows greater charity.[30] This is not the case

---

[26.] Ibid., n. 91.
[27.] Congregation for Institutes of Consecrated Life and Societies of Apostolic Life, Instruction, *Faciem tuam, Domine, requiram*, 11 May 2008, n. 9.
[28.] Ibid., nn. 13–14.
[29.] Ibid., n. 20.
[30.] Ibid., nn. 20, 26.

where what is commanded is immoral or is manifestly in contrast to God's will or the laws of the institute; then there is no duty to obey.[31]

The manner in which members of each institute are to observe the evangelical counsels is to be laid down in the constitutions of the institute. These apply to the institute as a whole; each house in the institute will usually be governed by particular statutes, which are to be in accordance with the Church's general law (as in the Code) and with the institute's constitutions. These are to define the way in which the counsels are to be observed on the basis of the character of each institute, its proper purposes and its way of life (c. 598 § 1), their members then to live their consecrated life on the basis of their proper law (constitutions and statutes) to strive for the perfection of their state of life (c. 598 § 2), which those laws are to foster and their observance should facilitate.

Fraternal Love (cc. 573 § 2, 602)

One of the developments in the Code is the association of the evangelical counsels with the community of love of God and of neighbour, which they are to serve and to promote. It remarks on the 'charity to which they lead' (c. 573 § 2); the counsels are not an end in themselves. The Code attaches a canon on fraternal charity (c. 602) to those on the counsels (cc. 598–601). It highlights the 'fraternal life (or way of life) proper to each institute', which is an instance of subsidiarity, since the community life of enclosed religious is bound to differ from that of more active congregations and again from institutes where many live and work as individuals, where some form of fraternal care and action needs to be built in. It is to 'unite all the members in a special family in Christ' (in prayer and cooperation with one another). It is to be defined in such a way that it proves of mutual assistance to members to fulfil their vocation, rooted and based in charity, and it is to be an example of reconciliation in Christ.

Different Types of Institute of Consecrated Life (c. 577)

The religious life is not the only type of consecrated life, but it is one special form of that life. All institutes of consecrated life 'follow Christ more closely' (c. 577), an allusion to the 'new and further consecration' (c. 573 § 1), by 'praying' (contemplative institutes), 'announcing the Kingdom' (apostolic institutes), 'doing good among people' (institutes of good works or certain types of apostolic institutes), 'living among them in the world, but doing the will of God' (secular institutes –

---

31. Ibid., n. 27.

c. 577). The Code seeks to provide ways in which both aspects of the life of any institute of consecrated life (what they have in common with one another in their fundamental vocation and mission and what is specific to the vocation and function of each) can be nurtured. For each institute it promotes a 'just autonomy', reflecting subsidiarity, linked to the specific gifts of God and to the specific vocation of its members (cc. 578, 586 § 1, 587 § 1). An example of this is that the law of each institute is to specify how the evangelical counsels are to be observed by members, according to the institute's purpose and function (cc. 573 § 2, 574 § 2, 598 § 1–2).

The Code distinguished various forms of consecrated life. There remains some lack of clarity since anchorites or hermits and virgins (cc. 603–604) appear in the norms governing all institutes of consecrated life, even though these groups are not part of any institute, except that some hermits may be attached to monasteries. *Vita consecrata* lists religious orders of monks and hermits (n. 6), contemplative institutes, institutes dedicated to apostolic work, subdivided into those of apostolic life or of missionary activity through public vows and a stable form of life, including mendicant (begging) orders, secular institutes, other associations of consecrated persons (such as orders of widows and of hermits), orders of widows being one of the new forms of consecrated life (c. 605) and clerical secular institutes (of diocesan clergy consecrated to Christ by the practice of the evangelical counsels). It notes societies of apostolic life, without commitment to the counsels, living them in different ways, but living the common life, as well as 'those individuals who give themselves to God most intimately in their heart by means of a special consecration'.[32] To discern whether new entities come from the Spirit and meet church criteria for the consecrated life, bishops should assess the life, orthodoxy and spirituality of the founders, together with their understanding of what the Church is, as well as the suitability of candidates for ordination, if applicable. A commission has been set up to help with this evaluation.[33]

Finally, the Code does not use the term 'charisms', since such particular gifts are not directly a matter of legal regulation, although there is a relationship between charism and institution in the Church and even though the same Holy Spirit guides both.[34] To avoid 'charism' being interpreted too individualistically, John Paul II presents it in

---

[32.] John Paul II, *Vita consecrata*, nn. 2, 6, 8–11.
[33.] John Paul II, *Vita consecrata*, n. 62; cf Gambari, *I religiosi*, 22–5.
[34.] *Lumen gentium*, n. 12.

an institutional context, as the specific purpose of its founder and its specific spiritual or apostolic character, which ought to guide the institute and be reflected in its constitutions and statutes.[35]

3. Institutes of Consecrated Life and Societies of Apostolic Life: Particular Norms

After examining canonical norms which apply to all institutes of consecrated life, we turn now to particular norms which apply to different types of institute of consecrated life and to societies of apostolic life. Most canons here deal with religious institutes of consecrated life, fewer applying to secular institutes, and fewer still directly to societies of apostolic life. Matters treated include the erection and governance of institutes and societies, admission, formation, and rights and duties of members, and separation from these bodies.

a. Definitions and Distinctions in Institutes and Societies

In all institutes of consecrated life members profess the evangelical counsels. Distinctions have to be made between religious and secular institutes and within religious institutes between monastic and mendicant, between contemplative and apostolic. Secular institutes profess the evangelical counsels, but live them from within the world, not apart from it. Societies of apostolic life have the apostolate at the heart of their life and work; some observe the evangelical counsels in some way as part of their way of life. We see these key distinctions and their implications in the canons in Tables 9C and 9D.

The Code gives special attention to religious institutes because of their importance in the history of the Church, their numbers in relation to the other groupings and their nature. The religious life is presented as one form of the consecrated life and is no longer simply identified with it.[36] The language of total dedication (consecration, sacrifice of the whole person, of themselves, of their whole existence) indicates the religious life, as a particularly striking form of the continuous worship which the Church as a whole offers to God in Christ. It is not a life of isolation, not just because of common vows and living, but because this Christocentric religious consecration is both a divine act and a wholehearted human act of perfect worship or self-giving

---

[35.] John Paul II, *Vita consecrata*, n. 36; Ghirlanda, 'Vita consacrata', *Nuovo dizionario de diritto canonico*, 1142–3.

[36.] Gambari, *I religiosi*, 108–9.

to God in Christ, a union analogous to marriage, 'consummated' in the total self-giving to God, being also an eschatological sign of the eternal values of the Gospel.[37]

In secular institutes members do not take public vows, nor do they make a public profession of the evangelical counsels, but they truly profess the counsels which they undertake to observe (cc. 713 § 1, 714), a profession received in the name of the Church and they give public witness to the counsels in their consecrated life. Recognition of these professions of the counsels by the Church is considered by some to involve a kind of 'public' status for the professions themselves.[38] Members are to live the consecrated life in the world (c. 713 § 1), not separated from it. Lay members are to do this sharing the Church's mission 'in the world and from within the world', by their witness and their fidelity to their consecration, animating the world by Gospel values, cooperating with the church community (c. 713 § 2). Clerical members witness to their consecration within the body of priests (*presbyterium*) and further the sanctification of the world by their sacred ministry (c. 713 § 3). Although not bound to the common life (some live alone or in families), some members of secular institutes live in common, some in fraternal groups (c. 714).[39]

Members of societies of apostolic life neither take vows nor make a profession, even if some of them undertake to live by the evangelical counsels. There is a bond, which is neither a vow nor another type of sacred bond, as in the consecrated life, even though they resemble the latter, but one 'defined in the constitutions' (c. 731 § 2). However, in these societies all commit themselves to the common living in fraternal charity and to the apostolic purpose of their society, again as specified in the constitutions of each society (c. 731 § 1).

b. Houses of Religious Institutes and of Societies of Apostolic Life

The establishment ('erection') of houses is not a feature of secular institutes, since they are not obliged to the common life. In the case of religious institutes, monastic, mendicant or apostolic, a house of the institute (order, congregation) or society may be established in certain

---

[37.] Ibid., 109.

[38.] J-P. Durand, 'Les instituts de vie consacrée et les sociétés de vie apostolique' in P. Valdrini *et al.*, *Droit canonique*, 2nd edn, Dalloz, Paris, 1999, 67–104 at 80.

[39.] J. A. Coriden, *An Introduction to Canon Law*, 2nd revised edn, Paulist, New York, Mahwah, 2004, 100.

Table 9C

Religious and Secular Institutes / Societies of Apostolic Life

Religious Institutes of Consecrated Life	Secular Institutes of Consecrated Life	Societies of Apostolic Life

Religious life 'as:
– a *consecration* of the whole person, manifests the *marriage* established by God as a sign of the world to come. Religious … *consummate* a full gift of themselves as a *sacrifice* … to God, so that their *whole existence* becomes *a continuous worship of God* in charity.'   (c. 607 § 1)
	'A *secular institute* is an: institute of *consecrated life,* in which
	  Christ's *faithful*
	  living in the world
	  strive for the perfection
	  of charity and
	  contribute to the
	  sanctification of the world
	  especially *from within.'*
	                   (c. 711)
		'Societies of the Apostolic Life: resemble institutes of consecrated life.' Members do not take religious vows, but pursue the Society's *proper apostolic purpose,* living a *fraternal life* in *common,* striving for the *perfection of charity,* by observing the constitutions.'
		                (c. 731 § 1)

'A religious institute is one in which members' according to their own law, make 'public vows', permanent or temporary (renewable) and who 'live a fraternal life in common'.
            (c. 607 § 2)
	'Members … are to express and exercise their special consecration *in apostolic activity, …* (endeavouring) to permeate everything with an apostolic spirit …' (c. 713 § 1)
	Lay members share the Church's mission in the world and 'from within the world' by
	  witness to Christian life
	  fidelity to consecration
	  help directing temporal affairs
	  to God
	  animating the world with the Gospel;
	all according to 'the secular manner of life proper to them'. (c. 713 § 2)
	Clerical members, by the witness of their consecrated lives, especially in the priesthood, support their colleague by distinctive charity and further the sanctification of the world through their sacred ministry.
	                (c. 713 § 3)
		Among (these societies) are some whose members 'through a bond defined in the constitutions, undertake to live the evangelical counsels.'
		                (c. 731 § 2)

'The public witness religious are to give to Christ and to the Church involves separation from the world, proper to the character and purpose of each institute.' (c. 607 § 3)	The Constitutions are to define the sacred bonds by which the evangelical counsels are undertaken by the institute. (c. 712)	

Table 9D

Schema of the Canons 573–746

Book II of the Code. The People of God

Part III: Institutes of the Consecrated Life and Societies of Apostolic Life

Section I: Institutes of Consecrated Life cc. 573–730
– General Norms for all Institutes cc. 573–606
– Religious Institutes cc. 607–709
– Secular Institutes cc. 710–730
Section II: Societies of Apostolic Life cc. 731–746

	Institutes of Consecrated Life		
	Religious Institutes	Secular Institutes	Societies of Apostolic Life
Definition	c. 607	cc. 710–716	cc. 731–732 (cc. 578–602, 606)
Houses	cc. 608–616		c. 733
Governance (cc. 617–633)	cc. 617–640 cc. 708–709	cc. 716–718	cc. 733–734, 741
Admission	cc. 641–645	cc. 720–721	c. 735 (cc. 642–645)
Formation	cc. 646–661	cc. 722–725	c. 736
Rights and Duties	cc. 662–672	cc. 711–712, 715, 719	cc. 737–740, 743
Apostolate	cc. 673–683	cc. 713–714	c. 737 (cc. 679–683)
Separation	cc. 684–704	cc. 726–730	cc. 742–746 (cc. 694–704)
Religious raised to the Episcopate	cc. 705–707		
Conferences of Major Superiors	cc. 708–709		

circumstances and, when this is done, this entails particular rights and duties. A 'lawfully established' religious house is required to make possible the life of religious in community (cc. 608, 610 § 1). This has to be done under the authority of a lawfully designated superior, with the prior written consent of the diocesan bishop, by the competent authority according to the constitutions (c. 609 § 1). It has to be able to provide for the needs of the members of the house: their material sustenance, well-being, as well as the conduct of the religious life in that place, which implies that the number of members must make that life tenable in the house (c. 610 § 2), and, where it is a house of cloistered nuns, with the prior permission of the Apostolic See (c. 609 § 2). Although the consent of the diocesan bishop is necessary, once that consent is given, this entitles the institute by law to have in that house an oratory in which the Eucharist is to be celebrated and also reserved, so that the Eucharist may truly be the centre of the community and of its life (c. 608), to live a life according to the character and purpose of the institute (c. 611), to engage in works of the institute, following any conditions attached to the consent (c. 611), but specific permission from the bishop is needed for works in the house not specific to the character and purpose of the institute (c. 612). Clerical religious institutes (those presuming the exercise of sacred orders) may have a church and exercise sacred ministries, according to law (c. 611), that is only with the consent of the diocesan bishop, which he may give only after consulting the council of priests and rectors of neighbouring churches to verify that this would be for the good of souls (c. 1215 § 3). Although such institutes have a right to have a church (c. 611, n. 3), the conditions here relate to their having a church in a particular place, in which they conduct public functions. The essential features of these canons are reflected in the norm applying to societies of apostolic life, whose competent authority (major superior) may establish a local community and a house, with the prior written consent of the diocesan bishop (c. 733 § 1). Once that consent is given, it carries with it automatically (by virtue of this canon) the right for the community of the society in that house to have an oratory in which the Eucharist is celebrated and reserved (c. 733 § 2).

The purpose of these norms is to ensure both that the diocesan bishop is properly involved in the establishment of houses within the territory for which he has responsibility and in permitting any works which are not of the institute but which pertain to his pastoral responsibility and also to ensure that there is no interference in the work of the institute or in its operations within the house.

The erection of a religious house is a 'juridical act', an administrative act with juridical effects (cc. 124–128). In particular such acts are invalid if, when consent is required, it is not obtained; consent means the agreement of the person(s) concerned and not merely their advice or opinion, as with consultation (c. 127). Since the act, as here, concerns the external forum, it must be in writing (c. 37). Hence the prior, written consent of the bishop of the diocese within whose bounds the house is to be established, is necessary for the validity of the act of erecting a religious house (cc. 611–612), even if the institute is of pontifical right (and for houses of societies of apostolic life, c. 733). The act must also conform to the constitutions which govern the institute or society.[40]

The suppression of a house, in the case of an autonomous house of monks or canons regular (such as Augustinians), is a matter for a general chapter of the order (cc. 613, 616 § 3). For the suppression of a house of any other religious institute or of a community of apostolic life it requires that the relevant superior consult the diocesan bishop, whose consent is not necessary (cc. 616 § 1, 733; 127), although only the Holy See can suppress the sole house of an institute (c. 616 § 2) or the house of an autonomous monastery of cloistered nuns (cc. 614, 616 § 4).

c. Governance

Superiors

Superiors have their authority 'from God through the ministry of the Church' (c. 617). This is to be exercised for the good of the Church and of the community, in a spirit of service, with reverence for the dignity of the person, so as to foster voluntary obedience, but still leaving the superior with real authority to make decisions (cc. 617–618).[41] Superiors (moderators) are at three main levels: for a house (now sometimes called 'local superior'), for a collection of houses in a province ('provincial', sometimes called 'regional superior') and for the institute as a whole ('general' or 'superior general' or 'supreme moderator'). Their authority is to be exercised according to the law (universal, mostly in the Code), of the institute as a whole (constitutions) and of the local house (statutes), according to their office,

---

[40.] J. Beyer, *Le nouveau droit ecclesial: Commentaire du Code de droit canonique: livre II – troisième partie: Le droit de la vie consacrée*, Tardy, Paris, 1988, 16–18.

[41.] Congregation for Institutes of Consecrated Life and for Societies of Apostolic Life, Instruction, *Faciem tuam, Domine, requiram*, n. 28.

lawfully held (cc. 620–622). According to the nature of each society of apostolic life, governance is to follow cc. 617–633, as determined by the constitutions of each society (c. 734), which implies local, regional or provincial and general levels, where societies were extended across parts of the world. For diocesan societies, the superior of the main house relates to that diocesan bishop, as superior general of the society.

Superiors are to be appointed or elected, according to universal law (the Code) and their particular law (constitutions), reflecting their purpose and charism. No one can be appointed or elected validly as superior unless they have been perpetually or definitively professed for a time determined by their own law (c. 623). Elections for major superiors are presided over by the bishop of the principal house and the election of other superiors has to be confirmed by the major superior before the appointment is valid (cc. 625, 164–179). In election to office and in other appointments to office, the good of the Church and of the institute is to be observed, avoiding all lobbying or other abuse (c. 626). It is still possible for some superiors to be elected for life (c. 625), which can avoid dangers of instability and pressure groups.[42] The present Code allows superiors to be elected more than twice in succession, if the constitutions so provide.[43]

For secular institutes, the indications are vague and largely left to particular law. Members are to play an 'active role' in the institute, being 'united with other members of the same institute' (c. 716). The constitutions are to determine periods of time, but the implications of c. 717 are that there are to be moderators in office for a specified time and a supreme moderator of each institute, who must have been 'definitively incorporated into the institute' (c. 717 § 2). Definitive incorporation is not specified here for other moderators, but particular law would probably require it. Moderators are to protect the spirit of the institute and foster the active participation of members (c. 717 § 3). For societies of apostolic life, their constitutions are to specify methods of governance always according to cc. 617–640, so that what is said for religious institutes needs to operate here too (c. 734).

For the exercise of authority superiors are to have councils. Apart from what is in the Code, their own laws are to lay down when consent is necessary and when consultation is necessary for the validity of their acts, something often required for certain types of financial transaction (cc. 627, 127). Since authority is to be exercised as service, with respect for the members and for the character of the institute (c.

---

42. Beyer, *Le droit de la vie consacrée*, 38–40.
43. Durand, 'Les instituts de vie consacrée ...', 90,

617), there are to be regular visitations, in which all individuals are to have free access and the right to express their true opinion without pressure or interference (c. 628). Superiors are never to jeopardize the freedom of conscience of members in respect of the sacrament of reconciliation or spiritual direction (c. 630 § 1). They are to ensure that there are suitable confessors available besides the ordinary confessors required, after consulting the community and with the approval of the diocesan bishop; for orders of enclosed nuns confessors are designated, but there is no obligation on members to make use of such ordinary confessors. No superior is to hear the confession of a subject unless freely asked to do so (c. 630 § 2–4), nor is a superior to ask a member to reveal his or her conscience to the superior (c. 630 § 5). These norms reflect the Code's concern to distinguish the internal and external fora. These regulations apply also to societies of apostolic life, since cc. 617–640 largely apply to them (c. 734). Members are subject to their own moderators (superiors), according to the constitutions and to the diocesan bishop in matters of public worship, care of souls, and other apostolic works which are not specific to the society's apostolate, according to the constitutions (cc. 738 § 1–2).

Chapters

The word chapter comes from '*caput*' or '*capitulum*' or 'head'; general chapters and provincial chapters of institutes are to take place. (It came to be used for headings, sub-divisions of books, often written by monks; chapter rooms in monasteries were rooms where 'chapters' from the 'rule' were read).[44] Chapters are to operate according to the particular laws of their institutes, having delegates elected from the various houses, meeting usually every three or six years, to elect superiors general, to ensure that the 'charism' or patrimony of the institute is maintained and to state how they may be preserved and developed (c. 578), to consider the needs of the institute as a whole and for particular areas, including erection or suppression of provinces (cc. 631–633). A general chapter is the main authority for the institute, under the Church's supreme authority; this chapter is to be chosen so that it truly represents the whole institute (c. 631 § 1). Once more subsidiarity is at work, in that the detail of the operations of chapters is to be settled by the constitutions of the various institutes.

[44.] Coriden, *An Introduction to Canon Law*, 102–3.

Financial Administration

This section (cc. 634–640) applies the norms of Book V of the Code to religious institutes of consecrated life. As juridical persons, institutes have the right to acquire, possess, administer and alienate temporal goods, in line with the purposes for which the Church has use of such goods, but, given their vocation and the counsels they profess, they are to avoid the appearance of luxury or gain (cc. 634–635, 640). There are to be financial administrators at all levels (local, regional, general), distinct from the superiors under whose direction they are to work (c. 636 § 1) – the principle of the separation of the powers can be seen here – regular accounts being provided (cc. 636 § 2, 637). Their own laws are to detail the limits of ordinary administration. Contracts, especially leading to debts, are not to be made where the institute cannot afford to repay them (cc. 637–638). The bursar usually has the power to undertake ordinary acts of administration, but the superior's consent, often with the advice or consent of his or her council would often be necessary for extra-ordinary acts. Further restrictions can be placed on ordinary acts to prevent undue expenditure without reference on acquisitions, repairs and such like.[45] For secular institutes, the norms of Book V of the Code and the institute's own laws apply, proper law defining responsibilities, especially financial, of the institute to its members (c. 718). Societies of the apostolic life, as juridical persons, may acquire, possess, administer and alienate goods, according to cc. 638–640 and their own law (c 741 § 1). Individual members may acquire, possess, administer and alienate goods, according to their own law (c. 741 § 2).

d. Admission and Initial Formation

The process for admission into an institute or into a society is concerned with the discernment by both the candidate and those responsible for formation of a divine vocation to the state of life in the particular institute or society.

Admission

The right to admit candidates to a religious institute belongs to its major superior (c. 641), to secular institutes to the major superiors with their councils (c. 720), both according to their own laws, and to a society of apostolic life, according to its own laws (c. 732).

Admission to the novitiate of an institute of consecrated life

---

45. Durand, 'Les instituts de la vie consacrée ...', 98–9.

(c. 642–645) or to probation in a society of apostolic life (c. 735) requires the following. For liceity no one may be admitted unless they have reached the required minimum age (particular law), are healthy,* have the right disposition, * have sufficient maturity to undertake the life of the institute or society, * (*qualities which may be established by experts, without damaging reputations (c. 220) c. 642), consulting the local ordinary if it is a secular cleric, and provided they do not have debts which they cannot meet (c. 644). For validity the following may not be admitted (c. 643): those not yet seventeen years old (1°), a spouse while the marriage lasts (2°), one already bound either by a sacred bond in another institute of consecrated life or admitted in another society of apostolic life (3°), one entering through force, fear or deceit (4°), one who has concealed his/her incorporation into an institute of consecrated life or society of apostolic life (5°). Documentary evidence required includes: proof of baptism by an authentic baptismal certificate (c. 645 § 1), proof of confirmation by an authentic baptismal certificate, which includes the details of the confirmation or a separate document proving confirmation (c. 645 § 1), a letter of free status, no more than six months old or a baptismal certificate which includes a statement that there is no evidence in the baptismal register of marriage, ordination or profession of vows, and letters of freedom from all the parishes in which the person has lived since the age of sixteen (the minimal canonical age for marriage for males) or fourteen (the minimal canonical age for females – c. 1083), stating that the person has never been married, ordained or perpetually professed, according to the registers of the parish and from the knowledge of the parish priest (c. 645 § 1). Also required is testimony from the local ordinary for those who had been clerics, from the major superior for those who had been clerics or others in an institute of consecrated life or society of apostolic life, from the rector for those who had been seminarians (c. 645 § 2). An institute's own law can require further proofs before granting admission to a novitiate (c. 645 § 3) or a society's own law can require additional proofs before granting admission to probation (cc. 735, 645 § 3). Superiors can seek other information, even secretly (c. 645 § 4).

In some ways these norms are similar to requirements for admission to seminaries. Proof of sacramental initiation is necessary, since baptism is the 'gateway to the other sacraments' (c. 849) and no other sacrament can be validly administered to anyone if they have not been validly baptized (c. 842 § 1). Such proof is needed not only where a person wishes to receive Holy Orders, but also where the desire is to join the institute, without ordination; full sacramental initiation into the Church as Catholics is required before the consecration of baptism and of confirmation can be deepened in the consecrated life. The other proofs are needed to verify the suitability of the person to be a candidate, to prevent those rejected or expelled from other institutes or societies or seminaries from inveigling their way into others and perhaps doing damage. Of course, there may be good reasons why someone may have left a previous institution, in good standing, and a further reflection on vocation has led them to make this request; then the documentary proofs will assist in making possible a positive response. For societies of apostolic life, the details of the procedures for admission are to be found in the particular constitutions of each society, but the norms for religious institutes in cc. 642–645 are always to be followed (c. 735).

Novitiate and Probation (cc. 646–653, 735)

A novitiate (for new candidates, usually after a time of 'postulancy' or asking to be considered) lasts usually for one year to ponder their own vocation, the vocation of the institute, the manner of life of the institute and their suitability; it includes 'testing' (c. 646), which is not to be arbitrary. It is to attend to theological and spiritual preparation, reflection on the life and purpose of the institute, the virtues, the evangelical counsels and the way they are lived in the institute and it should promote a love of the Church (c. 652 § 1–2). For validity a novitiate in a religious institute of consecrated life must take place in a house of the institute, designated for a novitiate, be for twelve months and not more than two years in the novitiate community (c. 648 § 1–3, cf. c. 656 § 2). A novice may leave or be dismissed, according to the institute's laws (c. 653 § 1). At the end of the novitiate a novice may make temporary profession of the counsels or may be dismissed as unsuitable or may have the novitiate extended by no more than six months, after which a decision must be made (c. 653 § 2).

In a secular institute the major superior (moderator) with his/ her council is to admit persons temporarily or perpetually (definitively) to assuming the sacred bonds of the evangelical counsels (c. 720). A person cannot be admitted validly to initial probation who is not yet of majority age (eighteen), is bound by sacred bonds in another institute of consecrated life or been admitted to a society of apostolic life, is a spouse while the marriage lasts (c. 721 § 1), lacks the maturity needed to live the life of the institute properly (c. 721 § 3), does not meet other requirements established by the constitutions for validity (c. 721 § 2). Initial probation of not less than two years (c. 722 § 3) is a time for the candidate and those responsible to discern a divine vocation, for training in the spirituality and life of the institute (c. 722 § 1), including how to apply this to the particular apostolate of the institute (c. 722 § 2). After this the person may leave the institute or must do so, if judged unsuitable, or may be admitted to a first incorporation in the institute (c. 723 § 1).

Probation in a society of apostolic life is determined by particular law and has a similar purpose to a novitiate in an institute of consecrated life; it is doctrinal and spiritual and must introduce candidates to the way of life of the society and to its mission (c. 735 § 1–3). Sometimes there is a period of first probation, analogous to the novitiate for institutes of consecrated life, and then a further period, after which the candidate is to be incorporated definitively into the society or dismissed, as determined by the society's constitutions.

One apparent oversight of the Code is that it does not require explicitly that there be a spiritual director for novices. There is the general norm, already noted, that those in religious institutes should have confessors available, members being free to choose a suitable one and superiors being forbidden to compromise the internal forum in respect either of confessors or of spiritual directors (c. 630). While it may be that the Code does not specify that a specific appointment be made of a spiritual director, clearly the implications of c. 630 and of the character of the novitiate is such that novices should have access to a suitable spiritual director and the prohibition against compromising the internal forum should extend to the novice master.[46] The same evaluation should be made about those seeking admission to a society of apostolic life and their superiors, especially during the time of their probation.

e. Profession of the Evangelical Counsels (cc. 654–658)

In a religious institute of consecrated life the novitiate, successfully completed, is followed by temporary profession by public vows of the evangelical counsels (c. 654), for no less than three and no more than six years (c. 655), unless extended by particular law in specific circumstances, but to a total of no more than nine years (c. 657 § 2). Their profession occurs through the ministry of the Church, their consecration to God, by their vows, which are public; thereby they are incorporated into the institute, giving them rights and duties, defined by law (c. 654). For validity temporary profession in a religious institute requires that the candidate be at least eighteen years old (c. 656 § 1),

---

[46.] Gambari, *I religiosi*, 239–40.

has made a valid novitiate (c. 656 § 2), admission has been granted freely and lawfully by the competent superior after a vote of his or her council (c. 656 § 3), the profession be explicit, without force, fear or deceit (c. 656 § 4) and be received by the lawful superior personally or through another (c. 656 § 5). In a religious institute of consecrated life, when the time of temporary profession, successfully completed, is followed by perpetual profession by public vows of the evangelical counsels (c. 657 § 1). This requires that the conditions of c. 656 § 3–5 obtain, that is that admission is freely granted by the lawful superior, after consulting his/her council, profession is explicit, without force, fear or deceit and is received by the lawful superior personally or through another, the person be at least twenty-one years old (c. 658 n. 1) and has already been temporarily professed for at least three years (c. 658 n. 2); perpetual profession may be anticipated by no more than three months (c. 657 § 3).

The detail of these canons shows the particular and serious level of commitment to religious consecration, the concern that there be proper and deep preparation through the novitiate both to familiarize the candidate with the life, spirituality and mission of the institute and to assess his/her suitability, with both candidate and those responsible assessing whether or not there is a divine vocation. The careful demands for the validity, even of temporary profession, underline the seriousness of this step; both candidate and superior must freely judge that this is right and the fact that force, fear and deceit which normally do not invalidate a juridical act (c. 125 § 1-2) would here precisely have an invalidating effect (c. 656 § 4; cf., c. 10) emphasizes what a major step this is.

Once the initial probation is completed for a candidate in a secular institute, he/she may be admitted to temporary incorporation by undertaking the sacred bonds of the evangelical counsels according to the institute's particular law (c. 723 § 1). This first incorporation must last for at least five years (c. 723 § 2), after which he or she may be admitted to definitive incorporation (c. 723 §), which has the same juridical effects as perpetual profession in a religious institute (c. 723 § 4) with continuing formation, human and divine (c. 724). Those in societies of apostolic life do not normally profess the evangelical counsels, although some do, according to the constitutions (c. 731 § 2).

f. Continuing Formation (cc. 659–661)

The formation of religious in doctrinal, spiritual, apostolic and practical matters, is to continue throughout the lives of all in the institute (cc. 659 § 1, 660-661), its nature and duration being laid down by the institute's own laws (c. 659 § 2). In a secular institute formation on human and divine matters continues after first incorporation (c. 724). Where there is a question of a man preparing for sacred orders, the universal law and the institute's own law, giving further specifications, apply (c. 659 § 3).

g. Incardination

Even for those in institutes of consecrated life and for those in societies of apostolic life, incardination occurs at diaconate ordination (c. 266 § 2). In a religious institute, incardination is normally into the institute itself; in a society of apostolic life, the society's own law determines whether it is into the society (usually it is) or into a diocese, in which case the inter-relationship of responsibilities is to be specified in the society's constitutions and/or statutes (cc. 736 § 1, 738 § 3). A clerical member of a secular institute is incardinated at diaconate ordination normally into the diocese, particular Church, although he could be incardinated into the secular institute itself, by a concession from the Apostolic See (c. 266 § 3). Those incardinated in a diocese are subject to the bishop in all except what pertains to the work of the institute; those incardinated in the institute are subject to him in the same way as religious (c. 715).

h. Rights and Duties of Persons in Institutes or in Societies

Religious Institutes

Spiritual

The supreme duty of all religious is the contemplation of God, divine things and constant union with him in prayer. Every day they should try to participate in the Eucharist, receive Holy Communion and adore Christ in the Blessed Sacrament. They should read and meditate on the Scriptures, pray mentally, have devotion to Our Lady, make an annual retreat (c. 663). They are to foster conversion of soul (c. 664: akin to the Benedictine vow of 'conversion of manners').

Residence and Cloister

They are to live in their own religious house (c. 665); the cloister is to be carefully and strictly observed for enclosed Orders (c. 667).

Evangelical Counsels

They are to avoid what might harm chastity (c. 666), observe perfect continence and avoid persons who might endanger their chastity and celibacy (c. 277). In regard to poverty, goods are to be ceded to others before first profession and before perpetual profession a will is to be made, if need be. All that the person acquires by work or through pensions belongs to the institute unless particular law states otherwise (c. 668). Where the nature of the institute is such that members cannot own goods at all, they are to renounce all goods before profession and, since they cannot acquire goods, any acts of theirs to the contrary are invalid (c. 668 § 4–5). As a sign of their consecration and their poverty, religious are to wear the habit; those in clerical institutes which do not have a habit are to wear clerical dress (c. 669). On obedience religious are not to undertake tasks outside their institute without permission of the lawful superior (c. 671). Religious are also bound by the duties to avoid anything unbecoming their state or what is unseemly, public offices or secular offices without permission (c. 285), active roles in political parties, trade unions, etc., unless superiors judge it necessary to defend the rights of the Church or the common good (c. 287), military service and other civil functions, taking advantage of exemptions offered (c. 289).

Formation

Formation in theology is to be continued by clerics (c. 279 § 2).

Apostolate

The primary duty is to the type of apostolate which is proper to the institute (c. 673). Hence, contemplatives can never be called on for pastoral ministries (c. 674), their apostolate is prayer, consecration. Institutes with an active apostolate have this as their primary focus; it stems from union with Christ and is to be conducted in the name of the Church and in union with the Church (c. 675). Lay institutes of men and women with corporal and spiritual works of mercy as their apostolate are to remain true to this (c. 676). Superiors and members are to preserve, but adapt the practice of the apostolate prudently, as need arises (c. 677), with cooperation between various institutes and with the diocese in the apostolate (c. 680).

Religious are subject to the bishop of the diocese in regard to the public exercise of divine worship and are to obey him sincerely (c. 678 § 1), as coordinator of apostolic works (c. 680), over works he has entrusted to religious, with written, agreed details (c. 681 § 2) and where he has made an appointment to an office, with the presentation or consent of the religious superior (c. 682). In matters concerning the institute members are subject to their proper superiors; the bishop is to insist on this (c. 678 § 2). For very grave reasons a bishop can refuse to allow a member of a religious institute to remain in his diocese, if the superior had been informed and failed to act; the Holy See is to be informed immediately (c. 679). Where the bishop is aware of abuses and the superior has failed to heed a warning, the bishop can act himself (c. 683).

Secular Institutes

Members do not change their status; they remain clerical or lay (c. 711). Constitutions are to define the obligations of the sacred bonds assumed in the consecration (c. 712). Lay members are to evangelize from within the world, directing temporal affairs and spreading the spirit of the Gospel in the world, cooperating with the Church as a whole (c. 713 § 2). Clerical members are to cooperate with the *presbyterium*, giving witness there to their consecration and furthering the sanctification of the world by their sacred ministry (c. 713 § 3). All are to live ordinary lives alone, in families, in groups in the world, according to their constitutions (c. 715). Members are to play an active part in their institute and are to foster unity and fraternity (c. 716). They are to be faithful to their vocation in Christ, their apostolate, prayer, reading Scripture, an annual retreat and other exercises, the (daily) Eucharist is to be the centre of their lives, confession and spiritual direction, which they may seek, if they wish, from their moderators (c. 719).

Societies of Apostolic Life

Incorporation includes rights and duties defined in the constitutions, the society being responsible for leading members in their vocation (c. 737). They are subject to their superiors, according to their constitutions, to the diocesan bishop in respect of public worship, care of souls and works of the apostolate not specific to the society (c. 738 § 1–2). Where a clerical member is incardinated in the diocese, the details of the relationship are to be agreed in writing (c. 738 § 3). They are bound by the common obligations of clerics, if they are clerics (c. 739; cf., cc. 273–289). They are to live in a lawfully constituted house/community and observe the common life of the society, according to their own law (c. 740). They have the right to acquire and dispose of their own goods, but whatever comes to them in regard to the society belongs to the society (c. 741 § 2).

i. Separation from the Institutes and Societies

There are three basic ways of parting from an institute of consecrated life or society of apostolic life, other than by dying:

Transfer

Perpetually professed members cannot transfer to another institute or society without the permission of the two major superiors, after each has consulted their respective councils (c. 684 § 1, cf., c. 745 on members of societies of apostolic life); after a probationary period in the new institute, if one is not professed or admitted, he/she is to return to the original institute (c. 684 § 2). Where this is a member of a society of apostolic life, he may return to the original society before definitive incorporation into the new one (c. 744). To transfer from one autonomous monastery to another of the same institute, the permission of the major superior of the new monastery, having consulted the chapter, is enough; no new profession is required (c. 684 § 3). To transfer from a religious institute to a secular institute or to a society of apostolic life or to transfer from a secular institute or society of apostolic life to a religious institute, the permission of the Holy See is needed (c. 685). In a time of vocational crisis for some institutes, care in evaluating and in forming one who wishes to transfer is important, as are financial adjustments, such as their wills, if transfer occurs. The provisions relate to perpetually professed, since those temporarily professed not intending to remain in an institute should not renew their profession.[47]

Departure

Those temporarily professed may leave before perpetual profession or definitive admission (cc. 686, 726). They must leave who are not accepted (lawfully) for further profession or definitive admission. Temporary indults of exclaustration can be granted by the relevant superior for grave reasons for a temporary absence from the institute (cc. 686–687, 727 § 1). Permanent departure can be granted for the perpetually professed by the competent authority, with dispensation from profession (c. 692), or for definitively incorporated by indult (c. 743). If the man is a cleric, he cannot obtain this indult until he has another bishop who has accepted him; he is incardinated in the new

---

[47]. Cf. F. G. Morissey, 'The Transfer of Religious and the Place of the Novititate', *Canon Law Newsletter*, 82, June 1990, 62–4; R. McDermott, 'Transfer Canons 684–685', Ibid., 64–9.

diocese after five years by virtue of the law (c. 693, 727 § 2, 743). Rights and duties cease once an indult has been issued lawfully (cc. 692, 728, 743).

Dismissal

A permanently professed religious who loses the Catholic faith or who attempts even a civil marriage is dismissed by virtue of the law itself (c. 694). For grave crimes against persons – external sins against the sixth commandment (c. 1395 § 1), sexual crimes against minors (c. 1395 § 2), murder or other grave damage to persons through fraud, force or fear (c. 1397), procured abortion (c. 1398), a member must normally be dismissed (c. 695 § 1), if these are grave, external, imputable, and judicially proven (c. 695 § 2) or for serious offences against the counsels or way of life of the institute, where these are similarly established (cc. 696 § 1, 697, 699–704). Analogous procedures apply to those in secular institutes (c. 729) and societies of apostolic life (c. 742).

4. Conclusion

After considering the structures of the Church in the longest book of the Code, we turn next to its teaching function in a much briefer book.

Chapter 7

The Teaching Function
of the Church
(Book III of the Code)

1. Introduction

Much of what we have seen so far has concerned the ruling function of the Church, not surprisingly in a study of law. In this chapter we examine the Code's treatment of the teaching function of the Church, by which it seeks to transmit faithfully the revelation of Jesus Christ. This relates to the Church's work of preaching, evangelizing and catechizing and to its teaching institutions. We have noted the theological approach to canon law which focuses on 'word' and 'sacrament', and on 'communion'. The structure of the Code reflects this; after the People of God in Book II, it treats the 'word' or teaching function in Book III and 'sacrament' or sanctifying function in Book IV, the ruling function appearing in all sections of the Code, although the criticism has been levelled that 'word' and 'sacrament' are juxtaposed rather than integrated in the way the Council's liturgical reforms had intended.[1] It is to the role of the law in regard to the 'word', the Gospel of Christ, that we now turn.

2. The Preliminary Canons

a. An Analysis of the Key Canon (c. 747)

The key canon for Book III of the Code (c. 747) indicates the main features of the Church's teaching function ('*munus*') in Book III (Table 10). First of all, the Church's right to preach and teach the Gospel is asserted as being 'inherent' (c. 747 § 1) and that of proclaiming

---

[1] L. Gerosa, *Le droit de l'Église*, St Paul, Luxembourg, 1998, 149.

Table 10

The Teaching Function of the Church

Canon 747 § 1

'It is the *obligation* and *inherent right* of the Church
   independent of any *human authority*
      to *preach* the *Gospel to all peoples*
         using for this purpose even its own means of social
           communication,

for it is *to the Church* that *Christ the Lord*
   entrusted the *deposit of faith*
      so that, by the *assistance* of the *Holy Spirit*, it might

         – conscientiously *guard revealed truth,*
         – *more intimately penetrate* it and
         – *faithfully* – *proclaim* and
              – *expound it.*'

Canon 747 § 2

'The *Church* has the *right always* and *everywhere*

   – to *proclaim moral principles*, even of the social order, and
   – to make *judgments* about any human situation

     insofar as this is *required* by

        fundamental rights or
        the *salvation of souls.*'

principles and judgments about moral matters is asserted as applying 'always and everywhere' (c. 747 § 2). The purpose of these asser- tions is to reiterate the Church's divine origin and its divinely given right and duty to spread the Gospel, which are not derived from human governments which, therefore, have no right to prevent the Church from discharging this role, fundamental to her existence and mission. This statement is said in part to reflect the '*ius publicum eccle- siasticum*' (ecclesiastical public law) and the Church's claim to be a 'perfect society' ('*societas perfecta*'), with the right to its own laws in a way which is analogous to the functioning of states. What this canon certainly does is to insist upon the core responsibility of all incorp- orated through baptism into the Church (the faithful) to spread the Gospel of Christ (cc. 204 § 2, 208–211).

The primary aspect of this responsibility is the proclamation of the 'deposit of faith', entrusted to the Church 'by Christ the Lord'. This means the 'full and living Gospel', of 'the words and deeds of Jesus ... the fullness of revelation', contained in and transmitted by the 'written books' (Scripture) and 'unwritten traditions'.[2] The task of proclaiming this living Gospel also explains the Magisterium's duty to guard revealed truth, penetrating it more intimately, and proclaim- ing and expounding it faithfully (c. 747 § 1).[3]

The two distinct paragraphs of c. 747 reflect the distinction between 'revealed truth' and its implications. Revealed truth includes moral truth, but some moral truth might be of natural moral law rather than revealed; nevertheless, as the second paragraph of this canon indicates, the responsibility of the Church's Magisterium extends to these areas too.[4] The assistance of the Holy Spirit is always at issue here; that assistance is of such a type that, in certain conditions, it operates as a guarantee that the exercise of Magisterium in regard to a

---

[2.] Second Vatican Council, Dogmatic Constitution on Divine Revelation, *Dei Verbum*, nn. 2, 7. Cf. H. Denzinger and A. Schönmetzer (eds), Decree on Sacred Books and on received traditions, Council of Trent, *Enchiridion symbolorum, definitionum et declarationum de rebus fidei et morum*, 36th edn, Herder, Barcelona, Freiburg-im-Breisgau, Rome, 1976, n. 1501; cf. J. Neuner and J. Dupuis (eds), *The Christian Faith in the Doctrinal Documents of the Catholic Church*, 2nd edn, Mercier, Dublin, Cork, 1976, n. 210, and the Dogmatic Constitution on the Catholic faith, '*Dei Filius*', First Vatican Council, Denzinger-Schönmetzer, Enchirdion symbolorum, n. 3006; cf. Neuner and Dupuis, *The Christian Faith*, n. 206.

[3.] Second Vatican Council, Dogmatic Constitution on the Church, *Lumen gentium*, n. 25.

[4.] *Lumen gentium*, n. 25; Second Vatican Council, Decree on Religious Liberty, *Dignitatis humanae*, n. 14.

precise point of faith or morals cannot be wrong. The definition of the First Vatican Council of papal infallibility, in regard to morals, did not intend to limit infallibility to mere principles of morality. The choice of 'on matters of faith or morals' (*'de rebus fidei et morum'*), rather than of 'on matters of faith and principles of morality' (*'de rebus fidei et principiis morum'*), was intended partly to ensure that judgments on more concrete moral matters were not excluded.[5] The subject matter may involve the social questions, questions of economics, science, bioethics, yet the Magisterium's competence to teach here does not include technical scientific facts as such, but 'insofar as' their moral aspects and implications are concerned, including how they affect the basic rights of persons (c. 747 § 2). Concern about different levels of magisterial teaching by which what is revealed and transmitted is authentically interpreted by the Church's Magisterium,[6] has led to an amendment in the preliminary canons to Book III, and in the corresponding canons of the Eastern Code. These we have noted when dealing with legislation in canon law.[7]

To conclude this introduction, we may note that c. 747 § 1 has been considered to furnish a structure for the rest of Book III through four 'key words': 'announcing', 'deepening', 'expounding' and 'guarding' the deposit of faith, specifying different, but related aspects of the Church's teaching function.[8]

b. The other Preliminary Canons and the Church's Magisterium

The preliminary canons (cc. 747–755) all concern the teaching function of the Church, specifically of 'guarding' the revelation entrusted to her by Christ (c. 747 § 1). This function of the College of Bishops (cc. 330, 331, 336), is crucial for the faithful transmission of the Gospel and for the Church's mission of spreading that Gospel rather than a diluted, distorted or contrary teaching.

---

5. This is clear from the '*Relatio*' of Bishop Gasser on the reason for the expression 'on matters of faith and *morals*' ('*de rebus fidei et morum*'), rather than 'moral principles' in the text of the Dogmatic Constitution, '*Pastor aeternus*', Denzinger-Schönmetzer, *Enchiridion symbolorum*', n. 3074); cf. Neuner and Dupuis, *the Christian Faith*, n. 839; cf. G. J. Woodall, *The Competence of the Magisterium in moral matters: A reflection based upon recent writing in English*, unpublished Licence tesina, P.U.G., Rome, 1984, 14–17.
6. Second Vatican Council, *Dei Verbum*, n. 10.
7. Cf. chapter 2, pp. 64–5.
8. Gerosa, *Le droit de l'Église*, 113.

The Proclamation of the Gospel and the Act of Faith as a Free Act

The Gospel cannot be imposed upon people (c. 748 § 2).[9] Although 'error' may not have rights, 'those in error' do have rights, which stem not from concessions by governments, but from the very fact that they are human beings, created in the image and likeness of God.[10] While denying that 'truth' is a matter of personal choice or is all relative, the Second Vatican Council insisted that our God-given freedom, an 'exceptional sign of the image of God in man',[11] entails a freedom to pursue the truth, to embrace the truth as it is understood (implying neither that it is right nor that it does not matter what it is), and to live by the truth thus embraced, provided it does not involve violating the rights of others or threatening the common good.[12] The Code summarizes this teaching (c. 748 § 1) and the consequence that there be no coercion in religious belief (c. 748 § 2).[13]

The Function of the Church's Authoritative/ Authentic Magisterium

This section presupposes an understanding of ecclesiology, which cannot be detailed here. In summary, the Church is not a collection of people who happen to agree upon certain opinions, but is the community of the faithful, of those baptized in Christ and thereby incorporated into his Church (cc. 96, 204). This implies faith, the acceptance of revelation, of Christ and of all that God has revealed to us for our salvation in him.[14] Although the faithful transmission and exposition of that deposit of faith is the task of everyone in the Church, the pastors of the Church, the Pope and the bishops in communion with him (the Magisterium), have the specific task of guarding, 'authentically' interpreting, and defending this truth.[15] The specific assistance of the Holy Spirit to the Magisterium (cf. Jn. 14:16–17, 26; 16:13; 17:14–19) relates to this task, crucial for the Church's service ('*ministerium*') of the Word of God.[16] Most of the time, this task of the Pope and of the bishops in union with him is carried on by their ordinary teaching and preaching. This 'authoritative' or 'authentic' Magisterium on faith and morals helps to preserve and foster the faith of the Church,

---

9. Second Vatican Council, *Dei Verbum*, n. 5; *Dignitatis humanae*, n. 10.
10. *Dignitatis humanae*, n .1.
11. *Gaudium et spes*, n. 17.
12. *Dignitatis humanae*, n. 2.
13. Ibid., nn. 2, 10.
14. *Dei Verbum*, n. 5.
15. *Dei Verbum*, nn. 8, 10; *Lumen gentium*, nn. 24–5; *Dignitatis humamae*, n. 14.
16. *Dei Verbum*, n. 10.

to maintain all of us in the Church in that truth of Christ, found in its fullness in the Catholic Church.[17] The moral implications of the Gospel of Christ, of what is required to 'repent and believe the Good News' (Mk. 1:14–15) or 'repent and be baptized' (Acts 2:38) along with faith, are the object of magisterial teaching, as the light of revelation is associated with the moral questions of the day.[18] In the name of Christ, with his authority and with the assistance of the Holy Spirit, the Pope and bishops in union with him teach authentically on faith and morals.

The Infallible Exercise of Magisterium

Against this background, we see that the assistance of the Holy Spirit to the Pope and to the bishops of the Catholic Church in union with him takes a particular form, operating as a guarantee against error in teaching a specific point of doctrine, when infallibility is at issue. This is not at issue unless this is clear (c. 749 § 3). Following the Council, the Pope teaches infallibly when, as Pope, as supreme pastor and teacher of the universal Church, he proclaims in a definitive act a doctrine which is to be held on faith or morals (c. 749 § 1). This 'definitive act' would be '*ex cathedra*' or from the chair of Peter; he would be acting precisely as Pope, as supreme Pastor of the universal Church.

The College of Bishops also teaches infallibly in two instances. It does so when, 'gathered in Ecumenical Council, as teachers and judges in faith and morals, they definitively declare for the universal Church a doctrine to be held on faith or morals'. It does so also when, 'dispersed throughout the world', but united 'among themselves and together with the same Roman Pontiff, authentically teaching matters of faith or morals, they concur in a particular judgment ('*sententiam*') definitively to be held' (c. 749 § 2). The first involves a collegial act of the bishops, with and never apart from the Pope, by which a doctrine is defined as dogma (defined to be part of revelation) or is taught definitively (absolutely and unchangeably). The second involves not a collegial act, but that the bishops, with and never apart from the Pope, judge and teach in their ordinary teaching across the world that a specific teaching is unchangeably and absolutely to be held by all.[19]

[17.] *Lumen gentium*, n. 8.

[18.] *Gaudium et spes*, nn. 33, 43.

[19.] For a discussion of the possible application of these conditions to a moral teaching which has been much disputed, see G. J. Woodall, *Humanae vitae forty years on: A new commentary*, Family Publications, Oxford, Maryvale, Birmingham, 2008, 181–93.

The Responses due to Magisterial Teaching

The response of the faithful to the teachings of the Magisterium of the Church ought to be one of openness and of acceptance of what is taught in the name of Christ, with his authority and with the assistance of the Holy Spirit. This ought to be the disposition of those seeking to live and proclaim the Gospel. It implies a readiness (docility), religiously motivated ('*obsequium religiosum*'), to seek better to understand, to accept and to abide by the teachings given. This religious adherence of mind and will includes taking care to avoid what is incompatible with that doctrine (c. 752).

With teachings not (yet) the subject of infallible Magisterium, but part of the authoritative or authentic Magisterium, the Pope or the College of Bishops do not engage the charism of infallibility. (Individual bishops, even diocesan bishops, on their own, do not possess the charism of infallibility).[20] The Pope, the College of Bishops and individual diocesan bishops for their dioceses, in their ordinary teaching, acting with the authority and in the name of Christ, enjoy the assistance of the Holy Spirit, but not the guarantee that they could not be wrong in a particular judgment even about faith and morals. The fact that they could not be wrong does not imply that they are wrong or that they are likely to be wrong; there is a presumption of truth attaching to this level of teaching. The response of religious adherence to the teaching in mind and will, of docility, openness, readiness to accept and follow it is greater depending on: how often the teaching is repeated, the type of document (an encyclical is a teaching document) and the manner in which the teaching is expressed, for instance whether something is rejected as 'intrinsically morally wrong'.[21] Here the person's will is directed to avoiding teachings which put the integrity of the Church's revealed truth in faith or morals in danger.[22] The religious motivation involves adhering to the faith and to the Magisterium's specific teaching role.[23]

Where a doctrine on faith or morals is defined by the Magisterium to be revealed, to belong to what Christ has revealed for our good and for our salvation, the very core of the Church's faith and of its

---

20. *Lumen gentium*, n. 25.
21. Ibid. cf. Woodall, *Humanae vitae* ..., 170–5, 197–201.
22. P. Valdrini, 'La fonction de l'enseignement de l'Église' in P. Valdrini *et al.* (eds), *Droit canonique*, 2nd edn, Dalloz, Paris, 1999, 218–43, at 223–5, n. 351.
23. G. Ghirlanda, *Il diritto nella Chiesa, mistero di comunione: Compendio di diritto ecclesiale*, 4th revised edn, San Paolo, Cinisello, P.U.G., Rome, 2006, 436, n. 531.

fidelity to Christ are at issue. The same is true when what is revealed by Christ is taught by the universal, ordinary Magisterium (the Pope and the bishops in union with him, even dispersed throughout the world (c. 750 § 1).[24] The charism of infallibility in teaching which the Magisterium possesses then guarantees that what is taught is true and so a response of divine and Catholic faith due to what is revealed by Christ is then required (c. 750 § 1). Given the infallibility operative here through this special assistance of the Holy Spirit to those specific pastors exercising their apostolic office, the obedience of faith or assent of faith is the only appropriate response.[25] Here the will of the person is called to protect the integrity of the deposit of faith as such. A deliberate refusal to accept what is proclaimed in this way to be the faith of the Church would entail one of the following sins and, if the conditions for imputability and obstinacy were met, also canonical crimes (c. 1364), of apostasy (rejection of the Christian faith altogether), heresy (rejection of one or more dogmas (defined doctrines) of the Catholic faith or schism (breaking communion with the Pope or with others subject to him – c. 751). Where a doctrine on faith or morals, though not solemnly defined as part of revelation, were taught or a judgment on faith or morals made in a definitive judgment ('*sententiam*') by the Magisterium, the response due would be not just to avoid what might endanger the Church's faith; it would entail excluding, 'shunning' ('*devitare*') and 'setting aside' any opposing doctrine (c. 750 § 1).[26]

This latter category of teaching has led to an important amendment to the Code, to incorporate into the Code a level of teaching noted in the Profession of Faith and Oath of Fidelity of 1989, not detailed in the 1983 Code. What is proposed by the Church's Magisterium 'definitively' on faith or morals, even though not stated to be divinely revealed, is to be 'firmly accepted and held'.[27] These truths are 'necessarily connected to revealed truths', either for 'historical reasons' or for 'reasons of logic', in such a way as to involve the Church's deeper understanding of revealed truth.[28] In consequence, the Pope ordered that the existing c. 750 become c. 750 § 1 and that an additional paragraph be included as § 2 to state that 'everything set forth definitively by the Magisterium on faith or morals must be firmly accepted

---

[24]. John Paul II, Apostolic letter, *motu proprio, Ad tuendam fidem*, 28 May 1998, n. 2.
[25]. Ghirlanda, *Il diritto nella Chiesa ...*, 434–5, nn. 528–9.
[26]. Valdrini, 'La fonction de l'enseignement ...', 223–5, nn. 351–2.
[27]. John Paul II, *Ad tuendam fidem*, nn. 3–4.
[28]. Ibid., n. 3.

and held', what is 'required for holy keeping and faithful exposition of the deposit of faith', such that anyone who rejects such teachings 'sets himself against the teaching of the Catholic Church' (c. 750 § 2).[29] It will be noted that here too the revealed truth of the Church's faith is at stake. This additional paragraph relates to the Church's teaching mission in terms of guarding and explaining revealed truth (cf. c. 747 § 1).

In an 'Explanatory Note' attached to this 'motu proprio' examples of various types of magisterial teaching are given by the Congregation for the Doctrine of the Faith. Revealed truths include the articles of the Creed, Christological dogmas, Eucharistic dogmas, the intrinsic immorality of the direct killing of the innocent, and so on.[30] Definitively taught doctrines not (yet) defined, but connected to revealed truth by logical necessity, include priestly ordination reserved to men, the illicit nature of euthanasia, and the immorality of prostitution and fornication. Definitively taught doctrines connected to revelation for reasons of historical necessity include the legitimacy of papal election, canonization of saints, and the invalidity of Anglican orders. Authentic, non-infallibly proposed teachings are various teachings on faith and morals.[31]

Another level of magisterial teaching, sometimes overlooked, is that of the individual diocesan bishops. They are not individually infallible, but they exercise authentic Magisterium when united to the Pope and to the other bishops in communion with him, on their own as diocesan bishops, they give judgments and teaching on faith and morals. Here the deposit of faith is not so directly at issue; it is the way the bishops teach and their own authority which affect the nature of that response (c. 753). When such diocesan bishops move on to issue statements or judgments about false opinions, they are exercising their governing or ruling function, not just their teaching function. At question here is the ordering of the way in which members of the faithful promote the teaching of the Church, how their activity affects the common good of the Church; it is not so explicitly or directly a matter of the faith itself.[32] Yet, insofar as they reinforce and defend the faith and authentic doctrine, they truly exercise their teaching role. Decrees or constitutions issued by legitimate superiors are to be

---

29. Ibid., n. 4.
30. Congregation for the Doctrine of the Faith, 'Explanatory Note to "Ad tuendam fidem"', n. 11.
31. Ibid., n. 11.
32. Valdrini, 'La fonction de l'enseignement ...', 224–5, n. 352.

obeyed (c. 754), where they touch the teaching of doctrine, proscribing erroneous opinions. This concerns especially the common good of the Church and is related to the Gospel in that the communion of the Church's faith and practice is protected from being undermined, (cf. cc. 209 § 1, 212 § 1. 218, 223).

This treatment of the Magisterium's role has been quite extensive, given the complex nature of what is involved. It is there to serve the Word of God in the discharge of the mission of the Church, to spread the Gospel of Christ.[33] We now turn to other aspects of this in the Church's teaching function.

3. The Ministry of the Word

Even before the Scriptures of the New Testament were written down, the task given by the Lord to the Apostles of preaching the Good News to the whole world was at the heart of the Church's mission. It constitutes the primary function of the ministerial priest, even though celebrating the sacraments, especially the Eucharist, is his principal task.[34] People need to be evangelized before they can be admitted to the sacraments and so preaching comes first in order of time, but the priest's sanctifying function, especially in the Eucharist, is his most important and central one; it is to be treated in Book IV of the Code.

The canons of Book III on the ministry of the word reflect the fundamental need for that ministry in the Church. Since the nature of faith is both 'believing from the heart' and 'confessing with the lips' (Rom. 10:9–10), St Paul outlines what is needed for faith to arise: 'They will not believe unless they have heard of him and they will not hear of him unless they get a preacher and they will not get a preacher unless one is sent ... So faith comes from what is preached and what is preached comes from the word of Christ' (Rom. 10:14–17). Preaching, then, is indispensable to the entire mission of the Church. It is based in the Sacred Scriptures and especially in Christ himself, not as an end in itself, but to stimulate and to foster faith, faith in Christ, to open people up to his life in the believing community of the Church.

This ministry of the word is of such importance that the Code details the responsibilities of different members of the faithful in its regard. The office ('*munus*') of preaching the Gospel has been committed (the implication being committed by Christ) for the Church as a whole,

---

[33.] *Dei Verbum*, n. 10; John Paul II, Encyclical letter, *Veritatis splendor*, n. 64.
[34.] Second Vatican Council, Decree on the Life and Ministry of Priests, *Presbyterorum ordinis*, nn. 4–5.

principally to the Roman Pontiff and to the College of Bishops (c. 756 § 1), for the particular Churches entrusted to them to individual bishops who are 'moderators of the entire ministry of the word in their Churches' (c. 756 § 2), and as cooperators with the bishops, especially to parish priests, but to all priests entrusted with the pastoral care of souls, who have the duty of proclaiming the Gospel (c. 757). Deacons also serve the People of God in the ministry of the word, not independently, but in union with the bishop and his *presbyterium*, the priests of his diocese (c. 757). Those in the consecrated life give special witness to the Gospel and so the bishop calls on them to help proclaim the word (c. 758), while the lay faithful, the baptized and confirmed, are witnesses to the Gospel by their lives and can be called to cooperate with bishop and priests in the ministry of the word (c. 759).

The Pope and College of Bishops are principally responsible for the ministry of the word in the Church as a whole, recalling the universal dimension of the ministry of the bishops. Yet, diocesan bishops exercise their function as moderators of the entire ministry of the word in their dioceses in that all others, especially priests, play their part as co-operators with the bishops. The Code treats the ministry of the word in two stages: preaching and catechesis.

a. Preaching

The present law represents a very significant change from the 1917 Code, where it was stated that only the diocesan bishop could grant faculties to priests, diocesan or religious, for preaching in his territory.[35] If preaching is the primary task of the priest in the sense just explained, or as the present Code puts it 'is among their principal duties' (c. 762), priests with responsibilities of pastoral care have that faculty now by the law itself. Priests and deacons have the faculty to preach unless specifically impeded by the particular law established in a specific diocese, province or territory of an episcopal conference (c. 763), although they need the permission of the rector or religious superior to exercise that right in a specific church (cc. 764–765). Since the function of preaching is inherent in the office of bishops, they have the right to preach even in churches of congregations of pontifical right, unless the local diocesan bishop forbids it in a given case (c. 763); priests and deacons exercise their preaching ministry in collaboration with the bishop, in communion with the local Church and with the universal Church, in proclaiming what is the faith of the Church,

---

35. Benedict XV, *Codex iuris canonici*, 1917, c. 1337.

in teaching only in accordance with its doctrine, including its moral doctrine.[36] The change in the canons on preaching compared to 1917 implies that every priest should be capable of preaching the word well; it implies further that a person should not be ordained who lacks the capacity to fulfil this, one of the fundamental responsibilities of priestly ministry.

Although the laity have a duty and a right to spread the Gospel (cc. 211, 225 § 1, 230 § 3) and can at times have a role, in union with the sacred ministers, in preaching (c. 759), permission for them to preach in a church or oratory 'if in certain circumstances it is necessary' or 'if in particular cases it would be advantageous' depends on norms issued by the episcopal conference, but 'without prejudice to', in other words, not contrary to c. 767 (c. 766). In other words, since the 'most important part of preaching' is the 'homily', which is 'reserved to a priest or deacon' (c. 767 § 1), they cannot preach the homily, which is a specific aspect of preaching, one which only a sacred minister may fulfil.[37] The Bishops' Conference of England and Wales promulgated a law specifying this further, that 'The homily is always to be given by a priest or deacon. If a lay person is to speak at Mass, this should take place after the post-Communion prayer.'[38] There is to be a homily on Sundays and holydays, except for grave reason (c. 767 § 2) and it is recommended at weekday Masses where there is a good number of faithful (c. 767 § 3). Its content is to be based upon 'the sacred text', the Scriptures, is to reflect the liturgical year, is to expound the mysteries of the faith, and, more precisely translated, the 'norms of the Christian life' (c. 767 § 1). Those who preach are to proclaim above all 'what must be believed and practised for God's glory and the salvation of all' (c. 768 § 1), explaining the teachings of the Magisterium on the dignity and freedom of the human person, the unity, stability and

---

[36.] Ghirlanda, *Il diritto nella Chiesa ...*, 440–1, n. 542.

[37.] Cf. 'The Inability of the Diocesan Bishop to Allow a Layperson to give a Homily' in L. G. Wrenn, *Authentic Interpretations on the 1983 Code*, Canon Law Society of America, Washington, DC, 1993, 41–3 at 41: 'Whether the diocesan bishop is able to dispense from the prescription of canon 767 § 1 by which the homily is reserved to priests and deacons' – response 'Negative'.

[38.] Bishops' Conference of England and Wales, on lay people preaching in a church or oratory (canon 767), *Briefing*, 19 April 1985, vol. 15, n. 8, p. 114; recognition granted on 3 May 1986, laws of their conference, once approved by the Holy See, being promulgated in *Briefing* with the date of promulgation being the last day of the month following their publication (can. 8 § 2), *Briefing*, 23 November 1984, vol. 14, n. 25, in J. Martin de Agar and L. Navarro (eds), *Legislazione delle conferenze episcopali complementare al C.I.C.*, 2nd edn, Coletti a San Pietro, Rome, 2009, 577 and 575 respectively.

duties of the family, social obligations and implementing God's will in the world (c. 768 § 2).

Once more, the integrity of the Church's faith, its fidelity to Christ and to all that he revealed to us, appears. The 'faith and morals' to be guarded and promoted are at the centre of 'what ought to be preached', especially at the Eucharist and in the heart of the Church's liturgy, which is an action of Christ and of the Church as such (c. 840). Where preaching is in the liturgy and particularly when it is in the Eucharist, it occurs in an action of prayer. The Code, emphasizing the proper and extensive content of preaching, reflects the important adage about all prayer, that it is to express and nurture the Church's faith (*'lex orandi, lex credendi'* – 'the law of praying is the law of believing') and not be at odds with it. The manner of preaching the homily is to be adapted to the hearers (c. 769). Priests, following the norms of their bishops, are to ensure that those who do not normally hear God's word may have it preached to them (cc. 770–772).

It is abundantly clear from these canons that very substantial content is to be expected from the homily; the manner of preaching refers to the manner of conveying this content, not to ignoring it or diluting it, much less to contradicting it. The Scriptures are the foundation of the faith and of the moral teaching of the Church, although they do not articulate all of it explicitly or directly; from the sacred texts, nevertheless, the range and depth of what is to foster and nurture the faith and practice of the faithful is to be expounded. This demands careful preparation through study in the seminary and afterwards, as well as careful preparation of each individual homily, and also a plan over time to meet the requirements succinctly summarized in these canons. This is not just to fulfil a law, but to ensure the rights of the faithful to be subjected neither to superficiality nor to wayward opinion and to receive the sustenance which is their due.

b. Catechesis

This is a matter of instructing those who have been evangelized; hence, unlike in the 1917 Code, it is treated after preaching rather than before it. The bishop has the duty of ensuring that there is catechesis and of directing it, but the parish priest has the key responsibility locally for seeing to it that all receive this attention generally, when preparing for the sacraments, when ill or disabled, and so on (cc. 776–770). Its content is extremely important, since it is to deepen the faith already embraced. People have a right to the truth of the Church's faith and doctrine to its systematic, positive presentation, one which does not exclude or distort that heritage.[39] It is to deepen their communion with Christ himself.[40] Catechesis is a 'sacred duty' of the Church, to which the baptized have an 'inalienable right'.[41]

'Pastors of souls' have a 'proper and serious duty' in regard to the catechetical formation of all Christians, so that, through doctrinal formation and living the Christian life, 'the living faith of the people may be manifest and active' (c. 773). A living faith is not just a matter of knowledge, but of practice, but, while catechetical formation is to be directed to all groups of the faithful (already evangelized and baptized) and adapted to people's age, capacities and circumstances (c. 779), it is to ensure that 'the faithful grow strong in learning Catholic doctrine more fully and in putting it into practice more widely' (c. 779). Parish priests are to ensure that there is a proper and effective programme of catechesis, especially for preparation for the sacraments, particularly for penance and first Holy Communion and for continuing catechesis thereafter (c. 777). Diocesan bishops are responsible for seeing that suitable persons are prepared to be catechists, that they receive continuing formation, know doctrine and the faith, as well as methods of catechizing (c. 780). They are to make sure that appropriate means are available for this work, in conformity with the Holy See and with catechetical programmes established by the episcopal conference, with the prior authorization of the Holy See, and may issue catechisms and establish catechetical offices to help them (c. 775).

In all of this the primary responsibility of parents for the catechesis of their children is to be recognized and fostered, a responsibility attaching to those who stand 'in loco parentis' and to godparents (c. 774 §2). Others may help parents in this role, but, in accordance with the principle of subsidiarity, may not remove from them their primary and inalienable right and duty to bring up their children especially in the faith.[42] By the same principle, but rooted in the fact that he is the 'proper pastor' (c. 773) of the diocese, the diocesan bishop may collaborate with others in the episcopal conference, but the latter cannot undermine or constrain him. The bishop and the parish priest are the 'pastors' with a 'proper and serious duty' for catechetics (c. 773). To say that the bishop is to ensure effective catechesis in the diocese and the parish priest has a serious duty to do so does not mean that they have

---

[39.] John Paul II, Apostolic exhortation, *Catechesi tradendi*, 16 October 1979, nn. 27, 30 on the need for 'integrity of content' in catechesis.

[40.] Ibid., nn. 4–5.

[41.] Ibid., n. 14.

[42.] John Paul II, Apostolic exhortation, *Familiaris consortio*, n. 37.

to do this alone. Collaborators are specifically commended, first of all other priests, these in institutes of consecrated life or in societies of apostolic life and lay people, especially catechists (c. 776).[43] The order in which those helpers are listed means that clergy and consecrated persons are not to be consigned to the background. The knowledge of doctrine, as well as lives being lived coherently with the faith and with the doctrines and discipline of the Church are essential, so that those living at odds with these are unsuitable as catechists.

Methodology is to be appropriate, but is not to predominate over the transmission of the Gospel in its fullest sense, including doctrine in its fullness. Where the influence predominates of a certain 'catechetical establishment', often the product of institutions which did not furnish an integral preparation and which centred upon methodology, where so-called national schemes which have never had the recognition from the Holy See required for an episcopal conference to compel their use reflect their priorities, they risk weaving a tangled web of confusion and the possibility of effective catechetics to which the faithful have an inalienable right is compromised. It is regrettable that in some instances such inadequacies have led some parents to set up 'home schooling', to assert their rights as primary educators, in the belief that catechetical and educational structures under the auspices of the Church are not reliable means of transmitting the faith and its implications to their children.

4. The Missionary Work of the Church and the Ministry of the Word

This is concerned with the Church 'planting itself' (not just being 'founded') where it is not yet in existence or where it is not strong (c. 786); this recalls the Second Vatican Council, which had spoken of missionary work as being that of people preaching the Gospel and 'planting it among people who do not yet know Jesus Christ'.[44] All the faithful share this duty through baptism and especially through confirmation (cc. 211, 781, 879); the Church is 'of its nature missionary' (c. 781). In this section the Code fully reflects Conciliar doctrine.[45] The Pope and the College of Bishops coordinate missionary work in the world; all bishops have a duty to assist in this (c. 782). Those mandated by the competent authority are 'missionaries' (cc. 784, 786),

---

[43] Valdrini, 'Le droit de l'enseignement ...', 230–1, nn. 363–4.
[44] Second Vatican Council, Decree on Missionary Activity, *Ad gentes*, n. 6.
[45] Gerosa, *Le droit de l'Église*, 126–7.

while local bishops are to promote and coordinate missionary work, working with missionary institutes (c. 790). Catechists have a special missionary role; they are to be trained and are to work under their direction (c. 785). Missionary work is to proclaim the Gospel through words and through the testimony of the lives of missionaries in sincere dialogue with those who do not believe (c. 787 § 1), draw people freely to embrace the faith, instruct them in it faithfully and integrally, so that, 'if they freely request it' (c. 787 § 2, 788 § 1), they may be prepared for baptism through the catechumenate, receiving the sacraments of initiation (c. 788) and be nurtured by word and sacrament thereafter (cc. 789–792).

5. Catholic Education

In terms of Gerosa's four categories, after the annunciation of the Gospel through preaching and its deepening through catechesis, comes education, although it might be better to think of the deepening of the Gospel through catechesis and education. In the realm of education parents have a special role.

a. Parental Responsibilities and Rights

The Church's long doctrinal and moral theological tradition has given prominence to the *'bonum prolis'* of matrimony. This 'good of the child' is the good of procreation, but it was never limited to procreation, always extending to the education of the child once born, in the very broad sense of upbringing, and always including as a crucially important element the child's religious upbringing or education (c. 1136). A recent magisterial text, too, insists that the primary duty for education, including religious education, rests with the parents.[46] This right and duty appear clearly in the Code (c. 793 § 1). Their right to receive assistance from society in this (c. 793 § 2) is an application of the principle of subsidiarity, leaving intact and safeguarding the primary right and duty of parents (c. 226 § 2). Education of the person is to be harmonious and holistic (c. 795), but special care is to be taken over the children's Catholic education. This touches the parents' right to choose institutions which will best assure this (c. 793 § 1), civil society's duty to assist them over the Catholic education of their children (c. 793 § 2), the duty of pastors to ensure that all the faithful have access to Catholic education (c. 794 § 2) and all on the

---

46. John Paul II, *Familiaris consortio*, n. 37.

basis of the Church's divinely established duty and right to educate because of the mission it has (from Christ) to enable the faithful to live Christian life fully (c. 794 § 1).

b. Catholic Schools

Since schools are not a substitute for parents, but the 'principal means of helping parents to fulfil their role in education' (c. 796 § 1), the Church has the right to establish and to run Catholic schools, under the authority of the diocesan bishop, even if operated by religious congregations (cc. 799–803, 806). Parents are to have a real choice of schools, to choose according to their provision of Catholic education (c. 797) and, if they cannot do this, they are 'bound to provide for their Catholic education outside the school' (c. 798). Schools, whether owned and run by the Church or not, are only allowed to use the term 'Catholic' if they are approved by the competent ecclesiastical authority, often the diocesan bishop (c. 803 § 3). Catholic schools and Catholic teaching are be based on Catholic doctrine and moral witness in uprightness of life (c. 803 § 2, 804 § 2), the diocesan bishop having the right to appoint or approve teachers, as also to remove or cause them to be removed for religious or moral reasons (c. 805). It may be a question as to whether the primary responsibility of parents for the religious education of their children justifies some of them removing them from, or refusing to send them to, official Catholic schools where they judge that the religious education does not provide the upbringing in the faith to which their children have an inalienable right in 'home schooling' projects.

c. Catholic Universities

The Church's right to establish and operate such universities (c. 807) rests on the same basis of the divine mandate to teach and to foster the Gospel. Once again an institution may only have the title 'Catholic' where it has been approved by the competent ecclesiastical authority (c. 808), teachers being appointed, apart from their technical abilities, for their doctrine and uprightness of moral life, with the authority being able to remove them if these are violated (c. 809). Those teaching theological disciplines must have a mandate to teach from the competent ecclesiastical authority (c. 812); this can be removed where c. 809 is at issue, where someone is systematically teaching contrary to Catholic doctrine. The bishop is to provide priests for the pastoral care of Catholic students in all places of higher learning (c. 813).

6. Social Communications

The Church recommends the use of modern means of communication to help in the spread of the Gospel, the ministry of the word, although she reserves the right for bishops to establish norms for those who speak on faith or morals on the radio or television, etc. (cc. 822, 823 § 1, 831 § 2).

In regard to books and other writings, the permission to print material on faith and morals is required from the bishop of the author or of the place of the publication (c. 824) in the following cases: the books of Scripture, including translations (c. 825), liturgical books, including translations, and prayer books (c. 826), catechisms, including translations, and other books of catechetical formation (c. 827 § 1), books on Scripture, theology, canon law, church history, religious or moral subjects, if they are to be used as textbooks (c. 827 § 2), with the recommendation that permission be sought even if they are not to be used as textbooks (c. 827 § 3), books or other writings to be displayed in churches and oratories (c. 827 § 4), collections of church decrees/acts, such as those of councils (c. 828).

Permission is valid only for the first edition and needs to be sought again for subsequent editions (c. 829). Bishops should appoint censors to advise on the suitability of any such material for publication. Since the bishop is to give the author the reasons if permission is refused (c. 830 § 3), the censor should advise him on this. The censor's task is to assess whether there is anything problematic in the material in the light of official magisterial teaching (c. 830 § 2); if not, his judgment is *'nihil obstat'* (there is nothing in the way) of publication. The bishop or other competent authority may then give permission to publish (*'imprimatur'*: 'it may be printed' or 'let it be printed'). An *'imprimatur'* means only that the material may be published, implying that there is nothing in the text contrary to official Catholic doctrine. It implies neither approval of contents or opinions, nor of shrines, alleged visions, messages, and so on, which may be discussed in it.

7. The Profession of Faith and Oath of Fidelity

The Creed (Nicene) must be professed and the oath of fidelity, as specified by the Apostolic See,[47] must be taken by: presidents, and delegates with deliberative or consultative votes at councils and

---

[47.] The current formula to be used is found with John Paul II's *'motu proprio'*, *Ad tuendam fidem*, 28 May 1998, Family Publications, Oxford, 1998, 23–4.

synods, cardinals, those to become bishops/those equivalent in law
to bishops (such as vicars Apostolic), diocesan administrators, vicars
general/episcopal vicars/vicars judicial ('*Officiales*'), parish priests,
rectors, professors of theology and philosophy in seminaries, when
taking up their offices (renewable on transfer), those to be ordained as
deacons, the local ordinary, rectors of ecclesiastical universities, and
lecturers in theological sciences there, when taking up office, superiors
of religious institutes/societies of apostolic life (c. 833).

As far as the profession of faith is concerned, the Church seeks to
protect the integrity of faith and morals, the faithful having a basic
right to receive orthodox teaching on such matters.[48] The protection
of the integrity of the Church's faith is a major responsibility of all
and of the Magisterium in particular.[49] An oath of fidelity, the anti-
modernist oath, had been required from the time of Pius X until 1967,
when it was replaced by a form of profession of faith. In 1989 John
Paul II introduced the oath of fidelity, much more positive than the
anti-modernist oath, to be taken by those who exercise office in the
name of the Church.[50] While a juridical requirement, this is related to
the Church's teaching office also; those teaching in official positions
and in the name of the Church are not to replace church doctrine with
their own, contrary opinions.

These procedures have given rise to some criticism in some quarters
on the basis of academic freedom. In part some of these concerns
relate to certain theologians being called by the Congregation for the
Doctrine of the Faith to explain positions they have adopted which
appear to be in contrast to the doctrine of the Church. In fact, new
procedures have been developed for handling cases.[51] These norms
specify details of procedures to be followed, including the involvement of the local bishop or bishops concerned, greater assurances for
the rights of the defence, but insist on greater respect for universal and
particular law. No appeal against *latae sententiae* penalties nor against
the final decisions of the Congregation in such a matter is permitted.[52]
It has to be said that teaching in an ecclesiastical institution, such as
a Catholic school, a Catholic university or a seminary, is analogous
to teaching anywhere else in the sense that there should be criteria of

---

[48] John Paul II, *Catechesi tradendae*, nn. 14, 30.
[49] Valdrini, 'Le droit de l'enseignement ...', 242, n. 383.
[50] Ibid., 243, n. 384.
[51] Congregation for the Doctrine of the Faith, *Agendi ratio in doctrinarum examine*, Acta
apostolicae sedis, 89 (1997), 830–5.
[52] J-L. Hiebel, 'La fonction de l'enseignement de l'Église', *Revue de droit canonique*, 49
(1999), 375–407 at 402–4.

suitability for appointment and for continuing in employment which pertain to the specific area of competence concerned. In such Catholic institutions, however, and even in the case of anyone teaching or writing as a Catholic theologian or canonist, there is in addition a serious responsibility to the fulness of Catholic doctrine, to the truth which it expresses or which is rooted in revelation. If an individual's opinions are such that he or she cannot affirm or indeed denies some truth, then it may be that there is a need to discuss the matter carefully with other experts, or with the Congregation for the Doctrine of the Faith. A theologian who finds his thought has been misunderstood, but who quite definitely does not disagree with a doctrine should state that clearly and show how his position is not in contradiction to the doctrine. Were someone to find himself or herself often or deeply at odds with the Church's doctrine, it could be a matter of conscience, but then that person would need to ask how they could continue to teach in the name of the Church, in a Church institution with a canonical mission or continue to write precisely as representative of the Church as such. Academic freedom implies freedom of research, thought and expression, but within the framework of the deposit of faith and of the doctrines on faith and morals which flow from it.[53] Opinions are not to be taken as automatically correct, much less so if it becomes a systematic dissent, fostering relativism and damaging the communion of the Church, but rather a certain humility is required, which in the end means submitting personal opinion to the truth taught by the Magisterium in the interests of the communion of the Church.[54]

Together with the mandate to teach (cf., cc 809, 812) and with the canonical mission associated with it, the profession of faith and the oath of fidelity constitute the ways in which the Church's Magisterium seeks to protect and guard the revelation it has received from Christ, to see that it is transmitted faithfully and integrally, and to ensure thereby that its mission of building up the communion of the People of God may be fostered.

8. Conclusion

Following this brief analysis of Book III of the Code, we have a good basis for the background to the next book on the sacraments. In the

---

[53.] Congregation for the Doctrine of the Faith, Instruction on the Role of the Theologian, *Donum veritatis*, 24 May 1990, nn. 11–12.
[54.] Cf. Ibid., n. 34.

inter-connection between them, the intimate link between 'word' and 'sacrament' emphasised by the Second Vatican Council is to be seen. The triple function of Christ, of the Church and of the faithful, according to their condition and relationship of communion with the Catholic Church (cc. 204–205, 207), of teaching, sanctifying and ruling is present; the Code as a whole articulates major aspects of the ruling function, as one of service to the communion of the Church with Christ and with one another as his people.

Chapter 8

The Sanctifying Function of the Church:

(Book IV of the Code)

Part I: Liturgy and the Sacraments in General

1. Introduction

The liturgy of the Church and its sacramental life were regulated by canon law from very early times. Not all canonical norms on the sacraments are to be found in the Code (c. 2); many are located in liturgical books, especially in the '*Praenotanda*' or 'matters to be noted beforehand', revised in the light of the doctrinal principles and liturgical reforms of the Second Vatican Council.

Early Church regulations often concerned liturgical matters, including the sacraments, particularly of baptism, Eucharist and reconciliation. Concern for 'good order' in the Church's articulation and celebration of its faith, according to the classical adage '*lex orandi lex credendi*' ('the law of praying is the law of believing') meant prayer according to Church's faith, the 'con-fession of the faith'. Liturgical prayer is not just public prayer, such as the rosary, but the official prayer of the Church, in which the Church both expresses and develops itself; it acts both in the name of Christ and in union with him (c. 834 §1) as head of the Church, under the action of the Holy Spirit, in actions which are actions of the Church itself (c. 837 § 1).

Book IV of the Code, on the sanctifying function or '*munus*' of the Church and of Christ, has to do with our becoming holy in response to our vocation in him. It deals with the core of our life as Christians. The centre of attention is the Church's sacraments, the seven saving signs which are simultaneously actions of Christ in and through his Church, the means by which the Church, in him and never apart from him, expresses itself and builds itself up. Canonically, they affect relationships within the Church, fundamentally through baptism, but also through Holy Orders in the presbyteral degree, the juridical status of persons arises or is developed in the Church (cc. 96, 204, 205–207), implying respective rights and duties.

2. Sacraments and Faith: Response to God's Word

a. Some Implications of Conciliar Teaching

Canon law goes beyond a sociological arrangement in which the Church regulates its community analogously to other societies ('*ius publicum ecclesiasticum*') or a mere voluntarism based on the sheer will of God, even were it capricious. It concerns those who believe in Christ. Canonical regulation of sacraments or worship makes no sense apart from faith.[1] 'Word' and 'sacrament' and 'communion' are key points of reference.[2]

In the New Testament the actions of Jesus sought to elicit a response of faith and of radical conversion or '*metanoia*' (Mk. 1:14–15), a response once he had returned to the Father which involved sacramental insertion into him: 'Repent and be baptized' (Acts 2:38), effecting a relationship which is transcendental, profound and all-embracing in a '*mysterion*' or '*sacramentum*' (Rom. 6:1–11). The inter-relationship between preaching, response of belief in Christ and life in him as a participation in the believing communion of the Church implies faith both as personal adherence to the Person of Christ ('*fides qua creditur*') and as acceptance of the truth he reveals ('*fides quae creditur*'), reflected in Rom. 10:8–17, esp. 9–10. This was summarized succinctly in the Second Vatican Council, where faith is presented as the response by which a person 'gives his entire self to God as he reveals himself'.[3] Specifically in respect of the sacraments, the Council insists on the necessary relationship with faith and on the communitarian and ecclesiological dimension of that faith:

> The sacred and organically structured character of the priestly community is brought into being both through the sacraments and through the virtues. Incorporated into the Church through baptism, the faithful are deputed by the character (it establishes) to the worship

---

1. L. H. Acevedo, 'Culto' in C. C. Salvador, V. De Paolis and G. Ghirlanda (eds), *Nuovo dizionario di diritto canonico*, San Paolo, Ciniselle, 1993, 319.
2. K. Mörsdorf, 'Wort und Sakrament als Bauelemente der Kirchenverfassung' in *Archiv für katholisches Kirchenrecht*, 134 (1965), 193–204; E. Corecco, ' "Ordinatio rationis" o "ordinatio fidei" ' in *Communio*, 36 (1977), 41–69.
3. Second Vatican Council, Dogmatic Constitution on Divine Revelation, *Dei Verbum*, n. 5.

of the Christian religion and, reborn as sons of God, they are bound to profess before men the faith which they have received from God through the Church.[4]

The ecclesial community, the Church, emerges from, and is built up through, the sacraments, although a personal response lived out in virtue is required. From baptism onwards, faith and sacrament are inextricably linked in the prayerful and sacramental worship of the Church as the believing community. The sacraments 'are directed to the sanctification of people, to building up the Body of Christ and so to offer worship to God'. They 'not only presuppose faith', but 'nourish, strengthen and express it' and so 'are said to be sacraments of faith', which confer grace and whose celebration 'disposes people in the best way' to receive that grace fruitfully, to worship God properly and to exercise charity.[5] These teachings imply that pastors of the Church should be concerned with more than the valid celebration of the sacraments (with the minimum needed for them to occur), but should foster their fruitful celebration, the proper disposition of people to receive their graces and the effective participation of people in the liturgy.[6] However, this should not be distorted; 'something more than' means something 'in addition to' and not 'instead of'. In other words, precisely because of the central importance of the sacraments for the life of the faithful and for the believing community of the Church as a whole, the greatest care needs to be taken that the sacraments are validly, lawfully and reverently celebrated (c. 840). Canon law interests itself in the sacramental, liturgical and prayer life of the Church because these sacred events are too precious not to be cared for. The Catholic faithful themselves have the right to receive them and the right to be properly prepared for them (c. 843 § 1–2).

b. The Church and the Liturgy

Apart from the sacraments, the prayer life and life of witness to Christ generally of all the People of God are part of the Church's sanctifying function or 'munus'. This includes the Liturgy of the Hours, listening to the Word of God, and daily living witness to Christ in the world (c. 839), which apply to every member of the faithful.[7] All have a right

---

4. ID., Dogmatic Constitution on the Church, *Lumen gentium*, n. 11.
5. ID., Dogmatic Constitution on the Sacred Liturgy, *Sacrosanctum Concilium*, n. 59.
6. Ibid., n. 11.
7. G. Ghirlanda, *Il diritto nella Chiesa; mistero di comunione: Compendio di diritto ecclesiale*, 4th revised edn, San Paolo, Cinisello, PU.G., Rome, 2004, 298–9, n. 297.

and duty in such ways to exercise the common priesthood of the faithful, for which purpose they were consecrated through baptism and many were sealed with the Holy Spirit in confirmation. Catholic members of the faithful have a right to the sacraments (c. 843 § 1); in the liturgy in general, the link with faith is such that Church ministers are called to nurture that faith especially through the ministry of the word (c. 836).

An individual, private prayer of a member of the Christian faithful can be an exercise of cult, which is regulated by canon law in that it has to conform to the faith of the Church ('*lex orandi lex credendi*') to be an authentically Christian prayer, which also explains the interest of canon law in prayer and worship in an ecumenical and inter-religious context. A public act of cult could be exercised by a number of such persons gathered and praying in a way which accords with the Church's faith; the diocesan bishop is to ensure that such prayers and other pious practices accord with the Church's laws (c. 839 § 2). A liturgical act of cult is never a private matter, but is always an official act of the Church as such (c. 837); properly speaking, it is an act which is both human and divine, since it is always an act of members of the Church and of God, of Christ himself.[8]

The Code of 1983, structured around the '*tria munera*' and here the sanctifying function, is the Code for the Latin rite of the Church (not only the Roman rite, but the Ambrosian and Mozarabic rites which involve very limited liturgical variations), as distinct from the Eastern Code of 1990 for the Eastern Catholic Churches. The latter gives a good definition of a rite as: 'a liturgical, theological, spiritual and disciplinary patrimony (inheritance) distinguished by the culture and by the asso-ciated elements of the history of a people which is expressed in their own way of living the faith of each Church *sui iuris*'.[9] Particular rites reflect the Church's concern for the celebration of its faith, the faithful 'handing on' or 'tradition' of all that it is in Christ and all that it has from Christ. This explains and justifies canonical regulation of prayer and liturgy and also explains the recognition of particular rites as proper ways of living out its relationship with Christ in the privileged actions of the liturgy, which are both his actions and those of his Church.

---

8. J-P. Durand, 'La fonction de sanctification de l'Église' in P. Valdrini *et al.* (eds), *Droit canonique*, 2nd edn, Dalloz, Paris, 1999, 244–306 at. 247–8, n. 387.

9. 'Ritus est patrimonium liturgicum, theologicum, spirituale et disciplinare cultura ac rerum adiunctis historiae populorum distinctum, quod modo fidei vivendae uniu-scuiusque Ecclesiae sui iuris proprio exprimitur.' (*Codex canonum Ecclesiarum orien-talium*, c. 28 § 1); cf. Durand, La fonction de sanctification', 248–9, n. 388; my transla-tion.

3. Preliminary Canons on the Church's Sanctifying Function

The Meaning of the Sanctifying Function

An analysis of the key canon on the sacraments, c. 840 (Table 11A), shows the close connection with the Second Vatican Council's teaching. Here the liturgy is presented as 'an exercise of the priestly function ('*munus*') of Jesus Christ', for our sanctification, using perceptible signs (here relating especially to the sacraments) as 'complete public worship', involving Christ's Mystical Body, Head and members, such that 'every liturgical celebration, insofar as it is the work of Christ the priest and of his Body which is the Church, is a sacred action, *par excellence*'.[10] The liturgy is both the 'summit' towards which the Church's work is directed to unite the baptized in deeper communion in the Church and the 'source' of God's grace, of power, of the work of sanctification and of apostolate.[11]

In c. 834 '*munus*' is translated as '*office*', but '*function*' might distinguish '*munus*' from the technical use of '*officium*', although fulfilling that function is a duty ('*officium*') for clergy and, indeed, the Liturgy of the Hours has long been known as the 'Divine Office'. The liturgy is a special way, though not the only way, of fulfilling the Church's sanctifying function, with the implications just noted for personal sanctification, for communion and for its mission.

The Church's supreme authority specifies the conditions necessary for a true, liturgical act, as part of its role of guarding and transmitting the deposit of faith. It is an action to be conducted or offered 'in the name of the Church' (thus, neither casually nor capriciously) 'by persons lawfully deputed' and 'through actions approved by ecclesiastical authority' (c. 834 § 2). This lies behind its specification of the ministers, matter (what is done or used) and form (what is said), especially for each sacrament.

The Sanctifying Function: Sacred Ministers and Lay Faithful

There follows a delineation of roles for the liturgy in general terms, reflecting the juridical status of each group.

---

[10] *Sacrosanctum Concilium*, n. 7.
[11] Ibid., n. 10.

Table 11A

The Sanctifying Function of the Church – Sacred Liturgy

Canon 834 § 1

('*Munus*' is translated as '*office*', but '*function*' might distinguish '*munus*' from the technical use of '*officium*'.)

'The *Church* carries out its *office of sanctifying* ('*munus sanctificandi*')
    in a *special* way through the *liturgy* (i.e not exclusively)
        which is an exercise of the *priestly office* ('*muneris*') of *Jesus Christ*.

In the liturgy...
    our sanctification is symbolized ('*significatur*') and ...
    brought about ('*efficitur*').

Through the liturgy a *complete public worship*
    is *offered to God* (*integer cultus Dei publicus*')
        by the *head*
        and *members*
            of the Mystical Body of Christ.'

Canon 834 § 2 states the conditions for this to occur:

'*This* (i.e. liturgical or complete public) *worship* takes place when:
    it is offered *in the name of the Church*
        by persons *lawfully deputed* and
            through *actions approved by ecclesiastical authority*.'

Bishops as Principal Dispensers of the Sacraments

The 'sanctifying *munus*' relates firstly to the bishops (c. 835 § 1), who have the 'fullness of the priesthood' ('high priests'). The responsibility for safeguarding and so for regulating the liturgy falls firstly upon them, the successors of the Apostles, the bishops, as the Church 'in her doctrine, life and worship, perpetuates and transmits to all generations everything that she herself is, everything that she believes'.[12] Hence, the bishops are the 'principal dispensers' of the sacred mysteries. If these mysteries are 'entrusted' to the bishops, this can only be by God, by Christ, so that they are moderators, promoters and guardians of these mysteries which are for our sanctification (c. 835 § 1). Christ is the supreme high priest of the New Covenant, the 'one sole Mediator between God and man' (Heb. 8:6; 9:11–15, 24–8) the real 'Pontiff' ('*Pontifex*' or 'bridge maker' between God and man). Bishops derive their sacred power from the sacrament of ordination in the episcopal degree, from Christ himself, as is clear from the form (required words) from the consecratory prayer at the ordination of a bishop: 'So now, pour out upon this chosen one the power which is from You, the governing Spirit whom You gave to Your Son, Jesus Christ, the Spirit given by Him to the Apostles.'[13] Since it is Christ's priesthood and sacred power which are transmitted in their fullness to the one ordained bishop, so, 'in the person of the bishops, to whom the priests render assistance, the Lord Jesus Christ, supreme high priest, is present in the midst of the faithful'. In 1917 the Holy See's exclusive competence meant that the role of the bishop was a matter of delegation by the Holy See in regard to the liturgy, which had been said to depend 'on the Apostolic See and, as laws may determine, on the bishop'.[14] The Council stated that the liturgy depends 'solely on the authority of the Church',[15] an expression taken up into the present Code, which speaks about regulation by the bishop, 'in virtue of the power conceded by law' (c. 838 § 1). This means not by delegation from the Holy See, but by the law itself, recognizing the implications of episcopal ordination and sacred power of the bishop, grounding his position in regard to the liturgy.[16] Likewise, his role as the

---

12. *Dei Verbum*, nn. 7–8.

13. 'Rite of Ordination of a Bishop' in *The Rites of the Catholic Church as revised by the Second Vatican Ecumenical Council* II, Pueblo, New York, 1980, English translation, 87–100, n. 26.

14. *Codex iuris canonici* (1917), c. 1257.

15. Second Vatican Council, *Sacrosanctum Concilium*, n . 22.

16. *Lumen gentium*, nn. 21, 24; cf., *Codex iuris canonici* (1917), c. 1257: 'Unius Apsotolicae Sedis est tum sacram ordinare liturgiam, tum liturgicos approbare libros': 'thus,

principal dispenser of the sacraments ('mysteries of Christ' – c. 835 § 1; 'mysterion': 'sacramentum') is rooted in the priesthood of Christ himself.[17]

The Second Vatican Council had insisted that 'no one, not even a priest, may add, remove or change anything in the liturgy on his own initiative';[18] bishops were to be consulted in the revision of liturgical books,[19] Latin was to be preserved in the liturgy,[20] but the vernacular may be used, the bishops' conferences deciding whether and to what extent it is to be used.[21] In regard to religious orders of pontifical right, the diocesan bishop was to regulate what pertains to pastoral care and public worship.[22] Bishops are the principal dispensers of the sacraments, but 'only' the supreme authority, the Apostolic See, is to 'order and regulate' the liturgy, diocesan bishops operating within what they are allowed to do by such laws (c. 838 § 1). Only the Apostolic See can issue liturgical books, approve their vernacular translations and seek to ensure that the liturgical norms are faithfully observed throughout the Church (c. 838 § 2). Episcopal conferences can prepare vernacular translations, but these need to be submitted for revision and approval ('recognitio') of the Holy See (c. 838 § 3).[23] Bishops may issue liturgical norms within their competence (c. 838 § 4), specifying how universal norms are to be more fully implemented or how pious practices are to be harmonized with the liturgy (c. 839 § 2). An important clarification of the role of bishops' conferences, after controversy and abuses in some places, has emphasized that bishops, and not the officials engaged to assist them, are to decide matters for which they are legally responsible and the assent of each diocesan bishop is normally necessary for something within the competence of a bishops' conference to become law. The only exception is where there is a two-thirds majority of the bishops with deliberative vote and approval after revision from the Apostolic See (c. 455 § 2).[24] This reinforces the role

---

ordering the liturgy and approving liturgical books is the task of the Apostolic See alone'; cf. Lumen gentium, nn. 21, 24.

17. Lumen gentium, n. 21.
18. Ibid.
19. Ibid., n. 25.
20. Ibid., n. 36.
21. Ibid., nn. 22, 36.
22. Second Vatican Council, Decree on the Pastoral Role of Bishops, Christus Dominus, n. 35.
23. Pontifical Council for Legislative Texts, 'La natura giuridica e l'estensione della 're-cognitio' della Santa Sede', 26 April 2006.
24. John Paul II, Apostolic letter, motu proprio, Apostolos suos, 21 May 1998, IV, nn. 1–2.

especially of diocesan bishops against the danger of their functions as Christ's high priests being usurped by officers assisting them or by other bishops imposing decisions upon them; rather, any decision of the bishops' conference has to be in full harmony with the Apostolic See, in the service of communion.

Priests, Deacons and Lay People and the Sanctifying Function

Others involved in the sanctifying function of the Church are priests (c. 835 § 2) who 'share the priesthood of Christ', meaning that, through the new and special consecration of their priestly ordination ('and are consecrated to ...'), they share in the ministerial or ordained priesthood of Christ, since they already share in his priesthood in respect of the common priesthood of the faithful. Sharing in the ministerial priesthood of Christ through this consecration (ordination) grounds their capacity and function as ordained priests, exercised 'under the authority of the bishop', to 'celebrate divine worship in the person of Christ ('*in persona Christi*') and to sanctify the people'. Deacons (c. 835 § 3) 'share in the celebration of divine worship according to law', not by a special consecration beyond the common priesthood of the faithful, since their diaconal ordination is for ministry ('*ad ministerium*') and not to priesthood ('*ad sacerdotium*'). Yet, their role in the liturgy is governed by canon law, for the reasons just outlined. Other members of Christ's faithful (c. 835 § 4) have 'their own part' in the 'sanctifying office' (function), 'each in his own way actively ('*suo modo actuose*') sharing in the liturgical celebrations'. Special mention is made of the role of parents in regard to living their married lives 'in a Christian spirit' and in providing for the Christian education of their children. This paragraph refers to the faithful as such ('*christifideles*': cf. cc. 96, 204 § 1), it means all the baptized and not just Catholics each 'having their own part' and sharing 'in their own way' means not only not taking the part of the ordained and especially of the ministerial priest, but also operating according to the norms of c. 205 which governs the exercise of rights by the faithful according to the degree of their communion with the Catholic Church, with particular reference to the profession of the faith, the validity of sacraments and ecclesiastical governance. These factors resurface in connection with the question of Catholics and other baptized Christians sharing sacraments ('*communicatio in sacris*').

A number of strengths have been identified in this presentation: the sacraments are treated under the Church's sanctifying function and no longer under 'things' ('*De rebus*') as in 1917 and the Christological and ecclesiological nature of the sacraments, in harmony with the

Council, appears which shows that they are not reduced to merely private celebrations or pious practices. However, some would have wished the sacraments to be linked more explicitly to the ministry of the Word and lay involvement in the sanctifying function of the Church extended in terms of the realization of their vocation in the Church.[25] In fact, there is some recognition of the lay role in terms of this function in regard to works of charity (c. 839 § 1) and the role of the word (c. 836).

4. The Sacraments in General

a. An Analysis of Canon 840

The key canon for the sacraments in general (c. 840) repeats the doctrine that all of the sacraments were instituted by Christ, 'the Lord' or 'Kyrios' (Table 11B) indicating the Risen Lord, whose saving action establishes and operates in the Church. They are not mere signs or symbols, although they are both, since they bring about or effect what they signify, precisely because they are 'actions of Christ', the Risen Lord. Since the liturgy as a whole is inseparably an action of Christ and of the Church (c. 834), so too are the sacraments, as privileged and special instances of liturgical action, 'actions of Christ and of the Church', whose purpose is again to express, but also to strengthen the Church's faith. Here it is not a question of the personal opinions about faith held by individuals, but precisely the faith of the Church as such, the deposit of faith or the revelation God in Christ has given for our salvation (c. 836), which is to be strengthened by the sacraments, as effective, salvific actions. In other words, they are to express and deepen in each individual member of the faithful the faith of the Church in the revelation communicated to us in Christ and indeed through these very sacraments. Being 'entrusted to the Church' (Divine passive) implies that they were so entrusted by Christ himself, an essential part of the one deposit of faith, revealed and given by Christ, expressed in Scripture and Tradition, transmitted in and by the Church and authentically interpreted by the Magisterium, to create and nurture the communion of the Church in him.[26]

As actions of Christ and of the Church, the sacraments express and bring about the authentic and perfect worship of God, impossible other than in Christ, 'through Him, with Him and in Him', so that

---

25. L. Gerosa, *Le droit de l'Église*, St Paul, Luxembourg, Cerf, Paris, 1998, 147–50.
26. *Dei Verbum*, n .10.

Table 11B

The Sacraments of the Church

Canon 840

'The sacraments of the New Testament were
  – *instituted by Christ (the Lord)* – *'a Christo Domino instituta'* and
  – *entrusted to the Church.'*

As *'actions*   – *of Christ* and
          – *of the Church*
they are   – *signs and means*
          – *by which faith*
                is *expressed* and *strengthened*
          – *(by which) worship* is offered *to God*
          – *(and by which) our sanctification* is brought about.'

Hence,   'they *bring about* in the greatest manner (*'summopere'*) the:
          – *establishment*
          – *strengthening* and
          – *manifestation (expression) of ecclesiastical communion'*.

Therefore, in their celebration
          'sacred ministers and
          all other members of Christ's faithful
                must show
                  – great *reverence* and
                  – *due care'*.

each member of the faithful worships God in and with other baptized persons in the Church in liturgical and especially sacramental actions only to the extent that he or she is indeed united to this action of Christ in the Church. Likewise, it is as actions of Christ through his Church that the sacraments not only signify, but effect or bring about our sanctification. Here, as with our worship of God, the extent to which each one of us is truly open to the action of the Risen Lord in the particular sacrament, affects the extent to which he or she is actually sanctified through it. Personal disposition notably affects whether or not this particular sacramental encounter with Christ bears fruit in us or not; this is why someone in a state of serious sin or living at odds with the Gospel and with church teaching is not to receive the (other) sacraments unless and until he or she has been reconciled to Christ through baptism or, thereafter, through sacramental reconciliation.

The sacraments stand in the service of the Church's communion, both of our communion with the Lord and, through our communion with him, our communion with one another in him. This they 'bring about' or 'establish' and, provided we are properly disposed, they 'strengthen' and 'express'. Sharing in a liturgical celebration would be false or untrue, were a person to be seriously at odds with the Gospel and its implications, incomplete and inadequate were that person to be incoherent with it even in a less drastic manner. Furthermore, as 'actions of Christ and of the Church', part of the liturgical action by which 'our sanctification is brought about' in a 'complete public worship offered by the head and members of the Mystical Body of Christ' (cc. 834 § 1; 840), they are the greatest instruments by which Christ effects this communion in the Church ('they bring about in the greatest manner'). Hence, they ought never to be treated causally or with disdain or reduced to expressions of popular desire or preference; they demand the greatest reverence both from sacred ministers (c. 835 § 1–3), and indeed from all the faithful (c. 840).

b. Equality of Status and Diversity of Function

The equality of status of all Christ's faithful (c. 208) derives from baptism (cc. 96, 204, 849), grounding their rights to have the Gospel faith preached and explained to them (cc. 213, 229), to participate in spreading the Gospel (cc. 211, 225 § 1), and, in principle, to receive other sacraments (cc. 213, 843 § 1), although only those in full communion with the Catholic Church (cc. 96, 205) actually have the right to receive most of the other sacraments. Any baptized person who validly marries another baptized person receives the sacrament of matrimony (c. 1055 § 2); the reception of other sacraments by those not in full communion with the Catholic Church, 'communicatio in sacris' (c. 844), will be treated later. Diversity of function also derives from the sacraments, especially from Holy Orders in the episcopal and presbyteral degrees. Bishops, priests and also deacons are sacred ministers, as distinct from those lay men formally instituted to the lay ministries of lector and acolyte (c. 230). Most of the sacraments depend upon the exercise of priestly power, either in the bishop or in the (ordained or ministerial) priest, by which these ministers participate by the grace of God in the unique priestly power of Christ himself, such that, when these priestly ministers act sacramentally, Christ's priestly power operates through them, he as principal minister, they as instrumental ministers.[27] The sacraments which do not require the exercise of priestly power, baptism and matrimony, therefore, either do not require a priest as the minister of the sacrament as an absolute condition of validity (as in baptism) or do not have a priest as the minister (as is the case in matrimony in the Latin Church). While the distribution of Holy Communion does not require absolutely the exercise of priestly power, to bring about the sacrament of the Eucharist does. This distinction of functions is not sociological, but sacred; precisely priestly functions, rooted in a new and further sacramental consecration in Christ, go beyond those grounded in baptismal consecration.

c. The Bishops' Role in the Sacraments and the Holy See

The Church's sanctifying function ('munus') 'is exercised principally by bishops', who, as 'high priests', are the 'principal dispensers of the mysteries of God' and 'moderators, promoters and guardians of the entire liturgical life entrusted to their care' (c. 835 § 1). What has been seen in detail above on the liturgy applies especially to the sacraments. The order and guidance of the liturgy depends 'solely upon the authority of the Church', on that of the Apostolic See (but not 'solely') and on that of the diocesan bishop, according to (the limits of) the law (c. 838 § 1). The Apostolic See is to regulate the liturgy of the universal Church, publish liturgical books, review ('recognoscere') translations (c. 838 § 3) and ensure that liturgical regulations are everywhere or universally observed, the Pope as moderator, promoter and guardian of the liturgy and sacraments, exercising this Petrine role 'since the sacraments are the same throughout the universal Church' and 'since

---

[27.] E. Besson, La dimension juridique des sacrements, P.U.G., Rome, 2004, 105–9.

they belong to the same deposit of faith' (c. 841). This also explains why 'only the supreme authority in the Church can approve or define what is needed for the validity of the sacraments' (c. 841), 'only' reinforcing 'validity' (c. 39).

Episcopal conferences are to prepare vernacular translations and may make appropriate adaptations as allowed by the liturgical books (c. 2). One adaptation permitted in German-speaking areas has been to select either the first or the second reading on Sundays and holydays, rather than having both read at Mass along with the Gospel. In England and Wales, there has been the inclusion of a form (words) of marriage, which serves not only Church requirements, but those of the State too. Episcopal conferences may publish translations of liturgical books, once reviewed and approved by the Holy See (c. 838 § 3).

The diocesan bishop can establish liturgical laws binding on all in the Church entrusted to his care (diocese), within the limits of his competence. The laws of the universal Church and those of the episcopal conference, properly established, bind also him (c. 838 § 4). Examples of diocesan liturgical laws might be the requirement (promulgated through an 'Ad clerum') for priests always to wear chasubles when saying Mass, to wear violet vestments when celebrating the funerals of those who are not children under seven, specifying diocesan feasts and memorias, and so on.

d. Other Norms for the Sacraments in General

Baptism is indispensable for the valid reception of any other sacrament (c. 842 § 1), so that someone not validly baptized does not receive any of the other sacraments, even if people were not aware of this at the time. Since baptism, confirmation and Eucharist are necessary for full Christian initiation (c. 842 § 2), no other sacrament can be received licitly unless all three have been received; penance or reconciliation is an exception to this (c. 914). Sacraments conferring a character, baptism, confirmation and order, in each degree, cannot be repeated for that reason (c. 845 § 1); they establish a new relationship with Christ which, even if not lived out or even rejected, cannot be said not to have been established.

All in the Church have a duty to treat the sacraments with reverence and care (c. 840). This implies that people are able to receive them (validly), may receive them (legally) and seek them 'opportunely' or in an appropriate way and at an appropriate time (c. 843 § 1), that they are both properly prepared to receive them and properly disposed to receive them (c. 843 § 2). Since the faithful have the right to receive the sacraments, it is especially incumbent upon sacred ministers and on all to ensure that they are validly (truly) received. Validity is an issue of whether the sacrament was or was not received, either whether anything took place at all or, where it appeared that it did so, whether it was in fact validly conducted, since, if it was not, no sacrament was received.[28] It is not enough to operate on the basis of a probable opinion; the safer course or 'tutiorism' ('*tutus*': safe, '*tutior*': 'safer') must be followed in such cases and so, in cases of real doubt which cannot be resolved, the sacrament is to be administered 'conditionally' (c. 845 § 2) or 'on condition that you have never been baptized/confirmed/ordained as … before'. This needs to be done in the case of sacraments conferring a character (c. 845 § 1). On the other hand, conditional baptism is not routinely to be given to those seeking full communion with the Catholic Church, since we do recognize the baptism of most other non-Catholic Christian Churches or ecclesial communities. Real doubt, though, may require conditional baptism; we shall look at these questions in respect of each of the sacraments. Suffice it to say here that sacred ministers especially have a duty to see to it that people are properly prepared; all the faithful have a role here of assistance, of evangelization and of catechesis (c. 843 § 2).

Other regulations are that ministers wear proper vestments when celebrating the sacraments (c. 846 § 1), celebrate them according to their own rite (c. 846 § 2), that priests use properly and recently (not over a year) blessed olive oil for sacraments involving holy oils (cc. 847, 999 § 2), that ministers seek nothing beyond an offering laid down by competent authority for such celebrations (cc. 847), avoid the crime of simony or appearing to 'sell' the sacraments (cf. c. 947), and avoid the poor being deprived of the sacraments (c. 848). The question of the lawful reception of sacraments by non-Catholic baptized persons and of Catholics receiving sacraments outside the Catholic Church (c. 844) will be treated later.

[28.] E. Olivares, 'Sacramento' in *Nuovo dizionario di diritto canonico*, 940–2 at 941.

5. The Valid Celebration of the Sacraments

a. The Distinction between Validity and Liceity

Something done unlawfully, illegally or illicitly may still be truly done (valid), whereas something done invalidly is more fundamentally flawed in that the action is null and void or nothing is in fact brought about. For a priest to say Mass without the proper vestments is unlawful; if he did not use bread, what he did would not only be unlawful, but it would be invalid too, so that he would not have consecrated bread into the Body of Christ and he would not have celebrated the Eucharist. Requirements for the valid celebration of the sacraments are not all that needs to be considered, since the lawful and reverent celebration of the liturgy requires that it be celebrated in a way which awakens and deepens faith and fosters both the communion of the Church and the apostolate of all its members. Nevertheless, their valid celebration is indispensable to the work of Christ's grace for his people as he intended.

b. The Conditions for Sacramental Validity in General

Christ is the principal cause of all sacraments, acting through such sensible signs to bring the Paschal mystery of salvation to people across the ages, through ministers who are their instrumental causes. External but effective signs of what he brings about, their basic meaning always remains, but where Christ did not specify them, the supreme authority of the Church specifies the matter and form or 'sensible' aspects through which each sacrament operates.[29] Thus, the conditions for the validity of the sacraments involve the following:

 – *matter:* what must be used, done and/ or be present
 – *form*: the words which must be used;
 – *minister*: one who is legally capable of administering the sacrament;
 – *intention of the minister*: the minister of the sacrament must intend (at least virtually – have intended this in the past and not revoked it, as with 'Whenever I ..., I shall intend to ....')[30] to administer a particular sacrament to a person/ certain persons; to 'do what the Church

---

[29.] Besson, *La dimension juridique...*, 196–201.
[30.] N. Halligan, *The Ministry of the Celebration of the Sacraments*: *Sacraments of Initiation and Union*, I, *Baptism, Confirmation, Eucharist*, Alba House, New York, 1973, 30–3.

does'. He does not need specifically to make an express intention: 'I intend to celebrate Mass, to consecrate bread and wine into the Body and Blood of Christ ...' every time he celebrates the Eucharist, but a virtual intention suffices, although he should renew it from time to time (for instance, at the Chrism Mass, on the anniversary of ordination as a priest).

– *intention of recipient*: This can be a factor in the validity of a sacrament, but it is not always. Thus, the Eucharist is 'confected' or brought about, without any intention on the part of (a) specific individual(s) to receive it being necessary to the validity of the consecration as such, although the priest himself is to receive Holy Communion and under both kinds at the Mass he celebrates for the integrity of the sacrifice. The baptism of an infant cannot involve the intention on the part of the infant, but the intention of at least his parent(s) or of the person baptizing that he receive it, be admitted to the life and faith of the Church is there. Normally, the fact that people come/ask for the sacraments is enough to presume their intention (the candidate intends to receive confirmation, the seriously sick or infirm person intends to receive the anointing of the sick, and so forth). However, there are some sacraments where the recipient's particular intention is also necessary for validity: the penitent must be sorry for his sins and intend to try to avoid them in future, this bridegroom must intend to marry this bride and *vice versa*, this candidate must intend to be ordained either a deacon or a priest or a bishop.

– *proper candidate(s)*: This can be a question of validity, it is not always. A person must be legally capable (c. 10) of receiving the sacrament or it is not validly celebrated, it does not occur. He does not receive it because he cannot do so: only a non-baptized person can be baptized; only a baptized person who has never been confirmed can be confirmed; only a man never ordained as a deacon/priest/bishop can be ordained to these orders (c. 845 § 1). With these sacraments, invalidity would arise from the fact that the sacrament had already been received and, since it confers a 'character' (a new relationship with Christ) 'cannot be repeated'; the act is invalid because the person is incapable of receiving that sacrament again. Only a baptized man can be validly ordained (c. 1024); the 'ordination' of a woman, therefore, would be invalid because, as a woman, she is incapable of being ordained.[31] Only a person already validly baptized can validly receive any other sacrament (c. 842 § 1). Thus, a non-baptized person's 'reception' of any other sacrament would be invalid (he would not

---

[31.] John Paul II, Apostolic letter, *motu proprio, 'Ordinatio sacerdotalis'*, 22 May 1994, n. 4.

in fact receive it) because such a person is incapable of receiving any other sacrament unless and until he is baptized. This is why baptism is called the 'gate to the sacraments' (c. 849). Only a person legally capable of marriage can marry validly, irrespective of whether or not this is a sacramental marriage (c. 1057 § 1). One without the use of reason (c. 1095 § 1) or otherwise incapable of assuming the obligations of marriage (c. 1095 § 3) would be incapable of giving marital consent or one suffering from permanent, antecedent impotence (c. 1084 § 1) would not marry validly because of being incapable of doing so. We saw from the general norms that validity is not at issue unless the law states that an act is null and that no law is incapacitating unless the law states persons to be incapable (c 10). The instances just quoted are examples of sacraments being invalidly administered (they do not take place) because the recipients are not capable of receiving them.

If a mistake is made, as where a bishop reads the prayer of consecration for the ordination of a priest or bishop when intending to ordain a man as a deacon, the man is not ordained at all, neither as a deacon because of lack of form – wrong words, nor as anything else because the intention was diaconal ordination.

It is necessary to underline here that none of what is said in this section detracts from the doctrine that the sacraments work through the action of Christ and by what is to be done being done ('*ex opere operato*') rather than depending upon the personal degree of sanctity or sinfulness of the one performing the action ('*ex opere operantis*'), the minister of the sacrament, usually the priest, or of the recipient, although the dispositions of the latter are necessary for any sacrament to be received fruitfully by someone with the use of reason. Rather, what is at stake when speaking of the validity of the sacraments is precisely the conditions which need to be present for the sacrament to take place ('*ex opere operato*'); putting it another way, when the conditions for validity are met, then the sacrament functions 'automatically' or by virtue of what is to be done being done (this is also what is meant by intending and doing 'what the Church does').

c. The Valid Celebration of the Sacraments in Particular

The summary of the conditions for validity of the seven specific sacraments of the Church is given in Tables 11C (for baptism, confirmation and Eucharist) and 11D (for reconciliation, anointing, Holy Orders and matrimony). These criteria will be seen later in relation to each of the sacraments in turn.

d. The Duty of Reverence and Due Care over the Sacraments

The responsibility of sacred ministers to show proper care and reverence for the sacraments (c. 840) includes the responsibility to prepare people well, by preaching, evangelization and catechesis, to receive the sacraments with understanding, faith and deepened spiritual appreciation (c. 843 § 2). It also means the duty to try to ensure that those seeking to receive the sacraments are proper candidates for the sacraments and that the proper matter and form are used to ensure validity to which people are entitled, since without this they do not receive Christ's sacramental gift of himself. They are also to ensure the lawful celebration of the sacraments, including liturgical laws and norms too, without personal innovations (cc. 841, 846 § 1).

e. The Conditional Administration of the Sacraments

One further aspect of the care due over the sacraments (c. 840) is that of their validity on occasions when there can be a genuine doubt as to whether someone has received baptism or another sacrament. Without scrupulosity, great care is needed here.

Conditional Administration with Doubts of Fact or of Validity

In the past, there was a requirement that anyone wishing to become a Catholic who had been baptized in a non-Catholic church reject their heresy or schism.[32] Although c. 845 § 2 of the 1983 Code is almost the same as the text in the 1917 Code, namely that, if there were a prudent doubt as to whether any of these three sacraments (baptism, confirmation, order – c. 845 § 1) had been administered or as to their validity if there had been a ceremony, there was a presumption until the ecumenical reforms of the Second Vatican Council that baptisms were probably invalidly conferred in non-Catholic churches and so those seeking to become Catholics were conditionally baptized.[33] Now, there is no such presumption about those seeking to be received into full communion with the Catholic Church. Indeed, the ecumenical movement has progressed in many ways on the basis of the common baptism we share (cc. 96, 204, 849). However, the proper concern for the careful and certainly for the valid celebration of the sacraments must be given. Therefore, where there is a real reason to doubt either

---

[32.] 'Vetitum est Sacramenta Ecclesiae ministrare hereticis aut schismaticis etiam bona fide errantibus eaque petentibus, nisi prius erroribus rejectis, Ecclesiae reconciliati fuerint', *Codex iuris* canonici (1917), c. 731 § 2).
[33.] Ibid., c. 732 § 2.

Table 11C

The Validity of the Sacraments in Particular I

	Baptism	Confirmation	Eucharist
Matter	Washing with (immersion in or pouring of) real water on the head (cc. 849, 853–854)	Anointing on the forehead with chrism, by laying on of hands (c. 880 § 1–2)	True bread, made of wheat, and uncorrupted and true fruit of the vine, uncorrupted (c. 924 § 1, 2 and 3)
Form	I baptize you in the Name of the Father and of the Son and of the Holy Spirit	Be sealed with the gift of the Holy Spirit	Take this, all of you and eat it. This is My Body, which will be given up for you (over the bread) Take this, all of you and drink from it. This is the cup of My Blood, the Blood of the new and everlasting covenant. It will be shed for you and for all, so that sins may be forgiven. Do this in memory of Me. (over the wine)
Ordinary Minister	Bishop, priest, deacon	Bishop (c. 882)	**(Confection of, bringing about, the Eucharist)** Only a validly ordained priest (c. 900) **(Distribution of the Eucharist)** Bishop, priest, deacon (c. 910 § 1)
Extra-ordinary Minister	Catechist/One deputed by the diocesan bishop, where there is no sacred minister or where he is impeded/ In emergencies, any other (preferably baptized) person (c. 861 § 2)	**(Other minister)** Priest, with faculties to confirm (c. 883)	**(Extra-ordinary Minister of Distribution of the Eucharist)** Man instituted as an Acolyte/ (c. 910 § 2) Temporarily deputed ministers (c. 910 § 2)
Minister's Intention	To baptize this person	To confirm this candidate	To change bread and wine into the Body and Blood of Christ (The matter is to be limited, for example, the bread/wine in the chalices, on the corporal).
Recipient's Intention	(If capable), to be baptized	(If capable), to be confirmed	–
Proper Candidate	Only a non-baptized person	A baptized, not validly confirmed person (cc. 842§1; 845§ 1)	Baptized person and ideally also confirmed

Table 11D

The Validity of the Sacraments in Particular II

	Reconciliation (Penance)	Anointing of the Sick	Holy Orders	Matrimony
Matter	Sins confessed (integrally) by penitent and any others, venial or forgotten by him/her (c. 960).	Oil of the sick – oil of the olive or of another plant, blessed by the Bishop (or, in real need by the priest himself), with sign of the cross on the forehead and then on each hand – or anywhere on the body in necessity, with an instrument in necessity, as where there is a contagion (cc. 847, 999– 1000 § 1–2).	Laying on of hands (on head) of a baptized man, as below.	The expressed internal matrimonial consent of a specific, baptized man and a specific baptized woman to marry one another (cc. 1057 § 1–2; 1104).
Form	I absolve you from your sins in the Name of the Father and of the Son and of the Holy Spirit.	Through this holy anointing may the Lord in His love and mercy help you with the grace of the Holy Spirit (anointing on the forehead). May the Lord who frees you from sin save you and raise you up (while anointing the hands). In necessity, the whole form is said when anointing the body (c. 1000 § 2).	The words given below, for ordination as a deacon (*), or as a priest (**) or as a bishop (***)	'I do', in response to the three questions posed by the Church's official witness who 'assists' (c. 1108).
Ordinary Minister	Priest, with faculties (cc. 965– 966, 968ff.), which includes any priest in danger of death (c. 976)	Only a priest	Only a validly ordained bishop	The couple themselves (Latin rite); priest (Eastern rite Catholics)

(continued)

Table 11D *(continued)*

The Validity of the Sacraments in Particular II

	Reconciliation (Penance)	Anointing of the Sick	Holy Orders	Matrimony
Official Church Witness	–	–	–	Bishop, priest or deacon able to 'assist' by law or delegation, to seek and receive the couple's consent (c. 1108)
Minister's Intention	– to absolve the sins confessed (and others, venial and/ or forgotten). With general absolution, only when permitted, to absolve the sins of all present who are sorry for them (cc. 961–962).	To anoint the sick person	EITHER to ordain this man as a Deacon * OR as a Priest ** OR as a Bishop. ***	To marry one another (Latin rite)
Recipient's Intention	sorrow for sins/ intention not to repeat them	(If capable), to be anointed	To be ordained EITHER as a deacon OR as a priest OR as a bishop	To marry one another
Proper Candidate	A baptized person	Only a baptized person, fully initiated, seriously ill or weak from age	Only a baptized man (c. 1024)	Two baptized persons legally capable of marriage

*   Lord, send forth upon them the Holy Spirit, that they may be strengthened by the gift of Your sevenfold grace to carry out faithfully the work of the ministry.

**   Almighty Father, grant to these servants of Yours the dignity of the priesthood. Renew within them the spirit of holiness. As co-workers with the order of Bishops, may they be faithful to the ministry that they receive from You, Lord God, and be to others a model of right conduct.

*** So now, pour upon this chosen one that power which is from You, the governing Spirit whom You gave to Your Beloved Son, Jesus Christ, the Spirit given by Him to the Holy Apostles, Who founded the Church in every place to be Your Temple, for the unceasing glory and praise of Your Name.

that a sacrament was administered at all or that it was validly administered, it is to be given conditionally (c. 845 § 2).

The form to use in the conditional administration of sacraments, where the doubt is about the fact or validity of their valid celebration is as follows:

Baptism: On condition that you have never been baptized before, I baptize you ....

Confirmation: On condition that you have never been confirmed before, be sealed ...

Holy Orders: On condition that you have never been ordained before as a deacon/priest/ bishop, ...

Conditional Administration and Doubts about the Person's State

There can be difficulties about the administration of the sacraments when someone is alive but unconscious, alive but not able to speak, or mentally disturbed. If someone is unconscious or too ill to receive Holy Communion or might not know what it is, they should not be given the Blessed Sacrament. If, though, someone is generally confused, but knows what they are receiving and can receive it without danger of desecration, they should receive it, as viaticum if they are dying. Where a person fully initiated into the Church is very ill and confused or is unconscious, the priest should say an act of contrition with them/for them for all their sins, give them absolution and administer to them the anointing of the sick. Where there is doubt as to whether or not someone is alive, although a dead person cannot receive the sacraments, the previous discipline of conditional absolution as to whether or not the person is alive and of conditional anointing in the same circumstances is no longer mentioned either in the new norms or in the 1983 Code and so it must be judged that this requirement has been removed; absolution and anointing (c. 1005) are now to be given absolutely or unconditionally.[34] In doubt as to whether or not a person

---

[34] Paul VI, Apostolic Constitution, *De sacramento unctionis infirmorum, Acta apostolicae sedis*, 65 (1973), 5–9; Congregation for Divine Worship and for the Discipline of the Sacraments, *Variationes in novas editiones librorum liturgicorum*, n. 15. Cf. F. R. McManus, 'The Sacrament of the Anointing of the Sick (cc. 998–1007)' in J. P. Beal, J. A. Coriden and T. J. Green (eds), *New Commentary on the Code of Canon Law: An Entirely New and Comprehensive Commentary on the Code of Canon Law by Canonists from North America and Europe with a Revised English Translation of the Code*, commissioned by the Canon Law Society of America, Paulist, New York, Mahwah, 2000, 1179–92 at 1190–1 on c. 1005. E. Caparros, M. Thériault and J. Thorn (eds), University of Navarre and University of Saint Paul, *The Code of Canon Law*, bilingual and annotated edition, note, under c. 1005, that the formula for conditional anointing in the earlier

is alive, it remains true that being alive is a condition of reception of the sacraments, but a conditional form is no longer used; quite simply, a dead person does not actually receive the sacrament.

6. Conclusion

This survey of the canons on the liturgy and on the sacraments in general will serve as a reference in all that follows on each of the sacraments in turn.

Ordo infirmorum of 1972, n. 135, has been completely suppressed in the *Variationes*, n. 15, so that the only form for anointing is the absolute one, where there is doubt as to whether or not the person is dead; McManus suggests plausibly that this was to avoid scruples on the part of the priest.

Chapter 9

The Sanctifying Function of the Church

(Book IV of the Code)

Part I: The Sacraments II:
The Sacraments of Initiation

1. Introduction

The fundamental importance of baptism in the life of the Church and in canon law, the basis for the juridical status of persons in the Church, as members of the faithful (cc. 96, 204) is now very clear. This chapter examines the sacraments of initiation (baptism, confirmation and Eucharist), beginning with baptism as the 'gateway to the sacraments' (c. 849).

2. The Preliminary Canons on Baptism

The canons distinguish between the baptism of adults and that of children and they distinguish baptism in normal circumstances and in case of necessity.

a. The Lawful Celebration of Baptism

The valid administration of baptism requires that a non-baptized person be washed in true water (by its being poured over the head or by immersion in it), while the minister of the sacrament says the Trinitarian formula (c. 854). The ordinary minister is a deacon, priest or bishop (c. 861 § 1), but an extra-ordinary minister, a catechist, another Catholic, a non-Catholic, non Christian or non-believer, can administer the sacrament validly in case of necessity, where the proper matter and form are used, provided he or she intends to do what the Church intends and does by baptism (c. 861 § 2).

Beyond these minimal conditions of validity, the lawful celebration of baptism involves using the 'rite prescribed in the approved liturgical books', except in case of necessity, when only what is required for validity suffices even for liceity (c. 850). Further conditions for the lawful celebration of baptism entail proper preparation for baptism (c. 851), the use of blessed water, except in case of necessity (c. 853), by pouring or immersion according to the norms of the episcopal conference (c. 854), using an appropriate name (c. 855), at the Easter Vigil or on a Sunday if possible (c. 856), normally in the candidate's proper church (cc. 857–860).

b. Revised Norms for Adult Baptism: Preparation for Baptism

The norms for adult baptism apply to anyone over the age of reason (c. 852 § 1). Norms for infant baptism apply to anyone under the age of reason (7) and to anyone lacking the use of reason, who is treated, canonically as equivalent to an infant in regard to baptism (c. 852 § 2).

The Catechumenate, Evangelization and Catechesis

The licit or lawful celebration of baptism of an adult presupposes that the adult is 'properly prepared', that he or she has been admitted to the catechumenate and brought through the stages of initiation, according to the 'Rite for the Christian Initiation of Adults', as adapted by the episcopal conference (c. 851, 1°). This norm reflects the duty of sacred ministers (c. 835 § 1) and of all of the faithful to ensure that the sacraments are celebrated with 'great reverence and due care' (c. 840). Adult candidates need to be evangelized and catechized in order to be able to understand and to appreciate what they are seeking and undertaking in being baptized (c. 206). However much the revised rites and steps in the catechumenate may have this aim, it remains a distinct obligation of sacred pastors, especially of the parish priest (cc. 530, 1°, 776, 777, 1°), to ensure proper preparation, a duty which is not automatically discharged by consigning someone to a 'process' or to other helpers.

'Proper preparation' (cc. 776–777, 1°, 852 § 1) includes catechesis in the truths of the faith, so that people may understand and commit themselves in faith to Christ.[1] The preamble or 'Praenotanda' of the 'Rite of Christian Initiation of Adults' calls baptism 'the sacrament of

---

[1] Second Vatican Council, Dogmatic Constitution on Divine Revelation, Dei Verbum, n. 5.

that faith by which ... we respond to the Gospel of Christ'.[2] In terms of the preparation required by canon law here, the Church 'believes that it is its most basic and necessary duty to inspire all, catechumens, children of parents still to be baptized, to that true and living faith by which they hold fast to Christ ...'[3] This basic and necessary duty corresponds to the fact that the 'primary duty' of a priest (first in order of time) is to preach the Gospel; it is 'among his principal duties' (c. 762).[4] In other words, this preparation must involve the communication of the faith by preaching and teaching about Christ and what he has revealed, the deposit of faith. Yet, the faith required for baptism is 'not a perfect and mature faith, but rather a beginning which needs to develop' afterwards.[5] This does not mean that a childish approach is to be adopted towards adults, who are to be brought to understand whom they are following and what they are embracing, to be able to respond in true faith, even if that faith will always need to be perfected. Since at issue is the 'faith of the Church', authentically interpreted and taught by the Magisterium,[6] the elements of that faith as content, as well as its relational dimensions towards Christ himself and as part of the community, must be sufficiently clear for the person not to be misled and to give an assent of faith.

Conversion and Preparation for Forgiveness of Sin

Embracing the faith of the Church implies a renunciation of the previous way of life, specifically of sin. Conversion or 'metanoia' is an intrinsic requirement of faith (Mk. 1:14–15); otherwise a person's real desire to be immersed in Christ (Rom. 6:12–11), to embrace the faith by which he will 'hold fast to Christ' for the rest of his life, would be in serious doubt and baptism could not proceed. Thus, preparation must help the catechumen to appreciate what is right and wrong in the light of the Gospel of Christ and to be converted through the forgiveness of sins, imparted by the 'cleansing waters of rebirth' in a remission of original and of personal sin.[7]

[2.] Congregation for Divine Worship, *Rite of Christian Initiation for Adults*, 6 January 1972, Vatican, 1972, 'Praenotanda', n. 3.
[3.] Ibid.
[4.] Second Vatican Council, Decree on the Life and Ministry of Priests, *Presbyterorum ordinis*, n. 4.
[5.] John Paul II, *The Catechism of the Catholic Church*, nn. 1253–4.
[6.] *Dei Verbum*, nn. 8–10.
[7.] *The Rite of Christian Initiation of Adults*, 'Praenotanda', n. 5.

Communion with Christ, Paschal Mystery: Faith and Prayer

Since baptism incorporates us into Christ and into the Church (cc. 96, 204, 849), the catechumen needs to be assisted to appreciate the Church as a living community of faith, prayer (especially liturgical prayer) and life. Baptism brings the gift of a participation in the life of the Risen Lord who has conquered death and in the Trinity. It unites the one who receives it to Christ such that he or she becomes capable of sharing his everlasting life; it offers personal holiness. The preparation of the catechumen should nurture this supernatural hope through reflection on the Scriptures, by prayer and by example, to facilitate a personal profession of the faith.[8] Baptism involves incorporation into Christ and, inseparably, into the communion of the Church of which he is the head.[9] The 'character' of baptism, its 'unchangeable effect' (c. 845 § 1),[10] is to unite the newly baptized person to Christ, to the Trinity and to all who share in this communion, symbolized in the Latin Church by the anointing with chrism after baptism (even where confirmation does not follow in the same ceremony, although it should with adults), to indicate their sharing through baptism in the threefold function of Christ as priest, prophet and king.[11] This involves simultaneous incorporation into the Church; partly for this reason, sponsors and others are involved in the preparation of adults for baptism.[12]

The Stages of the Catechumenate and the Status of Catechumens

The restoration of the catechumenate of the early Church was designed to make it clear that adult baptism is the canonical and liturgical norm for baptism and to bring out more clearly the close link between baptism, confirmation and Eucharist as the three sacraments of initiation.[13] There are four main stages in 'The Rite of Christian Initiation of Adults': the pre-catechumenate, including enquiry by candidates prior to enrolment in the 'order of catechumens', the catechumenate itself with various stages of catechesis and of rites, from enrolment to election, the stage from election until baptism (usually Lent) and post-baptismal enlightenment or deepening of the mysteries ('*mystagogia*').

---

8. Second Vatican Council, Dogmatic constitution on the Church, *Lumen gentium*, n. 10.
9. Ibid., nn. 5–6.
10. Ibid., n. 4.
11. L. G. Walsh, *The Sacraments of Initiation: Baptism, Confirmation, Eucharist*, Chapman, London, 1988, 66.
12. Second Vatican Council, Decree on Missionary Activity, *Ad gentes*, n. 14.
13. *Lumen gentium*, nn. 10–11; *Ad gentes*, n. 14.

The Council intended that Christian initiation of adults should 'not be a mere exposition of dogmatic truths and norms of morality', but should involve participation in the evangelizing work of the Church and an initiation into prayer and liturgy,[14] to promote the conversion needed to embrace forgiveness of sins.

The Council had wanted the place of catechumens to be recognized in the Code to be produced. As such catechumens do not enjoy the juridical status of the baptized who thereby are constituted 'persons in the Church' (cc. 96, 204). Their rights are 'analogous', they are 'linked to the Church in a special way'; by their desire in faith, hope and love they are 'joined to the Church' (c. 206 § 1). As distinct from the rights of the baptized which come from Christ through baptism, the Church, which has 'a special care' for catechumens, 'accords them various prerogatives' (c. 206 § 2). Thus, for funeral rites, they 'are to be reckoned among Christ's faithful' (c. 1183 § 1), since by their 'desire' (c. 206 § 2), not through actual baptism, they can be saved by Christ (through what is sometimes called analogously 'baptism of desire'): 'Baptism ... is necessary for salvation either by actual reception or at least by desire' (c. 849).

Baptism and the other Sacraments of Initiation

In the case of adult baptism, beyond the catechumenate, 'as far as possible' the person seeking baptism should 'be brought through the various stages to sacramental initiation in accordance with the rite of initiation as adapted by the episcopal conference and the particular norms issued by it' (c. 851 1°). This canon, in respect of the catechumenate, does not limit itself to baptism, but has in mind 'sacramental initiation', which implies also confirmation and Eucharist. This interpretation is reinforced by the statement later that, 'unless there is a grave reason to the contrary, immediately upon receiving baptism an adult is to be confirmed, to participate in the celebration of the Eucharist and to receive Holy Communion' (c. 866).

Some Delicate Cases

The priest needs to be involved in this process; he must know the person enquiring about baptism from whom he is to make prudent enquiries to ensure that there is no canonically irregular or otherwise problematic marital situation, which might prevent baptism or reception into full communion with the Catholic Church. If there is such a problem, it should be discussed with the vicar judicial ('*Officialis*') of the diocese.

[14.] *Ad gentes*, n. 14.

Ignoring this could make matters more complicated, for a valid non-sacramental marriage involving one baptized person would become sacramental by virtue of the baptism of the non-Christian (c. 1055 § 2).

b. Canonical Requirements for Infant Baptism

The Code treats adult baptism first in c. 851 before turning to infant baptism (c. 851, 2°), since, if infant baptism is more common, adult baptism is the norm theologically, liturgically and canonically. We recall that those 'incapable of personal responsibility' are to be treated as infants for the purposes of baptism (c. 852 § 2).

The renewal of the sacraments of initiation included a focus on catechetical and spiritual preparation. In the case of children, it is those who are responsible for asking for baptism and for the upbringing of the children who have the duty to be prepared for this sacrament. The family is the basic cell of society and the family of two baptized Christian spouses is a cell of the Church in miniature, a 'domestic church', and parents are the 'first heralds of faith to their children'.[15] Procreation and education, a good of marriage highlighted by Augustine, for Thomas one of its ends and for Paul VI on of its essential meanings, are not just a question of bringing children into the world, but of their upbringing, including their religious upbringing.[16] These responsibilities are clearly reflected in the Code (cc. 226 § 1–2, 774 § 2, 776, 851 2°, 1136) and they pertain to the proper preparation for the sacraments for which the parish priest, personally or through others, is responsible (cc. 835 § 1, 851 2°). Parents and sponsors 'are to be suitably instructed' about the meaning of the sacrament of baptism and the obligations attaching to it through pastoral advice, joint prayer, bringing families together for preparation and visiting each family, if possible (c. 852 § 1). Their instruction is to include what is central to the Catholic faith, including an explanation of some of the main points of the Creed which parents and sponsors are to profess on behalf of the child, as well as the significance of the baptism itself and of the explanatory rites.

As for obligations, parents, at least the Catholic parent, should be reminded of their duties to bring the child up to know and love the faith and to practise it by coming to Mass each week, at home and beyond, to go to a Catholic school if possible or otherwise to provide for an effective religious education. The importance of their own

---

[15.] *Lumen gentium*, n. 11.
[16.] John Paul II, Apostolic exhortation, *Familiaris consortio*, n. 37.

attendance at Mass and of their own commitment of faith emerges here; it is a time to urge parents whose practice is weak to resume it fully. The tendency, in regard to the religious upbringing and practice of children, to 'leave it until they are grown up' should be challenged, since example is irreplaceable and since doing nothing directly about faith for eighteen years is itself a powerful indication to children that it does not really matter. Those years are not spent in a vacuum and, in a secularized, often derisory society, children otherwise risk growing up hostile to faith and to the Church.

The positive endeavours by the Church, reflected in the Code, to promote a responsible attitude and practice by parents and sponsors to their duties in infant baptism are not to be made into terrible burdens. There need to be genuine and serious efforts, though, to fulfil these duties.[17]

d. Other Preliminary Norms for Baptism (Adult and Infant)

The Baptismal Name

Since baptism is a 'rebirth in Christ', it has been customary to take or to give a baptismal or Christian name to the child. The Code states that care should be taken that 'a name is not given which is foreign to Christian sentiment' (c. 855). This would exclude anything anti-Christian, anything directly expressive of a non-Christian religion or ideology, but it would seem also to exclude what is merely popular and fashionable as having no Christian significance. While a non-Christian name is not absolutely excluded, emulating a holy person, a saint, whose name is taken at baptism is to be encouraged.

The Timing of Baptism

Baptism is encouraged at the Easter Vigil, after the catechumenate and period after election, following the scrutinies and handing over of the Creed. Easter and Eastertide are very appropriate times for baptism, but otherwise, Sundays as the Day of the Lord's resurrection are particularly suitable (c. 856).

The Place of Baptism

The place of baptism should be a church or an oratory (c. 857 § 1; cc. 1214, 1219, 1225–1227), the parish church of the adult or of

---

[17.] J. M. Huels, 'Preparation for the Sacraments' in *Studia canonica* 28 (1994), 33–58 at 45–6.

the child's parents, the parish church of the place where they are domiciled (cc. 857 § 2, 862), at a font in the church (c. 858), ideally placed near the entrance to the church to symbolize the entrance into the communion of the Church of the person who is baptized or in another church or oratory nearer to where people live (c. 859). It should be with the permission of the proper parish priest (c. 862), who should not deny permission normally, since its purpose is to ensure that proper preparation takes place; it is not a licence to be obstructive. It should not take place in a private house, except in grave necessity, when permitted by the local ordinary (c. 860 § 1), nor in a hospital, except in emergency or for a pressing pastoral reason or where permitted by the local ordinary (c. 860 § 2). In case of necessity, baptism is permitted anywhere.

Baptism in Case of Emergency

In case of necessity, only the conditions for validity (washing with real water of a non-baptized person, with the use of the proper words – c. 849) must be met (c. 850). Where baptism has taken place in case of necessity, but where it later becomes possible, the explanatory rites or other rites which bring out or 'explain' the significance of the baptism itself are to be celebrated (anointing with chrism, if there has not been confirmation, clothing with the white garment, lighted candle, and perhaps the signing of the ears and mouth) with the liturgy of the word, and so on. This is a matter of liceity.

Children of Catechetical Age and Young Adults

Proper preparation of children of catechetical age (over the age of seven) is necessary to ensure that they know and accept some basic elements of the Church's faith, including the sacrament of baptism, and that they wish to be baptized. There must be the permission of at least one of their parents. The bishop should be approached for the baptism of adults and of all over fourteen who seek baptism, to allow him to confer baptism if he wishes, unless the diocesan laws provide otherwise (c. 863). Baptism is to be administered by an ordinary minister of baptism: bishop, priest or deacon (c. 861 § 1), in a church or oratory (cc. 857–860), using the full rites.

Proper Candidates for Baptism

Baptism is the fundamental sacrament, the 'gateway to the sacraments' and is 'necessary for salvation' (c. 849). 'Any unbaptized person and only such a person can be baptized' (c. 864). This canon effectively declares (by the term 'only' or 'unless') legally incapable of baptism (cc. 10, 39) any person already validly (truly) baptized, the character meaning it simply cannot be repeated (cc. 845 § 1, 849). An unbaptized adult should manifest the intention of being baptized, be adequately instructed, be tested over the catechumenate period, and be urged to have sorrow for personal sins (c. 865 § 1). An adult in danger of death may be baptized if he or she has some knowledge of the principal truths of the faith, has in some manner manifested an intention to be baptized, and promises to observe the requirements of the Christian religion (c. 865 § 2). There is a need for faith, conversion and the intention to be baptized in an adult. An intention might be manifested by the person having spoken with a relative of a wish to be a Catholic.

Parents should have the child baptized in the first few weeks after birth, contacting the priest beforehand to be themselves properly prepared (c. 867 § 1). An infant in danger of death should be baptized without delay (c. 867 § 2), with the consent of at least one of the parents/guardians (c. 868 § 1, 1°), where there is a 'well-founded hope' of them being brought up in the Catholic faith (c. 868 § 1, 2°), although in danger of death an infant of Catholic or even of non-Catholic parents may be baptized even without their consent (c. 868 § 2).

If the doubt cannot be resolved by diligent enquiry, a doubtfully baptized person is to be baptized conditionally (c. 869 §1). The Second Vatican Council emphasized our common faith in Christ and common baptism as the foundation of ecumenical cooperation. The presumption now is that the baptism in the Churches and ecclesial communities of the Reformation is valid (Orthodox baptism was always recognized as valid). Those baptized in non-Catholic ecclesial communities are not to be conditionally baptized, unless in a given case there are grounds to doubt the validity of the baptism, which should be checked out (c. 869 § 2). If it is necessary to baptize conditionally, this should be explained to the person concerned (c. 869 § 3).

Foundlings (abandoned children) are to be baptized, unless shown to have been baptized (c. 870). This shows care for the child's eternal salvation, but also recalls the fact that only an unbaptized person can be baptized (c. 864). Aborted fetuses are to be baptized if they are alive, 'insofar as is this is possible' (c. 871). This simplifies the earlier practice of conditional baptism; here the norm is that baptism be conducted absolutely. Nor is there any question here of obtaining parental permission, which might well be lacking in many instances. The canon shows a concern again for the salvation of the child. The essential condition that the child be alive reflects the fact that the sacraments cannot be given to the dead. In case of doubt, there should be a conditional baptism, but, as noted earlier, the condition is that the child is alive.

Canon law gives more attention to parents than previously. Their consent is normally needed for their children to be baptized (cc. 867 § 1, 868 § 1) and a proper explanation is required if baptism is conditional (869 § 3). Previously, parents had a very limited role; they might not even be in church and godparents took the main responsibility in the ceremony for the children.[18]

e. Sponsors at Baptism

Although the Code of 1983 reflects a more prominent role for parents in baptism, sponsors are still envisaged, as they present the child for baptism with the parents (c. 872). They have a major role in preparing adults for baptism. There need be only one sponsor, although two, one male and one female, are acceptable (c. 873).

However, there are important conditions for someone to be considered suitable as a sponsor (c. 874). Appointed by parents, guardians or the parish priest, sponsors must intend and must be able to fulfil their role, they must at least sixteen, although the priest can make an exception for a just reason, must be Catholic (not a baptized non-Catholic who can only be a witness – c. 874 § 2), who has been confirmed and has received the Eucharist, who lives a life of faith befitting the role of sponsor, is not under a canonical penalty, and who is not the father or mother of the person being baptized (c. 874 § 1). These criteria are important for safeguarding the faith and for the significance of the role of sponsor or godparent. To reduce this to a social role is wrong; one fulfilling this function must be able to be an example of (the Catholic) faith in its fullness; otherwise they could neither understand nor mean to assist the candidate or the parents of a child in professing and witnessing to the faith.

f. The Theological Significance of Baptism

Preparation of adults and of parents and sponsors of children who are to be baptized reflects baptism as a sacrament of faith and as a source of communion.[19] This insertion into Christ and into the Church, embraced in faith as the basis of our lives, is emphasized liturgically

---

18. M. R. Quinlan, 'Parental Rights and Christian Initiation of Children' in *Studia canonica*, 25 (1991), 385–401 at 391–3.

19. L. Gerosa, *Le droit de l'Église*, St Paul, Luxembourg, 1998), 180–1.

especially in the profession of faith and in the act of baptism.[20] The link with the other sacraments of initiation (c. 866) shows the orientation of baptism to a deeper participation in Christ and in the Church in confirmation and perfected in the Eucharist.

Our common faith in Christ and our common baptism constitute the foundation of a common, but as yet imperfect communion with one another in Christ, reflected in the prohibition of 'rebaptism' of those baptized in other ecclesial communities.[21] It has enormous significance for Christian unity.[22] It is worth noting, however, that some Protestants, focused on justification by faith alone, are very uneasy with infant baptism and some 'rebaptize'.[23]

g. Registration and the Baptismal Register

The baptismal register is one of the most important registers in the parish; it gives proof of baptism from at least one 'unexceptional' (reliable) witness (c. 875). In the absence of proof of baptism from a certificate based on the baptismal register, such proof can be given by one unexceptionable (reliable) witness or by the sworn declaration of the person himself if he is an adult (c. 876). The parish priest has the duty of registering the baptism carefully and without delay (c. 875).

The entry needs to contain the names of the baptized, the minister, the parents, the sponsors and, if there, the witnesses, the date and place of baptism (c. 877 § 1). With an unmarried mother, her name is to be entered, if the fact of her being a mother is publicly known or if she asks for entry to be made before witnesses or in writing and, similarly with the father; otherwise, only the child's name is to be entered (c. 877 § 2). For an adopted child, the names of the adoptive parents must be registered and, if locally registered in the civil register, the names of the natural parents are to be given (c. 877 § 3).

The baptismal register normally gives the names of the baptized, together with their confirmation details and details of their marriage, ordination in any and all degrees or perpetual profession of religious vows. In the case of ordination and/or of religious profession, the word 'marriage' can be crossed out in the baptismal register or, better, the margin can be used. Certificates are to show accurately all details

---

[20.] Walsh, *The Sacraments of Initiation*, 72–4.
[21.] Second Vatican Council, *Lumen gentium*, n. 15; Decree on Ecumenism, *Unitatis redintegratio*, n. 22.
[22.] Gerosa, *Le droit de l'Église*, 178–9.
[23.] Walsh, *The Sacraments of Initiation*, 85, 100–02.

in the register under baptism, including confirmation, marriage, ordination or profession. If there is no entry under 'marriage' in the baptismal register, a line should be drawn on that line on the certificate or 'Nothing recorded' written there; this then serves as a statement of freedom to marry for that person, as far as the baptismal register is concerned.

h. The Postponement or Deferral of Baptism

A new feature in the Code is the possibility of deferring baptism (c. 868 § 1, 2°). The earlier preoccupation with having children baptized as soon as possible to ensure forgiveness from original sin and to receive the life of Christ is still rightly reflected in the Code (cc. 867, 868 § 2, 870–871), but in the past it could have been reasonably expected that, in most cases, those seeking baptism for their children intended to and would bring them up to practise the faith. Where this is still a reasonable expectation, after preparation, there is no justification for deferring baptism. Where there is high lapsation and where any of those baptized are not brought up in the faith, there is reason to be more cautious, to avoid the sacrament being treated as an occasion for a party or as an empty ritual. This is why the Code envisages possibly deferring baptism, although it does not envisage absolute refusal. Only where a 'well-founded hope that the child will be brought up in the Catholic religion' is 'truly lacking' (c. 868 § 1, 2°), should baptism be 'deferred' (not refused), following local diocesan law if there is one, and the parents should be advised of the reasons for this. This is to cause parents to think again, to encourage them to come to the point where baptism can properly be administered. A sympathetic response where there are genuine problems can help to promote a more responsible attitude. To help people to think over what they are asking, so that they may be able to assume the responsibilities involved in good conscience, can also help.

The German bishops issued norms under which baptism may be deferred only where parents have refused to discuss their reason for not making more of a commitment and where not even godparents can or will assume real responsibility for bringing up the child in the faith. The parish priest has to consult the dean before such a decision; parents must be informed of it and of the reasons for it. An annual report to the bishop of such cases is to be made.[24]

---

24. Gerosa, *Le droit de l'Église*, 183.

3. The Sacrament of Confirmation

a. The Conciliar Background

The Second Vatican Council states that 'by the sacrament of confirmation the faithful are more perfectly bound to the Church, are 'endowed with the special strength of the Holy Spirit' and, 'as witnesses of Christ, are more strictly obliged to spread the faith by word and deed'.[25] It brings out the fact that this is a distinct sacrament from baptism, a 'true and proper sacrament'.[26] While the post-baptismal anointing with chrism signals sharing Christ's priesthood (common priesthood of the faithful), confirmation involves a specific gift of the Spirit and anointing with chrism to strengthen a baptized person to witness to the faith, defend it and spread it, sharing in this way in the Church's mission.[27]

b. An Analysis of Canon 879

This key canon states that: 'The sacrament of confirmation confers a character. By it the baptized continue their path of Christian initiation. They are enriched by the gift of the Holy Spirit and are more closely linked to the Church. They are made strong and more firmly obliged by word and deed to witness to Christ and to spread and defend the faith' (c. 879).

From this, it is seen that candidates for confirmation have to have been baptized already. Baptism is the 'gateway to the other sacraments' (c. 849) and confirmation is a furthering of baptismal incorporation into the Church; the baptized 'continue' the initiation begun in baptism, are 'more closely' linked to the Church and as a result are 'more firmly' obliged to give witness to the faith. The word 'confirmation' means a 'strengthening' (by God) of what has already begun. It is not the beginning of incorporation, but it 'complements' baptism (c. 842 § 2). For this reason, it can be received validly only by someone who has already been validly baptized (cc. 842 § 1, 889). This is why proof of baptism should be checked by sacred ministers, who have special care over the sacred mysteries (cc. 835 § 1, 841),

---

[25.] *Lumen gentium,* n. 11.

[26.] H. Denzinger and A. Schönmetzer, *Enchiridion symbolorum, definitionum et declarationum de rebus fidei et morum* 36th edn, Herder, Barcelona, Freiburg-im-Breisgau, Rome, 1936, n. 1628; cf. J. Neuner and J. Dupuis, *The Christian Faith in the Doctrinal Documents of the Catholic Church,* 2nd edn, Mercier, Cork, 1976, n. 1434.

[27.] L. Gerosa, *Le droit de l'Église,* St Paul, Luxembourg, 1998, 190–1.

before anyone is admitted to confirmation; normally, a valid certificate, signed and with a parish seal, is required; otherwise other proofs
should be obtained (cc. 875–878).

Confirmation is an action of Christ (c. 840) and of his Holy Spirit,
who comes as a specific 'gift' through this sacrament, this deepening
of uncreated grace producing the effect (created grace) of 'strengthening' the person who receives it and thereby enabling that person
to undertake the responsibilities in the Church which stem from it.
The sacraments are 'signs and means by which faith is expressed and
strengthened' (c. 840); confirmation strengthens those who receive it,
who are thereby 'more closely linked to the Church'.

Those who are confirmed have the duty to 'defend' the faith of the
Church and to 'spread' it 'by word' and 'deed' (c. 879). By confirmation they are strengthened, consecrated more fully, to enable them to
fulfil their task of being Christ's witnesses in the world. The use of
chrism in this sacrament represents their further consecration into
Christ's royal priesthood, the priesthood of the faithful, a more radical
relationship with him which can never be undone; this is the meaning
of the 'character' or 'seal' of confirmation (c. 845 § 1).

c. The Matter and Form of Confirmation

This sacrament was not initially clearly distinguished from the post-
baptismal anointing with chrism, but it was recognized as a distinct
sacrament from the fourth-century Council of Elvira. Anointing
with aromatic oil, chrism, became common in the Eastern Church
and spread to the West. The matter of the sacrament was described
as 'signing' or 'sealing' with chrism or at other times 'imposition
of hands' or 'confirmation'.[28] The matter of confirmation is the
'anointing on the forehead with chrism in a laying on of hands' by
the proper minister (c. 880 § 1). This means that the bishop (or priest),
having dipped his thumb into the sacred chrism, putting the other
fingers of his hand on the forehead, anoints the candidate with the
chrism he has on his thumb. The sacred chrism has to be that which
is consecrated by the bishop (c. 880 § 2), since, unlike the other holy
oils of catechumens and of the sick, this oil is specifically associated
with the priesthood of Christ. The consecration of sacred chrism is
thus reserved to the bishop, from the first Council of Toledo in 398, a

---

[28.] A. Mostaza, 'Confermazione' in C. C. Salvador, V. De Paolis and G. Ghirlanda (eds),
Nuovo dizionario di diritto canonico, San Paolo, Cinisello, 21993, 262–76 at 263.

reminder of the link to the bishop and to the apostolic succession.[29] The Holy See can grant a special faculty to a priest to consecrate sacred chrism, for instance where bishops are very scarce in areas of persecution or severe political repression. Whereas a priest can validly bless the oil of the sick himself in an emergency, he cannot validly consecrate chrism without such a special faculty. In confirmation 'Christians receive the spiritual anointing with the Spirit who is given to them'.[30]

The form of the sacrament is 'Be sealed with the gift of the Holy Spirit', said usually preceded by the person's 'confirmation name', while administering the chrism in the laying on of hands, as described. This was changed by Paul VI from 'I sign you with the sign of the cross and I confirm you with the chrism of salvation, in the Name of the Father ...'[31] A confirmation name should be a saint's name, someone the person will seek to imitate or to whom he or she will pray particularly in trying to live out the duties of confirmation and of the Christian life in general.

The proper place for confirmation to take place is in a church and the proper time is within the Eucharistic celebration. It can take place elsewhere for a good reason (c. 881), especially in danger of death.

d. The Minister of Confirmation

There has long been debate about whether the bishop is the only proper minister of confirmation or whether it is also the priest. The Council stated that the bishop was the 'originary minister' of confirmation, suggesting that he was not the only one.[32] To clarify the situation in the Eastern Catholic Churches, the Council stated unequivocally that the 'discipline going back to ancient times concerning the minister of Holy Chrismation is to be fully restored. Therefore, priests are to be able to confer this sacrament, using chrism blessed by the patriarch or

---

[29.] G. Sheehy et al., *The Canon Law: Letter and Spirit: A Practical Guide to the Code of Canon Law*, Chapman, London, 1995, 486, n. 1730.

[30.] 'Rite of the Blessing of Oils; Rite of Consecrating the Chrism', *The Rites of the Catholic Church*, II, Pueblo, New York, 1980, 302–12 at 303, n. 2.

[31.] Paul VI, Apostolic Constitution, *Divinae consortium naturae*, 1971, *Acta apostolicae sedis*, 63 (1971), 663, cited in Mostaza, 'Conformazione', *Nuovo dizionario di diritto canonico*, 264.

[32.] *Lumen gentium*, n. 26.

bishop'.[33] The Latin Code of 1983 uses the term 'ordinary minister' of the bishop (c. 882), although this is to be interpreted in a broad sense that he is the 'normal minister' of confirmation.[34] Those equivalent in law to a bishop have the faculty to confirm for the area of their jurisdiction (cc. 883 1°, 368, 412, 416). A priest can validly celebrate confirmation, but only when he has the faculty to confirm (c. 882), either by law if appointed as parish priest for his parishioners or by special faculty from the bishop (c. 883 2°), but only for adults he has just baptized or received into full communion (c. 885 § 2). If he has the faculty to confirm, within his territory, 'within the territory assigned to him', the parish of which he is parish priest, he may lawfully administer the sacrament to those from outside that territory (who are now in his parish), unless prohibited by their ordinary (c. 887). Those equivalent in law to the bishop may not confirm outside their jurisdiction, but, as with the diocesan bishop, may confirm within it those from elsewhere, unless their own bishop objects (c. 886 § 1).[35] A bishop needs the permission of the local diocesan bishop to confirm even his own subjects in another diocese or at least must be able reasonably to presume that permission (c. 886 § 2). Any validly ordained priest can validly confirm a proper candidate in danger of death (c. 883 § 3).

The duty to administer confirmation or to ensure that it is administered by another bishop is that of the diocesan bishop (c. 884 § 1). Either he or a priest with proper faculties to administer it may ask other priests to help in administering confirmation in given cases 'for a grave reason' (c. 884 § 1–2). His duty to confirm, or to ensure that confirmation is administered, relates to his subjects (not necessarily in his diocese at the time, perhaps during a diocesan pilgrimage elsewhere), who duly and reasonably ask for it (as proper candidates, properly prepared and disposed, at a reasonable time and in a reasonable place). That they 'ask for' the sacrament implies that they freely and willingly seek this sacrament (c. 885 § 1).

---

33. Second Vatican Council, Decree on the Eastern Catholic Churches, *Orientalium Ecclesiarum*, n. 13. Note Flannery's mis-translation of 'Holy Chrismation' as 'confirmation'. It is the same sacrament, but it is called 'chrismation' in the Eastern Churches and that is the term used by the Council: 'Disciplina de ministro S. Chrismatis', *Orientalium Ecclesiarum*, n. 13 (cf. A. Flannery, *Vatican Council II: The Conciliar and Post-Conciliar Documents*, Fowler Wright, Leominster, 1981, 445–6.

34. Ghirlanda, *Il diritto nella Chiesa* ..., 307–8, n. 309.

35. J. A. Coriden, *An Introduction to Canon Law*, revised edn, St Paul, Mahwah, NJ, 2004, 126.

e. The Proper Candidate for Confirmation

The proper candidate for confirmation is one who is baptized, but not confirmed: 'Every baptized person who is not confirmed, and only such a person, is capable of receiving confirmation' (c. 889 § 1), 'capable' meaning that anyone not baptized is incapable of being validly confirmed (cf. c. 10). For liceity or lawfulness, except in danger of death, it is further required that the person be suitably instructed, if he or she has the use of reason, properly disposed, able to renew his or her baptismal promises (c. 889 § 2), of the age of discretion or reason (c. 891) or of a higher age if the episcopal conference so decides. These are duties of the parish priest, in keeping with his responsibilities for catechetical instruction and for this sacrament (cc. 777, 2°, 890). Given the importance of the sacrament of confirmation as a sacrament of initiation, if there is an insoluble doubt about whether or not the sacrament was received or validly conferred, the sacrament is to be administered conditionally (c. 845 § 2). Conversely, since confirmation confers a character, it cannot be repeated (cc. 845 § 1, 879), which is why only a baptized person 'who has not been confirmed' is capable of receiving this sacrament (c. 889 § 1).

f. Reception into Full Communion with the Catholic Church

Remarkably little is said about this in the Code. However, those validly baptized in a non-Catholic church or other ecclesial community are not to be baptized even conditionally (c. 869 § 2), but are to be received into full communion with the Catholic Church, according to a special rite. This includes the public profession of the Nicene Creed and of their acceptance of all that is taught on faith and morals by the Magisterium of the Catholic Church.

There is some confusion about what is to be done with children who themselves wish or whose parents wish them to be received into full communion. If they are under seven, they are treated as infants and their parent(s) act on their behalf (c. 852). If they are over fourteen, they would be treated as adults in regard to baptism or changing rite in some instances (cc. 863, 111 § 2). At that age they could be received into full communion without parental consent, although the bishop should be consulted in any case to see if he wishes to confer the sacraments (c. 863) for those above fourteen years of age. Those who are between the ages of seven and fourteen can in fact be admitted to full communion, but only with the consent of at least one of their parents, except in danger of death (c. 891). In all cases baptism should be verified (by a baptismal certificate normally) and, except in danger of death, instruction in the faith appropriate to the age of the person should be given. Someone from an Eastern Church not in full communion with the Catholic Church will almost certainly have been confirmed at baptism and, since we accept the validity of orders in the Orthodox and other Eastern Churches, a certificate of confirmation is to be obtained; confirmation is not to be administered, but only the profession of faith and declaration of acceptance of Catholic teachings are to be made before giving First Holy Communion. For those from ecclesial communities stemming from the Reformation, no confirmation in their community can be accepted as valid since its validity depends on a validly ordained bishop or priest with faculties conducting it and confirmation is to be administered at the time of reception, by the bishop or by a priest with the faculty to confirm. The fact of reception is to be entered into a 'Register of reception into full communion' and the confirmation in the confirmation register, also for children between seven and fourteen, as well as those over fourteen treated as adults in this regard. It would be wise to issue all such persons with an official letter (or certificate) with relevant details, in case it is needed later for marriage, profession or ordination.

g. Sponsors at Confirmation

Sponsors are not required at confirmation, but they are recommended and, ideally, should be the baptismal sponsors (c. 892). Their function here would be to take care that the person confirmed behaves as a true witness and secondly that they fulfil the duties inherent in this sacrament (c. 892). Sponsors must be confirmed Catholics over sixteen years old, must be neither under a canonical penalty nor a parent of the candidate, and must be appointed by the candidate (cc. 874, 893).

h. Registration of Confirmation

This should be recorded in the parish confirmation register (cc. 894–896), the responsibility of the parish priest of the place of confirmation, and in the baptismal register if the person was baptized in that parish. Otherwise, the fact of the confirmation and other details are to be forwarded as soon as possible to the parish priest of the parishes in which the candidates were baptized, so that they may be added to the baptismal registers there (cc. 895, 896, 535 § 2).

i. Juridical Effects of Confirmation

Confirmation prepares the person for the full participation in the Eucharist which follows immediately when adults receive all three sacraments of initiation together or a person is received into full communion. With baptism, it confers the right and duty to participate in the life of the Church; such persons are 'appointed to the apostolate by the Lord Himself'.[36] They have rights to other sacraments, to share the ruling function of the Church in some ways, and to exercise actively their rights in the Church's life and mission (cc. 211–223).[37] Confirmation is a prerequisite for admission to a major seminary (c. 241 § 2), to a novitiate in an institute of consecrated life or to probation in a society of apostolic life (cc. 645 § 1, 735 § 2), to admission into an institute of consecrated life as well as professing the evangelical counsels (c. 597 § 1) and to sacred orders (c. 1033). Proof of confirmation is, thus, important. Confirmation and baptismal registers should be completed promptly as a matter of justice. Confirmation is also a prerequisite for being a sponsor to anyone else at baptism (c. 874 § 1) and/or at confirmation (c. 893 § 1). Ideally, a baptized Catholic should be confirmed before being married, but, while this is recommended, it is not indispensable (c. 1065 § 1).

j. The Timing of Confirmation and Sacramental Initiation

The order of the sacraments of initiation is baptism, confirmation and Eucharist. Over the last hundred years in the Latin Church confirmation has often come after the Eucharist, an unintended outcome of Pius X's efforts to encourage young children to receive Holy Communion at an earlier age. Yet, the practice has varied across the centuries. Even in the West it was administered at baptism, until the Church spread to rural areas and the bishop was not available. Medieval councils urged it for children below the age of reason; others saw the age of reason as key.[38] The 1917 Code made this a standard minimum age for those not in danger of death or where there were no other 'just causes' for early reception.[39] The recent experiment in the Diocese of Salford in England, with the permission of the Congregation for Divine Worship and for the Discipline of the Sacraments, allowed children to receive

---

[36.] Second Vatican Council, *Lumen gentium*, n. 33, Decree on the Laity, *Apostolica actuositatem*, n. 3.

[37.] Walsh, *The Sacraments of Initiation*, 156–9.

[38.] Mostaza, 'Confermazione', *Nuovo dizionario di diritto canonico*, 271–4.

[39.] Benedict XV, *Codex iuris canonici* (1917), c. 788.

confirmation at about the age of seven and subsequently to receive Holy Communion at a celebration in all parishes on Pentecost Sunday each year, the bishop giving the necessary faculties to the priests of the diocese and working in the diocese.

The importance of confirmation in the life of each member of the faithful and in the life of the Church as a whole is considerable. It should not be obscured by questions of secondary importance.

4. The Sacrament of the Eucharist

Through baptism people acquire personality in the Church (c. 96), are incorporated into Christ and into the Church (cc. 96, 204 § 1), and acquire the right in principle of access to other sacraments (cc. 213, 849, 889 § 1). Through confirmation their 'links with the Church' are rendered 'more perfect' (c. 879). In the final sacrament of initiation their incorporation is 'perfected' (c. 897).

a. The Nature of the Eucharist: The Preliminary Canons

The central and supreme importance of the Eucharist among all of the particular sacraments of the Church, is indicated its characterization as the 'source and summit' of all Christian life and worship (c. 897). It is the culmination of sacramental initiation into the Church, it reconciles and heals, it nourishes Christian spouses in their mission, and it fortifies the faithful in their common priesthood, as well as ministerial priests in their service of all.

An Analysis of the Key Canons (cc. 897–898)

A consideration of cc. 897–898 (Table 12) reveals the following features of note. The exceptional nature of the Eucharist emerges from the terms used: 'most venerable sacrament', 'summit and source of Christian worship and life', 'blessed Eucharist', 'highest honour', 'most august Sacrifice of the Mass', 'greatest adoration', since it 'contains the Lord Himself". All other sacraments and apostolic works are connected to it and directed towards it. 'The Eucharist' is co-terminous with the Mass, but not with Holy Communion. Holy Communion is not properly described as the Eucharist; it is part of the Eucharist or flows from it. The Eucharist as such is unique because of the unique presence of Christ stemming from the 'outpouring of the Spirit who works with absolutely unique power in the words of consecration'.[40]

---

40. John Paul II, Apostolic letter, *Dies Domini*, 31 May1998, n. 43.

Although he is omnipresent as God, present in those who pray in his Name, present through the Scriptures, Christ is not literally present there in the fullness of his humanity and divinity, as he is in the Eucharist, in which 'Christ the Lord Himself is contained' (c. 897). This canon encapsulates the truths of Eucharistic dogma, defined at the Council of Trent: the real change of the elements (bread and wine into the very Body and Blood of Christ), a change which may be called transubstantiation; the real presence of Christ brought about by that change; (hence he is 'contained' and, since he is really present, then in Holy Communion he is 'received'), and thirdly, the sacrificial nature of the Eucharist, as a real sacrifice (hence he is 'offered'), through a sacramental (un-bloody) and not physical sacrifice. Hence, the Eucharist is not a repetition of Calvary, but a sacramental re-presentation of the Paschal Mystery.[41] As a 'memorial' ('anamnesis'), the Eucharist is a 'calling to mind'[42] of the death, resurrection and ascension of Christ, but not as a mere memory of a historical event. Nor is it just like that of the Jews recalling the Exodus events at the Passover, recalling and identifying themselves with those events, in a sense 'becoming part' of them by that memory (cf. Dt. 26). The 'anamnesis' at the Eucharist is radically deeper than all of these. Christ makes himself truly and fully present through the action of the priest at the consecration of the Mass and the entire event of our salvation, the Paschal Mystery in all its fullness, is truly rendered present before us on the altar.[43] Nor is the Eucharist merely a symbolic or spiritual representation of the Paschal Mystery, as with the Calvinists, nor a combination of bread and wine present along with the Body and Blood (Lutheran consubstantiation), nor some presence which somehow disappears when the celebration is over. Christ is present in all his mystery as our salvation. It is not just that a new meaning can be seen in the bread and wine ('trans-signification'), nor just that these elements have a new purpose of providing spiritual rather than merely bodily nourishment ('trans-finalization'), but there is a new meaning and/or a new purpose precisely because of a real change ('transubstantiation'), by which Christ is rendered present as God and man in the Body and Blood in which he conquered death and by

---

[41.] Decrees on the Eucharist and on the Holy Sacrifice of the Mass, Council of Trent, in Denzinger and Schönmetzer (eds.), *Enchiridion symbolorum*, nn. 1635ff., especially 1651–61 and 1738ff., especially 1751–9; cf. Neuner and Dupuis, *The Christian Faith*, 2nd edn, Mercier, Cork, 1976, nn. 1512ff., especially 1526–36 and 1545ff., especially 1555–63.

[42.] Paul VI, *The Roman Missal*, Eucharistic Prayer III.

[43.] J. Quinn, *The Eucharist*, Mercier, Cork, Dublin, 1973, 44–7.

Table 12

The Sacrament of the Eucharist

Canon 897

'The *most venerable sacrament* is the blessed Eucharist in which *Christ Himself* is
- *contained*
- *offered* and
- *received*

and by which the *Church grows*.

The Eucharistic *Sacrifice*
the *memorial* of the death and resurrection of the Lord
in which the *sacrifice of the Cross* is for ever *perpetuated*
is the *summit* and the *source*
of all *worship*
and *Christian life*.

By means of it
the *unity* of *God's people* is
signified and
brought about, and
the *building* of the *Body of Christ is perfected*.

The *other sacraments* and
all the *apostolic works* of Christ
are *bound up with* and
directed to the blessed *Eucharist*.'

Canon 898

'*Christ's faithful* are
to *hold* the blessed *Eucharist in the highest honour*.
They should:
- take an *active part in*
the most august *Sacrifice of the Mass*
- *receive* it
with *great devotion*
and *frequently*, and
- *reverence* it *with* the *greatest adoration*.
Pastors of souls
in *explaining* the *doctrine* of this sacrament
are *assiduously* to *instruct* the *faithful* in this regard.'

Canon 899 § 1

'Christ the *Lord*
    through *the ministry of priests*
        – *offers himself*
           substantially present
                under the *appearance* of *bread* and *wine*
                to God the Father

        – and gives *himself*
           as *spiritual nourishment*
              to the *faithful*
                who are *associated* with him in his *offering*.'

Canon 899 § 2

'In the Eucharistic assembly the *People of God*
    are *called* together
        under the *presidency*
           of a *bishop* or of a *priest* authorized by him,
              who acts in the *person of Christ* ('*in persona Christi*')

All the *faithful* present,
    whether *clerics* or *lay* people
        participate in their *own way*
           according to their various *orders*
              and *liturgical roles*.'

Canon 899 § 3

'The *Eucharistic* celebration is to be so *organized* that
    all the *participants* derive from it
        the *fruits*
           for *which Christ* the Lord
              instituted the Eucharistic *sacrifice*.'

which he communicates his risen life; the new meaning and purpose depend entirely on this.[44]

Since the Eucharist is the 'source and summit of Christian life',[45] nothing is more important in the Christian life than the Eucharist; hence the obligation to attend and participate on Sundays and holydays of obligation (cc. 1246–1248).[46] As 'source' of Christian life, the Eucharist should be valued, since we are incapable of the conversion, fidelity and witness to which we are called without the constant stimulation of Christ's word and constant replenishment with his life, without the interior operation of his Holy Spirit.[47] These benefits are for those faithful whose condition allows them to participate in the Eucharist and to receive Holy Communion. As the 'source and summit of worship', the Church expresses all that she is and also grows in Christ, so that the Eucharist is the way Christ ensures that the Paschal Mystery is 'forever perpetuated', that he is with the Church 'until the end of time', that its 'unity ... is signified and brought about' (c. 897). Both in the deeper communion of individuals with Christ and in him the strengthening of the communion of the Church as such, the building up of the Church, which 'continually lives and grows' through the Eucharist, is 'perfected' (c. 897).[48]

The Eucharist, as summarized in cc. 897–898, involves a number of inter-related aspects which are not to be separated from one another. It is a memorial, a real sacrifice, a perfecting of Christian initiation, and an occasion to call to conversion, greater devotion, apostolate and mission. It is a 'calling together of the People of God' ('ecclesia'), a sacrament, signifying and effecting (bringing about) what it signifies, establishing deeper communion of individuals with Christ and in him of the Church as a whole.

Juridically, too, the perfecting of Christian initiation gives rise to rights and responsibilities of the faithful more fully united to Christ. Full initiation makes possible access to the sacraments of anointing, matrimony and Holy Orders, as well as to the profession of the evangelical counsels in a religious institute or admission to a society of apostolic life. Hence the 'other sacraments and all the apostolic works of Christ are bound up with ... the blessed Eucharist' (c. 897). Since

---

[44.] Paul VI, Encyclical letter, 'Mysterium fidei', 3rd September1965, Acta apostolicae sedis, 57 (1965), 753–74, at 766.

[45.] Lumen gentium, n. 11.

[46.] John Paul II, Dies Domini, nn. 46–9.

[47.] ID., Encyclical letter, Ecclesia de Eucharistia, 17 April 2003, nn. 16, 19–20, 60.

[48.] Ibid., nn. 21–4.

all depend for their effective living out upon Christ, all are equally 'directed to the blessed Eucharist'. Canonical conditions of access to these various aspects of church life stem from this theological (and canonical) appreciation of the centrality of the Eucharist.

Frequent reception of Holy Communion, urged here (c. 898), recalls Pius X's efforts to make the Mass and Holy Communion more deeply appreciated and accessible, to assist people in living out their vocations in the Church. Its frequent reception must be rooted in faith, devotion and a proper disposition. Pastors have the duty (c. 898) to explain this doctrine to the faithful and instruct them assiduously as to their duties in relation to it (c. 898), something to which they have a right (cc. 213, 229). As 'source and summit of worship', the Code insists that no other aspect of liturgy is as central or as important, no other prayer can compare with the Eucharist and no non-liturgical prayer or pious devotion ought ever to displace it or to have priority over it. In the Eucharist the whole Paschal Mystery is re-presented.

b. The Celebration of the Eucharist: General Aspects

As for other sacraments, the Eucharist is 'an action of Christ and of the Church' (c. 899 § 1), by which faith is 'expressed and strengthened, worship is offered to God and our sanctification is brought about' (c. 840), for which bishops and other pastors have a specific duty of care (cc. 835 § 1–2, 840). The real change in the elements at the consecration makes Christ 'substantially present' and the Eucharist as both sacrifice and communion (c. 899 § 1) underline the core truths of this mystery. The indispensable place of Christ's action and presence is brought out by the two Christological titles (Acts 2: 38): 'Christ ('Christos': the anointed One') the Lord' ('Kyrios': the Risen Lord'). He brings us the whole power of the Paschal Mystery in the sacramental offering of the Eucharist, re-presenting the sacrifice of Calvary and giving himself to us in his life-giving Body and Blood as 'spiritual nourishment to the faithful who are associated with him in his offering' (c. 899 § 1).

The Eucharist builds up and expresses the Church (c. 899 § 2). The 'faithful' (laity and clergy), exercise their common priesthood based on baptism by sharing in Christ's offering, in the summit of all we do as Christians. The ordained priesthood, different in kind, is essential since the Eucharist can only be brought about by the ministry of priests (cc. 899 § 1–2, 900).[49] In the Eucharist the faithful are 'called together' (c. 899 § 2) not of their own will, but by a vocation from

---

49. Ibid., n. 29.

Christ,[50] which requires a response of faith and conversion affecting the whole of our lives.

The Eucharist both manifests the Church and enables it to grow. Participation depends upon baptism, but is to take place 'according to orders and liturgical roles' (c. 899 § 2). A bishop or priest is needed for the Eucharist to occur, deacons having a role as sacred ministers, but not as ministerial priests. The common priesthood of the faithful is exercised as we all offer ourselves to the Father in, with and through Christ. The distinction between 'orders' and 'liturgical role' emphasizes that liturgical roles are not orders. The ministries of reader and acolyte and the functions of cantor, bringing the gifts, servers, and such like, have a proper place as the Church expresses herself in this distinction, within a common unity of joining Christ in his perfect prayer to the Father.

The Eucharist is a sacrament since it was instituted by Christ (cc. 840, 899 § 3). The 'real fruits intended' are that our Christian lives may be nourished and sustained, to pursue the apostolate more effectively, draw closer to Christ personally and grow as a church in greater unity in him with one another (cc. 897-898). Although the Eucharist is validly celebrated, receiving these fruits depends on the disposition of the recipient. The consecration is truly brought about even if the priest himself is in a state of serious sin, if he does what the Church intends, since he acts in the person of Christ, who activates the grace of his ordination as a priest ('*ex opere operato*') and so Christ acts through it, whatever the disposition of the priest.[51] Fruitful reception of Holy Communion by anyone of us depends on whether we are in a state of grace and properly disposed ('*ex operare operantis*'). To receive this sacrament in a state of mortal sin is to add sin to sin, not to grow in grace. Its purpose is that we grow in grace, which we do when we receive it properly disposed: 'The good eat, the bad eat, but their fate is unequal, life or ruin. Death is the fate for the evil, life for the good; see how, from consuming the same food, the outcome is so different.'[52]

[50.] Congregation for Divine Worship and the Discipline of the Sacraments, Instruction, *Redemptionis Sacramentum*, 25 March 2004, n. 42.

[51.] John Paul II, *The Catechism of the Catholic Church*, n. 1128.

[52.] Sequence for the Solemnity of Corpus Christi, *Lauda, Sion, Salvatorem*': 'Summunt boni, summunt mali, sorte tamen inaequali, vitae vel interitus. Mors est malis, vita bonis; vide paris sumptionis quam sit dispar exitus' (my translation).

c. The Valid Celebration of the Eucharist

For validity the matter must be 'wheaten only' bread 'recently made' to avoid the danger of corruption (c. 924 § 2) and wine which is 'natural, made from grapes of the vine and not corrupt' (c. 924 § 3). The use of any other grain than wheat or any admixture renders the matter invalid and there must be no admixture to the wine, which must be pure.[53] Wine which has not fermented properly – 'must' – is illicit, although, since fermentation has begun, it is valid matter.[54] It must be wine and not water with a little wine added; the contents must be mostly wine or it is not valid matter. The form to be used for the consecration is that given, in two parts in Table 12. The minister is a validly ordained priest only (c. 900 § 1). His intention must be to do what the Church intends in consecrating bread and wine into the Body and Blood of Christ, with regard to specified bread and wine (such as, the bread and wine here on the corporal). One useful practice is to intend to consecrate the bread/wine on the corporal and in the principal celebrant's hands or, where the matter cannot be seen by a concelebrant, this plus what else the principal celebrant intends to consecrate at that Mass. The intention may be virtual (that he intends to do this whenever he celebrates the Eucharist), but this should be renewed from time to time (for example, on the anniversary of his priestly ordination, Holy Thursday).[55]

d. The Licit Celebration of the Eucharist

Some General Norms

All the conditions necessary for validity are needed also for liceity. In addition, there is to be a little water added to the wine (c. 924 § 1), the bread is to be unleavened (c. 926), one element is not to be consecrated without the other (c. 927) and, if a priest dies or suddenly becomes too ill to continue, another priest must be found to continue the consecration and complete the Mass. It is to be celebrated in Latin, which is always permitted, unless a concelebration has been planned in the vernacular,[56] or according to approved translated texts, with sacred ministers not prohibited by law (c. 900 § 2), wearing the

---

53. *Redemptionis Sacramentum*, nn. 48–50.
54. D. Mussone, *L'Eucaristia nel codice di diritto canonico: Commento ai canoni 897–958*, Libreria editrice Vaticana, 2002, 109–10.
55. E. Besson, *La dimension juridique des sacrements*, P.U.G., Rome, 2004, 193–4.
56. *Redemptionis sacramentum*, n. 112.

sacred vestments prescribed (c. 928), on any day permitted (c. 931) – not Good Friday or Holy Saturday before the Vigil – and in a church, chapel or, in necessity, other setting which is reverent (cc. 932–933). The liturgical norms are always to be followed (cc. 925, 928, 930). A validly ordained priest and no one else is necessary for validity (c. 900 § 1), but, for liceity, he must not be prohibited by law: suspended, dispensed or removed from the clerical state (c. 900 § 2).

Individual Celebration and Concelebration

A priest may celebrate Mass 'in an individual manner', but not while there is another Mass being celebrated in the same oratory or church at the same time. He may concelebrate (c. 902). Concelebration emphasizes the unity of the presbyterate and symbolizes the unity the Eucharist expresses and fosters. This is a development in the light of the theology of communion at the Second Vatican Council; previously, concelebration was only permitted at the ordination Mass of a priest or of a bishop.[57] The permission to celebrate the Eucharist 'in an individual manner' ('individuali modo') could mean to be the only celebrant or it might mean that also he is permitted to celebrate on his own, even without a congregation of anyone. The previous Code said he should not do so without someone to respond to the Mass.[58] It remains forbidden as a general practice (he 'may not' celebrate the Eucharist 'without the presence of at least one of the faithful'), but that is 'unless there is a good and reasonable cause for doing so' (c. 906). Thus, it is not absolutely forbidden and, indeed, its legitimacy seems to be implied when priests are urged to celebrate the Eucharist 'frequently', indeed 'daily', since, 'even if it is not possible to have the faithful present', it is 'an action of Christ and of the Church', by which the 'work of redemption is continually carried out' and in it he fulfils his 'principal function' (c. 904).[59] Daily celebration, which is the tradition of the Latin Church, is thus strongly urged. A priest who does not concelebrate for a good reason, but who is present at the Mass, is to wear choir dress or at least a cassock and cotta.[60] This is to reduce the abuse of some priests wishing not to 'appear different' from those of the faithful who are not priests.

---

57. *Codex iuris canonici* (1917), c. 803.
58. Ibid., c. 813.
59. Cf., J. Gaudemet, *Le droit canonique*, Cerf, Fides, Paris, 1898, 50.
60. *Redemptionis sacramentum*, nn. 113, 128.

The 'Celebret'

Permission for a priest to celebrate or to concelebrate the Eucharist, though, depends on him either being known to the priest in the place where he goes or on his presenting to the priest there a recently issued document from his bishop or other superior, verifying that he is a priest not prohibited by law from celebrating the Eucharist. A priest with such a document ('celebret': 'Let him celebrate') who comes at any reasonable time, must be allowed to celebrate or to concelebrate the Eucharist (c. 903).[61] Abuses by people masquerading as what they are not do occur. It should be verified that one who presents himself is a Catholic priest in good standing; a recent celebret constitutes such proof.

Celebration of the Eucharist more than once a Day

A priest is normally not to celebrate the Eucharist more than once in the same day, although he may do so twice, even three times on a Sunday or holyday for pastoral reasons (c. 905). He should celebrate the Eucharist on a Sunday or a holyday, even if he has done so already, if, otherwise, people would not be able to participate in the Eucharist as such on a day of precept.

> The lay faithful have the right, barring a case of real impossibility, that no priest should ever refuse to celebrate Mass for the people or to have it celebrated by another priest, if the people would not be able to satisfy the obligation of participating at Mass on a Sunday or on another day of precept.[62]

This reflects the fact that the care of souls is the supreme norm of canon law (cc. 213, 1752).

Certain Liturgical Abuses

A priest is to say the parts of the Eucharist, especially of the Eucharistic prayer, proper to him; no one who is not a priest to say any part of those sections reserved to the priest nor to perform those acts proper to the priest (c. 907). The parts in which the other members of the faithful are to say in the Eucharistic prayer are the responsorial elements (responses to the introduction to the preface, the Sanctus, the Eucharistic acclamation and especially the 'Great Amen'), as an affirmation by all of everything that is said and done on their behalf

---

[61.] Ibid., n. 111.
[62.] Ibid., n. 163.

by the priest.[63] The priest should prepare himself for celebrating the Eucharist by prayer and should make a thanksgiving after Mass (c. 909). He is never to concelebrate with priests or ministers of Churches or ecclesial communities not in full communion with the Catholic Church (c. 908). To do so is one of the more serious canonical crimes ('*graviora delicta*'), where it is with ministers who do not have valid orders recognized by the Catholic Church.[64]

e. The Minister of Holy Communion

Although only a validly ordained priest or bishop can confect or bring about the Eucharist, through the consecration, the ordinary minister of Holy Communion is a validly ordained bishop, priest or deacon (c. 910 § 1). The fact that the officially instituted acolyte is mentioned first, and is the only one to be specifically designated, as an extra-ordinary minister of Holy Communion (cc. 910 § 2, 230 § 3) shows that, where an ordinary minister is not available or where ordinary ministers are not sufficient to avoid a prolonged delay in the Eucharist or to bring Holy Communion to the sick, the instituted acolyte is the one who should fulfil this function (c. 911 § 1), although others properly prepared and deputed as 'extra-ordinary ministers of Holy Communion' may fulfil that role on a temporary basis in accordance with canonical norms (c. 910 § 2, 911 § 2).[65] They are not to be called 'extra-ordinary' or 'special ministers of the Eucharist', since they are not such and calling them such 'would improperly broaden their role'; they are 'extra-ordinary ministers of Holy Communion'.[66]

f. The Administration of Viaticum

Viaticum ('*via tecum*': 'with you on the way') is Holy Communion given to the dying person to sustain him on the journey to the next world.[67] The parish priest, assistant priest, chaplain (priest chaplain) or the priest superior in a house of an institute of consecrated life or

---

[63] Ibid., nn. 52–4.
[64] Ibid., n. 172c; John Paul II, Apostolic letter, '*motu proprio*', '*Sacramentorum sanctitatis tutela*', 30 April 2001, *Acta apostolicae sedis*, 93 (2001), 737–9; cf., B. A. Ferme, ' "Graviora delicta": the Apostolic letter: "*Sacramentorum sanctitatis tutela*" ' in Z. Suchecki (ed.), *Il processo penale canonico*, Lateran University Press, Rome, 2003, 365–82 at 375–6.
[65] *Redemptionis sacramentum*, nn. 154–60.
[66] Ibid., n. 156.
[67] J. A. Coriden, *An Introduction to Canon Law*, 128.

society of apostolic life has the 'duty and right' to administer viaticum (cc. 911 § 1, 922). In the absence of such persons, the deacon, the acolyte or another extra-ordinary minister of Holy Communion may administer this sacrament to such a person (c. 911 § 2), but those who are not priests are incapable of absolving sins and are incapable of administering the sacrament of anointing of the sick, even in such extreme circumstances. The sick in such circumstances may receive and should receive Holy Communion, even if they have received it earlier in the same day (c. 921 § 1–2); they should receive Holy Communion daily in such circumstances, if possible (c. 921 § 3).

g. Participation in the Eucharist

The Basic Principle

The basic principle is that 'any baptized person not forbidden by law may receive Holy Communion' (c. 912). Baptism and confirmation, as sacraments of initiation, are orientated towards the Eucharist (c. 866) and there is a right to the sacraments (cc. 213, 843 § 1). However, the exercise of this right is limited by the 'condition' of the faithful (cc. 96, 204 § 1), based on the fullness of the profession of faith, whether or not they have other valid sacraments (depending on the validity of Order) and whether or not they are in full communion with the Catholic Church by their faith, practice and discipline and on whether or not they are under lawful ecclesiastical sanction (c. 205).

Children and Holy Communion

Once they have reached the age of reason (c. 914), are able to understand the basics of the faith, especially about the Eucharist, if they are properly prepared and disposed, children may receive Holy Communion (c. 913 § 1) after having made their sacramental confession (c. 914). Pius X sought to make this great sacrament available to them to assist them in their faith and Christian living. In the case of those who are disabled and/or those in danger of death, they may receive Holy Communion once they can distinguish the sacred species from ordinary food (c. 913 § 2). Parents and the parish priests especially are to ensure that children are properly instructed and prepared (c. 914); coming to Mass on Sundays would be an important indication of being otherwise prepared.

State of Grace

No one conscious of grave sin may receive Holy Communion until they have been absolved, unless they have no opportunity, but then they must make an act of perfect contrition and that includes the firm intention to go to confession as soon as possible (c. 916). Those under excommunication or interdict and others obstinately persisting in grave sin may not receive Holy Communion until they have been absolved from both sin and censures (c. 915).[68] The divorced and remarried, living in a state objectively in contradiction to church teaching on marriage, its fidelity and indissolubility cannot receive Holy Communion, unless living as brother and sister and where there is no scandal. They are to be encouraged to live their lives as Catholics as fully as possible, including prayer, participation in the Eucharist without receiving Holy Communion, with the support of proper pastoral care.[69]

Other Norms for Holy Communion

A Catholic other than priests may receive Holy Communion a second time in the same day, if that person participates in a full Mass a second time (c. 917). They are encouraged to receive Holy Communion when they share in the Eucharist (c. 918). They are not permitted to receive a second time if this is at Holy Communion outside Mass, nor are they ever permitted to receive Holy Communion a third time in the day, except as viaticum (c. 921). They are to fast from food and drink, other than water and medicine, for an hour before Holy Communion (c. 919 § 1); the elderly and the sick being exempt (c. 919 § 3). After first Holy Communion, they are obliged to receive at least once a year, ideally about Easter time (c. 920). Priests must receive Holy Communion at any Mass which they celebrate or concelebrate. They are allowed to drink and eat something in between Masses after the first one, where they have to say two or three Masses (c. 919 § 2). Catholics may receive Holy Communion in any Catholic rite (c. 923).

Communion under both kinds is permitted, but is not compulsory, except for the priest celebrating or concelebrating who must receive under both species from what is consecrated at that Mass.[70] The faithful must receive under the form of bread, except where a person is incapable of taking the host, when the precious Blood may be administered (c. 925). They may receive under the form of wine as

---

68. John Paul II, *Ecclesia de Eucharistia*, nn. 36–7.

69. ID., *Familiaris consortio*, n. 84; Congregation for the Doctrine of the Faith, Letter to Bishops on the reception of Communion by the Divorced and Remarried, 14 September 1994, *Acta apostolicae sedis* 86 (1994), 974–9; Benedict XVI, Apostolic exhortation, *Sacramentum caritatis*, 22 February 2007, n. 29.

70. *Redemptionis sacramentum*, n. 98.

well if they freely choose to do so, provided this can be done reverently and safely and the norms are followed. The precious Blood may be received either by drinking from the chalice or by a tube or by intinction (dipping the host into the precious Blood – in which case it must be administered on the tongue and never in the hand, with the host being strong – c. 924). The amount consecrated as precious Blood is to be limited, to avoid danger of spilling it, worthy chalices are to be used and never jugs, and it is all to be consumed at that celebration of the Eucharist, never thrown into the sacrarium and never reserved.[71]

h. The Reservation of the Blessed Sacrament

The Blessed Sacrament under the appearance of bread is to be reserved, under the appearance of wine it is not to be reserved, in a church, oratory or chapel, never in a private house (cc. 934–936). Someone is always to be responsible for its safety and for reverence and Mass is to be celebrated there at least twice a month (c. 934 § 2). This reservation is to be in a tabernacle, in a distinguished place, suitably adorned and conducive to prayer, immovable and secure, with its key equally secure (c. 938). A lamp is to burn to honour Christ's presence. Such places should be open, if possible, to the faithful, exposition and benediction by a priest or deacon is recommended, with exposition and deposition being conducted by an acolyte, other extraordinary minister of Holy Communion or deputed person in special circumstances, as determined by the diocesan bishop (c. 943). Public adoration, even processions in honour of the Blessed Sacrament, are recommended (c. 944).

i. 'Communicatio in sacris'

This question of Christian faithful sharing in the sacraments is not limited to Holy Communion, but includes reconciliation and anointing of the sick too. It has two aspects: when Catholics may approach ministers of another Church and when baptized members of other Churches or ecclesial communities may approach Catholic ministers for these sacraments. Since the faithful have a basic right to spiritual sustenance by word and sacrament (c. 213), access should not be unnecessarily restrictive, but it depends on the condition of the individual members of the faithful (c. 205); it is not a matter of merely human sociability, but of sharing in sacred mysteries.

[71.] Ibid., nn. 100–7.

Normally, Catholic ministers may lawfully administer these sacraments only to Catholic members of the faithful and Catholic members of the faithful may lawfully receive them only from Catholic ministers, including those of other Catholic rites (cc. 844 § 1, 923). Exceptions may occur when there is: real spiritual advantage, no danger of error or indifferentism, Christ's faithful physically or morally cannot approach a Catholic minister (there is none anywhere near over a significant period of time). A Catholic member of the faithful may then lawfully receive Holy Communion, penance and/or anointing from 'non-Catholic ministers in whose Churches these sacraments are valid' (c. 844 § 2). Since the validity of these sacraments depends absolutely on their being celebrated by a validly ordained priest, these sacraments are only valid in Eastern Churches (Orthodox) or Old Catholic Churches. Hence, Catholics may not receive these sacraments from Protestant, Reformed or Anglican ministers. Orthodox and other Churches have their own regulations and may not admit Catholics to Holy Communion; their regulations are to be respected, for reasons of ecumenical cooperation.

Catholic ministers may lawfully administer these sacraments to members of the faithful of Eastern Non-Catholic Churches and of Churches the Holy See judges to be in the same position as them, such as Old Catholic, if they ask for them spontaneously (are not invited, much less urged), are properly disposed (not in serious sin nor in a state objectively at odds with Church teaching such as divorced and remarried – c. 844 § 3).

If they are in danger of death or judged by the ordinary or episcopal conference to be in some other 'grave and pressing need', Catholic ministers may lawfully administer these sacraments to other members of Christ's faithful not in full communion with the Catholic Church if they cannot approach a minister of their own community, demonstrate Catholic faith in regard to these sacraments, and are properly disposed (c. 844 § 4). The diocesan bishop or the episcopal conference is not to issue norms on c. 844 § 2, 3, 4 without consulting competent authorities in other Churches or communities (c. 844 § 5); norms issued by the bishops' conference would need the 'recognitio' of the Holy See before they would be valid.

Since the Code was issued, there has been some clarification. The 'Church of Christ subsists in the Catholic Church' means that it is found there truly with all the essential elements of the Church of Christ in it. A major distinction exists between Churches in which there are valid orders and those where there are not. The former Churches, 'while not existing in perfect communion with the Catholic Church, remain united to her by the closest bonds ... (of) apostolic succession and a valid Eucharist, and are true particular Churches', though they do not accept papal primacy. The latter are 'ecclesial communities, which have not preserved the valid episcopate and the genuine and integral substance of the Eucharistic mystery, are not Churches in the proper sense', although their members, as baptized, are incorporated into the Church and so 'are in a certain union, albeit imperfect, with the Church'.[72] The recognition in the Code (c. 844 § 3–4) that, 'under special circumstances' for 'individual persons' there might be possible admittance to these three sacraments was to try to take care of the salvation of souls and not to establish a means of promoting inter-communion, 'impossible until the visible bonds of ecclesial communion are fully established'.[73] In fact, 'no dispensation can be given' from the conditions required in the Code. Thus, in a person seeking these sacraments, the denial of one or more of the truths of the faith about these sacraments 'and, among these, the truth regarding the need for the ministerial priesthood for their validity, renders the person ... improperly disposed to legitimately receiving them'.[74] All of the conditions stated must be present together.[75]

A document on this question issued by the Bishops' Conferences of England and Wales, Ireland and Scotland, giving further norms, claims to give 'norms for individual cases rather categories of situations', with 'no intention to present a type or precedent for apparently similar cases'.[76] They envisage a 'unique occasion, ... of its nature unrepeatable, a "one off" situation', but then they give examples of Christian initiation, a funeral, marriage or ordination.[77] It is not clear how this squares with their recognition of the norms (c. 844) requiring 'grave spiritual necessity', with 'no chance of recourse to their own community' (such as when scattered in a largely Catholic community), in 'grave and pressing need', nor how these situations can be regarded as 'one off' when they refer to events which may be regarded as in some way 'typical'.

---

[72] Congregation for the Doctrine of the Faith, *Dominus Iesus*, n. 17.
[73] John Paul II, *Ecclesia de Eucharistia*, n. 45.
[74] Ibid.
[75] *Redemptionis sacramentum*, n. 85; cf., Pontifical Council for Christian Unity, *Directory for the Application of Principles and Norms on Ecumenism*, Vatican, Rome,1993, nn. 130–2.
[76] Catholic Bishops' Conferences of England and Wales, Ireland and Scotland, *One Bread, One Body*, Catholic Truth Society, London, Veritas, Dublin, 1998, n. 107.
[77] Ibid., 108–9.

j. Offerings for Masses

A priest may offer the celebration of the Eucharist for a particular need or intention and is encouraged to do so (c. 945 § 2), although the Eucharist of its nature is destined to honour God and secondarily the saints, as well as being of its nature for the benefit of all the living and those in Purgatory. He may accept an offering for saying Mass for this particular intention (c. 945 § 1), by which the faithful contribute to the good of the Church and the upkeep of its ministers (c. 946). Obligations attaching to this are not to traffic or trade or appear to do so over Mass offerings (c. 947), to say a Mass for each intention and offering accepted (cc. 948–949), to base the number of Masses on an official diocesan Mass offering, in cases where the money received is not linked to a specific number of Masses (cc. 950, 952), not to retain more than one offering per day; if more than one Mass has been said with an offering on the same day, the others are to be sent to the diocese, to be used as the bishop decides (cc. 950–951). He is not to accept any offering for a second Mass said on the same day where he concelebrates (c. 951), not to accept more Masses than he can say in a year and to say Masses thus requested in a year or to transfer them to other priests (with the offerings), who, agreeing to say them, accept the obligation of doing so and receive the relevant offerings (cc. 953–956). He is to have a book of his own, where he records requests for such 'manual Masses', the amount of the offerings, and the dates the obligations were fulfilled; and to have such a book in each parish or house (cc. 955 § 4, 957–958), open to diocesan inspection. The recent practice of having multiple intentions from the one Mass, if this is understood and accepted by those who make the offering, could perhaps be allowed (for one Mass only in a day in the parish for all on that list), but then only the standard diocesan offering should be kept, the rest going to charity, to avoid any abuse;[78] other Masses would be said for individual intentions offered and accepted as such.

Foundation Masses, arising from sums of money left in wills or otherwise, are to be regulated by the diocese and the number of Masses required each year to be said. If over time the value of money has changed significantly the bishop may undertake a 'reduction', using the then current diocesan offering to determine how many are to be said; this practice should properly be made known to those making bequests or the like (c. 1308).

The bishop of the diocese is obliged to say Mass for the people of the

---

[78.] Ghirlanda, Il diritto nella Chiesa, 316–17, n. 321.

diocese ('*Missa pro populo*') every Sunday and holyday of obligation (c. 388) and the parish priest has the same obligation for the people of his parish (cc. 534, 543 § 2), one Mass if he is parish priest or moderator of a number (c. 517 § 1). They may not take an offering for that Mass, but if they request another priest to say it (on a rare occasion), they should give him an offering.

k. The Extra-Ordinary Form of the Mass

Mgr Lefevbre was associated with a refusal to accept the reform of the liturgy undertaken after the Second Vatican Council and in particular the Missal of Paul VI of 1970 or to accept that the centuries-old form of the celebration of the Eucharist (made normative, with the exception of rites of centennial custom, by Pope St Pius V in 1570 after the Council of Trent and often known somewhat misleadingly as the Tridentine rite) should not be celebrated henceforth. In fact, he and his followers refused to accept two documents of the Council itself, so that the question of the 'Latin Mass' was never the only issue which divided them from the mainstream of the Church. In 1988, in advancing age, Mgr Lefevbre sought to provide for his own succession as the self-appointed leader of what was called the Society of St Pius X by ordaining four priests as bishops, obviously without papal permission. Such an episcopal ordination or consecration would be valid, but not only illicit, but also a canonical crime, since it directly fractures the unity of the Church, being of its nature a schismatic act (c. 1382). It carries the penalty of automatic excommunication for the ordaining bishop and for any bishops ordained without the pontifical mandate. This automatic excommunication was declared in the '*motu proprio*' '*Ecclesia Dei*' of 1988;[79] in other words it was rendered public, to dissuade people from joining or remaining with a schismatic group, to urge acceptance of the Church's Tradition, including of the Second Vatican Council, and to foster unity in the Church.[80]

The aim of the '*motu proprio*' was to safeguard the unity of the Church in another way too. Pope John Paul II recognized that quite a number of people who had attached themselves to this group or who attended their Masses did so not in order to damage the Church, but out of attachment for the liturgy known as the Tridentine rite. In some places, such as England and Wales, there had already been an indult from the Holy See, a regular exception to the law as distinct from a

---

[79] John Paul II, Apostolic letter, *motu proprio, Ecclesia Dei*, 2 July 1988, n. 4.
[80] Ibid., n. 5.

dispensation which applies to an individual case only, to permit the celebration of the Mass according to the former rite if the local diocesan bishop granted permission. A few years before *Eccelsia Dei* John Paul II had made this a universal norm, so that this liturgy could be celebrated throughout the Church, if the local bishop gave permission, in order to avoid schism and in order to attract back to full communion those who had gone astray. The Congregation for Divine Worship and the Discipline of the Sacraments issued the relevant indult in 1984, which John Paul II, in 1988, urged bishops to apply generously.[81] A Pontifical Commission set up a little earlier was to help re-integrate priests from the St Pius X Society into the Church.[82]

In 2007 Pope Benedict XVI issued another *motu proprio, Summorum Pontificum* with the same purpose, convinced that the longer a schism continued, the more difficult it was to heal and to attempt all that could be done to effect reconciliation. This document recognizes the benefits of the liturgical reforms of the last forty years and designates the liturgy as reformed by Paul VI the 'ordinary form' of the Roman rite and what is known as the Tridentine rite, according to the 1962 Missal, as the 'extra-ordinary form of the Roman rite', there being thus 'two usages of the single Roman rite' ('*duo usus unici ritus romani*').[83] The 1962 Missal, the marginally reformed Missal in use at the time the Second Vatican Council opened, may be used by any priest of the Latin rite by virtue of this *motu proprio*. Thus, it is no longer necessary to seek the permission of the local bishop to celebrate that Mass; this permission is given in this text under universal law, by which all bishops are bound. However, that applies to a priest saying Mass himself, to which other members of the faithful may come if they so choose; this form being allowed also to institutes of the consecrated life and societies of apostolic life, where their communities so decide, in their own oratories.[84] For the use of the 'extra-ordinary form' with the people, it is necessary that a number of them ask for this to be available and also that the priest agree freely.[85] The priest must be capable of celebrating that rite with sense and dignity, which implies that he understands and can use Latin.[86] The bishop can neither forbid nor impose the use of this rite, but, as the principal dispenser of the sacraments, he has the

---

[81.] Congregation for Divine Worship and for the Discipline of the Sacraments, Letter, *Quattuor abhinc annos*, 3 October 1984, *Acta apostolicae sedis*, 76 (1984), 1088–9.

[82.] John Paul II, *Ecclesia Dei*, nn. 5–6.

[83.] Benedict XVI, Apostolic letter, *motu proprio, Summorum Pontificum*, 7 July 2007, art. 1.

[84.] Ibid., art. 2–4.

[85.] Ibid., art. 5 § 1.

[86.] Ibid., art. 5 § 4.

right to moderate its use, to intervene if there are abuses.[87] Examples of this might be if a priest is using the rite who simply does not know Latin sufficiently well to be able to do so or where a priest presumes to replace a parish Mass in the *Novus Ordo* rite of Paul VI with this Mass where many of the faithful find it imposed upon them. It would be wrong for the bishop to ignore such abuses; it would also be wrong for him to intervene in this area while not intervening to remedy more serious abuses in the ordinary form of the Latin rite, which he is also to moderate. The diocesan bishop can establish a 'personal parish', which uses the extra-ordinary form as its normal form of the Roman rite, if circumstances warrant it and make it possible.[88]

Benedict XVI has recently sought to reduce further the obstacles to members of the St Pius X Society being reunited with the Catholic Church by causing the excommunications incurred in 1988 to be lifted after receiving written indications that the four bishops of the Society who had been ordained illegally by Mgr Lefebvre wished to be reconciled.[89] In fact, an excommunication must be lifted when there is evidence of repentance. This measure was obfuscated by the public discussion of the opinions of one of those bishops, denying the extent of the holocaust of Jewish victims of Hitler, an irresponsible and dangerous personal opinion, which does not constitute a crime in canon law any more than it does in the civil laws of most states, to which, therefore, the excommunication had and could have no relevance.

With these attempts to heal the schism, Benedict XVI has also made it quite clear that the issues which continue to divide are not over the Latin Mass nor over canonical penalties, but over doctrine. Members of that Society must accept the doctrines taught by all Popes from John XXIII onwards, as well as all of those taught by the Second Vatican Council, before reconciliation can occur. Hence, canonically, that Society 'has no canonical status in the Church and its ministers cannot legitimately exercise any ministry' in it, unless and until they are reconciled on that basis.[90] Since the matters which remain are doctrinal, the Pope has placed the body which has been responsible in

---

[87.] Ibid., art. 5 § 1.

[88.] Ibid., art 5 § 10; cf. c. 518.

[89.] Benedict XVI, Letter to the Bishops of the Catholic Church, 10 January 2009, www.vatican.va/holy-father/benedict-xvi/letters/2009/documents/hf-ben-xvi-1..., accessed 8 July 2009.

[90.] Benedict XVI, Apostolic letter, *motu proprio, Ecclesiae unitatem*, 2 July 2009, n. 4, www.vatican.va/holy-father/benedict-xvi/apost-letters/documents/hf-ben-xvi, accessed 16 July 2009.

the Holy See for promoting reconciliation under the Congregation of the Doctrine of the Faith, the Prefect of that Congregation now being also the President of that body, *Ecclesia Dei*.[91]

5. Conclusion

After treating the sacraments of initiation, we shall consider the sacraments of healing next, those of reconciliation and of anointing of the sick.

---

91. Ibid., n. 5.

Chapter 10

The Sanctifying Function of the Church

(Book IV of the Code)

Part I: The Sacraments
III: The Sacraments of Healing

1. Introduction

In this chapter we shall examine the sacraments of reconciliation and anointing of the sick. Both sacraments have seen notable changes in recent years, which have had their effect on the Code of Canon Law. Abuses over reconciliation have resulted in legal clarifications in the last few years. The sacrament previously known as extreme unction was often associated only with anointing those on the point of death. The law reflects changes here too.

2. The Sacrament of Reconciliation

a. Doctrinal Foundations of Canonical Norms on Reconciliation

Biblical and Historical Perspectives

Whether we speak of confession, penance or reconciliation, this sacrament needs to be understood first of all in relation to the underlying Gospel virtue of penance: 'Repent and believe the Good News' (Mk. 1:14–15). Discipleship entails a wholehearted turning away from former values in lifelong conversion to Christ ('*metanoia*'), implied by the baptismal incorporation of people into him and into his Church (Acts 2:38; 1 Cor. 6:1–10, Col. 3:1–17, Gal. 5:16–26). Forgiveness was part of prayer (1 Jn. 2:1; James 5:13) and was to be practised (Mt. 5:38–41; 18:21–35; Lk. 6:36–8; 15:11–32; 17:3–4). It was at the heart of Christ's ministry and of all discipleship (Mt. 18:21–35; Lk. 6:36–8;

17:3–4; Rom. 3:21–6; 5:6–11, 15–21; 2 Cor. 5:18–21; Eph. 2:11–18; Col. 14–15).

Some in the early Church thought there was no post-baptismal forgiveness for sins. However, Jesus had instituted a sacrament of forgiveness which seemed really distinct from that obtained in baptism and his teachings seemed to imply that post-baptismal forgiveness was possible and was willed by him. Some evidence of this may be seen with the man guilty of incest (1 Cor. 5:1–13), who was excluded from the community or excommunicated; references to 'grave sin', 'handed over', 'not associate with', Paul instructing 'with authority' and 'in the Name of the Lord Jesus' and 'by the power of the Lord Jesus' show how serious it was. The call for reconciliation of a sinner who has been punished sufficiently (2 Cor. 2:5–11) may or may not refer to this case, but it certainly speaks of reconciliation after baptism. Without itself being an instance of sacramental reconciliation, it does indicate post-baptismal reconciliation. Paul says: 'I have forgiven' the one 'you have forgiven', adding that 'what has been forgiven' by him for their sake is forgiven 'in the presence (or person) of Christ'(2 Cor. 2:10), the divine passive and the reference to the presence of Christ reinforcing this interpretation.

The sin which cannot be forgiven (1 Jn. 5:16) and the sin of blasphemy against the Holy Spirit (Mt. 12:31) differ from mortal sins that can be forgiven, if the penitent is truly sorry for them. These sins cannot be forgiven though where the person rejects God's offer of forgiveness and dies impenitent, persisting in a 'radical refusal of forgiveness, conversion and salvation'.[1] This is not to be confused with someone who may not have had the opportunity to go to confession before death, but who is in fact sorry for their sins.

The transmission of the power to forgive sins is linked to the institution by Jesus of confession, penance or reconciliation as a specific sacrament (Mt. 16:17–19; Mt. 18:15–18 and Jn. 20:19–23). Mt. 16 deals with Peter and the 'keys'; 'closing' and 'opening', 'binding' and 'loosing' indicate complete authority. Mt. 18 refers to 'the disciples', probably indicating the Twelve. 'Binding' and 'loosing' could refer to teaching, but also to excommunication. The whole section before insists upon the duty of all Christians to forgive; 'binding' and 'loosing' could indicate an authoritative conversion and restoration to the communion of the Church. The use of the divine passive 'shall be considered bound, ... loosed, in heaven' is a typical way of referring to the action of God in Matthew, without mentioning his Name and

---

[1.] John Paul II, Encyclical letter, *Dominum et vivificantem*, 18 May 1986, n. 46.

suggests the sacrament of reconciliation. Also Jn. 20 uses the divine passive and 'retain' seems to refer to the forgiveness of those already baptized. The Council of Trent saw these texts as indicating God's action operating through the words and actions of the Apostles, a biblical basis for the sacrament of reconciliation.[2]

At first it was thought that Jesus's teaching meant forgiveness could be granted once only after baptismal forgiveness, which led to people delaying confession until almost the last moment. The sacrament was administered after lengthy, often public penance, at the Easter Vigil; communal and penitential aspects were prominent. With the Celtic monks, auricular confession became the practical norm in Ireland and then elsewhere, penances, often severe, coming after confession and absolution. The practice allowed more attention to the needs of the individual penitent and the administration of the sacrament by priests, not just or primarily by the bishop. Irish penitential books had a 'tariff list' of penances for particular sins, augmented or diminished according to a person's place and role in the Church.

The Council of Trent specified the key elements of the sacrament as contrition for sins, the integral (complete) confession of all mortal sins of which the penitent was aware and absolution by the priest.[3] This was not new, but it clarified the by then long-standing practice of individual confession to a priest, which could be received many times in a person's lifetime. This approach favoured personal attention to penitents, but confession might be reduced to a fairly 'automatic' listing of faults. The liturgical and communitarian aspects were somewhat obscured and the place of Scripture limited, if not often absent.

The Second Vatican Council and the Sacrament of Reconciliation

The Second Vatican Council wished to renew confession or penance to bring out 'the nature and effect of the sacrament'.[4] Those who receive it 'obtain pardon from God's mercy and, at the same time, are reconciled with the Church which they have wounded by sinning and

---

2. Council of Trent, Decree on the Sacraments of Penance and Extreme Unction, H. Denzinger and A. Schönmetzer (eds), *Enchiridion symbolorum, definitionum et declarationum de rebus fidei et morum*, 36th edn, Barcelona, Freiburg-im-Breisgau, Rome, 1976, nn. 1670, 1703; J. Neuner and J. Dupuis (eds), *The Christian Faith in the Doctrinal Documents of the Catholic Church*, 2nd edn, Mercier, Cork, 1976, nn. 1617, 1643.

3. Council of Trent, *Enchiridion symboroum*, D.S., nn. 1676–83, 1689–93, 1701ff., esp. 1704; Neuner and Dupuis, *The Christian Faith*, nn. 1622–6, 1630–3, 1641ff., esp. 1644.

4. Second Vatican Council, Dogmatic Constitution on the Sacred Liturgy, *Sacrosanctum Concilium*, n. 72.

which works for their conversion by charity, example and prayers'.[5] More broadly, it had called for the faith of members to be nurtured on the basis of the Gospel,[6] and for all sacraments to be renewed also by integrating the Scriptures into their liturgical celebration.[7] Thus, the ecclesial dimension of the sacrament is strongly present in terms of the damage done by sin, the communitarian prayer of the Church for the growth in holiness of each and all of its members, and the effects of bringing about the sinner's reconciliation with the Church. The Council thus favoured a revised rite of penance which would integrate the Word of God and bring out these aspects.

The revision led to the elaboration of three rites. The first rite is that of individual confession and absolution; with the recommendation that an extract of Scripture be used; this rite is essentially that which has operated in the Church for centuries. The second rite envisages communal preparation for the sacrament, with individual confession and absolution. The third rite is an extra-ordinary rite of general absolution, where there are large numbers of people and the impossibility of them being able to reach a confessor for a long period of time mean that neither of the first two (ordinary rites) can be used.

The revised prayer of absolution notes that this sacrament is rooted in the Paschal Mystery ('through the death and resurrection of Your Son'), by which the 'Father of mercies' has brought about our redemption, our reconciliation ('has reconciled the world to himself'). Through this sacrament, this blessing of reconciliation is bestowed upon us (he has 'sent the Holy Spirit among us' precisely 'for the forgiveness of sin'). Christ brings about our reconciliation, through the Spirit (operating 'through the ministry of the Church', bringing us 'pardon and peace') by means of the ministry of the ordained priest who, acting in the person of Christ by the grace of his priestly ordination, absolves the penitent ('I absolve you from your sins in the Name of the Father and of the Son and of the Holy Spirit').

b. An Analysis of Key Canons (cc. 959–961)

The revision of the Code of Canon Law aimed to link word and sacrament in the liturgical aspects of law and, more generally, to reflect the Council's doctrines. These features can be detected in its treatment of reconciliation (Tables 11C, 13).

[5.] ID., Dogmatic Constitution on the Church, *Lumen gentium*, n. 11.
[6.] *Sacrosanctum Concilium*m nn. 9–10.
[7.] L. Gerosa, *Le droit canonique*, 2nd edn, Dalloz, Paris, 1999, 147–53.

The opening canon (c. 959) distils church doctrine on this sacrament. It calls it the sacrament of penance, but confession and reconciliation are specifically mentioned, marking the three characteristics of what is involved. It can apply only to the 'faithful', the baptized, (cc. 96, 204, 849) and so relates to sins committed 'after baptism', since baptism forgives sins committed earlier, if the conditions necessary in a penitent over the age of reason are met. The three conditions required in the penitent for the valid reception of the sacrament are: confession, contrition (sorrow for sins) and satisfaction (manifesting the purpose of amendment). The lawful minister is only a validly ordained priest (c. 965) with valid faculties to hear confessions (c. 966 § 1). Absolution is to be 'given by that minister' (c. 959). Conciliar theology is reflected: through absolution by the priest God forgives a penitent's sin, simultaneously he is 'reconciled with God and with the Church' (c. 960).

The three possible rites of reconciliation are treated in cc. 960–961, but they are not on an equal footing. The 'sole ordinary means' of this reconciliation with God and with the Church, excused only by cases of 'grave necessity', is through 'individual and integral confession and absolution' (c. 960). An act of perfect contrition (with sincere sorrow for having offended God), but only on condition of there being the real intention to make a sacramental confession to a priest as soon as possible, is sufficient for the forgiveness of even mortal sins in such cases of impossibility.

The 'sole ordinary means' of reconciliation refer to the first two of the revised rites of the sacrament, the revised rite of individual confession and absolution and the new second rite of communal preparation for the sacrament, with individual confession and absolution. The rite of general absolution, the third of the revised rites, is, therefore, an extra-ordinary rite and it 'cannot be given to a number of penitents together, without prior individual confession, unless certain conditions apply' (c. 961 § 1). These conditions are that the number of penitents is too numerous for the number of priests available to hear their confessions properly (c. 961 § 1, 1°), that these penitents would, otherwise, be deprived of absolution and Holy Communion for a considerable period of time (c. 961 § 1, 2°), that penitents must be resolved to confess all mortal sins to a confessor individually as soon as possible afterwards (c. 962 § 1) and that all are to be informed of these conditions and all are to be urged to make individual acts of contrition, if time permits (c. 962 § 2). Physical impossibility might mean that someone is in an imminent situation of disaster, earthquake, shipwreck, terrorist outrage, and such like, while moral impossibility

Table 13

The Sacrament of Penance (Reconciliation)

Canon 959

'In the sacrament of penance
    the *faithful* who
        – <u>*confess*</u> their sins
            to a lawful minister
        – are <u>*sorry*</u> for those sins and
        – have a <u>*purpose of amendment*</u>
            receive *from God*
                through the <u>*absolution*</u> *given by that minister*
                    forgiveness of sins they have committed *after baptism*
            and at the same time
                they are *reconciled with the Church*
                    which, by sinning, they have wounded.'

Canon 960

'*Individual confession* and (individual) *absolution*
    constitute the *sole ordinary means*
        by which a member of the *faithful*
            who is *conscious of grave sin*
                is *reconciled*
                    with God and
                    with the Church.
Physical or moral impossibility alone
    excuses from such confession,
        in which case
            reconciliation may be obtained by other means also.'

Canon 961 § 1

'*General absolution,*
    without prior individual confession,
        cannot be given
    unless
        1° *danger of death* threatens
            and there is not time for the priest(s)
            to hear the confessions of the individual penitents
  (and)   2° there exists *a grave necessity,*
            that is, given the number of penitents, there are not enough confessors
            available properly to hear the individual confessions within an appropriate
            time, so that, without fault of their own, the penitents are deprived of the
            sacramental grace or holy communion for a lengthy period of time.'

Canon 987

'In order that the faithful
    may receive the saving remedy of this sacrament,
        they must be so disposed that,
            – *repudiating* the *sins* they have committed and
            – having the *purpose* of *amending* their *lives,*
              – they *turn back to God'*.

might be where someone in a very remote area could not gain access to a priest for a very long time.[8]

These norms for general absolution without prior individual confession were restated in the apostolic exhortation following the Synod of Bishops on reconciliation. The first form is not to be allowed to fall into disuse or to be neglected, since it is 'the normal and ordinary way of celebrating the sacrament'. The second form, although in its preparatory stages gives greater emphasis to communal aspects, nevertheless 'is the same as the first form in its culminating sacramental act' and so 'can be regarded as equal to the first form as regards the normality of the rite'.[9] It is noteworthy that this culminating sacramental act is described as 'namely, individual confession and individual absolution of sins', a clarification that the absolution, as well as the confession, has to be individual. The third form 'is exceptional in character' and 'is therefore not left to free choice, but is regulated by special discipline'.[10]

It should be added that confessions are to take place in a church or oratory (c. 964 §1), in a confessional, with a fixed screen (c. 964 § 2), with the penitent's anonymity being protected if he or she wishes it, unless there is a just reason for another arrangement (c. 964 § 3). The priest can insist upon using a screen or a grill.[11] Awareness of the danger of penitents being abused or of priests being falsely accused in this regard makes this a wise provision; visible, but soundproofed confessionals are advisable, for the protection of all involved.

c. Abuses in the Sacrament of Reconciliation

Abuses Treated in the *'motu proprio'*, *'Misericordia Dei'*

Since the revision of the liturgy of reconciliation, a number of abuses in its celebration have occurred, which John Paul II's *'motu proprio'*, *'Misericordia Dei'* of 2002 was issued expressly to correct. The practice of some priests urging penitents to mention only one or two token sins, violating the requirement of material integrity (for mortal sins), is condemned: 'any practice which restricts confession to a generic accusation of sin or of only one or two sins judged to be more important

---

[8.] G. Ghirlanda, *Il diritto nella Chiesa: mistero di comunione: Compendio di diritto canonico* 4th revised edn, San Paolo, Cinisello, PU.G., Rome, 2006, 319–20, n. 323.

[9.] John Paul II, Apostolic exhortation, *Reconciliatio et paenitentia*, 2 December 1984, n 32.

[10.] Ibid.

[11.] ID., Abuses in the Sacrament of Reconciliation, Apostolic letter, *'motu proprio'*, *Misericordia Dei*, 7 April 2002, n. 9.

is to be reproved'.[12] Given the call of all to holiness, the confession of even venial sins is recommended.[13] The two conditions for the extra-ordinary rite (rite 3) with general absolution, without prior individual confession, have to be met together and not just separately for this rite to be used (It is not enough for there to be too many penitents for their confessions to be heard worthily, but they would need also to be deprived of confession for a long time).[14] Norms are to be elab-orated by episcopal conferences and reviewed by the Apostolic See before rite 3 is used. The firm intention on the part of the penitent to confess all mortal sins to a confessor as soon as possible afterwards (c. 962 § 1) and before receiving another general absolution (c. 963) is to be explained to penitents if time permits (c. 962 § 2); this intention of theirs is a condition of validity of the absolution,[15] which therefore must be considered as conditional absolution.

Circumstances where rite 3 might be very appropriate would be in the face of a terrorist outrage and major accident or epidemic, where large numbers of persons were in imminent danger of death and where there were not enough priests to hear their confessions properly, where enough priests could not be found in the very limited time many of them were likely to live. Another example might be where large numbers of people were in a territory with a very marked shortage of priests, where a priest could not be found for months at a time, where there were not enough priests to be found for the numbers.[16] Where this was combined with a general situation of conflict such that death in the meantime was an imminent possibility, a genuine danger, the conditions for the third rite would exist. On the other hand, in the absence of imminent danger of death, the condi-tions of physical or moral impossibility entailing a 'grave necessity' and 'depriving people of sacramental grace for a long time' are not met when a time less than a month was envisaged.[17] The time for priests to hear confessions worthily does 'not' mean time for 'a more extended pastoral conversation',[18] but the time needed to hear, assess and absolve sins. Such circumstances are not to be engineered ficti-tiously or contrived, for example by failing to make available the other

---

12. Ibid., n. 3
13. Ibid., n. 3
14. Ibid., n. 4 b.
15. Ibid., n. 7 a.
16. Ibid., n. 4 a.
17. Ibid., n. 4, b, d.
18. Ibid., n. 4 c.

two rites of the sacrament.[19] Norms from diocesan bishops, based on norms of the episcopal conference, up-dated in the light of these legal clarifications, are to be sent to the Apostolic See, where it is thought the requirements necessary for the use of rite 3 (general absolution without prior individual confession) are met.[20]

Other Abuses in the Sacrament

Although 'Misericordia Dei' covers a number of abuses, it did not treat all. In some places, it has become not uncommon, with the use of the second rite, that of communal or collective preparation and individual confession and absolution, for a number of abuses to arise. After the communal preparation, involving reflection on Scripture, with a homily, and the use of a common form of examination of conscience, some or all of the following occur in some places: the confession of a token sin to be proposed or to be made (condemned in *Misericordia Dei*). The proclamation of a common penance to be recited or sung in common later (such as a 'Hail Mary' or a hymn) ignores the requirement that penances be individual and appropriate (c. 981). The practice of not giving absolution individually to each penitent, but of waiting until all are together after the individual confessions when all confessors together would give 'absolution' jointly, is certainly illicit and arguably even invalid. Whether the word 'individual' in the Code applied not only to 'confession', but also to 'absolution' (c. 960), seemed to need further clarification, although John Paul II seemed to apply 'individual' explicitly also to 'absolution'.[21]

The question of the last two of these abuses of the second rite of reconciliation (the first not being limited to this rite and having been addressed explicitly in *Misericordia Dei*) was raised with the Pontifical Council for the Interpretation of Legislative Texts in a private letter

---

[19.] Ibid., n. 4 e.

[20.] Ibid., nn. 5-6.

[21.] John Paul II, *Reconciliatio et paenitentia*, n. 32: ' ... The second form – reconciliation of a number of penitents with *individual confession and absolution* – even though in the preparatory acts it helps to give greater emphasis to the community aspects of the sacrament, is the same as the first form in the culminating sacramental act, namely *individual confession and individual absolution*' (my emphases). The difficulty is that the Latin text of c. 960 is *'cum confessione et absolutione singulari'* and the second *'qui confessio est atque absolutio singularis'*, which means that 'individual' (*'singularis'*) is not repeated in the Latin, although, coming at the end of the phrase in each case and directly after 'absolution', it must be intended to apply also to *'absolutio'*; otherwise, it would have come after *'confessio'* only. The text does not say *'cum confessione singulari et absolutione'* nor *'confessio singularis ... atque absolutio'*, which it would have to do if the intention were to limit 'individual' to 'confession'.

of 2004. After two weeks the rescript received from this Pontifical Council stated that the law as such was clear and the questions were rather matters of application. The competent authority for the application of these laws was the Congregation for Divine Worship and for the Discipline of the Sacraments, to which the questions had been forwarded by the Pontifical Council.[22] After examining the matter carefully, the Congregation replied that the practices were abuses which were illegal and reprehensible. It clarified perfectly that the word 'individual' in c. 960 did apply both to 'confession' and to 'absolution', since John Paul II had stated as much in a statement of 1998. As to the question of validity, this would depend upon the individual disposition of the penitent; one who was not sorry for their sins would not receive absolution.[23]

This, of course, is true and helpful. However, the precise question also concerned rather the specific intention of the minister who might be involved in such a 'general absolution' after communal preparation and individual confession. Taking the intention of the minister of the sacrament, the question is whether that intention needs to be at least the virtual intention to absolve (only) the sins confessed to that minister (cf. c. 959). The intention cannot be to absolve sins with no specification whatsoever. In baptizing the intention cannot be 'un-delimited', as if it referred to anyone at all, but would have to be to intend to baptize the specific person or persons, in confirmation, anointing and Holy Orders to confirm, anoint or ordain the specific baptized person or persons, in marriage for this spouse to intend to marry this specific spouse, in the Eucharist to consecrate this specific (delimited) bread and wine (even if in the sense of all the altar breads in the hands of the chief celebrant and/or on the corporal). Likewise, it would seem that an intention to absolve could hardly be without delimitation. No doubt, if a priest participating in a 'general absolution' in rite 2, as above, intended to absolve only the sins confessed to him by the penitents who had made their confession to him, that absolution would be valid from the point of view of his intention. Where this were not the case, where a priest gave no thought to what

---

[22.] Rescript from the Pontifical Council for the Interpretation of Legislative Texts, containing a private response to these questions posed in a letter of 12 February 2004, to Cardinal Herranz, Prefect of the Pontifical Council, rescript N. 9180/ 2004 of 20 February 2004.

[23.] Rescript from Cardinal Arinze, Prefect of the Congregation for Divine Worship and for the Discipline of the Sacraments, responding to the questions transmitted to them by the Pontifical Council for the Interpretation of Legislative Texts (as in the preceding footnote), rescript N. 397/ 04/ L of 7 March 2005.

he was doing or where he imagined he was absolving all and sundry, he could not have exercised the judgment about whether or not he should absolve, in regard to those penitents who had made their confession to other priests.

It is true that the third rite of reconciliation does envisage absolution which is valid, on condition of the penitent's sorrow and determination to confess mortal sins individually as soon as possible thereafter (c. 962 § 1). This conditional absolution 'cannot be given ... unless ...' (c. 961 § 1) excludes the circumstances in which the second (ordinary) rite operates. Such 'general absolution' with the second rite is 'an illicit practice' and 'is to be eliminated'.[24]

d. The Minister of Reconciliation and Confessional Faculties

Only a validly ordained priest is capable of absolving from sins (c. 965). All validly ordained priests can absolve validly if the penitent is in danger of death (c. 976). Otherwise, a priest cannot validly absolve unless he has faculties to hear confessions either by virtue of the law itself (as where they are attached to an office to which he is validly appointed, for as long as he is in that office) or by special grant of faculties from the local ordinary or other competent superior (c. 966 § 1 and 2). Faculties are not to be granted to priests unless their suitability to hear confessions has been established by a faculties examination or other means (c. 970). They are to be given in writing, if habitual (c. 973), and are not to be revoked without a grave reason (c. 974 § 1). All validly ordained priests, whatever their situation or legal status in the Church, wherever they are, dispensed or not, when the penitent is in danger of death, absolve not only validly, but lawfully, even if a priest with faculties is present (c. 976). They have the right and duty to exercise their sacred power of priesthood for the pastoral care of the one(s) in danger of death (cc. 976, 1752). The canon refers to priests 'even if they lack the faculty to hear confessions', which really means even if 'otherwise' they lack this faculty; they have the faculty by virtue of this canon.

Faculties to hear confessions can be acquired (only) by validly ordained priests (c. 965). The law itself provides them to the Pope throughout the world, without any limitation possible (c. 967 § 1), cardinals anywhere in the world, unless impeded by the Pope; no bishop can impede a cardinal from hearing confessions (c. 967

---

24. Ibid.

§ 1),[25] bishops everywhere (c. 967 § 1), unless impeded by the local ordinary, other local ordinaries within their jurisdiction (c. 968 § 1), a canon penitentiary in the diocese (c. 968 § 1), a parish priest in his parish (c. 968 § 1), one equivalent in law to a parish priest, such as a moderator over a group of parishes or a parish administrator (c. 968 § 2), superiors of religious institutes of consecrated life in regard to members of an institute of consecrated life and those who live day and night in a house of an institute of consecrated life, superiors of clerical societies of apostolic life of pontifical right in regard to members of the society of apostolic life and those who live day and night in a house of a society of apostolic life (c. 968 § 2). Those with confessional faculties either from their office or by grant have them everywhere, unless impeded by the major superior in a given case (c. 967 § 2-3). This is a change from previous law, which restricted faculties to the diocese; greater mobility and the demands of pastoral care explain the change.

Apart from the Pope who has unrestricted faculties by divine law and apart from cardinals and bishops, others have faculties within the diocese, parish or other entity, but these faculties last only as long as they continue to hold that office (c. 974 § 2), being lost if the office is lost, if the priest is excardinated or if he loses domicile (c. 975). Where faculties are granted by one competent to grant them (cc. 966 § 2; 969), this is to be in writing if they are given habitually (c. 973), although this is not needed if they are given just for a particular occasion. This can be from the local ordinary either of the place where the priest is incardinated or where he has a domicile (c. 967 § 2) to any priest incardinated or domiciled in the territory over which that ordinary has jurisdiction, provided that the priest is suitable (c. 970) and he has consulted that priest's local ordinary, if possible, if the faculties are to be given habitually rather than for an occasion or brief time (c. 971). Priests in religious institutes may exercise that faculty only with the permission, either expressly given or properly presumed of their own superior (c. 969 § 1). Faculties may be granted by the superior of a religious institute of consecrated life, the superior of a clerical society of apostolic life of pontifical right to any priest who is suitable (c. 970); by implication, this should only be after consulting that priest's local ordinary, if possible, if the faculties are to be given habitually rather than just for an occasion or brief time (c. 971), for hearing confessions of subjects as noted above (c. 969 § 2).

Faculties acquired by virtue of the law last as long as they are not revoked by the competent higher authority or through a legitimate

---

[25.] Ghirlanda, *Il diritto nella Chiesa ...*, 321, n. 327.

canonical penalty entailing their loss and the priest continues to hold the office by which they were acquired; they cease once he loses that office either by expiry of the office or by transfer or by removal. Faculties acquired by concession or grant last until they expire, if they were granted only for a specific time (c. 972), or are revoked by the competent superior, if they were granted indefinitely, although this has to be for a serious reason (cc. 972; 974 § 1). If a priest has faculties habitually to hear confessions from the local ordinary of where he is incardinated or where he is domiciled, he has faculties everywhere, unless another local ordinary impedes him (c. 967 § 1). If he loses the faculties in that diocese because of loss of office, loss of incardination or loss of domicile (c. 975) or if faculties are revoked by the local ordinary of incardination or of domicile who granted them, he loses them everywhere (c. 974 § 2), except for danger of death (c. 976). If they are revoked by another ordinary, they are lost only in the diocese of that ordinary (c. 974); that ordinary is to inform the priest's proper ordinary or competent superior in a religious institute (c. 974 § 3). Similarly, if faculties are revoked by his own major superior, the faculty to hear the confessions of members of the institute is lost everywhere; if by another superior, the loss applies only to the subjects of that superior (c. 974 § 4).

Common error (c. 144) does *not* apply to ignorance which results from neglect nor from crass ignorance of what a priest ought to have known. However, cases of genuine 'common error' over confessional faculties might occur and, if this happens, the Church supplies the priest concerned with faculties which he thought he had on some other basis, but in fact did not have. This means not that he hears confession without faculties, but that, despite not having faculties on the basis of office or grant, he does have them through the Church supplying him with faculties through the provisions of common error (c. 144). Examples of such common error over confessional faculties might be: a priest given faculties with a time limit, where he thought the expiry date was later than it was; a priest going to a diocese where the local ordinary had impeded priests visiting from hearing confessions without express faculties from himself; where the priest was unaware of this restriction through no fault of his own.

e. Responsibilities of Confessors

The duties of priests who have faculties to hear confessions are to act as judge (of the matter or facts presented to him by the penitent), to assess its gravity, the degree of imputability, and whether or not absolution can be granted, as a minister of God's justice and mercy (c. 978 §1). He is to act as healer (St Augustine called this sacrament the '*medicina salutis*' or 'medicine of salvation'), as a minister of God's mercy (c. 978 §1).[26] He is to act as minister of the Church ('through the ministry of the Church, may God grant you ...'), which requires that he adhere faithfully to the teaching of the Magisterium and to the norms laid down by competent authority (c. 978 § 2). This involves a ministry to the truth of the Gospel, according to the teaching of the Church. Never must a minister of reconciliation contradict, advise or endorse behaviour contrary to the moral teaching of the Magisterium; rather all that he says must be based upon it and be compatible with it. The 'law of graduality' means supporting someone who has failed, but who acknowledges and strives to keep to church teaching, in the efforts they are making without proposing or endorsing what dilutes or contradicts that teaching (the 'graduality of the law'). The 'graduality of the law' is never legitimate, the 'law of graduality', carefully applied, is good pastoral practice to foster its positive fulfilment.[27]

The confessor is to ask questions prudently and with discretion, of the penitent, with consideration for his age and condition. He is not to ask the name of a partner in a sin (c. 980). Such questioning is not to be an interrogation, but it is only to be undertaken for purposes of clarification about what has been said, so that the priest understands properly what has been confessed and so is able to judge the matter presented to him, as just noted. Where there is no doubt about the penitent's sorrow and disposition of amendment absolution is neither to be denied nor deferred (c. 980). If there is doubt, prudent enquiry may help to elicit the true disposition. The confessor should try to bring a penitent to a situation in which absolution is possible (acting as healer as a well as judge). If the penitent is not properly disposed and is unrepentant or intends not to try to amend his ways, or is living in a state objectively at odds with church teaching which he cannot or will not change, absolution cannot be given.

The confessor is to impose salutary ('salvific', 'healing', 'helpful', not 'harsh') penances. These are to show the person's willingness to try to amend his ways. The penance is necessary, part of the satisfaction (c. 959) required of the penitent. It is not to be confused with pastoral advice for the future and it should be clear and practicable, so that a person is not left worried about whether or not it has been properly completed.

[26.] Cf. cited in John Paul II, *Reconciliatio et paenitentia*, n. 31 II; cf., footnote n. 180.
[27.] ID., Apostolic exhortation, *Familiaris consortio*, 22 November 1981, nn. 9, 34.

The confessor is to preserve the integrity of the internal forum and the protection it affords the penitent; a novice master or the rector of a seminary or other institution is not to hear the confessions of students living in the same house unless a specific student asks him to do so on a given occasion (c. 985).

Priests have the duty to provide confessions at any reasonable time and to give the faithful opportunity to make individual confessions at times and on days which suit them (c. 986 § 1). This does not exclude hearing confessions 'even during Mass if there are other priests available to meet the needs of the faithful'.[28] In urgent need every confessor is bound to hear the confession of a member of the faithful and in danger of death every priest is obliged to do so (c. 986).

f. Offences against the Sacrament of Reconciliation

The major offences are the following: attempting to absolve an accomplice in a sin against the sixth commandment – 'attempting' because the absolution is invalid – (cc. 977; 1378 § 2), soliciting in the confessional, either while hearing confession or on the pretext of hearing confession, is to try to bring the penitent to commit a sin against the sixth commandment with the confessor (c. 1387) and violating the seal of the confessional (c. 1388 § 1).

The deliberate violation of the seal entails the deliberate or culpably negligent revelation both of the sin confessed and of the identity of the penitent. As deliberate, it is a canonical crime, with a *'latae sententiae'* penalty of excommunication, reserved to the Apostolic See (cc. 983; 1388 § 1). Where it is violated only indirectly, it is a canonical crime, for which there is to be a just penalty (c. 1388 § 1). An interpreter is bound by the seal of confession and commits a canonical crime if he violates this, for which there would be a just penalty, not excluding excommunication (cc. 983 § 2; 1388 § 2). The duty on the confessor is a strict one because he is an interlocutor in a sacred conversation between Christ and the penitent; the duty of the seal is absolute, even at the cost of personal suffering for the confessor. The danger of disclosure from careless chatter should be appreciated; the best advice is: 'nothing ever to anyone!'

Another offence is using any information discovered through the confessional to the detriment of a penitent (c. 984 § 1), especially in external governance (c. 984 § 2). This emphasizes the duty to keep the internal and external fora quite distinct.

[28.] ID., *Misericordia Dei*, n. 2.

g. The Duties of the Penitent

This section recalls the essential elements of Tridentine dogma of contrition, confession and satisfaction (c. 987, Table 13). Only the 'faithful', the baptized, can receive the specific sacrament of post-baptismal reconciliation. In restoring such a person fully to a state of living in Christ and of being fully reunited to the Church, it is a 'saving remedy', the 'medicine of salvation'. The dispositions required in the penitents which make possible and which require absolution (c. 980) are that, repudiating the sins they have committed and, having the purpose of amending their lives, they turn back to God' (c. 987). This 'turning away from (repudiating) sins' ('aversio a peccatis') and 'turning back to God' ('conversio ad Deum') is the exact opposite of sin as 'turning away from God' ('aversio a Deo') and 'turning in upon oneself' ('conversio ad se') or 'turning in upon the creature' ('conversio ad creaturam').[29] The minimal conditions for receiving God's healing grace in Christ in this sacrament are contrition (for love of God) or at least imperfect sorrow or attrition (fear of punishment, hell), which is rendered perfect (contrition) through the grace of the sacrament.[30] This implies a readiness and determination to amend one's life (conversion or 'metanoia'), a readiness manifested in satisfaction.[31]

Given these dispositions for the valid reception of absolution, those 'living in a habitual state of sin and who do not intend to change their situation cannot validly receive absolution'.[32] Even in general absolution in rite 3, the intention to confess all mortal sins individually is a condition additional to the basic dispositions required for confession and for valid absolution; such an individual confession is to be made before receiving another general absolution, where someone is in a state of grave sin.[33]

The third aspect of the penitent's disposition required at Trent and in the Code is that the penitent is 'bound to confess all grave sins committed after baptism', by 'number and kind', of which he is 'aware after a careful examination of conscience' and not yet confessed in individual confession (c 988 § 1). It is 'recommended to confess also venial sins' (c. 988 § 2). Once they have reached the age of discretion

---

[29.] Cf. ID., Reconciliatio et paenitentia, n. 14.
[30.] ID., The Catechism of the Catholic Church, nn. 1452-1453.
[31.] ID., Reconciliatio et paenitentia, n. 31 III.
[32.] ID., Misericordia Dei, n. 7 c.
[33.] Ibid., n. 7, a, d.

(reason – seven years old), people have the obligation to confess their grave sins at least once a year (c. 989). Someone unable to speak the language of the priest may use an interpreter, provided that there is no scandal and provided that the interpreter accepts being bound by the seal of confession (cc. 983 § 2; 990). Confession may be made to any priest of choice, even of another rite (c. 991) and for whatever reason.

h. Indulgences

Catholic teaching and practice on indulgences cannot be understood apart from the sacrament of reconciliation, to which they are intrinsically linked. In this sacrament a person's sins are truly forgiven by Christ through the priest, provided that the penitent's dispositions are correct and the absolution is validly bestowed. However, the damage done by our sins can be enormous, even if we are truly sorry for them and even if they have been forgiven by God, who does not forgive partially or half-heartedly. The damage done by sin (such as the ruination of a person's livelihood through serious theft or fraud or the destruction of a family resulting from murder or adultery) is not simply wiped out; people suffer as a result. Even less dramatic or evident sins damage our relationship with others and wound the Church. The duty to make amends by reparation for the damage done remains as a task for the person in this life and/or in Purgatory. In the early centuries the Church imposed often heavy penances before absolution at Easter, 'temporal punishment due to sin', as distinct from God's eternal punishment were sins not forgiven. With frequent and individual confession, the penances were imposed to be done after confession. Penances could be 'commuted' to lengthy prayers, pilgrimages, demanding acts of charity, even gifts to the Church. While sin was forgiven ('*reus culpae*') through absolution and so eternal punishment due to it removed, the temporal punishment due to sin ('*reus poenae*') could be remitted when someone performed an extra-ordinary act of prayer or charity with the right intention of true conversion, the Church remitting the punishment it had imposed. Apart from the temporal punishment or penance to be done, making satisfaction for the harm caused by our sin, insofar as this is demanding or difficult, can also be experienced as 'punishment'. Forgiveness through sacramental reconciliation releases the penitent from the eternal consequences of those sins ('eternal punishment due to sin'). The penitent is no longer responsible for the eternal fault (is no longer '*reus culpae*'), but is still accountable for doing his penance (is still *'reus poenae'*) and for making reparation for the damage his sins have caused.[34]

Various ways in which people collaborate with God's grace in Christ to repair this temporal punishment and damage have been recognized; they include prayers, pilgrimages, fasting, works of charity. An indulgence is an unusual or special way of penance due to sin being remitted and by which reparation for sin can be made, but only in collaboration with the merciful action of Christ who forgives us through the sacrament of reconciliation. Here it is really a prayer to the Lord, made with confidence in his merciful forgiveness, that there be such remission of temporal punishment by him. One who is 'properly disposed' (and only provided the person is so disposed) may gain an indulgence with the help of the Church (c. 992). This sincere intention of conversion and purpose of amendment of life, manifested in sacramental confession and sincere reception of Holy Communion, are required for an indulgence; without this, no indulgence is obtained.

With an indulgence the redemptive act of Christ's saving death and resurrection, operating through the sacrament of reconciliation, is embraced by the one who seeks the indulgence on his or her own behalf or (through a special act of love of neighbour) for the dead in Purgatory. In full union with Christ, in the prayer of the Church which is in full harmony with the Father's will, precisely for this deep and sincere conversion to the Lord, such a person intercedes on their own behalf or on behalf of those in Purgatory and implores the prayers of the saints for the same purpose. This is why the Church, as 'minister of the redemption' (c. 992) is confident that the prayer is heard. On the basis of all these factors, fulfilling the specific conditions attached to gaining the particular indulgence in question, a person may acquire an indulgence (c. 992). The capacity to gain an indulgence demands that a person be baptized, not be excommunicated, be in a state of grace (c. 996 § 1), intend to gain the indulgence and fulfil the prescribed works at the time and in the manner stated (c. 996 § 2), abiding by other special norms (c. 997), such as the regulations of the Apostolic Penitentiary on indulgences. An indulgence is partial if it removes part of the temporal punishment due to sin (makes some reparation), plenary if it removes all of it (makes total reparation – c. 993); it can be applied to the person themselves or 'by way of suffrage to the dead', on behalf of those in Purgatory (c. 994). Indulgences can be granted

---

[34] Cf. M. Schmaus, *Dogma 5: The Church as Sacrament*, Sheed and Ward, London, 1975, 245–52.

only by the supreme authority of the Church, except where acknowledged by the law or granted by the Pope (c. 995).

Hence, the question of indulgences is far removed from any of the
abuses prior to the Reformation associated with their 'sale' and is not
in any way a matter of Pelagianism. They rest on the Paschal Mystery
of Christ, his action through the sacraments, especially reconciliation,
embraced in faith, hope and love. Indulgences are 'an exceptional act
of the mercy of God'.[35]

3. The Sacrament of the Anointing of the Sick

a. The Significance of the Sacrament of the Anointing of the Sick

The sacrament of the sick used to be called 'extreme unction' or the
'last anointing'.[36] It was usually administered to people almost when
they were dying, after sacramental confession or conditional absolution and, ideally, prior to Holy Communion given as viaticum, as
food for the journey to God. As part of the 'last sacraments' or 'last
rites', it had and still has an important place; it should be given to
those baptized, who are dying, after absolution and before viaticum.[37]
However, it is a sacrament not only for those on the point of death, but
for the sick. Priests are to administer it, and others caring for them are
to call priests to administer it 'in good time' (c. 1001) to the dangerously sick or to those who begin to suffer from a dangerous condition
(cc. 1004 § 1, 1005). This was said also in the 1917 Code.[38] The proper
function of this sacrament was not always understood. This needs to
be rectified.

The sacrament of the sick in some ways reflects the general, healing
purpose and work of Jesus, a major part of his public ministry. From
the beginning he sought out the sick, blind, lame, leprous, dying. This
was to show them God's love, often to heal physical ailments, and
restore them to the human community from which they had often been
excluded, their illness judged a sign of personal sin or of their parents'
sin and so of their rejection by God (cf. Jn. 9:1ff.). Jesus's healing
miracles or signs were never limited to compassion and reinsertion

---

[35.] I. Fucek, Canon Theologian to the Apostolic Penitentiary, at the time of the proclamation of the Holy Year of the Jubilee of the year 2000.

[36.] Benedict XV, *Codex iuris canonici* (1917), c. 937.

[37.] *Sacrosanctum Concilium*, nn . 74–5.

[38.] *Codex iuris canonici* (1917), c. 940.

into human society, but were associated with his forgiveness of sin, since illness, though not a sign of the degree of direct personal sin, was connected to sin more generally. His signs brought to the sick and those around them the wonders of the Kingdom of God present and operative in himself (Mk. 1:14–15; Jn. 9:1–3).[39] The compassionate ('suffering along with') love of God in Christ triumphant over suffering, death and sin in the resurrection is a real, eternal, irreversible source of hope to human beings.[40] These are the blessings of the Paschal Mystery, bestowed on the faithful through the sacrament of the sick.

Sickness, a reminder of the severe limitations of human existence, a forewarning of death of the sick person and to those around, then as now, provokes serious questioning about the meaning of life, suffering and death. It can both open people up to faith, as Jesus sought to do, or it can provoke a crisis of faith. This is why Jesus's healing ministry is so firmly linked to spiritual healing, seeing with the eyes of faith, hearing his word and responding to it in belief. This ministry of Jesus was so central to his work that it is unthinkable that he did not intend it to be continued among his people in the Church. In fact, the collaboration of the Apostles in that work indicates that intention; they were sent to 'heal' (Mt. 10:7–8; Lk. 9:1–2) and to anoint the sick with oil (Mk. 6:13), 'laying hands on the sick' while praying for them and anointing them with oil (James 5:13–16). The focus is not just on physical healing, but that the prayer made in faith will save the sick man through Christ's Paschal Mystery.

The reality of the sacrament of the sick is that it unites the gravely ill and the dying to Christ in his passion, death and resurrection. As such it is a source of hope beyond what any human beings could offer or achieve, a specific gift of Christ to those of his faithful in such a predicament. It can forgive venial sin and can at times be associated with physical healing, but its proper purpose and effect is the spiritual healing which comes from this specific union with Christ, by which, if a person dies, he dies not alone (even on this journey he makes with no human aid), but surrounded by, filled with, the omnipotent love of Christ and fortified by that life which has conquered death and sin; he dies in Christ to rise with him.[41]

Serious illness and the real prospect of dying can involve a crisis of faith and the risk of despair; it is precisely then that we need this

---

[39.] J. Galot, *Le mystère de l'espérance*, Lethielleux, Paris, 1973, 68–71

[40.] ID., *Il mistero della sofferenza di Dio*, Cittadella, Assisi, 1975, 164–70.

[41.] F. Bourassa, *L'onction des malades*, P.U.G., Rome, 1970, 6.

supernatural help of Christ and of his sacraments. The Church's pastoral care of the sick at these times is not just to bring compassion, but to nurture faith and hope, to help the person to complete or consummate his or her love of God in a free, total and final gift of self to the Father with Christ through the Spirit. The sacrament of the sick brings to that person the almighty strength of the One who has conquered death and who is the Lord of eternal life.[42]

b. The Introductory Canon (c. 998)

We notice that the sacrament is called the 'sacrament of the sick' rather than extreme unction (last anointing) because, although highly appropriate for the dying (c. 1004 § 1), it is also a sacrament for 'the faithful once they begin to be dangerously ill, that they be supported and saved by Christ the suffering and glorified Lord' (c. 998). Thus, this sacrament can only be given to a baptized person (hence the reference to the 'faithful'), since no other sacrament can be given validly to a non-baptized person (c. 842 § 1). The form of the sacrament recalls key aspects of this canon, referring to the 'help' to be provided to the sick person by 'the Lord' and to the fact that this sacrament is concerned with that person being 'saved'. Being 'saved' goes beyond physical healing and human capacities; it is an action of Christ the Lord, precisely through this sacrament. The ecclesial and communitarian aspect of this sacrament is reflected in the Church commending the sick to the Lord.[43] Nor is it an accident that the canon uses the messianic titles 'Christ' ('Christos'), the One who even in his humanity was anointed with the fullness of the Spirit, the true Messiah or 'anointed one' and 'Lord' ('Kyrios'), designating him precisely as the Risen Lord, conqueror of suffering, sin and death. In this capacity he comes to save the afflicted person. The expression 'the suffering and glorified Lord' (c. 998) not only emphasizes the gift of the risen life, but the participation through this sacrament, by its recipients, in the passion and resurrection by which Christ overcame the suffering, sin and death, against which those in the Church still have to struggle ('all that remains to be undergone by the Church to make up what is lacking in the sufferings of Christ' – Col. 1:24). This refers to the suffering of people in the Church in the course of history, in every generation, especially at issue in a person who may be a proper candidate for the sacrament of the sick. This Code avoids the restrictive terminology of

---

42. Ibid., 51–2.
43. *Lumen gentium*, n. 11.

the Code of 1917, that extreme unction cannot be given to the baptized after coming to the age of reason 'unless' they are 'in danger of death' through illness or old age.[44] This reflects Trent, although that Council had presented this sacrament as not just of the dying, but of the sick, 'especially' (not 'only') for those in danger of death.[45]

c. The Administration of the Sacrament of the Sick

The matter of the sacrament is the oil of the sick applied to the forehead and to the hands (palms) of the proper candidate, although it may be applied just to the forehead or to any part of the body in emergencies (as when bandages cover the hands or head). The use of an instrument rather than the hand of the minister to apply the holy oil is permissible where it is impossible or dangerous (through danger of contagion or infection) to use the thumb (c. 1000 § 2). The form of the sacrament (that given in Table 11D), is said while anointing on the forehead and on the hands or, when anointing those areas is not possible, the whole form is said while anointing another part of the body (c. 1000 § 1).

The only minister of this sacrament is a validly ordained priest (c. 1003 § 1); it depends on priestly orders. Thus, anyone else pretending to administer it does not confer it, but rather 'simulates the sacrament' and commits a canonical crime. A priest administers this sacrament to those entrusted to his pastoral care: Catholic parishioners of a parish, or in the hospital where he is the chaplain (c. 1003 § 2), the norms of c. 844 applying to other members of the faithful.[46] For practical purposes, such priests should keep one another informed, so that there is no confusion and especially so that no one in need is overlooked. Any validly ordained priest may and should administer this sacrament to proper candidates, where he has the consent of their proper pastor or where, if there is urgent need, it can be presumed (c. 1003 § 2). A priest may carry the oil of the sick with him to be able to administer this sacrament in case of necessity (c. 1003 § 3).

---

44. *Codex iuris canonici* (1917), c. 940.

45. Decree on Penance and on Extreme Unction, Council of Trent, in H. Denzinger and A. Schönmetzer (ed.), *Enchiridion symbolorum*, n. 1698: 'Declaratur etiam esse hanc unctionem *infirmis* adhibendam, illis vero *praesertim* qui tam periculose decumbunt, ut in exitu vitae constituti videantur' ('It is also declared that this anointing is to be given to the *sick*, *especially* indeed to those who decline so dangerously that they seem to be brought to the point of leaving this life.' - my emphases); J. Neuner and J. Dupuis, *The Christian Faith.*, n. 1638; Gerosa, *Le droit de l'Église*, 218–19.

46. See the treatment of '*communicatio in sacris*', pp. 287–9.

The proper candidate for this sacrament is a member of the faithful (baptized), since no one who has not been baptized can validly receive any other sacrament, one who (normally) has been fully initiated into the Church through confirmation and Holy Communion. Certainly, one who has not been initiated in this way should (if conscious and able to speak) make a sacramental confession, be confirmed and, if possible (if conscious), receive Holy Communion before receiving the sacrament of the sick; one who has attained the age of reason or who has sufficient understanding (c. 1004 § 1) and who is dangerously ill or who has begun to be in danger of death through illness or through the infirmity brought on by age should receive it (c. 1004 § 1). The significance of this part of the canon is that the sacrament is not confined to those who are in actual danger of death, but 'danger of death' remains a relevant criterion in that someone must have 'begun to be' in such danger to be a proper candidate for the sacrament, which is not to be loosely offered to anyone who feels unwell. Someone may begin to be in such danger who is diagnosed as gravely or as terminally ill, even if their death is not thought to be at all imminent, if they are to undergo surgery, especially serious surgery. It may be repeated if the condition recurs or deteriorates (c. 1004 § 2); again this is a change from 1917, which did not allow for extreme unction to be repeated, other than where someone was in actual danger of death from the same condition, having recovered after a previous anointing or where they came to be in danger of death later on from another cause.[47] It may be given to those who are senile or otherwise not in full possession of their faculties, if they had asked for it earlier or if, implicitly, they would have asked for it (c. 1006).

However, the sacrament of the sick is not to be given to anyone 'obstinately persisting in manifestly grave sin' (c. 1007). A person who is repentant needs to receive sacramental absolution first and then may receive the sacrament of the sick. One who obstinately persists in manifestly grave sin cannot be given absolution unless and until there is repentance.

The 'greatest reverence and due care' to be shown in the celebration of the sacraments (c. 840) means that special care must be taken to ensure that those who receive this sacrament in a communal celebration are proper candidates and are properly disposed (c. 1002). There should never be a general invitation to anyone who is sick to come for this sacrament, nor should there be any practice in the liturgy which confuses this sacrament with non-sacramental or non-liturgical

---

[47.] *Codex iuris canonici* (1917), c. 940 § 2.

'anointings' with oil. The advantages of the communal celebration are that it can help all the parish to pray for the sick, especially if conducted in the context of the Eucharist, and it can assist the sick to have the spiritual support of the parish expressed communally and especially in the context of the supreme act of Christ and of his Church, the Eucharist.

No one can receive the sacrament of the sick validly unless they have been baptized; doubt about baptism, if proof cannot be found, requires that the person be baptized, if wishing this or if parental permission has been given or even if not. If there is doubt about a baptized person having reached the age of reason or being danger-ously ill or being dead, they should be anointed (c. 1005), after having received sacramental absolution and, if not already confirmed, after having been confirmed; we have seen that the anointing is not condi-tional any longer, but absolute. A baptized infant who is gravely ill is not a proper candidate for this sacrament, but is to be confirmed and, if capable of distinguishing the Eucharist from ordinary food, is to receive the Eucharist.

The oil of the sick is blessed by the bishop, usually at the Chrism Mass, or by those equivalent to him in law (territorial prelate, vicar or prefect apostolic, apostolic administrator – cc. 381 § 2, 368), but in urgent need it can be blessed by the priest during the course of the celebration of this sacrament, if he has no blessed oil left or with him (cc. 847 § 1; 999).

4. Conclusion

Following the sacraments of healing, it is time to consider Holy Orders, after which there will be a treatment of marriage in canon law.

Chapter 11

The Sanctifying Function of the Church

(Book IV of the Code)

Part I: The Sacraments
IV: The Sacrament of Holy Orders

1. Introduction

In this chapter it is necessary to recall what has been said about orders and the difference of function between the ministerial or ordained priesthood and the common priesthood of all the faithful, as well as its significance for the juridical status of people in the Church. The sacrament of order is of considerable importance for the life of the Church, for its proclamation of the Word of God, the Gospel, for its liturgical and sacramental life and so for its entire mission in the service of Christ, the Lord. It is intended here to highlight those features relevant to church law in the service of its communion of faith and its mission in the world.

2. An Analysis of the Key Canons (cc. 1008–1009, 1012)

These canons condense the rich theology of the sacrament of order, encapsulating both the defined dogmas of the Tradition and the insights of the Second Vatican Council (see Table 14). The divine institution of the sacrament of order emphasizes that this is a sacrament, since such cannot exist unless instituted by Christ, and so the orders of bishop, priest and deacon are not an arrangement of sociological convenience for the well-being (*'bene esse'*) of the Church, a human structure set up to facilitate its functional operation and efficiency at the human level, but something belonging to the very nature (*'esse'*) and purpose of the Church as such, willed and established by the

Table 14

The Sacrament of Holy Orders

Canon 1008

'By *divine institution*
    some *among Christ's faithful,*
        through the *sacrament* of *Order*
           – are marked with an *indelible character*
           – and are thus *constituted* as *sacred ministers;*

thereby they are *consecrated* and *deputed*
    so that, each according to his own *grade,*
        they fulfil in the *person of Christ* the Head
           the offices ('*munera*') of
                – *teaching*
                – *sanctifying and*
                – *ruling*
           and so they *nourish* the *people of God.'*

Canon 1009 § 1

'The *orders* are
    – *episcopate*
    – *priesthood* and
    – *diaconate'.*

Canon 1009 § 2

'They are conferred by
        – the *imposition of hands* (*matter*)
        – and the *prayer of consecration* (*form*)
           for each grade.'

Canon 1012

'The *minister* of *sacred ordination,*
    is a *consecrated bishop.'.*

Canon 1024

'Only a *baptized man* can *validly* receive *sacred ordination.'*

Lord. However, these 'sacred orders', although of divine institution, are not above or apart from the other members of the Church, but are selected from 'among Christ's faithful'. Here the inter-relationship and also real difference between the common priesthood of the faithful and the ministerial priesthood is evident. The Second Vatican Council never used the Lutheran term 'priesthood of all believers', intended to deny the truth of the ordained or ministerial priesthood, but its doctrine proclaimed the common priesthood of the faithful, of all baptized in Christ.[1]

Those in sacred orders, bishops, priests and deacons (c. 1009 § 1), are 'constituted sacred ministers' by their sacramental ordination (c. 1008), by the action of Christ through the ordaining bishop. This is true even though not all such ministers have the ministerial priesthood, since deacons as such do not. All sacred ministers remain members of the faithful and are to exercise the common priesthood of the faithful in which they continue always to share through their baptism and confirmation in praying in union with Christ for their own salvation. What they do as sacred ministers is not primarily concerned with their own personal salvation, but is to serve the rest of the faithful as a whole in a specific type of sacred, ministerial service. St Augustine's statement: 'With you I am a Christian, for you I am a priest' reflects this inter-relationship and distinction.

The long-standing theological question of the inter-relationship between the priest and the bishop emerges. In the early Church the specifically distinct 'priest' was not so evident; the bishop as the successor to the Apostles was the key figure. The Council states that 'the bishops have by divine institution taken the place of the Apostles as the pastors of the Church'.[2] As priests were ordained as co-workers with the bishops, as the Church soon expanded, there were two theological tendencies, one seeing episcopal ordination as a sacrament and the other seeing the culminating and critically important sacrament as that of priestly ordination (the climax of seven orders, in parallel to the sacraments), since nothing could be added to such sacred power, only the greater juridical power of the bishop.[3] The Code, and the Council before it, clearly teach that the sacrament of order is a true sacrament

---

[1.] Cf. J. Wicks, *Luther and his Spiritual Legacy*, Dominican Publications, Dublin, 1983, 91, 96–7.

[2.] Second Vatican Council, Dogmatic Constitution on the Church, *Lumen gentium*, n. 20.

[3.] H. Vogrimler, *Sacramental Theology*, Liturgical Press, Collegeville, Minnes., 1992, 253–5; original German: *Sakramenaltheologie*, 3rd edn, Patmos, 1992.

in each of its three grades.[4] The Council taught that 'the fullness of the sacrament of orders is conferred by episcopal consecration'.[5] This opinion that even a priest had the power to ordain to the priesthood, even though he could not exercise this sacred power, may have ceded to the tradition that only the bishop, with the fullness of priesthood, could do so. The Council's perspective led to the reform of 'minor orders' and of 'major orders', with the focus on the 'three grades of order' of episcopate, presbyterate and diaconate (c. 1009 § 1). The minor orders were abolished, the positions of porter and of exorcist were abolished as stable positions and those of lector and acolyte became 'lay ministries'. Entry into the clerical state, which used to occur at 'first tonsure' (now transformed for those preparing to be secular clergy into 'admission to candidacy'), occurs at ordination to diaconate (c. 266 § 1–2) and is one of the juridical effects of diaconal ordination.[6]

The nature of priesthood is reflected in both its dimensions, the ordained chosen 'from Christ's faithful' (c. 1008), are constituted by this sacrament as 'sacred ministers', the word 'minister' meaning someone who is to be of service, to the Gospel, to the believing community of the Church. Ministerial or ordained priests are consecrated through Christ's gift of the sacramental grace of order in this particular degree (c. 1008) in a way which enables them to fulfil 'in the Person of Christ the Head' the nourishment of the People of God by preaching, sanctifying and leading them in the Gospel (c. 1008). Both the common priesthood of the faithful and the ministerial priesthood are connected to one another, but both are rooted in the priesthood of Christ himself.

All priesthood rests on that of Jesus Christ the one true priest (Heb. 7:13–16; 9:11) and sole Mediator (Heb. 8:6; 9:15) between God and man. As human beings, incapable of achieving our own salvation, we depend absolutely upon Christ whose priesthood is the surpassing fulfilment of the Old Testament priesthood.[7] Instead of mere signs and desires on the part of human beings to be with God, Christ, true God

---

[4.] J-P. Durand, 'La fonction de sanctification dans l'Église' in P. Valdrini et al. (eds), Droit canonique, 2nd edn, Dalloz, Paris, 1999, 302, n. 468.

[5.] Lumen gentium, n. 21.

[6.] Paul VI, Apostolic letter, motu proprio, Ministeria quaedam, 15 August 1972, on the reform of first tonsure, minor orders and sub-diaconate, Acta apostolicae sedis, 64 (1972), 529–34; ID., Apostolic letter, motu proprio, Ad pascendum, 15 August 1972, Acta apostolicae sedis, 64 (1972), 534–40

[7.] A. Vanhoye, La structure littéraire de l'épître aux Hébreux, 2nd edn, Desclée de Brouwer, Clannecy, 1976, 137–8, 238.

and true man, actually bridged the gap (is the true bridge-builder or *'pontifex'*) between God and man in his own body, sacrificing himself literally in an act of total consecration to the Father and for our salvation, replacing the Old Testament sacrifices, signs and gestures, repeated every year, but entirely incapable of removing sin, with his 'one single sacrifice', his 'perfect sacrifice' (Heb. 9:14), which 'once and for all' (Heb. 9:12, 24–8) did away with the power of sin, and death (Heb. 9:15–16) as the 'Eternal High Priest'.[8] The Paschal Mystery, effected 'once and for all' is mediated by Christ through his eternal intercession as our supreme High Priest from heaven, where he is 'living for ever to intercede' on our behalf (Heb. 7:25). This continues through the action of ministerial or ordained priests in a way which is related to, but different from, the common priesthood in kind and not just in degree. The ordained, ministerial priest in the Church acts 'in the person of Christ', not for himself alone, but on behalf of all. This one eternal mystery of Christ is made present in the Eucharist and its blessings are truly and effectively granted to the faithful properly disposed to receive them through the sacraments of the Church.

The role of the diaconate and the restoration of the permanent diaconate, instigated by the Council, are reflected in the Code. The possibility was envisaged, 'should the Roman Pontiff think fit', of married men being ordained as 'permanent deacons', but only if of a more mature age, younger men being held to the discipline of celibacy in the Latin Church (c. 1031, § 2).[9] Ordination to the diaconate is not ordination to the priesthood, but ordination 'for service as deacons' (*'ad ministerium'*, not *'ad sacerdotium'*), service of the Church and in particular of the bishop. This service reflects the *'tria munera'* and might include liturgical service in baptism, matrimony, distribution of Holy Communion, a teaching function in preaching and catechesis, and a pastoral function in the service of charity.

These orders concern those called by divine vocation. They are not to exercise them according to their own wishes, but in teaching, sanctifying and ruling the People of God, on the basis of the particular grade of order they have received and the particular functions or offices they have been given in the Church. Those in sacred orders, especially in priestly orders, fulfil their ministry neither by their own doing, nor by human arrangement, but by the divine power and capacity given through the sacrament of order to each.[10]

---

8. Ibid., 238.
9. *Lumen gentium*, n. 29.
10. Durand, 'La fonction de la sanctification', 302, n. 468.

Those who are ordained are 'marked with an indelible character' (c. 1008), which means that it is impossible for the sacrament to be repeated (c. 845 § 1). It is precisely the ontological change brought about by Christ through the sacrament, working through the ordaining bishop, which constitutes the character, the 'new and further (sacramental) consecration' beyond those of baptism and confirmation, which can never be undone and hence can never be repeated. With priestly order, the character involves consecration to Christ in this new conformity to Christ such that Christ acts through the priest who acts in his person for the good of the Church, in the service of its mission.[11] The abiding nature of the sacrament, of what is brought about by Christ, as distinct from the personal state of grace of the recipient, underpins the '*ex opera operato*' of sacraments depending on priestly orders. Since it is the needs of the community of the Church which are at stake, the intention of Christ to nourish them through the abiding sacrament of the Eucharist implies the abiding nature of priestly ordination and hence its sacramental character.[12] This aspect of 'nourishing' the People of God emerges very strongly in the Code, not only in regard to the sacraments, in respect of all three functions of sanctifying, teaching and ruling (c. 1008). This reinforces the Council and the Code's association of 'Word' and 'Sacrament' to lead the faithful into deeper communion with Christ and, in him, with one another to facilitate the mission of the Church.

Of course, since the sacrament of order has three grades, a man who has been ordained a deacon who is later ordained a priest and one already ordained a deacon and priest is ordained a bishop, does receive the sacrament of order 'again', but it is in a different degree 'for service', 'for priesthood', and 'to the fullness of priesthood', so that the sacrament as such is not repeated.

3. The Celebration of Holy Orders: Conditions of Validity

There are very few conditions laid down for the valid conferring of Holy Orders. This is to be explained by the need of the Church to ensure a proper supply of priests to meet the needs of the faithful. In situations of urgent need, requirements which were too stringent would make it difficult to ensure that pastoral care which is the

---

[11.] J. Galot, *the Theology of the Priesthood*, 198–212.

[12.] C. E. O'Neill, *Sacramental Realism: A General Theory of the Sacraments*, Dominican Publications, Dublin, 1983, 194–7.

supreme purpose of the Church's law (c. 1752). For the validity of sacred orders, the candidate must be male and must be baptized (c. 1024). No other sacraments are valid unless someone has been baptized (c. 842 § 1).

As for the candidate having to be male, the question of whether or not Our Blessed Lady enjoyed the priesthood was examined in the Middle Ages and it was decided that she did not. The Tradition of the Catholic Church has been that ordination to the priesthood is reserved to Catholics of the male sex; the Orthodox and other Eastern Churches not in full communion with the Catholic Church have retained the same tradition. Females are said to have been admitted to 'priestly orders' in other ecclesial communities, in Protestant and Anglican communities, but these communities lack the apostolic succession and their orders, even for males, are not valid in the eyes of the Catholic Church.[13] Hence they do not act '*in persona Christi*' and sacraments celebrated by them which depend for validity upon priestly orders (confirmation, Eucharist, reconciliation, anointing of the sick and Holy Orders) are not valid in the eyes of the Catholic Church. Furthermore, many of them do not recognize priesthood as a specific sacrament and so talk of 'priests' or 'ordination' does not mean the same as it does in the Catholic Church and Orthodox Churches.[14]

In communities which the Catholic Church recognizes as 'true particular Churches', Churches in the full sense, those with apostolic succession and valid orders, ordination of women to the priesthood has never been practised and is not valid.[15] Jesus was male; hence, sacramentally, the sign value of priesthood is effectively represented by a male, not a female. The fact that Jesus recognized and promoted the equality of women in ways which contemporaries found shocking, but did not make them Apostles as one of the Twelve, seems to indicate the divine will that priesthood be restricted to males. The text resulting from an examination of the question stated not only that women had

---

[13.] Leo XIII, Apostolic letter, issued *motu proprio*, *Apostolicae curae*, 13 September 1896, H. Denzinger and A. Schönmetzer (eds), *Enchiridion symbolorum, definitionum et declarationum de rebus fidei et morum*, 36th edn, Barcelona, Freiburg-im-Breisgau, Rome, 1976), nn. 3315–19; J. Neuner and J. Dupuis, *The Christian Faith in the Doctrinal Documents of the Catholic Church*, 2nd edn, Mercier, Cork, 1976, nn. 1722–8.

[14.] Galot, *The Theology of the Priesthood*, 252-253; cf. his footnotes nn. 7–8 to this chapter on the Russian Orthodox Church's reaction, along the same lines, to the World Council of Churches' decision at Nairobi in 1975 to be more open to women's ordination, Ibid., 265.

[15.] Congregation for the Doctrine of the Faith, Declaration on the Unicity and Salvific Universality of Jesus Christ and the Church, *Dominus Iesus*, 6 August 2000, n. 17.

not been ordained priests and that the Church chose not to ordain them as priests, but that 'the Church, in fidelity to the example of the Lord, does not consider herself authorized to admit women to priestly ordination'.[16] This is reflected in c. 1024.

Recent positions adopted by the World Council of Churches and practices of various communities belonging to it and the Anglican Communion's acceptance of the ordination of women as 'priests' and very recently as 'bishops' have compromised seriously the ecumenical progress of recent decades.[17] In the face of such tendencies, John Paul II's major statement in 1994 rejected claims 'in some places' that the doctrine was 'open to debate' or might 'have a merely disciplinary force'. Rather it is fundamental: 'in order that all doubt may be removed regarding a matter of great importance, a matter which pertains to the Church's constitution itself ...',[18] to note that the doctrine that priestly ordination is reserved solely to males is not a mere, historical accident, nor just a matter of a disciplinary rule which the Church could alter, but, reflecting *'Inter insigniores'*, is based on the fact of Christ being male, on his deliberate selection only of males as members of the Twelve and on the constant doctrine and practice of the Church's Tradition.[19] It is a doctrine belonging to the Church's 'fundamental constitution' or to its essence and 'does not proceed from sociological or cultural motives', nor is it a temporary prudential judgment; it is a doctrine the Church has not changed and cannot change;[20] it is 'definitive' and 'cannot be altered'.[21] Thus, it belongs to the category of doctrines not (as yet) defined but definitive, which cannot be denied without setting oneself against Catholic doctrine, a category now expressly incorporated into the Code of Canon Law.[22] According to the Doctrinal Note of the Congregation for the Doctrine of the Faith, this doctrine reserving priestly ordination to males, based on Scripture and Tradition, is to be

---

[16.] Sacred Congregation for the Doctrine of the Faith, Declaration on the Admission of Women to Priestly Ordination, *'Inter insigniores'*, 15 October 1976, *Acta apostolicae sedis*, (69), 1977, 98–116, Introduction and n. 4.

[17.] Paul VI, letter to Donald Coggan, Archbishop of Canterbury, 30 November 1975, *Acta apostolicae sedis*, 68 (1976), 599–600.

[18.] John Paul II, Apostolic letter, *Ordinatio sacerdotalis*, 22 May 1994, *Acta apostolicae sedis*, 86 (1994), 545–8, at 548, n. 4.

[19.] Ibid., n. 2.

[20.] Ibid., n. 4.

[21.] John Paul II, Apostolic letter issued *motu proprio, Ad tuendam fidem*, 18 May 1998, *Acta apostolicae sedis*, 90 (1998), 543–8.

[22.] Ibid., n. 5; Congregation for the Doctrine of the Faith, Formula for the Profession of Faith and Oath of Fidelity, with an attached Doctrinal Note, *Acta apostolicae sedis*, 90 (1998), 457–61, n. 11.

held definitively and is taught infallibly on the basis of the universal ordinary Magisterium of the Church.[23] This c. 1024 states succinctly, saying only a baptized man can be validly ordained.

Other conditions of validity, which would apply to any ordination, are the following. The minister of the sacrament has to be a validly ordained bishop (c. 1012), the matter of the sacrament is the laying on of the hands of the bishop on the head of the candidate (c. 1009 § 2), and the form, for diaconal, presbyteral or episcopal orders, is the section of the consecratory prayer specified for validity for each grade (c. 1009 § 2). In addition, the minister must intend to ordain the specific candidate to a specific degree of order and the candidate must intend to be ordained to that degree of order; canons 1026, 1029, 1036 express conditions of liceity as to how the latter's intention is to be assured (Table 11D).

4. The Liceity of Ordinations

In addition to what is required for validity, there are further canons on what is needed for an ordination to be licit or lawful.

a. Laws Applying to Ordinations in all Degrees of Sacred Order

Ordinations are to take place normally on Sundays or holydays of Obligation, but for pastoral reasons can take place on other, even ferial days (c. 1010). They should be conducted during the Eucharist (c. 1010), normally in the cathedral, but for pastoral reasons in another church or oratory (c. 1011 § 1), in the presence of other clerics and of other members of the faithful (c. 1011 § 2). The purpose of these canonical norms is to highlight in the very celebration the intimate relationship between Eucharist and Holy Orders, between the latter and the communion of the Church; it does not envisage any ordination outside of the context of the Eucharist. The days of precept and the cathedral would emphasize the solemn nature of the celebration, the latter bringing out the link between ordination and diocese (especially significant with diocesan clergy). Ordinations ought not to occur outside a church, it being already a concession to pastoral reasons that an ordination would not be taking place in the cathedral; although there could be situations of dire need, where priests might need to be

---

[23.] Doctrinal Note attached to the Profession, n. 11.

ordained clandestinely or for other reasons of urgent pastoral need. The participation of the faithful as a whole is facilitated by these days and place settings, to indicate that sacred orders are to serve the People of God as a whole and the inter-relationship between the common priesthood of the faithful and the ministerial priesthood.[24] Even if a bishop is the ordinary of the candidate for ordination (whether as a deacon or as a priest or as a bishop), he may not ordain this man outside his own diocese without the permission of the local ordinary of the diocese in which the ordination is to take place (c. 1017).

b. Further Laws Applying to Ordination to the Episcopate

There must be a pontifical mandate before anyone is ordained as a bishop (c. 1013). This is essentially a question of the communion of the bishops with one another in union with the Holy Father in the College of Bishops. This communion is indispensable not for the validity, but for the liceity, of the episcopal ordination. It concerns not only the newly ordained bishop, but also the ordaining or consecrating bishop's belonging to the College of Bishops (cf. cc. 336, 375 § 2). To ordain someone as a bishop without a pontifical mandate or to be ordained as a bishop without such a mandate having been issued is a canonical crime, perpetrating schism. Both of these bishops would be excommunicated 'latae sententiae', its absolution being reserved to the Apostolic See (c. 1382). This is what occurred in 1988 with Archbishop Lefebvre and with the bishops he ordained without pontifical mandate and against the express precept of the Congregation of Bishops; the excommunication was then publicly declared, the excommunications of those ordained then being lifted in 2009.[25] There are to be two co-consecrating bishops in an episcopal ordination (c. 1014), unless

---

[24.] Ghirlanda, *Il diritto nella Chiesa: mistero di comunione: compendio di diritto ecclesiale* 4th revised edn, San Paolo, Cinisello, P.U.G., 2006, 328–9, n. 343.

[25.] John Paul II, Apostolic letter, *motu proprio, 'Ecclesia Dei'*, 2 July 1988, *Acta apostolicae sedis*, 80 (1988), 1495–8 at 1496, n. 3: This action 'is a very grave one and is truly of the greatest significance for the unity of the Church ... For this reason, such disobedience – which in itself implies a real rejection of the Roman Primacy – constitutes an act of *schism*'. Despite a warning from the Prefect of the Congregation for Bishops of 17 June, the illicit ordination went ahead and so Archbishop Lefebvre and four (named) priests 'have incurred the grave penalty of excommunication, already established by ecclesiastical discipline'. Cf. Benedict XVI, Lettera ai vescovi della Chiesa Cattolica riguardo alla remissione della scomunica dei 4 vescovi consacrati dall'Arcivescovo Lefebvre, 10 March 2009; www.vatican.va/holy_father/benedict_xvi/letters/2009/documents/hf_ben-xvi.

there is a dispensation from this requirement from the Apostolic See, although all bishops present are encouraged to participate.

c. Further Laws on both Diaconal and Presbyteral Ordinations

A man to be ordained to the diaconate and/or priesthood is either to be ordained by his proper bishop or has to have dimissorial letters issued by his proper bishop, to allow him to be ordained by another bishop (c. 1015 § 1). The proper bishop of a candidate for ordination to the diaconate for the secular or diocesan clergy is the bishop of the diocese in which he is domiciled or the bishop of the diocese in which he intends to be incardinated at diaconate (c. 1016). The proper bishop of a deacon who is to be ordained as a priest (to the presbyteral degree of order) is the bishop of the diocese in which he was incardinated by the diaconate (c. 1016). We recall that incardination occurs automatically at diaconate, into the diocese for which a man is ordained to serve in the secular clergy, into an institute of consecrated life, or into a society of apostolic life or secular institute which has the faculty to incardinate or into a personal prelature (cc. 265–266, 295) and, if this has not been established, into the diocese in which in fact the ordination took place. Hence it is obvious that the proper bishop of a deacon is the bishop of the diocese in which he was incardinated and not that of his earlier domicile. If the incardination had changed since diaconate ordination, unlikely but not impossible (cc. 267–269), the proper bishop would be the bishop of the diocese in which the deacon is incardinated at the time he is to be ordained a priest. The Code is precise about this to avoid the problem of wandering clergy ('clerici vagi') and also to specify which bishop has the right and responsibility to conduct an ordination and, by implication, which bishops do not.

d. The Ordaining Bishop

For validity, the ordaining bishop has to be a validly ordained or consecrated bishop (c. 1012). In addition, for liceity, he must be the proper bishop of the candidate or have dimissorial letters from the proper bishop of a candidate who is being ordained or from the one lawfully able to issue them, have the permission of the local diocesan bishop to conduct an ordination in that bishop's diocese, if he is not ordaining a man in the diocese of which he is the diocesan bishop (c. 1017), ensure that all other conditions necessary for licit ordination are met, and ordain the man who is his own subject, unless there is a lawful reason for not doing so (c. 1015 § 2). He is not to ordain a man who is of Oriental rite without an indult (an exception to the law by way of concession) from the Apostolic See (c. 1015 § 2). He may ordain a man, if he is a bishop who is able to issue dimissorial letters (c. 1015 § 3), but he cannot ordain a man if he is able to issue dimissorial letters in virtue of being equivalent in law to a diocesan bishop, such as a diocesan administrator, but if he is in fact not a bishop; this is because episcopal orders are necessary for ordination to be valid (c. 1012).

e. Dimissorial Letters

Where the ordaining bishop is not the proper bishop of the man being ordained, it is required for liceity that dimissorial letters ('letters which have been sent') have been properly issued to allow this bishop to conduct the ordination of this man to the diaconate or to the priesthood in the presbyteral degree (c. 1015 § 1). For the good order of the Church, it is obvious that bishops are not permitted to ordain anyone, just as they wish, without reference to the proper bishop or to the superiors of the institute, society or prelature which the man to be ordained is to serve. Those able lawfully to issue dimissorial letters to allow someone to be ordained by one other than his proper bishop are, for the secular clergy, the man's proper bishop himself (c. 1018 § 1 1°) or, for a lawful reason (cc. 1015 § 2; 1018 § 1), an apostolic administrator, or a diocesan administrator, in the latter case with the consent of the college of consultors (c. 1018 § 1, 2°). This means that a diocesan administrator would issue these letters invalidly if consent was not sought and obtained (c. 127 § 1) and, furthermore, he is not to issue such letters where the diocesan bishop has already refused to ordain the candidate (c. 1018 § 2, 2°). A pro-vicar or a pro-prefect of a territory not yet established as a diocese, with the consent of the council he must have, consisting of at least three missionary priests (cc. 1018; 495 § 2), can issue dimissorial letters, but they would be invalidly issued if consent were not sought and obtained (c. 127 § 1). It should be noted that c. 495 § 2 refers only to consultation of this council on more serious matters, but c. 1018 § 1, 2° makes this a matter of consent for the issuing of dimissorial letters. The pro-vicar or pre-prefect is not to issue dimissorial letters where the administrator or prefect has already refused to ordain the man (c. 1018 § 2, 2°).

For members of clerical religious institutes of consecrated life of pontifical right and for members of clerical societies of apostolic life of pontifical right, the superior of those institutes or societies in regard to their proper subjects (for diaconate or priesthood), who are perpetually professed (institutes), in accordance with the Constitutions or who have been definitively incorporated (societies), in accordance with the Constitutions, is to issue dimissorial letters (c. 1019 § 1). For all other members of any other institute or society (those which are not clerical religious institutes and / or are not of pontifical right), the laws applying to dimissorial letters relating to secular clergy apply (c. 1019 § 2). For members of personal prelatures, since these do not depend upon the diocesan bishop and since their prelate can promote men from their members to orders and incardinate them into the prelature (c. 295), and for members of secular institutes of pontifical right where they have the faculty to incardinate into the society (c. 266 § 3), there is a process analogous to that for religious institutes and societies of pontifical right (c. 1019 § 2).[26]

Dimissorial letters are to be issued only when all the testimonials and other documents have been obtained (cc. 1020; 1050–1052), and sent to a bishop in communion with the Catholic Church (not to a schismatic nor to one otherwise excommunicated by law) and who is of the Latin rite (c. 1021) or to a bishop in communion with the Catholic Church (not to a schismatic nor to one otherwise excommunicated by law) of a rite other than the Latin rite, but only where an apostolic indult has been granted for this (c. 1021). The ordaining bishop has to check that the dimissorial letters he has received are authentic (c. 1022), that they have not been revoked by the person who lawfully issued them or by his successor, although they do not lapse if the one who issued them simply ceases to be in office or if his authority otherwise ceases before the ordination occurs (c. 1023). For a bishop to ordain a man and for a man to be ordained without dimissorial letters having been properly issued is a canonical crime (c. 1383). Those who commit this crime, if it is imputable, incur the penalty of not being allowed to ordain for a year (for the ordaining bishop) and of being suspended from the order illicitly conferred 'ipso facto' (for the one ordained).

These norms are detailed, but they are essential to protect the People of God from those not proper candidates and from irresponsible persons being ordained and to ensure the communion of the Church. They are important, too, for ensuring that those who may be proper candidates in time are not 'rushed through' by irresponsible or negligent superiors before they are properly formed or even when they are not properly sponsored under an authentic canonical entity such as a diocese or a canonically erected entity of an institute

---

[26.] Ghirlanda, *Il diritto nella Chiesa*, 332–3, n. 351.

or society.

f. Proper Candidates for Sacred Orders

The very limited conditions laid down for the validity of ordination, beyond the minister, the intentions both of the ordaining bishop and of the candidate, the matter and form, are that the candidate be male and be baptized (c. 1024). These minimal conditions are to ensure a proper supply of priests, even in circumstances of dire need, persecution or grave discrimination, where ordination and the exercise of priesthood may have to be clandestine.

Beyond validity, the licit conferral of the sacred orders of diaconate and priesthood demands that the proper bishop (c. 1016) or competent superior (c. 1019) verify that the candidate has the necessary qualities, is free from all impediments and irregularities, has fulfilled the requirements which are to precede ordination, that all the documents required are at hand and that the necessary investigations have been made (c. 1025 § 1). They are to judge that the candidate's ordination would be beneficial to the Church's ministry (c. 1025 § 2). A bishop is to be certain the candidate will actually be attached to another diocese if he is ordaining his own subject for service in another diocese (c. 1025 § 3). The Church's long-standing desire to avoid unattached, acephalous or wandering clergy is again evident. If a bishop ordained someone who had not been accepted for another diocese which then refused to take him, he would be incardinated in the diocese of the ordaining bishop. Apart from incardination, the concern is that clergy are to serve the needs of the Church, to fulfil a foreseeable canonical mission and are not to be ordained for reasons of prestige or favour. This is why religious orders, other institutes of consecrated life and societies of apostolic life consider the needs of the community, institute or society in judging whether or not more deacons or priests should be ordained. Where there is an abundance of clergy diocesan bishops need to judge whether and how the ordination of further men would benefit the Church.

Beyond these general considerations (c. 1025 § 2 and 3), the details of the demands of c. 1025 § 1 are treated in the subsequent canons:

Requirements in the Candidate for Ordination

Freedom

Ordination always involves recognizing a personal vocation from Christ. Part of the discernment of that vocation is the direct and irreplaceable acknowledgement of such a vocation and free acceptance of it by the man himself. No one can do this for him; nor must he allow himself to be pressurized into being ordained, if he does not judge that he has such a vocation or if he does not freely embrace it. Apart from the act of faith itself, this vocational decision will profoundly affect the rest of his life, determining all else, since it is his decision of life or life option.[27] The responsibility for this recognition and acceptance rests with him. It cannot be handed to family or to those who have encouraged, assessed or supported a vocation. Nor must a sense of obligation be allowed to become a pressure constraining personal freedom. One reason for the abolition of 'minor orders' and that no one become a cleric until diaconate was to facilitate the free, irrevocable response to a vocation from the Lord.[28] The Code rightly insists that 'It is absolutely wrong to compel anyone, in any way or for any reason whatsoever, to receive orders' (c. 1026). While no one is to be pressurized into becoming a priest, it is also wrong to turn away anyone who is 'canonically suitable' for ordination (c. 1026).

Preparation for Ordination according to Law

Without repeating what has been said on the admission and formation of candidates for ordination (cc. 232–262), preparation should be 'careful' and 'in accordance with law' (c. 1027). Only for very serious reasons should there be any dispensations from parts of it by the proper bishop or competent superior who are to ensure that candidates are 'properly instructed' both about the 'order itself' and about the 'obligations' it entails before ordaining someone (c. 1028).

Specific Qualities of Candidates for Ordination

The Code lists as key qualities, without which a man is 'not to be ordained': sound faith, a right intention, the knowledge needed, a good reputation, moral probity and proven virtue, the physical and psychological qualities appropriate to the particular order to be received (c. 1029). It would be dreadful to ordain someone who lacked faith or for

---

[27.] Cf. K. Demmer, *Die Lebensentscheidung: Ihre moraltheologischen Grundlagen*, Schöningh, München, Paderborn, Wien, 1974, 148–64, 236–48.

[28.] Paul VI, *Ministeria quaedam*, 1972 .

someone to allow himself to be ordained who did not believe and love the Catholic faith. The moral qualities listed are not meant to exclude all but the perfect, but those whose moral standards and behaviour are at odds with the Gospel and with the teaching of the Church, whose ordination might constitute scandal. The physical and psychological qualities are not detailed, but a man who is ordained has to be able to preach and administer the sacraments according to the order received. In the past men who were blind or deaf and mute would have been seen to lack minimal physical qualities for priestly ordination. The present Code does not specify these; for instance, if effective means of artificial voice projection work in a given case (verified by expert assessment), the ordinary might well permit ordination.[29] An ordinand has to have the basic stability and commitment to live out a life option faithfully in a way which is in harmony with the Gospel. The conditions or qualities are the minimal needed for him to function in the order concerned; without these, a man could not lawfully be ordained.

If a proper bishop or competent superior knows of a 'canonical reason' why someone could not be ordained, even if this were 'occult' (not known nor capable of becoming known publicly), he is not to ordain the man (c. 1030). The good of the Church is at issue here; a vocation is a calling, not a right. Such a person could not serve the true good of the Church and must not be ordained.

Canonical Age for Ordination

For priestly ordination a man must be: over twenty-five years of age, with sufficient maturity, with at least six months between diaconate and priestly ordination (c. 1031 § 1). For diaconal ordination, intending to be ordained priest, a man must be over twenty-three (c. 1031 § 1). For ordination as permanent deacons, those who are not married must be over twenty-five (c. 1031 § 2), while those who are married must be over thirty-five and have the consent of their wives (c. 1031 § 2). Episcopal conferences may establish a higher age for priesthood and for permanent diaconate (c. 1031 § 3). Dispensation from canonical ages for ordination may be given up to a year by the local ordinary, for more than a year only by the Apostolic See (c. 1031 § 4).

[29.] Ghirlanda, *Il diritto nella Chiesa*, ,339–41, n. 361.

Studies and Formation

Those intending to be ordained priests may be ordained to the diaconate only after completing five years of a curriculum of studies in philosophy and theology (c. 1032 § 1). Between diaconal and priestly ordination such deacons are to spend a time settled by their bishop or competent superior exercising the diaconate and the pastoral ministry (c. 1032 § 2). No one is to be ordained as a permanent deacon until he has completed the period of formation (c. 1032 § 3), according to the provisions of the local episcopal conference (c. 236).

Confirmation

For liceity confirmation is necessary (c. 1033), indeed all the sacraments of initiation should have been received. Confirmation involves the specific gift of the Holy Spirit to render someone capable of, and responsible for, giving witness to Jesus Christ; it is highly appropriate that it should have been received by someone intending to devote the rest of his life to proclaiming the Gospel.

Lay Ministries and Admission as Candidates for Ordination

A candidate for the diaconate should have received admission as a candidate for sacred orders from his proper bishop or competent superior or one deputed through dimissorial letters to admit him, after having written in his own hand and signed a petition to be admitted and after this petition has been accepted by the proper bishop or competent superior (c. 1034 § 1). This reinforces the importance of the person seeking orders being free. This rite involves the formal recognition by the candidate that he (believes that he) is called to sacred orders by Christ and commits himself publicly before the Church to such official preparation and also the formal recognition by the Church, through these authorities, that he is a suitable person to be accepted to prepare for such orders.

This does not apply to a person who has made vows in a clerical institute (c. 1034 § 2), which implies that those entering a secular institute or those entering a society of apostolic life where they do not take vows, but make some other form of commitment, should be admitted as candidates. Those in a clerical society of apostolic life, where they have taken formal vows as such, it is judged by some, would not be required to be admitted as candidates.[30] Those preparing

---

30. M. P. Joyce, 'The Sacrament of Order' in M. P. Joyce *et al.* (eds), *Procedural Handbook for Institutes of Consecrated Life and Societies of Apostolic Life,* Canon Law Society of America, Catholic University of America, Washington, DC, 2001, 219–40 at 219.

for orders are to have been instituted as lay ministers, lectors and acolytes (c. 1035) and exercise these ministries 'for an appropriate time'. Insofar as the primary function of a priest is preaching the Gospel and the principal function is celebrating the sacraments, especially the Eucharist, this is highly appropriate. It does not undermine the lay character of these ministries, but emphasizes the fact that those preparing for sacred orders are still lay men, not yet definitively committed as clerics and still free to assess this vocation (c. 1026).

Request for Ordination and Life-Long Commitment

A candidate for the diaconate or priesthood is to ask his proper bishop or competent superior for ordination in his own hand and under his own signature (c. 1036). This written request must contain his commitment to the order for life; it is a free and irrevocable commitment to serve the Church in that order.

Promise of Celibacy

In the Latin Church the commitment of life-long celibacy is required from those entering the priesthood, made as a declaration of commitment prior to ordination and formally in the liturgy of diaconate ordination itself (c. 1037). This obligation, to be made 'publicly and before the Church', applies to those who are intending to be ordained to the permanent diaconate who are not married and to those intending to proceed to priestly ordination. A man 'is not to be admitted to the order of diaconate unless ...' he has made that promise in this way. The only exception is for those who have taken perpetual vows in a religious institute (c. 1037), which means that those belonging to secular institutes and to societies of apostolic life must promise celibacy in this way.[31]

A Spiritual Retreat

This is to be at least five days long, the ordinary settling its place and form; the ordaining bishop has to verify that this has been made (c. 1038).

The Transitional Diaconate

If a man has been ordained as a deacon, in view of priestly ordination and then decides not to proceed to the priesthood, the ordinary may not refuse to let him exercise the diaconate, unless there is a canonical

---

[31.] Ghirlanda, *Il diritto nella Chiesa*, 343–4, n. 364 e.

irregularity or a reason judged by the bishop or competent major superior as grave (c. 1038).

g. Canonical Irregularities and Simple Impediments

A simple impediment is one which is not perpetual; an impediment which is perpetual is an irregularity (c. 1040). Either a simple impediment or an irregularity can prevent someone from being ordained (preventing the reception of orders) or can prevent an ordained man exercising the order he has received.

Irregularities for the Reception of Orders (c. 1041)

A man is irregular for the reception of orders by reason of:

Insanity or Psychological Infirmity (1°), on the basis of which, according to the judgment of experts, he would be incapable of fulfilling the sacred ministry. This is analogous to c. 1095 § 1 and 3 on incapacity for marriage, both in its statement and its implications and in the need for an expert opinion to be sought to establish the incapacity. This is a canon which might well be invoked in respect of those with the disorder of paedophilia.

Canonical Crime, where a man has committed the canonical crime of apostasy, heresy or schism (2°).

Attempted Civil Marriage when himself prevented by a prior bond of marriage or by a sacred order or by a public perpetual vow of chastity or who attempted marriage with a woman validly married to someone else or who was bound by such a vow herself (3°).

Willful Homicide which he himself has committed wilfully or in which he has cooperated positively (4°).

Procured Abortion where he has actually procured an abortion or has positively cooperated in this (5°).

Grave Mutilation or Attempted Suicide where he has gravely and maliciously mutilated himself or someone else or where he has attempted suicide (5°).

Improper Exercise of Priestly or Episcopal Orders where he has exercised an act of order reserved to those in the presbyterate or episcopate while not having that order or while barred from its exercise by a canonical penalty (6°).

Simple Impediments to the Reception of Orders (c. 1042)

This involves a man who has a wife, unless he is seeking the permanent diaconate, a man who exercises an office or administration forbidden to clerics, of which he has to give an account (until he ceases to hold that office or administrative responsibility or has given an account and so the impediment has ceased), a neophyte (recent convert or recently received into full communion), unless sufficiently tested in the view of the ordinary.

Canonical Irregularities for the Exercise of Orders (c. 1044 § 1)

These concern those who are already ordained. They affect one bound by an irregularity who is ordained (1°), one who commits apostasy, heresy or schism publicly (2°), one who committed any of the crimes in c. 1041 3°, 4°, 5° or 6° (c. 1044 § 1 3°).

Simple Impediments to the Exercise of Orders (c. 1044 § 2)

These affect one bound by an impediment to orders who is ordained (1°), one suffering from insanity or other psychological infirmity as in c. 1041, n. 1, until, on the basis of an expert's assessment, the ordinary allows the order to be exercised (2°).

General Remarks on Irregularities and Simple Impediments to Orders

The faithful are obliged to reveal impediments to the reception of sacred orders of which they are aware to the ordinary or parish priest (c. 1043). Irregularities and impediments are incurred even if people are ignorant of them (c. 1045). They are multiplied if they arise from different causes, but not if they arise from the same cause, unless it concerns wilful homicide or actually procured abortion (c. 1046). Thus, two sources of insanity prior to ordination gives rise to only one irregularity, whereas two actual abortions result in two irregularities.

It can be seen that this rather technical section of the Code treats of matters of major importance for the common good of the Church, including people's esteem for the priesthood. People with knowledge of impediments, but especially of irregularities, are to make them known. Of course, there has to be some evidence for such serious allegations; the bishop or other superior to whom the allegation was reported or referred would have a duty to investigate to see if it were verified in fact.

Dispensations from Irregularities and Impediments

Dispensations Reserved to the Apostolic See

This applies to any and all irregularities: this is reserved to the Apostolic See alone, if the facts on which they were based have been brought into the judicial forum, that is brought to trial (c. 1047 § 1). Also reserved to the Apostolic See are irregularities arising from the offences in c. 1041, 2° (apostasy, heresy, schism) and 3° (attempted marriage), if public (c. 1047 § 2, 1°), any offence under c. 1041 4° (wilful homicide, actually procured abortion, positive cooperation in either), public or occult (c. 1047 § 2, 2°), a man with a wife, unless seeking permanent diaconate (c. 1047 § 2, 3°; cf. c. 1042 § 1), for the exercise of orders relating to c. 1041, 3° (attempted marriage), but only if public (c. 1047 § 3), for the exercise of orders relating to c. 1041, 4° (wilful homicide or actually procured abortion or positive cooperation in either), even if occult (c. 1047 § 3).

Dispensation not reserved to the Holy See

All other irregularities and impediments may be dispensed by the Local Ordinary (c. 1047 § 4).

Dispensation in Urgent, Occult Cases

Where the case is not in the public domain and is not capable of being known there, it is occult, In cases of urgency, for such occult cases, or for the crimes of attempted marriage, wilful homicide or actual abortion or for positive cooperation in these latter (c. 1048), the ordinary or the penitentiary should be contacted in the diocese. If neither can be approached and there is imminent danger of serious harm or loss of reputation, a person irregular for the exercise of order may exercise it, but he has to have recourse afterwards to the ordinary or penitentiary, anonymously and through a confessor (c. 1048).

Petitions for Dispensations

Petitions are to mention all irregularities and impediments. A general dispensation is valid if one irregularity or impediment is omitted in good faith (though not if in bad faith), unless it concerns wilful homicide or actually procured abortion or positive cooperation in either or unless it is in the judicial forum (c. 1049 § 1). The number of offences must be mentioned where wilful homicide or abortion are involved – for the validity of the dispensation (c. 1049 § 2). Importantly, a general dispensation for the reception of orders applies to all orders; it does not have to be obtained again for presbyterate and episcopate, if once granted to render diaconal ordination valid and licit (c. 1049 § 3).

h. Ordination and Homosexual Persons

The recent Instruction of the Congregation for Catholic Education states that those with deeply rooted homosexual tendencies are not to be admitted to seminaries, nor are they to be ordained to sacred orders. Specifically, it states that the Church, 'while profoundly respecting the persons in question, cannot admit to the seminary or to holy orders those who practice homosexuality, present deeply rooted homosexual tendencies or support the co-called "gay culture" '.[32] It considers that the situation of those with transitional homosexual tendencies, such as those which can be experienced in adolescence, to be different, but 'nevertheless, such tendencies must be clearly overcome at least three years before ordination to the diaconate'.[33] The candidate himself must evaluate his vocation in all honesty of conscience in a realistic way and must be open with his spiritual director and confessor about his situation; the latter, operating of course in the internal forum, where there is homosexual practice or where there are deep-rooted homosexual tendencies, must dissuade the individual from proceeding to ordination.[34]

This text does not constitute the addition of a further canonical impediment to ordination, since the Congregation lacks the capacity to establish such; that would require the Pope to approve a text 'in forma specifica', not, as here 'in forma ordinaria'.[35] It does underline, however, the very serious responsibilities not only of the individual and of those assisting him in the internal forum, but of the rector and of the external forum formation staff, as well as of the bishop or other superior in discerning a vocation. The question goes beyond homosexual persons and demands more careful attention at all levels to the assessment of a person's affective maturity, even where he is heterosexual. In the case of transsexual persons, it would have to be said

---

[32.] Congregation for Catholic Education, Instruction concerning the Criteria for the Discernment of Vocations with regard to Persons with Homosexual Tendencies in view of their Admission to Seminary and to Holy Orders: Text and Commentary, 4 November 2005, n. 2; www.vatican.va/roman_curia/congregations/ccatheduc/documents/rc_con_cath'

[33.] Ibid.

[34.] Ibid., n. 3.

[35.] G. Ghirlanda, 'Persone con tendenze omosessuali e ammissione al seminario e agli sacri ordini – aspetti canonici', Seminarium, XLVII, n. 3, 2007, 815–38 at 819.

that the very grave disturbances of one convinced that he/she is truly female/male in contrast to the bodily appearance to the contrary is liable to fall under the category of those impeded by reason of serious psychological imbalance.

i. Documentation and Investigations Required for Ordination

The following documents are needed: certificate of studies, relating to c. 1032 (c. 1050 1°): for ordination to priesthood certificate of diaconal ordination (c. 1050 2°); for ordination to diaconate certificates of baptism, confirmation, the ministries of lector and acolyte, the certificate in his own hand seeking the order freely (c. 1050 3°); for ordination to the permanent diaconate, if the candidate is married, a certificate of marriage and testimony of the wife's consent (c. 1050 3°). Furthermore, there needs to be a certificate from the rector of the seminary or house of formation on the qualities of the candidate, as listed above. This should be based on the 'scrutinies' which the rector is to make, after consultation with the formation staff at each stage of progress through the seminary and especially in relation to lectorate, acolyte, admission to candidacy for orders, diaconate and priesthood itself (whether there were reservations, delays and so on, and with reasons), as well as a certificate of the candidate's physical and psychological health (c. 1051 1°), with further evidence sought by the bishop or major superior, if needed (c. 1051 2°).

These documents are to be at hand for the diocesan bishop who ordains his own subject and there needs to be a statement of the candidate's suitability for ordination, positively established (c. 1052 § 1). For another bishop ordaining a man on behalf of his own bishop, he must have dimissorial letters stating that those documents are at hand and that the candidate's suitability has been established (c. 1052 § 2). For members of institutes of consecrated life and societies of apostolic life, there needs to be, in addition, verification in these dimissorial letters that the candidate has been definitively incorporated into the institute or into the society (c. 1052 § 2).

Despite all of these checks, if the diocesan bishop or major religious superior has definite reasons for doubting the candidate's suitability for ordination, he is not to be ordained (c. 1052 § 3).

j. Registration and Proof of Ordination

This is essential for all concerned, to know who is ordained. A special register is to be kept in the Curia of the place of ordination, to include: the name(s) of all ordained, the name of the ordaining bishop, and the place and time of ordination (c. 1053 § 1). All relevant documents are to be kept in that archive. The newly ordained man is to have a certificate of ordination, issued by the ordaining bishop (c. 1053 § 2). Where dimissorial letters have been issued, candidates are to give the certificate to their proper ordinary, for registration in a secret archive (c. 1053 § 2). The local ordinary (for secular clergy) or major superior of an institute of consecrated life and society of apostolic life is to send a record of the ordination to the parish priest of the place of baptism of the one ordained and that parish priest is to ensure that the ordination is recorded in the baptismal register. (c. 1054).

5. Conclusion

This brief treatment of the sacrament of sacred orders can seem complicated. Basically, it reflects the Second Vatican Council's renewed ecclesiology and sacramentology, as well as the reforms of the preparation and formation of the clergy introduced in the years following the Council. It brings out the key position of the bishop, the cooperative character of the presbyterate and the renewed understanding of the diaconate. The particular norms reveal a great sensitivity to the pastoral needs of the Church, which are especially served by those in sacred orders. This explains the detail in particular laws concerning the candidates for orders, including the detailed requirements and efforts to verify their suitability for ordination. Many problems have arisen because of vincible ignorance and neglect by superiors and by others; when the law is observed, the good of the Church and of all concerned is better assured.

Chapter 12

The Sanctifying Function of the Church

(Book IV of the Code)

Part I: The Sacraments

V: The Canon Law of Marriage – The Nature of Marriage

1. Introduction

In the next three chapters we shall examine the canon law of marriage, an area which comes to mind for many people whenever there is mention of canon law. This chapter will present the theological background needed to understand the Code before specifying what marriage is in the eyes of the Church. The next chapter will look at impediments to marriage and at the consent which brings a marriage into being which 'makes the marriage', together with defects which render that consent invalid. Then we shall consider canonical form or how a marriage is to be conducted, followed by various questions such as legal separation, dissolution of the bond of marriage and the nullity of marriage. This should help to provide a clear understanding of a complex area, which touches the lives of so many, since it is the vocation of most people in the Church.

2. A Historical Perspective on Marriage

a. Roman Law and Marriage

In the Roman Empire the head of the family ('*paterfamilias*') decided on marriages. However, Roman lawyers elaborated definitions of marriage which became classic. For Modestinus, it was 'the union of a man and a woman' in 'a sharing of the whole of life', while for Ulpian, it was the 'union of a man and a woman' involving a 'single sharing of life'.[1] These definitions deal with what marriage is (*'matrimonium in facto esse'*), rather than what brings marriage into existence (*'matrimonium in fieri'*).[2]

b. Augustine and the Good of Marriage

In the later Roman Empire the dualistic, Manichaean heresy disparaged anything to do with matter, the body and sexuality, judging it to come from an eternal source of evil. St Augustine, a former member of the sect, wrote against them and against exaggerated presentations of virginity which might have suggested something was wrong with marriage as such. His brief, classic text, expressed in its very title the Christian truth that marriage as such is something good. This he specified in three distinct, but inter-related goods (*'tria bona'*). The good of children (*'bonum prolis'*) was not just procreation or bringing children into the world, but included their upbringing or education in the broadest sense of that term; it entailed their religious re-birth in baptism and their religious education in the faith.[3] The good of fidelity (*'bonum fidei'*) is the marital relationship as exclusive to the husband and wife, one which precludes all adultery.[4] The third good was the good of the sacrament (*'bonum sacramenti'*); this reflects the relationship of Christ and his Church in Christian marriages, but Augustine considered that the three goods, including this one, applied to all true marriages (not only Christian marriages) and here he meant the good of the life-long bond (*'vinculum'*) between the spouses which could only be ended by the death of one of them and which precludes all divorce.[5] He saw marriage also as a way of protecting against concupiscence, understood as the disordered inclination, here sexual, resulting from original sin.[6]

---

1. Modestinus: 'coniunctio maris et feminae et consortium totius vitae'; Ulpian: 'viri et mulieris coniunctio, individuam consuetudinem vitae continens', quoted in T. Mackin, *Marriage in the Catholic Church, I, What is Marriage?* Paulist, New York, Ramsey, 1982, 73–4.
2. C. J. Scicluna, *The Essential Definition of Marriage According to the 1917 and 1983 Codes of Canon Law*, University Press of America, Lanham, New York, London, 1995, 24.
3. St Augustine, *De bono coniugali*, cc. 9–10.
4. Ibid., c. 4.
5. Ibid., c. 7.
6. Ibid., c. 5; ID., *De nuptiis et concupiscentiae*, I, cc. 6, 8.

c. Disputes over Consent and Consummation

By the twelfth century, when canon law developed as a specific science, traditions in Germanic parts of Europe, where having children was seen as important not only for the continuation of the species, but also for questions of inheritance, came into conflict with the Roman law tradition that 'consent makes the marriage' ('*consensus facit matrimonium*'), which had been sustained by Ives of Chartres.[7] Hugh of St Victor and then Peter Lombard had strongly defended the consensual basis for marriage, the latter emphasizing that it was consent between the partners about the present ('I take you now') rather than about the future ('I will marry you ...') which established a marriage.[8] In the Germanic sphere, Hincmar of Rheims had argued that consummation was what mattered.[9] Gratian said that there was no proper marriage between a couple unless it had been sexually consummated.[10] What he then explained was that, with consent a marriage is 'begun', but only with consummation is it 'perfected'.[11] These debates are more about how marriage comes into being ('*matrimonium in fieri*') than about what it is as such.[12] The Church judges that consent makes marriage, but consummation makes it absolutely indissoluble.

d. St Thomas Aquinas

St Thomas followed Peter Lombard in arguing that matrimony was one of the seven sacraments of the Church. He accepted also Augustine's goods of marriage, but in what was a sketch of his theology of marriage, since he died before completing it, he presented marriage in terms of 'ends' ('*fines*'), which were objective, metaphysical, underlying or essential purposes of all marriages (not the subjective, accidental reasons why particular people chose to marry, although these he accepted, provided that they were compatible with the former). These ends were related to the second level of natural inclinations which are found in all human beings, to which natural moral law corresponds, whereby we tend to ensure the propagation of the species.[13] Of the

---

[7.] Yves of Chartres, letter to Daimbert, Archbishop of Sens, cited in G. Mathon, *Le mariage des chrétiens, I, Des origines au Concile de Trente*, Desclée, Paris, 1993, 179.

[8.] Peter Lombard, *Quattuor libri sententiarum*, IV, dist. 27, c. 3; 28, c. 4.

[9.] Yves of Chartres, *Le mariage des chrétiens*, I, 149–53.

[10.] Gratian, *Concordia discordantium canonum (Decretum Gratiani)*, II, C. 27, q. 2, cc. 16, 39.

[11.] Ibid., II, C. 27, q. 2, c. 39.

[12.] Scicluna, *The Essential Defiintion of Marriage ...*, 31-33.

[13.] St Thomas Aquinas, *Summa theologiae*, I-II, q. 94, a. 2.

ends or purposes of marriage, he judged that the most fundamental was not what lasted for a time, but what endured.[14] Its primary end, therefore, was the procreation and education (or rearing) of children, while there were two essential secondary ends, the mutual help ('*mutuum adiutorium*') of the spouses in practical terms in general and in caring for their children in particular and the remedy or cure for concupiscence ('*remedium concupiscentiae*'), following St Paul and St Augustine by which disordered sexual desire is properly channelled.[15]

e. The Council of Trent and the Roman Catechism

The Council of Trent defined matrimony as one of the seven sacraments of the Church.[16] It also taught the indissolubility of marriage, condemning those who said the Catholic Church was wrong when it said that Matthew's Gospel did not contain any true exception to the prohibition of divorce, thus condemning Protestant, Reformed and Anglican doctrine, but not the Orthodox, who, while holding a different opinion on this, had never condemned Catholic doctrine on the matter.[17] The Roman Catechism recognized that the natural love existing between a Christian couple was strengthened by sacramental grace.[18]

f. Magisterial Interventions prior to the Second Vatican Council

The Reformation view that marriage was a matter for the State and not for the Church had a deleterious effect over the centuries. Leo XIII insisted that marriage involves more than merely human decisions, but the plan of God and that the Church by right legislates on

---

14. Ibid., I, q. 98, a. 1.
15. Ibid., III, Supplement, q. 41, a. 1 ad 1; q. 49, a. 1 ad 3, q. 65, a. 3; ID., *In quattuor libros sententiarum commentarium*, IV, dist. 27, q. 1 a.1; q. 26, q. 1 a. 1.
16. Council of Trent, Decree on the seven sacraments in general, H. Denzinger and A. Schönmetzer (eds), *Enchiridion symbolorum, definitionum et declarationum de rebus fidei et morum*, 36th edn, Herder, Barcelona, Freiburg-im-Breisgau, Rome, 1976, n. 1601, on the sacrament of matrimony, nn. 1797–812; cf. J. Neuner and J. Dupuis, *The Christian Faith in the Doctrinal Documents of the Catholic Church*, 2nd edn, Mercier, Dublin, Cork, 1978, nn. 1808–19.
17. Denzinger-Schönmetzer, *Enchiridion symbolorum*, n. 1807; Neuner and Dupuis, *The Christian Faith*, n. 1814.
18. *Catechismus ex concilii Tridentini ad parocchos*, 9th edn, Tauchnitz, Leipzig, 1587, II, c. VIII, q. 2–15.

marriage.[19] With the codification of canon law in 1917, the teaching of the ends or purposes of marriage, with its hierarchy and subordination of ends was stated: 'the primary end of marriage is the procreation and education of children, the secondary end is the mutual help and remedy for concupiscence'.[20] The primary end is reflected in the object of consent: 'Matrimonial consent is the act of the will by which each party hands over and accepts the right to the body for acts suitable in themselves for the procreation of offspring.'[21] Pius XI's encyclical on marriage, a very positive text, centred around the three Augustinian goods, taught the primacy of procreation, 'the offspring holds primacy of place'.[22] While love should pervade marriage and can cause people to marry, objectively the primary cause and reason for marriage is the procreation and education of children.[23] Pius XII warned against two distortions, one being so to emphasize the primary end as not to recognize the secondary ends and the other to claim that the secondary ends were equal to or superior to the primary end.[24]

There was much unease about the limited place given to love in these texts. Procreation could not actually occur from every conjugal act; some couples were sterile or too old for children and marriage involves building up a relationship between the couple themselves, an I-Thou union of two in one.[25] It was felt increasingly that this aspect needed to appear in doctrine on marriage.

[19.] Leo XIII, Encyclical letter, *Arcanum divinae sapientiae*, 10 February 1880, Denzinger-Schönmetzer, *Enchiridion symbolorum*, nn. 3124–46 at n. 3144; Neuner and Dupuis, *The Christian Faith*, n. 1821.

[20.] Benedict XV, *Codex iuris canonici* (1917), c. 1013 § 1.

[21.] Ibid., c. 1081 § 2.

[22.] Pius XI, Encyclical letter, *Casti connubii*, 31 December 1930, Denzinger-Schönmetzer, *Enchiridion symbolorum*, nn. 3700-3724 at n. 3704; Neuner and Dupuis, *The Christian Faith*, nn. 1824–33 at 1826.

[23.] Ibid., *Enchiridion symbolorum*, n. 3707; Neuner and Dupuis, *The Christian Faith*, n. 1829.

[24.] Pius XII, Allocution to the Sacred Roman Rota, 3 October 1941, *Acta apostolicae sedis*, 33 (1941), 421–6 at 423; ID., Allocution to Italian midwives, 29 October 1951, *Acta apostolicae sedis*, 43 (1951), 838–52 at 848–9.

[25.] Cf. H. Doms, *Du sens et de la fin du mariage*, Desclée de Brouwer, Paris, 1937, 68–70, 105–6; D. Von Hildebrand, *Il matrimonio*, Morcellana, Brescia, 1931, 26, 46–7; ID., *Gesammelte Werke*, III, *Das Wesen der Liebe*, Habbel, Regensburg, Kohhammer, Stuttgart, 1971, 75–82.

3. The Second Vatican Council and its Aftermath

There has been a notable development of doctrine on marriage in the Council, by Paul VI and by John Paul II. A brief synthesis of this is needed to appreciate the material in the Code of 1983 on marriage.

a. The Second Vatican Council

Gaudium et spes stated that marriage is: 'an intimate partnership (communion) of life and love ... established by the partners, ... by their irrevocable personal consent, ... by the human act by which they mutually surrender themselves to one another, involving a 'covenant', with its echoes of God's relationship with Israel and Christ's with the Church, as distinct from a 'contract' (n. 48).[26] Not only is love mentioned, but the mutual self-giving love of the couple implies much more than mere mutual help. Procreation is not the only focus, although it is implied in the intimacy of this relationship. Not only the communion of love but the communion of life, as well as the irrevocable nature of the consent, indicate the permanence of marriage. The consent which makes a marriage is irrevocable, implying indissolubility. Mutual self-giving is not confined to procreation; 'giving and receiving one another mutually' does not mention 'rights over the body for acts suitable for procreation', although such would be included in what is a much richer, personalistic and more complete presentation.

Love is directly treated for the first time by the Magisterium (n. 49). It is distinguished from selfishness, mere eroticism, mere emotion, casual, conditional relationships and appears as mutually affective, generous, committed (in that it is rooted in the will), mutually self-giving, expressed physically in 'acts proper to marriage' (n. 49) and as open to procreation (n. 50). This 'love' retains the depth of New Testament 'agape', but has an implicit orientation to procreation. Children are not an afterthought, but the 'crowning glory' and 'supreme gift of marriage', which is 'ordered' to children 'by its very nature' (n. 50).

Reflected in the texts of the Council's *Gaudium et spes* are Augustine's goods and two of Thomas's ends: God as the author of marriage has endowed it with various 'goods' and 'ends' (n. 48). Thus, marital love implies 'mutual fidelity' (n. 49), especially when strengthened

---

[26.] Second Vatican Council, Pastoral Constitution on the Church in the Modern World, *Gaudium et spes*.

by Christ as a sacrament between the baptized; this love remains faithful, enduring, in good times as well as difficult times (the good of the sacrament, n. 49). The 'unity', which is a property of marriage, 'distinctly recognized by Our Lord' (n. 49) refers to the bond of marriage between the two specific spouses. The next section opens by saying that 'marriage and marital love are by nature (*'indole sua naturali'*) ordered to the procreation and education of children' (n. 50). There is an allusion to all three goods: the intimate union of marriage and the 'good of the children' calling for 'fidelity' and an 'unbreakable bond' (*'sacramentum'*) between them (n. 48). As for Thomistic ends, God had 'various goods and ends in view' (n. 48). There is no treatment of the *'remedium concupiscentiae'*, but there is an allusion to the *'mutuum adiutorium'*, as the married couple, being a couple, 'help and serve each other by their marriage partnership' (*'mutuum sibi adiutorium et servitium'*, n. 48). The consideration of love (n. 49) and the treatment of procreation (nn. 50-52) shows the close connection between them in the Council's teaching.

The Council was not to pre-empt the decision of Pope Paul VI on responsible parenthood, a matter he had reserved to himself as Pope (n. 50). The Council says: 'While not making the other ends of marriage of lesser account', marriage and family life are 'structured to cooperating valiantly with God to give new life' (n. 50), alluding to the end of procreation. The Council did not reassert the primacy of procreation or the hierarchy of ends, since *Gaudium et spes* was a pastoral document and was to avoid much technical language, but it did not intend to deny earlier teaching on the primary end.[27] Building upon *Casti connubii*'s positive spirituality of marriage, the Council made major progress too in identifying the marriage between two baptized Christians not only as sacramental, but as a vocation (n. 48).[28] Beyond the three goods of Augustine, it spoke of the 'good of the spouses themselves', not called a fourth good explicitly as such, but there nonetheless (n. 48).

[27.] M. Zalba, 'Num concilium Vaticanum II hierarchiam finium matrimonii ignoravit, immo et transmutaverit', *Periodica de re morali, canonica, liturgica*, 68 (1979), 613–35 at 629–31.

[28.] Second Vatican Council Dogmatic Constitution on the Church, *Lumen gentium*, nn. 11, 35.

b. The Magisterium of Paul VI and of John Paul II

Paul VI's encyclical, *Humanae vitae,* builds upon *Gaudium et spes* in these doctrines. He summarized the characteristics of marital love as human (both of the sense and spiritual), total, faithful, exclusive and fecund or fruitful and specified criteria of responsible parenthood (nn. 9–10, 14, 16).[29] There is a development of doctrine in the encyclical with the statement of two essential meanings of the conjugal act and, by implication, of marriage itself, as unitive and procreative (nn. 8, 12); it tends of itself, essentially, to unite the spouses together not just physically or sexually, but equally its procreative meaning is also part of the essential ordering of the conjugal act and of marriage itself. The Pope states that these two essential meanings of the conjugal act may never be deliberately separated from one another by the couple (n. 12).[30] This doctrine was reiterated by John Paul II, who represented it in terms of the inter-personal giving of the spouses in and through the language of the body.[31]

Paul VI's teaching regarding this principle of inseparability,[32] fundamental for questions of responsible parenthood and of assisted procreation, is relevant to the developing perspective of what marriage itself is and involves. Not only the conjugal act, but marriage, involves both unitive and procreative meanings, which is not to say that there is always an actual procreative effect (there can be sterile couples, not every conjugal act can or will result in a conception) nor that couples automatically grow in union with one another, but that marriage is essentially about both uniting of the couple to one another throughout their lives and their being open to children, at least in not deliberately seeking to exclude them.[33]

These rich approaches to the theology of marriage in the Catholic tradition across the centuries are reflected in the canons on marriage in the Code of 1983.

---

[29] Paul VI, Encyclical letter, *Humanaae vitae,* 25 July 1968, nn. 9–10, 12.

[30] G. J. Woodall, *Humanae vitae forty years on: A new Commentary,* Family Publications, Oxford, Maryvale, Birmingham, 2008, 47–67, 83–9, 202–4.

[31] John Paul II, Apostolic exhortation, *Familiaris consortio,* 22 November 1981, n. 32.

[32] G. J. Woodall, *The Principle of the Indissoluble Link between the Dimensions of Unity and Fruitfulness in Conjugal Love: A Hermeneutical Investigation of its Theological Basis and of its Normative Significance* excerpt, P.U.G., Rome, 1996, 67–71.

[33] Scicluna, *The Essential Definition,* 180–1; Ghirlanda, *Il diritto nella Chiesa,* 360–1, n. 395–6.

4. Biblical Indications and the Canonical Doctrine of Marriage

The canon law of marriage reflects not only these approaches which have emerged in the course of history, but more fundamentally their biblical and especially New Testament roots. Therefore, a brief and highly selective review will be given here.

a. The Old Testament

The priestly tradition in the Pentateuch presents the creation of the world by God in seven days, its climax on the sixth day being the creation of man, 'male and female' in his 'image and likeness', with the vocation to 'multiply and subdue the face of the earth' (Gen. 1: 26–8). The sexual differentiaton and complementarity indicated here are fundamental to society as a whole and to marriage in particular. Marriage, as a special relationship between a man and a woman, open to children and the foundation of society can be rooted in this text. The Yahwishtic tradition focuses on the creation of Adam who, despite being responsible for sub-human creation and despite having a relationship with God, experiences a solitude in which he is 'incomplete' and 'dissatisfied'. This points to a vocation of love and in the creation of Eve from his side, showing in a different way from the priestly authors the essential sexual differentiation and complementarity, he finds a 'helpmate', a source of fulfilment at the human level, 'bone of my bone and flesh of my flesh' with the vocation that the two 'become one flesh' (Gen. 2:23–5). Beyond the generic need of human beings to support one another and the social dimension of our humanity, this text reflects also the unique, intimate communion of the married couple as such and marriage being a mutual help. Procreation occurs just after (Gen. 4:1).

Exodus (Ex. 20:14, 17) and Deuteronomy (Dt. 5:18, 21) provide the context of God's liberation of his Chosen People from slavery and the gift of the Covenant, within which the precepts of the Decalogue, which forbid both adultery, which is so destructive of marriage, and the lustful or covetous desire which threatens to undermine it. Deuteronomy notes the reality of divorce (Dt. 24:1–4), a 'permission' only for a man to 'send away' his wife.

Hosea and Isaiah focus on God's dealings with his people in terms of the marital relationship (Hos. 2:20–3: 1; Is. 62:2–5), as does Tobit (Tob. 9:1–10:13). This background symbolism to the Christian sacramental understanding of marriage brings out the dignity of marriage, since the husband-wife relationship is judged suitable for comparison with that of God with Israel. The Song of Songs indicates, but modifies the erotic aspect of marital love; the love of bride and groom is not to be a matter of lust. This same appears in Tobit (Tob. 8:7), speaking of the life-long union of husband and wife at their betrothal (Tob. 7: 9–15; 8:5–10).

Adultery and polygamy were common in the Old Testament, at least before the Exile, which is one reason why the prophets attack such infidelity to Yahweh as strongly as they do. Yet, even in earlier times, one wife was the norm, even if concubines were tolerated, and, where there was polygamy, the first wife was normally predominant.[34] Fidelity and exclusivity were not always practised, but they were normative.

b. The New Testament

Marriage as Permanent or Indissoluble: (Mt. 19:1–10; 5:32; Mk.10; Lk. 16)

This teaching on marriage and divorce is one of the most important moral teachings of the New Testament, considered to go back to Jesus himself. In the context of an academic Rabbinical debate as to whether the permission of Moses applies only in the case of adultery (Shammai school) or, more broadly, after any offence caused by the woman (Hillel school),[35] Jesus relativizes Moses's teaching as a concession to the fact that people were 'so unteachable', so that this concession is not the pristine moral truth on the issue. The authentic will of God, revealed 'in the beginning', is found in a conflation of the two traditions of Genesis in a synthesis radically new in Jesus:[36] the priestly tradition that 'in the beginning God made them male and female' and the Yahwistic tradition that 'this is why a man leaves his father and mother and clings to his wife and the two become one flesh'. Not only is this stated as God's will, but it is God who joins the bride and groom together in marriage, which means that 'What God has joined

---

[34.] E. Schillebeeckx, *Marriage: Human Reality and Saving Mystery*, revised edn, Sheed and Ward, London, 1976, 89–91.

[35.] W. Schrage, *The Ethics of the New Testament*, T. & T. Clark, Edinburgh, 1988, 94–5: original German, *Ethik des neuen Testaments*, Vandenhoeck & Ruprecht, Göttingen, 1982; T. Mackin, *Marriage in the Catholic Church*, III, *The Marital Sacrament*, Paulist, New York, Mahwah, 1989, 62.

[36.] I. Fuček, *La sessualità al servizio dell'amore: Antropologia e criteri teologici*, Dehoniane, Rome, 1993, 48–9.

together man must not put asunder' (Mt. 19:6; Mk. 10:9).[37] The force of this teaching is brought out by the fact that a Mosaic 'divorce' does not permit a man to marry another woman, especially by characterizing such a 'remarriage' as adultery, a major sin (cf. 1 Cor. 6:9; Jn. 8:1–11). It is in fact a logical consequence of indissolubility that such a 'remarriage' is adulterous.[38] This teaching is applied to both men and women equally in the Marcan redaction, in stark contrast to the Mosaic law; nor may a woman divorce her husband or, if she does and she then 'marries' another, she commits adultery. The shock among Jesus's disciples is not about celibacy, but about his teaching on the indissolubility of marriage: 'If that is so, it is better for a man not to marry' (Mt. 19:10). It underlines the novelty and reality of his teaching on the permanence or indissolubility of marriage, which is not a relationship established merely by two human beings who may then put an end to it, but it is a divine institution and its bond between the spouses is an indissoluble one.[39] This is true not just in general, but applies to every true marriage, such that it is beyond the competence of husband and wife to end it.[40]

The Matthean 'exceptive clauses' (Mt. 5:31; 19:9 – 'except in the case of adultery – πορνεια/porneia)' need to be interpreted consistently with Jesus's teaching. The Greek Orthodox and Protestant view that they constitute a true exception does not make sense, since Jesus would simply have been agreeing with the Shammai school in the Rabbinical debate and his position would not have been as controversial as it was.[41] The idea that Matthew introduced the clauses to soften Jesus's teaching is hardly likely, since he would hardly have deliberately distorted the Lord's teaching. Thirdly, Jerome's solution is that this is not a true exception, but refers to 'incomplete divorce' or to mere separation, but the text does not indicate this at all. The most likely solution is that Jesus was indicating that he was talking about those cases which were not even marriages according to Jewish law, but cases of concubinage due to violating laws on consanguinity; there would be no 'second marriage', since the one at issue was null. This interpretation, usually favoured by Catholics, leaves Jesus's teaching intact and is compatible with the reaction of the disciples.[42]

[37.] Mackin, *Marriage in the Catholic Church*, I, 53.

[38.] P. Adnès, *Le mariage*, 2nd edn, Desclée and Co., Tournai, 1963, 22.

[39.] Ibid., 21.

[40.] Mackin, *Marriage in the Catholic Church*, I, 53.

[41.] However, this is the interpretation of Mackin, *Marriage in the Catholic Church*, III, *The Marital Sacrament*, 62–4.

[42.] Adnès, *Le mariage*, 24–7.

Marriage as Permanent and Indissoluble: the Pauline Corpus

Paul presents Jesus's teaching on divorce and remarriage as 'from the Lord, not from me' (1 Cor. 7:10–11); an example of moral teaching in the Tradition, reflected in Scripture in an exercise of moral Magisterium in the New Testament itself. Paul teaches that a man must not divorce his wife, that, if he does so, he must not marry another woman and that, if he does, he commits adultery with her, that a woman must not divorce her husband, that if she does so, she must not marry another man and, if she does, she commits adultery with him. Marriage is then a life-long, permanent and indissoluble relationship of husband and wife. At least, this is so where the spouses are both baptized.

However, Paul concluded that Jesus's teaching was meant to apply to marriages between Jews and between Christians, but not necessarily to marriages involving pagans, since these had not been envisaged by Jesus in his teaching nor by Moses in his concession. He distinguishes this from the Lord's teaching ('this is from me, not from the Lord'), but this development of doctrine he gives with full apostolic authority and it too is an exercise of moral Magisterium (1 Cor. 7:12–16). Paul is careful to keep as close to Jesus's teaching as he can even in this hermeneutical application. If the pagan is content to live in peace (will allow the newly converted Christian spouse to practise his or her faith), they should not separate. Only where the pagan will not let the Christian live in peace (practise his or her faith) does Paul say that they may separate; he does not say anything about allowing either to marry anyone else.

This teaching is the basis of the canonical Pauline privilege, which would permit marriage here 'in favour of the faith'. It relates also to the distinction between sacramental and non-sacramental marriages.

The Unity, Exclusivity and Fidelity of Marriage

Jesus had condemned remarriage as adultery, a major sin, which is an implicit assertion of the unity of marriage or of its monogamy.[43] This means that marriage is a relationship between two specific persons, one particular man and one particular woman, a relationship as such exclusive to them ('let each man have his own wife and each woman her own husband' – 1 Cor. 7:2), which would apply not only to the marriages of Christians, but to any true marriage.[44] This same truth recurs in Paul's faithful rendition of the Lord's teaching on the unique

---

[43.] Ibid., 29.

[44.] Cf. W. E. May, *Sex, Chastity and Marriage: Reflections of a Catholic Layman, Spouse and Parent*, Franciscan Herald Press, Chicago, 1981, 37.

relationship of husband and wife in marriage, which makes adultery so serious a sin. This position, grounding the '*bonum fidei*', is implied in Paul's teaching on divorce and in his direct condemnation of adultery (1 Cor. 6: 9).

Marriage as a Remedy for Concupiscence

After noting the danger of adultery, prostitution and even incest, Paul recognizes the impact of disordered sexual desire or concupiscence (1 Cor. 7:2, 9). Anxious for people to be ready for the imminent second coming of the Lord, he sees another value of marriage in its directing sexual passion into legitimate channels, as a remedy for concupiscence (Aquinas's secondary end). Even in marriage disordered desire can be problematic; spouses should only abstain from intimate relations by mutual consent and for prayer, lest Satan tempt them (1 Cor. 7:5), and so live their vocation more fully and easily.[45]

Marriage 'in the Lord' and Sacramentality

Indications of the sacramentality of marriage in the New Testament need to be read against the Old Testament comparison between God's relationship with Israel and the husband-wife relationship. Jesus's teaching that what 'God' had joined together man could not put asunder refers to all true marriages, but the fact that God makes marriage also gives a basis for sacramentality. The wedding feast association of marriage with an eschatological sign of the Kingdom in super-abundant wine, (Jn. 2:12ff) recalls the 'wedding feast' of heaven and can be seen too in references to Jesus as 'bridegroom' and the Church as 'bride' (cf., Mk. 2:18–21; Mt. 9:14–17; Lk. 5:33–5; Apoc. 21:2). Paul tells Christians who wish to marry to marry 'in the Lord' (1 Cor. 7:39). In the condemnation of going with prostitutes, the baptized person is reminded of being a 'temple of the Holy Spirit', whose body is 'for the Lord' (1 Cor. 6:12–20), with the implication that the baptized person who marries can sanctify his or her spouse (1 Cor. 7:12–16). This may be a further basis for sacramentality in marriage in Pauline theology.[46]

The letter to the Ephesians (Eph. 5:21–33) uses the imagery of the God-Israel relationship and recasts it in terms of Christ and the Church, the 'great sacrament'.[47] It is clearly a husband and wife who are baptized ('washed with a form of words') who are in mind. The

---

[45] Mackin, *Marriage in the Catholic Church*, I, 57.
[46] Ibid., III, 64–5, 68–9.
[47] Ibid., 69–76.

husband is to love his wife 'as Christ loved the Church and gave himself for her to make her holy', to imitate the self-sacrificing love of Christ on the Cross. This is the very opposite of any domineering treatment of his wife which might be inferred from a superficial reading of this passage. The wife's love for her husband, to 'obey' or 'submit to' her husband is again 'as the Church submits to Christ', not slavishly, but in wholehearted, self-sacrificial love. This mutual self-giving love[48] is to be rooted in Christ's love for the Church and is to bear fruit.

The Church's recognition that Christ instituted the sacrament of matrimony stems in part from such passages. That the love of a Christian husband and wife for one another can reflect Christ's love for the Church and can bear fruit is due to their love being grounded in, and sustained by, his love.[49] This is reflected in other passages from the household codes, which often have a broader perspective, including parental child relationships (cf. Col. 3:18–21; 1 Tim. 2:14–15; Tit. 2:5–6, 1 Pet. 3:1–7).[50] There are aspects of these passages which do not apply literally (as with cultural presuppositions of female inferiority), yet, in many ways, a basic equality emerges from these texts. In their fuller, radical sense they indicate the importance of the Christian faith for marriage, and of the special role the marriage of two Christians has in the Church, which was recognized in time in the specific sacrament of matrimony.

Marriage and Procreation

These passages coincidentally indicate the significance of procreation in marriage in the New Testament (Eph. 5:21–33; Col. 3:18–21; 1 Tim. 2:15; Tit. 2:5). It is not highlighted in the time of Jesus, not least perhaps because of the expectation of an imminent parousia. The fact that marriage is also about being open to children from God was so fundamental that it was taken for granted. It is no accident that pericopes about marriage are followed often by those on children (Mt. 19:1–15; Mk. 10:1–16; Eph. 5:21–6:4; Col. 3:18–21). The *'bonum prolis'* of Augustine and the primary end of Thomas are based also here.

[48.] Cf. *Gaudium et spes*, nn. 48–9.

[49.] W. Kasper, *Theology of Christian Marriage*, Burns and Oates, London, 1980, 28–31: original German, *Zur Theologie der christlichen Ehe*, Matthias Grünewald, Mainz, 1977.

[50.] Schrage, *The Ethics of the New Testament*, 275–6.

Marriage and Life in Heaven

Although the wedding feast was a sign of abundant life with God, marriage was not a reality in heaven itself: 'at the resurrection men and women do not marry'. (Mt. 22:30). Sexuality is a created reality and is not a means of exerting pressure on God.

Some Concluding Remarks

This biblical synthesis shows the unity and indissolubility of marriage, the goods of procreation, fidelity and permanence, the ends of procreation, mutual help and remedy for concupiscence, as well as the importance of the intimate union of the spouses, the bases for marriage as a vocation and, between two baptized persons, as a specific sacrament. Theology and canon law reflect this as they present the vocation of most Christians and people in the world.

5. The Preliminary Canons on Marriage

a. The Need for Pastoral Care for those Marrying and for the Married

The key canons on marriage (cc. 1055, 1057) condense this teaching into a rich synthesis (Table 15). The canon law of marriage can seem complicated, but the situations of those seeking the Church's help over marriage is often complex. Proper pastoral care will always involve some consideration of canonical questions.[51] It is not enough to be kind, welcoming and sympathetic, although these are surely necessary; it is also necessary to be just, as people are entitled to receive proper pastoral care, in preparation for marriage and within marriage. They should not be misled or wrongly directed by priests on something like marriage, which profoundly affects their lives. Inaccurate or wrong advice, even if sincere, is an injustice to those directly concerned and perhaps to others. Canon law is designed to protect the People of God and all with whom it deals from such injustice. Parish priests first of all, but others too, have the duty to prevent such injustice and give people what is their due.

Pastoral responsibility for marriage preparation and care of the married involves taking care to discover the truth of a situation, judging accurately what needs to be done, seeking expert advice

---

[51.] J. MacAreavey, *The Canon Law of Marriage and the Family*, Four Courts Press, Dublin, 1997, 62–4.

where necessary, and requesting relevant dispensations/permissions from the right person in good time (c. 1066). This is in addition to proper instruction, spiritual preparation and preparation of the liturgy (c. 1063). The marriage of two baptized persons to one another, if it is valid, is a sacrament; in a special way it bears the mark of God's gift of faith to the two persons, reborn in Christ, who have not renounced that relationship (c. 1055 § 2).[52] This implies the further responsibility attaching especially to 'sacred ministers' to ensure that the sacraments are celebrated with 'great reverence and due care' (c. 840), that they and others try to arouse and foster faith, especially through the ministry of the word, so closely linked to the sacraments (cc. 835–836). People are to be prepared for the sacraments remotely by preaching and catechesis and more specifically according to norms (cc. 843 § 2, 1063), even with non-sacramental marriages out of respect for the institution of marriage established by God and as a matter of justice to all.

b. The Canonical Nature of Marriage

The 1983 Code retains the perspective of the Second Vatican Council; the key canon, c. 1055 § 1, states that: 'The marriage covenant ... is of its nature ordered to the good of the spouses and to the procreation and education of children'. Clearly, procreation and education (or upbringing/rearing) of children remain as an essential aspect, dimension or meaning of what marriage is, rooted in natural law or in the 'natural character of marriage itself' ('indole sua naturali'), reflecting the good, end and meaning seen above. The 'good of the spouses' ('bonum coniugum') is much broader than 'mutual help' ('mutuum adiutorium'), as the secondary end expressed it, including and presupposing a readiness to help one another in all spheres of their marital life.[53] The 'remedium concupiscentiae' does not appear in this Code. The term 'covenant' ('foedus'), rather than 'contract' ('contractus'), in Vatican II was deliberately personalistic and elicited echoes of the biblical covenant especially in Christ.[54] Its use in the Code (c. 1055 § 1) incorporates this rich symbolism. Yet, the Code also uses 'contract' as a verb (cc. 1058, 1073, 1085 § 2, 1086 § 3, 1089, 1095, 1096, 1098, 1101 § 2,

---

[52.] J. M. Serrano Ruiz, 'Fede e sacramento' in AA.VV., Matrimonio e fede, Libreria editrice Vaticana, 2004, 19–30 at 26–30.

[53.] Woodall, Humanae vitae, 55–61.

[54.] Gaudium et spes, n. 48.

Table 15

The Canon Law of Marriage

Canon 1055 § 1 (*'matrimonium in facto esse'* - 'marriage as it exists in fact')

'The marriage *covenant*
     by which a *man* and a *woman*
         establish between themselves a *partnership* of their *whole life*

            which *of its very own nature* is *ordered* to
                 – the *well-being* (*good*) of the *spouses* and to
                 – the *procreation* and *education* of children

            between the *baptized* has been raised by *Christ the Lord*
            to the dignity of a *sacrament*.'

Canon 1055 § 2

'*Consequently*, a <u>*valid*</u> marriage *contract*
     cannnot exist
         <u>*between baptized*</u> persons
            without its being, *by that very fact* a *sacrament*.'

Canon 1056

'The *essential properties* of marriage are
     unity and
     indissolubility.'
         strengthened in Christian marriage by the *sacrament*.

Canon 1057 § 1 (*'matrimonium in fieri'* - 'marriage as it comes into being')

'A marriage is *brought into being* by the
     lawfully manifested consent of
         persons who are *legally capable*.
            a consent which cannot be supplied by any human power.'

Canon 1057 § 2

'Matrimonial *consent* is an *act of the will*
     by which a *man* and a *woman*
         by an *irrevocable covenant*
            mutually give and receive *each other*
                for the *purpose* of establishing a *marriage*.'

Canon 1058

'All can contract marriage who are not prohibited by law.'

Canon 1061 § 1

'A *valid* marriage between *baptized* persons is said to be
    – merely *ratified,* if it is not consummated;
    – *ratified and consummated,*
        if the spouses have in a human manner, engaged *together*
        in a *conjugal act in itself apt* for the generation of offspring

To this act marriage is *by its nature ordered* and
by it the spouses *become one flesh.'*

Canon 1108 § 1

'*Only* those marriages are *valid*
    which are *contracted in the presence of*
        – the Local *Ordinary*
        – or *parish priest*
        – or *priest* or *deacon*
            <u>*delegated*</u> by either of them,

who
        in the *presence* of *two witnesses*
           assists' (at the wedding)
               'according to ... the following canons'.

Canon 1108 § 2

'*Only* that *person* who,
    being present,
        asks
            the *contracting parties*
                to *manifest* their *consent*
    and,
        in the *name* of the *Church,*
            receives it
                is understood to *assist at a marriage'*.

1102 § 1, 1104 § 1, 1106) and as a noun (cc. 1055 § 2, 1097 § 2).[55] Without denying the legal value of the term 'contract', the use of 'covenant' in both key canons (cc. 1055 § 1, 1057 § 2) evokes the divine institution of marriage, marriage as an image of God's dealings with his People, and the allusion to the sacramentality of the marriage of two baptized Christians.

Marriage is the 'covenant by which a man and a woman establish between themselves a partnership of their whole life' (c. 1055 § 1). It cannot be established other than by a man and a woman. This aspect of the canon refers both to creating a marriage and to the fact that marriage is a state which of its very nature is, and can only be, a heterosexual union. The term 'of its very nature' relates not just to procreation and education, but to the good of the spouses. The 'partnership' ('*consortium*') means that the heterosexual nature of marriage refers not just in the capacity to consummate a marriage and to be open to children, but in the very heterosexual relationship itself more broadly, to a sharing of the 'whole of their life'. Thus, '*consortium*' ('partnership' or 'sharing') was seen as equivalent to '*communio*' ('communion') and to '*coniunctio*' ('joining' – of the couple to one another).[56] It might also evoke the principle of inseparability of the unitive and procreative dimensions of marriage, both entailed in the very nature of marriage. The partnership of marriage (c. 1055 § 1) can be interpreted to imply a sharing of every aspect of their lives with one another as a couple, reflecting their mutual giving (c. 1057 § 2) in both unitive and procreative dimensions, and also a partnership or communion for the whole of their lives in the life-long bond, '*vinculum*' or '*sacramentum*'. This is what distinguishes marriage from any other human relationship. This unique and indissoluble union between a specific man and a specific woman as marriage partners is reinforced by the essential properties of marriage (c. 1056), excluding polygamy and polyandry in a relationship which cannot be ended by the parties themselves. These properties apply to any true or valid marriage.

[55.] In the case of c. 1086 § 3 '*contracti*' could be taken to be either a verb or a noun, but the official English translation of Collins is probably right to take it as a verb (Canon Law Society of Great Britain and Ireland, *The Code of Canon Law: An English Translation*, Collins, London, 1983): 'Si pars tempore *contracti* matrimonii tamquam baptizata ...' This could be translated as 'If, at the time of the *contract* of matrimony, the baptized party ...' or 'If, at the time of contracting matrimony, the baptized party ...' (in the latter case, literally , 'If at the time of the marriage *having been contracted*, the baptized party ...').

[56.] Scicluna, *The Essential Definition of Marriage*, 297.

The specific sacramentality of marriage is also indicated in c. 1055, where the marriage of two baptized persons is said to have been raised by Christ our Lord to the dignity of a sacrament (cc. 1055 § 1–2; 1056). This emphasizes the divine institution of the sacrament of marriage. Here we see the distinction between a sacramental marriage, between 'two baptized persons' (c. 1055 § 1–2) and a non-sacramental marriage, which is one between two non-baptized persons or one between a baptized person and a non-baptized person. That 'a valid marriage contract cannot exist between baptized persons without its being by that very fact ('eo ipso') a sacrament' (c. 1055 § 2) might not be obvious. The (indirect) institution by Christ of this sacrament (c.1055 § 1), implies a divine gift. He transforms the natural reality of marriage, the exchange of consent between the partners being the sign which produces the enduring bond between them, a reality subsumed and penetrated by the specific sacramental grace of matrimony, through which Christ is at the heart of the marriage to strengthen and sustain the couple, enabling them at the same time to reflect and embody his abiding union with the Church.[57] The reality of the two being baptized and where the baptismal relationship has not explicitly been rejected are a sufficient basis for this doctrine.

Thus, the valid marriage between two Catholics (of whatever rite), between two Orthodox, between a Catholic and a baptized non-Catholic Christian (Orthodox or otherwise), between two baptized non-Catholics with one another, whether the latter is celebrated in a non-Catholic church or chapel or in a register office before officials of the state, is a sacrament. Even if the non-Catholic ecclesial community denies the sacramentality of marriage, the Catholic Church recognizes such a marriage as sacramental. The valid marriage of a Catholic with a non-baptized person is not a sacrament, even though it will have been celebrated in a Catholic church before a Catholic bishop, priest or deacon. Since any valid marriage implies unity and indissolubility, even though the Catholic Church recognizes the validity of a marriage between two non-Catholics in a register or state office, we do not recognize their divorce; the State can never end a marriage. A valid marriage, then, is intrinsically indissoluble (it cannot be ended by the parties – from within the marriage); a marriage which is valid, sacramental and consummated is also extrinsically indissoluble (it cannot be ended by anyone external to it, but only by the death of one of the parties – c. 1141).

---

57. Cf. J-P. Schouppe, *Le droit canonique: introduction générale et droit matrimonial*, Story Scientia, Bruxelles, 1991, 137–8.

c. Matrimonial Consent

The saying 'Consent makes the marriage' expressed a key truth about bringing marriage into existence ('*matrimonium in fieri*'). It emphasizes that the persons marrying one another themselves cannot be ignored, taken for granted or overridden when it comes to their marriage, since without their personal consent no marriage can be established between them. That consent has to be '*de praesenti*' or a consent to marry one another here and now, not just an agreement or consent '*de futuro*', betrothal or engagement, to marry one another later.

Consent in the 1983 Code is not specified narrowly in relation to 'an exchange of the right over the body for acts *per se* suitable for the generation of children', as in 1917, but bears upon marriage as a whole.[58] The first paragraph of the key canon on consent in the 1983 Code (c. 1057) is identical to its equivalent in 1917: 'A marriage is brought into being by the lawfully manifested consent of persons who are legally capable. This consent cannot be supplied by any human power' (c. 1057 § 1). The second paragraph refers to its object: 'Matrimonial consent is an act of the will by which a man and a woman, by an irrevocable covenant, mutually give and receive one another for the purpose of establishing a marriage' (c. 1057 § 2).

The need for consent to be an 'act of the will' of the parties means that it has to be a human act in the sense of a deliberate and intentional act, knowingly and freely undertaken.[59] The object of consent is not only acts suitable for procreation; the couple 'mutually give and receive one another', recalling the mutual self-giving of the Council, 'to establish a marriage' (c. 1057 § 2); there is no use of the technical term '*finis*' to justify translating this as 'for the purpose of'; establishing a marriage includes openness to procreation, but is not limited to it. To say that the object of matrimonial consent is 'marriage' is a tautology, but the Code speaks here of the couple's consent to mutual self-giving, the 'rights and duties' which are treated later (c. 1095 § 2–3).[60] The term 'covenant' is used here, but it is said to be 'irrevocable' (c. 1057 § 2).[61] It concerns all true marital consent, not only that between two baptized persons. The irrevocability underlines the life-long nature of marriage.

[58.] *Codex iuris canonici* (1917), c. 1081 § 2.
[59.] Cf. John Paul II, Encyclical lettter, *Veritatis splendor*, 6 August 1993, n. 78, which speaks of the moral object of the human act as 'rationally chosen by the deliberate will'.
[60.] Scicluna, *The Essential Definition of Marriage*, 293.
[61.] Cf. *Gaudium et spes*, n. 48.

The 'marital act' or 'conjugal act' or act of sexual intercourse between the spouses is not treated under consent, but in relation to consummation, which occurs when the spouses have married and then engage together 'in a human manner in a conjugal act in itself apt for the generation of offspring' (c. 1061 § 1). In other words, it is an act between the spouses themselves ('with one another') as 'spouses' (after marriage to one another), 'in a human manner' (not through violent imposition), of itself 'apt' or 'suitable for procreation' (it must be the conjugal act itself and not a perversion of it).[62] The 'ius in corpus' (right over the body) of the 1917 Code had been criticized as restrictive, although it originated in St Paul (1 Cor. 7:2–5), but it does reflect a key aspect of what marriage is about, the sexual union of the couple as 'two in one flesh'. This aspect of what marriage is, reflecting a unitary anthropology, is rightly presented in the 1983 Code in more personalistic terms.[63]

Consent has to be between persons (canonically) 'legally capable' of marriage, which means in terms of factors such as age, baptismal status, degrees of relationship. These will be examined in dealing with impediments to marriage. It should be recalled that 'only the supreme authority of the Church' (the Pope or the College of Bishops) can establish 'incapacitating laws' (c. 10), laws which specify that certain persons are legally incapable of particular acts (here that of consent to marriage). Were such persons to go through the wedding rite and 'exchange consent' as far as those present were concerned, the marriage would be invalid because they would not be capable of marrying.

Even where the persons concerned are both legally capable of giving consent, they still need to do so in a way which is valid. Consent needs to be both true consent and lawfully manifested (the form of marriage or where, how and before whom it occurs). True consent involves each spouse actually intending what they say; their internal consent to marriage is essential and 'cannot be supplied by any human power' (c. 1057 § 1). The presumption is that what they say externally does express their true internal consent (c. 1101 § 1), but, if someone deliberately states that they consent to marriage, but in reality deny their internal consent to marriage as such or to some essential part of it,

---

[62.] Cf. L. Örsy, *Marriage in Canon Law: Texts and Comments; Reflections and Questions*, Dominican Publications, Dublin; Fowler Wright, Leominster, 1986, 68.

[63.] Cf. J. Vernay, 'Le droit canonique du mariage' in P. Valdrini *et al.* (eds), *Droit canonique*, 2nd edn, Dalloz, Paris, 1999, 307–62 at 316–17; cf. *Gaudium et spes*, n. 14; John Paul II, *Veritatis splendor*, n. 50.

that consent is said to be simulated or a pretence and the marriage is invalid because of this grave defect of consent (cc. 1101–1103). Consent must also be to what marriage is in its essentials, not just to whatever pleases the couple, 'for the purpose of establishing marriage' (c. 1057 § 2). If it is not, true marital consent is not exchanged (cc. 1095, 1098–1099).

The consent which makes a marriage is crucially important for the bringing into being of a marriage ('*matrimonium in fieri*'). Not only is the supreme authority of the Church (Pope or College of Bishops) alone able to establish incapacitating laws, but the same supreme authority alone is able to establish invalidating laws (cc. 10, 1075). These are the laws which establish the minimal conditions necessary for the act of consent to be a true act of consent, to be valid consent. If the consent is not valid, no marriage is created, the consent is null and void. The exchange of consent is a juridical act, an act with juridical effects; it has to be undertaken by persons capable of such an act and the act must be valid or nothing is brought about (c. 124).

d. Further Comments on the Preliminary Canons

Consummation

Properly exchanged consent of the parties to marriage establishes a true or valid marriage, even between two non-baptized persons and, if it is between two baptized persons, it is a valid and sacramental marriage (c. 1055 § 2); this marriage would be called a '*matrimonium ratum*' or a merely 'ratified marriage' (c. 1061 § 1). If a valid marriage between two baptized persons, a ratified marriage, were consummated, it would then become a '*matrimonium ratum et consummatum*' or a 'ratified and consummated marriage' (c. 1061 § 1). Such a marriage, ratified and consummated, could never be dissolved; even the Pope would not and, according to most canonists, could not dissolve such a marriage.

Looking at Jesus's teaching on divorce, in the way the Catholic Church rightly has taken it, to be a true and exceptionless prohibition of divorce, the question remains as to which marriage that teaching applies. St Paul's teaching and practice took it not to apply to the marriages of one baptized person with a non-baptized person, where the baptized person was prevented from practising their faith, giving rise later to the so-called 'Pauline privilege'. Other situations arose in history where there was the exercise of a Petrine privilege (the Pope acting as Supreme Pastor of the Church) to dissolve non-sacramental marriages in some instances. The Petrine privilege was used to dissolve some non-consummated marriages; although valid and, if between two baptized persons, also sacramental, these had not been 'perfected' by being expressed in the unique conjugal act of the two spouses becoming 'two in one flesh'.

Consummation is the act by which, after their wedding, husband and wife give themselves to one another through the intimate act of sexual intercourse. It involves at least three elements (erection of the husband's penis, penetration of the wife's vagina and ejaculation of seminal fluid into her vagina); since this is to be done 'in a human manner', it cannot be the result of violence.[64] Consummation is presumed to have taken place once the couple have lived together after marriage (c. 1061 § 2). Thus, strictly speaking, the marriage which can never be dissolved by anyone is one which is 'valid, sacramental and consummated' ('ratum et consummatum').

The Extent of the Binding Power of Ecclesiastical Law

In 1917 ecclesiastical law applied to all, Catholic and non-Catholic Christians alike; the 1983 Code is clear that it applies only to Catholics (c. 11). This is the general norm. In other cases, ecclesiastical law applies also to those non-Catholics who marry Catholics or who wish to marry Catholics (c. 1059). Ecclesiastical laws, of course, are those canon laws which are established by being properly promulgated by a legitimate superior for his proper subjects (c. 7). Such laws are merely human laws and are contrasted with natural laws, which are divine laws. Natural law, part of divine law, is also part of canon law; strictly speaking, the Church's lawgivers declare what natural laws are rather than make them, whereas they make or create ecclesiastical laws. Those laws which are of natural law cannot be dispensed precisely because they are divine and not human laws. Ecclesiastical laws can be dispensed by the competent authority on certain conditions (cc. 85, 90 § 1).

The Role of Civil Law

Although the state has no right to prevent the Church from regulating marriage, the Church recognizes that there are important consequences for people as to whether or not they are married, also in the eyes of the state. For example, they may have different rights over taxation, travel and passport rights, working and residence rights,

---

[64.] G. Sheehy *et al.* (eds), Canon Law Society of Great Britain and Ireland, *The Canon Law: Letter and Spirit: A Practical Guide to the Code of Canon Law*, Chapman, London, 1995, 577, n. 2073.

and so on. Such civil effects of marriage (c. 1059) are important for people and are a matter of justice to them. Hence, there is a responsibility to ensure that people are married validly not only in the eyes of the Church, but also in the eyes of the state.

In some cases, the state simply recognizes the validity for the state of marriage in the Catholic Church (for instance, in the Irish Republic). In other instances, there are conditions: obtaining a certificate or licence from the register or state office, stating that the couple may marry one another in a specific church within a particular time (twelve months in England and Wales) of the issue of the certificate and requiring the presence of a registrar or authorized person and full civil registration of any wedding. In some countries, the state does not recognize the validity of any (France) or of some (Italy) marriages in church and insists by civil law, in such cases, on state weddings for civil validity. In France, in view of the practical impossibility of doing otherwise, since a church wedding as normal would be a crime under state law, the Church has arranged an indult, an indulgent act of mercy, relaxing the Church's ecclesiastical law to the extent of allowing the couple to go through the state procedures (so-called 'civil wedding'), although without recognizing it as valid, and then allowing them to marry, perhaps the next day, in the church. In all countries the Church requires that what is necessary for couples to enjoy the proper recognition of civil law, to enjoy the civil effects of marriage, is to be observed.

The Status of an Invalid Marriage

An invalid marriage needs to be investigated and declared by the Church's Tribunals to be invalid. Marriage is not a private reality, but is of its nature a public and very significant public reality. Where there are good reasons to think that a marriage may be invalid, there is a right to have that marriage investigated for nullity by the Church's tribunals. Where a marriage is thought to be valid in good faith by at least one of the parties, but is in fact invalid and may be known to the other party to be so, the marriage is said to be a putative marriage, is 'thought to be a marriage' (c. 1061 § 3)

The Question of a Promise of Marriage

Consent has to be about the present, not just for the future as in an engagement, or marriage is not brought into being. In some societies even now, a promise to marry is very serious and cannot always be swept aside easily. The Code recognizes that there can be some responsibilities of justice deriving from such promises, relating to land, money or gifts of value which have been exchanged and there might be a duty of restitution. However, no such agreement can ever create a true right to marry (c. 1062 § 2).

6. Conclusion

From this analysis of the key canons on marriage (cc. 1055, 1057), much is already known about the canon law of marriage. There are three main aspects of canon law to be considered in what follows: the implications of what marriage is and so the obstacles or impediments to marriage, the consent needed to bring marriage into being and defects of consent rendering marital consent null and void, and the form of marriage (where and how it is to be conducted). We shall now proceed to treat these three areas in turn.

Chapter 13

The Sanctifying Function of the Church

(Book IV of the Code)

Part I: The Sacraments

VI: The Canon Law of Marriage (Impediments to Marriage and Matrimonial Consent)

1. Introduction

In this chapter we shall examine some implications of the nature of marriage, namely what is incompatible with true marriage or what prevents or impedes it from being established. We shall also consider the implications of the need for true internal consent to marriage. We turn first to impediments.

2. Impediments to Marriage in General

a. The Meaning of a (Diriment) Impediment

An 'impediment' is a 'hindrance' or an 'obstacle', which 'prevents' something from being done. The Code of 1917 distinguished between merely 'impedient impediments' (obstacles or impediments rendering an act merely illicit or unlawful, but not invalid) and 'diriment impediments' (obstacles or impediments rendering an act not merely illicit or unlawful, but also invalid).[1] The words '*dirimere*' (to 'divide' or 'separate') and '*irritum*' or '*inritum*' ('not right', 'incorrectly done', 'not truly done') express the fact that a diriment impediment keeps the couple divided, stops a marriage being created. In the 1983 Code there are no 'impedient impediments'. The impedient impediment under the 1917 Code of mixed religion no longer exists as such; the Code

---

[1.] Benedict XV, *Codex iuris canonici* (1917), c. 1036.

now states simply that there must be a 'permission' for the marriage to take place and specifies the conditions necessary for this (c. 1125). Although this is similar to an impedient impediment, no dispensation is needed because there is no impediment from which to dispense. Permission is needed for liceity.

All matrimonial impediments in the 1983 Code are diriment impediments. A diriment impediment 'renders a person incapable of validly contracting marriage' (c. 1073). The Church is not interfering here, but merely specifying what is a true marriage and what is not. Given the basic right to choose a state of life, including marriage (c. 1058), 'an impediment has its source in a fact or in a defect which, affecting the person of the future (potential spouses), renders them juridically incapable of contracting a valid marriage'.[2]

b. The Declaration and the Establishment of Impediments

Only the supreme authority of the Church can create or state what is a diriment or invalidating impediment (cc. 1075, 1077 § 2); only laws stated to be invalidating or incapacitating laws are such (c. 10). Thus, no individual bishop nor other ordinary is capable of establishing or declaring diriment impediments to marriage (cc. 1073, 1075 § 1–2, 1077 § 2). Only the supreme authority can establish other impediments for the baptized (c. 1075 § 2), as distinct from the declaration of impediments, also reserved to the supreme authority (c. 1075 § 1). Canon law consists of divine law, revealed or natural, and merely ecclesiastical law. Since the Church is bound by divine law, it claims only to declare what that is, whereas ecclesiastical laws are human laws established by their promulgation by the legitimate authority for its proper subjects (c. 7). Normally, merely ecclesiastical laws bind only Catholics (c. 11) and in the 1983 Code Catholics of the Latin rite (c. 1). The diriment impediments to marriage in general distinguish impediments declared by the supreme authority (divine laws) from those established by the supreme authority (of ecclesiastical law).

Since the Church recognizes that non-Christians can marry validly and even have a right to marry (all can marry who are not prohibited by law from marrying – c. 1058) and since it recognizes that marriage is of divine institution even at creation, such marriages are governed

---

[2] J. Vernay, 'Le droit canonique du mariage' in P. Valdrini *et al.*, *Droit canonique*, 2nd edn, Dalloz, Paris, 1999, 307–62 at 327, n. 500: 'Ainsi, un empêchement a sa source dans un fait ou un défaut qui, affectant la personne des futurs, les rend juridiquement inhabiles à contracter un mariage valide'.

by divine law. Hence, impediments of divine law are declared (c. 1075 § 1). Most of these apply to all marriages; they state what is necessary for a marriage to be valid and for a person to be capable of marriage, irrespective of whether or not that person is Catholic or even baptized, whether the marriage is between two Catholics, two baptized persons, one baptized person and a non-baptized person, or two non-baptized persons. Ecclesiastical laws normally apply only to Catholics and here of the Latin rite (cc. 1, 11). However, the supreme authority alone can establish other impediments (of ecclesiastical law) which apply to all the baptized (c. 1075 § 2), not only those who marry Catholics, but in some respects even the marriages of two baptized non-Catholic Christians with one another, whether conducted in a non-Catholic church or even in a register office. In fact, this will not become a practical issue unless one of these persons wishes to marry a Catholic or unless one or both of them become Catholic.

The local ordinary can prohibit a specific marriage for a limited time for grave reasons and only as long as the reason persists (c. 1077 § 1). This does not allow him to establish an impediment, not even an impedient impediment. Rather, it is a pastoral device allowing him to delay a marriage which seems to be very unwise or which might be invalid, to ensure that matters are clarified, that there is proper preparation. This capacity is limited to his own proper subjects, wherever they are or to those actually present in the territory for which he has proper responsibility.

c. Dispensation from Impediments to Matrimony

A dispensation is a relaxation of a law in a given or particular case (c. 85); in such a case, the person could marry validly. However, not all impediments to marriage can be dispensed. Impediments of divine law, which only the supreme authority can declare (declares them, but does not establish them, since they are established by God), cannot be dispensed even by the supreme authority.[3] Those of ecclesiastical law can be dispensed, but only if certain conditions are met and they can only be dispensed by certain persons.[4] Thus, if the conditions required for dispensing are not met or if someone other than a person capable

---

[3.] G. Ghirlanda. *Il diritto nella Chiesa, mistero di comunione: Compendio di diritto ecclesiale* 4th revised edn, San Paolo, Cinisello, P.U.G., Rome, 2006, 373, n. 413.

[4.] J. A. Coriden, *An Introduction to Canon Law*, revised edn, Paulist, New York, Mahwah, NJ, 2004, 135; cf. Vernay, 'Le droit canonique du mariage', 328, n. 502.

of dispensing attempts to dispense or if the act of dispensation does not follow requirements for validity in other respects, the dispensation itself will be invalid and so the marriage conducted on the basis of it will be invalid (cc. 88–93).

Dispensation from impediments, then, concerns ecclesiastical law. Some impediments can be dispensed only by the Apostolic See (c. 1078 § 1), namely those of sacred orders, a public, perpetual vow of chastity in a religious institute of pontifical right and crime (cc. 1078 § 2, 1090). With these exceptions and noting that dispensations from consanguinity in the direct line and up to the second degree of the collateral line are never given (c. 1078 § 3), the local ordinary is usually the person who grants dispensations, often through a person in the diocese designated by the bishop for that purpose and given the necessary faculties; this could be the chancellor. (This needs to be checked in the diocese where a priest or deacon works or is to conduct a wedding.) The vicar general of the diocese can grant such dispensations, since he exercises ordinary power vicariously or on behalf of the diocesan bishop by virtue of his office throughout the diocese. An episcopal vicar can grant such dispensations within the area of the diocese for which he has been given specific responsibility by the diocesan bishop. The local ordinary only has such power of dispensation within his own diocese or for his own proper subjects (c. 1078 § 1). Any such dispensation must be for the spiritual welfare of the faithful (c. 88) and only for a 'just and reasonable cause' (c. 90 § 1), with 'strict interpretation' as to circumstances, the law in question (cc. 90 § 1, 92) and only as long as the motivating reason persists (c. 93). This affects not only liceity or lawfulness, but validity, when the legislator himself does not grant the dispensation (c. 90 § 1), although in doubt as to the sufficiency of the reason, the act of dispensation is lawful and valid (c. 90 § 2). Thus, dispensation for a Catholic to marry a baptized non-Catholic in a non-Catholic Church ceases immediately if the non-Catholic becomes a Catholic in the meantime, precisely because the condition (non-Catholic) has ceased.

In case of danger of death, the local ordinary (c. 1079 § 1) or even, when he cannot be approached other than by telephone (c. 1079 § 4), a parish priest or a sacred minister already properly delegated for the wedding (cc. 1079 § 2; 89) can dispense from all impediments of ecclesiastical law, except for impediments stemming from sacred orders (c. 1079 § 1-2) and a confessor can dispense from the same impediments in the internal forum, if they are occult – not capable of being known publicly (c. 1079 § 3). The case of danger of death is not restricted to the literal fact of danger of death, but includes serious surgery, air crashes, being in a war zone;[5] the situation of a terrorist outrage might be added.

Similar powers of dispensation, again except from sacred orders and from a perpetual vow of chastity in a religious institute of pontifical right, are possessed by the local ordinary and, when he cannot be approached, by the parish priest and by a properly delegated sacred minister, if an impediment is discovered at the last moment and the wedding cannot be deferred without the likelihood of grave harm (c. 1080 § 1–2). These powers in danger of death or when all is prepared do not extend to a person delegated to assist at a wedding who is not a sacred minister (cc. 1079–1080), since both canons expressly limit the power to dispense even in these extreme cases to sacred ministers. (This is distinct from the Church's official witness to the wedding; remember that in the Latin Church the ministers of matrimony are the bride and groom). Thus, not even a lay person, properly delegated as the Church's official witness in the unusual circumstances of c. 1112, could ever validly dispense from any impediment; only bishops, priests or deacons can ever dispense and then only as specified above, with conditions strictly interpreted. It is further to be noted that powers of dispensation concern a particular wedding (c. 1078 § 1; cf., cc. 88–93).

Where a dispensation from a diriment impediment to marriage is validly given in such a situation of emergency, the local ordinary is to be informed immediately, where it concerns a dispensation in the external forum and the dispensation is to be recorded in the church marriage register (c. 1081). Where the impediment is occult (cannot be established in the external forum) and where the dispensation is granted in the internal non-sacramental forum, it is normally to be recorded in a special book in the secret archives of the diocesan curia (c. 1082), unless the apostolic penitentiary determines otherwise.[6] This is limited to the non-sacramental internal forum, since the sacramental internal forum is the sacrament of reconciliation and any such record would inevitably entail the violation of the seal of the confessional. Since a dispensation can be given even there, in the case of danger of death and then, obviously, precisely by the confessor (c. 1079 § 3), as c. 1082 clearly implies, this is never to be recorded.

---

5. Ghirlanda, *Il diritto nella Chiesa*, 373–4, n. 415.
6. Ibid., 374–5, n. 417.

3. Particular Impediments to Marriage

With these general points in mind, we turn to the specific impediments.

a. Age (c. 1083)

A woman may not marry before her fourteenth birthday and a man may not marry before his sixteenth birthday (c. 1083 § 1); the Code uses 'man' ('*vir*') and woman' ('*mulier*'), not 'boy' and 'girl'. It is precisely the fact that, in earlier times, this was the age at which they would have been regarded as becoming adults, at least in terms of being marriageable, which lies behind this canon and this usage. The reason for this impediment is that it settles a minimum age before which a valid marriage cannot be established. It is based upon the developing physiological and sexual maturity of the young. In some ways, the understanding of marriage and of matrimonial consent in terms of the '*ius in corpus*' lies behind this canon, reflecting the capacity of those at that age to engage in marital intercourse. It also reflects the generally earlier and more rapid development of the female as compared to the male.

Two other factors are to be considered in this connection. First of all, the episcopal conference, but not individual bishops, can establish a higher minimum age for marriage for purposes of lawfulness or liceity, but not for validity (c. 1083 § 2; cf. cc. 1075, 1077 § 2).[7] This may be judged wise in the light of the growing number of difficult marriages and of marriages which break down these days, as well as of the increased pressures upon the young from society, the media and peers in ways which do not reinforce, but rather threaten, marital stability. Early sexual and physiological maturity does not go together necessarily with maturity of life and of responsible decision-making, especially in regard to marriage (cf. c. 1095 § 2).[8]

The other factor is that the civil law of a country may well have a different and higher minimum age for the validity of marriage. In this instance, the Church would not wish to encourage and celebrate marriages which were illegal in civil law, with all directly involved thereby committing a criminal offence; hence the episcopal conference would be wise to set a higher minimum age for the lawful canonical exchange of marital consent. Indeed, the local ordinary must be

---

7. Vernay, 'Le droti canonique du mariage', 330–1, n. 506.
8. McAreavey, *The Canon Law of Marriage*, 81–2, nn. 199–200.

consulted before any marriage is celebrated which would not be recognized by or which could not be celebrated in accordance with civil law (c. 1071 § 1, n. 2). This is one reason why pastors are to dissuade the young from marrying before the age customarily accepted in the region (c. 1072), although the other is that they need in any case to appreciate what they are undertaking in marrying and need to be able to assume the responsibilities involved (c. 1095 § 2–3). In England and Wales the episcopal conference has set the minimum age for marriage, for liceity, at sixteen also for a woman, to correspond to the requirements of civil law.[9]

b. Impotence (c. 1084)

The question of impotence is sometimes presented as a hangover from looking at marriage based on the '*ius in corpus*'. It is a mistake to see it just in that way. However much personalism has rightly influenced our understanding of marriage, it does not remove the reality that part of the purpose and meaning of marriage is the expression by the spouses of their love to one another in a mutually self-giving genital union of the 'two in one flesh'; this is not all that marriage is, but it is part of what marriage is. Thus, if one or other or both parties were to be incapable of this, what would be undertaken would not be marriage. Legitimate expectations of marriage would be severely dashed.

Impotence means the incapacity to perform the conjugal act of genital intercourse. It is not the same thing as infertility or sterility, which has to do with whether or not that act can be fruitful in the sense of generating a new life. Sterility does not render a marriage invalid (c. 1084 § 3), but impotence does so if it is antecedent (present before and at the time of the wedding and not the result of an accident afterwards, which would mean that the marriage was valid) and permanent or perpetual (not temporary, resulting from a lesser accident, an operation, medication, and the like, but which can cease). If impotence is temporary, it does not prevent the couple from

---

[9.] Statement of Bishops of England and Wales: 'In conformity with c. 1083 § 2 for the lawful celebration of marriage in England and Wales, the civil law requirements concerning age are to be observed (age 16).' in E. Caparros, M. Thériault and J. Thorn (eds), *Code of Canon Law Annotated*, Wilson & Lafleur, Limitée, Montréal, 1993, 1337; J. M. Agar and L. Navaaro (eds), *Legislazione delle conferenze episcopali complementare al C.I.C*, 2nd revised edn, Coletti a San Pietro, Rome, 2009 on c. 1083 § 2, 580, based on *Briefing*, 29 June 1986, 16, n. 13, 158–9, following the *recognitio* of 3 May 1986 (note 9 in Agar and Navarre, 580).

being truly married, from becoming 'two in one flesh' through the act of intercourse; it does not prevent them from consummating their marriage. Impotence is considered to be perpetual if it is incurable or curable only by immoral means or by surgical means which are extraordinary.[10] Where there are certain deformities, where functionally one of the essential conditions can never be met, there is impotence.[11]

Permanent, antecedent impotence renders a marriage null or invalid whether it is absolute (this person could not consummate any marriage with anyone) or whether it is relative (these two persons cannot be united in conjugal intercourse with one another). The latter might occur because their genital organs are completely incompatible by reason of physical size (as between a person of restricted growth and a very large person). Impotence, even invalidating (permanent, antecedent) impotence, can arise from psychological factors, where a woman's reaction is always so traumatic that she cannot receive her husband in the conjugal act ('vaginismus')[12] Invalidating male impotence involves one or more of the following being impossible, permanently and antecedently: erection of the penis, ejaculation of sperm and depositing seminal fluid ('true sperm elaborated in the testicles' is not required)[13] in the vagina of his wife; vasectomy does not constitute this impediment if all three remain possible. Female impotence occurs where there is no vagina or not one large enough to receive the husband's penis, or where there is permanent, antecedent vaginismus or dyspareunia.[14]

The impediment of impotence is not to be presumed; the presumption is that persons are potent unless and until the opposite is clear. In a case of doubt, the marriage is not to be prohibited (c. 1084 § 2). In a case of real likelihood of invalidating impotence, it is important to consult the diocesan authorities, especially the vicar judicial, for advice before making a decision.

[10.] L. G. Wrenn, *The Invalid Marriage*, Canon Law Society of America, Washington, DC, 1988, 8–9.

[11.] Ibid., 10–11.

[12.] Ibid.

[13.] Sacred Congregation for the Doctrine of the Faith, Decree, *Circa impotentiam quae matrimonium dirimit*, 13 May 1977, in Congregatio de cultu divino et disciplina sacramentorum, *Collectanea documentorum ad causas pro dispensatione super 'rato et non consummato' et a lege sacri coelibatus obtinenda*, Libreria editrice Vaticana, 2004, 115, n. 44.

[14.] Wrenn, *The Invalid Marriag*, 8–15, especially the decree from the Sacred Congregation for the Doctrine of the Faith of 1977 and the decree of nullity of the Roman Rota of 1986 that this does not constitute impotence where erection, ejaculation and penetration of the vagina are possible.

c. Ligamen - *Bond of a Previous Marriage (c. 1085)*

This impediment arises in connection with the essential properties, unity and indissolubility, of marriage (c. 1056) and that a marriage *'ratum et consummatum'* is dissolved only by the death of one of the parties (c. 1141). If one of the parties is already married to another person and the bond of that union still exists, they cannot validly marry someone else. This is so even if the first marriage was never consummated (c. 1085 § 1). Furthermore, the public reality of marriage and the relevance of marriage for family and for society are such that, even if a marriage is invalid, it must be declared null and void by the Church tribunals before any 'further' marriage is attempted; otherwise the latter is illicit (c. 1085 § 2).

A prior bond of marriage applies to a previous valid or putatively valid (c. 1061 § 3) marriage of two Catholics, a previous valid or putatively valid marriage of a Catholic and a baptized, non-Catholic Christian or a previous valid or putatively valid marriage of two baptized, non-Catholic Christians. In all of these cases the bond involved is a sacramental bond, since the valid marriages of the baptized are of their nature sacramental marriages (c. 1055 § 2). It also applies to a previous valid or putatively valid marriage of a Catholic with a non-baptized person, a previous valid or putatively valid marriage of a non-Catholic Christian with a non-baptized person, whether this took place in a church or in a register office (before the state), a previous valid or putatively valid marriage of two non-baptized persons in a religious ceremony or in a register office (before the state). In these cases the bond is a non-sacramental, natural bond.

Where a marriage is declared by the Church's tribunals to be null and void, this means no marriage ever existed. Where a marriage bond (one which is not *'ratum et consummatum'*) is dissolved by the Pauline privilege, non-consummation or in favour of the faith through the Petrine privilege (cc. 1142-1143), the person would be canonically free to marry from this point of view, since the impediment of the prior bond (c. 1085) would no longer exist. These points will be examined later.

The question of a prior bond of marriage, sacramental or natural, is one reason why, in the preliminary care of those intending to marry, it is important to establish the freedom to marry of both parties. They need to be asked about any previous marriage in any way to anyone else and, if so, where and when (Information for Marriage Form). It is necessary to obtain a recent baptismal certificate (within six months of the wedding is usual) from the Catholic party (parties') church of baptism, which should state whether or not the individual has been married, been ordained or made perpetual vows. Where the episcopal conference or diocese has the practice of proclaiming or of publishing by posting on the church board banns of marriage or where such forms are available, this too is a further check on freedom. (These are still to be used in England and Wales in the parish in which the Catholic party or parties reside.)[15] The priest should obtain letters of freedom to marry from the parish priests of all the parishes where the Catholic(s) has (have) lived since the age of fourteen/sixteen, confirming that they have not been married in their parishes and letters of freedom to marry from responsible persons who have known the individual non-Catholic party (and Catholic if the parishes do not provide them), stating who the writer is, how they know the person, where and for how long and confirming that the person has never been married. If all else fails, the party is to be asked to swear an affidavit or oath that he/she has never been married before.

Where there is a civil certificate or licence needed for a marriage to occur, this should also be checked to see that there is no previous marriage (divorce). Where the Information for Marriage Form or the couple themselves independently of this reveal that one (or both) of them has been married before, and where the spouse is said to have died, it is necessary to have an authentic death certificate of that former spouse before proceeding and this certificate must be kept with the marriage papers. Where the Information for Marriage Form or the spouses independently reveal that there has been a previous marriage and the spouse is either certainly alive or cannot be proven to be dead, advice should be sought from the vicar judicial.

Where there is any prior bond, before there can be any wedding to another person, the freedom of the one seeking marriage now must be established. There must be either a decree of nullity of the previous union with no limitation on the party now wishing to marry from doing so or a decree of nullity of the previous union with a *vetitum* or prohibition on the person now wishing to marry from doing so without the permission of the bishop and also written permission for the person now to marry (showing that the *vetitum* has been lifted)

---

15. Statement of the Bishops of England and Wales: ' In accordance with c. 1067, ... marriage banns should continue to be published at least in the Catholic's present parish of residence, except when, in the judgment of the priest, there is good reason to omit publication. In Caparros *et al.* (eds), *Code of Canon Law Annotated*, 1337; Agar and Navaaro (eds), *Legislazione delle conferenze episcopali* on c. 1067, 579–80, based on *Briefing*, 19 April 1985, 15, n. 8, 114–15, following the *recognitio* of 9 November 1985 (note 8 in Agar and Navarre, 579).

or a decree of the dissolution of the former bond of marriage, issued from the Holy See or a decree of dissolution of the bond on the basis of the presumed death of the former spouse, issued from the diocese or from Rome (and a letter of permission from the civil authorities in which the presumed death is accepted and the present wedding is permitted). In all cases where former unions were recognized by the state, there needs also to be a decree absolute of divorce before any wedding proceeds, to avoid the danger of celebrating a marriage which would be bigamous in civil law and, as such, would be an offence in civil law. This again is why it is important to check with the vicar judicial (*Officialis*) or the chancellor before proceeding.

d. Disparity of Cult/Worship (c. 1086)

The impediment of disparity of cult (or of worship) concerns the marriages of a Catholic with a non-baptized person. From the time of St Paul, the difficulties of such unions, the danger of pressure on the Christian spouse not to practise the faith and/or on any children, rightly have made the Church especially sensitive to the question of such unions. The impediment to such unions (c. 1086 § 1) covers: those baptized in the Catholic Church and those received into full communion with it, provided, in neither case, that they have defected from it by a formal act, and where they wish to marry a non-baptized person. It is to be emphasized that this impediment is not to do with the permission of mixed religion, between a Catholic and a baptized non-Catholic Christian, even though the same promises and information are required for that permission to be granted lawfully (cc. 1125–1126). The dispensation from disparity of cult is a more radical matter, since it involves a non-baptized person. A formal act of defection from the Catholic Church (cc. 1086, 1117, 1124) differs from virtual defection deduced from someone's behaviour as where someone publicly defected from it (c. 194 § 1 2°), where they are still bound in some way by ecclesiastical law. Formal defection occurs only when someone internally decides to leave the Catholic Church in a way which involves heresy, schism or apostasy and puts that decision into effect by manifesting it in writing, and that decision is accepted by the competent ecclesiastical authority to whom it has been manifested. [16]

[16.] Pontifical Council for the Interpretation of Legislative texts, *Actus formalis defectionis ab Ecclesia Catholica* Prot. N. 10279/2006, 13 March 2006, nn. 1–2, 4–5; www.vatican. va/roman_curia/pontifical_councils/intrptxt/documents/rc_pc_intr. Cf Appendix 2 on the change in the law, 2009, on formal defection and marriage.

For the impediment of disparity of cult to apply, it is necessary not only that the Catholic party's position be clarified in the manner outlined above, but that the other person must never have been baptized at all or must have gone through a 'baptismal ceremony' where the 'baptism' was invalid (cc. 849, 854). Jews and Muslims would be particular examples of non-baptized persons, to whom the impediment of disparity of cult would apply. Catechumens are non-baptized persons (c. 206); as long as they remain so, a dispensation from disparity of cult is needed for them to marry a Catholic validly.[17] If they were to be baptized in the meantime, there would no longer be an impediment of disparity of cult; if they were baptized Catholic, there would be a marriage of two Catholics; if non-Catholic there would need to be a permission from mixed religion, (for liceity or lawfulness, but not for the validity of the marriage).

Dispensation from this impediment is possible, but only where the conditions for it are properly met. The Catholic party must promise both to do all in his or her power to preserve their Catholic faith and to do all in their power to have all children of the marriage baptized and brought up as Catholics; the non-baptized party must be aware of these promises and both parties are to be instructed about the purposes and essential properties of marriage (cc. 1086 § 2, 1125–1126). (The Bishops' Conference of England and Wales has established that these promises may be made either in writing by the Catholic party signing the promises in the presence of the priest or deacon, who also signs them, or orally, with the priest or deacon recording the fact and completing the required form.)[18] This is a change from the 1917 Code, where, even for what was then the impedient impediment of mixed religion, as well as for the diriment impediment of disparity of cult, the Catholic had to make these promises and the non-Catholic had to be warned to allow the Catholic to practise his or her faith and to allow all the children of the union to be baptized as Catholics and brought up as practising Catholics; the priest had to be morally certain this would be done.[19]

e. Sacred Orders (c. 1087)

Anyone who is ordained as a bishop, priest or deacon, even a married

---

17. McAreavey, *The Canon Law of Marriage*, 87, n. 221.
18. Statement of the Bishops' Conference of England and Wales, Caparros *et al.* (eds), *Code of Canon Law Annotated*, 1337–8 on c. 1126.
19. Benedict XV, *Codex iuris canonici* (1917), cc. 1061, 1071.

permanent deacon, is incapable of marrying validly. Those in sacred orders 'invalidly attempt marriage' (c. 1087); the word 'attempt' underscores the fact that no marriage is established because the person is incapable of marriage.

This impediment is connected to the practice of celibacy for priests in the Latin Church, which has been almost universally the law since the early Middle Ages.[20] After the restoration of the permanent diaconate, the Church permits the ordination of married men to the diaconate, provided that they are not intending to proceed to priesthood, but they may not marry anyone else if their wife dies and so they are conditionally committed to celibacy and actually so committed if she does indeed die. Those ordained to the permanent diaconate who are not married are to make a promise of life-long celibacy at their diaconate ordination, as are those being ordained to the diaconate with a view to priesthood. Such deacons, priests and bishops are permanently bound to celibacy (cc. 1037, 277 § 1, 291) and are under an impediment of sacred orders for marriage.

Although this impediment is of ecclesiastical law and since celibacy as an obligation for clergy is of ecclesiastical law, dispensation from the impediment of sacred orders is reserved to the Apostolic See (c. 1078 § 2) and, in fact, is never given.[21] The Apostolic See never dispenses a cleric so that he may marry and continue to function as a cleric. If he loses the clerical state, through the commission of a canonical crime and the imposition of a just canonical punishment, or if his request for release from its obligations is granted, a dispensation from celibacy would still be needed; he would then already be deprived of the clerical state and could not exercise his ministry. If a cleric attempts marriage, he automatically loses the clerical state and any ecclesiastical office he holds (c. 194, 1394 § 1); again he cannot function as a cleric if he attempts marriage while a cleric and without dispensation from celibacy. The dispensation from celibacy which is given to those whose request for release from the duties of the clerical state has been granted or to those deprived of the clerical state, allows them to marry, but they cannot thereafter function as clerics. They are not dispensed as clerics to continue as such and to marry; since they are no longer in the clerical state, the impediment has ceased to exist.

---

[20]. J-P. Schouppe, *Le droit canonique: Introduction générale et droit matrimonial*, Story Scientia, Brussels, 1991, 157–8.

[21]. Ghirlanda, *Il diritto nella Chiesa*, 379, n. 425.

f. Perpetual, Public Vow of Chastity in a Religious Institute (c. 1088)

This is not a question of temporary vows, since these do not engage a person irrevocably to a particular state of life. A perpetual vow does involve such a life-long commitment, relevant here insofar as it involves the public vow of chastity in a religious institute (this does not apply as such to those in secular institutes nor to those in societies of apostolic life, although priests in these institutes and societies are bound by the impediment of sacred orders – c. 1087).[22] This impediment is not limited to priests, but concerns those committed in the way described to a life of consecrated chastity. A vow is a solemn promise made to God (c. 1191). A perpetual vow of chastity is made to God for the rest of the person's life and requires total continence; hence someone who has made a perpetual, public vow of consecrated chastity in a religious institute is bound to a way of life for the rest of his life which is incompatible with the consummation of marriage.

Once again this impediment is of ecclesiastical law. The dispensation is reserved to the Apostolic See, except in danger of death (cc. 1078 § 2, n. 1, 1079) if the religious institute concerned is of pontifical right; the local ordinary can dispense those in institutes of diocesan right. Strictly speaking, the dispensation is not granted in reality. Rather, a person may be released from their vow of chastity, which means that the impediment no longer exists.[23]

g. Crimes (cc. 1089–1090)

The crimes which constitute diriment impediments to marriage are:

Abduction or Detention (c. 1089)
Where a woman has been abducted or detained to pressurize her into marrying a man against her will, unless, after release, she has freely consented to marry him.

Murder (c. 1090)
A person who murders the spouse of the person he or she wishes to marry or their own spouse to marry another (coniugicide) attempts marriage invalidly (1090 § 1), as would a couple who mutually caused, even morally (through others), the death of the other's spouses (c. 1090

[22.] Vernay, 'Le droit canonique du mariage', 334–5, n. 511.
[23.] Ghirlanda, Il diritto nella Chiesa, 380, n. 426.

§ 2). Again the dispensation is reserved to the Apostolic See, except in danger of death (cc. 1078 § 2, n. 2, 1079).

h. Relationships (cc. 1091–1094)

Consanguinity (c. 1091)

This impediment is of both divine and ecclesiastical law. It is of divine law insofar as it concerns the marriage of very close blood relatives to one another, but the details of how far the impediment stretches is a matter of ecclesiastical law, which means that these details have varied considerably over the years.[24] The various health and other genetic factors which we now know more precisely reinforces the recognition of old that close inter-relationships and inter-marriage are damaging and can be dangerous for people. The Code of 1983 has adopted the Germanic system of computing degrees of consanguinity rather than the Roman system of 1917 and before. All marriages conducted since 27 November 1983 are under this newer system; marriages conducted before that date are considered under the Roman system, the law operative at the time of the exchange of consent. In any case involving consanguinity, the vicar judicial or the chancellor of the diocese should be consulted before proceeding.

Consanguinity (blood relationship) is now calculated, under the Germanic system, by going back to the common ancestor and counting each level between persons via that common ancestor. A dispensation is never given in the direct line, the line from which a person is actually descended or from which he or she has progeny or successors (mother-son, father-daughter, father-grandmother, grandmother-grandson ...); this is of divine and natural law (certainly in the first degree of the direct line and possibly in these other degrees) and cannot be dispensed (c. 1091 § 1, 4; cf., c. 1078 § 3).[25] This impediment is not confined to those in legitimate marriages, but affects those related by blood even naturally (c. 1091 § 1). This reflects the fact that it is inter-breeding which is especially damaging, the question being one of blood relationships, not marriage as such.[26]

In the collateral line (where people are descended from the same common origin but not from one another, such as brother and sister, cousins, aunts, uncles); the impediment exists up to four degrees (c. 1091 § 2). A dispensation is never given up to the second degree

---

24. Ibid., 381, n. 429.
25. Ibid.
26. Schouppe, *Le droit canonique*, 161, n. 180.

in the collateral line, but can at times be obtained from the local ordinary in the third or fourth degrees of the collateral line (c. 1091 § 4). Dispensation in the third degree (aunt and nephew/uncle and niece) is given only for very grave reasons, while in the fourth degree (first cousins), it is more usual. Often medical advice is sought on these matters.[27] Since consanguinity is so serious, in case of doubt about the existence of the impediment in the direct line or up to the second degree of the collateral line, being perhaps of divine law, ecclesiastical law insists that no dispensation be given (cc. 1078 § 3, 1091 § 4), even though doubts of fact about other impediments will lead to the marriage being permitted (c. 90 § 2; cf. c. 1084 § 2). Examples of computation of consanguinity are as follows:

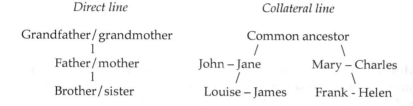

Direct line

Grandfather/grandmother
1
Father/mother
1
Brother/sister

Collateral line

Common ancestor
/ \
John – Jane   Mary – Charles
/ \
Louise – James   Frank - Helen

Grandparents and grandchildren are related in the second degree of the direct line. Counting the numbers of relationships (marked / and \) through the common ancestor, Louise and Frank are related in the fourth degree of the collateral line (first cousins), while James and Mary (nephew and aunt) are related in the third degree.

Affinity (c. 1092)

This is the impediment which exists with in-laws and the impediment exists in all degrees of the direct line, but there is no impediment in the collateral line. Thus, a man cannot marry his former wife's mother or daughter, nor a woman her former husband's father or son.[28] Note that the impediment does not exist between two in-laws only related to one another by each of them being married to two others who are the ones truly related to each other. (Affinity does not exist canonically between a man's brother and his wife's sister; it arises from the relationship between spouses or cohabitants (c. 1093) but not between families.) This is a change from the 1917 Code; there is no impediment now of affinity in the collateral line and the dispensation from affinity

---

[27.] McAreavey, *The Canon Law of Marriage*, 92–3, nn. 237–41.
[28.] Coriden, *An Introduction to Canon Law*, 141.

in the direct line, which had been reserved to the Apostolic See, is now given by the local ordinary.[29]

Spiritual Relationship
(relationships with godparents)
This no longer an impediment to marriage.

Public Propriety (c. 1093)
Where there is an invalid marriage or a notorious or public concubinage, there is an impediment in the first degree of the direct line between the man and those related by consanguinity to the woman and vice versa. If the relationship ends, the man cannot marry his former partner's mother or daughter, nor a woman her former partner's father or son.[30]

Legal Relationship (Adoption) (c. 1094)
Those legally related by adoption cannot marry one another validly in the direct line or up to the second degree of the collateral line. Under the present law an adopted person cannot marry his adoptive parents (direct line), nor can he marry his adoptive sister (second degree of the collateral line). He cannot marry a girl adopted by the same parents either (second degree of the collateral line). He can marry his adoptive aunt or niece.[31]

4. The Nature of Matrimonial Consent

We have considered what makes people legally capable ('*iure habiles*') or incapable of marrying (c. 1057 § 1). The former were either never under any impediment to marriage or are no longer under such an impediment, because they have been validly dispensed from it in order to marry validly. Given that 'consent makes the marriage' ('*consensus facit matrimonium*'), those legally capable of marrying need to exchange consent to marriage, to what marriage is (c. 1057 § 2) and to marrying one another.

Medieval debates had led to the recognition that the consent which makes marriage is not consent about some future possibility ('*consensus de futuro*'), as when a couple become engaged, but consent given at present ('*consensus de praesenti*'), to marry one another from

---

29. Schouppe, *Le droit canonique*, 161–2, n. 181.
30. MacAreavey, *The Canon Law of Marriage*, 94–5, n. 249.
31. Ibid., 95, nn. 250–1.

this moment onwards. No promise of marriage, no engagement to marry, no betrothal, creates an obligation or a right to marry (c. 1062 § 2).

The consent which brings a marriage into being (*'matrimonium in fieri'*) has to be consent to what marriage really is, to what marriage is in itself (*'matrimonium in facto esse'*, c. 1055), 'for the purpose of establishing a marriage' (c. 1057 § 2; cf. c. 1101 § 1). It cannot be consent to anything other than marriage.[32] Hence, consent has to be: for this particular man to marry this particular woman (c. 1055 § 1), to establish a marriage (c. 1057 § 2) with one another in a partnership for the whole of life (*'consortium totius vitae'*, c. 1055 § 1), in an 'irrevocable covenant' (c. 1057 § 2), for the good of the spouses themselves (*'bonum coniugum'*, c. 1055 § 1), for the procreation and education of children (*'bonum prolis'*, c. 1055 § 1), involving sexual intercourse with one another (c. 1096), in a marriage which is faithful (cc. 1056, 1101 § 2) and also permanent or indissoluble (cc. 1056, 1057 § 2, 1101 § 2).[33] Consent has to be consent between the two who marry one another; it 'cannot be supplied by any human power' (c. 1057 § 1), between a particular man and a particular woman (cc. 1055 § 1, c. 1097 § 1), legally capable of marrying one another (c. 1057 § 1), who exchange this consent irrevocably (c. 1057 § 2), even if through an interpreter (c. 1106), even if by proxy (cc. 1104, 1105 § 1).

The consent to marriage which is exchanged has to be 'lawfully manifested' (c. 1057 § 1), something we leave for later consideration of the form of marriage. However, the consent to be lawfully manifested has to be true consent or there is no marriage. Consent is not just a feeling, but is an 'act of the will' (c. 1057 § 2); it is what each of the parties to the marriage actually intends. Since they do not consent to what they deliberately exclude from their willing or intending, it is their true and internal consent which makes a marriage. If deliberately, 'by a positive act of the will' (c. 1101 § 1), they intend something else and lie at the external exchange of consent, no marriage comes into being. Canon law presumes that the external or lawful manifestation of consent does correspond to the true, internal consent of each of them (c. 1101 § 1), but, without it, there is no marriage. The conditions for the valid exchange of true consent are not to be such that most people could not meet them. Quite the opposite! It is only when these minimal conditions are truly lacking that valid consent is not exchanged. The importance of this consent makes it all the more

---

[32.] Schouppe, *Le droit canonique*, 168–70, nn. 188–9.
[33.] Scicluna, *The Essential Definition of Marriage*, 294–5.

necessary for priests especially to take great care of those intending to marry and to foster in them a proper understanding of marriage, so that they may in fact exchange true consent and may enter a marriage which fulfils their hopes and, in the case of two baptized persons, in which they may live out happily their vocation in the Church.

5. Defects in Matrimonial Consent

Here we consider those defects which render matrimonial consent invalid or null, so that the couple would not in fact be married. The presumption of church law is that those who express external consent to marry one another do in fact do so (c. 1101 § 1) and, since marriage enjoys the favour of the law (c. 1060), a declaration of the nullity of a union (that it was never a true marriage at all) is neither automatic nor presumed; the opposite is presumed. Unless and until procedures envisaged by law establish otherwise with moral certainty (c. 1608), both parties to a marriage are legally incapable of marrying anyone else validly by reason of the prior bond of marriage between them ('ligamen', c. 1085). We shall now consider in turn the defects of consent for matrimony.

a. Incapacity to Exchange Consent (c. 1095)

There are three categories of person who are considered to be incapable of giving matrimonial consent: those who lack sufficient reason to know what they are doing (c.1095 § 1); those who suffer from a grave lack of discretionary judgment, such that they do not grasp what is involved in consenting to marriage (c. 1095 § 2); and those who are incapable (for reasons of a psychic nature) of fulfilling the essential rights and duties of marriage and who, therefore, could not validly consent to them (c. 1095 § 3). This canon (c. 1095) has come to be the basis of many nullity investigations in recent decades, especially on the basis of the second and third paragraphs. It is important to understand what is at stake here and so to ensure a careful, effective preparation of those intending to marry, to seek to promote what can enable couples to consent truly to marriage.

Incapacity for Marriage through Lack of Sufficient Reason (c. 1095 § 1)

In the past a distinction was made between those who were completely irrational (suffering from 'amentia') and those whose reason was seriously lacking, but not absolutely so (suffering from 'dementia'). The present canon refers generally to those who lack sufficient reason for marriage. It concerns those whose mental disability is so severe that they are incapable of performing a human act. As consent is an act of the will (c. 1057 § 2), it has to be a human act, knowingly and willingly performed, and not just an act of a man. There has to be a minimum of knowledge and freedom; otherwise it would not be a deliberate or a voluntary act, it would not be an act of the will. Someone so mentally disabled as not to know where he or she is or what they are doing or to know it only in a seriously distorted manner, could not marry validly.[34]

In the case of a wedding by proxy, if the mandator (intending to marry and mandating another to speak on his or her behalf) becomes insane after signing the mandate and before the wedding, the marriage is invalid, even if the other party is unaware of this at the time of the wedding (c. 1104 § 4). This reinforces the indispensable role of true consent at the time of exchange of consent, which 'no human power can supply' (c. 1057 § 2).

Not only those rendered incapable of a voluntary act through serious mental disability, but those who, at the time of consent, do not know what they are doing (through alcohol or drug abuse or because of a head injury), either regular and operative at the time of the wedding or temporary at the time of the wedding, could not validly exchange consent to marry. No wedding should proceed if either party is in such a condition at the time. In some ways, c. 1095 § 1 is covered also by c. 1095 § 2 in the sense that the second paragraph deals with grave lack of due discretion for marriage, the result of the condition indicated in the first paragraph and the reason why consent would not be valid.

Grave Lack of Due Discretion for Marriage (c. 1095, § 2)

This is still dealing with those 'incapable of contracting marriage', which applies to all parts of c. 1095. It is not intellectual ability as such which is at issue, although, canonically both intellect and will are required for consent (an act of the will – c. 1057 § 2), but the assessment, evaluation and choice which are implied in consent.[35] People who are never going to be the most able academically can and do know what they are doing, can will to get married and do so. This is the normal state of things. On the other hand, it can be that a great intellectual does not grasp in anything like an adequate manner what is implied in marriage. No generalizations are to be made on the basis

---

[34.] Vernay, 'Le droit canonique du mariage', 318, n. 489.
[35.] Wrenn, *The Invalid Marriage*, 25.

of intellectual ability or lack of it. Nor is it the case that an exhaustive knowledge of the theology or canon law of marriage is needed; people should not be ignorant of the fact that marriage implies sexual relationships (c. 1096), but extensive theoretical knowledge is not required for people to be able to marry validly.

What is at stake here (c. 1095 § 2) is more of an evaluative or critical knowledge, an awareness of the importance of what is being undertaken, an appreciation of the significance of what is being done in getting married, at least to a minimal extent. When even that minimum is lacking, judgment or discretion is seriously defective, matrimonial consent is not exchanged. People are not expected to be able to foretell the future or to plan it in rigorous detail; it is marriage as such which is at stake. The following might be examples of what is at stake in c. 1095 § 2, the sort of issues which should be addressed in marriage preparation, to help couples to prepare well for marriage.

A level of responsibility about life appropriate to the person's age is expected. The age of reason in general is seven (c. 97 § 2) and the minimum age for the validity of canonical marriage is fourteen for a woman and sixteen for a man (c. 1083) as previously stated. People, though, are to be discouraged from marrying too young (c. 1072). This is partly to ensure that they have thought about what they are undertaking sufficiently to appreciate properly what they are doing. A person's sense of responsibility which does not correspond to the age they have reached is likely to be reflected in a pattern of behaviour, drunkenness, drug abuse, squandering money, inability to hold down a job for reasons of irresponsible behaviour, sexual promiscuity, aggressive and/or criminal activity. Here it is not an isolated incident which is at issue (unless especially serious and then it would betoken or reveal a much deeper problem), but precisely a pattern of behaviour gravely at odds with someone entering adult life and seeking to embrace the married state. Where a person were habitually and seriously irresponsible in these matters or in a combination of them, his or her capacity to understand and consent to the responsibilities of marriage would be in question.

How such a person could consent to looking after a spouse and family, share responsibility for finances, for long-term commitments might be at stake. A person with a pattern of entering and leaving sexual relationships might lack an adequate appreciation of the meaning and implications of fidelity. Someone with a habit of intense commitments, but without perseverance might not grasp the implications of permanence. Someone so utterly self-centred as to care for no one but himself or herself might not grasp the demands of the intimate, loving relationship of marriage. A person who had no time at all for children might not appreciate that openness to children is an essential part of what marriage is about. More generally, consent might be defective if the attention given to what is a decision about what to do with the rest of a person's life were to be entered into with no reflection or thought measuring up to the significance of such a life option (as where marrying were treated like buying a car or a computer). These concerns have to do with marriage itself, as such or in regard to its essential properties or elements; they are not marginal matters. Where they were verified in a serious way, consent, based upon such a defective perception, would not be true consent to marriage. There can be love at first sight, but, then proper thought and preparation are needed to ensure that the commitment of the will in the exchange of consent is real. Thinking through the implications of marriage during preparation promotes due discretion and facilitates true consent.

Another cluster of questions might relate to the time of consent. Consent might be gravely defective if the judgment brought to bear upon it were in no way proportionate to its importance for the life of the two people directly involved. This can happen if a person gives his or her time and attention to everything other than their intended spouse and preparation for marriage. It can happen if someone marries in a hurry, especially if there has been a devastating family illness or bereavement, loss of a previous close friendship (even engagement) and the decision to marry someone else is taken suddenly and recklessly. A person marrying under severe pressure might not see any way out of the situation other than through marriage; this could occur at times with a young girl becoming pregnant, especially if pressurized by parents and others. A person who lacks the internal freedom to make any other choice than to go through with a marriage he or she does not want to undertake would not bring to bear on this important decision the due discretion, the minimal level of critical judgment and would not consent to marriage.[36] Where there is a question of an arranged marriage, this does not mean that consent is automatically lacking, but it means extra care is needed to ensure that consent is genuine and free.

In all of these cases it is not to be presumed that consent is defective. From the standpoint of preparation for marriage, greater care is needed and probably more time to help the couple to prepare well. The preparation should include giving deliberate attention to potential pressures, to help the couple to reflect on what they are proposing to

---

[36.] Schouppe, 172, n. 193.

do and so to marry freely and validly and also, beyond these minimal canonical requirements, to marry well.

Inability to Assume/Fulfil the Essential Obligations of Marriage (c. 1095 § 3)

The last paragraph of this canon is not directly centred upon the judgment made in marrying by one or both parties (although it can be that this is affected also by the particular type of inability). Rather, it concerns the ability to take on or assume the essential duties of marriage and the basic capacity to fulfil them. A person cannot validly consent to what lies beyond their means, according to the classical adage of moral theology: '*Ultra posset nemo tenetur*' – 'No one is obliged beyond what they can do' or '*Ad impossibilia nemo tenetur*' – 'No one is obliged to do the impossible.' The question here is not that a person states or fears that they are not able to live a married life; factors of a psychic nature causing a true inability normally need to be identified and established, in a report of an expert, such as a psychologist (cc. 1680, 1574–1575).

Serious pathologies which might result in the inability which would render consent defective, might be severe forms of clinical depression, of obsessive-compulsive behaviour, paranoia or schizophrenia. Other causes 'of a psychic nature' (c. 1095 § 3) would include serious psycho-sexual factors, such as transsexualism or deep, non-transient homosexuality; in the latter case, a person might understand well what marriage is, but would still be incapable of marriage, which is of its nature a deeply inter-personal, heterosexual reality.[37] There could be incapacity and defective consent, if these are established to have been present at the time of consent and in such a severe form as to render the person unable to take on the essential marital duties.[38] The onset of a condition later would not necessarily prevent true consent to marriage from having been given. In a given instance, if it could be proven that the condition was severe and inevitable, such that its later emergence or its later, more forceful emergence, was inevitable at the time of consent, the consent would not be valid. Deep-rooted personality disorders are in mind, but there is a need to verify the degree of the problem and either that it was operative at the time of consent or that its later emergence was inevitable at the time of consent.

The question of incapacity or inability has to be distinguished from mere difficulties, even serious ones, which people have to confront in

---

[37.] Vernay, 'Le droit canonique du mariage', 321, n. 491.
[38.] Wrenn, *The Invalid Marriage*, 73.

life, not of struggling with the commitment which is an indispensable part of any marriage. It relates to something much more radical, and of a psychic nature, such as to render the person incapable of living out the basic or essential responsibilities of marriage. Since these are not specified in c. 1095 § 3, they are to be inferred from the other canons. Thus, the person must be incapable of accepting children (different from impotence c. 1084) and/or of ensuring their care, of fidelity, of permanence or indissolubility, or of the inter-personal, heterosexual relationship 'between and man and a woman' (cc. 1055 § 1, 1057 § 2, 1101 § 2, 1135).

There must be no confusion between the full attainment of human development as a goal to be sought through marriage and the minimum necessary to contract marriage validly.[39] Again, as distinct from difficulties in marriage, at issue here are deep-seated factors which 'substantially vitiate the capacity of the individual' to undertake marriage or its essential elements.[40] With inability to assume and fulfil the essential obligations of marriage, an expert report is never enough; rather, a pattern of behaviour or specific episodes at or before (and at times after) the time of consent are needed, to prove that a cause of a psychic nature did or does render this particular individual incapable of marriage or of its essential duties and, therefore, of consenting to marriage.

From the standpoint of preparation for marriage, where there is good reason to think that these factors may have been at work, it is highly desirable that the vicar judicial (*Officialis*) be consulted and his advice followed. The aim would be to establish whether or not a person does possess the minimum necessary to discharge the main responsibilities of marriage as in sharing the whole of one's life with one's spouse, being open to and bringing up children, fidelity, indissolubility.

b. Ignorance (c. 1096)

Since consent, as an act of the will, involves knowingly and deliberately willing something and, in this case, marriage, it is not surprising that ignorance is a defect of consent. Someone who does not know what they are undertaking cannot intend it. On the other hand, there is not a very high threshold of knowledge. A minimal knowledge,

---

[39.] John Paul II, Allocution to the Roman Rota, 'Unacceptable Anthropology', 5 February 1987, in W. H. Woestman (ed.), *Papal Allocutions to the Roman Rota, 1939–2002*, Faculty of Canon Law, St Paul University, Ottawa, 2002, 192–7 at 194.

[40.] Wrenn, *The Invalid Marriage*, 26–7.

enough to know basically what is being done, pertains to three points listed in this canon, of which the contracting parties 'at least should not be ignorant': that marriage is a partnership between a man and a woman, ordered to procreation, through some form of sexual cooperation (c. 1096 § 1). These are such basic features of marriage that it would be surprising for someone to be ignorant of them. However, were they to be truly ignorant of them, that ignorance would be so basic as to entail a fundamental error on their part of what it was they were entering or taking on; this is why, stemming from this ignorance, their consent would be invalid.[41] Such ignorance 'is not presumed after puberty' (c. 1096 § 2). By the time a man and a woman (c. 1096 § 1) have reached the minimum canonical age to be able validly to marry (c. 1083), they are presumed to know these very basic facts about marriage.

c. Error of Person and of Quality of Person (c. 1097)

Marital consent is not just consent to be married, but for a particular man to marry a particular woman (cc. 1055 § 1, 1097, 1105 § 1). If consent were exchanged and it were discovered that it involved the wrong man or the wrong woman, the consent would be invalid by reason of error of person (c. 1097 § 1). This could happen, for example, if one of the parties were blind or if there were a proxy wedding (c. 1105). The one making the error would not have intended to marry the one mistaken as the intended spouse and so would not have done so.

When the error is not about the person as such, but about some particular quality of the person (the person being married is the correct person, but some major aspect about them is mistaken), this does not automatically mean that consent is invalid. Consent is still valid, unless this quality was the decisive reason for the one making the error marrying the other, unless this quality is 'directly and principally intended' (c. 1097 § 2). This follows the general norm that a juridical act (such as matrimonial consent) is valid, even if there is an error, unless that error concerns the substance of the act or unless it amounts to a condition *sine qua non* (c. 126).[42] A condition *sine qua non* means a condition 'without which it would not have been done'. Had the truth been known, the person would not have performed the act; he or she only performed the act because of their (erroneous) understanding of such a key fact.

---

41. Vernay, 'Le droit canonique du mariage', 322, n. 492.
42. MacAreavey, *The Canon Law of Marriage*, 111, nn. 292–4.

Examples of serious error about the quality of a person, which might render the act of matrimonial consent invalid, if 'directly and principally intended' (c. 1097 § 2), would be the following. If a man intended marriage to a particular woman and very definitely to have children and had thought her to be capable of having children, only to discover that she was past the menopause, there would be no marriage. A couple might have married only because of a pregnancy, one of them or both of them believing the groom to be the father of the child, only to find that this was not so. Often the reaction of the one in error to discovering the truth is of critical importance where a quality of the other person is truly the object of an error which is directly and principally intended by the first in marrying.[43] An error about the quality of a person does not normally render consent invalid (cc. 1097 § 2, 126). A simple error, that someone was not in such a good state of health, was a year or two younger, was not as able academically or practically as had been imagined, had less money than was believed, and so on, would not render consent null and void.

d. Deceit (c. 1098)

This canon is new in the 1983 Code, having no equivalent in that of 1917. In principle it is a matter of ecclesiastical law (c. 11), not of natural law, and so is not retro-active (c. 9).[44] It is a canon dealing with consent; what may be surprising at first sight is that it does not operate in the person who does the deceiving (the deceiver's consent is not defective, despite the grave immorality being perpetrated on the other party). Rather, it is the consent of the person who is the victim of the deceit which is defective (the deceived), since the latter, not knowing the truth of the matter, consents to something which is not the case, which is false.

In canon law deceit does not normally or automatically render an act invalid (c. 125 § 2). Nor does deceit in relation to marital consent render that consent automatically or normally invalid (c. 1098). However, when all of the following conditions are met, matrimonial consent entered into by reason of deceit is invalid, namely when a person (the one being deceived) 'enters marriage', is 'inveighled'

---

[43] Ibid., 111–12, nn. 295–6.

[44] Rescript from the Pontifical Council for the Interpretation of Legislative Texts, 8 February 1986, on canon 1098: 'The Consultation is inclined to regard the wording of Canon 1098 as of merely positive law and, therefore, as *nonretroactive*', as translated and given in Wrenn, *The Invalid Marriage*, 229–30 (emphasis in Wrenn).

into it (by the deceiver) 'by deceit', 'perpetrated' (by the deceiver) 'in order to secure consent' (from the deceived) 'concerning some quality of the other party' (the deceiver) 'which of its very nature can seriously disrupt the married life'. The issue is that the deceiver knows or believes that something about himself (or herself) is so contrary to the other's desires, wishes, dreams or beliefs that, if the truth about them (the deceiver) were known (to the deceived), the latter would refuse to marry the deceiver. Therefore, wanting marriage, for whatever reason of love or other sort, it is realized that the only way of obtaining the other's consent to marriage is to deceive them about this crucial matter because, if they knew the truth, they would refuse to go through with it. This matter or quality of the deceiver has also to be so fundamental that, were it to become known, it would, of its nature, seriously threaten the marriage itself.[45]

Examples might be that the deceiver knows the other absolutely will not marry anyone who is not a virgin and deliberately deceives them about this (that he is a virgin, when he is not) or that a woman knows that the man she wishes to marry definitely would not marry someone who had had an abortion (which she has had and so she deceives him about it) or that someone incapable of having children (the deceiver knows he or she is sterile) wishes to marry someone who especially wishes to marry to have a family (and they deliberately deceive the other about their sterility), all to gain the other's consent which, it is known, otherwise will not be forthcoming. In these examples consent on the part of the one deceived is defective because they are in fact consenting, as a result of the deceit, to marry someone very significantly different from the person they understand them to be, deceived on a matter so serious as, of its very nature, to jeopardize the marriage itself.

---

45. In a case of nullity, relating to a marriage of 1966, on the ground of 'dolus' (deceit), coram Woodall, 2004, in the 'in iure' (section on the law), it is argued that the precise point over which deceit was involved in the given case was of natural law, so that the correct presupposition of the law as such (c. 9) and of the authentic response from the Pontifical Council for the Interpretation of Legislative Texts (as reported in Wrenn, here in the preceding footnote), that c. 1098 is a matter of positive or merely ecclesiastical law and so not retro-active (i.e., does not apply to marriages celebrated before the entry into effect of the new Code in Advent, 1983), is, in fact, overturned in this instance – affirmative decision at First Instance (Nottingham), ratified at Second Instance (Westminster).

e. Radical Error Determining the Will (c. 1099)

This canon is not concerned with errors about the persons exchanging consent, whether about the person as such or about a quality of person, whether spontaneous or the result of deceit by the other, but it concerns error about what marriage is. To that extent it is perhaps connected more to c. 1096 on ignorance of the basic aspects of marriage. It not just a matter of an error at the intellectual level, about the doctrine of what marriage is. The main point of c. 1099 is to stress that such an error does not render marital consent invalid, even though it concerns the unity or indissolubility or sacramental dignity of marriage. Why this is so emerges from the condition: 'provided it does not determine the will' (c. 1099). It is quite possible for someone to hold that marriage is not of its nature indissoluble, that it can be ended by divorce, but in his or her own mind and intention in marrying actually to intend to marry the other for the whole of life. It is quite possible for someone, mistakenly, to hold that fidelity is not essential to marriage as such and to marry themselves intending total fidelity to their spouse. In these cases, their intellectual or theoretical or doctrinal error about the nature of marriage would not have determined (settled) their own will in their exchanging of consent at their own wedding and, since consent is 'an act of the will' (c. 1057 § 2), they would have married validly, with true consent, despite their error.

On the other hand, where a serious error about the very nature of marriage was held and where it did determine the will, the consent would be defective and the marriage invalid. This is the exact implication of c. 1099. This is not a minor error, but a serious or radical (deep) error about the essential properties of marriage (unity and indissolubility) and/or about the sacramental nature of marriage. These are the three indicators of radical error given in the canon, which, if they determine the will, vitiate marital consent. With radical error we are not dealing with a deliberate refusal or restriction of consent by one of the parties (c. 1101), but with a seriously flawed understanding of the very nature of marriage, which determines their will, in the sense that, had they appreciated the truth of the matter, they would not have married. In contemporary Western society a serious misunderstanding of what marriage is could arise more easily than in the past, given the way people live married lives, the presentation of marriage in the media and even in text books, and so on. If a person genuinely believed that marriage was a reality brought about by the consent of the parties, but only as long as they both found it fulfilling or satisfactory, if divorce were a real way out compatible with marital consent in their view, this would constitute a radical error about the nature of marriage. If, further, it was only this erroneous view which led them to marry and they would not have married unless this 'get out' was part and parcel of marriage, then this radically erroneous understanding of marriage would have determined that person's will and his or her consent would have been vitiated. No true marital consent would have been exchanged.

Again, in Western societies or, in a predominantly Muslim culture, a man might believe that marriage meant being able to have more than one wife or someone who knew he or she could have only one spouse, might believe that being married to that person did not exclude intimate sexual relationships with someone else, but genuinely incorporated such a possibility. If the person only married because of such a misunderstanding of the essential property of unity or the good of fidelity and would not have married otherwise, then this radical error would have determined the will, the consent would have been vitiated and the marriage would be invalid.

The question of the 'sacramental dignity of marriage' (c. 1099) is important and controversial. Any valid marriage between two baptized persons is of its nature sacramental (c. 1055 § 2). Such a marriage is merely '*ratum*' (ratified), if it has not been consummated (and is internally indissoluble); if consummated ('*ratum et consummatum*'), it is both internally and externally indissoluble (c. 1061 § 1). However, without denying these truths, a baptized person whose faith is weak and/ or who is not practising their faith might believe that marriage was just a human arrangement, with some general reference to God, but might well believe that it is not a sacrament at all. This would be erroneous and radically so, since, although only a valid marriage can be sacramental, its sacramentality is not just a religious adjunct, an optional extra, but is 'a component which transforms that essence (of marriage) itself'.[46] If this radically erroneous understanding were the only basis on which that person would have married, this radical error would have determined his or her will in marrying, the consent would have been vitiated and the marriage invalid.

f. Simulation of Consent (c. 1101)

This is a case neither of someone being incapable of consent nor of ignorance, nor of error, but of a knowing, deliberate exclusion, 'by

---

[46.] M. F. Pompedda, former Dean of the Roman Rota, cited in McAreavey, *The Canon Law of Marriage*, 117, n. 310.

a positive act of the will' (c. 1101) of marriage or of some essential property of marriage. The lawful manifestation of consent in words, or, exceptionally, in equivalent signs (cc. 1101 § 1; 1104 § 2), is presumed to express the true internal consent of the will (c. 1101 § 1). What is done externally, what is expressed publicly, has to be a manifestation of true (true internal) consent, if it is to bring a marriage into existence (c. 1057 § 2).

When this presumption is not verified, when the words or signs used externally do not conform to, but are actually contradicted by, the internal will of the person who expresses them, it means that one or both parties to a union are lying in what they say through the words (or signs) used externally. They deliberately mean the opposite of what they say, either totally or in regard to one of more of the essential elements. Instead of a lawful, manifestation externally of true internal consent; there is in the external expression a deliberate untruth, a lie and so there is no marriage: 'If ... either or both of the parties should, by a positive act of the will, exclude marriage itself or any essential property, such a party contracts invalidly' (c. 1101 § 2).

This is not a requirement that a man and a woman at their wedding deliberately think of all the details of canon law. Rather, when they answer the questions posed to them by the Church's official witness (c. 1108 § 1 and 2) or, for those not bound by canonical form, by other official witnesses, they mean what they say. If a person deliberately wills, by a 'positive act of the will', not to enter into marriage with the person whom they are saying they will marry, there is a sheer pretence or simulation of consent to marriage; the internal will is not to marry. This deliberate (wilful) exclusion of marriage altogether is a total simulation of consent. This might happen if someone wanted to go through a wedding ceremony only because, by being officially 'married' to the other, they would gain a passport, residence or citizenship in a country, which otherwise would not be possible or which would be very difficult. That this was their real intention of the will, that they did not consent to marriage to the other person at all, would probably be shown by their departure soon after gaining what they wanted. Of course, a cause for marriage or a motive for marriage, even such as gaining residence in a country, otherwise impossible or difficult, does not of itself mean that there is no true consent. A person wanting citizenship who did truly consent to marry the other, would give real, internal consent and there would be a true marriage. In the former instance, though, there would be total simulation of consent. A desire to legitimate a child about to be born out of wedlock is compatible with true internal consent to marriage, but, if it caused someone only to go through the externals of a ceremony with a real internal intention not to be married to the other parent, there would be total simulation.[47]

The deliberate exclusion of consent, by an interior, positive act of the will of an essential property of marriage would mean that whatever the person was consenting to was something less than marriage through a partial simulation of consent. Partial simulation arises from the deliberate exclusion of one or more of the essential properties of marriage, taken in jurisprudence to include the deliberate exclusion of one or more of the essential elements of marriage. The essential properties of marriage (c. 1056) are those of unity (or fidelity of this particular man to this particular woman, the 'bonum fidei'), indissolubility or permanence ('bonum sacramenti'). The essential elements of marriage (c.1055 § 1) are the good of the spouses ('bonum coniugum'), implying the fidelity and permanence just noted also as essential properties, the good of the offspring ('bonum prolis') in a readiness to be open to the transmission of new life and to the education and upbringing of any who are born and, for two baptized persons, the specific good of the sacrament of Christian matrimony (also part of the 'bonum sacramenti'). The deliberate exclusion of all of these is involved in total simulation of consent, the deliberate exclusion of any one of them would mean its partial simulation.

Examples of the exclusion of the 'bonum prolis' might be the intention never to engage in the conjugal act with one's spouse (a refusal to consummate the marriage might indicate an intention 'contra bonum prolis', an intention against the good of children). It might be indicated by a refusal to engage in the conjugal act unless contraceptives were always used, that any child conceived would be aborted or deliberately neglected in order that it die, if born. Partial simulation of consent through an intention 'contra bonum fidei' (an intention against the good of fidelity) might be indicated where someone intends to keep on with another relationship of an intimate nature, to frequent prostitutes or live promiscuously.[48] Partial simulation of consent through an intention 'contra bonum sacramenti' might be indicated where someone reserves the right to divorce if the marriage does not work out as wished. Such simulation which excluded the sacramentality of marriage between two baptized Christians might be indicated where a person, though baptized, was lapsed and resentful, intended to marry, but rejected any Christian meaning or implication in what they

---

47. Vernay, 'Le droit canonique du mariage', 324–5, n. 496.
48. MacAreavey, The Canon Law of Marriage, 122–7, nn. 324–41.

were doing, marrying in the Church perhaps for other reasons. Partial simulation through an intention *'contra bonum coniugum'*, against the good of the spouses or against the communion of their life with one another (*'contra consortium totius vitae'*) has only very recently been pleaded successfully in the Roman Rota.[49]

Simulation of consent, whether total or partial, occurs only if there is a positive act of the will to exclude marriage itself or an essential part of it (c. 1101). There is no simulation of consent implicitly, where someone just 'does not want', 'wish' or 'like' something; they may consent reluctantly.[50] Finally, simulation of consent, total or partial, refers to what is done at the exchange of consent on the wedding day. The mere fact that someone did not fulfil what they promised means neither that they did not intend it (c. 1101), nor that they were incapable of fulfilling it (c. 1095 § 3), nor that they did not grasp its basic implications (c. 1095 § 2). A person who commits adultery fails to be true to marital unity, the good of fidelity, while one who divorces fails in the duty of permanence or indissolubility, the good of the sacrament as the life-long bond. This does not imply that such a person entered marriage deliberately, intending to exclude such goods from their consent.

g. Conditional Consent (c. 1102)

The medieval debates about consent as the cause of marriage had to resolve when consent to marriage was properly exchanged, distinguishing it effectively from an engagement. Nowadays, canon law has to consider a different aspect, namely whether consent is true marital consent if there is a condition attached to it. If the condition were about something in the future, the 1917 Code stated that the consent was true consent, but that the marriage only came into being if the future condition was actually fulfilled.[51] This has been eliminated in the 1983 Code; consent of its nature is 'irrevocable' (c. 1055 § 1), not conditional. A condition about the future renders consent invalid (c. 1102 § 1). A condition about the past or the present is possibly compatible with true marital consent (c. 1102 § 2), but it then depends on whether or not the condition is based in fact. If a man marries a

---

[49] A. Mendonça, 'Recent Developments in Rotal Jurisprudence on Exclusion of the *bonum coniugum'*, *Canon Law Society of Great Britain and Ireland: Newsletter*, n. 140 (Dec., 2004), 32–69.

[50] Schouppe, *Le droit canonique*, 181, n. 203.

[51] *Codex iuris canonici* (1917), c. 1092.

woman on condition that the child she is carrying is his child (she is not deceiving him, but believes that the child is his), the marriage is valid if the child is indeed his. For liceity, such a condition as to the past or present must not be attached to matrimonial consent without the bishop's permission (c. 1102 § 3).[52]

h. Force and Grave Fear (c. 1103)

As in the case of deceit, the mere fact of force imposed from outside (c. 125 § 1) or the fact of grave fear unjustly caused (c. 125 § 2) do not normally render a juridical act (an administrative act intended to have juridical effects) null and void. Thus matrimonial consent, as an act intended to produce the juridical effect of the couple being married, is presumed to be true consent, despite force or fear. However, if the force imposed from outside (not the pressure of internal tensions) is such that the victim is 'quite unable to resist it' (c. 125 § 1), an act is invalid. These general norms are significantly nuanced in the canons on marriage. The general norm on grave fear says an act is presumed valid 'unless the law provides otherwise' (c. 125 § 2). The law on force and fear in regard to marital consent does provide otherwise: 'A marriage is invalid which was entered into by reason of force or grave fear, imposed from the outside, even if not purposely, from which the person has no other means of escape other than by choosing marriage' (c. 1103). The reason for this canon is to protect those entering marriage from such severe pressure that they have no way out of the circumstances other than to marry someone whom they do not wish to marry. The force or fear has to be imposed or threatened from outside and grave enough to cause the victim to enter a marriage they do not want and would otherwise have avoided; they lack the internal freedom to give true consent. This is why a dispensation from crime resulting from abduction or kidnapping can only be given if the person freely chooses marriage after release from the pressure of those circumstances (c. 1089). It can be a real question in arranged marriages.

i. Knowledge/Opinion about Nullity of a Union (c. 1100)

A person may know or believe that their marriage is invalid either because of an impediment which was not dispensed (such as disparity of cult) or because of lack of canonical form (the marriage, involving a

---

[52.] MacAreavey, *The Canon Law of Marriage*, 128–9, nn. 342–4.

Catholic, was in a register office). This does not necessarily mean there was not true consent to marriage. If there was, this can make it easier to 'rectify' matters through convalidation or sanation

j. Consent in Difficult Circumstances

Consent makes the marriage or brings it into being. The questions of how someone can give consent to marriage if they are deaf and/or dumb, or if there is a problem of a foreign language in the exchange of consent, and of how people may consent to marry one another if they are not physically present to one another at the time of the wedding, are real ones.

Consent making use of Interpreters

In the case of foreign languages, canon law requires that the parish priest, and by implication the priest or deacon who validly assists at the wedding as the Church's official witness (c. 1108 § 1 and 2), be certain of the trustworthiness of the interpreter (c. 1106). This would preclude just asking at the last minute for someone to interpret; it would need settling beforehand, with the careful advice of the chancellor or vicar judicial. Furthermore, it should be noted that it would not be enough to proceed through an interpreter, even trustworthy, if the ceremony included the elements necessary for the civil validity of marriage, as in England and Wales. What was done would have to harmonize with the civil law; usually the non-English speaker needs to know enough to utter the exchange in English (or, in Wales, perhaps Welsh).

In the case of deaf and/or dumb people (c. 1104 § 2), the use of an interpreter who knows 'sign language' is possible (cc. 1101 § 1; 1104 § 2), with the same provisos.

Consent by Proxy (c. 1105)

The law requires that those intending to marry one another normally be present together and with two witnesses and with the Church's official witness (cc. 1104 § 1, 1108). However, it provides for the exchange of consent through a proxy, in which case the couple are said to 'be present together ... by proxy' as opposed to being together 'personally' (c. 1104 § 2). Cases where proxy consent can be exchanged might be where people are separated geographically for a long time or even for a short time, but unexpectedly, as where a spouse has become very ill or been injured to the point of not being able to travel to the wedding, or where one of them is in prison.

However, for a wedding by proxy to be valid, all the following conditions must be met:

1. A 'mandate' is to be prepared, a document authorizing a named person to act as proxy to give consent on behalf of the spouse who is absent to marry the specific person of the other spouse (c. 1105 § 1, 1°), the proxy being specifically designated for this by the mandator (c. 1105 § 1, 2°).
2. (For validity, the mandate must be: EITHER drawn up and signed by the mandator (absent spouse) – c. 1105 § 2. If the mandator cannot write, this fact is to be noted in an addendum to the mandate and another witness (besides those listed below) is to be added; this witness must sign the mandate or it is invalid (c. 1105 § 3) and either the parish priest of the place where the mandate is given* or the local ordinary of the place where the mandate is given* or the priest delegated by either of them or two other witnesses (c. 1105 § 2) (*not necessarily the domicile of the mandator) OR it must be drawn up in a document authentic in civil law (c. 1105 § 2).
3. The mandated person must give this exchange in person (c. 1105 § 1, 2°), which means that it cannot be given via a further proxy. It is to be noted that, if the mandator revokes the mandate or becomes insane before the exchange of consent takes place, the mandate is invalid, even if the other spouse and the proxy and others do not realize that it has been revoked (c. 1105 § 4). This emphasizes that it is the true consent of the parties at the time of exchange of consent which alone brings a marriage into being, a consent which 'cannot be supplied by any human power' (c. 1057 § 1).

6. Consent and Preparation for Marriage

Matrimonial consent is crucially important; it makes the difference between a marriage being valid or not. The purpose of this section is not to look for cases where consent may have been defective to the point where a union was null and void. If there is a genuine suspicion that this has been the case, consult the vicar judicial of the diocese and follow his advice. Here, the purpose is to underline how important it is that the parish priest or other priest responsible for the preparation for a couple for marriage take great care to ensure that they are not ignorant of what marriage is or of its essential properties and elements, that they consider the implications of what they are contemplating and undertaking, that any erroneous conceptions are corrected and that they are not marrying under such pressure that their consent would be vitiated. Helping prospective spouses in these areas is all the more important when marriage is increasingly disparaged and misunderstood. Suitable married couples among the faithful can do much to help prospective spouses to think about some practical aspects of married life and are to be encouraged actively to assist in preparation for marriage (c. 1063). This should supplement and not substitute for the careful, even if time-consuming, task which the parish priest especially owes to each couple (c. 1063 § 2), with assistance organized in the diocese too (c. 1064). This preparation is also to help them, if Christian, to understand something of the vocation to matrimony to which they are called in Christ.

Specific norms were issued by the Bishops' Conference of England and Wales in 1985, concerning marriage preparation. These require :

(a) a specific course of instruction dealing with the meaning, purpose and obligations of marriage, its unity and permanence, as well as on the vocation and role of Christian spouses and parents,
(b) avoiding 'invalid and injudicious marriages' by following the Pre-Nuptial Enquiry Form and verifying that there are no impediments, that the couple are marrying freely and that they understand and accept the essential obligations of marriage,
(c) that there be independent confirmation of the fact that there are no impediments and that the freedom of the couple to marry be established, and
(d) that banns continue to be published, at least in the Catholic's present parish of residence, unless there is a good reason to omit this.[53]

7. Conclusion

Having assessed what is needed for people to be legally capable of marrying and the conditions for such persons validly to consent to marriage, we turn next to the way they are to manifest that consent lawfully, to the form of marriage. We shall then examine other features of canon law on marriage.

---

[53] Agar and Navaaro (eds), *Legislazione delle conferenze episcopali.* on c. 1067, 579–80, based on *Briefing,* 19 April 1985, 15, n. 8, 114–15, following the *recognitio* of 9 November 1985 (note 8 in Agar and Navarre, 579).

Chapter 14

The Sanctifying Function of the Church

(Book IV of the Code)

Part I: THE SACRAMENTS
VII: The Canon Law of Marriage –
Canonical Form and Other Questions

1. The Canonical Form of Marriage

In the last chapter we examined what was necessary for people to be legally capable of marrying and the conditions necessary for them to exchange valid consent in marrying. We turn now to the question of how that consent is to be 'lawfully manifested' (c. 1057 § 1) and to what is known as the canonical form of marriage. We shall then treat briefly some situations relating to marriage including legal separation, nullity and the dissolution of the bond.

a. The Origin of Canonical Form

In the early Church, there was no special form of marriage. Rather, people married according to the customs of the Roman Empire. While there was an exhortation that Christians should not marry without the blessing of the bishop, this was not an absolute requirement.

What caused people to judge that there was a need for a specific form of marriage was partly the large number of clandestine marriages taking place in medieval Europe. When it was acknowledged that consent makes the marriage, if that consent could be exchanged between the two partners without anyone else knowing it, there would be real problems, since marriage and family are the foundations of society. Apart from inheritance rights of land and titles, if a couple's marriage were not recognized in a locality, their lives would be difficult and the legitimacy of their children would be brought into question. The problem of consanguinity, very sensitive and more extensive in the range of forbidden degrees of marriage than nowadays, was a very real one, but it would be hard to know who was really related to whom. Again, a man might abandon his wife and 'marry' another woman in secret, basically living in bigamy.

The Fourth Lateran Council in 1215 had tried to resolve the problem of clandestine marriages, requiring marriages to be conducted with the involvement of the priest, having checked that there are no impediments, also through proclaiming banns of marriage.[1] In fact, clandestine marriages continued in many places and were regarded in principle as being valid, even though illicit. Difficulties continued and the need for some public exchange of consent was increasingly recognized; Luther thought it a matter for the state. The Council of Trent dealt with the problem by insisting on a canonical form of marriage, no longer just for liceity, but for the validity of marriage. Even at Trent some queried this innovation, prior to the decision, since they argued that the bodies of the couple were the matter of the sacrament of matrimony, their exchange of consent its form and the contracting parties themselves its ministers.[2] Trent's decree, *'Tametsi'*, made it clear that, having checked freedom to marry, the priest was to receive consent in church before two or three witnesses and, otherwise, the couple were incapable of marriage (*'inhabiles'*) and the marriage would be invalid and null.[3] However, *'Tametsi'* was not promulgated in some parts of Europe and so did not become law there. Pius X made its provisions part of the Church's universal law through the decree *'Ne temere'* of 1907, which came into force in 1908: 'Only those marriages are valid which are contracted before the parish priest or the ordinary of the place or the priest delegated by either of them and at least two witnesses.'[4] This is the basic position of c. 1108 of the 1983 Code, except that deacons may be delegated to assist at a wedding.

---

1. Chapter 51 'On the Penalty for contracting Clandestine Marriages', Fourth Lateran Council, 1215, Denzinger-Schönmetzer, *Enchiridion symbolorum, definitionum et declarationum de rebus fidei et morum*, 36th edn, Herder, Barcelona, Freiburg-im-Breisgau, Rome, 1976, n. 817.
2. J. Vernay, 'Le droit canonique du mariage' in P. Valdrini et al., *Droit canonique*, 2nd edn, Dalloz, Paris, 1999, 307–62 at 338–40, nn. 518–19.
3. Canons on the Reform of Marriage, *'Tametsi'*, Council of Trent, Denzinger-Schönmetzer, *Enchiridion symbolorum ...* , nn. 1813–16, esp. 1816.
4. Pius X, Decree, *'Ne temere'*, 2 August 1907, Ibid., n. 3469: 'Ea tantum matrimonia valida sunt quae contrahuntur coram parocho vel loci Ordinario vel sacerdote ab alterutro delegato et duobus saltem testibus'.

Protestants and Reformers denied any right to the Church to 'interfere' with marriages, which they saw as essentially a secular reality, specifically denying any sacramentality. One aim of Trent on canonical form was to reject these claims and, indirectly, to defend sacramental marriage of the baptized.

b. The Key Canon on the Form of Marriage (c. 1108)

The key canon on this topic, c. 1108 (Table 15), confirms that canonical form of marriage is a matter of validity ('only' those marriages are 'valid ...') It entails the manifestation of their consent by the contracting parties, not secretly, but publicly before two witnesses (other than the bishop, priest or deacon who 'assists'). This has to be an exchange of consent, asked for and received by the one who 'assists', 'in the name of the Church'.

Since the local ordinary (diocesan bishop, vicars general, episcopal vicars and so on) and the parish priest can assist at marriages by virtue of their office, there are essential conditions attaching to their capacity to assist at weddings, which will be explained below. The Church's official witness is to 'ask for' and to 'receive' the consent of the couple 'in the name of the Church'; he has to be present at the time that this exchange of consent takes place (c. 1108 § 2).

c. Official 'Assistance' at Weddings

The one who 'assists' at a wedding as the Church's 'official witness' in this way is one of the following:

The Local Ordinary or the Parish Priest (by their Office)

It is the exchange of consent between the couple themselves, both legally capable of marrying, done in the correct form, which brings a marriage into existence. In the case of a marriage of two baptized persons, it is the couple themselves who are the ministers of the sacrament of matrimony. Thus, the bishop, priest or deacon is not the minister, as such, nor is he on a par with the other two witnesses (c. 1108 § 1) who need to verify that the wedding took place and between whom. Rather, he is the Church's official witness.

For persons validly to assist at marriages, the local ordinary or the parish priest must be in office at the time ('by virtue of their office, they validly assist at marriages', given certain conditions – c. 1109).

They have the ordinary faculty to assist at weddings.[5] They must not have been transferred elsewhere prior to the date of the wedding; otherwise they are no longer in office, no longer the local ordinary or the parish priest. It must not be before the date on which their appointment is effective or they are not yet in office, not yet the local ordinary or parish priest. They must not be under a canonical censure of excommunication, interdict or suspension from office (c. 1109); otherwise, they do not assist at the wedding unless they are delegated by one who does hold one of those offices at the time of the wedding. 'As long as they validly hold office', the local ordinary or parish priest 'can delegate priests or deacons to assist at marriages within their territory', c. 1111 § 1). They have to be within their jurisdiction (c. 1109), the local ordinary (in his diocese in the case of a diocesan bishop or vicar general, in the area for which he is responsible for an episcopal vicar) and not outside it (or he needs delegation), the parish priest in the parish to which he has been appointed validly as parish priest and not in another (or he needs delegation).

Other priests who are equivalent in law, for marriage matters, to a parish priest and who, therefore, could assist validly at marriages by virtue of their office (to which they have been validly appointed) would be the moderator of a group of priests officially appointed as responsible for a number of parishes in a 'team ministry' and each of the priests appointed to that group ministry for each parish within the group (c. 517), one appointed as administrator of the parish when the parish is vacant or impeded (c. 540), a priest caring for a parish in the absence of the parish priest, if the bishop has given him the necessary faculties (c. 533 § 3).[6] In the latter case, it is sometimes presumed that the bishop will normally furnish the requisite faculties, but this is by no means always done and, unless it is done explicitly and in writing, then the priest lacks the capacity to assist at weddings, unless he receives proper delegation. Any marriage at which he attempted to assist would be invalid by reason of lack of canonical form.

The Delegation of other Bishops, Priests or Deacons

Delegation is needed for any bishop or priest not in one of the offices just noted or not in the place where he validly holds that office and it is needed by deacons. It is needed by any such priest who wishes to

---

[5.] G. Ghirlanda, *Il diritto nella Chiesa, mistero di comunione: Compendio di diritto ecclesiale*, 4th revised edn, San Paolo, Cinisello, P.U.G., Rome, 2006), 289, n. 447.

[6.] J. McAreavey, *The Canon Law of Marriage and the Family*, Four Courts Press, Dublin, 1997, 137, n. 370.

assist at a wedding as the Church's official witness, soon after ordination, by an assistant priest, a deacon.

Delegation can be general delegation to assist at any / all weddings in the parish (given by the local ordinary or by the parish priest) to assistant priests appointed to that parish or to deacons appointed to that parish, or even to other priests and deacons, provided the parish priest permits this in given cases. The general delegation does not mean that an assistant priest or a deacon has a right to assist at any or all weddings in the parish; the parish priest has that right (c. 530, 4°); it merely means that he has the capacity to do so. Any general delegation is to be given in writing (c. 1111 § 2).

Delegation can be for individual weddings, special delegation, in which case it can be given orally, although it is always better to have it in writing; it must be given to a specific person and for a specific wedding (c. 1111 § 2). It is a good idea to record the fact in the church marriage register, putting 'delegated' in brackets when signing that register as the Church's official witness. For validity any delegation must be given to specified persons, not to 'any priest or deacon' (c. 1111 § 2). Sub-delegation can take place, where a bishop, priest or deacon, already validly delegated, passes the delegation on to another bishop, priest or deacon (c. 137 § 3), but this sub-delegated person cannot further sub-delegate (c. 137 § 4). Sub-delegation can only be for one specific wedding and cannot involve a general delegation to assist at a number of weddings.[7] Allowing deacons to assist at weddings and allowing general delegation other than to an assistant priest holding office in a parish, are new since the Second Vatican Council.[8]

The Church's Official Witness – Unusual Circumstances

Always attentive to the pastoral care of its people, the Church has provisions in law for very unusual circumstances, which can exist at times in some parts of the world.

Delegation of Lay Persons as Official Church Witnesses (c. 1112)

Where there are no priests or deacons, diocesan bishops (not priests) can delegate lay persons to assist at marriages, but only if both the episcopal conference has given approval and the Holy See has given permission (c. 1112 § 1). This canon contains conditions, necessary

---

7. Ghirlanda, *Il diritto nella Chiesa* ..., 289–90, n. 448.
8. Vernay, 'Le droit canonique du mariage', 343, n. 524.

for validity, which rightly are very restrictive.[9] The Holy See will not currently give such permission for Europe, since there are enough members of the clergy to provide proper care for assistance at marriages. Such lay persons are to be suitable, especially, they are to be able to give proper instructions on marriage and be able to conduct the liturgy fittingly (c. 1112 § 2).

Extra-Ordinary Form of Marriage before only Two Witnesses (c. 1116)

So far we have examined the ordinary canonical form of marriage. Even its celebration before delegated lay persons (c. 1112), in the exceptional circumstances given, constitutes an ordinary form of marriage in the sense that the Church's canonical form is actually observed. Here we turn to an extra-ordinary form of marriage.[10] Here the Code envisages a situation in which no one capable of assisting validly at a marriage can be there without 'grave inconvenience'. This might occur either in danger of death (c. 1116 § 1 1°) or (without danger of death) where it is prudently foreseen that this lack will continue for at least a month (c. 1116 § 1, 2°). Given the overriding duty of pastoral care, which canon law serves (c. 1752), where people would not be able to marry because no priest or deacon (or even delegated lay person, c. 1112) was or could be available, two witnesses would suffice. Such an exception had been made, for example, during the French Revolution, to enable people to marry validly.[11] Notification and registration need to be ensured, even here (c. 1121 § 2). Such a provision was envisaged even at Trent in its 'Tametsi' decree.[12] This is a case in which canonical form as such does not apply.[13] The marriage is valid only insofar as all the provisions and conditions of the specific canon are properly observed: '... can validly and lawfully contract ...' (c. 1116 § 1), the 'prudently foreseen' impossibility for 'at least a month' not being loosely interpreted. This canon, though, does provide for the pastoral care of couples in such unusual circumstances. While this extra-ordinary form of marriage in such emergencies does not require canonical form, it would preserve some real element of a canonical form: the couple who 'intend to enter a true marriage' would in this way 'contract' or exchange true consent

---

[9.] J-P. Schouppe, *Le droit canonique: Introduction générale et droit matrimonial*, Story-Scientia, Bruxelles, 1990, 191, n. 216.

[10.] Ibid., 192, n. 218.

[11.] Vernay, 'Le droit canonique du mariage', 342, n. 521.

[12.] Ibid., 341–2, n. 521.

[13.] MacAreavey, *The Canon Law of Marriage*, 139, n. 375.

'in the presence of witnesses only' (implying two witnesses); there would not be a clandestine marriage.

d. Further Requirements of Liceity and the Official Church Witnesses

Whoever is the official church witness, the one who by office or by delegation validly assists at a wedding has the following duties. He is to ensure, if possible, that the couple have been well prepared for their marriage by himself or by another priest, with the help of suitable lay persons and according to diocesan arrangements (c. 1063 § 2), that each one of the parties is marrying freely (cc. 1113, 1114 §1), if he has a general delegation, that he has the parish priest's permission to assist at this wedding (c. 1114 § 2), that he has the permission of the parish priest of the parish of the Catholic's domicile, if the wedding is conducted elsewhere (c. 1115), that the liturgy is well prepared and celebrated in such a way as to bring out the participation of the (baptized) couple in the loving and fruitful communion of Christ and the Church (c. 1063 § 3). The liturgy is to be celebrated according to the liturgical rites (cc. 1119–1120) and in the church, if both are Catholic or if one is Catholic (c. 1118 § 1) or elsewhere if the local ordinary permits it (c. 1118 § 2 and 3) and civil law allows it (c. 1071 § 1, n. 2). This aspect concerns the place of the wedding and the rite used. He is to ensure that he completes the church marriage register accurately and promptly after the wedding (c. 1121 § 1) and also enters the details in the baptismal register, if the wedding is of a Catholic from that parish (c. 1122 § 1) and that he notifies the parish priest of the parish(es) of the Catholic(s) if not (c. 1122 § 2). The proper registration of weddings is very important for proof of people's status and the exercise of their rights.

e. Those bound by the Canonical Form of Marriage (c. 1117)

We have seen the historical reasons behind canonical form. Equally, we know that for centuries there was no universal law requiring the celebration of marriage with the involvement of a priest. Hence, the norms on canonical form, although essential because they are now a matter of validity, are norms not of natural law, but of positive, ecclesiastical law. According to the present Code, 'merely ecclesiastical laws bind those who were baptized in the Catholic Church or received into it … , unless the law expressly provides otherwise' (c. 11). Yet it is not quite as simple as that, since marriage involves two parties. Therefore, the canonical form of marriage (described above) is binding where both parties to the marriage are Catholic or where even one of the parties is Catholic. This is an instance where the law expressly provides (c. 11) that ecclesiastical law binds: canonical form binds 'if at least one of the parties …' was baptized in or received into full communion with the Catholic Church and has not by a formal act defected from it (c. 1117).

The implication of this canon is that someone who has defected from the Catholic faith by a formal act is not bound by the canonical form of marriage obligatory for Catholics. He or she is treated in this regard like a non-Catholic person, even though in other regards he or she is bound by ecclesiastical law (c. 11).[14] If such a person wanted to marry a Catholic, though, he or she would be bound to canonical form because of the person he or she wished to marry being Catholic (c. 1117). However, such a marriage is not to be celebrated without the permission of the bishop (c. 1124), precisely because of the defection from the Catholic faith and because it would be difficult to see how the person such an individual wished to marry would be able to fulfil the promises mentioned in c. 1125. What is to count as defection from the Catholic faith by a formal act (cc. 1117, 1124) is not specified in the Code, but has been clarified by an authentic interpretation from the Pontifical Council for the Interpretation of Legislative texts, as explained in the last chapter.[15]

Thus, the canonical form of marriage binds in any marriage between two Catholics, a Catholic and a baptized non-Catholic, and a Catholic and a non-baptized person, and is to be observed for validity (c. 1108 § 1), except in the case of a Catholic marrying a baptized non-Catholic Christian of Oriental rite, where canonical form binds only for liceity, although, for validity, a sacred minister must be involved (c. 1127 § 1). This is a requirement of such non-Catholic Churches of Oriental rite, since the priest has to be present as a requirement of their own canonical form. In this case, the sacred minister is not required to ask and receive consent, as is required in our canonical form; it is enough in these circumstances that a canonical form be observed.[16] The reason why the Latin Code makes canonical form, in principle, a question of liceity, not validity, for a Catholic marrying a non-Catholic Christian

---

[14.] Ghirlanda, *Il diritto nella Chiesa*, 393, n. 454. Cf appendix 2 on changes to the law on this point in 2009.

[15.] Cf. the treatment of the impediment of disparity of cult and footnote 16 of chapter 13.

[16.] Ghirlanda, *Il diritto nella Chiesa*, 398–9, n. 459.

of Oriental rite is that the canonical form of that Church is obligatory in that Church and it necessarily involves a sacred minister. The
other exceptions are in the case of a validly granted dispensation from
canonical form (c. 1127 § 2) or where cc. 1112 or 1116 apply. Otherwise,
without such a dispensation, the marriage is invalid. Thus, any
marriage in a register office, involving a Catholic, is invalid and any
marriage in a non-Catholic church, involving a Catholic, which does
not meet the requirements of c. 1127, is invalid.

Since canonical form only binds where at least one of the parties
is Catholic (c. 1117), marriages involving two non-Catholics, whether
celebrated in a non-Catholic church or in a register office, are in
principle valid. We recognize their marriages (and do not claim that
they are living in sin), but we do not recognize their divorce, since
marriage is of its nature for life. This is why Catholic priests need to
take great care pastorally. If a person was married in a register office
who was not bound by canonical form, the marriage is valid, unless
proven to be otherwise and the union declared null by the tribunals
of the Catholic Church. Hence, such a person now wishing to marry
a Catholic cannot do so because of the impediment of a prior bond
('*ligamen*') of marriage (c. 1085 § 1). A civil divorce does not end that
first marriage!

f. Mixed Marriages (c. 1124–1125)

These are marriages between two baptized Christians, one of whom
is Catholic, through baptism or reception into full communion with
the Catholic Church, provided he or she has not defected formally
from the Catholic faith (c. 1124). It would be a sacramental marriage.
As a fruit of the ecumenical movement, such marriages are no longer
subject to a formal impediment, unlike the diriment impediment of
disparity of cult (c. 1086 § 1) to marriages of a Catholic to a non-baptized
person. For a Catholic to marry a baptized non-Catholic Christian,
one who 'belongs to a Church or ecclesial community not in full
communion with the Catholic Church' (c. 1124), a mixed marriage, it
is necessary to have express permission from the competent authority
(cc. 1124, 1125). The competent authority is the local ordinary or his
equivalent in law (Vicar General, Vicar Apostolic); in England and
Wales the capacity to grant this permission has also been delegated by
diocesan bishops to parish priests, but not to other priests.

However, for any of these to grant this permission of mixed religion,
the following conditions must be met. There must be proof of the
baptism of both and the Catholic party has to promise to do all in his

or her power within the union of the marriage to avoid defecting from the (Catholic) faith, to do all in his or her power to have all the children of the union baptized and brought up as Catholics. The baptized non-Catholic must be aware of these promises and of the obligations they imply for the Catholic. Both parties are to be instructed about the nature and essential properties of marriage, which are not to be excluded by either of them (c. 1125). There needs to be a just cause for the permission (c. 1124), such as the lack of Catholics in the area, the spiritual welfare of the couple or of the Catholic.

These promises are required because the faith is not a matter of barter nor is there to be indifferentism or relativism. The Bishops' Conference is to settle how the promises are to be made and communicated to the non-Catholic Christian (c. 1126). In England and Wales, they are either signed by the Catholic party in the presence of the priest or read to him with signatures added.[17] This reflects both the reality of a sacramental marriage of the baptized (cf. Eph. 5:21–33), brought out ecumenically, and the need to preserve the faith.

Dispensation from Canonical Form (c. 1127 § 2)

As noted, it is possible for there to be a dispensation from canonical form; this is not a right nor is it automatic. It can only apply to mixed marriages, marriages between a Catholic and a baptized non-Catholic and can only apply to their marrying in a non-Catholic Christian church, before the non-Catholic Christian minister according to the rites of that ecclesial community, provided there is a true exchange of marital consent. Before such a dispensation can be granted by the local ordinary (not by the parish priest), it is necessary that all the conditions noted above on mixed religion already be fulfilled, that there be a just cause ('grave difficulties in the way of observing the canonical form', c. 1127); 'just because the other church looks nicer' will not do. Examples of when this dispensation might properly be sought (remembering that it might not be granted) are where the non-Catholic party is a regular practising member of his or her faith community or where he or she is the child of the local minister of that church. There is to be no semblance of a second blessing either in the ceremony or after it, nor are the Catholic and the non-Catholic minister to ask for and seek to receive consent from the couple in the same ceremony (c. 1127 § 3). For validity of the dispensation and

---

17. Cf. J. M. Agar and L. Navarro (eds), *Legislazione delle conferenze episcopali complementare al C.I.C*, 2nd revised edn, Coletti a San Pietro, Rome, 2009 on c. 1126, 580–581, based on *Briefing*, 9 April 1985, 15, n. 8, 114, following the *recognitio* of 9 February 1985 (note 10 in Agar and Navarre, 580).

so of the marriage, the fact of there being a Catholic and a baptized non-Catholic Christian is essential. If, before the wedding, the non-Catholic were to be received into full communion with the Catholic Church, the dispensation would immediately become invalid. Two Catholics would be marrying one another and canonical form would be binding (c. 1117), without possibility of dispensation. The Catholic parish priest of the place of the wedding is responsible for ensuring the registration of the wedding (including note of the dispensation) in the Catholic marriage register and in the baptismal register of the Catholic party's parish of baptism (c. 1121 § 3).

It should be noted that the permission for mixed religion (c. 1124) includes an '*ad cautelam*' (precautionary) dispensation from disparity of cult (c. 1086). This means only that, in case the non-Catholic party's baptism had actually been invalid, this dispensation comes into effect so that this person, in fact a non-baptized person, may still marry the Catholic validly and licitly. This does not mean that parish priests in England and Wales have the power to dispense from disparity of cult; they do not! Any such 'dispensation' by them where they are certainly dealing with a non-baptized person is invalid and so is any marriage celebrated in consequence of it.

g. The Secret Celebration of Marriage (cc. 1130–1133)

Enough has been said to show why this is highly undesirable and not normally possible. For a grave reason a local ordinary could permit such a wedding to be registered in a secret diocesan archive. All involved formally would be bound by the secret, except that the local ordinary would be released from it if future danger of scandal arose. This is to be made known to the parties prior to the wedding. Any priest faced with a request for a secret wedding must not proceed without the local ordinary's permission (cc. 1130–1133).

h. Registration and Proof of Marriage (c. 1121)

Many details of what is required have been given in the course of this chapter. The importance of making these entries and of making entries in the baptismal registers of Catholic spouses, or notifying their parish priests so that this may be done, cannot be over-emphasized. Such entries are to be made promptly and carefully. Any dispensations should be noted in the margin of the register, with the protocol number. Registration is not a matter of mere legalism; it affects the status and rights of the couple and perhaps of others.

2. Other Features of Marriage Law

a. The Effects of Marriage

Properly speaking, this section treats of the canonical effects of marriage, which concern primarily those who are married in the Catholic Church, whether their marriage be sacramental or non-sacramental. However, since we recognize the validity of the marriages of those who are not bound by canonical form, but who do exchange true consent to marriage, there is a sense in which there can be said to be canonical effects of civil marriages or of marriages in non-Christians religions, always provided that these are valid marriages according to our canon law.

The Civil Effects of Marriage

The Catholic Church has denied the claim, going back to the Protestant and Reformed challenges of the sixteenth century and of the secular state since the nineteenth century, that marriage is nothing to do with the Church and with its law, rejecting the view that marriage is only a civil matter. This does not imply that the state has no legitimate interest in marriage nor right to regulate certain aspects of it. In fact, canon law requires that proper heed be taken of such legitimate concerns (cc. 1059, 1062 § 1). Episcopal conferences may set higher minimal age limits, for liceity but not for validity, for marriage on the basis of the civil laws operative in their areas (c. 1083 § 2). Parish priests are not to proceed with marriages which would be invalid in civil law without the local ordinary's permission (c. 1072 § 1, n. 2). Not only does the Church recognize legitimate, if limited, state rights in regard to marriages taking place, but it also recognizes that there are civil as well as canonical effects arising from it. These would include marital status, taxation status, housing and benefit, legitimacy of children, and so on.

The Canonical Effects of Marriage

The Lifelong Bond of Marriage

Marriage brings into being a bond between the couple which is lifelong, normally dissoluble only through the death of one of the parties (c. 1141), 'a bond of its nature permanent and exclusive' (c. 1134). Any valid marriage is intrinsically indissoluble (c. 1056) and 'what God has joined together man may not put asunder' (Mt. 19:6; Mk. 10:9), reinforced by a sacramental bond if between two baptized persons (cc. 1055 § 2, 1056). Once such a marriage is consummated, by divine law it is intrinsically and extrinsically indissoluble (c. 1061 § 1), until the death of one of the parties (cc. 1134, 1141). The Church does not consider that it has the power to alter its teaching and practice for this reason.[18]

Communion of Life of the Spouses/ their Mutual Rights and Duties

Marriage creates a communion of life between the spouses. The marriage established by the true and lawfully manifested consent of persons legally capable (c. 1057 § 1) involves not only a lifelong bond between the spouses, but it constitutes their 'state of life' (c. 1134). It entails 'a partnership of the conjugal life – *consortium vitae coniugalis*' (c. 1135), which goes beyond mutual help of a merely practical order to embrace fully the true good of the spouses ('*bonum coniugum*', c. 1055 § 1) and to enable that to grow. This state of life and this communion or partnership of life and love entail mutual duties and rights between the spouses, which are equal (c. 1135). These are not limited to the '*ius in corpus*', but concern 'whatever pertains to the partnership of conjugal life' (c. 1135). Duties and rights of the couple, deriving from their marriage to one another, include the duty and right to consummate the marriage in a human manner (c. 1061), not violently imposed, and, morally speaking but not as a condition of canonical validity of consummation, also un-contracepted. There is the fundamental dignity and equality of the spouses themselves (c. 1135), the mutual duties and rights to fidelity, to permanence, to the conjugal act also after consummation, to openness to children in each and every conjugal act, the mutual and primary duty and right to educate their children, including in regard to their religious education.[19] They include the duty and right to lifelong fidelity. Also included are the mutual duties and rights to cohabitation (suspended for reasons of military service, legitimate work abroad), to communicate truthfully and caringly with one another on all matters of importance to the marriage and family, to consideration in regard to opinions expressed on such issues, to affection and to care, especially when ill or in particular need, to material care and well-being, including providing

---

[18.] Ghirlanda, *Il diritto nella Chiesa*, 400, n. 463.

[19.] Cf. J. Hervada, *Studi sull'essenza del matrimonio*, Giuffrè, Milano, 2000, 195, 199, in which he locates the '*bonum fidei*', '*bonum sacramenti*' and '*bonum prolis*' as the essential conditions of the '*bonum coniugum*', which he does not consider to be a fourth good of marriage.

money through work, unless unavailable. There is the mutual duty and right to spiritual care, to support to be able to attend Mass and the sacraments without opposition.[20] Not all of these duties and rights would necessarily be strictly juridical duties and rights, although all of them constitute moral duties and rights, arising from marriage.[21]

Parental Duties and Rights

In regard to the 'bonum prolis' (c. 1055 § 1), marriage has the following effects. While not implying a duty and right to have children as such, since children are not an object or commodity and since God is the author of life,[22] it does imply the mutual duty and right of the spouses to cooperate with God in the transmission of new life, through their conjugal acts; they have the mutual duty and right to be open to the gift of children through these conjugal acts, exclusive to them.[23] The mutual 'grave duty' and 'primary right' to bring up, educate, the children born to them physically, socially, culturally and morally (c. 1136; cf. cc. 774 § 2; 793 § 1 and 2; 796 § 2; 797; 798). The mutual 'grave duty' and 'primary right' to ensure the religious upbringing of those children born to them (c. 1136) are inalienable duties and rights; the Church and civil authorities support parents, but do not replace them. Where they are incapable of fulfilling their duties, subsidiarity allows and requires others to step in.[24]

Paternity

The man in a lawful marriage is presumed to be and 'is to be identified as' the father, unless it is proven that he is not such (c. 1138 § 1).

[20.] Ibid., 322.

[21.] Ibid., 335–40.

[22.] Congregation for the Doctrine of the Faith, Instruction, Donum vitae, 22 February 1987, II, B, 8.

[23.] Ibid., II, A, 1–3; II, B, 4, b. This text refers to the 'right' of the child to be conceived and born through marriage; properly speaking, this must be understood to mean that parents have the duty to ensure that this is the only way that a new human being is conceived and brought to birth, since a 'not-yet-existing being' cannot have rights as such. The recent Instruction, up-dating Donum vitae in the light of new dimensions of bioethical issues, does not repeat this expression. Cf., Congregation for the Doctrine of the Faith, Instruction on Certain Questions of Bioethics, which speaks more appropriately of the morally unacceptable dissociation of procreation from the fully personal context of the conjugal act and of human procreation as a personal act of the couple, male and female, which admits of no form delegation or substitution, Dignitas personae, 8 September 2008, n. 15.

[24.] MacAreavey, The Canon Law of Marriage, 169, nn. 468–9.

Legitimacy and Legitimation of Children

This sensitive question concerns one of the most important canonical effects of marriage. Legitimate children are those born of a valid marriage or of a putatively valid marriage – one entered into in good faith and thought to be valid by at least one of the spouses, until both are certain it is null (cc. 1061 § 3, 1137). Presumed to be legitimate are those born at least 180 days after the wedding or within 300 days from the dissolution of the conjugal life, from the separation of the spouses (c. 1138 § 2). The first envisages a very premature birth, the latter an extended pregnancy and late birth. Legitimated children are children who were illegitimate; by canon law they are 'legitimated' or rendered officially legitimate either by the subsequent marriage of their parents, where that marriage is truly valid or only putatively so (entered into in good faith and thought to be valid by at least one of the parties, until both are certain it is null – c. 1061 § 3), or by a rescript from the Holy See, a written document from the Holy See declaring the child legitimated, in response to a request that this be done (c. 1139). There is no difference in regard to canonical effects between legitimate and legitimated children, unless expressly stated otherwise (c. 1140).

b. The Rectification of Invalid Unions

Marriages may be null and void because of an impediment which cannot be dispensed or which has in fact not been dispensed, because of a defect of consent or because of lack of canonical form. Where impediments cannot be dispensed, such unions cannot be rectified. In the other cases, it may be possible to rectify them, but this is neither automatic, nor always straightforward. The possibilities are twofold: simple validation (sometimes called simple convalidation) and 'sanatio in radice'.

Simple Validation

Here there is a renewal of consent. What is required depends on the reason why the former union was invalid. The law requires the following. Where the original union was invalid through an undispensed impediment, it is necessary that either the impediment have ceased or it be dispensed and that the party aware of the impediment renew consent (c. 1156 § 1). This is necessary for validity of the convalidation, even if the original consent of the two had not been withdrawn by either of them (c. 1156 § 2). This must be a 'new act of the will', where the renewing party knows or thinks the marriage was invalid from the start (c. 1157) or by both if both know or think the original invalid (c. 1158 § 2). If the impediment is occult, cannot be proven publicly, this renewal of consent can be done in secret (c. 1158 § 2), but if it is public (can be proven publicly, even if it is in fact not known as yet), the renewal of consent must be in the canonical form (cc. 1158 § 1, 1108ff.).

Where the original union was invalid through a defect of consent, convalidation occurs by the party who did not consent now consenting, provided that the consent of the other party perdures or continues (c. 1159 § 1). Again, if the defect of consent is occult, cannot be proven in public, consent can be renewed in secret by the one who did not consent (c. 1159 § 2), but if the defect of consent is public (can be proven in the public forum, even if it is not (yet) actually known), consent must be renewed in the canonical form (c. 1159 § 3).

Where the original union was invalid through a defect (lack) of canonical form, consent must be given again in the canonical form, unless a dispensation from canonical form has been granted validly according to c. 1127 (c. 1160).

The renewal of consent by one of the parties is possible only provided that the consent of the other party, though not renewed formally, perdures or continues. This is essential since it is precisely the consent which makes the marriage. If that consent were lacking and the person refused to renew consent, there could be no convalidation; in fact; a 'convalidaton' would itself be invalid.

'Sanatio in radice' (Radical Sanation or Retro-active Validation)

This is a different approach to rectifying an invalid union, one which is used when a normal validation is impossible, because one party refuses to renew consent or it is judged futile even to ask him or her to do so. It is called a 'radical healing' or 'healing at the root' ('sanatio': healing; 'radix': root), since it is one of the rare instances in canon law of something operating in some respects retro-actively, impossible unless the law expressly provides otherwise (c. 9), as it does here (cc. 1161ff.). A 'sanatio in radice' is a healing of an invalid union without the actual renewal of consent (c. 1161 § 1), needing the permission of the competent authority (which is the Apostolic See (c. 1165 § 1) or the diocesan bishop, but only for a particular marriage and provided it does not concern an impediment reserved to the Apostolic See under c. 1078 (c. 1165 § 2), involving a dispensation from any impediment of ecclesiastical law (c. 1161 § 1, cc. 1165 § 2, 1078) and a dispensation from canonical form if it had not been observed (c. 1161 § 1), with the canonical effects of the 'sanatio' being retro-active (c. 1161 § 1). The validation takes effect from the time the favour (the sanation) is granted, but the effects of the sanation go back to the moment the marriage was originally celebrated; hence a radical sanation (c. 1161 § 2).

The following types of case may arise. Where there was a defect of consent, no sanation (retro-active validation) can be granted, whether there was never any consent from the start or whether consent given at the original celebration has since been withdrawn; this is in either or both parties (c. 1162 § 1). Since the consent which makes the marriage is lacking, any attempted validation would itself, be invalid. Provided there was no consent at the original celebration of the union, but such consent was given later, a radical sanation can be given (c. 1162 § 2). This presumes the consent of both perdures or continues, even though not expressed at this later time; otherwise, the consent of one or other or both is lacking and no *sanatio* is possible (c. 1162 § 1) for that reason. Where there is an undispensed impediment, a radical sanation or retro-active validation can be given, provided the consent of both parties perdures or continues (c. 1163 § 1). However, a marriage invalid because of an impediment of natural law or divine positive law can only be validated or radically sanated retro-actively after that impediment has ceased (c. 1163 § 2). Where there is a defect (lack) of canonical form, a retro-active validation or radical sanation can be granted, provided the consent of both parties perdures (c. 1163 § 1).

It is clear from these summaries that the key condition for any valid 'sanatio in radice' is that the consent of both parties is in existence, perdures or continues, without which no sanation is possible. In a sanation consent is not formally renewed or externally manifested, but it must exist. Such a sanation can be validly given even if one or both parties is unaware of it (c. 1164). This latter might be the case where a series of marriages were invalid by reason of a defect of form or through an undispensed or invalidly dispensed impediment. In such a case, only the Holy See could grant the sanation, since it concerns more than an individual marriage (c. 1165 § 1). On the other hand, no sanation is ever to be granted, unless it is probable that the couple are intending to persevere in the conjugal life (c. 1161 § 3).

c. The Separation of the Spouses

There are three different types of separation of spouses: legal separation where the bond of marriage remains (they are still married), the dissolution of the bond of marriage and where a union is declared null and void.

Legal Separation with the Bond of Marriage Remaining

Here a properly married couple might not just separate in fact, but one of them or both of them might wish that separation to have legal status, in civil law, in canon law, or in both. There would need to be a grave reason for this to be sanctioned in canon law, since marriage is for life and spouses have the duty to maintain the conjugal life (c. 1151). However, there can be situations in which one of the spouses is violent or otherwise abusive to the partner and/or to the children (c. 1153). Such grave reason is judged to operate if there is a grave danger to the soul of the spouse or children or if one spouse makes the common life unduly difficult (c. 1153). The case of separation due to grave danger to the soul of a spouse lies behind St Paul's permission for separation in 1 Cor. 7:12–16. To protect such innocent spouse and/ or children, the bishop could even be asked to permit a civil divorce, provided it were understood clearly that this does not and cannot end a marriage.

The case of one of the spouses committing adultery was the occasion of Jesus's strong teaching condemning divorce, the reason the Catholic Church does not acknowledge divorce as ending a marriage. The Church urges the innocent spouse to seek to forgive the guilty even after adultery (c. 1152 § 1). Agreeing expressly with the other's adultery, being the cause of their adultery or committing adultery themselves or tacitly condoning the other's adultery by willingly engaging in marital life with them after becoming aware of the adultery would preclude any legal separation by the Church (c. 1152 § 1–2). The innocent spouse is presumed to have condoned the other's act if they have not brought a case to the Church's authorities within six months of becoming aware of the adultery (c. 1152 § 2)

If the innocent spouse ends the conjugal life as a result of the other's adultery, he or she may bring the case to the church authorities. These are to consider whether the innocent spouse can be brought to condone the other's fault and so end the separation (c. 1152 § 3). If not, that spouse's right to sever the conjugal life is recognized (c. 1152 § 1). Such legal separations and even any separations legalized in civil law, even a civil divorce, mean that the bond of marriage actually remains. The innocent spouse may separate for the sake of peace and maybe for greater legal protection, but neither can marry another person, since there would be the impediment of the prior bond (c. 1085 § 1).

Dissolution of the Bond

The indissolubility of marriage, we have seen, is an essential property of marriage (c. 1056). St Paul considered Jesus's condemnation of divorce and remarriage to apply properly to Jewish marriages and Christian marriages, but not necessarily to marriages between pagans, where one had become baptized. Any valid marriage is intrinsically indissoluble, a marriage which is valid, sacramental and consummated is both intrinsically and extrinsically indissoluble until the death of one of the partners (c. 1141).

Where all three conditions are not verified together, some marriages can be dissolved in certain circumstances and under certain conditions.

Dispensation from Non-Consummated Marriages

A non-consummated marriage either between baptized persons or between a baptized and an unbaptized person, a sacramental or a non-sacramental marriage, can be dissolved by the Roman Pontiff, but only for a just reason (c. 1142); at the request of one or both parties. A just cause might be that the spiritual welfare of the parties can be provided for in no other way, that the breakdown due to non-consummation is irreversible. This comes under the so-called 'Petrine privilege', the power of the keys, to bind and loose, given to Peter and his successors by Christ. It is a favour or privilege, not a matter of justice and rights. The proof of non-consummation is essential; it can arise from the couple not having had the time to consummate their marriage (*'per coarctata tempora'*), if one was in prison or, after a proxy wedding, they had never met; from physical proof of virginity and/or from moral arguments that there was no consummation (cc. 1697–1706).

Although some people think that this approach reflects the *'ius in corpus'* approach of 1917, it is rather insisting that a ratified marriage has not been perfected, that the bodily, sexual union of the couple is not an optional extra, but is part of what marriage is about (cc. 1061; 1096); it reflects the unitary anthropology developed since the Second Vatican Council. It has been specified since that consummation 'in a human manner' (c. 1061§ 1) means, canonically, that it was 'a human act on the part of both', it being 'sufficient that this be a virtually voluntary act', in other words 'provided it was not elicited by violence'.[25] In other words, only where the only act of intercourse after consent is shown to have been imposed by violence against the

---

[25.] Sacred Congregation for the Sacraments, Circular Letter 'De processibus super matrimonio rato et non consummato', 20 December 1986, in Congregatio de culto divino et disciplina sacramentorum, *Collectanea documenta: ad causas pro dispensatione super 'rato et non consummato' et a lege sacri coelibatus obtinenda*, Libreria editrice Vaticana, 2004, n. 50, 119–24 at 120, introduction: 'ad habendam consummationem oportet ut actus sit humanus ab utraque parte, sed sufficit ut sit virtualiter voluntarius, dummodo non violenter exigitus'.

will of one party would a dissolution on the basis of non-consummation be possible following a post-nuptial sexual act; otherwise, the absence of such an act must be established.

At issue here is a dispensation from the law of indissolubility, since such non-consummated unions are intrinsically, but not extrinsically, indissoluble. Indissolubility here would be of divine natural law and not of divine positive law, as with a valid, sacramental and consummated marriage, which is extrinsically as well as intrinsically indissoluble (c. 1141). Since the Pope has the authority to interpret divine natural law, a dispensation is possible, since it concerns a secondary precept of natural law.[26] The other case in which a non-consummated marriage was capable of being dissolved in the past was where one of the parties made a solemn profession of vows in a religious order; this possibility has been abolished with the 1983 Code.[27]

The Pauline Privilege

This was not what St Paul himself allowed, but it is a development from the official separation he permitted when a pagan spouse refused to allow the newly baptized Christian spouse to 'live in peace', to practise their faith. The Pauline privilege envisages the Catholic spouse, whose partner will not allow this peaceful practice of the faith (by this fact the unbaptized is considered to have departed – c. 1143 § 2,), not only to separate, but to marry someone else (such departure being a condition of validity of the second marriage – c. 1144 § 1). At the moment of the establishment of the second union, the first is by that fact dissolved (c. 1143 § 1). This can only occur after the non-baptized party has been 'interpellated', asked if he or she is willing to be baptized and whether he or she is willing to live at peace with the other, although the local ordinary can dispense from this interpellation if it is judged to be useless (c. 1144). There must be proof in the external forum of some form of interpellation (c. 1145 § 3). In the case of negative replies or in the absence of replies in the requisite time, the baptized party has the right to contract a new marriage (c. 1146) with a Catholic or, even, with the permission of the local ordinary and with the provisions for mixed marriage being observed (c. 1125), to marry a non-Catholic baptized person or even a non-baptized person (c. 1147). The Pauline privilege involves, therefore, the dissolution of a non-sacramental marriage.

[26.] Ghirlanda, *Il diritto nella Chiesa*, 401, n. 464.
[27.] Vernay, 'Le droit canonique du mariage', 351–2, n. 541.

The Petrine Privilege and Polygamous Unions (c. 1148)

Where an unbaptized man had many wives in a polygamous society or an unbaptized woman many husbands in a polyandrous society, if it would be hard for them to stay with the first spouse, he may keep one of the wives or the woman one of the husbands (c. 1148 § 1). After the baptism of the person just mentioned, the marriage is to be celebrated according to canonical form (c. 1148 § 2). The local ordinary is to ensure that responsibilities of justice relating to other 'spouses' and to children are met (c. 1148 § 3). The origins of this practice go back to the time of Spanish and Portuguese colonization of what is now Latin America and stem from the practical need to deal with such cases. Pope Paul III had allowed a man to choose one of his wives, with whom to remain and to whom he was to be married (she did not have to become a Catholic), if the man could not remember which woman was his first wife. Pius V allowed a man to choose a woman as his wife from among those to whom he was polygamously united on the basis that she would agree to be converted, even if he knew who his first wife was.[28] This type of case, too, would be one of the dissolution of a non-sacramental marriage.

Separation through Captivity or Persecution (c. 1149)

Where a person is baptized in the Catholic Church, but that person is and remains separated from their unbaptized spouse in captivity or under persecution, even if the spouse from whom they are separated in the meantime is baptized, the first spouse can marry someone else. This is without prejudice to c. 1141, which says that only death can end a marriage which is valid, sacramental and consummated. The point is that a sacramental marriage was never consummated between the two spouses.

Dissolution of a Non-Sacramental Marriage

In the case of a non-sacramental marriage, it is possible for a dissolution to be granted by the Pope on the basis of the non-baptism of a person who wishes to marry a Catholic, to marry 'in favour of the faith'. This does not feature in the Code as such, although the statement that 'in cases of doubt the privilege of the faith enjoys the favour of the law' (c. 1150) can be seen as a basis for it. In fact, this procedure under the Petrine privilege has been operative for almost a century. Proof of non-baptism is required and the person seeking

---

[28.] Ibid., 354–5, n. 546.

the favour or privilege must not have caused the breakdown of their previous union.

In none of the cases given above are we dealing with a valid, sacramental and consummated marriage, which can only be dissolved by the death of one of the parties (c. 1141). Rather, it is either the case of the dissolution of a sacramental or of a non-sacramental marriage which was not consummated or it is the case of the dissolution of a non-sacramental marriage, consummated or not.

Declaration of the Presumed Death of a Spouse (c. 1707)

Only death dissolves a valid, sacramental and consummated marriage (c. 1141). Where one of the spouses is believed dead, but death cannot be verified directly, it is not enough that a long time passes, even if in civil law this is the standard used. In canon law proofs have to be such as to establish the person's death with moral certainty. Then a declaration that death is presumed to have occurred is to be issued (c. 1707), which means that the marriage is dissolved by that death; since it is the truth of the matter which counts, if after all the spouse were alive, the marriage would still be in existence and any new union would actually be null by reason of that prior bond. A case of presumed death can be examined in the diocese and the bishop then makes the declaration, but, in complex cases, the Congregation for Divine Worship and for the Discipline of the Sacraments should be consulted by the vicar judicial of the diocese and their advice followed.

The Declaration of the Nullity of a Union

Here we are not treating of the dissolution of a valid marriage. Rather, there is a grave reason to suspect that there was either an undispensed impediment to marriage or there was a grave defect which meant that true consent was not given (and so no marriage was established) or there was a lack of canonical form which renders the union invalid. Where there is such a serious reason to suspect invalidity, a spouse (c. 1674 1°) or the promoter of justice in some instances (c. 1674 2°) may approach the Church's tribunals, to ask for the matter to be investigated to 'challenge the validity' of the union, to see whether or not the union was null and void. This would mean, if verified, that no true marriage had really existed, even if one or both thought there had been.

The nullity enquiry will be opened if there is a clear basis in law for suspecting nullity, if there is a 'fumus nullitatis', that is if this case has the smoke or perhaps smell of nullity about it (c. 1677 § 2). If the evidence gathered proves nullity with moral certainty (c. 1526

§ 1), there has to be an appeal to a tribunal of second instance for the judgment to be ratified before a declaration of nullity can be issued (c. 1682 § 1). If it is not confirmed or ratified, the case has to go to a third instance tribunal, whose judgment will stand, since it will be true that two tribunals have concurred in the same judgment on the same ground of nullity. There can be a restriction (a 'vetitum') added to a decree of nullity, stating that a particular person is not to marry in the Catholic Church without the permission of the bishop; in such a case, the vicar judicial is to be consulted before making any arrangements about a wedding.

Nullity is not dissolution, nor is it divorce; it declares that what was thought to have been a marriage was not in fact really a marriage. Since marriage enjoys the favour of the law (c. 1060), proof to the contrary, proof of nullity, has to be with moral certainty; otherwise the judges are bound to state that the case for nullity has not been established (c. 1608 § 4).

Chapter 15

The Sanctifying Function of the Church

(Book IV of the Code, Parts II and III)
VII: Other Acts of Divine Worship

The sacraments of the Church constitute the overwhelming bulk of the material of Book IV of the Code, part I of that book. In this brief chapter we shall examine non-sacramental acts of worship (part II of Book IV) and sacred times and places (part III of Book IV).

1. Non-Sacramental Acts of Worship (Book IV part II)

a. Sacramentals

Sacramentals are sacred signs, symbolizing certain effects, brought about through the intercession of the Church (c. 1166), established, interpreted, suppressed only by the Apostolic See (c. 1167 § 1), with rites and formulae to be observed when celebrating sacramentals (c. 1167 § 2). They are mostly to be administered by clerics, though by lay persons with the right qualities, may administer some of them if the local ordinary judges this to be appropriate, always using the prescribed liturgical books and under his authority (c. 1168). In fact, sacramentals, as with the use of all objects, are ordered to persons; they are to help people to prepare for the sacraments and to grow in holiness.[1]

Dedication and consecration are to be celebrated by the bishop or by a priest permitted to do so by law or lawful grant (c. 1169 § 1). Blessings may be given by priests, unless reserved to the Apostolic See or to bishops (c. 1169 § 2). Deacons may impart only those

---

[1.] G. Ghirlanda, 'Sacramentale' in C. C. Salvador, V. De Paolis and G. Ghirlanda (eds), *Nuovo dizionario di diritto canonico* , 2nd revised edn, San Paolo, Cinisello Balsamo, 1993, 939–40.

blessings expressly allowed to them by law, those he is permitted to give within a liturgical function (c. 1169 § 3). This latter norm is of universal law and cannot be set aside by bishops or others. Blessings are mostly to be bestowed upon Catholics, but can be given to non-Catholics, unless specifically prohibited (c. 1170). Sacred objects set aside for divine worship by dedication or consecration are to be revered and not used in a secular or inappropriate way, nor are they to be owned by private persons (c. 1171). Thus, the altar of a church is especially set apart for the Eucharist and is not to be used for signing marriage registers.

At issue here is an exercise of the sanctifying function of the ministerial priesthood for the most part and especially that of the bishop. Where it pertains to a dedication or consecration, these are always 'constitutive', as is the case too with a blessing which is 'constitutive' or 'imparted' (one which renders holy what is blessed). Hence, consecrations are limited for validity to the bishop and to priests he may delegate. Blessings are limited for deacons who do not act in the person of Christ and of the laity; where they are allowed, they involve an exercise of the sanctifying function rooted in the common priesthood of the faithful and are invocations of or requests for God's blessing.[2]

Exorcisms may only be lawfully performed with the express permission of the bishop (c. 1172 § 1), to be given only to a priest of piety, knowledge, prudence and integrity of life (c. 1172 § 2).

b. The Liturgy of the Hours

Exercising the priestly function ('*munus*') of Christ, the Church celebrates the Liturgy of the Hours, listening to God speaking to his People, recalling the mystery of salvation, praising God without ceasing in song and in prayer, interceding with him for the salvation of the world (c. 1173). Clerics are obliged to recite the Liturgy of the Hours (c. 276 § 2–3) every day (c. 1174 § 1). This involves priests and deacons preparing for the priesthood saying the whole of the Divine Office each day (Office of Readings, Morning Prayer, Prayer during the Day, Evening Prayer and Night Prayer); the duty in regard to Morning and Evening Prayer is grave matter, for the other Hours it is light matter. Permanent deacons are obliged to recite those parts laid down by the Ordinary. Other members of the faithful are invited to take part in the Liturgy of the Hours as an action of the Church (c.

---

2. Ibid., 940.

1174 § 2). The Hours should, where possible, be said at the appropriate times of the day (c. 1175).

c. Funerals

Christ's faithful who have died are to be given a church funeral, according to the norms of law (c. 1176 § 1), according to the liturgical books, praying for the spiritual support of the dead, honouring their bodies, comforting the living with hope (c. 1176 § 2). Burial is preferred, but 'the Church does not forbid cremation' on condition that it is not chosen for reasons contrary to Christian teaching (c. 1176 § 3). Funerals are to be celebrated normally in the church of the dead person's proper parish (c. 1177 § 1) or the church of the parish where he died (c. 1177 § 3) or another church with permission of the priest there and notification of the death to the person's parish priest (c. 1177 § 2). The funeral of a bishop should be in the cathedral, unless he has chosen another church (c. 1178), of religious and members of societies of apostolic life in their proper church or oratory, by their superior (c. 1179). Burial is to be in the cemetery of the parish church, if there is one, or in another cemetery (c. 1180). Offerings made are to be treated according to law (c. 1264); the poor are to receive proper funeral rites (c. 1181). Deaths are to be registered in the parish register (c. 1182).

In addition to members of the faithful, funeral rites are to be allowed for catechumens, treated in this regard as the faithful are treated (c. 1183 § 1), children whose parents intended to have them baptized, but who died before baptism (c. 1183 § 2), baptized persons of a non-Catholic church or ecclesial community, if their own minister is not available and if the local ordinary judges this prudent, unless they do not want this (c. 1183 § 3).

Funeral rites are to be denied to the following unless they showed signs of repentance before death: notorious apostates, heretics or schismatics, those choosing cremation for anti-Christian motives, other manifest sinners who could not be given a church funeral without causing public scandal to the faithful (c. 1184 § 1). The local ordinary's judgment should be sought and followed in doubt (c. 1184 § 2); indeed, if ever there is a question of possibly denying someone a funeral, it would be wise to consult the diocesan bishop or another local ordinary first.

d. The Cult of Saints: Images and Relics

To foster the sanctification of the People of God the Church commends the special veneration of the Blessed Virgin, the Mother of God, whom Christ constituted Mother of us all, the cult of other saints on the basis of their example and their intercession (c. 1186). Public cult is only for those beatified or canonized (c. 1187). Sacred images may be displayed in churches, but in moderate numbers and in a suitable way, to avoid disturbing people and to foster only appropriate devotion (c. 1188). The written permission of the ordinary is to be sought for their restoration and he is to seek the advice of experts before giving it (c. 1189). They are not to be sold (c. 1190 § 1); distinguished relics and images greatly venerated by the faithful are not validly alienated or transferred without the permission of the Apostolic See (c. 1190 § 2 and 3).

e. Vows and Oaths

A vow is a deliberate and free promise to God about some good which is possible; it is to be fulfilled on the basis of the virtue of religion (c. 1191 § 1). It must be made freely and concern a good and it must be practicable. It can only be made by one with the use of reason (c. 1191 § 2). If made through unjust force, fear or deceit, it is invalid (c. 1191 § 3). Since a vow is a firm decision to fulfil what is promised, it requires the capacity to understand its implications and the ability to fulfil it; it is of its nature ordered to what is good and has no effect if its object is not good.[3] The criteria at work here are closely comparable to those which apply to the exchange of matrimonial consent.

A vow is public if accepted by a superior in the name of the Church, otherwise, private (c. 1192 § 1); solemn if recognized by the Church as such, otherwise, simple (c. 1192 § 2); personal if it requires action by the one who made it, real if it promises something; mixed if it involves both (c. 1192 § 3). It only obliges the one who made it (c. 1193) and ceases to oblige if the time for its fulfilment expires, a substantial change occurs in the matter promised (it is no longer what it was), a condition on which it depended ceases, it is dispensed by one with the power from the Apostolic See or from the local ordinary (c. 1196), is commuted or changed to something else (c. 1194) equivalent or better

---

3. J. M. Huels, 'Other Acts of Divine Worship (cc. 1166–1204)' in J. P. Beal, J. A. Coriden and T. J. Green (eds), *New Commentary on the Code of Canon Law: An Entirely New and Comprehensive Commentary by Canonists from North America and Europe, with a revised English Translation of the Code*, study edition, Paulist, New York, Mahwah, NJ, 2000, 1400–23 at 1416–17.

by the one who made it, or to something less by one with power over vows (c. 1197), it is suspended by one with authority over vows (c. 1195) or through making religious profession (c. 1198).

An oath invokes God's Name as a witness to truth; it can only be taken in truth, judgment and justice (c. 1199 § 1); oaths required by canons cannot be taken by proxy (c. 1199 § 2). One who freely swears an oath is bound to fulfil it by the virtue of religion (c. 1200 § 1); if extorted by force, grave fear or deceit, it is invalid (c. 1200 § 2). A promissory oath depends for validity on the nature of the promise (c. 1201 § 1); one which directly threatens harm to others, to the public good or to salvation is not reinforced by an oath (c. 1201 § 2). Any duty ceases if it is remitted by the one favoured by it, there is a substantial change (for instance, it becomes evil, irrelevant or a hindrance to a greater good), the purpose or condition under which it was made ceases, it is dispensed or commuted (c.1202) by those able to dispense from vows, unless remitting would tend to harm others and they refuse this, in which case only the Apostolic See can remit it (c. 1203). An oath is to be interpreted strictly according to law, the intention of the person taking it or, if the latter is deceitful, the intention of the person in whose presence the oath was taken (c. 1204). It is very clear from these canons that the moral theological doctrines on vows and oaths and even on promises pertain, such that a promise, oath or vow to do what is immoral has no validity precisely because its object is immoral; there is no duty to fulfil it and indeed, there is a strict duty not to fulfil it in such a case. The example of Herod's promise and the assassination of John the Baptist is the classic case of an invalid oath (Mk. 6:22–9), which ought never to have been implemented.

2. Sacred Places and Sacred Times (Book IV, Part III)

a. Sacred Places

Sacred Places in General

A place dedicated or consecrated for worship is a sacred place (c. 1205). It is not enough that a liturgical action occur somewhere; for somewhere to be a sacred place it must be 'set apart' from profane use for worship or for burial of the faithful through a liturgical act of dedication or of blessing.[4] Such dedication or consecration is performed

---

[4] L. H. Avecedo, 'Luogo sacro' in Salvador, *et al.* (eds), *Nuovo dizionario di diritto canonico*, 645–55.

liturgically by the bishop in dedicating a church, or an ordinary in dedicating another sacred place or at times a priest he delegates for this purpose (c. 1207). Such places are to be used exclusively for divine worship, except where the bishop gives permission for other use, but this must not contradict their sacred purpose (c. 1210). Where a sacred place has been the scene of scandalous behaviour, no worship is to take place in the desecrated place until the bishop can conduct a penitential rite (c. 1211).

Churches

A church is 'a sacred building intended for divine worship, to which the faithful have the right of access for divine worship' (c. 1214). It is to be built only with the 'express, written consent of the diocesan bishop' (c. 1215 § 1), to be given only after consulting – after having heard the views of ('*audito* ...') – the council of priests and rectors of local churches, and then judging that a new church would serve the needs of souls and the means are there to build it and to provide for divine worship (c. 1215 § 2). Consultation does not imply consent, but failure to consult renders the act invalid (c. 127 § 1).[5] This is necessary even where religious institutes already have the diocesan bishop's consent to establish a new house, which entitles them in law to have a church where the Blessed Sacrament is reserved, since this does not give a right to establish a church in a particular place, especially without the bishop's permission (cc. 1215 § 3; 611, 3°). The requirement of express written consent from the diocesan bishop (not any other local ordinary) means that any priest or group acting to build a church otherwise would be acting invalidly and seriously misusing church funds, even if this were a parish where the project was agreed and where funds were available.[6]

In building or restoring churches, experts are to be used and the principles of the liturgy followed (c. 1216). New churches are to be dedicated, or at least blessed (c. 1217 § 1), cathedrals and parish churches especially in a solemn rite (c. 1217 § 2), with a title of dedication (c. 1218). Any church is a place where all acts of divine worship may be celebrated, but rights of parishes have to be respected (c. 1219); churches are to be kept clean and have only those ornaments which are in keeping with its sacred character (c. 1220). At hours of sacred functions entry to churches is to be open and free of charge (c. 1221).

---

5. J. M. Huels, 'Sacred Places and Times (cc. 1205–1253)' in Beal *et al.* (eds), *New Commentary*, 1424–48 at 1429.
6. Ibid.

If a church cannot be used properly for divine worship any longer the bishop may allow it to be used for a secular, but not unbecoming purpose, but, having consulted, heard the opinion (*'audito ...'*), of the council of priests, he must have the consent of those with rights relating to the church and must ensure that the care of souls will not be damaged (c. 1222). [7]

Oratories and Private Chapels

An oratory is a place for divine worship, with the ordinary's permission for a specific group of the faithful, such as a religious community, a society of apostolic life, a school, a university, a hospital, but to which other members of the faithful may have access with the relevant superior's permission (c. 1223); it differs from a church, to which the faithful have a right of access for worship (c. 1214).[8] Permission for an oratory is to be given only if it is a place which is suitable (c. 1224 § 1). The bishop's authority is needed for it to be converted to secular use (c. 1224 § 2). A school chapel ought never to be used as a classroom or office. A private chapel is a place set aside for divine worship, with the local ordinary's permission, for the convenience of one or more physical persons (c. 1226); bishops can set up their own private chapel, which has the same rights as an oratory (c. 1227). His permission is needed for Mass and other sacred functions to be celebrated in a private chapel (c. 1228). Chapels differ from oratories precisely in that the latter are for a specific group, the former are private (cc. 1219, 1226).[9] Oratories and chapels may be blessed; they must be reserved for divine worship and not be used for domestic purposes (c. 1229).

Shrines

A shrine is a church or other sacred place, approved by the local ordinary, where the faithful come as pilgrims for special devotions (c. 1230); the approval of the episcopal conference is needed for it be a national shrine and of the Apostolic See for it to be an international shrine (c. 1231). These bodies settle its statutes, which decide its purpose, the rights of the rector, ownership and administration of property (c. 1232). Shrines should help to bring the means of salvation to the faithful, especially through the celebration of the Word of God,

---

[7]. J. A. Coriden, *An Introduction to Canon Law*, revised edn, Paulist, New York, Mahwah, 2004, 151.

[8]. F. D'Ostilio, *Prontuario del codice il diritto canonico: tavole sinottiche*, 3rd revised edn, Libreria editrice Vaticana, 1996, 452.

[9]. Huels, 'Sacred Places', 1435.

the Eucharist and penance, and approved forms of popular devotion (c. 1234). These features stem from the Church's concern to foster pastoral care of the pilgrims who come to such places, their provision and availability being serious responsibilities.[10]

Altars

The altar or table ('*mensa*') on which the Eucharist is to be celebrated is fixed or movable; in a church it should be fixed (c. 1235), ideally of stone or, if the episcopal conference decides, some other suitable material, although the base can be of any material (c. 1236). Fixed altars are to be dedicated; movable ones dedicated or blessed, the ancient practice of inserting the relics of saints into the altar is to be retained (c. 1237). An altar is to be reserved exclusively for divine worship, (the meaning of 'dedication'/'consecration'), excluding any secular usage (c. 1239 § 1). It is entirely wrong ever to allow (marriage) registers to be signed on the altar. No corpse may be buried beneath an altar (c. 1239 § 2).

Cemeteries

Ideally, churches should have their own blessed cemeteries, reserved for the faithful (c. 1240 § 12); otherwise graves are to be blessed in other cemeteries (c. 1240 § 2). Only the Roman Pontiff and cardinals and, in their own churches, bishops (even retired) are to be buried in churches (c. 1242).

b. Sacred Times

Sacred Times in General

Only the supreme authority (Pope or College of Bishops) can establish, transfer or suppress holydays or days of penance for the universal Church (c. 1244 § 1); bishops may do so for their own dioceses, but only on special occasions (c. 1244 § 2). This arose because of the excessive spread of feast days under episcopal direction.[11] A parish priest, in individual cases, under the diocesan bishop's regulations, can dispense from holydays of obligation or days of penance or commute the latter to another pious work. The superior of a pontifical clerical religious institute or society of apostolic life can do this

---

[10.] L. H. Avecedo, 'Santuario' in Salvador *et al.* (eds), *Nuovo dizionario di diritto canonico*, 954–55.

[11.] ID., 'Festa, giorno di' in Salvador *et al.* (eds), *Nuovo dizionario' di diritto canonico*, 502–4 at 503.

for his own subjects or those who live day and night in the house (c. 1245).

Feast Days

The Lord's Day, on which 'the Paschal Mystery is celebrated, is by Apostolic tradition to be observed in the universal Church as the primary holyday of obligation.' (c 1245 § 1). Other holydays of the universal Church to be observed are the Nativity of Our Lord, the Epiphany, the Ascension, Corpus Christi, Mary, Mother of God, the Immaculate Conception, the Assumption, St Joseph, Ss Peter and Paul and All Saints (c. 1246 § 1). The episcopal conference, with prior approval of the Apostolic See, may suppress certain hoydays or transfer them to a Sunday (c. 1246 § 2), as has been done with the Epiphany, the Ascension, and Corpus Christi recently in England and Wales, as well as the decision to transfer holydays falling on Saturday or Monday to the nearest Sunday, with the exception of Christmas Day. On Sundays and other holydays, the faithful are obliged to assist at Mass (c. 1247), at any Catholic rite; on the day or its eve (c. 1248 § 1) and to abstain from work/business which would inhibit the worship of God, inhibit the joy proper to the Lord's Day or inhibit due relaxation of body and mind (c. 1247). Where assistance at Mass is impossible because of the lack of priests or for some other grave reason, the faithful are urged to attend a liturgy of the word (according to norms), to pray as families or as groups of families (c. 1248 § 2).

Days of Penance

All the faithful are obliged by divine law to do penance. To make this a communal matter, certain days are prescribed for penance, for prayer, works of piety or charity, self-denial, fulfilling other duties more fully, fasting and abstaining as the canons prescribe (c. 1248). Every Friday and the season of Lent are days and times of penance for the universal Church (c. 1250). Abstinence from meat (or other food determined by the episcopal conference) is to be observed on Fridays, except when a solemnity occurs on a Friday (c. 1251). Abstinence and fasting are to be observed on Ash Wednesday and Good Friday (c. 1251). Abstin-ence is binding on those over fourteen years of age (c. 1252); fasting binds those over eighteen and under sixty (strictly until their fifty-ninth birthday 'until the beginning of their sixtieth year', although others are to be encouraged to under-stand its meaning and to practise it, even if it is not a strict duty for them (c. 1252). Episcopal conferences can determine substitutes or other ways of fasting or doing penance (c. 1253), such as attending

Mass, adoring the Blessed Sacrament, doing a work of charity, on a Friday.

There is also the Eucharistic fast of one hour from all food and drink, other than water and medicine, before receiving Holy Communion (c. 919 § 1), which does not apply to those who are elderly or sick (c. 919 § 3), nor to a priest who says two or three Masses on the same day, before the second and third Mass (c. 919 § 2).

3. Conclusion

This brief treatment of other acts of worship and of sacred places and times completes the analysis of Book IV of the Code, largely on the sacraments. It is the second longest book of the Code, after Book II on the People of God. In the last three chapters, we shall consider very diverse topics, the temporal goods of the church, penal law and procedural law. The latter (Book VII) is also a long book, but its detail is necessary mostly for experts and our treatment of it will be somewhat selective.

Chapter 16

The Temporal Goods of the Church
(Book V of the Code)

1. Introduction

Temporal goods are goods of this world, goods of this time (*'tempus'*) or age, as distinct from spiritual goods, such as grace, salvation and the like. We may think that the Church ought to have nothing to do with temporal possessions, money, land, buildings and so on. Such an over-simplification might not take adequate account of the practical implications of the Church's mission, especially in terms of recognition and proper protection for its legitimate work. It is worth looking back at the New Testament itself, to assess what, if any, are the proper interests of the Church in temporal goods.

2. Scripture and Church Involvement with Temporal Goods

The following gives a brief summary of some relevant indications which may be derived from the New Testament:

a. The Missionary Work of the Church (2 Cor. 8:1–5; 9:1–9)

St Paul's second letter to the Corinthians may appear to lack the theological depth of the letters to the Romans and Galatians and the directly pastoral solicitude of his first letter to the Corinthians. This is partly because its central part asks for generous, financial means for his preaching the Gospel elsewhere. In these sections of the letter, however, St Paul's practical preoccupation is inextricably bound up with what is the Church's very *raison d'être*, to preach the Gospel to all the nations of the world (cf. Mt. 28:19). His evident desire to involve all Christians in that missionary endeavour explains his delight that the Macedonians, though poor, wish to be part of that work (2 Cor. 8:1–5). Yet he asks the Corinthians to give not just themselves, but of their resources (2 Cor. 8:2–4; 9:1–9), not from their necessities, but from their surplus, to meet the need of other churches (2 Cor. 8:11–15), to do so freely and generously, with an understanding of and participation in the Church's mission and of the communion between the churches (2 Cor. 8:1–15; 11:8–10).

b. Support for the Clergy (2 Thess. 3:7–9; 2 Cor. 11:7–11)

While pleading for funds for missionary work, Paul not only states his duty to preach the Gospel, but asserts his right as an Apostle to remuneration from the Church for this work, a right he chooses to forego (2 Thess. 3:7–9; 2 Cor. 11:7–9). This expresses the responsibility to sustain the Church and its pastors in its proper purpose of spreading the Gospel.

c. Facilitating works of Charity (Acts 2:42–7; 4:32–5)

The Acts of the Apostles provides an evident expression of the Church's responsibilities to those in need (a form of 'preferential option for the poor') within an early expression of community living. Also evident is the sense of duty which the Church and its members have to do this in an effective way (Acts 2:44–5; 4:34–5).

d. Temporal Goods and Worship

These above texts show why the temporal goods of the Church are important for the work of the Church, which is of a specifically spiritual character. One feature of that work which does not emerge so clearly is the need and right to own temporal goods for the purpose of facilitating the worship of God. The texts from Acts both refer to meeting in one another's houses and the 'breaking of bread' is an allusion to the Eucharist, celebrated in the 'churches' of people's houses, both a protection in times of persecution and a means of preserving the sacred mysteries from misunderstanding and abuse from Jews and non-believers.

e. The Need for Accountability and the Prevention of Abuses

New Testament indications on temporal goods are few, but significant, valuable not only for what they imply as positively useful or necessary, but also for an awareness of potential problems and abuses:

Accountability and the Problem of Fraud (Acts 5:1–11)

The organization of collections to sustain the missionary work of the Church would lead to large sums of money coming into the hands of the Church. From the start Paul was alert to the possibility of abuse and/or of the impression of malpractice. Such a large fund needed to be handled properly, not only to do the right thing in God's sight, but to be accountable also in the sight of men. To avoid scandal and allegations of injustice, Paul had the assistance of Titus (2 Cor. 8:19–22). This is an early example of the Church striving to be transparent, open and accountable in its use of gifts and resources donated by the faithful; spending money on the purpose for which it was given.

The case of Ananias and Sapphira is an early example of the fraudulent use of goods destined for the Church. They had agreed to sell land and to give the proceeds to the Church, but Sapphira held back some of the money with the connivance of her husband. What may have been theirs to do with as they wished had become property to which the Church had a right, through their gift.

The Crime of Simony (Acts 8:14–24)

Simon Magus (or the magician) wished to emulate the Apostles' work of transmitting grace through what would become known as the sacrament of Holy Orders. His sin was to try to obtain this by bribery. One of the most serious crimes, 'trafficking' in God's grace or sacraments, has its roots here (called 'simony' after him).

Thus, we see from the New Testament some of the key justifications for the Church's owning and/or using temporal or worldly goods, but note also the potential and actual pitfalls for the Church in undertaking such a role.

3. Historical Perspectives on Temporal Goods

One reason why temporal goods in the Church are so sensitive a matter stems from difficulties over their possession and use which have arisen in history. One interpretation had been that the Church needed both goods and a real political role and influence to be able to provide security for its spiritual work. In fact, Italian unification and the loss of the Papal States have proven to be a source of strength rather than of weakness for the Church in the conduct of her mission. The much more restricted role and aspirations of the Vatican City State do not imply a major political role so much as the minimal foundations for the Church's mission, including a properly moral influence in the world. Nevertheless, caution remains necessary, as allegations of incompetence and worse made in the 1980s about the role of the Institute for Religious Works (Vatican Bank) remind us.

Apart from temporal goods being associated with an expressly political role of the Church, in the Dark and Middle Ages of providing ecclesiastical (church) offices and trying to ensure the proper upkeep of the cleric appointed by granting him land or the right to revenues from his 'living' (the 'benefice' connected to the 'office', the *benefi-cium* to the *officium*) often gave rise to the suspicion that the benefice was more important than the office, that what a priest could gain from an appointment was what concerned him above all. The fact that the Church possessed large amounts of land as a result of this and of endowments of monasteries, and the like, gave rise to great hostility, which manifested itself in the anti-clericalism of the last two hundred years.

The remains of the 'benefice system' were to be dealt with, and as far as possible, eliminated or at least radically reformed in a way which would bring out the primacy of the office to be fulfilled as distinct from the benefit derived by the holder.[1] Since the benefice system had been recognized in concordats between the Holy See and certain states, the question of abolition or of radical reform of the system was closely debated when the Code was being revised.[2] In the end, partly because of concordats, it was decided that the system is to be 'regulated' where it still exists, but in a way that the income and even capital from those sources be progressively part of the fund for the support of the clergy in the diocese (c. 1272). In effect, the term 'benefice' remains, but its reality is being changed. The reforms required by the Code are to be under the care of the episcopal conference, since coordination is needed between individual dioceses and any state where the system involves civil authorities, but to be approved by the Apostolic See. Especially significant is the fact that the income is not really regarded any longer as belonging to the individual who holds an office because of the transfer to the fund for support for the clergy.[3] Thus, the reforms are tending towards eventual abolition and the office becoming more important than the benefice.

[1.] Second Vatican Council, Decree on the Life and Ministry of Priests, *Presbyterorum ordinis*, n. 20.

[2.] V. De Paolis, 'Beneficio' in C. C. Salvador, V. De Paolis and G. Ghirlanda (eds), *Nuovo dizionario di diritto canonico*, San Paolo, Cinisello, 1993, 91–5 at 93–4.

[3.] Ibid., 93–5.

4. The Second Vatican Council and Temporal Goods

Although not much space is devoted to this question, the Council did furnish some principles on the subject, especially in its text on the life of priests. Quite starkly it states the most fundamental of all principles in this area: 'Priests, whose "portion and inheritance" (Num. 18:20) is the Lord ought to use temporal goods only for those purposes to which the teaching of Christ and direction of the Church allow them to be used.' 'Ecclesiastical property', managed according to its nature and church laws, with the help, if possible, of skilled laymen, is to be applied 'always to those purposes for the achievement of which the Church is allowed to own temporal goods'. These purposes are based in the Christological and ecclesiological perspectives we have seen and were stated to be: the organization of divine worship, decent support for clergy and works of the apostolate and of charity, especially to the neediest.[4]

Beyond this statement of principle, it is specified that priests are to have a 'decent and fitting livelihood', to be properly remunerated, by the faithful, if from no other source, a 'real obligation ... arising from the fact that it is for the benefit of the faithful that priests are working'. This underlines the obligation priests have to work, which most do. There is to be 'due provision ... for decent support for ... all who hold or have held any office in the Church' (which could, it seems, cover lay persons too to some extent, where they may hold office, and which would include support for the retired or sick priests, those who 'have held' office). Priests' remuneration should be such as to allow them to pay those who aid them, to give something to the needy and to have a proper holiday each year. 'It is however to the office that sacred ministers fulfil that the greatest importance should be attached.' As noted, the system of benefices is to be 'abandoned or else reformed' such that the 'benefit' is seen to be of secondary importance. In future an office 'should be understood as any office conferred in a permanent fashion to be exercised for a spiritual purpose' (c. 145 § 1).[5] In the Code 'office' was not defined as 'permanent', but as 'stable', to avoid suggesting that holders might not be transferred.

Beyond the key principles and provisions outlined above, everything to do with temporal goods of the Church needs to be grounded in a profound attention to justice as a persevering disposition and

---

4. *Presbyterorum ordinis*, n. 17.
5. Ibid., n. 20.

practice or virtue, which requires that it proceed from a deep personal integrity on the part of all involved.

5. The Preliminary Canons on Temporal Goods

The key canon, c. 1254, is to be considered in the light of the foregoing remarks (Table 16).

The Church's assertion of its 'inherent right' over temporal goods, 'independent of any secular power' (c. 1254 § 1) brings to mind the '*ius publicum ecclesiasticum*', but it is true that an inherent or innate right is not an acquired right, granted by anyone else. It asserts the right to use what is needed for the mission of the Church, implicit in the mission itself, a right which could be said to be divine, but whose specifications would often be human. That right is asserted in relation to acquiring, retaining and administering, and alienating temporal goods, these being the titles of the chapters into which Book V is divided. These 'proper objectives', of course, are the spiritual purposes rooted in the New Testament and of which the Council had spoken; they are principally for divine worship, the fitting support for the clergy (not just priests) and for other ministers (not other office holders), for the apostolate and for charity (c. 1254 § 2). The Code's list of such purposes is not exhaustive, but indicative.

The preliminary canons specify those entities involved with temporal goods in the Church and those to which the norms of Book V apply: the universal Church, the Apostolic See, particular churches, all other public juridical persons and (all other) private juridical persons 'alone' may acquire, administer and/or alienate the Church's temporal goods (c. 1255). They include moral persons (the universal Church and the Apostolic See – c. 113 § 1), as well as public juridical persons such as dioceses (particular churches) and others (parishes, institutes of consecrated life) and even private juridical persons (such as the SVP Legion of Mary). Since only these groups are capable ('*capacia*') of discharging juridical acts in regard to temporal goods, others, such as private members of the faithful, including priests in their own right, are not capable of such acts (cf. c. 10). Thus, any attempt by such individuals to act in that way would be invalid and could have serious financial and other consequences for the individual concerned. Even those able to act in this way are to do so only 'in accordance with the law' (c. 1255).

Although all of the above may acquire such temporal goods for the purposes specified, only the moral persons of the Apostolic See and the universal Church and public juridical persons possess these goods, administer and alienate them as ecclesiastical goods or goods

Table 16

The Temporal Goods of the Church

Canon 1254 §1

'The Catholic Church has the *inherent* right,
    independent of any secular power,
        – to *acquire*
        – *retain*
        – *administer* and
        – *alienate*
           temporal goods
               in pursuit of its *proper objectives*.'

Canon 1254 § 2

'These proper objectives are *principally*:
    – the regulation of divine worship
    – the provision of *fitting support* for
        – the *clergy*
        – and *other ministers*
    – carrying out *works* of
        – the *apostolate*
        – and of *charity*, especially for the *needy*.'

Canon 1291

'The *permission* of the *authority competent by law* is required for
    the *valid* alienation of goods which
        by *lawful assignment* belong to the
           stable patrimony of a *public juridical person*
        whenever their value exceeds the sum determined by law.'

of the Church as such (c. 1257 § 1). It is these bodies that the canons of Book V concern, even the term 'Church' in this Book being restricted to these groups, unless otherwise expressly stated (c. 1258). In an application of subsidiarity, norms governing the temporal goods of private juridical persons are not those of Book V, but their own statutes (c. 1257 § 2).[6] This decision was taken after much debate; the distinction in this Code between public and private juridical persons (c. 116) had led some to think that the latter too should be regulated directly by the canons of the Code. However, public juridical persons are established by church authority, for a specific purpose of the common good of the Church, and they act in the name of the Church, whereas private juridical persons lack at least one of these three criteria (c. 116 § 1). In respect of those temporal goods of the Church which are ecclesiastical, the issue at stake was who would be responsible for the acts undertaken in acquiring, administering and alienating them. The limitation in c. 1257, then, is also a way of restricting liability for such acts, so that the Church as such is responsible for these acts only as to moral and public juridical persons; private juridical persons, operating under their own statutes, are responsible for such acts as pertain to their own temporal goods.[7] Religious institutes of consecrated life are public juridical persons, with the capacities listed in cc. 1255ff., but the constitutions of such institutes can restrict or remove that capacity; often restrictions apply to the capacities of individual houses of an institute, leaving some elements or all of those capacities at provincial or other higher level (c. 634).[8] This indicates who is responsible for debts, upkeep, interest, and so on. The other point to note is that the Church's innate and inalienable right to acquire, administer and alienate temporal goods for its proper purposes (c 1254 § 1) is actually exercised, and can only be exercised, through the moral persons and public juridical persons, it being precisely in and through them that the Church as such acts.[9]

[6.] J. A. Coriden, *An Introduction to Canon Law,* revised edn, Paulist, New York, Mahwah, NJ, 2004), 175–6.

[7.] V. De Paolis, 'Beni ecclesiastici' in *Nuovo dizionario di diritto canonico,* 99–107 at 99–100.

[8.] Ibid., 102–3.

[9.] Ibid., 102.

6. The Acquisition (and Retention) of Temporal Goods

a. Natural Law and Positive Law

Canon law's relationship to and dependence upon moral theology are brought out by the need for acquisition of temporal goods to accord with natural law and positive law, the latter meaning both canon law and respective civil law (c. 1259). Methods sanctioned by natural law would include sale and purchase, loans, gifts and bequests, but the manner in which these were effected would involve observance of local civil laws on procedures. Natural law would legitimate retention of lost property where the owner could not be traced, again where any conditions of civil law had been observed. There would have to be acquisition in good faith, since any items coming into the possession or use of the Church from dubious sources (such as theft, robbery, deceit, fraud) would be immorally and illegitimately acquired. Any goods obtained in good faith which proved not to have been the donor's to give would have to be returned (restitution) or, if that were not possible, compensation would have to be made, if possible.

To say that temporal goods can be acquired by the Church 'by any just means' ('*omnibus iustis modis*') of natural or positive law (c. 1259) not only excludes immoral methods, but demands attention to the purposes for which such goods may be held.[10] It implies that those with private titles to temporal goods be prepared to forego such rights at times to ensure that they serve the Church's mission. Such had been urged at the Second Vatican Council.[11] This is one reason why sacred goods belonging to public juridical persons may not be alienated to private individuals (c. 1269).

b. Donations from the Faithful

General Parish Offerings/Collections

The giving of funds by the faithful to support the mission of the Church had long been presented as a matter of obligation. Indeed, one of the 'six commandments of the Church' had been that people should support their pastors. In the recent *Catechism of the Catholic Church* this duty has not been classified technically as a precept of the Church (the

---

[10]. J-C. Périsset, *Les biens temporels de l'Église*, Tardy, Paris, 1995, 68–71.

[11]. Second Vatican Council, Pastoral Constitution on the Church in the Modern World, *Gaudium et spes*, nn. 63, 73.

other five are listed as such, but this is added, without that label, to state that they are to support their clergy, according to their ability to do so.[12] The duty to support the clergy and the work of the Church was already stated in the Code (cc. 222, 1260–1262). The duty to give financial support to the Church in response to appeals, according to norms of the episcopal conference (c. 1262), gave a canonical foundation in universal law to custom in England and Wales, not further specified by the bishops.[13]

Diocesan Collections

Normal Taxes (Quotas)

The diocesan bishop may levy normal taxes (or quotas) on parishes and other public juridical persons subject to his authority (not religious institutes or societies of apostolic life other than of diocesan right, nor international bodies erected by the Holy See), for the needs of the diocese, if they are moderate, related to their income, after having consulted, heard the opinions of ('auditis'), both the diocesan finance committee and the council of priests (c. 1263), since the one has competence to advise on finances, the other on its pastoral implications.[14] The consultations are necessary for validity (c. 127 § 1) or there is no obligation to pay the tax. They should verify how real the need of the diocese is, as well as the other factors mentioned and, if it is to be a standard, repeated tax, the consultation should be repeated whenever it is renewed.[15]

Extra-ordinary Taxes (Quotas)

The bishop may raise extra-ordinary, but moderate taxes from all physical and juridical persons (all individual Catholics and juridical persons, including private juridical persons) for a grave necessity, again only after consulting the two bodies mentioned above (c. 1263).

12.John Paul II, *The Catechism of the Catholic Church*, nn. 2042–3.

[13.] Cf. J. M. Agar and L. Navarro (eds), *Legislazione delle conferenze episcopali complementare al C.I.C*, 2nd revised edn, Coletti a San Pietro, Rome, 2009, on c. 1262, 584–5, based on *Briefing*, 19 April 1985, 15, n. 8, 114, following the *recognitio* of 9 February 1985 (note 16 in Agar and Navarre, 585).

[14.] Périsset, *Les biens temporels*, 82–4.

[15.] R. T. Kennedy, 'Book V: The Temporal Goods of the Church (cc. 1254–1310)' in J. P. Beal, J. A. Coriden and T. J. Green (eds), *New Commentary on the Code of Canon Law: An Entirely New and Comprehensive Commentary from Canonists from North America and Europe with a revised English Translation of the Code*, study edn, Paulist, New York, Mahwah, NJ, 2000, 1448–525 at 1463–5.

This cannot be a regular tax or quota, not even to meet regular needs of the diocese.[16]

Collections authorized by the Diocesan Bishop

Apart from any rights of mendicant orders ('begging orders': Franciscans, Dominicans, Augustinians, Carmelites) to beg, no one else has any permission to raise any money for whatever good or religious purpose or cause without the written permission of the bishop (c. 1265 § 1). This gives some responsible control and has the advantage of shielding people from exploitation by unscrupulous persons or groups, who might otherwise make appeals and keep money for themselves. Those making appeals, including mendicant orders, are bound by norms drawn up by the episcopal conference (c. 1265 § 2).

The role of the diocesan bishop and of the episcopal conference here and more generally in respect of money-raising for Church gives some degree of order, to stop people being subjected constantly to demands for money. Collections authorized by the diocesan bishop for other worthy causes may be made (c. 1266), often by special or 'second collections' for the missions, for the Ecclesiastical Education Fund (vocations) and such like. Taxes or dues for the Apostolic See, for such things as the erection of a diocese, the bull of nomination of a bishop, dispensations granted by the Apostolic See, are to be set by the meeting of the province of bishops with the approval of the Apostolic See (cc. 1264 § 1, 1271); this seems to relate to costs of executing those acts at diocesan level, since the Roman Curia has its own taxes for the concession of the rescript concerned.[17] The involvement of the episcopal conference can provide some coordination for congregations making appeals. It is useful, too, given different systems of raising money in different countries affected by differing civil laws.[18] The French Law of Separation of 1905 and the present constitution allow money to be raised only for purposes of cult, while the German state has church taxes (*Kirchensteuer*) for church purposes and in Britain various forms of fundraising and covenant are permitted.

On the other hand, there needs to be great responsibility in sanctioning such collections. When 'planned giving' was introduced into many dioceses of England and Wales, it was said that this would give all a reliable expectation of what was to be given and received and that the number of second collections would be reduced. The number of

---

[16.] Ibid.

[17.] Périsset, *Les biens temporels*, 90–2.

[18.] Ibid., 75.

the latter crept back up to the point where there was a 'rationalization' some years ago to combine a number of them. Whether individually enumerated or called a 'National Catholic Fund', the costs of supporting a vast bureaucracy for the conference and increasingly numerous and very expensive staffs related to diocesan curial bodies are very burdensome and gaps in 'second collections' after rationalization are all too quickly filled with more of the same. While there are some excellent, highly competent people in such bureaucracies, there are others who are not so. In any case, in a country with reduced Mass attendance and an increasingly aged population less able to pay, a serious, radical overhaul is needed to see what is essential and what can be afforded; otherwise, diocesan bankruptcies are likely to increase and people will not be justly treated in the demands made upon them.

Offerings (formerly Stipends, 'Stole Fees')

These are offerings to priests on the occasion of requests for Masses for particular intentions (Mass stipends), when sacraments ('stole fees') or sacramentals are celebrated (such as blessing a house). The meeting of the province's bishops is to set the standard amount for offerings on these occasions (c. 1264 § 2). If a large sum is offered for an unspecified number of Masses, the number of Masses to be said is to be worked out from the rate set, the intentions are to be recorded and the Masses are to be said, or caused to be said, by the priest who accepts them (cc. 1264 § 2, 945–955).[19]

Other Offerings

Offerings, more generally, made to an administrator of a juridical person (parish priest, superior of an institute of consecrated life) are given to the parish or institute, not to the administrator (c. 1267 § 1). Hence, they may not normally be refused, unless it is suspected that they come from an unjust or other immoral source (c. 1267 § 2). They are to be used for the purpose for which they were given (c. 1267 § 3).

c. Sacred Objects and Goods

These goods, owned by private persons, may be acquired by other private persons, but are not to be used for secular purposes, unless they have been 'de-consecrated'; this is to protect against disrespectful or even sacrilegious abuse. Those belonging to a public, ecclesiastical,

---

[19.] D. Mussone, *L'Eucaristia nel codice di diritto canonico: commento ai can. 897–958*, Libreria editrice vaticana, 2002, 168–9, 173.

juridical person may only be acquired by another public, ecclesiastical, juridical person (c. 269). This is to protect against the same sort of abuse, but also to prevent parish or diocesan property or the property of an institute of consecrated life from being 'lost' to them, to prevent administrators such as parish priests from doing away with what they have a duty to protect and preserve. Sacred objects are those which are ordered to worship, dedicated or consecrated by the bishop (c. 1171). Not even when owned by private individuals (physical persons) are they to be put to secular or inappropriate use (c. 1171). These are not all ecclesiastical goods, since they can be owned even by individuals, but their use and alienation are to avoid all abuse (c. 1269).[20]

Prescription

Under Roman law, to avoid a situation where no one knew who owned or had rights to use certain goods, 'prescription' was introduced. It is analogous to lost property becoming the property of the finder if no one claims it, but here specified time limits are involved. For immovable goods (buildings, land) or movable goods (such as a chalice, painting, statue) judged precious by reason of historical or artistic value (cc. 1189, 1292 § 2), those belonging to the Holy See are prescribed after 100 years, those to public juridical persons after thirty years (c. 1270); someone in possession of or exercising rights uninterruptedly over them acquires them after that time, if the original ownership or right is not asserted.[21]

d. Wills and Foundations

Gifts may be made to parishes or to pious foundations (such as shrines) quite apart from any church initiative as with collections. They may be made '*inter vivos*' (between living people or while the donor is still alive) or '*mortis causa*' (on account of death); this could mean upon death or prior to and approaching death, perhaps without a formal will (c. 1299 § 1). Normally, civil law is to be followed (cc. 1299 § 2ff), a case of the 'canonization of civil law' (c. 22). This is because most structures of civil law do not recognize canon law, conditions vary from place to place and the Church cannot establish detailed, uniform practice; hence it gives general norms and requires observation of civil law where necessary. If civil law is ignored, there is a risk of constant litigation and of donors' wishes not being fulfilled because they were

---

[20.] De Paolis, 'Beni ecclesiastici', 100–1.
[21.] Ibid., 101.

not recognized in civil law.[22] Such gifts are to be carefully preserved and protected and the specific wishes of the donors are to be observed. The ordinary is responsible for seeing that these things are properly done.

7. The Administration of Temporal Goods

The key concept in this section of the Code is that of 'stewardship', responsibility for the proper care, repair and use of the temporal goods of the Church. Two extremes are to be avoided: self-indulgence by an administrator, such as a parish priest arranging for fine refurbishment of the presbytery with parish money and, on the other hand, neglect of repair and care, which would lead to deterioration of church resources, with consequent danger to health, greater expense later or actual loss of goods.

a. Responsible Administrators

The Holy Father has overall responsibility and certainly could intervene anywhere in an emergency (c. 1273), recalling that juridical persons own goods 'under the supreme authority of the Roman Pontiff' (c. 1256). Ordinaries, major superiors (c. 1276 § 1), those appointed by law as administrators, such as parish priests, rectors of seminaries (c. 1279 § 2) or those to whom the goods belong (c. 1279 § 1), are responsible for the administration, for good stewardship, of the Church's temporal goods. Ordinaries have this duty with regard to all public juridical persons subject to them (c. 1276 § 1), which, in a diocese, would mean all the parishes, a diocesan seminary, diocesan centres, institutes of diocesan right, and they are to supervise the administration of all ecclesiastical goods according to law (c 1276 § 2). The ordinary is not 'the supreme administrator and dispenser' of ecclesiastical goods as is the Pope for the universal Church (c. 1273), but is the primary person responsible for exercising oversight ('*episkopé*') over their administration. This supervision is exercised through the decrees he issues in regard to temporal goods (c. 48), through precepts directing individuals to comply with laws and decrees (c. 49), approving statutes of public juridical persons (c. 94) and approving the statutes and supervising the administration of public associations of the faithful (c. 319) in his pastoral visitation to parishes and to other bodies, through ensuring that accounts are

---

[22.] Ibid., 104–5.

inspected of public juridical persons for which he is responsible. It is exercised directly by such visitation and inspection of those accounts or indirectly, through others.[23] Other responsible administrators would be parish priests, rectors of seminaries, superiors of institutes of consecrated life and of societies of apostolic life, according to their own particular laws.

b. Administration and Finance Committees

Diocesan Council for Economic Affairs

The bishop is obliged to have a diocesan finance committee, often called in England Trustees, for reasons of civil law, but properly a diocesan finance committee (c. 1277). The bishop is to regulate the financial administration of the diocese and of public juridical persons for whom he is responsible. For 'ordinary acts of administration', which in the light of the financial situation of the diocese, are of major importance he must consult ('audire debet': 'must hear') both this diocesan council for economic affairs and the college of consultors, the former about the financial situation of the diocese, the latter given the importance to the diocese of such a decision at that time. The term 'must hear', implies a strict obligation of consultation with these bodies; should he not consult both bodies, his subsequent act would be invalid (c. 127 § 1). For acts of extra-ordinary administration he needs the consent of both of those bodies, also a matter of validity (c. 127 § 1). What constitutes extra-ordinary administration also varies, but limits are to be set by the bishops' conferences (c. 1277), an upper limit of expenditure for acts of ordinary administration and a further upper limit for those of extra-ordinary administration. The canon remains vague, not fixing limits as does c. 1292 on alienation.[24]

The diocesan council for economic affairs is to be consulted, along with the college of consultors, for the appointment of a diocesan financial administrator (c 494 § 1). His tasks are to administer the goods of the diocese under the authority of the bishop and according to a diocesan plan (c. 494 § 3) and to give an annual account to the council for economic affairs of income and expenditure (c. 494 § 4). The bishop may entrust to him also (c. 1278) the task of supervising the administration of goods by public juridical persons subject to him as bishop (c. 1276 § 1) and of intervening to act as or to appoint an administrator of

---

[23.] Périsset, Les biens temporels, 151.
[24.] Ibid., 153–5.

such entities where none exists (c. 1279 § 2). The position of financial administrator can be given to a lay physical person who is competent in financial matters and a person of integrity. He could not be a vicar episcopal for financial matters, since any position of ordinary presupposes sacred power, but a lay person would be cooperating in the exercise of the ordinary power of the bishop (c. 129 § 2) in the discharge of executive power.[25]

c. Administration of Goods in General

Ecclesiastical goods are administered by the one with direct power of government over a juridical person, although the ordinary is to intervene where there is neglect (c. 1279 § 1) or where there is no administrator provided (c. 1279 § 2). Every juridical person is to have its own finance committee or else is to have at least two counsellors to assist in the administration of its goods (c. 1280). This would include parishes, which is why parish finance committees are compulsory. Administrators act invalidly when they go beyond the limit or manner of ordinary administration, unless they have the written faculty to do so from the bishop (c. 1281 § 1). Thus, a parish priest who goes beyond the limit of expenditure set by the diocese for ordinary administration or who acts beyond what he is allowed to do as parish priest in relation to temporal goods acts invalidly. This could expose him to action by the bishop, even in civil courts, which might have serious personal financial or other consequences. The sale or gift of ecclesiastical goods, the re-ordering of the church, without the requisite authority might be examples of going beyond ordinary administration in terms of the manner of acting.

This is an especially important point, applying to all administrators of ecclesiastical goods. If the act is invalid, then the public juridical person is not responsible for any damage done (c. 1281 § 3), which would leave the administrator personally responsible. Since many acts relating to ecclesiastical goods pertain to civil as well as to canon law, as we have seen, it would not be impossible for those who considered themselves damaged by these actions to have recourse in the Church against the administrator, or even to pursue the administrator through church tribunals or through civil courts for damages. If the act were illicit but valid, the administrator would not be responsible for the damage done as such; he could still be sued for damages by those believing themselves damaged (c. 1281 § 3). Civil law could not

---

[25.] Ibid., 156–9.

normally be used against an administrator, provided he had acted in accordance with the regulations or procedures of the entity he administered (which is how civil law might regard canon law), but anyone acting invalidly or even illicitly could be in difficulty; the Code expressly states that all who are lawfully involved in administering ecclesiastical goods 'are bound to fulfil their duties in the name of the Church, in accordance with law' (c. 1282).

Before taking up office, administrators are to swear an oath before the ordinary or his delegate to perform their office well (often at a ceremony of installation), draw up an inventory of all goods (with values) to be certified, keep a copy and give a copy to the curia, both to be updated (c. 1283). General responsibilities of administrators are to take care of goods for which they are responsible (insurance), ensure ownership is protected also through civil law, follow civil and canon law on donors, and so on, avoiding damage to church interests from not observing civil law, seek goods (such as rents which are due) at the right time and see that proceeds are properly used, pay interest when due and repay capital (on loans), use surplus money, with the ordinary's permission, for the good of the juridical person, keep accurate records of income and expenditure, give an annual account of administration, and keep safely titles to goods, with copies to the curia (c. 1284 § 2). An annual budget is recommended (c. 1284 § 3). They are to give an annual report to the diocese or other superior (c. 1287), make contracts of employment with employees, observing church social teaching and also civil law (c. 1286 § 1), and ensure their employees receive a 'just and honest wage ... sufficient to provide for their needs and those of their dependents' (c. 1286 § 2). Within the limits of ordinary administration, they may make gifts for pious purposes or to charity from movable goods, but not from stable patrimony such as buildings or land (c. 1285). They are bound to give an account to the faithful of what they have given to the Church (c. 1287 § 2). They are not to engage in legal proceedings against others or as defendants without the written permission of the ordinary (c. 1288).

d. Fund for the Support for the Clergy

The intention radically to reform and to phase out benefices meant that the Church had to consider how to provide support for the clergy. Various possibilities exist. The German state tax system means diocesan clergy are in some respects equivalent to employees of the state, with contracts, salaries and social security. In England and Wales, diocesan clergy are supported by the contributions of the faithful, allowed to take a minimal salary from the parish (£66.00 per month at present), but have their housing, utility bills and food paid out of parish funds, as well as social security contributions which give them rights to access the health system and the state pension. All of this is to be declared on personal tax return forms, for which the individual is responsible, as he is for any taxes to be paid. What is less clear is the situation he would be in were he to retire. A diocesan fund for sick and retired clergy would provide some support, but he would no longer have a house in which to live, since he would no longer be in office. Provision of accommodation for retired diocesan clergy has been very erratic, compared to institutes of consecrated life and societies of apostolic life, where some houses have often been converted to make such provision.

Different circumstances in various parts of the world makes universal provision difficult, but the Code lays down an obligatory norm, if nothing else is provided. This is that each diocese is to establish a fund to gather 'offerings and temporal goods' for the support of the clergy, 'unless they are otherwise provided for' (c. 1274 § 1), the fund into which the income from benefices, where they continue, is to be placed (c. 1272). The episcopal conference is to set up another fund to provide 'adequate social security for the clergy' in cases 'where there is as yet no properly organized system of social provision' (c. 1274 § 2). If needed, the bishop is to set up a reserve fund to meet obligations towards others who serve the Church (c. 1274 § 3). Dioceses may combine to make these various provisions (c. 1274 § 4), but in all cases what is done is to be such as to be recognized also in civil law (c. 1274 § 5).

8. Alienation of Temporal Goods

a. The Role of Contracts

The treatment of the temporal goods of the Church provides one of the clearest cases in the Code of the 'canonization of civil law'. This is especially evident over contracts, where the Code enjoins observance of local civil law (c. 1290), which, therefore, becomes canon law in those limited respects. This would be relevant to any sales, leases, loans, bequests, and such like. The Church is rightly anxious that whatever arrangements it makes be secure in civil law, since otherwise its sales or purchases would always be open to dispute and this could easily lead to the loss of what it needs for the pursuit of its proper objectives, on the basis of which its own law permits the acquisition, possession, administration and alienation of temporal goods (c. 1254 § 1).

b. The Key Principle for the Alienation of Goods

The Church needs to ensure proper protection of its temporal goods for the purposes for which it may legitimately hold them. This includes ensuring that administrators do not exceed their powers, improperly sell, or otherwise provoke the loss of what belongs to the juridical person, of which they are the proper representatives. These concerns are at the heart of c. 1291.

The question concerns the valid alienation of property. To sell or give away by bequest or other means the temporal goods of the Church where these are of a value greater than that stipulated, for instance, by diocesan law, the norms of the episcopal conference or a major religious superior, is invalid. It might be difficult to ensure that this would be upheld always in the civil courts of various countries if, otherwise, the transaction were licit in the respective civil law, but the fact that, in canon law, the administrator would be alienating what did not belong to him and what he had no right to alienate, would probably cause the civil courts to enforce canon law here. Anyone considering themselves damaged by such action might seek damages through ecclesiastical tribunals.

The canon refers to goods to which the juridical person has a lawful title, so that this would exclude any possessions obtained in unjust or immoral ways, or obtained in good faith, but actually truly belonging to someone else. The canon applies only to public juridical persons, such as a diocese, parish, institute of consecrated life, seminary, not to private juridical persons. The limit stipulated by law would refer to laws or regulations of the diocese, bishops' conferences, where the amount in question fell between the minimum and maximum limits set by the conference (c. 1292 § 1). Beyond the maximum sum, as well as for any alienation of goods pertaining to a vow or artistically or historically precious, the permission of the Holy See is required (c. 1292 § 2). Between the minimum and maximum sum, the bishop's conference must give permission, whereas below the minimum sum, the general laws and procedures of the Code on alienation apply and no further special permission is needed. In England and Wales the minimum sum was fixed at £100,000.00 and the maximum at £1,000,000.00, linked to the cost of living index and subject to periodic review.[26] The 'stable patrimony' of the public juridical person means

---

26. Cf. Agar and Navarro (eds), *Legislazione delle conferenze episcopali*, on c. 1292 § 2, 585, based on *Briefing*, 19 April 1985, 15, n. 8, 114, following the *recognitio* of 9 February 1985 (note 18 in Agar and Navarre, 585).

that what is at issue is not small items, but enduring possessions, such as a church, school, presbytery, land, capital for a specific purpose. Of course, for the competent authority to give permission, it must itself observe the canonical norms, which, for validity require the consent of the relevant finance committee (in a parish the parish finance committee, in the case of the diocese the diocesan council for economic affairs and also the college of consultors (cc. 1276 § 1, 1277, 1297).

These same conditions apply to any action which would jeopardise the stable patrimony of the juridical person (c. 1295), which means for validity in the same sense as above.

c. Further Norms

Except for items of truly small value, goods may not be alienated to members of the family of administrators, up to the fourth degree of consanguinity in the collateral line (c. 1298; cf. c. 108). This is to protect against forms of nepotism, an abuse of the past, but one not impossible today. For the alienation of goods of any value, proper valuations are to be obtained and, except in special circumstances, alienation is not to be made for sums lower than valuations obtained (cc. 1293–1294). This is to protect the Church, in its public juridical persons, from being manipulated or to prevent administrators irresponsibly, even when well motivated, from damaging the nature or value of the goods and, as a result, perhaps impairing the work of the Church in its proper objectives. Money obtained is to be used for the good of the Church (c. 1294 § 2), not for any private person. Once again this brings us back to the fundamental reason for the Church's possession of temporal goods in the first place.

d. Advice and Specific Regulations

Although there are not specific norms in the Code, often diocesan regulations or those of other competent ecclesiastical authorities and / or civil law require the following. Even if they do not, they are sensible practices.

Administrators are to keep clear records of all income and expenditure, bank statements and 'paying in' records. These are to be entirely distinct from personal accounts, where clear records of income and expenditure, bank statements and 'paying in' records are recommended to be kept. Diocesan clergy are responsible personally for their own tax returns. These are probably best prepared with professional advice, with diocesan guidelines on taxes and benefits being followed carefully. Parish (or other public juridical person) accounts are to be audited annually, according to regulations in many dioceses and according to civil law in many places. It can be advisable for personal accounts to be audited similarly by professionals (the priest is to pay for this audit of his own accounts, not the parish), so that everything is not only properly done, but seen to be properly done. Very careful attention should be paid to diocesan regulations (or those of other juridical persons) as to what may be used or retained by the administrator and by other clergy. For example, a car may belong to the priest personally, but petrol may be charged to the parish only for truly parish expenditure, or it may belong to the parish and be used by the priest personally only if he pays for his own use of petrol. Diocesan regulations (and those of institutes of consecrated life, which will be different) should be checked carefully and should be scrupulously observed, not least since these will have been arranged with civil law requirements also in mind. They will include keeping detailed records of usage and distance. Analogous records and receipts for any travel by public transport on parish business and charged to the parish should be kept carefully. Specific regulations from diocese (or other public juridical person) about procedures and alternatives concerning the retention or otherwise of Mass offerings and offerings in relation to sacraments and sacramentals, should be followed scrupulously. Advice will be available from diocesan finance offices and from bursars of institutes of consecrated life. It should be sought and followed.

e. A Problematic Development

The burgeoning of diocesan bureaucracies and of those of episcopal conferences in recent decades has already been noted. Many of those working in such structures are qualified and competent, but others are not. The vast expansion of these structures involves a massive cost to the Church and where, as in England and Wales, the Church depends upon the offerings of parishioners very directly, the danger of operating like big business is all the more problematic. A major overhaul, with serious reductions, would seem to be called for also on the basis of falling numbers, especially of those most able and willing to support the Church financially. An episcopal conference should not be able to make demands which are then simply underwritten by diocesan bishops and passed on to the parishes.

Another worrying feature of current thinking and practice relates to the confusion between canon law and civil law in regard to the relationship between diocese and parishes. Whereas civil law regards them as all part of the one entity, in canon law each parish is a distinct public juridical person. Although the parish must follow diocesan regulations and laws relating to temporal goods, these can never violate the universal law of the Church or they are invalid and not only need not be followed, but ought not to be followed. On the one hand, parish priests who do not follow diocesan regulations by submitting proper financial returns are in violation of the law and risk compromising the diocese also in civil law. On the other hand, the diocese cannot simply seize or even solicit the funds of parishes; the division of parish goods into two halves following upon certain transactions, half to remain in the parish and half being required or solicited by the diocese, seems to raise very serious difficulties. The reality would seem to be one public juridical person (the parish) alienating goods to another (the diocese), the claim that they actually remain the property of the first (the parish) being something of a fiction in the sense that the diocese and not the parish would be gaining interest on them in the meantime. It might also be asked whether such an operation were not, in fact, a way of imposing a further tax or quota. This would be in violation of the canon forbidding the exaction of ordinary taxes from parishes and other public juridical persons subject to the bishop except where these are moderate (c. 1263), since half the proceedings of a major alienation could hardly be called moderate, or of the same canon forbidding the exaction of extraordinary taxes from physical and juridical persons which can be done only if the tax is moderate, and then 'only in a grave necessity' (c. 1263), in other words not on a permanent or extended basis, not even to meet the normal needs of the diocese. Perhaps, clarification from the Pontifical Council for the Interpretation of Legislative Texts and/or recourse, eventually hierarchical recourse, to the Congregation for Clergy, which deals with temporal goods, may be necessary.

9. Temporal Goods and Pious Foundations

Mention has already been made of pious foundations and of the possibility of people making donations for them.

These donations are to be made with respect for the current civil law and also the money or gifts provided are to be used for the purpose for which they were donated (cc. 1299–1300). Any difficulty arising from physical or moral impossibility would normally be resolved by, and in consultation with, the ordinary, who must be satisfied about their origin, purpose and any relevant conditions (c.

1302). Any pious foundations involving long-term obligations must be approved by the ordinary, who is not to accept them unless he has satisfied himself also about the possibility of fulfilment of their purposes (c. 1304–1307).

There is a distinction between autonomous pious foundations, set up for specific purposes by the proper authority (such as foundation Mass funds, for Masses to be said over a (long) period of time for particular intentions) and non-autonomous pious foundations set up in connection with an existing juridical person it is intended to serve.

Although in principle donations are to be used for the purposes for which they were intended, it could become impossible or highly impracticable for them to be fulfilled as originally planned. In such a case, the ordinary has the main responsibility to amend the arrangements, such as where income from funds for foundation Masses is significantly reduced to the point where there could be serious difficulty about the Mass intentions being fulfilled (c. 1308 § 2, § 3 and § 4) or when reduced income or other non-culpable cause prevents the effective or proper fulfilment of the intention for which a foundation was made (c.1310). Mass intentions are usually 'manual' Masses, where priests are asked to celebrate Masses for particular intentions and offerings are given into his hand ('*manus*'), whereas 'foundation' Masses are multiple Mass requests associated with a fund (autonomous pious foundation).

10. Conclusion

The norms in Book V of the Code may seem technical on the one hand and very brief on the other. Yet, they are crucially important for the effective stewardship of temporal goods, needed by the Church to pursue its proper spiritual objectives (c. 1254). They are necessary to protect the People of God, to serve their needs in the Church. They guard against injustices, small and very grave, and warn against any negligence.

These days there are many more regulations at diocesan level. Where such laws are followed and where people adhere to procedures, especially diocesan procedures or those of a religious or other institute of consecrated life, the likelihood of serious malpractice is much reduced. It remains true that a combination of a real commitment to the virtue of justice and a genuine personal integrity are the real moral prerequisites for the proper and effective observance of these canonical norms. Without that, a serious misunderstanding of the role of temporal goods can arise, which can be a matter of scandal for the Church. These virtues need to be fostered in all who are called to be administrators of temporal goods in the Church for the sake of her spiritual mission and proper objectives.

Chapter 17

Penal Law: Sanctions in the Church

(Book VI of the Code)

1. The Reason for Penal Law in the Church

Although it may appear at first sight that the Church should be able to function without any penal law (laws providing for penalties or punishments for crimes), a little reflection will show that this is not possible, nor would it be right. The Church is both holy and yet is always to be made holy ('*simul sancta et sanctificanda*'),[1] in the sense that, as its members, we are not (yet) living with the perfect goodness of Christ. This brings us face to face with the reality of sin. However, the Church's law cannot treat all matters of sin, not least because it cannot have access to purely internal sins of the mind. Yet, the damage done by what is seriously at odds with the Gospel can be considerable; it can put people off the Church and be an obstacle to their embracing or persevering in the life of faith.[2] The damage done within the Church to people's faith and its practice, to those whose rights are violated, to the communion of the Church in discharging its mission require the protection of law, even penal law, aiming to facilitate conversion and reconciliation.[3] The enormous damage done by priests abusing young people and children demonstrates this. If serious wrong and injustice in the Church itself were ignored, it would not assist, but would impair our capacity to let the voice of Christ be heard. Some acts are so wrong that to leave them unheeded, or without official reaction, provokes real scandal and injustice. This is a key context for the Church's penal law.

[1.] Second Vatican Council, Dogmatic Constitution on the Church, *Lumen gentium*, n. 8.
[2.] ID., Pastoral Constitution on the Church in the Modern World, *Gaudium et spes*, n. 19.
[3.] A. Borras, 'Un droit pénal en panne?: sens et incidence du droit pénal canonique', *Revue de droit canonique*, 56 (2009), 139–61 at 139–44, issue dedicated to 'Le droit penal et l'Église: histoire, philosophie, pastorale, droit comparé'.

The danger of scandal, that grave wrong might be thought legitimate or tolerable, was a concern from the earliest days of the Church. Scripture gives indications of what lies behind Church penal law. Where a disciple, a 'brother', does wrong to another brother, the latter should persuade the former to change and, if necessary, two or three members of the community are to attempt this; if he refuses to alter, the offender is to be 'treated like a pagan or a tax collector', is to be excommunicated (Mt. 18:15–18). Corinthian tolerance of incest led Paul to tell them to 'banish this evil-doer from among you' (1 Cor. 5:1–13). Perhaps with reference to the same offence, once a man has been punished sufficiently, he is to be forgiven, lest he become discouraged and be lost (2 Cor. 2:5–11). These instances show that the purpose of penal law in the Church is to give a person a shock, so that he realizes the error of his ways, changes and is restored to communion. The purpose of sanctions is medicinal, their aim is reconciliation.

The New Testament has examples of serious sins, which are now canonical crimes: simony (Acts 8: 9–24), apostasy (cf. 1 Cor. 6:9; 1 Tim. 1:19–20), heresy (2 Tim. 2:17–18; 1 Jn. 4:2–3), and abuse of office (Acts 5:1–11). The methods and stages of correction in Mt. 18 seem generic, but these procedures are associated with the exercise of church authority (Mt. 18:18).

The early Church used penal action to preserve the integrity of the faith, to protect the communion of the Church, to safeguard its common good, to rectify injustice and to repair the damage of scandal, all within a perspective of mercy and conversion, reflecting the parables (Mt. 18:23–35; Lk. 15:11–32). This medicinal aim of reconciling the offender to Christ and to the Church is the object of church penal law in the service of the 'salvation of souls'.[4]

2. The Nature of Canonical Crimes and of Canonical Penalties

Confusion about what is meant by canonical crimes and penalties is partly explicable because of canonical punishments used in the past and because of the term 'automatic' to refer to some penalties even today. First of all, the Code insists that church penal law applies irrespective of any civil law, based on a right which derives from no

---

4. V. De Paolis, 'Sanzoni penali, rimedi penali e penitenze nell'ordinamento canonico' in D. Cito (ed.), *Processo penale e tutela dei diritti nell'ordinamento canonico*, Giuffré, Milan, 2005, 165–208 at 166–7. Cf. M. Metzger, 'Une Église peut-elle excommunier?', *Revue de droit canonique*, 56 (2009), 7–32 at 16–20, 22–4.

human power but from God. Punishments can only be applied to the faithful (baptized) who have committed a canonical crime (c. 1311). Where a law changes after an offence, the lighter penalty applies (c. 1313 § 1); where a law or a penalty is removed after an offence, the law lapses (c. 1313 § 2). No penalty which has to be imposed ('*ferendae sententiae*') applies until it has been properly imposed (c. 1314). Only those able to legislate may impose penalties. Apart from the universal law itself, other legislators may do so only as follows (cc. 1315 § 1, 1317–1320), imposing penalties within the limits of their authority (c. 1315 § 1), adding penalties for existing crimes where there is grave necessity, or determining penalties which higher law leaves undetermined (c. 1315 § 3) and where diocesan bishops seek to ensure uniformity of penalties in a given area (c. 1316). Dismissal from the clerical state cannot be laid down by particular law, but only by the universal law itself (c. 1317). A legislator may only threaten automatic censures ('*latae sententiae*' punishments) where crimes are malicious or more serious through scandal or where '*ferendae sententiae*' punishments are ineffective (c. 1318). Where a legislator can impose precepts, he may threaten a determined penalty, but not a perpetual expiatory penalty (c. 1319 § 1), but he may only do this after careful consideration and after following the norms of cc. 1317–1319. A local ordinary may apply penalties to religious where they come under his authority (c. 1320).

We recall that a law is established by being promulgated by a legitimate superior for his proper subjects (c. 7) and it is general in that it applies to all subjects in a given area or of a particular group of subjects, whereas a precept is a particular command, lawfully issued, from a legitimate superior to (a) proper individual subject(s), urging observance of a law by requiring that something be done or something not be done (c. 49).

3. The Subjects of Canonical Penalties

The key canon here (c. 1321) states the limits of those to whom canonical penalties can apply. All penal laws are to be interpreted strictly (c. 18).

a. An Analysis of Canon 1321

The reluctance of the Church to have recourse to sanctions appears as the Code emphasizes what cannot be done; 'no-one is to be punished ... unless ...' It reiterates the need for a canonical crime before there can be a canonical penalty, which means that there has to be an infraction of a 'law', specifying a crime, by proper subjects (all the Catholic faithful for universal laws) or of a precept validly imposed upon a proper subject or subjects by the legitimate superior, whose purpose is to urge observance of a law. It has to be an 'external violation' of the law or precept, since no merely internal sin (one not expressed in an external act) can constitute a canonical crime. Thus, it is deemed that a crime against doctrine has not been committed if no one perceives the declaration or other manifestation (c. 1330); not only has the sin to be external, but there would be neither scandal nor unjust damage to faith or morals, if no one knew of it, which is why no crime technically exists in this instance. An exterior act constitutes the 'objective' dimension of crime. An external act, however, in violation of a law or precept carrying with it a canonical penalty, is still not sufficient to give rise to a sanction, since personal imputability must first be established in regard to the violation, as the subjective dimension of the crime.[5] Unlike many civil laws, canonical penal law is very limited. Ignorance of a sanction does not mean there is no crime, but the punishment is attenuated (cc. 1324 § 1, n. 9, 1341).[6]

b. The Question of Personal Imputability

For any person to be guilty of a canonical crime and liable to canonical penalties, it must first be established that he or she has committed a mortal sin in this act; in addition to the grave matter (which there would be), there must have been sufficient knowledge that this was gravely morally wrong and true consent: even under pressure, a person can be responsible for deliberately choosing to do what they know to be morally wrong.[7] This needs to be assessed.

Thus, lack of age for canonical crime, under sixteen years of age (c. 1323 1°), invincible ignorance (2°), grave force or an unforeseeable or irresistible circumstance (3°), grave fear (4°), using moderate force in self-defence (5°), lack of reason (6°) would so reduce or eliminate moral responsibility for the wrong action that the person would not be subject to canonical penalties (c. 1323). The action would not be imputable for one or more of the reasons given. Where an action is not imputable, the canonical penalty does not apply, even if it is a 'latae

---

5. A. Borras, *Les sanctions dans l'Église*, Tardy, Paris, 1990, 15–18ff.
6. De Paolis, 'Sanzioni penali', 175.
7. John Paul II, *The Catechism of the Catholic Church*, nn. 1731–3, 1749, 1858–9; ID., Encyclical letter, *Veritatis splendor*, n. 78.

sententiae' or 'automatic' penalty. There must be 'grave imputability' (c. 1321 § 1) and canon law states where such does not exist (cc. 1322, 1323).[8] However, whereas if there is 'mere' or 'slight' negligence, 'lack of due diligence', the penalty does not apply (c. 1321 § 2), but serious, crass (hence culpable) negligence does not excuse, while malice aggravates matters.[9] With an external violation of a penal law, imputability is presumed, unless the opposite appears to be the case (c. 1321 § 3) from one of the factors just noted (cf. Table 17A).

The Diminution of Penalties

In line with this criterion, those habitually lacking the use of reason are not capable of committing an offence (c. 1322); they would not be capable of judging and deliberately acting in the gravely morally wrong manner stated; the action would not be gravely imputable to them. Here imperfect use of reason, acting through drink or passion, doing what is intrinsically morally wrong through fear or force, a minor over sixteen years of age, not responding moderately in self-defence, reacting to unjust provocation, being unaware that a penalty attached to a crime might reduce imputability without removing it (c. 1324 § 1). One with imperfect use of reason would not be bound by a *'latae sententiae'* punishment (c. 1324 § 3).

These factors, like those in c. 1323, are impediments to voluntariety, which affect either the understanding or the will to the point where responsibility is excluded or diminished, factors traditionally considered in moral theology in assessing personal responsibility for good or ill. Crass or supine ignorance (what ought to have been known or what could only be unknown through gross irresponsibility) does not excuse (c. 1325). Drunkenness or passion do not remove or diminish responsibility where these have been willingly embraced or pursued to facilitate committing the crime (c. 1325).[10] This applies the moral theological principle of *'voluntarium in causa'* ('voluntary in cause'); a person who has deliberately performed an act which was wrong or has negligently performed one which in principle was good, as a result of which or on the basis of which another occurs (here a canonical crime) cannot be excused from the latter on the basis of the former.[11]

[8.] Borras, *Les sanctions*, 17.

[9.] W. H. Woestman, *Ecclesiastical Sanctions and the Penal Process: A Commentary on the Code of Canon Law*, Faculty of Canon Law, St Paul University, Ottawa, 2000, 26–7.

[10.] Ibid., 35.

[11.] Cf., St Thomas Aquinas, *Summa theologiae*, II-II, q. 64, a. 8.

Table 17A

The Nature of Penal Law

Canon 1311

'The Church has its *own inherent right*
    to *constrain with sanctions*
        Christ's faithful
           who *commit offences.*'

Canon 1312 § 1

'The *penal sanctions* of the Church are
    1° *medicinal penalties or censures* – cc. 1331–1333
    2° *expiatory penalties.*' – c. 1336

Canon 1312 § 2

'The law may determine *other expiatory penalties*
    which deprive a member of Christ's *faithful*
        of some *spiritual* or *temporal good*
    and which are *consistent with the Church's supernatural purpose.*'

Canon 1312 § 3

'Use is also made of
    penal remedies
    and *penances;*
  the former are
    primarily *to prevent offences,*
  the latter are
    to *substitute for*
    or to *augment*
        a penalty.'

The Aggravation of Penalties

If certain factors may at times eliminate or reduce imputability for a canonical crime, others may increase or aggravate it. Once a penalty has been declared (this refers to a *'latae sententiae'* penalty in the external forum, since a *'ferendae sententiae'* penalty is imposed and not declared and since a *'latae sententiae'* penalty in the internal forum is not declared), if the person 'obstinately persists' (*'pertinacia in mala voluntate conici potest'*) in the crime, an additional penalty may be added by a judge (c. 1326, § 1, 1°, § 2). Other aggravating factors are where someone abuses a position of dignity or of authority or an office to commit a crime (c. 1326, 2°) or where someone guilty of a crime (*'reus'*) does not take normal care to avoid a crime, to which he knows a penalty has been attached (c. 1327, 3°). Particular laws may add excusing or aggravating circumstances and may determine circumstances in a precept which diminish or aggravate the penalties it contains (c. 1327). Where someone has not carried a crime out to the full, but involuntarily stopped short of this (for reasons beyond his control), he is not to be subjected to a penalty unless the law or precept says otherwise (c. 1328 § 1); the fact that the crime was not completed is the key here. Where acts or omissions of their nature lead to a crime, the offender may be given a penance or penal remedy, unless he has of his own will stopped short of fulfilling the offence once begun; if scandal or serious harm results, he may be subjected to a just penalty, but a lesser one than for the completed crime (c. 1328 § 2).

Accomplices in Canonical Crime

Accomplices in crime are to be punished with the same or lesser *'ferendae sententiae'* penalties (c. 1329 § 1). If *'latae sententiae'* penalties apply to the main offender, they apply also to the accomplices (provided their involvement was necessary for the crime to be committed), if they can be affected by them (only clerics can be suspended). If the same penalty cannot apply, *'ferendae sententiae'* penalties may be imposed (c. 1329 § 2). Accomplices in some crimes, such as simony, would almost necessarily be willing accomplices.[12] This canon seeks equity among those responsible for the same crime.

[12.] Woestman, *Ecclesiastical Sanctions*, 38–9.

4. Types of Penal Sanction

a. Censures

There are four types of penalty, the first two of which are punishments proper (cf. Table 17B). Censures are medicinal penalties, aiming directly and mainly at the reform of the offender (c. 1312 § 1), although the differences are ones of emphasis or of primary focus, since censures and expiatory punishments contain within them all the functions of canonical sanctions, of correcting the offender, repairing scandal and restoring justice (c. 1341).[13] There are three types of censure: excommunication, interdict and suspension. Previously, only excommunication could be a censure; interdict and suspension being expiatory.[14] Aiming at the correction of the individual concerned, a censure is related not just to the crime, but to an attitude of obstinacy or contumaciousness in the individual, to the point where, if this element is lacking, it 'cannot be validly imposed' (c. 1347 § 1). For censures which are imposed for the violation of a law or of a precept ('*ferendae sententiae*'), there has to be at least a prior warning given to the person to avoid or to amend his ways, without which the imposition of the penalty is invalid. Where penalties are 'automatic' or imposed in virtue of the law itself ('*latae sententiae*'), whether publicly declared or not, knowledge of the penalty is presupposed for it actually to apply and, hence, the element of obstinate, contumacious or pertinacious refusal to heed the warning exists there too. It is this obstinate refusal to amend their ways which requires the medicinal penalty of a censure. Such refusal remains an issue after, since this attitude has to end, as one sign of repentance, for a censure to be lifted (c. 1347 § 2, 1358 § 1).[15]

Excommunication

There is often confusion because some people think that excommunication means that a person is excluded from the sacraments, forbidden to be buried in holy ground and is damned for all eternity. This is not the case. A censure is a medicinal penalty, aiming at the reform, conversion and reconciliation of the perpetrator (cf. Mt. 18:15–18; 1 Cor. 5:1–11). An excommunicated person is forbidden to exercise any ministerial role in the Eucharist or other public worship

---

13. Borras, 'Un droit canon en panne?', 147.
14. ID, *Les sanctions*, 61–4.
15. Ibid., 64–6.

Table 17B

Subjects of Penal Sanctions

Canon 1321 § 1

'No-one can be punished by
    a penal *law*
    or (penal) *precept*
        unless it is *gravely imputable* by reason of
            malice
            or *culpability*.'

Canon 1321 § 2

'A person who *deliberately violated*
    a *law*
    or a *precept*
        is *bound by* the *penalty prescribed*
            in that law or precept.
If, however, the violation was *due to* the *omission of due diligence*,
    the person is *not punished*,
        unless the law or precept says otherwise.'

Canon 1321 § 3

'Where there has been *external violation*,
    imputability is *presumed*,
        unless it appears otherwise.'

(c. 1331 § 1, 1°). This would apply particularly to clergy, those formally instituted in the lay ministries of lector and/ or acolyte and those performing temporary duties in an extra-ordinary ministerial role. An excommunicated person is also forbidden to celebrate sacraments or sacramentals, to receive the sacraments (c. 1331 § 1, 2°) or to exercise any ecclesiastical offices, ministries, functions, or acts of governance (c. 1331 § 1, 3°). As distinct from a person not in communion with the Church (c. 205), an excommunicated person remains externally in the Church, but their spiritual growth is compromised by their sin and by the limitations stemming from the penalty.[16]

Censures may be declared ('*latae sententiae*' penalties in the external forum) or imposed (always '*ferendae sententiae*' penalties in the external forum) or neither declared nor imposed (internal forum). If an excommunication is declared or imposed (hence, not if it is neither of these), where someone intends to act against c. 1331 § 1 1°, he is to be removed or the liturgical act is to be suspended, except for a grave reason (c. 1331 § 2 1°). Such a person acts invalidly in respect of acts of governance under c. 1331 § 1, 3° (c. 1331 § 2, 2°), is forbidden to benefit from any dignity already granted (3°), cannot validly assume any dignity, function or office in the Church (4°) and loses the titles to any dignity, office, function or pension in the Church (5°). However, the validity of the sacraments celebrated by an excommunicated priest or bishop is not altered; his celebration of these is completely illicit, but remains valid, including reconciliation outside of the case of danger of death, provided he retains confessional faculties, since excommunication as such does not remove these.[17]

Interdict

An interdict is liable to be misunderstood if it is thought of in terms of its operation in the Middle Ages and, less often, until the last century. Some medieval popes used a local interdict (interdict of place) to bring pressure on rulers to abandon a canonical crime, Innocent III using this most extensively against Philip Augustus of France, King John of England and against the rulers of Leon and of Navarre in the early thirteenth century. An interdict often precluded the celebration of any sacraments for anyone in a given territory or in respect of a group of persons.[18] Now it is a less drastic penalty than excommunication; indeed, the Eastern Code calls it a 'lesser excommunication' (c. 1452),

---

[16.] Woestman, *Ecclesiastical Sanctions*, 42–3.
[17.] Borras, *Les sanctions*, 69–77.
[18.] Ibid., 80–1.

calling the Latin Code's 'excommunication' a 'major excommunication' (c. 1451). Under the Code of 1983 a person under an interdict may not exercise any ministerial part in the Eucharist or other act of public worship, may not celebrate the sacraments or sacramentals and may not receive the sacraments (c. 1332). In other words, an interdict does not necessarily affect offices, governance and functions (c. 1332). However, if the interdict was imposed ('*ferendae sententiae*') or declared ('*latae sententiae*' in the external forum), but not if it is in the internal forum only, and if the offender intends to function ministerially in the Eucharist or in any act of public worship, he is to be removed or the liturgical act suspended unless there is a grave reason not to do these (cc. 1331 § 1, 1°; 1331 § 2, 1°; c. 1332).

Suspension

This 'can only affect clerics' (c. 1333 § 1), although it would have been possible for the Code to have applied it to lay persons holding office.[19] There are various possibilities with suspension and care is needed to grasp what is at stake in a given case. A suspended cleric is forbidden (c. 1333 § 1) to perform all or some acts of order, to be specified (1°). Suspension cannot deprive someone of order itself, but only of its exercise or of some acts of order (c. 1338 § 2), of the performance of all or of some acts of governance (c. 1333 § 1), to be specified (2°), or of the exercise of all or of some rights or functions attaching to an office, to be specified (3°). A law or precept may prescribe that, following a judgment, imposing or declaring a penalty of suspension, the suspended cleric cannot validly perform acts of governance (c. 1333 § 2). However, suspension never affects offices or powers of governance not within the power of the one imposing the penalty (1°), a right of residence a suspended person may have by virtue of an office (2°) or the right to administer goods attaching to an office held by the suspended cleric where the penalty is '*latae sententiae*' (3°). On the other hand, if a suspension carries with it (states) a prohibition against receiving benefits, stipends or pensions, and if these are received, there is a duty of restitution (c. 1333 § 4). A law or precept or a decree imposing suspension, should lay down the extent of the suspensions (c. 1334 § 1). A law, but not a precept, may lay down an undetermined '*latae sententiae*' suspension, which has all the effects of c. 1333 § 1 (c. 1334 § 2). Although suspension does not affect the validity of sacraments celebrated by priests, it can affect the validity of acts of government, where he is suspended from office and, indi-

---

[19.] Ibid., 86.

rectly, it means that he cannot assist validly at weddings, since this is attached to the office of diocesan bishop or parish priest.[20]

We see the key canonical principle of the pastoral care of souls (c. 1752) in operation again, where a censure is suspended to allow a suspended cleric to attend to the spiritual needs of a person in danger of death (c. 1335). A non declared '*latae sententiae*' censure (one operative only in the internal forum) is also suspended where a member of the faithful asks the suspended cleric for the sacraments. This assures that person of their spiritual rights and does not render public the occult censure, thus protecting the good name of the cleric concerned.

Although all canonical punishments imply the three aspects of such punishment, of correcting the offender, of repairing the scandal and of repairing the injustice, the focus of emphasis of censures is on the former, and of expiatory penalties on the latter two. Censures are a peculiarity of canon law, which is concerned not just with expiation, nor only with reform of the criminal in his or her dealings with others as is civil law, but necessarily has to do with salvation. However, beyond the moral theological level of the perception of sin and the need for sacramental reconciliation, the positive specification of what constitutes canonical crimes, without which no penalty can be inflicted, limits sanctions to those same matters. With censures, the failure to avert crime leads to an attempt to pressurize the individual to confront his or her grave wrong through the deprivation of the goods noted, specifically those which would be of assistance to that person's eternal salvation. This is why censures are not applied except as a last resort.[21]

b. Expiatory Penalties

These punishments aim primarily and directly at the reparation of scandal or of the injustice perpetrated, depriving a member of the faithful of a spiritual or temporal good, consistent with the Church's purpose (c. 1312 § 2), whereas censures are essentially concerned with the reform of the offender. They can be very serious; they can be for a limited period or they can be permanent (c. 1336 § 1). They consist of a prohibition of or obligation of residence in a particular territory (c. 1336 § 1, 1°). A prohibition of residence can affect clerics and religious; an order to reside in a particular place can affect secular clerics and

---

20. Ibid., 85–7.
21. De Paolis, 'Sanzioni penali ', 173–5, 179–82.

(within the limits of the constitutions) religious (c. 1337 § 1), but an order imposing residence must have the agreement of the ordinary of the place, unless it is a house of penance intended also for those outside of a diocese (c. 1337 § 2). It can involve deprivation of power, office, function, right, privilege, faculty, favour, title, insignia, even just honorary (c. 1336 § 1, 2°), but only to the extent that they are under the power of the superior imposing the penalty (c. 1338 § 1). There can be a prohibition of the exercise of any of the things mentioned in 2°, entirely or limited to a particular place (c. 1336 § 1, 3°), but only to the extent that they are under the power of the superior imposing the penalty (c. 1338 § 1). Such orders are suspended for the pastoral care of souls, on the same bases as c. 1335 (c. 1338 § 3, re. c. 1336 § 1, 3°). Other possibilities are penal transfer to another office (c. 1336 § 1, 4°) or dismissal from the clerical state (c. 1336 § 1, 5°). The law may establish other expiatory penalties (c. 1336 § 1). However, only the prohibition of the exercise of power, office, function, and so on (c. 1336 § 1, 3°) can be incurred 'automatically', 'latae sententiae' (c. 1336 § 2), so that those removing from the office as such have to be 'ferendae sententiae', which implies a process, preferably judicial.[22] It is important to recall that expiatory penalties do not include deprivation of order itself, but only apply to its exercise or to some acts of order. Nor can they include deprivation of academic degrees (c. 1338 § 2). Even expiatory penalties cannot and do not neglect the reform of the offender. They are intended to bring the individual to face the wrong done and its implications for his or her eternal salvation, provoking a response of sorrow and of repentance, which implies a true readiness to repair the injustice perpetrated and any scandal caused.[23]

With censures and with expiatory penalties, there is more than a sinful action with consequent loss of grace, even with an 'automatic' censure. It is not true that a person excludes themselves from the Church's communion; beyond their relationship with God and with the Church by sin and reconciliation, there is a further reality of a crime and a penalty which either the legitimate superior declares or imposes or the law itself imposes, involving deprivation of some good or goods of the Church for the purposes stated.[24]

[22.] Borras, *Les sanctions*, 93–5.
[23.] De Paolis, 'Sanzioni penali', 179–82.
[24.] Ibid., 191–3.

c. Penal Remedies

These are not punishments, in the strictest sense, but aim at the prevention of crimes (c. 1312 § 3) or at the correction of an injustice. Where a person is in proximate danger of committing an offence or there are sufficient grounds for serious suspicion that an offence has been committed, he or she may be given a warning (c. 1339 § 1); where behaviour has caused scandal or grave harm to public order, the one responsible is to be corrected, according to his situation and to the circumstances (c. 1339 § 2). In both instances, there must be proof of the warning or correction, kept in a secret archive (c. 1339 § 3). Penal remedies are less drastic than censures and expiatory penalties. They entail a retreat, a pilgrimage, a fast, some work of service. These may be used where a person has done serious wrong, but where lack of full proof or imputability, hence, where found 'not guilty' or where a penalty has not been imposed (c. 1348).[25]

Penal remedies arose in relation to the sacrament of penance in the past and were often public penances for serious offences, which distinguished them from more usual sacramental penances and which associated them more with penal law. They are not canonical punishments, since often no crime has been proven to have been committed (c. 1348). They seek either to prevent a crime, where admission or evidence indicates that such risks being committed (such as the risk of apostasy, heresy or schism from associating with anti-Catholic groups, encouraging schism or disobedience to the Pope or bishop or heresy through homilies). Where a crime has been committed and there has been a preliminary investigation, but there is a lack of proof or of moral certainty; the aim then is to warn the person of the penalty if proof emerges and/or to prevent a recurrence of such a crime.[26] Penal remedies require that a warning be given, 'after a preliminary investigation' (c. 1339 § 1) to verify the facts and, more seriously, can involve issuing of a 'correction' to the person concerned, which presupposes that a warning has been given.[27] This correction is a formal and official one from a legitimate superior, in relation to a pattern of behaviour which risks provoking scandal, even if not a crime. Failure to heed such correction is a factor indicating pertinacious or contumacious obstinacy (c. 1341).[28]

---

[25] Cf. Woestman, *Ecclesiastical Sanctions*, 63.
[26] G. P. Montini, 'I rimedi penali e le penitenze: un'alternativa alle pene' in Z. Suchecki (ed.), *Il processo penale canonico*, Lateran University Press, Rome, 2003, 75–101 at 77–85.
[27] De Paolis, 'Sanzioni penali', 193–9.
[28] Montini, 'I rimedi penali', 88–90.

d. Penances

These are substitutes for or increases to punishments as such (c. 1312, § 3). A penance which is imposed in the external forum is a work of religion, piety or charity (c. 1340 § 1). It cannot be a public penance if the offence is occult or not publicly known (c. 1340 § 2). An ordinary may add a penance to a penal remedy of a warning or a correction (c. 1340 § 3). Such penances are distinct from sacramental penances insofar as they are in the external forum and in that they are specifically designed to repair scandal and/or injustice. They differ from expiatory penalties in that they have to be accepted by the individual.[29] This does not mean that they are pleased to accept them, but that they do in fact accept them. Penances can exist on their own, as when someone was prevented from committing a crime only by factors outside of his control impeding him (c. 1328) or when he was absolved from a crime on the basis of a technicality, but clearly committed a grave offence imputable to him (c. 1348). Penances can substitute for a punishment, often when there are extenuating circumstances or they can be added to punishments where there are aggravating factors, such as where a 'latae sententiae' penalty is declared.[30]

5. The Application of Penalties

Having seen which penalties may be applied by church law for canonical crimes, we turn to when and how this is to be done. The key canon here refers to the declaration or imposition of penalties, which means that this has to do with the external forum, relating to declared 'latae sententiae' penalties or to 'ferendae sententiae' penalties being imposed. This also explains why it is the ordinary who has to initiate a process. The Church's law favours a judicial process (it is mentioned first in c. 1342), since it protects better the rights of the accused (c. 221). The ordinary must first be clear that less drastic approaches (fraternal correction, reproof, pastoral means – c. 1341) have been exhausted or that the issues are so grave that scandal, justice and reform of the offender cannot properly be assured by such approaches; initiating a process is a last resort. In listing these three features, the Code recalls the three key functions of punishment (restoring justice or retribution, deterrence and reform).

The ordinary must first satisfy himself, directly or through a judge

---

[29] De Paolis, 'Sanzioni penali', 199.
[30] Montini, 'I rimedi penali', 92–5.

Table 17C

The Application of Penalties

Canon 1341

'The *Ordinary* is *to start*
    a *judicial*
    or *administrative procedure*
        for the *imposition*
        or *declaration of penalties*
only when he perceives that
    neither by *fraternal correction* or *reproof*
    nor by any *methods of pastoral care*
        can
                the *scandal be* sufficiently *repaired*
                    justice restored
                    and the *offender reformed*.'

who conducts an investigation, that there is evidence that a crime has been committed and that a particular person appears to be responsible for it, that there is a case to be answered (c. 1717). If he judges that there is, he must decide upon a judicial process (trial) or an administrative process (cc. 1341, 1718 § 1). Some have thought an administrative process less problematic or more convenient, but the law very clearly favours a judicial process and there must be good reasons for not following it, which must be stated if an administrative process is adopted (cc. 1342, 1718 § 3). A judicial process gives the accused a fairer hearing, greater opportunities to defend his rights and justice is more clearly seen to be done, whatever the outcome. This is why canon law favours the judicial process and why the relevant Congregation might overturn a guilty verdict or any penalty if an ordinary has effectively denied or failed to observe such rights by opting without grave reason for an administrative process. This principle has been qualified by the norms on clerical abuse of minors and by very recent norms approved by the Pope granting to the Congregation for the Clergy 'special faculties', which include using an administrative process in cases where current law has proven inadequate to repair scandal, restore justice or reform the offender.[31] The specific cases will be noted later.

Since censures are medicinal penalties, aimed at the reform of the offender, even if a judicial or an administrative process establishes that a canonical crime (delict) has been committed, penalties cannot be imposed (*'ferendae sententiae'*) until the person has been warned and/or given an opportunity to make amends ('purged contempt') and has contemptuously (*'a contumacia'*) refused to do so (c. 1347 § 1). Someone who has repented and has made or has promised to make amends is considered to have purged contempt (c. 1347 § 2).

Pastoral care and the principle of the revision of the Code that automatic penalties in penal law be reduced led to greater attention being given to individual circumstances in applying penalties, to an 'individualization of penalties'.[32] This cannot be pressed too far, given

---

[31.] Congregation for the Clergy, Letter to the Bishops of the Catholic Church on special faculties granted to the Congregation, 18 April 2009, Prot. N. 2009/ 0556, n. 5: 'However, one must acknowledge that situations of grave lack of discipline on the part of some clergy have occurred in which the attempts to solve the problems by the pastoral and canonical means foreseen in the Code of Canon Law are shown to be insufficient or unsuitable to repair scandal, to restore justice or to reform the offender.' The faculties were granted on 30 January 2009.

[32.] O. Échappé, 'Le droit pénal' in P. Valdrini *et al.* (ed.), *Droit canonique*, 2nd edn, Dalloz, Paris, 1999, 374–96 at 388, n. 626.

the need for justice and equity (parity of treatment for similar crimes), but where the law allows the judge to apply or not to apply a penalty, he may modify it or impose a penance instead (c. 1343), where the law or precept uses 'obligatory words', he may defer the penalty if grave harm might otherwise be caused (c. 1344 § 1) or impose a lesser penalty or impose a penance as a substitute for the penalty, if the offender has repented, repaired the scandal or has been or is foreseen to be likely to be sufficiently punished by the civil law (c. 1344 § 2), or he may suspend the penalty for a first offender, who is repentant and where the scandal has been repaired, but only on condition that this is done so that a further offence brings both penalties to apply (c. 1344 § 3). A judge can refrain from imposing penalties where the offender's voluntariety was clearly not complete through drunkenness, grave fear or force, and the like. (c. 1345). Where for accumulated offences, cumulative penalties seem excessive, he may modify them equitably (c. 1346), not arbitrarily, but based on the real situation.[33]

This attenuation of punishments, combined with the conditions already noted for the verification that a canonical crime has been committed, may give the impression that the Church is not serious about such matters, that any excuse may suffice to reduce or avoid sanctions actually applying. Such an impression can be justified when those responsible for applying the Church's laws do not know what they are doing or are negligent and this itself is a real cause of scandal at times. Properly understood, the canons we have summarized do not entail any evasion of this sort nor any diminution of justice, but the risk in practice of penal law not being effective and so of resultant scandal is real.

Penal law in the Church is concerned with the reform of the offender, the avoidance or repair of scandal and the reparation of justice. The first stems inevitably from the Gospel. Reconciliation, as a requirement for all disciples and on the Church, is an indispensable characteristic of the love preached and manifested by Jesus, which goes much deeper than the rehabilitation of criminals in modern penal systems. Since a canonical crime of its nature implies that a grave sin has been committed, this requires from the sinner the repentance necessary for forgiveness and from the Church attention to that person's salvation through sacramental reconciliation.[34] Reservation of the remission of canonical penalties for some crimes to the bishop or to the Holy

---

[33.] Woestman, *Ecclesiastical Sanctions*, 71–2.
[34.] G. Lo Castro,'Responsabilità e pena: premesse antropologiche per un discorso personalistico nel diritto della Chiesa' in D. Cito (ed.), *Processo penale*, 3–31 at 29–31.

See is not a matter of obstructing this process, but of ensuring that it occurs under conditions which show there has been real repentance, with a firm intention not to repeat the crime. Nevertheless, this alone is not sufficient, since real sorrow for the crime implies a readiness to repair both the injustice perpetrated and the scandal given. Expiatory penalties specifically concern these two dimensions of canonical crimes.[35] A real tension can exist between the purposes of reconciliation and of reparation inherent in canonical penal law, but the one is not to be suppressed in favour of the other. Where a superior may reduce, defer or substitute a punishment in the ways outlined, he is not to do so unless there has not only been repentance, but where this damage has already truly been repaired or is certainly being repaired by the offender. The damage done by some crimes, both through the specific injustice committed and further by the scandal given (leading some to imagine that such behavior is licit which could lead others to sin and/or that such conduct is tolerable or compatible with the demands of Christian living) may be at times so grave that, even if there is personal repentance and some reparation, the injustice and scandal cannot be repaired adequately without serious punishment being undertaken, declared or imposed.[36] There has been real neglect by some superiors, at times wanting the benefits of subsidiarity without its difficulties, to the point of leaving it to the Pope or to the Holy See to attend to matters they themselves ought to have addressed. This has itself caused scandal and has aggravated the injustice. The opposite reaction of rushing into action risks injustices of another kind.[37]

When, in fact, a penalty applies, it applies everywhere, unless otherwise expressly stated (c. 1351), but the prohibition of receiving sacraments or sacramentals is suspended as long as danger of death persists (c. 1352 § 1) and a 'latae sententiae' penalty (not declared) is suspended if the offender is in a place where the offence is not known and if its revelation would risk causing grave scandal or harm to his good name (c. 1352 § 2). A penalty is suspended during an appeal against a guilty judgment from a judicial process or during recourse against an administrative decree (c. 1353). When penalties are imposed on a cleric (other than dismissal from the clerical state), his 'worthy support' is to be provided for (c. 1350 § 1) and, even if he has been

---

[35.] J. Llobell, 'Contemperamento tra gli interessi lesi e i diritti dell'imputato: il diritto all'equo processo' in D. Cito, *Processo penale*, 63–143 at 76–83.

[36.] Ibid., 80–1.

[37.] Ibid., 90–3.

dismissed from the clerical state but is in real need, the ordinary is to 'provide for him in the best possible way' (c. 1350 § 2).

One way in which a bishop can try to address the problem of a cleric's serious misbehavior or the danger of his committing a canonical crime is by imposing upon him a penal precept, commanding him to do something or forbidding him to do something specific (c. 1319 § 1), but this can only be done where there is real necessity (c. 1317) and the facts of the matter have been 'very carefully considered' (c. 1319 § 2). The penal precept needs to state the canonical penalty which may be incurred should the crime be committed or its commission be proven, as laid down by the law, or must specify the penalty where it is indeterminate. However, no penal precept can threaten permanent expiatory penalties or the dismissal from the clerical state (cc. 1319 § 1, 1317). Apart from not being able to threaten such a penalty, precisely the penalty envisaged by the special faculties of the Congregation for the Clergy, it also means that the right of defence by the one suspected or eventually imputed is not assured.[38]

6. The Cessation of Penalties

Expiatory penalties with a time limit attached cease on expiry of that time limit or on the death of the person punished.[39] Other penalties, meaning censures or medicinal penalties, cease upon their being remitted. They may not be remitted unless the person has repented and has repaired or promised to repair injustice and/or scandal (cc. 1347 § 2, 1358 § 1), but, once he has, they must be remitted as a matter of justice (c. 1358 § 1). Remission is normally in the external forum by decree, but can be in the internal sacramental forum (confession) by way of exception (c. 1357). Censures are absolved; expiatory penalties are usually remitted by a decree (external forum); their remission where they do not cease by death or by the expiry of a time limit, is not a question of justice, but of an act of favour.[40]

For declared censures and for expiatory penalties, the ordinary who declared or imposed the penalty can remit it, as can the ordinary of the place where the offender is domiciled, although only after consulting the ordinary who imposed it (c. 1355 § 1). Other penalties can be remitted by those who can impose them or dispense from them or by

---

[38.] Borras, 'Un droit pénal en panne?', 157–60.
[39.] Échappé, 'Le droit pénal', 388–9, nn. 626–7.
[40.] Ibid., 388–9, nn. 627–9.

those delegated by these (c. 1354 § 1–2), provided they are not reserved to the Apostolic See (c. 1354 § 3).

In the internal sacramental forum (confession), those with faculties for confession may absolve from sins reserved neither to the diocesan bishop nor to the Apostolic See. For absolution from censures which have been neither declared nor imposed, absolution and an appropriate penance may be given where there is repentance and injustice and/or scandal have been repaired, if it is difficult for the penitent to remain in a state of grave sin until there has been recourse (c. 1357 § 1). If the penalty is lifted or remitted on this basis, it must be on condition that the penitent or the confessor has recourse to the appropriate person (canon penitentiary of the diocese if there is an excommunication or interdict whose absolution is reserved to the bishop, even himself to transmit to the Apostolic Penitentiary in Rome or to do so through the canon penitentiary, cases reserved to the Apostolic See) within a month under pain of the penalty applying once more (c. 1357 § 2). A similar procedure is to be followed by those who absolve from such penalties or who remit expiatory penalties in danger of death (c. 976). If recourse is had through the confessor, it is to be anonymous (the sin and the name of the penitent are not to be identified together, since this would be a violation of the seal of confession). Here the priest making the recourse to the canon penitentiary of the diocese or to the Apostolic Penitentiary in Rome needs to write along the lines that 'on ... date penitent X' (saying whether male or female) 'confessed the sin of ... The following were the circumstances' (to be given clearly, including the number of offences, the degree of responsibility). He/she has manifested true sorrow and has attempted (or intends) to repair the damage done by .... He/she has incurred the penalty of ... *latae sententiae*. Absolution from the sin and remission of the penalty have been given under c. 1357. A rescript is now requested from the Apostolic Penitentiary, confirming the same.' The penitent should be told to return to the confessional in a month's time and to check who the confessor is (to ensure it is the same one) and to make themselves known, to receive this verification.

In this context, it is important to remember the implications of the fact that someone who has confessional faculties from his proper superior has them throughout the world unless specifically impeded in particular dioceses. In dioceses in England and Wales, the faculty to absolve from the *latae sententiae* excommunication where it has been incurred for the crime of abortion (c. 1398) has usually been given to all priests who have received confessional faculties from their bishop. However, those priests do not have that faculty if they hear confession elsewhere in the world; the censure is reserved to the local diocesan bishop, to whom or to whose canon penitentiary recourse would need to be had. The following *latae sententiae* censures are reserved to the Holy See, for which recourse to the Apostolic Penitentiary is necessary: desecration of the Blessed Sacrament (c. 1367), physical violence against the Roman Pontiff (c. 1370 §), the attempt to absolve one's accomplice in a sin against the sixth commandment (cc. 977, 1378 § 1), episcopal ordination without a pontifical mandate (c. 1382), and the direct violation of the seal of confession (c. 1388 § 1).

7. Particular Crimes and Particular Penalties

The simplification of penal law in the 1983 Code, sought in the principles for the revision of the earlier Code, appears from the removal of certain penalties (denying ecclesiastical burial is no longer a canonical penalty) and reducing the number of particular crimes with penalties from 101 canons to 36.[41]

a. Offences against Religion and against the Unity of the Church

Apostasy, heresy and schism

Apostasy is the total abandonment of the faith, heresy a denial of one or more dogmas of the faith and schism is the violation of the communion of the Church. These crimes carry a '*latae sententiae*' excommunication (c. 1364 § 1); for a cleric there follows loss of office by virtue of the law itself (c. 194 § 1, n. 2), with the possibility of prohibition, compulsory residence, loss of power, function, faculties, and the like. (c. 1336 § 1–3), with further penalties not excluding loss of the clerical state if contempt or scandal warrants it (c. 1364 § 2).

One guilty of participation in prohibited religious rites is to suffer a just penalty (c. 1365). This canon includes the prohibition of a Catholic priest from 'concelebrating' with a minister of a non-Catholic church or ecclesial community not in full communion with the Catholic Church (c. 908). This more specific crime has since been stated to be one of the more serious crimes against the sanctity of the sacraments and is reserved to the Apostolic See (see below).

Parents and those taking their place having their children baptized in a non-Catholic church and/or bringing them up as non-Catholics are subject to a just penalty (c. 1366).

---

41. Ibid., 390, n. 630.

Throwing away the sacred species or taking/keeping them for a sacrilegious purpose involves a *'latae sententiae'* excommunication, reserved to the Apostolic See; for a cleric other penalties may be added, not excluding dismissal from the clerical state (c. 1367).

b. Offences against Authorities and the Freedom of the Church

One laying violent hands on the person of the Holy Father suffers a *'latae sententiae'* excommunication, reserved to the Apostolic See; for a cleric other penalties may be added, not excluding dismissal from the clerical state (c. 1370 § 1). Laying violent hands on a bishop entails a *'latae sententiae'* interdict and, if a cleric, also a *'latae sententiae'* suspension (c. 1370 § 2).

Laying violent hands on a cleric or religious out of contempt for the faith, the Church, ecclesiastical authority or ministry entails a just penalty (c. 1370 § 3).

One who teaches a doctrine condemned by the Roman Pontiff or Ecumenical Council or one who 'obstinately rejects' (*'pertinaciter respuit'*) the teaching in c. 752 and, warned, does not retract (c. 1371, 1°) or one who refuses to obey a command/prohibition of the Apostolic See or ordinary or superior and who, being warned, persists in disobedience suffers a just penalty (c. 1371, 2°).

One who appeals against a decision of the Roman Pontiff to an Ecumenical Council or to the College of Bishops suffers an unspecified censure (c. 1372). This reflects the rejection of Conciliarism (the idea that a General Council is above the Pope or that he is accountable to such a body).

c. Offences of Usurpation of Office or Abuse of Office

Attempting to absolve an accomplice in a sin against the sixth commandment is a gross abuse of the office of a priest and of the role of a confessor; it involves a *'latae sententiae'* excommunication, reserved to the Apostolic See (cc. 977, 1378 § 1). One who is not a validly ordained priest, attempting to celebrate the Eucharist suffers a *'latae sententiae'* interdict or, if a cleric, *'latae sententiae'* suspension (c. 1378 § 2, 1°); other penalties, not excluding excommunication, may be added, according to the gravity of the situation (c. 1378 § 3). Anyone other than a priest attempting to absolve or hear a sacramental confession suffers a *'latae sententiae'* interdict or, if a cleric, *'latae sententiae'* suspension (c. 1378 § 2, 2°) to which other penalties, not excluding excommunication, may be added, according to the gravity of the situation (c. 1378 § 3). Celebration or reception of a sacrament with simony involves interdict or suspension (c. 1380); other penalties, not excluding excommunication, may be added, according to the gravity of the situation (c. 1378 § 3). Usurping or unlawfully retaining an ecclesiastical office, for instance refusing to leave after being lawfully removed or transferred, entails a just penalty (c. 1381).[42] Consecrating a bishop or being consecrated a bishop, without a pontifical mandate incurs a *latae sententiae* excommunication, reserved to the Apostolic See (c. 1382). A bishop ordaining someone without dimissorial letters is prohibited from conferring orders for one year; the recipient is automatically suspended from the order received (c. 1383). Anyone exercising the office of a priest or another sacred ministry in any other way from those just mentioned suffers a just penalty (c. 1384).

Trafficking in Mass offerings involves a censure or another just penalty (c. 1385). Someone using gifts or promises to cause another who exercises an ecclesiastical office to do something or to omit something (bribery or attempted bribery) is punished by a just penalty, as is the one accepting such gifts or promises (c. 1386). Solicitation in the confessional (in confession or under the pretext of confession), inciting someone to commit a sin against the sixth commandment (c. 1387) entails suspension, deprivation, prohibition, in more serious cases dismissal from the clerical state (c. 1387). Direct violation of the seal of confession (revealing the identity of penitent and the nature of the sin) involves *latae sententiae* excommunication, reserved to the Apostolic See, while the indirect violation of the seal entails a just penalty (c. 1388 § 1). Interpreters and anyone else bound by the seal, who directly violates it, are subject to a just penalty (c. 1388 § 2).

d. Offences of Falsehood

False denunciation of a confessor over 'solicitation' incurs a *latae sententiae* interdict and, if a cleric, also suspension (c. 1390). Falsifying an ecclesiastical document or using a false document or falsified ecclesiastical documents involves a just penalty (c. 1391).

e. Offences against Special Obligations

Clerics or religious who engage in trade (c. 1392) are to be punished according to the gravity of the crime. A person violating obligations

---

[42.] Cf. A. Calabrese, *Diritto penale canonico*, Libreria editrice Vaticana, 2006, 293–4.

imposed by a penalty can be punished by a just penalty (c. 1393). A cleric who attempts marriage suffers a *'latae sententiae'* suspension, with further penalties if he persists, not excluding dismissal from the clerical state (c. 1394 § 1). A religious (not a cleric) in perpetual vows, who attempts marriage (even civil) suffers a *'latae sententiae'* interdict (c. 1394 § 2).

A cleric living in concubinage or in some other external violation of the sixth commandment suffers suspension, with further penalties if he persists, not excluding dismissal from the clerical state (c. 1395 § 1). A cleric engaging in other violations of the sixth commandment, if committing the crime with one or more of these aggravating factors – with force, with threats, in public or with a minor under sixteen years of age suffers just penalties, not excluding dismissal from the clerical state, if the case warrants it (c. 1395 § 2). This canon has been amended, so that the crime involving a minor is now operative, as an exception in canonical penal law, up to eighteen years of age. Furthermore, it is one of the more serious crimes, reserved to the Apostolic See under the exclusive competence of the Congregation for the Doctrine of the Faith, operating as a tribunal (see below). The grave violation of duty of residence attaching to an office entails a just penalty, not excluding, if it persists after a warning, deprivation of office (c. 1396).

f. Offences against Human Life and Liberty

Murder or abduction, imprisonment, mutilation, grave wounding with force or by fraud incur deprivations and prohibitions (residence, office, functions, faculties, or their exercise) according to the gravity of the offence (c. 1397). The murder of the Pope incurs a *'latae sententiae'* excommunication, reserved to the Apostolic See (cc. 1397, 1370 § 1). If the murder is of a bishop, it entails a *'latae sententiae'* interdict (cc. 1397, 1370 § 2); if the murderer is a cleric there is also a *'latae sententiae'* suspension (c 1370 § 2). If the murder is of a cleric or religious there is a just penalty (cc. 1397, 1370 § 3).

Procured abortion: this means where 'a person actually procures an abortion' (not an attempted abortion which did not take place), but it includes those having an abortion, conducting an abortion, arranging an abortion, pressurizing someone into an abortion where the abortion was carried through; it entails a *'latae sententiae'* excommunication (c. 1398).

It must be remembered that imputability must be established (all the conditions for mortal sin must be met and prior knowledge of the existence of a canonical crime) before there is any 'automatic' penalty, though there is a presumption of imputability unless there are clear factors against it (c. 1321 § 3).

g. A General Norm (c. 1399)

This canon is new in the 1983 Code and is controversial because it does not give a specific crime to which a canonical penalty is attached; it serves rather as a 'catch all', a canon which would allow the Church's authorities to proceed against someone, where a violation of divine law or of canon law were of 'special gravity' and where there was a real need to 'repair or prevent scandal'. A just penalty applies (c. 1399). It has been criticized for going against the principle of 'no punishment without a crime',[43] but it would allow the Church to act in an instance of grave scandal not covered by any other canon specifying particular crimes.

In fact, this canon is involved in one of the three special faculties recently granted to the Congregation for the Clergy, as will be seen below.

8. 'More Serious Crimes' ('graviora delicta')

In recent years the scandal of the sexual abuse of minors by clerics has drawn a great deal of attention to this very serious canonical crime. It is listed as a crime in c. 1395 § 2; the age limit, the competent tribunal and the procedures have been amended by the *motu proprio* on protecting the sanctity of the sacraments.[44] It is to these 'more serious crimes' that we now turn.

The Congregation for the Doctrine of the Faith had responsibility for centuries for surveillance over faith and morals when it operated as the Roman Inquisition and later as the Holy Office. In the norms for the operation of the Roman Curia (not in the Code itself, but in the Apostolic Constitution, 'Pastor bonus' of 1988), its overriding competence was stated to extend to all matters touching faith and morals 'in any way'.[45] Its competence in these areas as a tribunal of the Church

---

[43] J. A. Coriden, *An Introduction to Canon Law*, revised edn, St Paul, New York, Mahwah, NJ, 2004, 189.

[44] John Paul II, Apostolic letter, *motu proprio*, 'Sacramentorum sanctitatis tutela', 30 April 2001; cf. B. E. Ferme, ' "Graviora delicta": the Apostolic letter M.P.; "Sacramentorum sanctitatis tutela" ' in Z. Suchecki (ed.), *Il processo penale canonico*, 365–82 at 370, n. 7.

[45] John Paul II, Apostolic Constitution, *Pastor bonus*, 28 June 1988, art. 48: 'Proprium Congregationis pro doctrina fidei munus est doctrinam de fide et moribus in univer- so catholico orbe promovere atque tutari; proinde ipsi competunt ea, quae hanc ma-

was further specified: 'It judges crimes against faith and the more serious crimes against morals whether in the celebration of the sacraments or as they come to be notified to it and, according to the case, it proceeds to declare or to inflict canonical sanctions according to the norms of the law, whether common or proper.' (art. 52).[46] Thus, more serious crimes ('*graviora delicta*'), established or clarified in '*Sacramentorum sanctitatis tutela*', are:

a. Crimes against the Eucharist

Desecration of the Blessed Sacrament and taking or keeping the sacred species with sacrilegious intent (c. 1367): excommunication and, if a cleric, further penalties (not excluding dismissal from the clerical state). The attempted celebration or simulation of the Eucharist (c 1378 § 2): for those not priests, '*latae sententiae*' interdict; for clerics '*latae sententiae*' suspension. The Code did not reserve these crimes to the Apostolic See, but the norms of '*Sacramentorum sanctitatis tutela*' seem to do so.[47] Concelebration of the Eucharist 'with ministers of ecclesial communities which do not have the Apostolic succession and which do not recognize the sacramental dignity of priestly ordination' is also such a crime. Although c. 908 prohibits any concelebration with any minister of a church or ecclesial community not in full communion with the Catholic Church and although c. 1365 renders this a canonical crime, '*Sacramentorum sanctitatis tutela*' creates a new norm. The older canons remain, but now in addition (only) those who concelebrate with ministers from communities which do not have Apostolic succession and do not recognize the specific sacramental status of the ordained priesthood commit this graver crime, now reserved to the Apostolic See with a '*latae sententiae*' excommunication and suspension.[48] Consecrating one element of the matter of the Eucharist without the other in the Eucharistic celebration or consecrating either

---

teriam quoquo modo attingunt': ('The proper function of the Congregation for the Doctrine of the Faith is to foster and to protect doctrine on faith and morals throughout the Catholic world; therefore, those things belong to its competence which touch this matter in any way').

[46.] Ibid., art 52: 'Delicta contra fidem necnon graviora delicta tum contra mores tum in sacramentorum celebratione commissa, quae ipsi delata fuerint, cognoscit atque, ubi opus fuerit, ad canonicas sanctiones declarandas aut irrogandas ad normam iuris sive commune sive proprii, procedit'.

[47.] Ferme, 'Graviora delicta', 375, n. 3.1.2.

[48.] Ibid., 375–6, n. 3.1.3. The information on this crime comes from Ferme's article, since the detailed norms relating to '*Sacramentorum sanctitatis tutela*' were occult; he has based his analysis upon a letter which gives a summary of them: ibid., 370, n. 7.

element outside the Eucharistic celebration 'with sacrilegious intent', acts already seriously prohibited in the Code (c. 927), are now a crime reserved to the Apostolic See; punishment involves the question of 'sacrilegious intent' in doing what is already gravely wrong 'even in extreme circumstances' (c. 927).[49]

b. Crimes against the Sacrament of Penance

Absolution of an accomplice in a sin against the sixth commandment (cc. 1387 § 1, 977): '*latae sententiae*' excommunication, reserved to the Apostolic See. Soliciting someone in the confessional or under the pretext of confession into a sin against the sixth commandment (c. 1387) is a crime too. The norms in '*Sacramentorum sanctitatis tutela*' do not include all the categories of solicitation noted in c. 1378, but the 'more serious crimes' of this *motu proprio* concern only those where the solicitation in the act of confession, on the occasion of confession or under the pretext of confession, is for the penitent to engage in those acts with that confessor himself. Although c. 1387 gives a variety of canonical punishments for solicitation in general, it says that 'in more serious cases he is to be dismissed from the clerical state' (c. 1387). It could be, though it is not stated as such, that the implication of '*Sacramentorum sanctitatis tutela*' on this point is that such a priest would be dismissed from the clerical state.[50] Direct violation of the seal of confession (c. 1388) entails '*latae sententiae*' excommunication, reserved to the Apostolic See.

c. Crime with a Minor

The crime of sexual abuse against a minor had been listed as the '*crimen pessimum*' ('worst crime'; 'very bad crime') in special norms of 1962 and is condemned by c. 1395 § 2 of the 1983 Code. Recent confusion about whether it was reserved to the Congregation for the Doctrine of the Faith, is now cleared up by the norms of 2001 ('*Sacramentorum sanctitatis tutela*'), which reserves this to the exclusive competence of that Congregation, meaning that the Roman Rota cannot be an appeal tribunal in such a case and that a different 'court' within the Congregation for the Doctrine of the Faith would have to hear appeals. The other very significant change introduced by these norms is that the age of a minor for the purposes of this crime is raised from sixteen to eighteen years of age.

[49.] Ibid., 376–7, n. 3.1.4.
[50.] Ibid., 378–9, n. 3.2.2.

A cleric found guilty of such a crime could be punished by dismissal from the clerical state or by dismissal from office.[51] One advantage of reserving this crime to the Apostolic See would be the possibility of greater consistency of treatment in processes and of the guilty, but whether or not it will mean delays in processes remains to be seen.

There are various matters relating to the rights of the accused, which will be considered in the next chapter. Here it might seem to some that the intricacies of the Church's penal law may seem to militate against effective action against a perpetrator or sexual abuse against a minor. One reading of penal law might suggest that imputability is difficult to establish, while varieties of penalty even under c. 1395 § 2 might seem to afford a possibility of leniency to a perpetrator found guilty of the crime. Those in religious institutes of consecrated life, found guilty of murder or forcefully or fraudulently kidnapping, abducting, mutilating or gravely wounding another (c. 1397) or of procured abortion (c. 1398) or of sexual abuse with force or fear or threats or with a minor (c. 1395 § 2) 'must be dismissed' (c. 695 § 1), unless, in regard to c. 1395 § 2, this is judged not absolutely necessary and the scandal can be repaired in some other way. Furthermore, we should recall that imputability is presumed where there is an external perpetration of such a crime. The divergence in penalties might allow for a proper distinction to be made between someone found guilty of inappropriate touching and someone found guilty of much more intrusive, sexually abusive behaviour. Despite initial impressions, perhaps, canon law does have the capacity to deal effectively with perpetrators of sexual crimes against minors and it is the intention of the norms of 2001, that this should be done.[52]

9. Special Faculties of the Congregation for the Clergy, 2009

The special faculties which the Congregation for the Clergy sought and received from Pope Benedict XVI on 30 January 2009, according to the letter from the Congregation to all the bishops of the Catholic Church (signed by the Prefect, Cardinal Hummes, and by the Secretary, Bishop Mauro Piacenza) on 18 April 2009, concern the following:

I. Clerics who have attempted civil marriage and, admonished, persist in an irregular and scandalous life (c. 1394 § 1) and of clerics guilty of grave sins against the 6th commandment (c. 1395 § 1 and 2).

[51.] Ibid., 380, n. 3.3.

[52.] A. McGrath, 'Is canon 1395 a cause of disrepute for the Church?', *Irish Theological Quarterly*, 68 (2003), 51–60.

II. Clerics who violate c. 1399, the canon which is the generic penal canon concerning any external violation of divine or canon law in a specially grave manner, and where there is 'need or urgency to avoid an objective scandal'.

III. Clerics who have freely abandoned the ministry for ... more than five consecutive years', persisting 'in such freely chosen and illicit absence from their ministry'.[53]

In the first case, the special faculty involves the Congregation treating the matter and presenting it to the Holy Father for his approval *in forma specifica* and for his decision to impose on the cleric the canonical sanction of dismissal from the clerical state, releasing him from the obligations of that state and from the obligations of celibacy.[54] Although the Code deals with these crimes, it foresees a 'just penalty not excluding dismissal from the clerical state', the latter requiring a judicial trial. In fact, suspension and irregularities have often failed to make any impact; hence, the need for this special faculty for there to be an administrative process, instructed by the bishop according to the norms of the Code and with the right of defence assured. Where this shows that discipline has been gravely breached, that there is real scandal and that the situation is likely to continue, dismissal from the clerical sate can be sought and, if granted, the dispensation from its obligations and from that of celibacy would be granted.[55]

The second instance concerns a canon which, in itself, foresees only the imposition of a 'just penalty' (c. 1399), but the special faculty obtained here grants derogation from cc. 1317, 1319, 1342 § 2 and 1349 'with respect to the application of perpetual penalties'. In other words, those canons do not permit threatening, imposing or declaring perpetual penalties, but this special faculty now permits that, although it states that this is to be applied to deacons 'only for grave reasons' and to priests 'only for the gravest of reasons', again where the Holy Father gives approval *in forma specifica* and decides that such a penalty is to be applied.[56] Where a bishop asked the Congregation to intervene or where it intervened directly itself, again an administrative process, with the right of defence of the cleric assured, would be followed and again, if granted by the Pope, this would be with release from the obligations of the clerical sate and also of those of celibacy.[57]

[53.] Congregation for the Clergy, Letter to bishops ... on special faculties, 18 April 2009, stating the faculties granted by the Pope on 30 January 2009, I, II and III.

[54.] Special faculties granted by Benedict XVI, ibid., I.

[55.] Congregation for the Clergy, Letter concerning special faculties, n. 6.

[56.] Special faculties granted by Benedict XVI, II.

[57.] Congregation for the Clergy, Letter concerning special faculties, n. 7.

The third case of clerics who have abandoned the ministry and persist in such freely chosen absence for over five consecutive years envisages their dismissal from the clerical state, with the removal of all obligations deriving from that state and from the obligations of celibacy.[58] The fact that clergy who have abandoned their ministry have often not sought dispensation from the obligations of the clerical state and also from celibacy, where they have committed no canonical crime and could not be dismissed, leaves the Church with a serious problem of objective counter-witness often in the midst of people aware of the situation. Indeed, part of the reason for the request of the special faculty in this case is to avoid people being led into a common error about the meaning of the sacraments (Holy Orders). The emphasis on the cleric having left the ministry voluntarily and remaining away from it freely is to distinguish this from cases where a cleric was removed from an office as unsuitable. In this instance 'The Dicastery ... may declare the dismissal from the clerical state, with dispensation from the obligations consequent to ordination, including that of celibacy, for the cleric involved.'[59]

If a bishop chooses to act over a cleric in regard to problems over celibacy or abandonment of ministry, he may do so according to existing law and the cleric's right of recourse remains. If a bishop seeks the Congregation's involvement under these faculties, he must follow the procedures of the Code and of these norms, trying to resolve the matter first without penalties and assuring the right of defence. Any issue of clerical abuse of minors, even as the basis for abandonment of ministry, must be referred to the Congregation for the Doctrine of the Faith. The Congregation for Clergy has the right, under these norms, to intervene directly. In other words, it would seem that this would be where a bishop was unable or unwilling to tackle a problem causing scandal of the kinds noted.

The procedures envisaged in the case of the cleric abandoning the clerical state are that there be a request from the ordinary of incardination, an investigation which involved the promoter of justice which establishes with moral certainty the irreversibility of the abandonment of the ministry from the cleric, witnesses or public knowledge, the ordinary giving his *votum* (opinion), the promoter his observations, and all the Acts being sent to the Holy See, which may seek further information before deciding whether to grant the request through a rescript.[60]

[58.] Special faculties granted by Benedict XVI, III.

[59.] Congregation for the Clergy, Letter concerning special faculties, n. 8.

[60.] Ibid., art. 1–8.

Both these special faculties and, in some instances, the 2001 norms on sexual abuse of minors entail a change in penal law to the extent that the principle that dismissal from the clerical state can only follow a judicial process has been altered. The right of defence is not so easily nor clearly upheld in an administrative process.[61] Where the special faculties lead to dismissal from the clerical state by the Holy Father *in forma specifica*, there is no right of recourse, since no act of the Pope can ever be impugned (cc. 331, 1405 § 2, 1629 § 1, 1732). These limitations on the principle and practice envisaged in the Code seem regrettable, but grave matters cannot continue not to be ignored or left unattended. It is hard to understand why church laws should be promulgated which are occult; the law needs to be known, understood and applied. Knowing that new procedures exist and not being able to find them is frustrating. Transparency, even on sensitive matters, is better than secrecy which could give some the impression that there is something to hide. Whether through inability or through reluctance, bishops have some real responsibility for the situation in which the Holy See has judged it necessary to alter the law and to proceed in these ways. Apparently, the Holy See is examining some aspects of penal law and of its procedures, to see what might need to be updated or, at least, clarified to make it more understandable and more effective in the face of realities which the Church has to confront.

10. Conclusion

Having considered the nature of canonical crime and canonical punishment, we have attended to the complexities of assessing responsibility and of the applications of sanctions. The recent norms on graver crimes from the Apostolic See have given further clarification to these matters. The particular difficulty of combatting injustice and scandal effectively and of its impact on clearly established canonical rights is an area of real debate and tension. Conversely, the many mitigating features of the Code's penal law, in the light of the very optimistic views of the Second Vatican Council and of the Commission for the Revision of the Code, may cause some to wonder whether canonical crime can be effectively combatted and punished within its present framework.

[61.] Cf. K. Martens, Les délits les plus graves réservés à la Congrégation pour la doctrine de la foi', *Revue de droit canonique*, 56 (2009), 201–21 at 218–20.

Chapter 18

Procedural Law

(Book VII of the Code)

1. The Importance of Procedural Law

Although procedures in any legal system are complex, some clear and fair procedures are indispensable for justice to be done. Otherwise, laws might look good on paper, but fail to achieve their purpose of serving the common good. There is always a need to avoid mere legalism, but the Church's mission would not be assisted, but impeded, by an absence of such procedures. In particular, those who seek to vindicate their rights in the Church need equitable access to effective justice. Procedural laws need adaptation to changing needs and improvement in the light of experience, but their role in the service of justice in the Church is vital. Canon law serves the Church as the communion of Christ's faithful in the pursuit of the mission entrusted to it by him. That noble vocation needs practical ways of being promoted and implemented.

It is not intended here to give a detailed analysis of all the procedures and processes in Book VII. The aim will be to give an understanding of the key principles and practices involved. Qualified, trained canonists should be consulted before embarking upon some procedure or before advising others to do so.

Book VII deals with trials in general (part I), with the contentious (disputed) trial (part II), and then with special processes (part III), which largely treats matrimonial processes, but also the process for nullity of ordination, how to avoid trials, and the penal process (part IV), ending with certain administrative procedures concerning parish priests (part V).

2. Trials in General (Part I)

a. Some General Remarks

Judgments or trials leading to judgments in the Church are 'to promote and defend the rights of physical or juridical persons or to make judgments of juridical facts' (c. 1400 § 1,1°) or, as regards crimes, to judge the punishment which is to be imposed or declared (c. 1400 § 1, 2°). Disputes about the exercise of administrative power are a matter exclusively for the superior or for an administrative tribunal (c. 1400 § 2). Here we see the fundamental distinction between the judicial process and the administrative process, further reflected in the fact that only a challenge to a judicial decision can involve an appeal, challenge to an administrative act involving recourse to the superior or to an administrative tribunal, not an appeal, since there is no judgment against which to appeal.

The Church asserts 'its own and exclusive right to judge' cases involving spiritual matters or matters touching upon the spiritual, the violation of ecclesiastical laws, whatever contains an element of sin, and to impose its own judgments and penalties (c. 1401), independently of any secular power. It seeks to avoid conflicts, especially between Christians (1 Cor. 6:7); hence, procedures to see whether the parties can be reconciled or why, only if they cannot be reconciled, a case may proceed. The norms of Book VII apply to all church tribunals, except for special laws for pontifical tribunals (c. 1402) and for the causes of saints (c. 1403).

b. The Competent Forum

A trial cannot take place simply where people wish; a tribunal (Church court) has to be competent to deal with and to judge a particular case; otherwise, the whole action could be challenged and could possibly result in the action and decisions being declared null and void. The 'first see', the Apostolic See, 'is judged by no one (c. 1404) and, if any process is begun against the Pope or against the Apostolic See, 'the acts and decisions are invalid' (c. 1406 § 1). Cases which can be brought to trial (c. 1401) are exclusively to be judged by the Roman Pontiff if they involve, Heads of State, cardinals, legates or, in penal cases, bishops or any other case which the Pope has reserved to himself (c. 1405 § 1). A judge cannot review any act or instrument which the Pope has confirmed 'specifically' ('*in forma specifica*'), as distinct from what he has confirmed or underwritten in a generic way ('*in forma ordinaria*'), without his prior mandate (c. 1405 § 2), nor is there any appeal or recourse against a judgment or decision of the Roman Pontiff (cc. 1629, 1732). Only the Roman Rota may judge contentious (disputed) cases involving bishops, abbots of monastic congregations or moderators of institutes of pontifical right or institutes with no superior but the Pope (c. 1405 § 3). These restrictions of competence protect against Conciliarism and reflect papal primacy and the Pope's pre-eminent ordinary power (cc. 331, 333 § 1). For all cases in this canon, 'the non-competence of all other tribunals is absolute' (c. 1406 § 2).

Apart from these cases, the competence of the tribunal is based on the place of domicile of the Respondent, to facilitate his or her right of defence (cc. 1407 § 3, 1607 § 2), the domicile, quasi-domicile or residence of the parties (cc. 1408–09, 1673 § 2–3), the place where most of the evidence lies concerning a dispute (cc. 1410–11, 1673 § 4 l), the place where the crime was committed in a penal case (c. 1412). Where two tribunals are equally competent, the first one to have acted has competence and, in cases of dispute, the matter is to be settled by the appeal tribunal of both or, if they have different appeal tribunals, by the Apostolic Signatura (cc. 1415–1416). The logic of these norms is evidently to facilitate a fair trial in the most suitable place.

c. Grades or Instances of Tribunals

A case heard at first instance may go on appeal to the respective tribunal of second instance. In a matrimonial trial (a dispute about the fact of validity or nullity of the marriage), for there to be a judgment (sentence) which is valid, there has to be a 'concordant sentence' of two tribunals, a judgment on the matter on which two tribunals are agreed (cc. 1682, 1684 § 1). If the first instance and second instance tribunals give different judgments (discordant sentences) on the same issue, the case goes to third instance (often the Roman Rota); that sentence, since it will normally agree with one of the two preceding sentences, will usually settle the matter.

The Apostolic Signatura is the highest tribunal in the Church. Other tribunals of the Apostolic See include, for '*graviora delicta*', the Congregation for the Doctrine of the Faith, as a tribunal; given its exclusive competence in these matters, the Apostolic Signatura does not function as the highest court for them. Any member of the faithful can have a case heard in any instance by the tribunals of the Apostolic See, if they wish (c. 1417). Tribunals are also to cooperate with one another, in interviewing witnesses, supplying documents and the like (c. 1418).

d. The Judicial Process – Procedures for Contentious Trials

The Tribunal Officials and the Trial at First Instance

The bishop is the judge in his diocese for most cases not reserved to the Apostolic See, although he usually delegates this duty to a vicar judicial or *Officialis* (cc. 1419–1420). Judges are to be appointed, normally priests, but a lay person may be appointed, but all are to have a doctorate or at least a licentiate in canon law. This requirement should be obvious, since no one would entrust a case to an unqualified person in the secular world; the clear risk of injustice to those whose causes are entrusted to the tribunal is evident. Vicars judicial and judges remain in office when a bishop dies and may not be removed by a diocesan administrator, but they need to be confirmed by the new bishop. They are appointed for a limited term, which is renewable. (cc. 1420–1422). Tribunals are usually collegial (with three judges or even five per case), although there can be a single judge in some situations (cc. 1424–1425). Regional tribunals can be set up, if circumstances warrant it, with the approval of the Apostolic Signatura (c. 1423). A first instance tribunal can operate under an abbot or supreme moderator where there is a dispute between two houses of the same religious institute of pontifical right; for disputes between other institutes or between one institute and another institute or entity, it is the local diocesan tribunal that is competent (c. 1427).

Auditors are to instruct the case by gathering evidence under the direction of the judge. The vicar judicial is to appoint a *ponens* or *relator* or principal judge for a trial, who must lead discussion between the judges and write the official sentence (judgment) on the case (cc. 1428–1429). The bishop is to appoint a promoter of justice, who is to defend the common good in contentious cases and for penal cases (cc. 1430–1431, 1435–1436). He is to have a doctorate or licentiate in canon law and be of good character; he can be a lay person. Also the bishop is to appoint a defender of the bond, who is to produce all reasonable arguments in favour of the bond in marriage cases; he is to have the same qualifications and qualities as the promoter of justice and can hold both positions, though not in the same case (cc. 1432–1436). Where they should intervene, the acts are invalid if they have not been summoned, unless, despite that, they have actually intervened as they should (c. 1433). A notary is to authenticate all acts or they are invalid (c. 1437).

The Second Instance Tribunal

The second instance tribunal, for appeals by plaintiffs or as required by law, is the metropolitan tribunal for all dioceses in the province, a second instance tribunal for each of them being arranged with the Apostolic See, the Signatura. A second instance tribunal operates under the abbot general of a monastic order, where the abbot provincial had overseen the first instance and the supreme moderator of a religious institute of pontifical right where the first instance was under a provincial (c. 1438). For regional first instance tribunals, the episcopal conference must arrange second instance tribunals through the Signatura (c. 1439). A second instance tribunal must be collegial if the first instance was under a single judge (c. 1441).

Tribunals of the Apostolic See

The Pope is supreme judge of the whole Catholic world, exercising this role himself, through the Apostolic tribunals or through delegates (c. 1442).

The Roman Rota

This is the ordinary tribunal of the Apostolic See (c. 1443). It acts in second instance for tribunals which send it appeals, but mainly it operates as a court of third and further instances. It functions in first instance for the cases noted in c. 1405 and in other cases where it accepts a request (c. 1444). Its judgments are normative for the jurisprudence of all Church tribunals; in other words, the judgments of the Rota are to be studied and their interpretations and applications followed in all tribunals.

The Apostolic Signatura

As the Church's supreme tribunal, it hears cases where a rotal judgment is alleged to be null and void, cases of status of person which the Rota has not accepted for re-examination, complaints against auditors of the Rota, and decides competence of all tribunals (c. 1445 § 1). It is the supreme point of reference for administrative actions or recourses, overseeing and making final decisions on the actions of the Roman Curia (c. 1445 § 2). It also oversees these tribunals, erecting tribunals, ensures that they have properly qualified personnel and, if these are not provided, could move to close such tribunals (c. 1445 § 3). The Congregation for the Doctrine of the Faith, in its function as a tribunal, is exclusively competent to deal with more serious crimes ('*graviora delicta*') since 2001.

The Apostolic Penitentiary

This tribunal deals with cases only in the internal forum, based on a petition from someone or on behalf of someone under a penalty, irregularity or an impediment. The decision, given in the internal forum, without the name of the individual, is valid in the external forum, a fact which is important, should the matter in fact become public knowledge.

e. The Discipline of the Tribunal

Judges and Tribunal Officers

Contentious or disputed cases are to be avoided as far as possible, bishops and others seeking ways of conciliation (c. 1446). Judges and other officers cannot exercise the same role in a further instance of the same case (c. 1447), nor are they to take part in any trial where there is personal interest, with relatives up to the fourth degree in the collateral line of consanguinity, close connections of favour or hostile, or financial connections (c. 1448–1451).

Cases brought by private individuals which concern only the private good are to proceed only at the behest of those persons, but cases involving the public good, however begun, are to proceed irrespective of a change of mind by an individual who may have brought a case (c. 1452). A norm not easy to implement recognizes that justice needs to be done within a reasonably brief time, within one year at first instance and six months at second instance (c. 1453), although this is not to be at the expense of justice. Officials are to take an oath to function 'properly and faithfully' (c. 1454) and oaths of secrecy are required to protect those involved or affected by cases (c. 1455). No gifts are to be accepted by officials of the tribunal on the occasion of a trial (c. 1456). Challenges or 'exceptions' to the judge or other officials, to the fact that the parties have reached agreement or to other peremptory exceptions are to be heard before the joinder of the issue, before, that is, the issue at stake is settled, if possible (cc. 1458–1464). Time limits for different parts of the process which are not laid down by law are to be set by the judge; they are neither to be extended nor ever shortened without the consent of the parties, to avoid undue protraction of the case; if the final day for some part of the process is a holiday, the time limit is extended to the next working day of the tribunal (cc. 1465–1467). As far as possible the tribunal should have an office, where the proceedings occur (c. 1468). The acts of the case are to be in writing and notarized, signed by the parties and witnesses where required (refusals to sign being noted and authenticated), interpreters being engaged and used where need be, but translations being provided (cc. 1470–1475).

The Parties to the Case

Those who can appear before the tribunal or court are any member of the faithful, with the use of reason, although a parent or a guardian, even appointed by the court, is to represent someone under fourteen years of age (cc. 1476–1479). Juridical persons are represented by their lawful representatives (parish priest for a parish, rector for a seminary, and so on). The diocesan bishop can stand in where the proper representative of a juridical person subject to his authority has failed to do so (c. 1480).

Advocates and Procurators

The parties to the dispute have a right to an advocate and/or of a procurator to assist them, the former to plead on their behalf, the latter to present documents, receive notifications on their behalf, either with the right to be present at interrogations (c. 1481). The advocate should have a doctorate or licentiate in canon law (c. 1483). Although the tribunal is to appoint an advocate, if one is not chosen, for the accused in penal trials (c. 1481 § 2) and is to appoint a legal representative, if one is not chosen, in most contentious trials involving the public good (c. 1481 § 3), this is not required of the tribunal in a matrimonial case (c. 1481 § 3), since the latter concern the good of the couple rather than the public good as such. The notary is to authenticate documents, verify that evidence was given, that a document is an authentic copy of an original, and so on. Where selected by the parties, the procurator and the advocate are to provide an authentic mandate (of appointment) before acting. Abuses by either can result in fines or suspension by the judge or removal from the case and even, for advocates, removal from the register of advocates (cc. 1484–1490).

Actions and Exceptions

An action occurs when one of the parties seeks a decision to defend a right; an 'exception' is an objection on the basis of the competence of the tribunal, of the judge being related or having a vested interest. Such matters are to be settled as far as possible before the issue is joined (cc. 1491–1500).

3. The Contentious Trial (Part II)

The main stages of an ordinary contentious trial (concerning a dispute) are as follows:

a. The Introduction of a Case

The Introduction of the Petition ('libellus')

A person who thinks he may have a case to be examined can approach a church tribunal, via his parish priest or the promoter of justice or directly. After an initial interview and assessment, he would present a formal petition, or 'libellus' (c. 1501), addressed to the bishop (ordinary) as the chief judge of the diocese, prepared by the vicar judicial and signed by the applicant, who is now the petitioner, that diocesan tribunal being competent in law to handle the case; if not, the case can be transferred to the tribunal competent to hear it. The petition must state the judge before whom the case is being introduced, what is being sought and from whom, the general nature of the facts and evidence, be signed by the petitioner or procurator and state the address of one of them, the petition being dated and specifying the domicile of the respondent (c. 1504). The petitioner is to be admitted or rejected by decree from the judge within a month, the petitioner having the right of appeal to the college if it was the presiding judge who rejected it or to the appeal tribunal within ten canonical days (c. 1506). Grounds for rejecting the petition are that the tribunal is not competent, that the petitioner has no basis to appear before that tribunal, that the requirements of the petitioner have not been met (they can be met and the petition reintroduced) or that there is no foundation for the plea, nor is one likely to appear (c. 1505).

The Citation of the Respondent

Here we see the concern for justice and rights at work, specifically the rights of the defence. Were someone to introduce a petition in a dispute about facts or rights of persons or allegations of canonical crimes (c. 1400 § 1) and the other party to the dispute not to be informed, this would necessarily impair their right to be heard and/or there would be a risk of a decision, a judicial sentence, being issued potentially affecting them very significantly, without their having been able to put their side of the case. Therefore, once a petition is introduced at a tribunal in a contentious case, the other party (respondent) must be informed officially by the tribunal ('cited') of the claim or allegation and asked if he or she wishes to participate in the proceedings; normally a copy of the petition should be enclosed (c. 1508). One who refuses to accept or avoids a citation 'is to be regarded as lawfully summoned' or cited (c. 1510). Once the summons has taken place, the parties are either to appear before the judge or the respondent is to reply in writing, as determined by the judge's decree (cc. 1507–1512).

Specification of the Point at Issue ('litis contestatio')

Both parties are to be informed and invited to give their views about the precise point of canon law which is at stake or at issue in the case (c. 1513). This is to be settled and a decree issued by the vicar judicial stating what it is. If a claim to property is disputed, the date of the joinder of the issue becomes important as the point from which a person eventually judged in unlawful possession not only has to restore the property, but has to pay compensation for damage on it (c. 1515). If the parties had not agreed the point of issue, they have ten days to appeal if dissatisfied (c. 1513 § 3). Once it is settled, the judge must set dates for gathering evidence (c. 1516).

b. The Instruction of the Case

The procedures followed here are not so well known in civil court systems based on common law, but they are akin to procedures used under codified legal systems, with a *'juge d'instruction'* or *'giudice istruttore'* gathering evidence.

The Beginning and the End of the Trial

The trial opens when both parties have been cited, but it can be brought to an end in different ways. It is ended by the judges issuing their concluding decision (c. 1517). If the litigant dies or changes status or ceases to be in an office by virtue of which he or she was acting for a juridical person, the trial is suspended if it has not been concluded (c. 1518 § 1), but if it has been concluded, the judges are to perform the remaining procedures, having summoned the procurator, heir or successor of the litigant concerned (c. 1518 § 2). If nothing is done by either party in respect of the case over a period of six months, the case is abated or 'perempted' by virtue of the law itself, although this is to be declared (cc. 1520–1521); this means that the case is ended. The 'acts of the process' or the procedural acts cease to have any standing (it is as if nothing has been done), although the 'acts of the case' remain and could be used in another instance between the parties (c. 1522), the parties bearing the costs unless it can be shown that the procurator or other official had not acted correctly. The case can be ended by the parties 'renouncing' or abandoning it in writing, if the renunciation is accepted by the judge (c. 1524).

Proofs in the Trial

The burden of proof lies with the one making the claim (c. 1526 § 1). Normally something admitted as true by both sides is presumed to be true, as is what the law presumes (c. 1526 § 2). Any useful and lawful proof may be admitted and the judge can depute others qualified to take evidence (cc. 1527 § 1, 1528). The judge himself, or through others lawfully deputed, may question the parties more closely to clarify what is in doubt and must do so where the public good is at stake or where one of the parties asks for this and is to ask about matters submitted by the promoter of justice or the defender of the bond (cc. 1530, 1533). Those questioned are obliged to answer. An oath to tell the truth should be administered where the public good is at stake and may be administered in other cases (cc. 1531–1532). A judicial confession is something confessed against oneself and relevant to the cause, made before a legally competent judge, is considered proven and, unless the public good is at stake, such a judicial confession relieves the other party of the burden of proof (cc. 1535–1536 § 1), but in cases involving the public good judicial confessions and other declarations of the parties do not have probative force unless other elements wholly corroborate them (c. 1536 § 2). The judge is to evaluate the worth of an extra-judicial confession (c. 1537), but a confession or any other declaration is 'devoid of all force' if it shown to be based on an error of fact or extracted by force or fear (c. 1538).

Documentary proof is admitted in all trials and, unless clearly shown otherwise, public ecclesiastical documents (drawn up by those responsible in the course of their duty and according to law) and public civil documents (in accordance with prevailing civil norms), all other documents being private, are 'acceptable evidence' in respect of what is 'directly and principally affirmed in them' (c. 1541; cf. cc. 1539–1540), provided they are originals or authenticated copies, officially lodged with the tribunal (c. 1544). Private documents are to be treated like extra-judicial confessions (c. 1542).

Witnesses can be admitted to all trials and are obliged to answers questions lawfully posed by the judge, except for clerics in respect of their ministry, and others where professional secrets are involved or those who might be exposed to serious danger or grave harm which might result for them or their relatives from doing so (cc. 1545–1546). Anyone can be a witness, except those excluded by law: minors under fourteen years of age or those of feeble mind, although they can be heard if the judge decrees it as necessary, the parties themselves or those who represent them, all officials in that case, priests in respect of anything heard in or on the occasion of confession (cc. 1547–1550). Witnesses are to be summoned by decree, questions for them being proposed within the time limits set by the judge, who can curb an excessive number of witnesses, their names being communicated to the other party at least before the publication of the evidence (cc. 1551–1554).

The manner of giving evidence is important. Witnesses are to be heard at the tribunal office, but cardinals, patriarchs, bishops or major civil dignitaries where they so choose, and, unless the judge decrees otherwise (c. 1558), in the absence of the parties, individually, in the presence of the notary, with the promoter of justice, defender of the bond, procurator and advocate being allowed to be present, but only to propose additional questions to the judge and not to the witness directly (cc. 1559–1561). The oath is to be administered and note made of refusal to take it, but questions should proceed (c. 1562). The identity of the witness, their relationship to the parties, the sources of their knowledge and the precise time of events they describe are to be elicited (c. 1563), questions being brief and not covering too many points at once, neither deceptive nor leading, nor offensive, relevant to the case (c. 1565). Evidence is to be written at once, or a tape used and immediately transcribed, the witness having their evidence re-read to them and having a chance to add or change points made (c. 1566–1569). Witnesses may be questioned further to clarify matters (c. 1570). The credibility of evidence is to be assessed on the basis of the condition and uprightness of the witness, whether knowledge was first hand, based on what was seen or heard personally, on rumour or hearsay (these latter being admissible in canon law, but to be evaluated carefully as just described), whether the evidence itself is consistent and how far it is consistent with that of others, whether what is asserted is corroborated (c. 1572). A single person cannot provide full proof, unless that person is qualified and giving evidence in an official capacity or 'unless circumstance of persons and things persuade otherwise' (c. 1573). Thus, there are clear criteria for the evaluation of evidence, which in some respects are less demanding than those in civil law, where hearsay evidence is inadmissible.

Other contributions to a trial can come from expert witnesses, such as a psychologist or a doctor, where relevant or required by law and decreed by the judge. Such an expert is to see the acts of the case, is to submit a report, stating how and on what basis his opinion is based (cc. 1574–1581). This is submitted to the judges, but cannot constitute a judgment in the trial itself. Places can be visited, if necessary for the trial (c. 1582). Presumptions of law do not need proof; the person without such presumption in his or her favour has the burden of proof (cc. 1584–1586). Presumptions of law are that marriage is valid until the contrary is established, the accused is innocent until proven guilty and so on. If an incidental matter is raised through a petition, the judge is to decide how relevant it is to the main issue, whether it needs to be decided beforehand and how to proceed (cc. 1587–1591). If the respondent does not answer the summons and does not offer a good reason, after a further summons, to ensure there was a lawful citation, he or she is to be declared absent from the trial and the case is to proceed (c. 1592), but may be heard later if not at fault, but without unduly delaying proceedings (c. 1593). A third party who wishes to intervene in a case can submit a petition to the judge, explaining the connection; the judge is decide to hear him or not. Where a third party is needed to settle a matter of relevance, the judge can require his presence, after speaking to the parties (cc. 1596–1597).

c. The Conclusion of the Case

When all the evidence is ready, the judge has to decree that the parties and their advocates inspect and comment upon those parts of it which they have not seen, although for a grave reason such as fear of violence, he can exclude certain parts, but only provided the right of defence remains intact (c. 1598 § 1). This procedure is crucial 'on pain of nullity' (c. 1598 § 1), which shows how strong is the right of defence in canonical trials. The parties may indicate other items of proof (c. 1598 § 2), and then, when the parties state that they have no more to add, when the time limit for producing evidence is reached or when the judge decides all the evidence necessary is present, the case is concluded by decree (c. 1599 § 3).

After this, the advocate for the petitioner presents his arguments on behalf of the petitioner (pleadings) and the promoter of justice (or in matrimonial nullity enquiries the defender of the bond) presents the points of law and observations (animadversions) on the quality of the evidence which the judges will need to bear in mind in judging the point at issue. Each party has a brief time to respond to these and the promoter of justice or defender of the bond has the right to reply to each point (cc. 1600–1603).

Judgment of the Case and Subsequent Procedures

The judge must have 'moral certainty about the matter to be decided (c. 1608 § 1), derived from the acts of the case and the proofs' (c. 1608 § 2), evaluating the evidence with regard to the law about the value of evidence (c. 1608 § 3) and, where such moral certainty is not to be had, he is to find that the petitioner's case is not established and find in favour of the respondent, except in cases which enjoy favour of the law, when he is to find in favour of the law (c. 1608 § 4). This would be in favour of validity in a case of nullity of marriage or in favour of the accused in a penal trial.

The judges each have a copy of the evidence, with the various observations, the 'Acta', and they prepare their own assessments in writing. Then the case is heard before the vicar judicial or his delegate ('ponens'). The decision has to be based on moral certainty by the judges (c. 1608 § 1) and must be either a unanimous or a majority decision, written up as a formal judgment ('sentence') by the main judge on the case ('ponens'). The decision is to be communicated to the two parties by the vicar judicial, informing the petitioner of his right to appeal if the judgment goes against his claim (cc. 1608–1618). In a matrimonial case, the petitioner must be informed of the tribunal's canonical duty, through the defender of the bond, to appeal against a decision it if it goes in his favour (c. 1682 § 2).

Nullity of the Judgment

A judgment of a tribunal can itself be null or invalid, either irremediably (it cannot be corrected) or remediably (can be corrected). Irremedial nullity stems from one of the following: the judge was absolutely non-competent, one gave judgment who had no power to judge in the given tribunal, or gave it under force or fear, the petition was drawn up neither by a person whose interests were affected nor by the promoter of justice, at least one of the parties had no right to appear before the court, someone acted in another's name without lawful mandate, the right of defence was not observed or the issue was not even partially decided (c. 1620). Simply remediable, within three months of judgment, would include a judgment which was null because the case was required to be tried before a college of judges (c. 1425 § 1) but was not, the decision is not motivated (reasons for it are not given in the sentence), it lacks either the signatures required by law or the date it was given as day, month and year, or it was grounded on an invalid juridical act not rectified or it was given against a party who was lawfully absent (c. 1622). In these latter cases, a petition of nullity can be made within three months and the matter can then be rectified (cc. 1623–1624).

Appeals against Judgment

The parties have the right of appeal against a judgment which they consider harms their interest (c. 1628), but there can be no appeal against a judgment of the Roman Pontiff himself nor against a judgment of the Apostolic Signatura, nor against a judgment which has become adjudged matter (c. 1629). An appeal is to be lodged within fifteen canonical days of the publication of the judgment (c. 1630).

For a decision to be final or adjudged matter ('*res iudicata*'), there have to be two conforming sentences, that is, two judgments which are the same, 'between the same parties, on the same matter and on the same grounds' (c. 1641 1°) or if there was no appeal within the canonical time limit (2°) or if the trial was abated (perempted) or abandoned by the parties (3°) or a definitive judgment has been given (c. 1629) against which there is no appeal (4°). The decisions and decrees are then issued by the tribunal of second instance. However, questions of the status of persons (married, single, celibate, and so on) are never adjudged matter. Hence, there can be recourse to an appeal tribunal any time to challenge even two conforming sentences, but then the question of whether there are serious grounds for hearing such a plea has to be settled within a month of the petition (c. 1644 § 1). In cases where the adjudged matter was based on false evidence such as to render the sentence untenable, where other documents are discovered requiring a new judgment, where deceit led to the judgment, where a non-procedural law was neglected or where the judgment goes against a preceding decision which has become adjudged matter, a plea for total reinstatement (overturning of the judgment) can be made (c. 1645).

Expenses

It is often thought that tribunals are very costly for people or that the rich obtain special favours in the Church. This has never been my experience. It is true that hiring advocates can be costly. This occurs when cases reach the Roman Rota, but then these are often lay people, needing to make a living. We know that the cost of paying civil solicitors and barristers in civil cases is enormous. In fact, most tribunals charge only a minimal amount, often only when a case is successful, and grant free access to the tribunals where costs cannot be met. Legal aid is possible (c. 1649). Well qualified people would never work for nothing as do so many tribunal personnel, even well qualified, something they do as a service to people in need in the community of the Church.

The Execution of the Judgment

Once there is adjudged matter, a decree is issued, often by the appeal tribunal, ordering the execution or implementation of the judgment (cc. 1650–1655).

d. The Oral Contentious Process

This is heard before one judge, who is to receive a petition. If he judges that there is the basis for a case, he is to send a copy of this to the respondent. The parties are to be summoned within thirty days, written submission can be made up to three days before the hearing, which is where the gathered evidence is discussed and people are questioned. The judge is to settle the matter at that hearing, if possible (cc. 1656–1670). This process cannot be used in matrimonial (c. 1690), nullity of ordination (c. 1710) or penal cases (c. 1728 § 1). It can be used to settle incidental causes and must be used to settle disputes about rights to appeal (c. 1631).

4. Special Judicial Processes or Types of Contentious Trials (Part III)

a. Matrimonial Processes I. Investigation of the Nullity of Marriage (Table 18A)

These follow the procedures laid down in section 3 above by and large.

Competence

Any matrimonial case involving the baptized is 'by right' a matter for an ecclesiastical judge (c. 1671), in other words for a church tribunal, contrary to claims in Protestant and Reformed as well as secular traditions that they are matters only for civil law. On the other hand, we have seen the importance of the civil effects of marriage, for people's status as married or single, as a citizen or resident in a country, and so the 'merely civil effects of marriage pertain to the civil courts' (c. 1672).

The tribunal competent to handle an enquiry as to whether a putative marriage is valid or null is the tribunal of the place of celebration of the marriage (c. 1673 § 1) or of the place where the respondent has a domicile or quasi-domicile (c. 1673 § 2) or the petitioner's domicile,

Table 18A

Procedures for an Investigation of Nullity of Marriage

Applicant	complete form (obtainable from parish priest or from tribunal), asking to open a nullity enquiry
initial interview	of applicant by tribunal by an auditor under oath
initial assessment	by tribunal to see if there is the 'smoke of nullity' (*'fumus nullitatis'*), a basis in canon law for thinking marriage may have been invalid
determination of point at issue	specification of grounds in canon law for the investigation
petition	prepared by tribunal, checked and signed by applicant, now petitioner, to the bishop asking for an enquiry on the grounds stated
citation of respondent	other party informed of enquiry and of the ground(s) to be examined, shown copy of petition, asked to participate by giving formal evidence, by writing to tribunal, etc
respondent	– interviewed (under oath), if willing; questions prepared by or confirmed by defender of the bond – submission accepted if writes to tribunal – sent reminder if does not reply and, if not further reply after a month (checking his/ her whereabouts), declared absent from the court; case ordered to proceed
witnesses	nominated by petitioner and/ or by respondent interviewed (under oath, if willing); questions prepared by defender of the bond
expert involvement	if necessary or useful, expert (eg. psychologist) may assess evidence or one or other party (if need be and if they are willing), providing a report only of expert evaluation (not whether the union is null and void)
evaluation of evidence	defender of bond and advocate(s) or procurator(s) for the parties assesses evidence for completeness, consistency, etc. If need be defender of bond poses further questions (or

	advocate asks for further questions to be proposed) to clarify and complete evidence
inspection of oneevidence	petitioner and respondent may examine all evidence of another and of witnesses under tribunal supervision and may make remarks about what is said, which are recorded
conclusion of case	declared by vicar judicial when all evidence completed
defender of the bond	prepares animadversions (observations) about quality, reliability, consistency of evidence and as to what favours the view that the marriage is not null, which the judges are to bear in mind in forming their judgment
advocate(s)	may prepare pleadings on behalf of the party he/ she represents
judges (usually three, of whom is the principal judge or *'ponens'*, but could be five, or even one)	receive all the evidence ('Acta') to evaluate, on the basis of which they are to judge whether the union is null and void or not; each must be morally certain of nullity or else must conclude that the case for nullity is not established
decision at first instance	judges meet with vicar judicial, defender, advocates to discuss their (independently reached) opinions and to conclude whether or not the union is null and void; a majority decision is sufficient
principal judge (*'ponens'*)	writes the formal sentence (judgment): summary of facts of the case, of the law relevant to the case, and of the application of the law to the case, giving the concluding judgment
second instance tribunal	– if first instance sentence states nullity is established, the defender of the bond must appeal against it by law; if it finds against nullity, the petitioner can appeal – if first instance states nullity is established, the second instance tribunal must decide whether it can simply 'ratify' their decision; if so, it does so and also concludes the union is null and void – it issues the decree of nullity – if second instance does not ratify first instance judgment, it examines the case formally again (ordinary process) and comes to a conclusion; if it finds nullity is established, it issues the decree of nullity

511

Table 18A (*continued*)
Procedures for an Investigation of Nullity of Marriage

	– if second instance finds against nullity where first instance found in favour or, where the petitioner appealed against a negative first instance judgment and second instance found in favour of nullity, there would be two discordant sentences and the petitioner would have to decide whether he/ she wished to go to third instance
third instance (normally Roma Rota For tribunals in England and Wales)	examines the case anew, seeks further evidence, if needed; judges the case and, if on the same ground(s) as in either of the prior instances, its sentence will conform with one or other that the case for nullity has/has not been established; if it has, the Rota issues the decree of nullity.
lack of canonical form	here the question for the (first instance) tribunal can be addressed usually through gathering relevant documents of baptism and of civil or other 'marriage' to show it invalid through lack of form. The tribunal has to check through all parishes where the couple lived from their 'wedding' until separation to have certificates from the parish priests to show that no convalidation or radical sanation of the union had taken place. If all documents are present and complete and give moral certainty of nullity, the vicar judicial can issue the decree of nullity.

provided both parties live in the territory of the same episcopal conference (England and Wales) and provided the vicar judicial of the respondent's domicile, after consulting the respondent, gives permission (c. 1673 § 3), or the place where most of the evidence relevant to the case is located (c. 1673 § 4). In these paragraphs we see the implications of the 'condition' of the person in terms of domicile, the concern for the rights of the defence or of the respondent and the need to gain access to evidence to establish the truth.

The Right to Challenge the Validity of Marriage

The spouses have 'the right' to question the validity of their marriage (c. 1674 n. 1), but so does the promoter of justice, if the nullity of the marriage has become public and it cannot or should not be convalidated (c. 1674, 2°). This is because the question, once public, is a question of the public good; a marriage which is null and void for reasons of an undispensed impediment or for lack of canonical form should not be convalidated if it is likely that there is a serious defect of consent or if the union is fragile in any case. The validity of a marriage can only be impugned while both spouses are alive, the marriage ending through the death of one of them (c. 1141), unless it is a question which needs to be settled to permit the resolution of another matter in canon law or in civil law (c. 1675 § 1). If a spouse dies during the investigation, the trial is suspended if it has been opened formally through the joinder of the issue and is still in progress, but, if it has been concluded, the subsequent procedures are to be completed (cc. 1675 § 2, 1518 § 2). The surviving spouse might wish to insist on clarifying the doubt raised about the validity of their union or a third party might have a legitimate interest, since this question might affect another cause in canon or in civil law.[1]

Procedural Matters Prior to and during the Trial

The law presumes that a marriage celebrated is a valid marriage (c. 1060). For nullity to be established, the evidence in the case has to demonstrate the opposite, namely that, despite all appearances, despite the exchange of consent heard or witnessed by others, the

---

[1] Pontifical Council for the Interpretation of Legislative Texts, Instruction on Procedures in Cases of Nullity of Marriage, *Dignitas connubii*, 25 January 2005, art. 143 § 1; K. Lüdicke and R. E. Jenkins (eds.), *Dignitas connubii: Norms and Commentary*, Canon Law Society of America, Alexandria, VA, 2006, 151–2: original German, *Die Eheprozeßordnung der katholischen Kirche: Text (Latein und Deutsch) und Kommentar*, Polylein, 2005.

union was actually null and void. It has to demonstrate this to the point where the judges are morally certain (c. 1608 § 1), that the case for nullity is established ('*constat de nullitate matrimonii in casu*'); otherwise they are bound to conclude that the case for nullity has not been established ('*non constat de nullitate matrimonii in casu*'). The Church does not 'annul' marriages; it does not render a valid marriage null. It merely makes a declaration of fact that a marriage has shown to have been null and void (not a true marriage) or it has not; this it does where a diriment impediment meant one of the parties was legally incapable of marriage, where lack of canonical form is proven or where a defect of consent is established; it is a statement about the time of consent and thus about what followed.

If there is hope of doing so, the judge should try to persuade the two parties to be reconciled, try to have their marriage convalidated (c. 1676). Where this is not likely or possible, if an applicant has been interviewed and there appears to be a real sign of nullity ('*fumus nullitatis*'), the presiding judge or '*ponens*' is to arrange the summons (cc. 1677 § 1, 1508). If neither side asks to meet to settle the joinder of the issue (the precise point or points of canon law under which the marriage might be thought to be null and void and which are, therefore, to be investigated and not just whether the marriage is null – c. 1677 § 3), he is to decide the point at issue by a decree within the following ten days and notify them of it (c. 1677 § 2) and, if ten days after being notified they have not objected, a new decree is to be issued ordering the case to be heard (c. 1677 § 4). We see how each stage of this initial process involves equal treatment for both sides and how it operates through decrees (cc. 48–58), each determining a decision with motivation and open to challenge within the canonical days indicated in c. 1677.

The defender of the bond and promoter of justice (if involved) and the advocates to the parties have the right to be present at the examination (questioning) of the parties, of witnesses and of experts and to see all the evidence and proofs (c. 1678), an important way of protecting the interests of the parties who cannot be present at the examination of anyone else. The judge should hear evidence as to the credibility of the parties (petitioner and respondent), unless unnecessary (c. 1679). In cases involving impotence or defect of consent through mental illness, experts are to be consulted, unless this would be fruitless (c. 1680). The expert doctor or psychologist or psychiatrist is to provide expert information which the judges could not be expected to know or to evaluate, but they are not to try to settle the question of nullity, a matter over which they are incompetent. For mental illness or incapacity, they are to try to give information as to a specific illness or disorder, how and when it was diagnosed, how serious it was or is and what its likely effect would have been upon the individual's capacity to make evaluative judgments or to take on and live out responsibilities involved in marriage.[2]

If the evidence indicates that it is likely that the marriage was not consummated, the nullity enquiry can be suspended by decree and an instruction of the case for submission for a dispensation from the Holy See can be prepared (c. 1681). However, this can only be at the request of one or both parties and, if even one of the parties refuses consent to the suspension of the nullity process, this must continue due to the right for them to have clarification of their personal status, as married or not.[3]

Judgment and Appeals

In discussing the case and the proofs, the judges are to give their opinions as to nullity on each of the grounds alleged in the petition, the reasons in law and in fact being elaborated in a formal judgment or sentence by the '*ponens*' which must give a summary of the persons involved and of the point at issue, the relevant law and its application to the case, and conclude with a response as to each ground of nullity alleged, state whether a *vetitum* is to be attached and state what is to be done about expenses.[4]

In the case of a decision that the nullity of the union has been established ('*constat ...*'), the defender of the bond has the duty, by law, to appeal against the decision (sentence) of the first instance tribunal to the appropriate second instance tribunal (c. 1682 § 1), within twenty days of the publication of the judgment. This is because of the fact that at stake here is the existence or otherwise of a marriage and, in the case of two baptized persons, also of a sacrament.[5] The second instance tribunal has to review the case and is normally able to ratify the decision of the first instance tribunal, issuing then a decree of nullity

---

2. *Dignitas connubii*, art. 203, 209; Lüdicke and Jenkins (eds), *Dignitas connubii: Norms*, 345, n. 1, 353–4, nn. 1–5.

3. *Dignitas connubii*, art. 153; Lüdicke and Jenkins (eds), *Dignitas connubii: Norms*, 263–4, nn. 4–5, 7.

4. *Dignitas connubii*, art. 250, 253 Lüdicke and Jenkins (eds), *Dignitas connubii: Norms*, 405–6, n. 2, 409-413, nn. 1–11.

5. O. Échappé, 'Le droit processuel de l'Église' in P. Valdrini *et al.* (ed.), *Droit canonique*, 2nd edn, Dalloz, Paris, 1999, 397–425 at 419, n. 715.

(c. 1682 § 2). If the objections raised and the review of the case cause the second instance tribunal not to be able to ratify the first instance decision, the case is to be put on to the ordinary process at second instance and the case re-examined fully, with the possibility of new evidence and even of new heads (grounds) of nullity, the latter being examined as of first instance (c. 1683). Then, if the tribunal concurs with the first instance tribunal on the same head of nullity, there are two conforming sentences and the decree of nullity is to be issued.

If the second instance tribunal finds against nullity where the first instance found in its favour, on the same ground, the petitioner has the right to appeal to a third instance tribunal (usually the Roman Rota), whose sentence, if on the same ground, will settle the question, either agreeing with the first or with the second instance decision and so giving the two conforming sentences needed for a judgment, whether this is in favour or against nullity. If a decree of nullity is issued and if the ground is established in one of the parties who wishes to marry in the Catholic Church, there may be a '*vetitum*' or 'prohibition' added by the tribunal, forbidding marriage in the Catholic Church without the bishop's permission (c. 1684 § 1). The reason for this might be that the person was found unable to fulfil the essential duties of marriage (c. 1095 § 3). In such a case, he or she would not automatically be able to marry another person, but would need counselling or further assessment to ensure that he or she could contract marriage validly. However, it is important to note that, strictly the *vetitum* is not a judicial decision, but an administrative one in the interests of the pastoral care of the parties. It does not have invalidating effects, since only the supreme authority of the Church can establish impediments to marriage. It might be said to be an impedient impediment in a particular case, which can be lifted by the bishop.[6] Of course, if a marriage is declared null and void because of an undispensed (diriment) impediment, the person concerned cannot marry until that impediment has ceased or has been validly dispensed.

There is the possibility of a nullity investigation by means of a documentary process only, where there is a matter not of examining the validity of the consent exchanged, as in the procedures discussed so far, but rather of establishing whether or not there was an undispensable or undispensed diriment impediment operative at the time or whether canonical form was lacking, without a valid dispensation or

---

[6.] *Dignitas connubii*, art. 251, 301; Lüdicke and Jenkins (eds), *Dignitas connubii: Norms*, 407–9, nn. 2-4, 6, 484–6, nn. 2, 4.

whether there was or was not a valid mandate for a proxy exchange of consent (c. 1686). In such cases, the necessary proofs (the relevant documents, checks to see whether or not there was a dispensation or a convalidation) need to be evaluated by one judge, who can issue a decree of nullity if the proofs show that the union was, in fact, null. However, the defender of the bond has to be involved and give his animadversions; he can appeal against the decision if dissatisfied as to the proofs (c. 1687).

In the case of a nullity investigation on the ground of lack of canonical form, proof of the baptism of the Catholic (baptismal certificate) and proof of the civil wedding as to the persons involved, the date and the place (wedding certificate) and a decree absolute of divorce are essential. Then, documentary proofs (certificates or authenticated letters) are required from the parish priest of every parish in which the couple lived between the time of the wedding and the end of the common life (their separation). Each one of these is to verify that the priest has searched the church marriage register between the relevant dates and that, on that basis, he confirms that this invalid union was never convalidated nor sanated. Once all of this evidence is present and, provided there are no gaps in it, nullity on the basis of lack of form is established and the decree of nullity can be issued.

b. The Legal Separation of Spouses

The legal separation of the spouses is not a divorce. It always involves the public good and so the promoter of justice must always be involved (c. 1696). If the couple cannot be reconciled (c. 1695) and if at least one of theme is baptized (c. 1692 § 1), the bishop by decree or a judge delegated by him by judgment can proceed, if the judgment will not have civil effects or if a civil judgment is foreseen which will not be contrary to divine law (c. 1692 § 2). If it will have civil effects, the bishop may give permission to function through the civil courts, provided it is foreseen that the judgment will not contradict divine law (c. 1692 § 3). Competence of the church tribunal is according to c. 1673 (c. 1694) and the oral contentious process is normally to be used (c. 1693).

c. Processes for Dissolution of a Non-consummated Marriage

This is not a trial. A petitioner applies to the bishop, who entrusts the investigation usually to the tribunal. Only the Apostolic See can decide the fact of non-consummation and the presence of a just reason for seeking the dispensation (c. 1698 § 1), but the Roman Pontiff alone can grant such a dispensation (c. 1698 § 2). The instruction of the case is ordered by the bishop who accepts the petition (c. 1700 § 1). It must involve the examination of the parties and of any other relevant witnesses, with guidance from the Apostolic See (Congregation for Divine Worship and for the Discipline of the Sacraments), and there must be animadversions from the defender of the bond (cc. 1701–1704). After the necessary investigations, the bishop must give an opinion on the merits of the case (c. 1705). This opinion as to the truth of the matter of non-consummation or otherwise, derived from the evidence gathered, is a matter for the diocesan bishop and cannot be handed over to the vicar general or an episcopal vicar except by special mandate; however given the gravity of the matter, the diocesan bishop should normally discharge this function himself.[7] The 'Acta' are transmitted to the Congregation for Divine Worship and the Discipline of the Sacraments, who also examine it and give an opinion, deciding whether to recommend to the Holy Father that he grant a dispensation to dissolve this union. Dispensation is by rescript (c. 1706).

d. Dissolution of a Non-sacramental Marriage

The Pauline Privilege

This is a development from the separation allowed by Paul where a pagan spouse would not let the baptized spouse live in peace (1 Cor. 7:12–16). Where the pagan refused to live in peace, it was decided later, the Catholic could marry another Catholic and at the point of doing so the former bond was said to be dissolved. The non-Catholic should be asked if he or she will be baptized or at least will live in peace, as

---

[7.] Response from the Commission for the Authentic Interpretation of the Code of Canon Law, 21 February 1984, 'affirmative' to the question: 'Can the dispositions of c. 134 § 3 be referred and applied to the opinion of the bishop *pro rei veritate* in causes *super rato*?'; Congregatio de cultu divino et disciplina sacramentorum, *Collectanea documentorum: Ad causas pro dispensatione super 'rato et non consummato' et a lege sacri coelibatus obtinenda*, Libreria editrice Vaticana, 2004, 118, n. 48.

a matter of validity, although the diocesan bishop can dispense from this (c. 1145–1147). 'Living in peace' has been taken to mean not being pressurized into acting immorally in the conjugal life or refusing to let the Catholic practise their faith, unless the latter has provoked this behaviour (c. 1143 § 2). More recently, the Pauline privilege has been extended so that the Catholic may marry a non-Catholic baptized person, but only after enquiries have established that this person would allow the Catholic to live in peace.[8]

The Petrine Privilege

As we have seen, this does not refer to any position taken by St. Peter himself, but to papal action under the power of the keys in granting a privilege. One is the case of a polygamist (man with more than one wife) or a polyandrist (woman with more than one husband) where the man in the first case and the woman in the second becomes baptized. They can have only one spouse, who should be the first one they 'married', but it may not be known who the first is or it may be hard to live with that person, in which case that intrinsically but not extrinsically indissoluble marriage can be dissolved (only) by the Pope 'in favour of the faith' to permit marriage to the one chosen, the others being dismissed, although the ordinary is to provide for them (cc. 1148–1149).[9] In the case where one party was baptized and the other received baptism, but the couple never came to live together after that as a baptized couple by reason of imprisonment or separation through persecution, their marriage as sacramental would not have been consummated due to lack of possibility and could be dissolved in favour of the faith. (c. 1149). Even in a case of doubt of nullity the privilege of the faith enjoys favour of the law and so a marriage could be dissolved similarly in that instance too (c. 1150).

The case of the dissolution of a non-sacramental marriage involving two non-baptized persons or of one baptized person with a non-baptized person, with dispensation from canonical form (c. 1086) if the baptized person is Catholic, is not found in the Code, which only speaks of the cases mentioned, but in fact dissolution in favour of the faith, for one or other to marry a baptized person is given, where non baptism is proven (through depositions from the person concerned and relatives), where there has been no consummation afterwards if the other is baptized, and the one petitioning

---

8. J. Schouppe, *Le droit canonique: introduction général et droit matrimonial*, Story Scientia, Bruxelles, 1990, 210–12, nn. 238–9.
9. Ibid., 212, n. 240.

for the favour was not the cause of the breakdown of the common life.[10]

e. Declaration of the Presumed Death of a Spouse

Where death cannot be proven from an authentic civil or ecclesiastical document (c. 1707 § 1), there needs to be an investigation. If the proofs gathered give 'moral certainty' that the other spouse is in fact dead (since 'the mere absence of the spouse, no matter for how long a period, is not sufficient' – c. 1707 § 2), a declaration of presumed death can be issued. In especially difficult cases the Congregation for Divine Worship and for the Discipline of the Sacraments is to be consulted (c. 1707 § 3); then the declaration would still normally come from the diocese, unless competence has been given to the Congregation. Since marriage is dissolved by the death of one of the parties (c. 1141), the other is then free to marry.

5. Procedures for the Declaration of Nullity of Sacred Orders

The case would have to come to the Congregation for Divine Worship and for the Discipline of the Sacraments (c. 1709 § 1) – a diocesan bishop or tribunal is not competent – with a petition from the cleric or from the ordinary of the diocese where he is working or where he was ordained (c. 1708). Once a petition is submitted, he may not exercise orders (c. 1709 § 2). The Congregation could give the case to a particular tribunal (c. 1710). It would follow the ordinary contentious process, as above. However, it is not likely to be used. More usually, such a matter would be dealt with by means of a different approach altogether, now under the Congregation for Clergy, that of seeking a dispensation from the obligations of the clerical state. Here a petition from the priest concerned, detailing his life also as a priest, the reasons which led to the crisis, the reasons why the situation is considered irreversible, along with relevant documents, including the scrutinies (judgments of staff) from the seminary or other house of formation of the priest, and testimony from others, including the opinion of the bishop, would all need to be submitted to the Holy See. The only time there is likely to be a declaration of nullity of orders is if there were a violation of the form of the sacrament which could be verified.

[10.] Ibid., 213, n. 242. Cf., Congregation for the Doctrine of the Faith, Instruction on the Dissolution of Marriage in Favour of the Faith, 6 December 1973.

6. Ways of Avoiding Trials

Arbitration, even through ecclesiastical judges making binding agreements, are recommended (cc. 1713–1714), but they must respect the norms of the Code on the alienation of ecclesiastical goods and should be compatible with civil law as far as possible (c. 1715 § 2). Where there would be divergence from civil law, the agreement has no canonical validity, unless it is confirmed by an ecclesiastical judge in the place where it was given (c. 1716 § 1).

7. Procedures in Penal Law (Part IV)

a. Judicial and Administrative Processes

The practical question of defending rights or of establishing what is just, of how to go about this, of what actually to do, is the subject matter of procedural law. Most of Book VII deals with trials, judicial procedures for such a matter and the preferred approach in canon law. An administrative process avoids a trial (c. 1718 § 1, 3°), in cases of penal law. Questions of strict justice, of precise duties and rights, are to be distinguished further from privileges (we have just seen some norms for privileges sought from the Apostolic See). There is no appeal in the case of a 'favour' or 'privilege' being requested, but, although there is no appeal against a judgment of the Supreme Pontiff, Ecumenical Council or Apostolic Signatura (cc. 1404, 1629, 1732), in judicial actions which are concerned with a point of justice as such (not a favour), the petitioner has the right of appeal against a judgment. Precisely this is lacking in an administrative procedure, there being no judgment against which to appeal; even though the person affected has the right of recourse (cc. 1400 § 2, 1732), there is not the same protection of their rights as in a trial. This is why a judicial process is preferred by law in criminal cases.

When someone is alleged to have committed a canonical crime or where the promoter of justice considers such needs to be examined for the common good, the following canonical procedures apply (Table 18B).

Table 18B

Procedures in Penal Law

Canon 1717 § 1 (Preliminary investigation)

'Whenever the *Ordinary* receives information which has at least the *semblance of truth*, about a offence (*crime*), he is to

enquire carefully
    either *personally*
    or *through some (other) suitable person*

        about the *facts*
        and the *circumstances,*
        and about *imputability,*

  unless this *enquiry* would appear to be entirely *superfluous.*'

Canon 1717 § 2

'*Care is to be taken* that this enquiry does *not call into question anyone's good name.*'

Canon 1720 1° (Extra-Judicial or Administrative Procedure)

'If the *Ordinary judges* that the matter should proceed by way of an *extra-judicial* decree, he is to

notify the accused

    of the *allegation*
    and the *evidence* ...,

    giving the accused the opportunity *to defend himself ,*

unless the accused,
    having been lawfully summoned,
        has failed to appear.'

Canons 1721 § 1, 1723   (The Judicial Process)
'If the *Ordinary* (has) <u>*decreed*</u> that a *judicial penal process* is to be initiated,

    (the Ordinary) is to pass the *acts of the investigation* to the *promoter of justice,*

    who (the promoter of justice) is to *present to the judge a petition of accusation ...*'
          (c. 1721 § 1)

Table 18B (*continued*)

Procedures in Penal Law

and the judge is to

summons (cite) the accused by means of a decree (c. 1723 § 1), invite him to nominate an advocate (for himself) (c. 1723 § 1)

or ...provide (nominate) an advocate for him ...
(until he nominates) one for himself.' (c. 1723 § 2)

Canon 1722   (Canonical Restrictions upon the Accused)

'At any stage in the process, (in order) to

prevent scandal
protect the freedom of the witnesses,
and safeguard the course of justice,

the *Ordinary can,*

after <u>*consulting*</u> *the promoter of justice*

and *summoning the accused* person to appear,

prohibit the accused from
the *exercise* of
sacred ministry
or some *ecclesiastical office (officium)*
and *position (function – munus)*
or *impose* or *forbid*
residence in a certain *place* or *territory,*
or even prohibit *public participation*
in the *Blessed Eucharist.*

If, however, the *reason ceases,*
all these *restrictions* are *to be revoked;*
they cease by virtue of the *law* itself
as soon as the penal process ceases.'

The Preliminary Investigation

The ordinary (diocesan bishop or major superior, but not vicar general or episcopal vicar, since they lack judicial power)[11] who believes that a crime has been committed, is to order a careful investigation of the facts and circumstances and of the imputability of the person suspected, appointing an investigator, either through his own tribunal or through another (c. 1717 § 1). This is to be done without damaging the reputation of the accused (c. 1717 § 2) and, to prevent prejudice, the investigator cannot be a judge in any subsequent trial which may occur (c. 1717 § 3). He is to ask a commission of judges whether there is a case to answer. If the evidence is such as to indicate that there has been a canonical crime and that a particular individual or individuals may be guilty of it, on the basis of the judges' opinion, the bishop is to decide whether to initiate a process to impose or declare penalties, whether this should be done in the light of the duty to move to this only after fraternal correction and reproof and pastoral efforts have been fruitless to effect his own reform and to repair the damage of scandal and of injustice (cc. 1341, 1718 § 4) and, if affirmative, whether through a judicial or administrative process (c. 1718 § 1). As noted, a judicial process is much preferred. a grave reason for choosing the administrative process instead is required. Unless needed for a trial, the acts of the preliminary investigation are to be kept in a secret archive (c. 1719).

The reluctance of the Church's law to engage in a penal trial stems from concern for reconciliation. Such an emphasis, along with the complexities and limited use of penal law, caused some to wonder whether the Church has become unrealistic and even irresponsible. Scandals over child sexual abuse by clergy have shown in part that avoiding trials has been misused, that penal remedies such as extended retreats have been employed to correct what many thought twenty years ago were merely moral errors in the offender. The recognition of psychological disorder in paedophiles led bishops to combine this with extended counselling or therapy, but it has come to be recognized that it is not usually curable. A reluctance to engage in penal procedures and especially by a trial stemmed also from a desire to avoid scandal for and about priests, a consideration which distorts the fact that not acting effectively through penal processes to deal with what is itself gravely unjust, abusive and thoroughly scandalous behavior by some clergy is itself a grave scandal. The reluctance to embark upon complex procedures, with dubious outcomes, with the fear of actions

---

[11.] W. H. Woestman, *Ecclesiastical Sanctions and the Penal Process: A Commentary on the Code of Canon Law*, Faculty of Canon Law, St Paul University, Ottawa, 2000, 157.

and decisions being overturned on appeal or after recourse did deter some bishops from acting sooner or more decisively in the way that they ought to have done.

Another factor which was misinterpreted was the role of the preliminary investigation. It does have to establish facts and circumstances and make a judgment about imputability, but it is quite distinct from the trial itself. It might be thought of as akin to the preliminary procedures of the director of public prosecutions; it is definitely not the trial itself and should not try to anticipate a judgment of a trial. Facts and circumstances are to be assessed to see whether it appears that a canonical crime has been committed as alleged and, if so, whether it is imputable to the one under suspicion not in terms of what needs to be evaluated at the later trial, but whether there are clear indications that this person appears to have been the perpetrator.[12] If so, a process should be opened to try the case. It need hardly be said now that mere penal remedies cannot substitute for this, cannot adequately repair the injustice done nor the scandal generated by the putative acts of a member of the clergy. The aim is to find the truth for the good of all concerned.[13]

The Course of the Penal Process

THE ADMINISTRATIVE PROCESS

If there are serious reasons for an administrative rather than a judicial process (a confession or a conviction in a civil case), the bishop is to summon the accused, making known the charge and the proof to provide the possibility of defence (c. 1720 § 1). Together with two assessors he is to evaluate all the evidence from prosecution and defence (c. 1720, 2°), and then issue a decree of condemnation or of acquittal, summarizing the arguments in law and in fact (c. 1720 3°).

THE JUDICIAL PROCESS

In the case of judicial process, the bishop has to give the case to the promoter of justice who introduces a petition before the tribunal and the case proceeds according to the norms for contentious cases (c. 1721 § 1). He gives the case to a judge, who is to summon the accused, give him the opportunity to select his own advocate (c. 1723 § 1) and, if he

[12.] C. Papale, *Il processo penale canonico: commento al Codice di Diritto Canonico Libro VII, Parte IV*, Urbaniana University Press, Vatican, 2007, 53–5.
[13.] Woestman, *Ecclesiastical Sanctions*, 156–7.

does not do so or until he does so, must appoint an advocate for him (c. 1723 § 2). The insistence on an advocate in a criminal trial to this extent is a way of ensuring proper defence. However, it presupposes that the advocate is qualified in canon law with a doctorate or at least a licence in canon law, preferably with knowledge and experience of operating in penal law. Certainly, if the advocate appointed or proposed is not qualified, the accused can and should exercise recourse to the one who nominated him, since otherwise there is no effective assistance in his defence. The accused, the advocate and/or the procurator for the accused always has the right to speak or intervene last in each stage of the trial (c. 1725). The accused is not bound to admit the offence, nor is an oath to be administered to the accused (c. 1728 § 2). The promoter of justice may resign from the case at any stage at the discretion or with the permission of the bishop (c. 1724 § 1), but, for validity, this must be with the consent of the accused (c. 1724 § 2). If, at any stage, it becomes clear that the accused is not guilty of the crime alleged, the judge must declare him acquitted in a judgment (c. 1726). If judged guilty, the penalties must be imposed (*'ferendae sententiae'*) or declared (*'latae sententiae'*).

THE RIGHT OF DEFENCE IN A PENAL PROCESS

The rights of defence in a case of someone accused of a canonical crime include the right to be told the charge and the essential elements of proof, the right to an advocate, one being appointed by the tribunal or by the diocese if he does not choose one for himself, the right not to be pressed to make a confession (indeed, to remain silent, without implication of guilt), the right not to be interrogated under oath (to avoid putting him a position where he might perjure himself), and the right to have the last word before judgment is made (c. 1728).[14]

Appeal or Recourse

The person convicted can appeal against a judicial sentence or have recourse against an administrative decision in accordance with law, even if the judge has reduced, suspended or substituted penalties (c. 1344) or if they are reduced because of factors lessening imputability (cc. 1345, 1727 § 1). The promoter of justice may appeal against the decision if he considers that the penalty does not adequately repair scandal or the injustice perpetrated (c. 1727 § 2). If there has been an administrative process, the right to have recourse against the eventual

---

14. Ibid., 174.

decision operates analogously. Again, the procedures aim at truth and justice, attending to the rights of accuser and accused.

b. Action for Restitution (Reparation of Damages)

A third party (perhaps an individual or a group or a juridical person) has the right to engage in a contentious process to obtain reparation for damages allegedly suffered as a result of the crime. This has to occur from the first instance of the penal case. The case for reparation of damages has to be suspended until the outcome of the penal case itself is clear (cc. 1729–1731).

c. Some Observations relating to Cases of Clerical Sexual Abuse of Minors

The Problem of Sexual Abuse in General

Sexual abuse in various forms stems from the effects of original sin and from the damaging effects of sexually disordered concupiscence or sexual desire which remain after forgiveness. The sexual revolution of the 1960s undoubtedly unleashed a libertine spirit, something aggravated by mass pornography, whose diffusion has been assisted by the advent of literacy and of sophisticated communications, deliberately exploiting the weaknesses of fallen human nature and appealing to weak, deviant people and posing a danger to the innocent, including children.[15] The human person, in his or her sexuality and bodiliness, is reduced to the level of a product to be marketed, enticed and debased.[16] Descriptions and images of debauchery available readily to large numbers of people through advertising, marketing and the Internet, expose the weak and young to exploitation, something hardly unconnected to the sexual abuse of recent decades.[17] Although caution is needed in that a relatively low direct connection between

---

[15.] Pontifical Council for Social Communications, *Pornography and Violence in the Means of Communication: A Pastoral Response*, 7 May 1989, n. 6; hereafter *Pornography and Violence*.

[16.] I Fuček, 'Pornografia e mass media: in margine ad un recente documento del Magistero cattolico' in ID., *La sessualità al servizio dell'amore: Antropologia e criteri teologici* (Dehoniane, Roma, 1993), 141–72 at 146.

[17.] Pontifical Council for Social Communications, *Pornography and Violence*, n. 9; ID., two brief mentions of the dangers of pornography for the family from the internet in two texts dealing also with much broader aspects: *La Chiesa e l'Internet*, 22 February 2002, n. 11; ID., *Etica dell'Internet*, 22 February 2002, n. 16.

pornography and child sexual abuse has been found, such materials can hardly fail to lower inhibitions and focus the mind on wrongful ways of treating others sexually.[18] Such images, deliberately sought and contemplated, develop and reinforce patterns of thinking, often associated with masturbation, which feed deviant behaviour in the depraved acts of sexual abuse of the innocent. Exploitation of the poor by organized criminal bodies and sex tourism are specific aggravations of this problem.

The sexual abuse of the human person is always seriously wrong. When perpetrated by a person working for the Church, especially by a priest, it is even worse. The abuse of a child's innocence is the specifically aggravating factor of paedophilia. Paedophilia has been called the 'sexual abuse of a child', 'any sexual activity with a child unable to express adequate consent',[19] or the use of a child 'by another person for his or her gratification or sexual arousal or that of others'.[20] Some abusers with another focus may abuse children casually or opportunistically, simply because a child happens to be available,[21] but paedophilia is more specifically a sexual preference for children over adults,[22] of an enduring character, deep rooted and resistant to change as far as can be gauged.[23] This can be orientated homosexually, heterosexually or, more rarely, bisexually, involving seeking intercourse with children, exhibitionism, exposure before children or sado-masochistic practices and so on. Deviant persons are more likely to act when inhibitions have been lowered.[24] A study of clergy sex

---

[18] R. Langevin, 'Who Engages in Sexual Behaviour with Children? Are Clergy who Commit Sexual Offences Different from Other Sex Offenders?' in R. K. Hanson *et al* (ed.), *Sexual Abuse in the Catholic Church*, 24–43 at 32–3.

[19] Russo, *Loc. cit.*, 225.

[20] This definition was used by the Law Reform Commission of Ireland in 1990 and in 'Children First: National Guidelines for the Protection and Welfare of Children (Department of Health and Children – Ireland, 1999). It was used as a working definition by the official enquiry commissioned by the Irish Government into clerical sexual abuse in the diocese of Ferns (Country Wexford) in the south-east of Ireland, under the presidency of a prominent state judge, Mr. Francis D. Murphy, *The Ferns Report, Presented to the Minister for Health and Children, October, 2005*, known as and hereafter referred to as *The Ferns Report*, 10. The Report refers to the earlier uses of this definition at this point.

[21] Ibid., 30, 34–5.

[22] This definition, quoted by Langevin, is that used by the World Health Organization in 1992 in 'The ICD-10 Classification of Mental and Behavioural Disorders: Clinical Descriptions and Diagnostic Guidelines', Author, Geneva, 1992, 25 and 41, note 1.

[23] Ibid., 25.

[24] Ibid., 33–6.

offenders (69% Catholic), compared to controls, found 83% of clergy had sexually assaulted male minors, with alcoholism being a problem for 33% of them (as with others), but a high rate of neurological factors and endocrine factors (diabetes).[25]

The Ferns Report lists types of behaviour which would constitute the sexual abuse of children, which coheres with what Langevin and Russo have stated, as follows: exposure of the sexual organs or any sexual act intentionally performed in the presence of a child, intentional touching or molesting of the body of a child for the purpose of sexual arousal or gratification, masturbation in the presence of a child or the involvement of a child in an act of masturbation, sexual intercourse with a child, oral, vaginal or anal, or sexual exploitation of a child by inciting, encouraging, propositioning, requiring or permitting a child to solicit for, or engage in, prostitution or other sexual acts. Sexual exploitation also occurs when a child is involved in the exhibition, modelling or posing for the purpose of sexual arousal, gratification or sexual act, including its recording (on film, video tape or other media) or the manipulation for those purposes of the image by computer or other means. It may also include showing sexually explicit material to children which is often a feature of the 'grooming' process by perpetrators of abuse.[26]

Paedophiles are often family members, successful professionals, very intelligent and able, often known to those they abuse, appearing as 'benign and admirable people'. Clerical abusers often seemed to be 'successful, spiritual and even caring human beings', even 'pious and holy'. Yet, an 'outstanding characteristic of paedophiles or ephebophiles' generally 'is their capacity to rationalize and normalize their sexual fantasies and activities', another being to associate with like-minded people and gain access to relevant literature.[27]

Seeing paedophilia and child sexual abuse as essentially a moral problem was common until two decades or so ago. In the Church this led to priests being moved to different parishes or dioceses, a practice now known to have exposed other children to abuse. Society generally saw it as a medical or a psychological problem which called for treatment or therapy and so the Church then tended to send priests for assessment and treatment. Now it is seen as too deep-rooted to be cured and, with a belated concern to attend to the victims and to

---

[25] Ibid., 39–40.
[26] *The Ferns Report*, 14.
[27] Ibid., 17–18.

prevent and protect others from becoming victims, there is perhaps a focus on seeking to prevent recidivism and on monitoring paedophiles more fully. The awareness of the dreadful trauma for victims of abuse and of the enduring scars it leaves has led to attempts to care for such victims and to institute policies to protect children and young people, including putting children first, the 'paramountcy principle' of the Nolan Report of 2001, a report commissioned by the Bishops' Conference of England and Wales to recommend how the Church should address this question there, recommendations which are now the policy of the dioceses of that bishops' conference.

Since abusers are often adept at gaining access to positions where they can be alone with children or young adults, it is especially important to check applicants for posts in the Church or volunteers for work in the Church. Screening for potential paedophiles is not always easy, but a structured interview about the number of moves since the person was eighteen, experience of working with children, hobbies, his or her family background are useful.[28] Questions relating to attitudes and judgments about risk situations, attitudes to adult-child sexual friendships, checking references in previous employments with relevant questions and a criminal records check are urged.[29] The Nolan Report 2001, recommends a reference for applicants for posts or volunteers and an interview which would explore experience of working with children, arranging a criminal records check and making any appointment conditional on successfully completing a probationary period.[30] References should be pursued and doubts expressed

---

[28.] R. K. Hanson and S. Price, 'Sexual Abuse Screening Procedures for Positions of Trust with Children' in R. K. Hanson *et al.* (ed.), *Sexual Abuse in the Catholic Church: Scientific and Legal Perspectives: Proceedings of the Conference 'Abuse of Children and Young People by Catholic Priests and Religious' (Vatican City, April 2–5, 2003)*, Libreria editrice Vaticana, 2004, 77–91 at 79, relating to work done by MacCormack, Selvaggio and Lanning in the 1980s in social work with children.

[29.] Ibid., 81–5.

[30.] Lord Nolan, *Review on Child Protection in the Catholic Church in England and Wales (The Nolan Report)*, First Report, London, April 2001, Executive Summary, 'Choosing the Right Paid Staff and Volunteers', nn. 7–11; hereafter *The Nolan Report*. This enquiry and Report was commissioned by the Bishops' Conference of England and Wales and its recommendations were fully adopted by the Conference; they are the basis of child protection policies in all dioceses of the Conference, although no '*recognitio*' has ever been sought for them from the Apostolic See, despite the requirement that this be done for any policy which is a national policy. The procedures in force under the Nolan Report were being reviewed by a group since October 2006 and the Cumberledge report was issued in 2008.

should also be followed up.[31] Other organizations have developed practices of having two adults together as much as possible on visits, trips, a code of practice, including instructions not to touch children in ways or parts of the body which could be interpreted as sexually sensitive, being visible as far as possible when talking to a child or vulnerable adult alone when it cannot be avoided, separated by a table or clear space, avoiding words, topics or gestures which could be threatening or sexually suggestive. A child protection officer in every parish was recommended by the Nolan Report, to whom allegations of abuse can be made in confidence and who is responsible for overseeing the implementation of diocesan policies in this area. Specific job descriptions for all posts in the parish are recommended and the samples given in the report include the responsibility 'to ensure the safety and well-being of the children (and young people)'.[32]

It makes sense also for clergy not to be in positions which could be compromising, if possible to avoid them. They should see children with their parents or with a responsible adult present. Responsibility about keeping a space between him and them, not saying or doing anything which could be misinterpreted are important, also for his own self-protection. Where there may be particular suspicion that a person may be problematic (perhaps after a telephone call to arrange a visit which gives rise to concern), it is best to speak to the person seated at the other side of a table and not to be alone in the presbytery. Friendliness and pastoral openness should never be confused with or lead to irresponsible behaviour or conversation.

In all of these respects the need to protect children from abuse is rightly a matter of priority and, in any doubt at all, a person should not be employed or allowed to act as a volunteer in any capacity in the Church where he or she might be with children. Similarly, in a seminary it is essential that allegations be investigated; allegations of grave abuse in St Peter's seminary, Wexford, were known by both rector and ordaining bishop, but they were ignored and a notorious paedophile went on for years to perpetrate abuse.[33] A priest on the staff of St Patrick's College, Maynooth, who urged the seminarians who lodged a complaint about another priest staff member to notify their bishops, which they told him they did, and who himself referred to it in a confidential document, was upbraided by another bishop

---

[31.] Ibid., Summary Recommendations, n. 6: 17–21.
[32.] Ibid., Annex two.
[33.] *The Ferns Report*, 86-100, 171–3.

who had gained knowledge illicitly of the latter, was persuaded to take sabbatical leave and found his post taken on his return; the priest who was the object of the accusations is said to have made a financial arrangement with an alleged victim with a confidentiality clause so that the latter did not cooperate in an official enquiry.[34] The need to be scrupulous about the qualifications and about the moral character and background of those appointed to seminary staff (c. 253) is clear.

The Nolan Report recommended that in every parish there be a child protection officer and a clear job description, including the duty of ensuring the safety and well-being of children, for all employed or voluntary workers with the Church. A member of the clergy ought not to be alone with a child, if possible, but should see a child with a parent and for anyone who might find himself alone with children, including all clergy, there should be not just a generic, but an enhanced, police check of any criminal background relating to children and young people. Such investigations have long been standard for teachers in some countries. Here the validity of the Nolan Report's 'paramountcy principle' emerges clearly. Proper supervision can provide a safeguard both for children and for those who work with them. Training for those involved, codes of practice or procedures for relating to children, with norms for accompanying children in cars, sleeping arrangements during visits away from home at weekends and the like are essential.

The Ferns Report specifically noted scandalous behaviour in a priest hearing the confessions of children prior to their confirmation. Ten girls reported having to go to confession to a specific priest 'on the altar', that is in the sanctuary, while the rest of the class were told to close their eyes and pray and it seems he abused a number of them sexually by causing them to touch him. The priest is now dead.[35] The norms issued (though not publicly) by John XXIII in 1962 dealt largely with the canonical crime of soliciting during confession, but they did include brief mention of the dreadful crime of child abuse, the 'worst crime' ('crimen pessimum'). For this crime to result in canonical penalties, it was necessary that there be 'any obscene external act, which is gravely sinful, committed or attempted in any way by a cleric with young persons of either sex or with brute animals', although it had been referred to initially as a crime with a person of his own sex.[36] In this instance using the confession to commit a

---

[34.] Ibid., 100–3, 182–3.

[35.] Ibid., 82–5.

[36.] Instruction from the Supreme and Holy Congregation of the Holy Office to Patriarchs, Archbishops and Bishops and other Diocesan Ordinaries 'even of the Oriental

sexual crime with the penitents, even if they did not commit any crime, would have aggravated the crime of sexual abuse, in that the priest would have been abusing minors, abusing his authority and office and abusing the sacrament too. From the priest's point of view, he is in a very privileged position when hearing confessions, but he is also in a vulnerable position. For his own protection, it might be better only to hear confessions in a confessional box, where actual contact with a penitent is limited by the structure. Confessions are to be heard in a church or oratory as the proper place and, 'except for a just reason ... not ... elsewhere than in a confessional' (c. 964 §1, § 3). For the protection of penitent and priest and to avoid misunderstandings, a Roman-type confessional or one fitted with strong glass so that the persons can be seen from outside it is advisable.

Penal Law and Sexual Abuse

One area of serious neglect has been the failure of church authorities to deal with sexual abuse, even though the norms of the Holy Office of 1962 had been circulated to bishops and even though bishops can seek advice from the Congregation for Bishops about their needs and concerns at any time. This neglect has been more culpable since clerical sexual abuse scandals erupted in the late 1980s and early 1990s. Procedures in England and Wales and in the United States seem not to have been followed, even in this latter period in any adequate way. One factor seems to have been the reluctance to act in a disciplinary fashion and to leave the odium of such action to the Holy See. Thus, it is a scandal that the Church in the United States could handle many thousands of nullity cases per year, but fail to handle penal cases, and the same can be said elsewhere.[37] Tribunals are not 'marriage' tribunals, but church courts. The consequence has been that scandals abounded to the point where the Holy See has had to intervene in an area where bishops and bishops' conferences could and should have functioned under subsidiarity. Asking the highly respected Lord Nolan to investigate the problem may have been wise, but to suggest that whatever he recommended would be implemented was irresponsible; no one can approve legal norms without seeing them. The final resolution of the Bishops' Conference of England and Wales, communicated in their

---

Rite' on how to proceed in cases of Sollicitation, *Crimen sollicitationis*, 16 March, 1962, Title V ('*Crimen pessimum*'), nn. 71, 73.

[37.] 100J. Llobell, 'Contemperamento tra gli interessi lesi e il diritto dell'imputato: il diritto all'equo processo', in D. Cito (ed.), *Processo penale e tutela dei diritti nell'ordinamento canonico*, Giuffré, Milan, 2005, 63–143 at 95–6.

news release, embraced Nolan's final recommendations of May 2001, and noted progress already made on implementing his framework recommendations. No hint is given in this resolution of any role for canon law nor of any need to seek the approval after revision or '*recognitio*' for norms for the area of the bishops' conference of the Holy See, a grave failure, which robbed the norms adopted of validity in canon law.[38] This deficiency has been rightly recognized in the Cumberledge Report of 2008 which reviewed the operation of the Nolan procedures and which has had to take the embarrassing step of urging the bishops' conference to seek that '*recognitio*', without which the Nolan recommendations 'and indeed our own … will not be binding on individual Bishops or Congregational leaders'.[39]

To turn to the procedures outlined above for penal processes, the first requirement when a bishop or other superior receives a complaint against a cleric of the sexual abuse of a child or young person (under eighteen) is urgently to establish a preliminary enquiry (c. 1717 §1), to facts, circumstances, and, imputability, to see whether the person has a case to answer. This is not to be confused with a full trial; advice given to Bishop Comiskey of Ferns seems to have led him to judge that he needed full proof of guilt before acting. This enquiry needs to establish precisely what is being alleged, in respect of which canon(s).[40]

The Nolan Report's 'paramountcy principle' from family court precedent, is justified in the areas of appointments, conduct and supervision of those who work with children and young persons in the Church. The Cumberledge Report claims that the principle of 'innocent until proven guilty' applies only during the stages of a criminal trial under civil law, which implies that it does not apply during the preliminary investigation (nor in any canonical process), when, instead, paramountcy would be operative. The request that the bishops' conference prepare a general decree on the bases of their recommendations and to apply to Rome for the '*recognitio*' involves an

---

[38.] Resolution of the Bishop's Conference of England and Wales on the Final Nolan Report, 16 November 2001, accessed on 10 November 2006, from www.catholic-ew.org.uk/cn/01/011116-4.htm

[39.] Working Party of the Canon Law Society of Great Britain and Ireland, *Responding to Allegations of Clerical Child Abuse: Recommendations for Harmonising the Nolan Report and the Code of Canon Law*, Canon Law Society of Great Britain and Ireland, London, 2004, introduction, p. 3; The Cumberledge Commission, *Safeguarding with Confidence: Keeping Children and Vulnerable Adults Safe in the Catholic Church: The Cumberledge Commission Report*, Catholic Truth Society, London, 2007, 89, n. 7.4.

[40.] Working Party, *Responding to Clerical Child Abuse*, 7, n. 5.

explicit request to recognize the 'paramountcy principle', listed first.[41] In fact, Nolan had recommended that, when an allegation was raised, the Child Protection Coordinator to be established in each parish should be notified and the statutory authorities and a priest against whom the allegations are made be urged to 'take administrative leave', analogous to 'suspension' on full pay for a lay person, but 'suspension' could not be used as a term here since, canonically, it is a penal sanction.[42] The recommendation of the Cumberledge Report confirms this and suggests that the civil and canonical preliminary processes be combined.[43] Since the bishop can nominate another person to conduct the preliminary enquiry, there being two assessors to help, this would be possible in theory. The argument that this avoids duplication might have some weight, but the specific question of evaluating whether or not there has been a canonical crime committed and whether or not the evidence indicates that the person suspected may have been responsible has elements specific to canon law which need attention. When Cumberledge states that those responsible should 'apply the civil standard of proof in the investigation and determination of any matter relating to the abuse of children and vulnerable adults',[44] it means that, in criminal proceedings, a judgment be formed 'beyond reasonable doubt', which is rightly equated with the canonical requirement of 'moral certainty'. Apart from criminal proceedings, it urges that a judgment be based on 'balance of probabilities', which indicates a judgment in a court or tribunal as to which version of events is found the more convincing.[45]

This latter consideration is advanced in relation to what Cumberledge calls the 'Church process' and envisages a situation in which an accused has been acquitted in a civil criminal case, in which a criminal enquiry does not lead to a criminal prosecution or in which an internal investigation found 'inappropriate conduct but not amounting to a crime'.[46] The report is very helpful in explaining that a decision by the Crown Prosecutions Service may decide not to bring a criminal prosecution either because 'there is insufficient evidence to justify a prosecution' or because a prosecution 'is not in the public interest', the latter meaning that a very young child, a

---

[41.] The Cumberledge Report, 90, n. 7.5 (i).
[42.] The Nolan Report, n. 3.5.1; recommendations 52–4, 65–6.
[43.] The Cumberledge Report, n. 4.21; recommendation 42.
[44.] Ibid., n. 4.21; recommendation 41.
[45.] Ibid., n. 4.46, and p. 132.
[46.] Ibid., n. 4.46.

disabled person, someone very ill, is unable to give evidence, but that, otherwise, there is sufficient evidence to warrant a prosecution.[47] It is perfectly true that someone may be acquitted in a criminal trial, who escaped conviction on a technicality or where the evidence adduced did not demonstrate a crime as such, but did demonstrate grave misconduct, even where a judge has obtained a confession of grave misconduct from the accused. Canonically, with or without such an admission, but depending upon exactly what grave misconduct had been involved, it would be extremely likely that the accused could be asked to accept a form of penance (c. 1340) and should be warned or given a reproof as a penal remedy (c. 1339), but the evidence may well be such to warrant action in a canonical trial or through an administrative procedure, given that there has been a civil trial, to impose or declare sanctions as such.

There is a danger of a real presumption of guilt, especially as Cumberledge denies presumption of innocence at this stage. One aspect of the preliminary enquiry is that the evaluation of evidence has to involve an evaluation of the credibility of witnesses. The 1962 norms on solicitation applied procedurally to sexual abuse of children, but they involved the examination under oath of witnesses as to the credibility of accuser and of accused.[48] This would not be possible very easily with children, but serious attention to this question is fundamental for justice.

It is regrettably true that grave cases of sexual abuse were overlooked in the past because it was judged either that priests could never do such things or to avoid scandal in the form of prosecuting them. The danger too of not believing what children say, especially if repeated, is not to be replaced by believing everything they say without further ado; in other words, some form of corroboration needs to be sought or at least some basis for credibility needs to be verified. This is a question of major importance, specifically for cases of child sexual abuse. The French judicial system has suffered a major shock in recent years because in the Outreau case (named after the main accused) seventeen persons were prosecuted for the sexual abuse of children at St Omer in spring 2004, the case having been opened in February 2001, on very weak charges in regard to most of the accused ('... *marquée par la fragilité des charges pesant sur la plupart des accusés*').

[47.] Ibid., nn. 39-40.
[48.] Holy Office, Instruction, *Crimen sollicitationis*, Title II, n. 33.

Seven were acquitted on 2 July 2004, the others appealing against their sentences ranging from an eighteen months' suspended sentence to seven years in prison. The Court of Appeal in Paris on 1 December 2005, took the exceptional step of acquitting all of them, on the basis of retractions from some of the accusers and of the inadequacies in the instruction of the case. Of the thirteen released, most had spent several years in prison awaiting trial, some had lost jobs, children had been taken into care, they suffered gravely from 'unfounded suspicions', there was also the suicide of one of the accused while awaiting trial in prison.[49] The attitude of some of the social services involved in the face of each new complaint from the children, the judgments of experts as to the credibility of the accusers and the claimed profile of sexual abuser in relation to fourteen of the original seventeen accused, and the way the case was instructed as a search for the guilty were all to blame.[50] The report presented to the French Chamber of Deputies urged that the right of defence be more effectively observed, that evidence adduced be available to the accused or at least to his lawyers, the lawyer informing the *juge d'instruction* of what he intended to show to his client, with the former having the right to object to that to avoid contamination of evidence, pressure on the victims, their lawyers and anyone involved in the process.[51] Indeed, the right of the defence formed the core of the first recommendation put forward for reform, urging that the lawyer of the accused have full access to the charges and evidence.[52] It is especially the neglect of the principle of the presumption of innocence of the accused which is targeted by the report of a French Parliament, which operates under a constitution which is, from its first article, very strictly that of a republic which is democratic and lay. Despite what they rightly state are excellent statements of principle, the reality is often different:

[49.] Documents issued on 7 December 2005: N. 2725 Assemblée nationale: *Rapport* (de M. Philippe Houillon, Député) ... *sur la proposition de resolution (n. 2722) de Mm. Jean-Louis Debré et Philippe Houillon tendant à la creation d'une commission d'enquête charge de rechercher les causes des dysfonctionnements de la justice dans l'affaire dite d'Outreau et de formuler des propositions pour éviter leur renouvellement*; http//www.assemblee-nationale.fr/12/rapports/r2725.asp, accessed 2 August 2006, Introduction.

[50.] Ibid., II B.

[51.] Report of M. Philippe Houillon to the French Parliament on the Outreau Case, n. 3125, http//www.assemblee-nationale.fr/12/rap-enq/r3125-tl.asp, accessed 24 March 2007, pp. 261–2.

[52.] Ibid., Recommendation 1, pp. 393–4.

We know that too often the presumption of innocence gives way before a presumption of guilt. Those who were shouting the loudest to complain against the imprisonment of innocent people in the Outreau case, were they not the very ones who were shouting the loudest to have them thrown in prison? In certain cases, the pressure of society is such in effect and the fear of not condemning the guilty is so strong, that we increase the risks of prosecuting and of imprisoning the innocent. And when there is no longer any place for reflection, when revulsion carries away reason, we come to the point of the disasters of the Outreau case.[53]

In the appeal, it was shown that 'evidence' had stemmed from one particular lady who had pressed the matter forcefully, that a number of the children had had access to one another and had made up part of their stories together, that the witnesses were so vague about when precisely the events occurred that they should have been doubted.[54] The young judge, Burgaud, received evidence from a number of children, all giving elements corroborating the story, but it turned out that the matter was blown up out of all proportion and was based on gossip; all were acquitted. The French Parliament has ordered a full review of its own judicial procedures to try to avert such a grave miscarriage of justice (*'immense erreur judiciaire'*) in the future.[55]

Recent attempts after Nolan to sensitize people in the Church to the reality and problems of clerical paedophilia have included some group sessions with seminarians, sometimes involving members of Child Protection authorities. Anecdotal accounts from seminarians involved in such a session outside Rome in the last few years recount a priest from the agency set up after Nolan who had come out from England as part of the group animating such a session, who allegedly stated to these seminarians that, in his view, after encountering a number of priests over the years, all against whom an accusation was levelled were guilty.

[53.] Ibid., p. 3: 'Hélas, la réalité est parfois loin des principes et l'on sait que trop souvent la présomption d'innocence cède le pas devant une présomption de culpabilité. Ceux qui criaient le plus fort pour dénoncer l'emprisonement des innnocentés d'Outreau, n'étaient-ils pas ceux qui avaient crié le plus fort pour qu'on les jette en prison? Dans certaines affaires, la pression de la société est telle en effet et la peur de ne pas condamner un coupable si fort, qu'on multiplie les risques de poursuivre et d'emprisonner des innocents. Et quand il n'y a plus d'espace pour la réflexion, quand la révolte l'emporte sur la raison, on en arrive à des désastres comme celui d'Outreau.'

[54.] Ibid., III A, pp. 59–63.

[55.] Rapport on the Outreau Case, n. 2725, 7 December 2005, II A.

Sufficient evidence to open a prosecution in any area does not guarantee sufficient evidence to gain a conviction; a decision not to prosecute because to do so is 'not in the public interest' does not entail that the accused is guilty of a crime of sexually abusing a child. The canonical preliminary investigation is not a trial as such, but an evaluation of whether there is a basis for a trial. Whenever an accusation is made, it needs to be examined. If it is manifestly false, it is to be discarded, in civil as well as in canonical terms. Otherwise, there needs to be some corroboration, some basis for credibility; the paramountcy principle should not in any way override these elementary requirements of justice. The accused person is innocent until proven guilty; hence the preliminary enquiry should not call into question anyone's good name (c. 1717 § 2) and should be conducted 'carefully' (c. 1717 § 1), both to ensure that the truth is as fully uncovered as possible to protect any victims of child sexual abuse and to protect the suspect from false allegations.

In a case where the bishop judges that there is sufficient basis to open a criminal process, he would be wise to consult two judges or legal experts (in canon law) about drawing up the decrees needed (c. 1718 § 3). It is to be noted that the Cumberledge proposal does not require canonical experts at this stage, but they are not to be overlooked. Moreover, a person against whom allegations have been laid would be advised immediately to seek proper canonical advice from an advocate qualified in canon law and through that advocate to challenge by recourse actions undertaken by the bishop or other superior which do not meet the requirements of canon law. This is not suggested to be obstructive, but as a way of ensuring that justice be done. The guidance, even to the point of providing samples of decrees, given by the Canon Law Society is very good,[56] but there have been serious aberrations. It seems a bishop appeared and required a priest's removal to another place within a matter of an hour, with neither decrees, nor written information, nor any detail as to alleged offences. In fact, the guidance the Society drew up and which Cumberledge saw makes it clear that c. 1722 does not constitute a single uniform measure to be adopted by bishops as Nolan and Cumberledge seem to wish, but 'a series of measures, each of which needs to be justified in a decree'.[57] We recall that a decree needs to be motivated (reasons given) at least in summary form or it is lacking in full legal force (c.

[56.] Working Party, *Responding to Clerical Child Abuse*, 33–5.
[57.] Ibid., 14, n. 16.

51). These guidelines indicate diocesan tribunals which are competent to hear certain cases, but cases of child sexual abuse, 'a delict against the sixth commandment of the Decalogue committed with a minor under eighteen years of age', are reserved to the Congregation for the Doctrine of the Faith.[58] We notice the age limit of eighteen years, increased from the standard sixteen years in the Code (c. 1395 § 2). Canon law, like many systems of law, but not the common law in Britain, has a statute of limitations on most crimes of three years or in some instances of five years (so that they cannot be prosecuted after that time), but these norms make this ten years and 'prescription begins to run from the day on which the minor completes the eighteenth year of age', allowing action not from the time of the crime, but until the victim is twenty-eight years old.[59] As in all penal cases where the accused are priests, all judges must be priests, with doctorates in canon law, but only priests can be judges as a matter of validity in the cases under the 2001 norms. In fact, the Congregation has the faculty to dispense from the requirement of doctorate and priesthood in specific cases, to allow the process to function as under c. 1421, according to amendments to these norms by John Paul II in February 2003.[60]

The Congregation may delegate a particular tribunal to handle the case at first instance or may choose to handle it itself; the second instance is always with the Congregation. As for the norms of c. 1722, the presiding judge of such a tribunal may exercise the power of the ordinary over these restrictions, at the request of the promoter of justice. It is not specified whether this is the promoter of the local tribunal or of the Congregation, but the former would be likely for urgent action, although the advocate of the accused would have the right to appeal to the promoter of the Congregation.[61] The 2001 norms reiterate the Code's position that graver crimes, reserved to the Congregation 'can only be tried in a judicial process'.[62] However, the amendments of 2003 permit two exceptions where the Congregation may dispense from this, one where 'grave and clear cases' may be referred directly to the Holy Father for *ex officio* dismissal from the clerical state and others which may be treated under the administrative process of c. 1720 when the ordinary considers that the accused

---

[58.] John Paul II, Apostolic letter *motu proprio, Sacramentorum sanctitatis tutela*, 30 April 2001, art 4 § 1.
[59.] Ibid., art 5 § 2.
[60.] Ibid., art. 8, 11, 12; amendments made by John Paul II, 7 and 14 February 2003.
[61.] Ibid., art. 15.
[62.] Ibid., art. 17.

should be dismissed from the clerical state and asks the Congregation to impose this by decree.[63] This is a limitation of the right to defence, which was especially protected through the judicial process where permanent penalties were in view, but it can only occur through a dispensation from the Congregation for the Doctrine of the Faith in pressing circumstances.

A vexed question is that of 'administrative leave', a concept unknown to canon law. Nolan and Cumberledge, and the Ferns Report too, all recommend the equivalent of suspending a lay person from a post on full pay during such an investigation. Such a person would normally have the assistance of family and of trade union support, not to conceal criminal paedophilia, but to ensure that his or her rights were observed. Cumberledge helpfully suggests either that funding legal assistance (for civil lawyers) comes from the diocese or that the legal aid services be involved, to help priests. Although describing this administrative leave as 'temporary', the fact is that it is much more public than most suspensions of employees, where a person's sudden absence may be capable of various interpretations, and it is extremely unlikely that a priest will ever return to such a position, since his reputation is inevitably destroyed in a fairly public way,[64] even through the desirable efforts to support the parish in such a crisis. A recent booklet summarizes these points, including 'temporary' absence from the parish, but there is no mention of how or when a priest might return or resume his ministry.[65]

It should be noted that the Code does not envisage any automatic application of the possible restrictive or prudential measures under c. 1722. It was to be a matter judged case by case, and still is such in penal cases generally. However, the presumption of this law has been changed by the norms of 2001. Where a preliminary investigation of allegations of child sexual abuse leads to a decision to pursue criminal process (in mind in the canon is a canonical process, but it could function for a civil criminal action), the suspect is to be subjected to the restrictions envisaged. Nevertheless, this does not dispense with the need to consult the promoter of justice, who, in the case of the promoter at the Congregation for the Doctrine of the Faith, has the

---

[63.] Amendment to art. 17, 2003.
[64.] Woestman, *Ecclesiastical Sanctions*, 157.
[65.] Catholic Bishops' Conference of England and Wales, *Directory on the Canonical Status of the Clergy: Rights, Obligations and Procedures*, Catholic Truth Society, London, 2009, nn. 19.1, 2, 5 (vi), 6 and (ii), 7, 8.

discretion to say otherwise, not to allow such measures or to allow some rather than others. The restrictions prohibit the exercise of the sacred ministry, of some ecclesiastical office or position, require or forbid residence in a certain place, or forbid public participation in the Eucharist. These restrictions end of themselves at the end of a canonical process (c. 1722), either because the person is acquitted or because there is a conviction, which may involve any or all of these being imposed or declared as sanctions.

These measures are designed for the time after the preliminary investigation. The tendency now is to seek to impose them all immediately upon receipt of an allegation. This has been assisted by the 2001 norms from the Holy See in response to the scandals and by the costs of damages in civil cases in many countries. The procedures currently in force, therefore, seem to offer fewer guarantees for the right of defence. Neglect of the Church's penal law for so long has meant both the most scandalous exposure of innocent children and young people to the predatory activities of clerical abusers and a weakening of the right of all accused, especially those innocent of crime.

The Cumberledge Report offers progress in seeking legal support for the accused, in urging the bishops' conference to observe its own Church's laws, in providing for an appeal by those considering themselves wrongly accused and treated through a review body, in trying to stop group psychotherapy for those under suspicion but not convicted. Like Nolan, it has the great merit of offering very much more effective protection to children and young persons through structures which are functioning. The legitimacy and need for the paramountcy principle in appointments and in procedures generally in church affairs is obvious and necessary. It is not right to place this above the effective right of defence which needs to be operative from the point when an allegation is made or, at least, once the preliminary investigation is under way. Paedophiles are a scourge, especially because of their dissimulation, but no child is in any way better protected from sexual abuse by the wrongful condemnation or exclusion (by indefinite administrative leave and restrictions) of a priest or other cleric who is innocent.

It is absolutely correct to say and to act on the basis that the absence of a conviction or even of a prosecution does not mean that there is no problem of sexual abuse; there can be, but there must be some evidence of this and not just conjecture. There is a difficulty with child protection bodies having such massive power over the lives of people accused or suspected when there is no trial, either civil or canonical. Canonical trials do admit hearsay evidence under certain conditions and could be effective where civil proceedings are not. What would be dangerous would be for people rightly committed to protecting children and the young, themselves not judges, to end up acting in effect as a court in circumstances where neither civil nor church courts are involved. The review body envisaged by Cumberledge is an improvement. However, when assessing these latter type of cases, it seems to me that, in addition to any counsel the suspect may have, such child protection panels ought to have someone qualified in civil or in canon law sitting on them to act as a critical evaluator of what the body decides in respect of such a suspect, to intervene where a judgment or proposed action appears to be rash or unfounded. Since no child is protected by the condemnation or exclusion of the innocent, such a provision would serve both to ensure justice to the suspect and to ground actions to protect children more solidly.

8. Recourse against Administrative Acts (Part V)

Recourse in General

We recall that a juridical act is an administrative act intended to produce juridical effects. Where such an administrative act, other than of a judicial trial and other than acts of the supreme authority (of the Pope, or of an ecumenical council) is considered to be unjust, to violate the rights of a physical or juridical person, the physical person or the one who properly acts on behalf of the juridical person has the right of recourse against this action (cc. 1732–1733 § 1). It is not an appeal because there has been no judgment in a judicial process.

a. Preliminary Recourse or Petition

The preliminary action is technically a petition made to the one responsible for the (allegedly unjust) administrative act, asking him to withdraw it or amend it (c. 1734 § 1), which has to be made within ten canonical days of receiving the decree (c. 1734 § 2). If he does so, the matter is resolved; if he refuses or does not reply (taken as implicit refusal), then a recourse to his hierarchical superior is possible. In fact, a procedure of mediation or arbitration, to settle the disputed matter is recommended, but is not compulsory (c. 1733).

Recourse to a Hierarchical Superior

Recourse to a hierarchical superior has to take place within fifteen days of the notice of the act or of the refusal or implicit refusal to reconsider it (c. 1735) and the time to exercise hierarchical recourse runs either from the issuing of the new decree or from the ending of the thirty days which indicates that there has been no response (c. 1735). It means recourse to the bishop for acts of a parish priest, episcopal vicar, vicar general, to the relevant Congregation against an act of the bishop, to the Apostolic Signatura, highest court in the Church, against an administrative act of one of the other Dicasteries; people have the right to go the Apostolic See without passing through the other levels. The person making the recourse has the right to an advocate, appointed by the relevant body, if he does not choose one himself, to assist him to present his case (c. 1738). With the Apostolic Signatura, a petitioner has the right to an advocate trained in the procedures of the Signatura, so that he is represented by someone of real competence and justice can be done and can be seen to be done. The one to whom recourse is made can revoke, confirm or amend the original act (c. 1739).

b. Special Acts of Recourse

Recourse against Removal of a Parish Priest

Where someone is removed from ecclesiastical office, this has to be for serious reasons. In the case of a parish priest, this might be when he cannot fulfil his duties through physical or mental ill health, he has badly mismanaged his responsibilities over the temporal goods of the Church, he is a cause of disruption to the communion of the Church or cannot get on with the parishioners in a serious way (c. 1741). The bishop has to consider the case with two priests agreed by the diocesan council of priests (c. 1742). If he judges that the parish priest ought to be removed, he is to be told so and why and he is to be given fifteen days to resign (c. 1742). If he disputes the decision, the bishop is to renew the request and extend the canonical time for a response (c. 1744). If he still refuses, the bishop must, for validity, let him see the acts of the case, ask him to put his reasons in writing, the bishop (and ideally the two priests) are to reconsider the case and, if they remain convinced that he should be removed, he is to be ordered to leave through a decree (c. 1745). If he does not respond to the bishop's initial request, it is to be repeated and a further time is to be given to the parish priest to respond. In the end, if the parish priest believes the decision is unjust, he may appeal to the Apostolic See (the Congregation for the Clergy, or possibly the Congregation for Institutes of the Consecrated Life and Societies of the Apostolic Life, if the removal is by his provincial). During this time a successor cannot be appointed, although a parish administrator can be (c. 1747 § 3). If the decision is upheld, the parish priest is to be supported still by the diocese (c. 1746) and helped especially if sick (c. 1747 § 2) and is to be given another appointment if suitable or helped to retire (c. 1746).

Recourse against the Transfer of a Parish Priest

As we saw earlier, where a parish priest is asked to transfer for 'the good of souls' or for the 'advantage of the Church', this is to be proposed to him in writing and the bishop is to try to persuade him to consent (c. 1748). This refers to a parish priest of a parish 'which he governs satisfactorily' (c. 1748) and not one where he needs to be removed because he is not operating satisfactorily for whatever reason (cc. 1741–1747).

If a priest whom the bishop wishes to transfer considers that he ought not to be transferred or, more precisely, where a transfer is decided in violation of the canonical procedures for the transfer of the said parish priest, he has the right to have recourse against the bishop's decision. He can ask him in writing to revoke the decision (c. 1749). If the bishop refuses, and if the procedures have been violated, the priest can have recourse against the bishop's decision to the Congregation for the Clergy. If the bishop has violated the procedures in regard to the parish being vacant before a new appointment is made, the transfer is null and void. If this is on the basis that the parish to which the transfer was being made was not canonically vacant at the time, the transfer is invalid and the office does not subsequently become vacant (c. 153 § 1). A removal of a parish priest under the guise of a transfer is invalid. The decision of the Congregation is binding on both bishop and parish priest.

9. Conclusion: The Pastoral Care of Souls (c. 1752)

This concludes our treatment of the canon law of the People of God, the teaching function of the Church, penal law and procedural law. The Code ends with a canon which is the key to its canon law, namely that the law of the Church is there to foster the eternal salvation of its members and, potentially, of all people. The 'care of souls is the supreme law' ('*salus animarum suprema lex*' – c. §1752). This does not mean that it sets aside other laws, since these are the ways in which that care is exercised and assured in the communion of the Church. However, this supreme law inspires and guides the understanding and application of the other laws in the Code and beyond it, which are designed for the good of the faithful, to help the Church to fulfil faithfully, effectively and justly the mission given to it by Jesus Christ.

Conclusion

This analysis of the Code after twenty-five years demonstrates that canon law is profoundly rooted in the mystery of God's revelation in Jesus Christ, whose saving Gospel it seeks not to supplant, but to express and to serve in support of the Church's mission. The common good of the specific society of the Church, in the service of that Gospel, is exposed to serious risk of arbitrariness and preference of persons, unless there is an instrument of law for the benefit of all and for the sake of the mission with which they are charged by Christ.

To lead us to his Father, Christ abides in the Church always through the Holy Spirit who renders it indefectibly holy as it responds to the Trinitarian call to perfect communion in them, but human beings who are members of the faithful through baptism do not always respond fully to that call of eternal love. Thus, the Church, insofar as it is composed also of sinners in its earthly pilgrimage, is always in need of being made holy.[1] In this study we have had cause to note that ignorance of the law, even by those who ought to know better, can damage the pastoral care of the faithful, whose service is the supreme norm of canon law (c. 1752), at times doing them real disservice and even harm. People's rights are not respected without determined, systematic effort to pass from good intentions to what objectively is required as a matter of justice. Whether it concerns preparation for sacraments, liturgical norms, parish registers, criteria for appointments, the administration of the Church's temporal goods, the observance of procedures, or the like, this is where justice, rights and the proper participation of all the faithful in the mission of the Church are encountered as practical realities, where principle is shown to be sincere and effective or where it is undermined or even betrayed. Canon law is an instrument of justice for people called to holiness, but as yet grappling with sin and failure.

Whether from ignorance, neglect or wilfulness, the violation of

---

[1.] Second Vatican Council, *Lumen gentium*, n. 8.

the law's provisions can cause exasperation, to the point where the solution may seem to be to make more of its provisions matters of validity and not just of liceity.[2] Such an understandable reaction might impede the Church's mission in other respects, a reason why conditions for validity are usually very limited. Perhaps, greater use needs to be made of procedures for recourse against illicit or even invalid juridical acts, where superiors act out of ignorance or refuse to attend properly to their responsibilities. The difficulty of living with them afterwards deters many from this course of action, but it may be necessary at times for the common good. Mere procedures will never be enough to ensure respect for canon law and for its function. What is needed in all the faithful and at every level is a genuine passion for justice in the Church in all its activities. Hopefully, this study may contribute in some way to fostering a greater appreciation of the value of canon law as an instrument of that justice in the Church, as she continues to strive to serve her Lord and the mission he has entrusted to her.

[2.] J. Beyer, *Le nouveau droit ecclésial: Commentaire du Code de droit canonique,* Livre II troisième partie: *Le droit de la vie consacrée, instituts et sociétés,* Tardy, Paris, 1988, 41.

Appendix 1

The Reception of Groups of Former Anglicans into Full Communion with the Catholic Church

(*Anglicanorum coetibus* and Complementary Norms)

In 2009 an Apostolic Constitution, *Anglicanorum coetibus*, was issued to erect new 'personal Ordinariates' for 'those Anglican faithful who desire to enter the full communion of the Catholic Church in a corporate manner', precisely as groups and not as individuals.[1] The reason for this seems to have been that groups of Anglicans have sought the possibility of entering into full communion as parishes, in part perhaps after the 'ordination' of known homosexual persons as Anglican bishops, perhaps more broadly following Anglican ordination of women and a general feeling that the Communion was increasingly departing from Apostolic Tradition and was in increasing danger of internal schism. Women are incapable of ordination and Anglican orders are themselves invalid, but the Holy See has judged that the practice of recent decades of receiving into full communion individuals who wished this and who were judged suitable and were properly prepared would not be an adequate way of confronting the present situation. It might be speculated that a refusal might be seen as total rejection and might jeopardize the salvation of many people who are undoubtedly deeply disturbed at recent trends within that Communion.

An Apostolic Constitution is an act of constitutive law in the Church, establishing or bringing into being a new reality, in this case

---

[1] Benedict XVI, Apostolic Constitution, Anglicanorum coetibus, 4 November, 2009, preamble, www.vatican.va/holy_father/benedict_xvi, apost_constitutions/documents/hf_ben-xvi, accessed 16 December, 2009.

the new Ordinariates. The Constitution does not address all aspects of receiving Anglicans into full communion as groups, but only the legal arrangements for this entity, which resembles a diocese, but without being located in a specific division of territory (the existing Military Ordinariates under a bishop for the Armed Forces are a model for this type of structure). Hence, it is essential that these legal provisions be read together with the Complementary Norms issued by the Congregation for the Doctrine of the Faith, which do deal with other critically important aspects of this new venture.

Anglicanorum coetibus allows new Ordinariates to be erected within the territory of the local Catholic Bishops' Conference, where the latter has been consulted (AC, I, § 1–2).[2] They would be composed of and would serve the needs of former Anglicans who enter into full communion with the Catholic Church or individuals who subsequently become Catholics through the ministrations of those belonging to the Ordinariates (AC, I § 4; CN, art. 5). Within this structure, there would be an ordinary, who would be a former Anglican who had become a bishop (of the Catholic Church) or who had become a Catholic priest and who was appointed by the Holy See (AC, IV; CN art. 4 § 1). Those who become members of such Ordinariates will be able to maintain many of the liturgical, spiritual and pastoral traditions they have known as Anglicans, using their liturgy of the Office and of the various sacraments (AC, III). Here it needs to be emphasized that the books which may be used will have to be checked, amended and approved by the Congregations for the Doctrine of the Faith and of Divine Worship and of the Discipline of the Sacraments, to ensure that they conform fully to Catholic doctrine; their ministers will become Catholic priests and so the sacraments depending on the power of order will be valid. The preparation of future priests would be conducted in conjunction with the local territorial diocese of the Catholic Church in a seminary, but the new Ordinariates may have a house of preparation to foster the spiritual and liturgical traditions they had known in Anglicanism (AC, VI § 5; CN, art. 10 § 1–5).

It is the Complementary Norms which specify that all those in such groups who wish to become Catholics would have to receive the sacraments of initiation. Here we recall that baptism conferred

---

[2.] The Apostolic Constitution is referred to as AC (Anglicanorum coetibus) and the Complementary Norms as CN; Congregation for the Doctrine of the Faith, Complementary Norms for the Apostolic Constitution Anglicanorum coetibus, 4 November, 2009, www.vatican.va/roman_curia/congregations/cfaith/documents, accessed 16 December, 2009.

by pouring water with the Trinitarian formula is valid; it does not depend on priestly orders and can be administered validly even by a non-Christian in urgent need. Thus, unless there were doubt about the actual validity of a baptism (e.g. water had not been poured or a non-Trinitarian form had been used), this sacrament would not and could not be repeated (c. 845). However, all seeking full communion would have to be confirmed and make their first holy communion (CN, art. 5 § 1), since these sacraments do depend on valid priestly orders, which *per se* are lacking in the Anglican Communion. It should be noted that, although these provisions concern groups of persons entering full communion, in fact, there is no 'group' initiation, but necessarily each individual needs to receive these sacraments. Both the Constitution and the Complementary Norms state unequivocally that the norm of doctrine for those entering full communion in this way is *The Catechism of the Catholic Church*, not any Anglican formula (I § 5). It is somewhat surprising that the brief formula recited by those entering full communion, after the recitation of the Nicene Creed, affirming acceptance of all that the Magisterium teaches on faith and morals, is not explicitly mentioned in these texts; it is to be hoped that the liturgical rite leading to confirmation retains it.

Any man who is currently an Anglican minister, who enters full communion through a group in the way outlined and who wishes to be a Catholic priest would need to have his vocation assessed in accordance with criteria agreed with the Holy See (CN, art. 6 § 1) and would need to be prepared before being ordained as a deacon and then as a priest (VI § 1). Any man ordained as a Catholic priest, however, who has since become an Anglican is expressly prohibited from exercizing sacred ministry, hence even as a deacon, in the Ordinariate; nor may Anglican clergy in irregular marital situations be accepted for ordination (CN, art 6 § 2). Ordination is absolute; it is not conditional, since Anglican orders are null and void; this is clear from the fact that a former Anglican bishop 'is to be ordained a priest in the Catholic Church' before he can undertake certain functions (CN, art. 11 § 1), a logic which applies to all who are to exercise priesthood. Here, of course, those men who are already married would need to seek and receive dispensation from celibacy from the Pope on an individual basis, as is already done with former ministers who have been received into full communion and who have become Catholic priests; the Ordinary himself can only admit celibate men for training as priests (AC, VI § 2). As we have seen, the exception foreseen here does not alter the norm on celibacy.

For those who are Anglican bishops, ordination to the diaconate and to the priesthood would operate as just outlined. It would be possible for a single man from this background to be ordained a bishop in the Catholic Church, but no ordination to the episcopate is possible for anyone who is married, as long as his wife remains alive; he could be appointed Ordinary, but 'in such a case he is to be ordained a priest in the Catholic Church' (CN, art. 11 § 1). Surprisingly, it is conceded that married Anglican bishops who are ordained Catholic priests but who cannot be ordained as bishops may use the title 'emeritus bishop' and may request permission to wear the insignia of a bishop (CN, art. 11 § 3–4). Why such external trappings should be remotely envisaged in what ought to be a major matter of conscience is hard to imagine. Moreover, emeritus bishops do have rights to function in and on behalf of bishops' conferences and even at synods; it is to be presumed that those who are in fact not bishops would be unable to operate in this way.

It can be seen that, on the one hand, former Anglicans who enter full communion in Ordinariates of this kind (they have to register as such following reception of the sacraments of initiation) may maintain many of their liturgical, spiritual and pastoral traditions and that they are provided with pastoral care specific to their needs in this regard. On the other hand, they must truly become Catholics, doctrinally and sacramentally. These Ordinariates are linked to the local bishops' conference and the ordinary is a member of it. There is to be collaboration between them and the bishops' conference and some pastoral collaboration is envisaged between priests of the Ordinariates and of the local diocese (AC, VI § 4; CN art. 9). The Ordinariate is to be governed by the Ordinary, together with a Governing Council of at least six priests, with powers analogous to those of the Presbyteral Council and of the College of Consultors, is to have a Finance Committee and a Pastoral Council, and the Ordinary is to make the *Ad limina* visit to the Holy See every five years along with others from the bishops' conference (AC, X–XI). After consultation with the local diocese, the Ordinary can erect personal parishes, a house of formation (in both cases he needs also the consent of the Governing Council – CN, art. 12 § 2) and institutes of consecrated life or societies of apostolic life (CN, art. 9 § 2). In each parish a finance committee and a pastoral council must be established (I CN, art. 14 § 1), the compulsory nature of the latter being a difference from the requirements of the Code for parishes in a diocese.

Where the number of Ordinariates within the territory of a given bishops' conference were large enough, especially given the presence of those proclaimed to be 'emeritus bishops', difficulties of integration and of undue preponderance might emerge. However, with good will and cooperation, it should be possible to work together in advancing the mission of the Church, with people who, hopefully, will feel at home in their new situation and who should be welcomed on that basis. It is worth saying that the new Ordinariates are not ritual Churches, like the Uniate Eastern Catholic Churches; they are part of the Latin Church, under the 1983 Code, and constitute a variation within it and, indeed, the permission to use their traditions is 'without excluding liturgical celebrations according to the Roma Rite' (III). The situation is to be monitored by the Congregation for the Doctrine of the Faith, in conjunction with other dicasteries of the Holy See (AC, II; CN, art. 1).

Appendix 2

Two Changes to the Code

(*Omnium in mentem*, 26 October 2009)

Whereas the arrangements for groups of former Anglicans entering full communion do not involve any change in the Code, two changes to that Code have just been introduced by the Apostolic letter, given *motu proprio*, 26 October 2009, *Omnium in mentem*, whose publication has just occurred. Prior to this, the only formal amendment to the Code had been *Ad tuendam fidem* of 1998.

1. The Sacrament of Orders

The text of c. 1008 had spoken about those ordained acting '*in persona Christi*', which was ambiguous in that deacons were not ordained as priests and did not in fact operate in the person of Christ; they were ordained for service ('*ad ministerium*'), but not to the priesthood ('*ad sacerdotium*'), as we have seen. Some concern about this arose after the first text of the Catechism had repeated this ambiguity and John Paul II ordered that the matter be clarified in 1998. It will be recalled that the inter-dicasterial instruction on the collaboration of the lay faithful of 1997 had sought to reduce confusion over the role of deacons and over other matters.

Under *Omnium in mentem*, the matter is clarified fully. C. 1008 is now amended to refer to the three grades of order, but the reference to '*in persona Christi*' is eliminated from the canon: '... are constituted sacred ministers, that is those who are consecrated and destined to serve the People of God, each according to his own grade, by a new and special title' (art. 1). A new, third, paragraph is added to c. 1009 (art. 2), stating that those constituted as bishops or priests through sacred orders act *in persona Christi capitis* ('in the person of Christ, the Head'), while deacons receive the capacity to serve the People of God in the liturgy of the word and of charity:

> Those who are constituted in the order of the episcopate and in that of the presbyterate receive the mission and the faculty to act in the person

of Christ the Head; deacons, on the other hand, are enabled to serve the People of God in the liturgy, of the Word and of charity. (c. 1009 § 3)

2. Formal Defection from the Catholic Faith and Marriage

The other change to the Code introduced by *Omnium in mentem*[1] concerns the canon, new in 1983, which spoke of formal defection from the Catholic Church. We have already seen that an authentic interpretation of this canon requires, for validity, that such formal defection be expressed in a formal document. Here the interest is in marriage, since the Code expressly refers to those who have 'formally defected from the Catholic Church' (cc. 1086, 1117, 1124) in that connection. Under *Omnium in mentem*, this phrase is suppressed in all three canons (arts. 3, 4 and 5 respectively). The aim of including the phrase in the Code, for marriage, had been to avoid people in such a position from entering invalid marriages. However, the experience of trying to understand what was implied and how these canons were to be applied had led to much confusion. After a widespread consultation of bishops across the five continents, there was a call for this phrase to be completely suppressed. Problems which emerged from this consultation included not wanting to treat these persons differently from baptized persons who had contracted civil unions, a wish to link matrimony more to the sacrament, problems in some areas over the civil effects of marriage and in some places worries about clandestine marriages.[2] There was even a concern that some who had defected were being encouraged to apostasize in countries where Catholics were a small minority.[3]

The Pontifical Council for the Interpretation of Legislative Texts had examined a question about formal defection from the Catholic Church in respect of the implications of Catholics in certain countries, such as Germany, refusing to pay the Church taxes (*Kirchensteuer*), which had led bishops to equate this to formal defection. The authentic interpretation of formal defection of 2006 excludes such an interpretation and, as we have seen, required a formal document

---

[1] Benedict XVI, Apostolic letter, motu proprio, 'Omnium in mentem', 26 October 2009, preamble, www.vatican.va/holy_father/benedict_xvi, apost_letters/documents/hf_ben-xvi, accessed 16 December 2009.

[2] Pontifical Council for Legislative Texts, 'The motu proprio 'Omnium in mentem': 'Reasons for the two Changes' 15 December 2009, accessed 16 December, www.vatican.va/roman_curia/pontifical_councils/intrptxt

[3] Benedict, XVI, *Omnium in mentem*, preamble.

of defection.[4] The Pontifical Council states that *Omnium in mentem* concerns formal defection and marriage, not taxation, although that dispute confirmed the wisdom of suppressing the phrase in these canons.

Those who have formally defected from the Catholic Church did not need a dispensation to marry a non-baptized person (c. 1086), were not bound by canonical form (c. 1117) and needed no permission to marry a baptized non-Catholic (c. 1124), whereas they will need a dispensation to marry a non-baptized person and will be bound by canonical form, both for validity, and will need permission to marry a baptized non-Catholic, for liceity, once the *motu proprio* comes into force, three months after its promulgation in the *Acta Apostolicae sedis*. In effect, the elimination of this phrase from these three canons means that the general norm of c. 8 applies also to those who have formally defected from the Catholic Church, that they remain bound by merely ecclesiastical laws. As the Pontifical Council notes, regularizing marriages which have occurred under these norms will mean obtaining dispensations and sanating unions, effecting retroactive validity, where such is possible.

[4.] Pontifical Council for Legislative Texts, Actus formalis defectionis ab Eccelsia Catholica, 13 March 2006, accessed 16 December 2009, www.vatican.va/roman _curia/pontifical_councils/intrptxt

Appendix 3

Procedures: Clerical Sexual Abuse of Minors and other Grave Crimes

Since the text of this book was completed almost a year ago, there have been some formal changes to canon law, which have been treated in the appendices 1 and 2. This last year has seen further, dramatic evidence of sexual abuse of minors by clergy, particularly from Ireland and from Germany. Pope Benedict XVI has repeatedly condemned these sins and outrages and has criticized those in authority in the Church where there were inadequate responses to complaints of abuse or where it was covered up. He has promised reforms to ensure both that unsuitable men are not ordained and that effective measures be adopted to protect children from such abuse.

The legitimate criticism that laws relating to clerical sexual abuse of minors were not known even by bishops who were responsible for their implementation and the understandable reaction of victims and of others to the more recent revelations led to the publication on the Vatican website of specific information on procedures relating to such abuse in April 2010. This includes an unofficial English translation of the hitherto secret 1962 norms, now superseded, and a summary of procedures operating under the auspices of the Congregation for the Doctrine of the Faith (from 2001, as amended in 2003 and in 2005). This summary on the website does not constitute law as such and is expressed in terms designed to make the content understandable to people generally, rather than always in precise legal language. The norms in force were said to be under review, for the purpose of updating them to make them more effective in the light of experience; the new norms were promulgated by Benedict XVI on 21 May 2010, as amendments to *Sacramentorum sanctitatis tutela* of 2001 and were made known generally on 15 July 2010.

The summary of procedures on the Vatican website of spring 2010, includes what amounts to a significant reinterpretation and application to the question of child sexual abuse of the precautionary measures which c. 1722 envisaged might be applied in certain circumstances for penal cases. Their imposition in full seems here to be required, even before a preliminary enquiry has come to a decision as to whether there are grounds for thinking that a canonical crime has been committed and that a specific individual has a case to answer in its regard. The local bishop (diocesan bishop) 'is encouraged to exercise' the authority he has 'to whatever extent is necessary to assure that children do not come to harm ... before, during or after any canonical proceeding' (Guide to Understanding Basic CDF Procedures concerning Sexual Abuse Allegations, part A, April 2010). Remarks made in this book will need to be read with this in mind. It does not mean a bishop can do as he pleases, but it does mean he can and should implement the provisions of c. 1722, measures which I believe were intended previously in the Code, to be adopted, in part or as a whole, by way of precaution, once a preliminary investigation had been completed and then where specific factors were verified. A suspect believing himself unjustly treated has the option of exercising recourse. Confirmation of this interpretation seems to come from the revised norms, which speak less in a mandatory than in a permissive tone: 'The possibility of taking the (pre-)cautionary measures foreseen in CIC can. 1722 and CCEO can. 1473 during the preliminary investigation is allowed' ; the bishop has this power ('*habet potestatem*'), but according to the conditions laid down in c. 1722 (*sub iisdem condicionibus in ipsis canonibus determinatis*' – art. 19).

A very helpful summary of procedures operated by the Congregation for the Doctrine of the Faith in such cases was written by the current promoter of justice, Mgr C. J. Scicluna in spring 2010 ('The Procedures and Praxis of the CDF ...') . It indicates specific procedural options when an accusation is made in a diocese or against a cleric in an institute of consecrated life, always involving an initial investigation, analogous to c. 1717. When the report of the preliminary investigation and any supporting evidence reach the Congregation, four options exist for non-consecrated clergy. No penal action may be required and some non-penal provision for the common good and for that of the suspect may be made. Where the investigation's report and evidence are so strong as to demonstrate clear guilt beyond doubt ('particularly grave cases in which the guilt of the cleric is beyond doubt and is well documented' – 'Options of the CDF', option b), an administrative procedure may be chosen to seek the cleric's dismissal from the clerical state *ex officio* by the Holy Father; the Congregation in practice asks the individual accused to petition the Holy Father for dispensation from the obligations of the clerical state, but, if he does not do so, the Congregation would then petition for his dismissal. The third option involves authorization by the Congregation of a penal administrative procedure (c. 1720); if the Ordinary considers that dismissal from the clerical state is warranted, he must refer the matter to the Congregation, which would decide the matter, appeal being possible to a higher instance of the Congregation as a tribunal. Finally, the Congregation may authorize the conduct of a penal trial or judicial procedure (c. 1720) either in the diocese or elsewhere under instruction from the Congregation or in the Congregation itself; appeal against the first instance judgment may be had either by the defendant or by the promoter of justice, but only to the Congregation in its capacity as a tribunal. For those in the consecrated life, the supreme moderator of the institute and his council must send the acts of the preliminary investigation to the Congregation for the Doctrine of the Faith, which will decide on a penal trial (analogously to what has just been said) or an administrative procedure, which could lead to dismissal from the institute and from the clerical state.

These provisions are incorporated explicitly into the revised norms of May 2010, under art. 21. Interestingly, this article confirms the Code's clear preference for a judicial trial; the most serious crimes 'are to be pursued through a judicial trial' (art. 21 § 1). Mentioned as exceptions, administrative procedures may replace the trial in individual cases (art. 21 § 2, 1°), and in the gravest of cases, where the crime is manifest, although even then while safeguarding the right of defence, the Holy Father may be petitioned specifically to dismiss the cleric from the clerical state or a dispensation from the obligations of the clerical state may be sought (art. 21 § 2, 2°), in the ways outlined above.

The revised norms are notable for the fact that they extend the crime of sexual abuse of a minor to those who, due to insufficient use of reason, are equivalent to a minor (art. 6 § 1). They introduce also as a specific 'more serious crime' the 'obtaining, keeping or divulging of pornographic images of minors under the age of fourteen, in whatever way or by whatever means this is done by the cleric' (art. 6 § 2). This would not easily have been covered by c. 1395 § 2, which refers back to an external sexual sin against the sixth commandment, and the generic criminal canon (c. 1399) has clearly been thought not to be ideal for dealing with the pornographic aspect, long since recognized as frequently involved in the background to acts of paedophilia. The limit of fourteen years of age is probably to be explained by the fact that paedophilia is technically sexual abuse of someone before puberty, although the crime persists up to eighteen years of age.

The revised norms extend the period of prescription for the crime of sexual abuse against minors to twenty years, to run from the date of the victim's eighteenth birthday (art. 6 § 1). Obviously, experience has shown that ten years was insufficient in many cases. The Congregation has the faculty to derogate even from the limit of twenty years in a given case (art. 7 § 1), so that its ability to deal properly with cases of child sexual abuse is not hampered.

Only the Holy Father may judge cardinals, patriarchs, legates, bishops and others (c. 1405), but these revised norms make explicit mention of the fact that he may mandate the Congregation to judge such persons in respect of more serious crimes, on a case by case basis (art. 1 § 2). There have been cases where bishops or cardinals have been accused of abusing children or youngsters; this provision gives a clear way forward for the Church to deal with such cases.

The Congregation has the faculty also to sanate merely procedural errors at a lower level in the preparation of a case, whether the Congregation was the first instance tribunal and this concerned a preliminary investigation conducted elsewhere or whether it concerns procedural errors at first instance elsewhere (art. 18); in other words, someone guilty of this crime would not easily be able to escape punishment on merely technical or procedural grounds, less so than in some civil jurisdictions.

The norms do not mention denouncing the crime to civil authorities, although the Holy See has made it clear that this can be done. It should be borne in mind here that in a number of states there is no legal obligation at all upon any private citizen to denounce even a serious crime of another, including murder (although often there is such a requirement upon public officials of the state who come to know of a crime committed). Nor do these norms refer to the 'paramountcy principle', favoured in recent years in family courts in England and Wales and urged by Nolan and Cumberledge; since these norms refer expressly to what is to be done when a crime is thought to have been committed (they are norms of penal law), this does not affect the legitimacy of that principle at the level of procedures to be followed by clerics and others to ensure that children and young persons are protected from abuse; this is discussed in the book.

The statement of the Bishops of England and Wales in April 2010, asking for prayers for victims of abuse, for acts of reparation for the grave wrong done by those clergy who have been responsible for sexually abusing minors, fitted in well with the Pope's call for penance in the Church. The statement rightly noted that considerable efforts have been made by the Catholic Church to introduce effective procedures to protect children in England and Wales from such abuse and will have reassured people that there is cooperation with state authorities on these matters.

In the light of extensive criticism of the Church, it cannot be denied that the Holy See has taken very strong action in recent years and that it is more than ready to adapt its procedures in the light of experience. It should not be forgotten that the Church lacks coercive powers and cannot compel testimony, nor that it is necessary to have proof before acting against someone who may be innocent. The fact that the Holy See will have sought supplementary information in a number of cases stems from the fact that evidence is often incomplete, unclear or contradictory. Mere suspicion or accusation does not constitute proof. It is for this reason that the Code's penal law stressed the Church's preference for judicial trials in penal cases. As can be seen here, the failure of so many bishops to implement the Church's laws over the years has led to measures being taken, reflected in what is said here, which may perhaps be more efficient, but which seem in some ways to prefer administrative procedures to judicial.

It should be added that a background paper on the history behind these laws on child sexual abuse, issued on 15 July 2010, when the text was made public situate the crime in the setting primarily of the crime of solicitation in the confessional. It was for this reason essentially that previous laws and procedures were occult. The *'crimen pessimum'* of the norms of 1922, updated in 1962, was actually priests engaging in homosexual acts, but considered particularly in the context of solicitation. Clerical abuse of minors was included in those texts too. However, it is clear, in addition to the discussions about penal law after the Council and the distaste for trials and penalties, many bishops and others wanted to act pastorally, to cure the offender, making use of increasingly popular psychological assistance. When the Code of 1983 was operative, the normal places for judicial trials relating to paedophilia would have been diocesan ecclesiastical courts, with the Roman Rota being the appeal tribunal, while requests for dispensations from the obligations of the clerical state were the competence of the Congregation for Sacraments and Divine Worship and, since 2005, of the Congregation for the Clergy. Only in 2001 did the Congregation for the Doctrine of the Faith became the exclusively competent tribunal for these matters, since when it appears to have been very active and effective; criticisms of the role of the then Prefect of that Congregation, Cardinal Ratzinger, now Benedict XVI, prior to 2001, seem to have been very misguided.

Surprisingly, the recent statement of the Bishops of England and Wales made no mention of canon law, nor was anything said about clergy wrongly accused or suspected of abuse. This latter question is as much as matter of justice as is that of attending to claims of abuse. It has to be said that the revised norms, just issued, do not seem to address this question explicitly. They do make reference to the right of defence, even in very serious cases, but the name of the person making the accusation may not be made known either to the accused or to his advocate at a trial, unless the former explicitly agrees (art. 24 § 1), although the tribunal must assess the credibility of the one making the accusation (art. 24 § 2).

These revised norms have been issued publicly, a major step forward, since law is for the common good and needs to be known both by those who might infringe it and by those who need to apply it and by the community who need to be protected by it. The updating of these norms shows a readiness to learn from experience in a very delicate area of the application of penal law. Those so badly abused by clergy do have means at their disposal to effect redress and those who are guilty of such outrages deserve to face the full weight of canon law.

Other than sexual abuse, these revised norms, in regard to other serious crimes, make the following changes. The crime of attempting to hear a confession or to impart absolution by one not able to do so (c. 1378, art. 4 § 1, 2°) is now a more serious crime, as is simulation of absolution (c. 1379, art. 4 § 1 3°), as well as even the indirect violation of the seal of confession (art. 4 § 1 5°). A further, new 'more serious crime' is introduced of attempting to ordain a woman or attempting to be ordained as a woman, for which the penalty is a *latae senten-tiae* excommunication (art. 5 § 1), or in the case of a member of an Eastern Catholic Church a major excommunication (art. 5 § 2) and, if one involved is a priest, he may be dismissed from the clerical state (art. 5 § 3). The word 'attempt' is used, since any such action would be *ipso facto* invalid (c. 1024). Some notorious cases in recent years lie behind this provision.

Index of Modern Authors

Adnès P. 354–5
Agar J. M. 221, 376, 379, 405, 415, 448, 457
Alfaro J. 117
Alvarez A. 70–1
Ardito A. S. 133
Arieta J. I. 15
Avacedo L. H. 232, 433, 436

Barraclough G. 24
Beal J. P., Coriden J. A. and Green T. J. 4, 52, 156, 253, 432, 434, 448
Besson E. 49, 243, 246, 281
Beyer J. 197–8, 548
Borgonovo G. 16, 113
Borras A. 463, 466–7, 470, 472–5, 482
Bourassa F. 315–16
Brown R. 4

Calabrese A. 486
Caparros E., Thériault M. and Thorn J. 15, 253, 376, 379
Cattaneo A. 16, 113
Cito D. 464, 480–1, 533
Corecco E. 16, 113, 124, 128, 139, 232
Coriden J. A. 4, 22, 33, 42–3, 52, 68, 93, 117, 154, 156, 193, 199, 253, 270, 284, 372, 385, 432, 435, 446, 448, 488
Cusack B. A. 156

Demmer K. 334
Denzinger H. and Schönmetzer A. 267, 275, 297, 317, 326, 347–8, 407

De Paolis V. 62, 70–1, 90–1, 147, 180, 232, 268, 429, 442, 446, 451–2, 464, 466, 474–7
Diaz J. 172, 175
Dieni E. 15
Doms H. 348
D'Onorio J-B. 143–4
D'Ostilio F. 149, 435
Dulles A. 129
Durand J-P. 193, 198, 200, 233, 323–4

Echappé O. 479, 482, 484, 515
Erdo P. 21–3, 27

Ferme B. E. 54, 61, 63–4, 132, 134, 284, 488–91
Flannery A. 92, 270
Fuček I. 314, 353, 527

Galot J. 315, 325–6
Gambari E. 184, 192, 203
Gasparri, Cardinal 28, 30–1
Gaudemet J. 16, 19, 23, 27, 95–6, 282
Gauthier A. 42
Gerosa L. 30–1, 128, 139–40, 210, 213, 224, 240, 264–7, 298, 317
Ghirlanda G. 17, 52, 60, 62, 70–1, 76, 82, 90–1, 113, 117, 131, 142–3, 147, 158, 160, 180, 182, 185, 192, 216–17, 232–3, 268, 270, 290, 302, 307, 329, 332, 335, 337, 341, 351, 372, 374, 382–4, 409–10, 413, 418, 425, 429–30, 442
Griffin B. F. 168

Grisez G. 10

Haligan N. 246
Hanson R. K. 100, 528–30
Heinschel D. E. 52
Herranz Cardinal 305
Hervada J. 15, 418
Hiebel J-L. 228
Houillon P. 537–8
Huels J. M. 261, 432, 434–5
Huizing P. 17

Jemolo C. 15
Jenkins R. E. 157, 513, 516
Joyce M. P. 336

Kafka M. P. 100
Kasper W. 357
Kelly D. 4
Kennedy R. T. 448
Kiely B. 100
Kitchen P. 165
Kondratuk L. 30

Lafleur 15
Langevin R. 528–9
Latourelle R. 117
Llobell J. 481, 533
Lo Castro G 480
Lombardía P. 15
Lüdicke K. 157, 513, 516
Lütz M. 100

MacAreavey J. 358, 375, 381, 385–6,
    394–5, 400, 402, 409, 411, 419
Mackin T. 345, 353–6
McGrath A. 4, 491
McManus F. R. 253–4
Marcuzzi A. 120, 133
Martens K. 494
Matthias 113
May W. E. 355
Mendonça A. 401
Metzger M. 464
Montini G. P. 476–7
Morrisey F. G. 4, 40, 208

Mörsdorf K. 15–16, 232
Mostaza A. 268–9, 273
Müller G. L. 86
Murphy F. 528
Mussone D. 281, 450

Navarette U. 129
Navarro L. 221, 376, 379, 405, 415, 448,
    457
Neuner J. and Dupuis J. 267, 275, 297,
    317, 326, 347–8

Ochoa X. 31
O'Collins G. 117
Olivares E. 149–50, 156, 160, 245
O'Neil C. E. 325
Örsy L. 17, 365

Papale C. 525
Périsset J. C. 164, 447–9, 453–4
Pfäfflin F. 100
Pompedda M. 398
Price S. 528–9

Quinlan M.R. 264
Quinn J. 275

Recchi S. 181
Redford J. 188
Renken J. A. 168

Salvador C. C. 62, 70–1, 90–1, 147, 180,
    232, 268 429, 436, 442
Schillebeeckx E. 353
Schmaus M. 313
Schouppe J. 62, 363, 382, 384, 386–7,
    391, 401, 411, 519–20
Schrage W. 353, 357
Scicluna C. J. 345–6, 351, 362, 364, 387,
    558
Serrano Ruiz J-M. 359
Sheehy G. 4, 31, 184, 269, 367
Smith G. N. 113, 147–8
Suchecki Z. 54, 132, 284, 488–9

Urrutia F. J. 67

Valdrini P. 22, 59, 68, 70, 81, 95–6, 127, 129– 30, 146, 150–1, 157–8, 160–1, 216–18, 224, 228, 233, 323, 365, 371, 407, 479
Van der Wiel C. 22–3
Vanhoye A. 129, 323–4
Vela L. 62
Vernay J. 365, 371, 375, 383, 389, 392, 394, 400, 407, 410–11, 425–6
Villemin L. 52
Vorgrimler H. 322
Von Hildebrand D. 348

Walsh L. G. 258, 265, 273
Werckmeister J. 16
Wicks J. 322
Wijlens M. 156
Wilson 15
Winroth A. 26
Woestmann W. H. 393, 467, 469, 472, 476, 480, 524–6, 541
Woodall G. J. 213, 215–16, 351, 359, 396
Wrenn L. G. 149, 221, 377, 389, 392–3, 395

Zalba M. 350

General Index

abduction 487, 491
abortion 10, 263, 338, 340, 487, 491
abrogation *see* laws abrogation
absenteeism 103, 147, 168, 487
absolution *see* penance
abstinence 437
abuse *see also* crimes
  of office 464, 485–6
  protection of children 530–9
  sexual, of minors 3–4, 99–100,
     463, 487, 490ff., 527ff., 533–43,
     557–62
Academy, Pontifical
  for Life 133
  of Science 133
accomplice,
  in canonical crime 469, 489
  in sin 310, 485–6, 489
acephalous *see* clergy, acephalous
acolyte 89, 92–3, 280, 284, 287, 323,
    336–7, 472
acquisition *see* temporal goods
act/acts, *see also* decree, precept,
    rescript 67–76
  administrative/executive 69–76, 118,
    496, 543–6
  collegial *see* Pontiff
  invalidity of 119
  judicial 67, 69, 118
  juridical 67–9, 444
  legislative 67–8, 118, 153
  liturgical *see* liturgy
  and canonical sanctions 470–5
Acta apostolicae sedis 63–4

Ad clerum 63–4, 244
adjudged matter 508
administration, Apostolic established
  137
'administrative leave' 535
administrative process *see* procedural
  law
administrator
  Apostolic 331
  diocesan 149–50, 157, 168, 331
  diocesan financial 453ff.
  parochial 168–70, 409, 454ff.
  responsible, temporal goods 452ff.
adoption 56, 386
adultery 345ff., 352–6
advice *see* consultation
advocate 501, 505–6, 511, 514
affinity 56, 385–6
age 53–5
  and consecrated life 54, 201, 203
  and crime 54, 465–7, 490–1, 559–60
  and marriage 54, 375, 389ff., 393–4,
    417
  majority 54, 465
  and office 54–5, 78
  and ordination 54, 335
agent *see* person juridical
alienation *see* temporal goods
altars 429–30, 436
amendment, to Code 64–5, 212,
    217–18, 554–6
amentia 55, 388–9
anamnesis 275–8
Ananias 441

Anglican 57, 288, 326–7, 347, 549–54
anointing of sick 171, 314–19
absolute/conditional 319
   extreme unction 316–17
   form 251
   intention of minister 252
   liceity 317–19
   matter 251, 316
   meaning 314–16
   minister 252, 317
   oil of sick 251, 319
   proper candidate 252, 316–19
   repetition of 317–18
   validity, conditions of 251–2, 317–19
apostasy 340, 380, 431, 464, 484
Apostles 111ff., 322
Apostolate see also mission 85–6, 275–9
   lay 170ff., 273
apostolic life see societies of
Apostolic Penitentiary see tribunals
Apostolic See see also Roman Curia 109,
   130–5, 144, 370–2, 381–3 409–10,
   421, 429, 432, 436–7, 442–51, 457–8,
   477–85, 496–500, 518–20
appeal
   no appeal against Roman Pontiff
      485, 496–7
   judicial trial see procedural law
appointment, to office see office,
   provision
Aquinas, St Thomas 10–12, 61, 260,
   346–7, 467
archbishop (metropolitan) 143, 149–52
archivist see notary
archpriest see vicar forane
Arinze, Cardinal 305–6
Armenian 57
Assemblée Nationale (France) 537–8
assent, of faith/to truths to be held
   216–9
assistance see form canonical
association
   clerical 105–6
   of faithful 84–5, 109–10, 171, 452–3
   right to 105
attrition see penance

auditor 498 ff.
Augustine 260, 309, 322, 345ff.
authority
   of Christ 111, 115–17, 296–7
   apostolic, of Paul 355
   supreme 111–35, 150, 313–14
   civil 117, 211ff.

banns, of marriage 405
baptism 3, 11, 13, 55–6, 81ff., 250–2, 317
   of adults 256–64
   and character 48, 179, 244–5, 263
   and consecrated life 178ff.
   conditional 253–4, 263
   deferral, postponement of 266
   and ecumenism 262–5
   of foundlings 263
   and indulgences 313
   of infants 260–4
   and other sacraments of initiation
      258–9, 265
   liceity 255–6
   and participation in liturgy 231ff.,
      264–5
   matter and form 250, 255
   and membership of Church 11–15,
      46–58, 113, 264–5, 287–9
   minster
      extra-ordinary 250, 255, 263
      ordinary 250, 255
   and mission in the Church 81ff.
   name 261
   and office 77–8, 142
   parents 260–4, 266
   person see person
   preparation 256–65
   proof of 201, 265–6
   proper candidate 262–4
   reverence and care 256
   registration 265–6
   sponsors 56, 260, 264–5
   time and place 261
   validity 250, 255
Barsabbas 113
Basilicas of St Peter and St Paul
   outside the Walls 136–7

beatification 65, 432
benediction 287
benefice 24, 76, 103, 442–4
bishop
    and acts of consecration 429–30,
        433–6
    auxiliary 143–4, 148ff.
    co-adjutor 144, 148ff.
    College of see College
    diocesan see also institutes/societies
        72–3, 109, 137–64, 167, 219–20,
        225–8, 288, 306ff., 330–2, 341–2,
        408–16, 421, 429–31, 433–6,
        442–4, 448ff., 457–61, 465ff.,
        477–84, 491–4, 496–8, 517–18
    emeritus 149
    ordaining 330–1, 342
    of Rome 115–16
    pastoral ministry 69, 145–8
    and the Pope 36–9, 137ff., 496–7
    and priests, relationship see priest
    principal dispenser of sacraments
        see sacraments
    and Roman Curia 134–5
    selection of 142–5
    and seminaries see seminary
    suffragan 151
    titular 149
blasphemy against Holy Spirit 296
Blessed Sacrament 287, 434, 438, 485,
    489–90
Blessed Virgin Mary 326–8, 432
blessings 429–30
bond see marriage, impediments
bonds sacred see also vows, profession
    178ff.
bonum ... see goods of marriage
books 227
Burchard of Worms 23
Burgaud 538
burial 431

Calvinist see also Reformers 275
canonization
    of civil law 451–2, 457–8
    process 65, 452

Canon Law Society
    of Australia and New Zealand 43
    Canadian 43
    of Great Britain and Ireland 4, 43–4,
        51, 534, 539–41
        Working Party re clerical sexual
            abuse 534, 539
canons
    of Councils 20–7
    penitentiary 78, 154, 161, 307, 340,
        374, 482–4
    regular 197
capacity
    legal 53–5, 77, 444
    for marriage see impediments, iure
        habiles
cardinals 24, 55, 119–21, 128–9, 143,
    228–9, 306ff., 496–7
catechetics 145–6, 222–4, 359
catechumens/catechumenate 54, 225,
    256–9, 261, 381.431
cathedral 144–5, 147, 328, 431,
'Catholic', name 85
celebret 283
celibacy 24, 97–100, 105, 142, 146, 179,
    382, 491–4
Celtic monks 297
cemetery 431, 436
censor 227
censures see sanctions
chancellor 149, 155, 372ff.
chapels 287, 435
chaplain 177, 284
Chappuis 28
chapter, of canons 143, 158, 161
    see also institutes of consecrated life
character see sacrament
charism 191–2
charity fraternal 105, 186–90,
Charlemagne 24
chastity 105, 179, 186
chrism 250, 267
Christ Jesus see also holiness
    presence, forms of 275–8
    sole Mediator, High Priest 231ff.,
        323–5,

Church 14,
  Apostolic 44,
  Catholic 12,
  Eastern 40, 64, 86, 269–70, 272,
    287–9, 331, 354
  in full sense 288–9
  Latin 12, 57, 84, 136ff., 347, 354
  marks of the 138–40, 185
  mission 76, 81ff., 180ff., 210ff., 224–5,
    273, 320ff., 439–40
  Orthodox 57, 263, 288, 326, 347, 354,
    413–14
  particular (diocese in Latin Church)
    44, 84, 93, 121ff., 134–5, 136–62,
    170
  particular *sui iuris* 57, 84–6, 234,
    326–8
  universal 111ff., 121, 134–5, 139
  visible structure and law 37–40
church, building 160, 262, 287, 328,
    429–31, 433–6
circumcision 2, 19
civil law *see also Corpus iuris civile,*
    marriage, 451–2, 464–5, 468, 495–7
clergy, cleric 51–2, 92ff., 158
  abandonment of ministry 491–4
  acephalous 93–6, 108, 330, 333
  and canonical crimes 485–8
  cleric and sacred order 51–2, 92ff.,
    320–43
  at diaconate 92–6, 330
  dimissorial letters 330–2
  dress 106
  excardination *see* excardination
  formation 96ff.
  incardination *see* incardination
  reforms after Vatican II 92–3, 323
  rights and duties *see* clerical state
clerical state 181ff.
  rights and duties 51–2, 92ff., 103–6,
    239–40
  loss of 51–2, 104–8
  dismissal from 107, 470–84, 559, 562
codification, of law 29–45
Code of Canon Law, 1917
    (Pio-Benedictine) (*Codex iuris*

canonici) 1, 16–17, 28–31, 40–1, 93,
    95, 107 178–80, 237–8, 249, 273,
    282, 314, 317– 18, 348, 364, 370–1,
    381, 401
Code of Canon Law, 1983 (*Codex iuris
    canonici*) 1–2, 16–17, 36–45
  revision of, principles 31–6, 67, 81,
    479–80
  structure 36, 40–1
Code of Canons for the Eastern
    Churches, 1990 (*Codex canonum
    ecclesiarum orientalium*) 2, 40–2, 64,
    213, 234
Code Napoléon 30
Code of Theodosius 20
Codex iuris canonici fontes (Gasparri)
    28
collections of laws
  Anselmo dedicata 23
  Antiochene 21–2
  Dacheriana 22
  Decretum (Burchard of Worms) 23
  Dionysiana-Hadriana 22
  Extravagantes 28
  Hispana (Isidoriana) 22
  Liber sextus; Liber septimus 28
  Libri duo (Reginald of Prüm) 23
  Tripartita, etc. (Ives of Chartres) 23
  Vetus Gallica 22
collegiality 44, 111ff., 122–8
College
  of Apostles 111ff., 320ff.
  of bishops 38, 111ff., 121–8, 213,
    219–20, 329–30, 485
  of cardinals 129
  of consultors 149–50, 157–8, 453ff.
Comiskey Bishop 534
Commission, Pontifical for revision of
    Code, *see* Pontifical Commission
common good
  of the Church 8–9 , 76, 85, 131, 152,
    320ff., 446, 464
  of society 85, 557–62
common life 180
communicatio in sacris 239, 245, 284,
    287–9, 317, 484, 489–90

communications and ministry of word
227
communion
canon law and 16, 48, 464ff.
Church as communion 44, 48–9,
111ff., 121ff., 137–40, 150, 170ff.,
329ff., 495
concept of 113,126–8, 139–40
of faith 138–40, 170, 220–1, 275–80
communion with the Catholic
Church 57–8, 77, 82–5, 275–9,
285–6, 330–2, 470
hierarchical 38, 51, 117–18, 126–8,
137–42
and liturgy 232ff., 275–80, 285–6
and marriage *see* marriage
consortium … 362
Communion Holy, see also
communicatio in sacris
fasting 286, 437–8
ministers of distribution of 284–5,
472
reception of, conditions 279–80,
285–7
as viaticum 284–5, 314ff.
communities, ecclesial 289, 326, 431
Conciliarism 126, 485, 497
conclave 118–21
Concordats 65, 78, 143
Concubinage *see also* crime 354, 487
condition 48, 53ff., 82–5,
age 53–5, 299
domicile / quasi-domicile 55–6, 262,
306–8, 497, 509
relationships 56, 384ff.,
reason 55, 299
rite 57
conference, bishops' 101, 109, 143,
151–2, 220–4, 238–9, 244, 259,
288–9, 410–11, 417, 437–8, 442–4,
447–50, 457–8
of England and Wales 221, 289,
375–6, 379, 381, 405, 437–8,
448–50, 457–60, 483–4, 530–4,
539–42, 560–2

*Directory on Canonical Status of
Clergy* 541
One Bread, one Body 289
and of Ireland and of Scotland 289,
534, 539–41
German 259, 266
of the United States 533
The Rites of the Catholic Church 45
confession *see* penance
confessor *see also* penance 97, 201, 341,
374
confirmation
sacrament of
and baptism 267
bishop as ordinary minister 250,
269
character 244–5, 267, 271
faculty to confirm 250, 269
form 250.268–9,
matter 250, 268–9
minister 250, 269–70
and mission in the Church 87ff.,
234, 268
name 269
place 269–70
and sacred orders 336
proper candidate 271–2, 319
and reception into full
communion, 271–2
registration 272
specific sacrament of initiation 267
sponsors 56, 272
timing of 273–4
of election 120
consanguinity
in collateral/direct line 56, 354,
384–5, 458
and marriage 56, 384–5, 407
consecrated life *see* institutes of
consecration
of chrism 268–9
in the life of Jesus 178–9, 320ff.
of life 178ff.
at Mass 275–8
non-sacramental, juridical 52, 83–5,
203–4

of objects, places 429–30, 433–6
sacramental 51–2, 82–5, 320ff.
conscience, forum of *see* forum internal
consensus facit matrimonium 346, 360,
    386, 421–2
consent
    and admission to institutes/societies
        201
    and marriage
        act of will, irrevocable 360, 364,
            387–8
        de futuro/ de praesenti 386–7, 402
        defects of 388–405
            conditional 401–2
            deceit 395–6
            error of (quality of) person
                394–5
            error, radical determining the
                will 396–7
            force and grave fear 402
            ignorance 393–4
            incapacity
                insufficient reason 388–9, 404
                grave lack of due discretion
                    389–2
                inability to fulfil duties 392–3
            knowledge/opinion of nullity
                402–3
            simulation of consent 365,
                398–401
                partial 400–1
                total 398–9
        internal and true 365, 387–403,
            420–2
        interpreter 387, 403
        nature of 386–8
        proxy 55, 387, 403–4
        public 406ff., 420–1,
        renewal of 420–1
        sanation of 421–2
    and personal prelatures 109
    and places of worship 434
    and validity of acts 75, 156–61, 164,
        196ff., 201, 448, 453–4, 458
consistory *see* cardinals
Constantine 20

constat (non constat) de nullitate
    matrimonii in casu 514–5
constitution/constitutions 111–12, 115,
    320ff.
    see also institutes/societies
consubstantiation 275
consultation 75, 149, 156, 158–61, 164,
    168, 196ff., 201, 434, 448–58
consummation *see* marriage
consultors *see also* College of 134
convalidation, simple validation of
    marriage 420–1
converts (neophytes) 19
cooperation, positive and irregularities
    /impediments to order 340
Corpus iuris civile 24, 31
Corpus iuris canonici 24ff.
Council of
    Arles 21
    Carthage 21
    Elvira 21, 268
    Jerusalem 2, 19
    Toledo 21, 268–9
    Nicaea 20–1, 142
    Second Lateran 26
    Fourth Lateran 27, 407
    Trent 28, 124, 142, 212, 275, 297, 317,
        347, 407–8
    First Vatican 30, 124, 212–13
    Second Vatican *see* Second ...
    Europe (Strasbourg) 9
Councils
    diocesan, of priests 72, 158–9, 164–5,
        448
    ecumenical, general 119–28, 215ff.,
        485
    episcopal 158–9
    parish pastoral *see* parish pastoral
        council
    regional 152
counsels, evangelical
    profession of 52, 82, 178–90
        chastity 186–8
        obedience 80, 189–90
        poverty 188
    context of charity 183, 190

creed 57
cremation 431
crime canonical *see also* law penal,
    procedural, sanctions
    concept of 464–5, 468, 471
    and deprivation of office 79, 471–2,
        474–5
    external violation of law/precept
        465–6, 471ff,
    in general 41, 463–84
    imputability 217, 466–82
    obstinacy 217, 469–75, 477–84
    and orders, irregularity 338
    particular crimes 484–94
        abuse of office 485–6
        against authorities, freedom of the
            Church 485
        against faith, unity of Church 217,
            284, 329, 332, 484–5
        attempting to absolve
            accomplice in sin against 6th
            commandment 484, 490
        clerics
            attempting marriage 486–7
            concubinage 486–7, 491–4,
            other sexual offences 486–7
            sexual abuse of minors 486–7,
              490–1, 557–62,
            crimen pessimum 486–7, 490–1, 561,
            graviora delicta 63–4, 132, 134, 284,
              488–91, 499, 557–62
            against the Eucharist 489–90
            against penance 490, 562
            with a minor 490–1, 557–62
            attempted ordination of a
             woman 562
            generic norm 488
            murder 487–8
            procured abortion 487–8
            usurpation of office 485–6
cult *see* worship
    disparity of *see* marriage
Cumberledge Report 534–6, 538–9,
    541–2
curia
    diocesan 153–62, 449–50

Roman *see* Roma Curia
custom 66

deacons *see* diaconate
deans *see* vicars forane
deaneries *see* vicars forane
death *see also* office, loss of
    danger of 250–2, 302–6, 312–14, 317,
        374–5, 472, 482–4
    presumed, and marriage 427, 520
deceit, *see also* defects of consent 75,
    204
de-consecration 433–6, 450–1
decrees
    general 69–70 , 151–2, 452–3
    particular, individual 70ff., 165–7,
        169, 452–3, 482, 505, 509ff.
    of Burchard of Worms, *see* Burchard
    of Gratian *see* Gratian
    of Vatican II *see* Second Vatican
        Council
decretals of popes 20–4, 27ff.
dedication 429–30, 433–5
defects of consent *see* consent
defection, formal from the Catholic
    faith 109, 380, 413–14, 555–6
defence, right of *see* law penal and
    procedural law
defender of the bond 498, 505–6, 511,
    514–15
delegation 237
    acts of consecration/dedication
        429–30
    general 237, 408–10
    special
        to assist at weddings 361, 407–10
        of executive, administrative
            power 237
    and sub-delegation 410
deposit of faith 211ff., 240, 244
deprivation of office *see* office
    deprivation
de rebus fidei et morum 64–5, 212ff.
derogation *see* laws derogation
diaconate/deacons *see also* orders 158,
    219–20, 239–40, 243, 285, 287,

320–8, 330ff., 361, 407, 429–30
permanent, 93, 103, 106, 382
transitional 93, 103, 106, 337–8, 382
suitability for 19, 92–103, 330–8
dicastery, of Holy See *see* Roman Curia
Dictatus Papae 24
Didaché 20
diocese 136–62
   portion of People of God 93, 136
   diocesan curia/structures 152–62
   particular Church *see* Church
   purposes 137–40
   sub-ubicarian 143
   entities equivalent in law to a
      diocese
      Apostolic administration
         established 137
      Apostolic prefecture 137
      territorial abbey 136–7
      territorial prelature 136
      vicariate Apostolic 137
directory *see* Roman Curia
   Congregations
disparity of cult *see* impediments
dispensations
   capacity (incapacity) to grant 73–4,
      288–9, 372–4
   concept and meaning 73–4, 372–4
   conditions for granting 73–4, 372–4,
      413–14, 520
   reserved to the Roman Pontiff 373,
      520
dissolution of the bond of marriage
   423–7
   of non-consummated marriages
      424–5, 518
   of non-sacramental marriage 426–7,
      519–20
   Pauline privilege 423–5, 518–19
   Petrine privilege 424–7, 519–20
divine office *see* Liturgy of the Hours
divine law *see* law divine
divorce 345–7, 352–6, 397–8, 400–1
divorced and remarried 286
doctrine, dogma, responses due 64–5
domicile/quasi-domicile *see* condition

dress *see* institutes habit, vestments
duties *see* rights and duties

Eastern Catholic Churches *see* Church,
   Code
Ecclesia Dei, 291–4
ecclesiastical law *see* law
ecclesiology 15–18, 36–40, 43–5, 121–8,
   138ff., 150, 181ff., 232–40
ecumenism 239, 263, 284, 287–9, 317,
   327, 347, 354, 484, 489–90
education 85–6, 225–6, 435
   Catholic schools 145–7, 226
   Catholic universities 226, 435
   parents and primary duty 223–6,
      260ff, 285, 419, 484
   subsidiarity 223–6
election *see also* office, provision 78,
   143, 159, 118–21
encyclicals *see* Pope
ends, of marriage 346ff.
   mutual help 347–51, 359
   procreation and education 346–53,
      357, 359–62, 387, 389–93
   remedy for concupiscence 347, 349,
      356, 359
   St Thomas 346–7
   in Vatican II and after 349–51
ephebophilia 529
episcopal vicar *see* vicar episcopal
episkopé 452
equality *see also* faithful 13–14, 82
error common 308
esse/bene esse 111, 185, 320
Eucharist 274–94
   celebration by priest more than once
      a day 282
   celebration with non Catholic
      ministers 489–90
   concelebration 282
   confection 51, 275–89
   daily 97, 279
   distribution of Holy Communion 284
   form
      for validity 250, 281
      ordinary/extra-ordinary 291–4

and Holy Communion *see also*
     Communion 274
intention of minister 250, 281
liceity *see also Redemptionis*
     sacramentum 281–4
link to liturgy of the word 233–5, 275
Mass for people 290–1
matter 250, 281
offerings Mass 290–1, 450, 461
and ordination 328
participation in 274ff., 285–6
principal duty of priest 257, 282
real change 275–9
real presence 275–9
reservation *see* Blessed Sacrament
sacrament 274–80
and sacraments of initiation 274
sacrifice 274–9
source and summit of Christian life
     274ff.
trans-finalization 275–8
trans-signification 275–8
transubstantiation 275–9
validity, conditions of 250, 281–2
evangelical counsels *see* institutes of
     consecrated life
evangelization
     in general 81ff, 210ff., 222–5, 256–8
     institutes of consecrate life,
     societies of apostolic life 206
     and Roman curia 133, 137
excardination 93–6, 306–8, 330
ex cathedra 215
exclaustration *see* institutes
excommunication *see* censures
exhortations Apostolic *see* Pope
ex opere operato (operantis) see
     sacraments
exorcism, exorcist 92–3, 430
experts,
     and suitability for office, 77, 89
     role in contentious trials 505–6, 510,
     514–15
expiatory penalties *see* sanctions
Explanatory Notes of C.D.F. *see* Roman
     Curia

exposition 287
Extravagantes 28

faculties
     and bishops 34
     for confession 306–8
     to incardinate 93
     by law / by grant 306–8
     limitations 220, 470ff.
     to preach 220
     special faculties of Congregation for
     2009 Clergy 479, 482, 491–4

faith 13,
     catechetics (integral presentation of
          faith) 85–6, 146, 222–4
     deposit of 256–7
     faith and doctrine 96–7, 109, 142ff.
     faith and morals 85–6, 109, 210ff.
     and grave illness 314–16
     fides qua/quae 232
     free from coercion 214
     and liturgy 232ff., 275–8
     and Magisterium 65, 85, 214–20, 257,
          484–5
     preaching 214, 220–3, 256–9,
     profession of 65, 84–6, 144, 155,
          227–9, 258, 285ff.
     unity of faith 285ff.
faithful ('*Christifideles*'), all the
          faithful
     constitution through baptism
          46–53, 276–7
     equality, but distinct function 48,
          50–1, 82ff., 242–3, 278–80
     rights and duties of all faithful
          47ff., 82ff., 231ff., 239–42,
          285ff. 317
     and selection of bishops 142
     lay faithful 87ff., 178ff.
          rights and duties 87ff., 231,
          239–42, 275ff.
falsehood, crime of 486
family/parents
     education of children 260ff.
fasting 437–8

favour,
  of faith *see* privilege
  remission of expiatory penalties
    482
fear *see* force and fear
feast days *see* holydays
Felici Cardinal 32, 34, 36
Ferns Report 528–33
fidelity *see* goods
finances *see also* temporal goods of the
    Church
financial administration, 452ff.
financial committees
  diocesan 448, 453ff.
  parish 454ff.
  public juridical person 454ff.
    consultation 448, 453
    consent 453
force and grave fear 75, 204, 402,
    465–7, 487, 491
form
  see each sacrament
  canonical form of marriage 406–17
    Tametsi 407
    Ne temere 407
    assistance, official at weddings
      408–12
    blessing by bishop 406
    clandestine marriages 406–7
    defect of 512–13, 516–17
    dispensation from 413–16
    extraordinary form of marriage
      411–12
    obligation of 412–14
    ordinary form of marriage
      408–11
    proof and registration 412, 416
    secret celebration 416–17
    and validity 406–8
    witnesses 412–14
  form of Mass, ordinary/
    extraordinary 291–4
formation
  see institutes of consecrated life/
    societies of apostolic life
  in seminary 96–7

forum
  competent *see* tribunals
  external, internal 3, 33, 70, 78, 97,
    101–3, 310, 340–2, 374, 472–84
foundations, pious 451–2, 460–1
fraud 441, 487
free conferral *see* office, provision
function (*munus*)
  collegial, primatial (of supreme
    authority), 115–18
  distinct from office (*officium*), 115
  legislative, executive (admin.),
    judicial, *see* acts
  teaching, sanctifying, ruling (*tria
    munera*) 47ff., 76ff., 82, 88–9,
    111, 140–2, 145–7, 166–77, 210ff.,
    231ff., 323, 429ff.
Fund
  Ecclesiastical Education 449
  National Catholic 450
funerals, and denial of 431–2, 470

Galloway, Diocese of 80
Gasser, Bishop 213
girovagi see clergy acephalous
giudice istruttore 503
godparents *see* baptism, sponsors
good, basic, integral 10
goods
  ecclesiastical *see* temporal goods of
    the Church of marriage
    Augustine (*tria bona*) 345
    of fidelity (*bonum fidei*) 345,
      349–55, 387, 389–93, 397,
      400–1
    of procreation (*bonum prolis*) 345,
      349–53, 357, 387, 389–93, 400
    of permanence (*bonum sacramenti*)
      345, 349–50, 356–7, 386–7,
      389–93, 397, 400–1
    of spouses (*bonum coniugum*) 350,
      359–62, 387, 389–93, 400–1
    Vatican II 349–50
Gospel, proclamation of 210ff.
governance
  in general *see* acts administrative

of diocese 140–2, 146–7
and canonical sanctions 470–5
see institutes of consecrated life
and societies of apostolic life
Gratian (*Decretum*) 24ff, 62, 346
graviora delicta see crimes

habit *see* institutes, habit
heresy 340, 380, 431, 464, 484
hermits 191
Hillel 353
Hincmar of Rheims 346
Hippolytus, *Apostolic Tradition* 20
history, of canon law 18–45
holiness,
    of Christ 14, 82, 178–9, 235, 237
    of the Church 82–5, 463
    of clergy 105–6, 145–8
    in consecrated life 178ff.
    and liturgy/sacraments, worship
        231–438
    universal call to 82–5, 145–8, 181
holydays 283, 328, 436–7
homicide, wilful 338, 340
homily 221–2
homosexuality/homosexual persons
    and admission to sacred orders
        99–100, 341–2
    and chastity 341
    and entry into seminary 99–100,
        341–2
    and marriage 392–3
house *see* institute/society

ignorance *see also* consent defects of 75,
    465–7
images 432, 435–6
impediments
    to marriage 63
        dispensations from, in general
            372–4
            local ordinary 373
            occult/public 373–4
            reserved to Apostolic See 373
            sacred minister 374
        in general 370–2

declaration/establishment
    371–2
diriment 370–2
(impedient) 370–1
meaning 370–2
particular
    age 375–6
    impotence, permanent and
        antecedent 376–7
    ligamen, prior bond 377–80
    disparity of cult 380–1
    sacred orders 373, 381–2
    public perpetual vow of chastity
        in religious institute 373, 383
    crime, 373, 383–4
        abduction 383
        murder 383–4
    relationships 384–6
        consanguinity, direct/collateral
            lines 373, 384–5
        affinity, direct line 385–6
        (spiritual relationship) 386
        public propriety 386
        adoption 386
    simple to orders 338–9
        admission to 339
        exercise of 339
        dispensation from 340–1
        judicial, occult, public 340–1
imprimatur 227
imputability *see* crime
incapacity *see* consent defects of
incardination 93–6, 108, 205, 306–8, 330
incest 464
incorporation,
    into Church *see* baptism
    into secular institutes *see* institutes
    into societies of apostolic life *see*
        societies
indefectibility 547
indissolubility, of marriage, *see also*
    marriage 345–7, 361–4, 423–7
induction *see* installation
indulgences
    abuses 314
    conditions 313–4

and redemptive act of Christ 313–4
partial/plenary 313
and 'punishment', temporal due to
sin 312–4
and reconciliation 312–4
and suffrage for dead 314
indult 208, 331–2
infallibility *see* Magisterium
infant 54
infirmity, psychological 338
in forma ordinaria/ specifica, see Pope
in loco parentis 223
in persona Christi, see priest
inseparability, principle of 351
installation 144, 150, 164–8
inter vivos 451–2
institutes of consecrated life *see also*
consecration
clerical 183–7, 193
religious 93, 178ff., 193ff., 336,
490
secular/lay 93, 178, 181–7, 193–4,
202–3, 336
admission and conditions of 194–5,
200–2, 273, 278
apostolate 206
and candidacy for orders 336
chapters, function 199
charism 190–2
churches, chapels of 196
common life in religious institutes
190–1, 194
confessional faculties, religious
institutes 306ff.
confessors, religious institutes 199
constitutions 194, 196ff., 203–4
and diocesan bishop 147, 196
dismissal 209
doctrine
of Vatican II, 181–2
of John Paul II 184–6
evangelical counsels 178–90, 194,
206
excardination incardination, *see*
excardination incardination
exclaustration 208

financial administration and
temporal goods 200
formation, initial/continuing 195,
202–6
governance 184, 195–200, 470–4
superiors, 197, 284, 331–2, 435, 497
appointment/election 198
major 198, 452ff., 496–7
proper 189–90, 470ff.
supreme moderator 198–9,
202–3, 497
habit 206
hermetic 191
holiness, vocation to 178ff.
houses, erection/suppression
193–7
incorporation, temporary/definitive
into 195, 203–4, 342
mendicant 190–2, 449
monastic 190–2
nature of consecrated life 178–90
novitiate 201–3
ordination, need for clergy 333
postulancy 202
profession, temporary/perpetual
203–4, 273
relationship to diocese, 194–7
and 'religious' 179–86
residence/cloister 205–6
rights/duties of members 194–5,
278
religious institutes 205–7
secular institutes 207
separation from 195, 208–9
spiritual directors 199, 203
state of life 183–6
statutes 184, 452ff.
and transfer 208
of parish priests 80
vows, *see* vows
irregularities
in relation to sacraments of initiation
259–60
to orders
admission to 338–9
exercise of 339

dispensation from 340–1
    judicial, occult, public 340–1
Italian lay school of canon law 15–16
iure habiles 360, 365, 371ff., 386–7
ius in corpus 348–9, 365, 375
ius publicum ecclesiasticum 7, 212, 232,
    444
Ives of Chartres 23, 346

Jerome 354
judicial process *see* procedural law
judicial vicar, processes *see* diocese and
    procedural law
juge d'instruction 503, 537
judges 498ff., 504–6, 511, 514ff.
judgment (sentence) *see* procedural
    law
juridical nature of 1983 Code 32–3
juridical status, in the Church 46–53,
    231–9, 495–6
jurisdiction *see* tribunals, competence
jurisprudence, 66, 389–93, 395–401, 499
justice,
    in the Church 7–11, 101, 158, 359,
        443–4, 463ff., 496ff.
    social 85, 101
Justinian 24–5, 28, 30–1, 40

Kirchensteuer 449, 455

laicization *see* dispensation from
    obligations of, dismissal from,
    clerical state
laity *see* faithful
Latin Church 40
    language and vernacular 238, 243–4,
        282, 291–4
'*Lauda Sion salvatorem*' 280
law
    abrogation 66, 143
    amendments to 64–5
    canon,
        function of 7–47
        sources of 18–29, 43–5
        collections of 20–9
        canons 20–4

civil 47, 56, 367–8, 375–6, 451ff.
decretals 20–4
derogation 66
divine 62–3, 81, 87, 111ff., 140–2, 371
ecclesiastical 6–32, 66–7, 128, 367,
    370ff., 395–6, 412–14
Fundamental ('*Lex fundamentalis*')
    40–3, 81
human 62, 447
incapacitating 66, 366, 371
interpretation 66, 71, 395–6
invalidating 371
jurisprudence *see* jurisprudence
liceity 66, 70, 77
natural 47, 346, 359, 367, 371, 447
of graduality 309, 371
particular 45, 66, 465
penal *see also* crime, sanctions 36, 41,
    48, 54, 79, 463ff.
procedural *see* procedural law
promulgation of 43–5, 61–4, 151–2,
    465
(non) retro-activity of 66, 395–6,
    421–2
Roman 344–6, 451
subjects of 63, 465ff.
superior legitimate and 465ff.
and theology 15–18, 111
universal 61–2, 465
validity 63, 66, 70, 77–80
lawgivers/lawmakers
    diocesan bishop 66
    episcopal conferences 150–1
    Pope as legislator for universal
        Church 61ff.
    Superiors *see* institutes/societies
Law (French) of Separation 449
lector(ate) 89, 92–3, 280, 323, 336–7, 472
Lefebvre, Mgr 58, 291, 329
Legate, papal 135, 143–4, 497
legitimacy/legitimation of children
    417, 420
letters
    apostolic and encyclical *see* Pope
    of appointment 155
    dimissorial 330–2, 342

lex orandi, lex credendi 222, 231, 234
ligament, see impediments
Lineamenta, see synods of bishops
liturgy
  abuses in 146–7, 283–4
  action of Christ and of Church
    231–9, 275–8
  and Apostolic See 237–8
  bishop, principal dispenser,
    moderator, of 145–8, 237–9
  and Second Vatican Council 232–4
  of Eucharist 274ff.
  of the Hours 233, 235
    obligations in regard to 106, 430–1
  and law 65, 231ff.
  and parish priest 171ff., 358–9
  Office (Pontifical) liturgical
    celebrations – *Sede Apostolica
    vacante* 120
  and canonical sanctions 470–5
Lombard Peter 26, 346
loss of office *see* office, loss of
L'osservatore romano, 68
Lutheran *see also* Protestant 275, 322,
  408

Magisterium 81, 85, 88–9, 117, 143,
  212ff., 227–9, 240–2, 328, 355
  authoritative/authentic 212–19,
    355
  definitive teachings 64–5, 212–13,
    215, 327–8
  infallibility and 117, 212, 215ff.,
    327–8
majority, legal *see* condition, age
mandate
  and marriage by proxy 403–4
  pontifical 329, 485–6
Manichaeans, 345
marks of Church *see* Church
Maronite 57
marriage
  assistance official at 361, 374, 408–12
  (attempted) civil 338–40, 363,
    378–80, 486–7
  biblical background, 352–8

and baptism 259–60, 360–1, 378–81,
  387–8
canonical effects 88–9, 417–18
capacity for *see iure habiles* /
  impediments
civil effects 367–8, 417, 509, 517ff.
and civil law 347–8, 367–8, 375–6,
  378–80, 404, 423ff., 509ff.
clandestine 406ff.
and conditions 401–2
and conjugal act/love 349ff., 365
consortium totius vitae 349–50, 360,
  362, 387, 400–1, 418–19, 423
consent 346, 360–1, 363–6, 386ff.
  lawful manifestation of, *see* form
    canonical
consummated/non-consummated
  346, 361, 366–7, 378–9, 424–7
  elements of consummation 367
contract/covenant 350ff., 359–62
dispensation *see* impediments
dissoluble/indissoluble 18–19,
  345–7, 353–7, 361–3, 378–80,
  387, 389–93, 397–8, 400–1, 423ff.,
  518–20
ends 346ff.
essential elements and properties
  360, 362–3, 387, 389–92, 398–401,
  404–5
form, canonical 360–1
and formal defection from Catholic
  faith 555–6
foundation of society 406–7
goods 345ff.
historical background 344–8
impediments to, *see* impediments
and inheritance 406–7
invalid 364–5, 378–9
meanings 351
and mission 88–9
nature canonical of 359–63
non-sacramental 361, 378–80, 397–8
pastoral care and preparation 358–9,
  372ff., 387–8, 404–5
place of 56
and post-Conciliar Magisterium 351

promise to marry 368
by proxy 403–4
putative 368, 378–9, 509
rights and duties of spouses 417–19
sacramental ('*ratum*') 346, 350,
    355–7, 360–3, 366, 378–80, 397–8
sacramental and consummated
    ('*ratum et consummatum*') 346,
    361, 366, 378–80, 397–8
and Vatican II 349–50
secret 412–14
vocation 352, 387–8
Mass offerings *see* Eucharist
of inauguration of new papacy 121
matrimonium in facto esse/in fieri 345–6,
    360, 366, 387
matter *see also* sacraments
and sin 430, 466ff.
medicina salutis 309
metropolitan, *see* archbishop
ministers
    extra-ordinary 250–2, 262
    of marriage (Latin Church) 408ff.
    ordinary of sacraments 246–7, 250–2,
        262
    original *see* confirmation
    sacred *see* orders/priest
ministries
    Apostolic *see* office
    Petrine *see* office
    stable lay 89, 92–3, 114, 279–80, 323,
        336–7, 472
    temporary functions 89
    and women 89, 92–3
    of word 210, 219–24, 234
minor
    age (canonical) *see* condition, age,
        crime,
mission
    of the Church *see* Church
    canonical 94, 140, 333
    to laity 105
missionaries 224–5
mixed religion 414–6
moderator
    bishop, of liturgical life *see* liturgy,

sacraments
    of diocesan curia 154–5
    of group of parishes (team ministry)
        166
    superior of institutes of consecrated
        life, societies of apostolic life
        497
Modestinus 20, 344–5
monks/monasteries *see* institutes of
    consecrated life
mortis causa 451–2
motu proprio 1, 63 *et passim*
Munich school 15–16
munus, see function
mutilation, grave 338, 487, 491
mutuum adiutorium, see ends
mystagogia 258

natural law *see* law natural
Navarre canonical school of 15–16
nepotism 56, 103, 142, 144, 458
Ne temere 407
nihil obstat 227
Nolan Report 3–4, 530, 532–5, 538–9,
    541
norms, general 46–80
notary *see also* chancellor
    diocesan 155
    of tribunal 498, 505
novitiate, novices *see* institutes/
    societies
nullity
    of acts 74–5
    of arbitration agreement 521
    declaration/decree of 517
    of marriage 427–8, 509–17
    of sacred orders 520
    of sacraments *see* sacraments
    of sentence 506–7
    procedures 509–17, 520–1
nuncio 143–4, 497
nuns, cloistered 196

oath
    of fidelity on assuming certain
        offices 65, 144, 155, 227–9

in general 227–9, 432–3
on assuming certain offices 500
of truth and secrecy in processes
500, 504–5
obedience
to proper ordinary 105
evangelical counsel, *see* institutes of
consecrated life
to the Pope 105
virtue 179
objects sacred 429–30, 432, 450–1
obsequium religiosum 216–19
obstinacy *see* crime
offerings Mass *see* Eucharist,
sacraments
office (*officium*) 24, 76–80, 83ff., 115
(*munus*, function) *see also* function
canonical crimes and 485–6
concept of ecclesiastical office 76–7,
442ff.
episcopal *see* bishop
incompatibility of 77–8
incompatible with clerical state 106
loss of 54–5, 78–80
and assistance at weddings
408–12
and celibacy 107–8
and confessional faculties 306–8
deprivation 79, 107, 474–5
removal 79, 107
resignation 78–9, 107
transfer 79–80, 107, 474–5
Petrine 111–21
provision (appointment I) 76–8, 105
election 78
free conferral 78
postulation 78
presentation 78, 143
and canonical sanctions 470ff.
suitability, criteria of 77, 88
suspension from 473–4
Officialis, see vicar judicial
oils, holy 245
chrism 250, 262, 268
of the sick 251, 317–19
blessing of oils 251

consecration of chrism 268–9
Old Catholic 288
Opus Dei 15, 108
oratory 261, 287, 435
orders holy 320–43
and baptism 252, 321, 323–8
candidacy for 323, 336–7
and celibacy 337
and character 244–5, 321, 325
conferred clandestinely 328–9
and confirmation 273
canonical crimes and 485–6
diaconal 39, 92–3, 321ff., 554–5
dimissorial letters, see letters
episcopal 52, 114, 137–42, 237–9,
321ff.
form – consecratory prayer 251–2,
321, 328
free request for/acceptance of 334,
337
fulness of priesthood, see priesthood
holy/sacred 39, 51ff., 82–5, 92–3,
137–42, 179, 274–80, 320ff.,
554–5
impediments, simple *see*
impediments
improper exercise of 338–9
intention
of candidate 252, 328
of minister 252, 321, 328
irregularities *see* irregularities
liceity 328ff., 333–8
and liturgical roles 279–80, 287
major/minor, abolition of 92–3, 114,
322–3, 334
male 252, 321, 325–8, 562
matter 251, 321, 328
minister of 252, 321, 328,
place 328
preparation, *see also* seminary 334ff.
presbyteral (priestly) 52, 82–5, 87,
162ff., 251–2, 277–80, 298ff.,
321ff., 554–5
proper candidate 252, 321, 333–8, 562
qualities required 334–42
registration and proof of 343

retreat canonical 337
sacrament 320ff.
time 328
and Vatican II 320–5
validity, conditions of 57, 251–2, 321,
325–8
and women 325–8, 562
ordinances 75–6
ordinariate, former Anglican
communities 547–62
ordinary 140–2
local 140–2, 262, 306–8, 329, 361,
375–6, 383, 408–9, 412, 414–16,
431, 433–4, 477–84, 521ff.
ordination
diaconal 93–6, 321ff., 330ff.
episcopal (consecration) 140–2,
321ff., 329–30,
presbyteral (priestly) 93–6, 321ff.,
330ff.
Otto the Great 24
Outreau case 536–8

paedophilia see abuse sexual
pallium 151
Papal States 441
paramountcy principle 530–3, 539
parenthood responsible 350–51
parents 223, 260ff., 419
parish
major alteration of 71–2, 160, 163–5
erection of 160, 163–4
finance committee, see financial
committee
full pastoral care of parishioners 165
and institute/society 165
nature of 162–6
part of diocese 162–3
pastoral council see pastoral council
personal 165
suppression of 71–2, 160, 163–4
territorial 162
parish priest (pastor)
assistance official at weddings
408–12
and pastoral needs of faithful 84,

164–6, 262, 358–9
full pastoral care of parish see
pastoral care 166
proper pastor 163–4
removal 168, 409, 544–5
transfer 71–2, 166–8, 409, 545
responsibilities 166–72, 227–9, 275ff.,
372ff., 452ff.
participation, active see also institutes/
societies in liturgy 239–40, 275–8
particular Church see Church
pastor proper see parish priest,
diocesan bishop 137, 223, 262, 317
supreme, of universal Church
(Pope) 115–17
pastoral care
and diocese 140–2
duty to provide 105, 145–8, 317,
435–6
of parish
full pastoral care, priestly orders
67, 105, 163
share in by others, conditions 173
supreme law 34, 133–4, 464, 545–6
pastoral council
diocesan 162, 448
parish 160, 172–3
paterfamilias 344–5
paternity 419–20
patrimony
liturgical 234
stable see temporal goods
Paucapalea 26
penal law see law penal, crime and
sanctions
penalties see sanctions
penance
days of 437–8
penal see sanctions
sacrament (reconciliation) 295–314
abuses 302–6, 310
absolution, 314–19
general 299, 301–6
individual 297–306
and canonical sanctions 482–4
anonymity 302

attrition 311
biblical, historical background
   295–7
communitarian dimension 297ff.
confessors
   responsibilities of 308–10
   suitability of 306
contrition, disposition of penitent
   297, 299ff., 309, 311–2
and dispensations for marriage
   374
faculties for confession 306–8
   by law 306
   by grant 306–8
form 251–2, 298–306
individual confession/absolution
   297, 299–306
intention of minister 252, 302–6
intention of penitent 251, 297ff.
internal forum 310
interpreter 310, 312
liceity 297–306
material integrity 297, 302–6
matter 297ff., 302–6
minister 252, 298ff., 306–8
nature of 297ff.
necessity of 286
penance and satisfaction 297,
   299–306, 309, 312–14
place of 302, 309–10
post-baptismal reconciliation
   296–7, 300
purpose of amendment 299–304,
   309–10
punishment due to sin 312–14
rites, ordinary (rites one and two)
   298–304
rite, extraordinary, 298–304
and canonical sanctions 470–84,
   489
seal of confession 310, 374, 472–4,
   482–4, 490
time 309–10
and Vatican II 297–8
and word of God 298
validity 251–2, 298–306

virtue 295–7, 310–2
penitent *see* penance, sacrament
penitentiary
   canon *see* canon
   Apostolic, *see* tribunals
peremption 503
periti, see experts 134
persons 41
   agent, of juridical person 59, 100,
     170, 451
   human 2, 46–7
   in the Church 46–61, 240–3, 274
   juridical, 58–61, 109–10, 496
     private 58, 60–1, 444–6, 457
     public 58.60, 157, 444–6, 448–52,
       457–8
   moral 58–9, 444
   physical 53–8, 448–51, 496
     and baptism 48, 53–8, 113, 139,
       210ff., 231ff.
     and holy order 51–2, 232–43
     and juridical status 46–53, 57–8
petitioner *see* procedural law
places sacred 433–6
pluralism 103
polyandry 362, 519
polygamy 353, 362, 426, 519
ponens 498, 511, 514
Pontifical Commission for revision of
   the Code 1, 31ff., 40, 59
Pontifical Councils 133
   for Christian Unity 133
     Directory ... Principles and Norms of
       Ecumenism 289
   for the Family 133
   for the Interpretation of Legislative
     Texts 66, 133, 149, 152, 157, 238,
     304–6, 380, 395–6, 518
     Actus formalis defectionis ab Ecclesia
       Catholica, 380, 555–6
     see also formal defection
     Dignitas connubii 157, 513, 515–16
   for Latin America 133
   for Pastoral Health Care 133
   for Social Communications
     The Church and Internet 527

Etica dell'Internet 527
Pornography and Violence 527
Pope (Supreme Pontiff)
acceptance of election 118–21
a bishop or to be ordained a bishop
118–21
and College of Bishops 111ff.
and collegiality 111–14, 116–18
death of 119
and ecumenical Council 119
and synod of bishops 119
and diocesan bishop 137ff.
election of 118–21
exercise of power and authority, *see
also* Roman Curia
in forma ordinaria/specifica 134,
496–7
and confessional faculties 306ff.
and marriage cases 518–20
and ministry of word 214ff.
and penal law 465ff., 496–7
power, see power
prerogatives of 119, 121
and primacy 111–17, 496–7
resignation of 119
Alexander III 25
Benedict XV 28, 30–1, 180, 220
Codex iuris canonici (1917), *see*
Code of 1917
Benedict XVI 119
Anglicanorum coetibus 549–53
De aliquibus mutationibus 120
Deus caritas est 50
Ecclesiae unitatem 293–4
L'antica e venerabile Basilica 137
Letter on divorced and remarried 293
*Special Faculties, Congregation for
Clergy* 491–4
Sacramentum caritatis 127, 286
Spe salvi 47
Summorum Pontificum 292–3
Boniface VIII 28
Clement V 28
Damasus 21
Gelasius I 21
Gregory VII 24

Gregory IX 24–5
Hadrian I 22
Innocent III 25
Innocent IV 25
John XXIII 1, 31
Crimen sollicitationis 532–3, 561
John Paul II 1, 119
Ad tuendam fidem 64–5, 217, 223,
227, 327
Allocution to Roman Rota 393
Apostolos suos 140, 151–2, 238
Catechesi tradendae 127, 223, 228
Catechism of the Catholic Church
257, 280, 311, 448, 466
Centesimus annus 9
Christifideles laici 87, 90, 127
Codex iuris canonici (1983), *see*
Code of 1983
*Codex canonum Ecclesiarum
orientalium*, *see* Code of 1990
Dies Domini 274, 278
Divinus perfectionis magister 45
Dominum et vivificantem 296
Ecclesia de Eucharistia 70, 278–9,
286, 289
Ecclesia Dei 291–2, 329
Ecclesia in Europa 50
Evangelium vitae 123
Familiaris consortio 127, 223, 225,
260, 286, 309, 351
Misericordia Dei 64, 302–6, 310–11
Omnium in mentem 554–6
Ordinatio sacerdotalis 247, 327
Pastor bonus 45, 75, 114, 126, 128,
131–4, 488,
Pastores dabo vobis 93, 96–7, 127
Pastores gregis 127, 139–40, 145–8,
151, 162
Reconciliatio et paenitentia 127, 302,
304, 309, 311
Sacrae disciplinae leges 1, 43–5, 64
Sacramentorum sanctitais tuela
54, 134, 284, 488–91, 540–3,
557–62
Sacri canones 64
Universi Dominici gregis 119–21,

126, 128–9
Veritatis splendor 219, 364–5, 466
Vetustissimam abbatiam 137
Vita consecrata 52, 127, 185–9,
    191–2
Leo XIII
    Apostolicae curae 326
    Arcanum divinae sapientiae 347–8
Paul III 426
Paul VI 31
    Ad pascendam 323
    De sacramento unctionis infirmorum
        253–4
    Divinae consortium naturae 269
    Ecclesiae sanctae 96
    Episcopi facultas 143
    Evangelii nuntiandi 127
    Humanae vitae 350–51
    Letter to Donald Coggan 327
    Ministeria queadam 92–3, 323, 334
    Mysterium fidei 278
    Ordo infirmorum 254
    Regimini Ecclesiae universae 130
    Romano Pontifice eligendo 129
    Sacerdotalis caelibatus 98
    The Roman Missal 275
Pius IX 30
Pius X 28, 30–1, 279, 285
    Ne temere 407
Pius XI
    Casti connubii 348, 350
Pius XII
    Allocution to Italian Midwives 348
    Allocution to the Roman Rota 348
    Cleri sanctitate 40
    Crebrae allatae 40
    Primo feliciter 180
    Postquam Apostolicis 40
    Sollicitudinem nostrum 40
pornography 527, 559
porter 92
possession *see also* poverty
    take possession of (installation in)
        office 144, 150, 164, 166, 168
    temporal goods (*see* temporal
        goods)

postulation, appointment to an office,
    see office
poverty *see also* evangelical counsels
    duty 105
    virtue 179
power
    administrative/executive *see* acts
    judicial *see* acts judicial
    juridical 52, 140
        delegated 140
        deprivation of *see* crime, office
        full 116
        immediate 116, 140
        loss of *see* crime, office
        ordinary 38, 116–17, 140ff.
        supreme 116–17
        universal, of Pope 38, 114–17
        vicarious 131, 154ff.
    legislative, *see* acts legislative
    sacred 39–40, 51–2, 94, 103, 105,
        238–9
prayer
    life of prayer of all the faithful
        231ff.
    liturgical 145–8, 231–6, 274ff.
    private 231
    public 231, 234
    special duties of, depending on
        vocations 105
preaching
    capacity for 221
    diocesan bishop 145–6, 219–20
    faculty by law 220
    and ministry of word 210ff., 220–2,
        359
    primary duty of priest 220–1, 257
precept
    in a single administrative act 72–3,
        452–3
    penal 465ff., 482
prelature, personal 93, 108–9, 330–2
presbyterate *see* priesthood
prescription
    of certain crimes 559–60
    of temporal goods 451
presentation *see* office, provision

priest
    assistant 174, 284
    and assistance at weddings 361
    and bishops, relationship 39–40,
        145–8
    chaplain 177, 284
    co-worker with bishop 166ff., 218–19
    functions 69, 166ff., 219, 274ff., 287
    operating *in persona Christi* 239,
        275–80, 324, 326
    ordination for service 93–4, 322ff.,
        333
    parish priest 166–74, 219–20, 223,
        284–5, 315–19
    rector 176–7, 220, 284
    rights and duties 166ff., 219–20, 257,
        274ff.
    remuneration *see* temporal goods
priesthood
    common, of all faithful (baptized)
        36–40, 48ff., 234–6, 267–9,
        274–80, 320, 322–5
    fulness of 140–2, 323
    ministerial (ordained as priests)
        36–40, 52, 57–8, 274–80, 298ff.,
        317, 320–5
    presbyterium of diocese 138–9, 145,
        162
    suitability for 19
privilege
    contra legem, praeter legem 73
    and canonical sanctions 475
    of faith
        Pauline 355, 366, 425–6, 518–19
        Petrine 366–7, 424–7, 519–20
probation *see* institutes / societies
procreation *see* ends / goods
procedural law
    importance of 495–6
    penal procedures *see also* tribunals
        521–7
        administrative procedure 478,
            521–2, 525, 559, 561
        advocate 501, 523
        appeal 481, 526–7
        judges 498ff.

judicial procedure 477–8, 521–3,
        525–6, 541–3, 559, 561
    penalties / sanctions 526
    precautionary restrictions 541–2,
        557–8
    preliminary investigation 479,
        522–5, 534–5, 560
    presuppositions 477–9
    promoter of justice 521ff., 540–1,
        558
    recourse 481, 496–7, 526–7, 543–6
    right of defence 479, 482, 496–7,
        506–7, 521, 523, 526, 559, 562
    sentence (judgment) 497, 526
    and sexual abuse of minors
        527–43, 557–62
    recourse, procedures for 543–5
    restitution, action for 527
    trials *see also* penal procedures,
        tribunal avoidance of 521
    contentious trial 502–9
        acts of case 500–1, 503
        acts of process 503, 506
        advocate 511, 514
        appeal 508, 515–17
        citation of respondent 502–3, 510,
            512–13
        conclusion of case 506, 515
        expenses 508
        instruction of case 502–6
        oral contentious process 509ff.,
            517
        petition 502, 510
        petitioner 502, 513ff.
        point at issue 503, 510
        proofs 504–5, 510–11
        respondent 502–3, 509–13
        right of defence 506–7, 509, 513
    in general 41, 79–80, 495–502
    and marriage 509–20
    and notary 500–1, 505
    parties, 501
    penal *see* above
    procurator 501, 505, 514–15, 526
    and sacred orders 520
    sentences (judgments) 500, 506

time, procedural 500, 505–6, 510, 514–15
profession
    of evangelical counsels *see* institutes of consecrated life
    of faith *see* faith, profession of
professors in ecclesiastical institutions 227–9
promises 432–3
promoter of justice 498, 514
promulgation *see* law
proofs *see* procedural law
Propaganda Fidei *see* Roman Curia, Evangelization of Peoples
property *see* temporal goods of the Church
propositiones see synods of bishops
pro-prefect 331
Protestants 57–8, 265, 288, 326–7, 347, 354, 408, 509
pro-vicar 331
province,
    ecclesiastical 143, 150–1
    of institute/society 197–8
    provincial, superior 197–8
psychological disorder 392–3, 510, 514–15
punishment *see* indulgences, *reus poenae*, sanctions
Purgatory 312–14

quotas, diocesan, see taxes

Raymond of Penyafort 27
reason *see also* condition, consent 466–7
reception into full communion 271–2, 380
recognitio
    revision of Code 31
    of the Holy See 45, 151–2, 224, 238, 243–4, 288, 376, 379, 405, 415, 448, 457, 534
reconciliation *see* penance
recourse
    and administrative acts, processes 70, 79–80, 496, 543–5

against removing a parish priest 544–5
against transferring a parish priest 545
    procedures 79–80, 495–7, 543–5
rector
    of a church 176–7, 220
    of a seminary see seminary 452ff.
Reformation 96, 263, 314, 347
Reformers 57–8, 275, 288, 347, 354, 408, 509
Reginald of Prüm 23
registers, for sacraments, etc.
    certificates 342, 378–81
    and freedom for marriage, profession, sacraments 342, 372ff.
    requirements of registration 265–6, 272–3, 343, 416–17
regulations 75–6
relationships *see* condition
relics 432, 435–6
religious *see* institutes of consecrated life
remedy for concupiscence (*remedium concupsicentiae*) *see* ends
removal, from office *see* office removal
remuneration 105
reparation for sin 311–4
reputation 85, 142–5, 522, 524ff.
rescript 71, 73–4, 518
reservation
    of Blessed Sacrament see Blessed Sacrament
    of canonical penalties 480–4
    of sins 482–4
residence 103, 147, 168, 474–5
resignation
    age recommended 78–9, 148
    acceptance of 78–9
    of diocesan bishop 148
    of Pope 79, 119
respondent *see* procedural law
retro-active *see* law
reus culpae/poenae 312–14
revelation, 210ff., 231–3, 240–2
right, innate (of Church) 210–12, 444–6,

464–5, 468, 496
right reason (*recta ratio*) 10–12
rights (and duties) *see also* clergy,
    institutes, societies
  of Eastern Catholic Churches 39–40
  human 46–7, 82
  of persons in the Church 35, 47ff., 57,
    81ff., 496ff.
    and diocesan bishop 145–8
    spiritual assistance from pastors
      84
    word of God 84, 210ff.
    sacraments 84, 231ff.
rite *see also* condition, Church '*sui iuris*'
  Ambrosian 57, 234
  Latin *see* Church, Latin
  Mozarabic 57, 234
  The Rites of the Catholic Church 237,
    269
  Rite of Christian Initiation for Adults
    256–9
  'Tridentine' see form, extraordinary
rites
  ordinariate within the Catholic Latin
    rite 549–53
  explanatory 262,
  of sacraments *see also* each
    sacrament 256ff.
Roman Catechism 347
Roman Curia, 65, 119, 131ff.
  Congregations of
  for Bishops 132, 144
    Directory for Bishops 69
  for Catholic Education 133
    *Orientamenti ... competenze
      psicologiche ...* 98–9, 103
    *Instruction ... Vocation ... Persons
      with Homosexual* 100, 341
  for Causes of Saints 132
    Sanctorum Mater 132
  for Clergy 132, 520
    Directory on Ministry ... of Priests
      69, 94
    Special faculties of ..., 2009 479, 482,
      491–4
  for Divine Worship and the

Discipline of the Sacraments
  132, 273–4, 292, 520
  *De processibus super matrimonii
    rato et non consumato* 377, 424,
    518
  *Institutio generalis:
    Missale Romanum ... recognitum*
    45
  Quattuor adhinc annos 292
  Redemptionis sacramentum 70, 91,
    132, 280–4, 286–7, 289
  *Rescript to a question about
    Reconciliation* 304–6
  *Variationes in novas editiones
    librorum liturgicorum* 253–4
  (Holy Office) procedures
    relating to *Crimen
    sollicitationis* 532–3, 536
  for the Doctrine of the Faith 132,
    294
    *Agendi ratio in doctrinarum
      examine* 228
    Communionis notio 121, 128,
      139–40
    *Complementary Norms to
      Anglicanorum coetibus*
      550–3
    *Decree attempted ordination
      women* 69
    Decree, 'Cum impotentiam ...'
      377
    Dignitas personae 419
    Dominus Iesus 58, 289, 326
    Donum veritatis 229
    Donum vitae 419
    *Instruction on dissolution of
      Marriage in Favour of the
      Faith* 520
    Inter insigniores 327
    *Letter on the Reception of Holy
      Communion by Divorced
      and Remarried* 286
    Orientamento per l'utilizzo ...
      98–9
    *Profession of Faith/ Oath of
      Fidelity* 227–9, 327–8

Responsio ad quaestiones 58
Explanatory notes on *Ad
    tuendam fidem* 218–19
for the Doctrine of the Faith as
    tribunal, *see* tribunals
for Eastern Churches 133
for Evangelization of Peoples
    133, 137
for Institutes of Consecrated
    Life and Societies of
    Apostolic Life 133
    *Directives on Formation in
        Religious Institutes* 188
    Faciem tuam, Domine, requiram
        189–90, 197
Secretariat of State 132
Congregations of the Roman
    Curia *Collaboration of the
    Non-Ordained Faithful* 173
Roman Rota *see* tribunals of Apostolic
    See

sacramentals 429–30
sacraments *see also* each particular
    sacrament
  absolute administration of 253–4
  and Apostolic See 236–9, 243–4,
      268–9
  catechesis and 170–1, 222–4
  character 48–9, 179, 244–5, 325
  Church and sacraments 138–40,
      231–428
  conditional administration of 249,
      253–4
  diocesan bishop,
      principal dispenser of 237–9
      responsibilities towards 145–8,
          243–4
  dispositions for reception *see* each
      sacrament
  effective signs of salvation 242, 268,
      275–8
  ex opere operato (operantis) 248, 280,
      325
  and faith 232–3, 275–8
  form 246, 250–2, 302–6

fruitful reception of 233, 280
in general 41, 231–54
intention
    of minister 246–7, 250–2, 302–6
    of recipient 247, 250–2, 302–6
licit celebration of 244–6
matter 246, 250–2, 304–6
minister of 246, 250–2
offerings related to 450
and parish priest 170ff.
preparation for 244–5
proper candidate 247–8
reverence and care 242–5, 249, 275–8,
    317
rights of faithful to 170ff., 273ff.
role of canon law in 20
and canonical sanctions 470ff.
seven sacraments, *see* each
    sacrament 347
validity of 233, 244–8, 250–2
St Thomas Aquinas *see* Aquinas
Saints *see also* beatification/
    canonization veneration of
salary (just) 188, 455
Salford, diocese of 273–4
salvation of souls, supreme law 34,
    133, 545–6
sanation
    of merely procedural errors 560
    radical, *sanatio in radice* 421–2
sanctification *see* holiness
sanctions, canonical *see also* crime, law
    penal in general 85, 109, 286, 463ff.
  aggravation of 465, 469
  application of 477–82, 491–4
  cessation of 482–4
  diminution of 466–7, 469
  effects of 310, 313, 329, 409,
      470–82, 491–2
  form of
      latae sententiae ('automatic')
          465–7, 469ff.
      ferendae sententiae ('imposed')
          465, 469ff.
  purposes of 463ff., 470, 477–82
  subjects of 465ff.

in particular *see also* crimes
  particular censures 465, 468,
    470–91
  excommunication 310, 313, 329,
    464, 562
  interdict 470
  suspension 469–70
  expiatory penalties 465, 468–70
  deprivation of office, etc.
    474–5
  dismissal from clerical state
    474ff., 490–1
  penances, penal 468–9, 477
  remedies, penal 468–9, 476
Sapphira 441
scandal 431, 463–4, 466ff., 491–4
schism 340, 380, 431, 464, 484
Scholastics 25
schooling, home 224
schools
  of canon law 15–6
  Catholic 224–6
scrutinies and preparation for Holy
  Orders 342
seal
  with Holy Spirit *see* confirmation
  of confession *see* penance
Second Vatican Council
    1, 16–18, 31, 36–40, 92–6, 111–14,
    124, 126–7, 137
  constitutions
    Sacrosanctum Concilium 92, 233,
      235, 237, 297, 314
    Lumen gentium 14–15, 18, 37–9, 52,
      113–14, 118, 139–40, 181, 191,
      212, 214–16, 233, 237–8, 258,
      260, 265, 267, 269, 273, 278,
      316, 322, 463, 547
    Dei Verbum 115, 186, 212–15, 219,
      232, 237, 240, 256–7
    Gaudium et spes 214, 349–50, 357,
      359, 364–5, 447, 463
  declarations
    Dignitatis humanae 47, 212, 214
    Presbyterorum ordinis 39, 76, 96,
      219, 257, 442–3

decrees
  Ad gentes 224, 258–9
  Apostolicam actuositatem 273
  Christus Dominus 38–9, 96, 114,
    137, 139–40, 238
  Optatam totius 17
  Orientalium Ecclesiarum 40, 270
  Perfectae caritatis 80, 182
  Unitatis redintegratio 139, 265
secrecy *see also* oaths 155
Secretariat of State *see* Curia Roman
secular institutes *see* institutes of
    consecrated life
  world/order/character 87ff., 106
see *see also* Apostolic see, diocese
  Apostolic 111ff., 151
  impeded *see* 149–50
  vacancy of 149–50
  vacancy of Apostolic See 119–21, 129
selection
  of bishops *see* bishops
seminary
  admission, selection of students,
    criteria 99–100, 273
  confessors 97, 102, 341
  celibacy *see* celibacy
  diocesan, 99–100
  formation 96–7, 100–3
  and internal/external fora *see* forum
  major/minor 96
  and personal prelature 108
  Pontifical 100
  and psychologists 101–3
  rector 97, 100–3, 341–2
  regional 100
  spiritual director 97, 102, 341
  staff and criteria of suitability 77,
    100ff., 341
Seminary, St Patrick's, Maynooth 531
Seminary, St Peter's, Wexford, 531
sentire cum Ecclesia 189
separation of spouses
  captivity or persecution 426
  dissolution of bond *see* dissolution
  legal 422–3, 517
servus servorum Dei 117

Shammai 353
shrines 435–6
Signatura, Apostolic *see* tribunals, Apostolic See
Simon Magus 441
simony 24, 142, 245, 441, 464
simulation of consent *see* consent
sin
    absolution from *see* penance
    damage done by 295ff., 463–4
    mortal 251–2, 297ff., 311–12
    personal 251–2, 296ff., 311–12
    punishment due to *see* indulgences
    remission of 251–2, 295ff.
    venial 311–12, 315
societas perfecta 8, 212
societies of apostolic life
    admission 195, 202, 273, 278
    and admission to candidacy 336
    apostolate 195–6, 207
    and bishop of dicoese 147, 196, 207
    and clergy 93
    common life 178ff., 190, 207
    confessional faculties 306ff.
    dismissal 209
    excardination/incardination *see* incardination/incardination
    financial administration 207
    formation 195, 203
    governance 195–6, 207
    incorporation into, definitive 195, 204, 342
    probation 195, 203
    nature 194–5
    ordination, need for clergy 333
    possessions 207
    rights and duties 278, 284
    separation from 195, 208
    superior (of Pontifical right) 331–2, 435
    transfer 208
Society of Pius X 293
spiritual director *see also* seminary 110, 203, 341
spiritual life 146–8
sponsors *see* baptism and confirmation

state
    of life 85, 103, 105, 181–6
    political 367–8, 417
status, juridical *see* Church
statutes *see also* institutes/societies
    of council of priests 159
    of episcopal conferences 151
stipends *see* Eucharist, Mass offerings
'stole fees' *see* sacraments, offerings related to
Strasbourg, canon law school 15–16
structure, hierarchical, of Church 111–35
Suarez F. 28, 62
subjects *see* law, subjects
subsidiarity, principle of 34, 188
succession/successor
    Apostolic 111–14, 140–2, 322, 489
    of Peter 111–17
suicide, attempted 338
suitability, criteria of *see* office, provision/appointment of
superior 61, 93–4, 178ff., 189–90, 220, 465ff., 496
supreme authority *see* authority, supreme
suum cuique 9
synod
    of bishops *see* synod of bishops
    diocesan 153, 160
    provincial/regional 150–1
synods of bishops
    and death of Pope 119
    and revision of the Code 32
    nature and purpose 123–8
    post-synodal documents *see also* Popes
        Ultimis temporibus 127
        Convenientes ex universo 127
    procedures 127
        Instrumentum laboris 127
        Lineamenta 127, 185
        Propositiones 127
    special/general 127
    themes of general synods 91–2, 126–7

Syrian 57

Tametsi 407
Taylor, Bishop Maurice 80
teaching *see also* education
  function of the Church 88–9, 142,
      145–8, 210–30
  doctorate, licence 143
  of erroneous doctrines 64–5, 146, 485
  of theology and canonical mission
      64–5, 85, 88–9
'team ministry' 165, 409
temporal goods of the Church 439–62
  acquisition of 110, 447–52
    conditions of 447
  administration of 435, 452–6
    extraordinary acts of 157, 159,
        454–5
    ordinary acts of 454–5
  alienation of 156–7, 159, 432, 454,
      456–60
  and apostolate 443, 445
  audits of, accounts and
      accountability 440–1, 453, 455,
      458–60
  benefices 442–4, 455–6
  bequests 451
  and canonization of civil law 448ff.
  charitable works 440, 445
  and civil law 156, 454ff., 458–60
  collections 447–50, 455–6
  concept 444–6
  contracts 456ff.
  expenditure, extraordinary/
      ordinary 156–7, 159, 457–8
  finance committee
    diocesan 56, 69, 156–7, 448, 457–8
    parish 173–4, 458
  financial secretary/administrator
      diocesan 149–50, 156–7, 453–4
  gifts 447, 455–6, 460–1
  goods, ecclesiastical 445–6, 451, 454
  innate right 444–6
  and juridical persons *see* persons
      160
  loans 447

and moral persons *see* persons,
    Apostolic See
objects sacred *see* objects
offerings of the faithful 440, 444–6,
    455–6, 460–1
possession 444ff.
purposes of 439–41, 445, 460–1
restitution 447
and Scripture 439–41
stable patrimony 445, 455
subsidiarity 446
support of pastors 85, 440, 442–6,
    455–6
taxes/quotas, diocesan 156–7, 160,
    448–50
  extraordinary/ordinary 448–9
and worship 440, 445
temporal order *see* secular order
  territorial structures in Church
    35
  abbacy/abbot *see* diocese,
      equivalent to parish *see* parish
      prelature/prelate *see* diocese,
      equivalent to
terna 144
times sacred 436–9
tonsure 92
transfer *see* office, loss of
trans-finalization *see* Eucharist
translations, of Scripture/liturgical
    books 227
transsexual persons 341–2
trans-signification *see* Eucharist
transubstantiation *see* Eucharist
tria munera see Church, functions
tribunals
  appointments to 77
  of Apostolic *See* Apostolic
      Penitentiary
        133, 313, 374, 482–4, 500
      Apostolic Signatura 80, 134, 497–9
      Congregation for Doctrine of the
          Faith 134, 490–1, 497, 499,
          540–3, 557–62
      Roman Rota 133–4, 400–1, 490–1,
          497, 499, 512, 516

competent forum 55, 490–1, 496–9, 509–13
 diocesan 498
 instances 497–500
 officials 498, 500–1
 procedures *see* procedural law
 regional 498
 reserved cases (to Apostolic See) 496–9
 rights and duties in regard to 85, 495ff.
tutiorism 245

ubi societas, ibi lex 7
Ulpian 20, 345
unction extreme *see* sacraments, anointing of sick
Uniate Greek, Russian, Ukrainian 57
universities, Catholic *see* education

vacany *see also* see
 of office 77, 79–80
vacatio legis 44, 64
vagus, cleric *see* clergy acephalous
Vatican I *see* Councils, First Vatican
Vatican II *see* Second Vatican Council
Vatican Bank (Institute for Religious Works) 442
Vatican City State 8, 132, 441
veneration of saints 432, 435–6
vestments 282
vetitum 516
viaticum see Holy Communion
vicar
 Apostolic 137
 of Christ 113
 episcopal 77, 149–50, 155, 159–61, 518,
 forane (dean) 166–8, 174–6
 general 70, 77–8, 149–50, 154, 159–61, 518
 judicial (*Officialis*) 77, 157–8, 259–60, 393, 404–5, 498, 509ff.
 parochial *see* priest assistant
 power (vicarious) *see* power, vicarious

violence against Pope, bishops, etc. 485
virtue
 of justice 9–11, 443–4, 461
 of penance 295–7, 310–12
 of religion 433
visit '*ad limina Apostolorum*' 131, 145, 147
visitation, canonical 109
 of bishop 147–8, 452
vocation
 Christian 46–53, 81ff.
 to consecrated life 52, 178ff.
 to permanent diaconate 334
 divine 334
 of all the faithful 146
 to marriage *see* marriage
 to priesthood 145, 334
 lay/secular 178ff.
voluntarium in causa 467
voting
 types of
  consultative 127–8, 151–2, 162
  deliberative 127–8, 151–2
 validity of
  in general 151–2
  in election of Pope 118–21
vows,
 in general 432–3
 religious 178–90, 383, 425

wage, just *see* salary
wedding *see* marriage
widows, 191
will (testament) 451–2
witness
 to Christ, confirmation 267
 of Apostles 113
 judicial 504–6
 to marriage
  Church's official witness 361, 374, 408–11
  by proxy 403–4
  two witnesses 361, 411–2
worship see also prayer 85–6, 231ff.
 cult of saints 432, 435–6
 images and relics 432, 435–6

public 432, 435–6
sacraments 137, 210, 231–428,
    239–40, 242–3, 275–8, 320ff.,
    435–6

word of God 137, 210ff., 232–3,
    320ff., 435–6